LABOR RELATIONS
Development, Structure, Process

LABOR RELATIONS
Development, Structure, Process

John A. Fossum
Industrial Relations Center
University of Minnesota

FIFTH EDITION

IRWIN
Homewood, IL 60430
Boston, MA 02116

Sponsoring editor: Kurt Strand
Project editor: Jean Lou Hess
Production manager: Bette K. Ittersagen
Designer: Robyn B. Loughran
Compositor: Better Graphics, Inc.
Typeface: 10/12 Electra
Printer: R. R. Donnelley & Sons Company

Library of Congress Cataloging-in-Publication Data

Fossum, John A.
    Labor relations: development, structure, process/John A. Fossum.—5th ed.
        p.   cm.
    Includes bibliographical references and index.
    ISBN 0-256-05824-5
    1. Industrial relations.   I. Title.
HD6961.F65   1992
331'.0973—dc20   91–18828

Printed in the United States of America
2 3 4 5 6 7 8 9 0 DOC 8 7 6 5 4 3

To all my parents
Peter, Almeda, Herb, and Jane

PREFACE

The fifth edition of *Labor Relations: Development, Structure, Process* is the first edition in the third decade of its use. Over this period of time, employment, and as a consequence, labor relations, has seen major changes. The preponderance of employment has moved from the production of goods to the provision of services. The relative number of occupations has moved from those requiring physical prowess and effort to those depending on cognitive abilities and their application. Simultaneously, the financial performance of organizations became increasingly critical and the economy became truly global.

Over the period of time covered by the five editions of this text, research has increasingly identified the effects of these changes on employers and unions, the effects of unions on firm performance, and the effects of unions on individual employees. During the same period, there has been *no* legislation at the federal level that has had any major effect on labor laws. Although, at the same time, the interpretation and enforcement of labor laws has been substantially different than in the past. As a result, organized labor has increasingly adopted new methods for representing employees.

Similar to the previous editions, this edition can be recognized as an evolutionary product. The basic topics remain much the same, with the exception of the incorporation of information on health care labor relations and equal employment opportunity into the text where appropriate, and the addition of chapters on employee relations in nonunion organizations and international and comparative labor relations. Changes within chapters include expanded treatments of the political activities of unions, updated evidence on the effects of unions on economic and noneconomic outcomes to firms and individuals, a completely revised chapter on union-management cooperation, the incorporation of substantial new research material on the grievance process, and an updating and greater information in the mock contract negotiation exercise.

I hope that you will see this book as presenting a balanced perspective—balanced from a labor or management viewpoint, and balanced from a behavioral, institutional, and economic perspective. In the development of this approach, I am indebted to many institutions and individuals—my graduate school professors at the University of Minnesota and Michigan State University; my colleagues over time at the University of

Wyoming, University of Michigan, UCLA, and now in the Industrial Relations Center at the University of Minnesota; and the many academics and practitioners from whom I have received ideas in academic meetings and conversations.

Specific acknowledgments are also necessary to credit those who have assisted me in the development of this book. The first edition was conceived in an act of faith with Jim Sitlington and Cliff Francis of Business Publications, Inc., an earlier subsidiary of Richard D. Irwin. The thorough reviews and helpful comments of Hoyt Wheeler of the University of South Carolina (and my first faculty industrial relations colleague at the University of Wyoming) and I. B. Helburn of the University of Texas significantly assisted me in the preparation of the first edition. The second edition was aided by suggestions and comments from Jim Chelius of Rutgers University, Sahab Dayal of Central Michigan University, and George Munchus of the University of Alabama at Birmingham. The third edition was aided by the reviews of George Bohlander of Arizona State University, Richard Miller of the University of Wisconsin, Edmond Seifried of Lafayette College, and Bobby Vaught of Southwest Missouri State University. The fourth benefited from comments and suggestions from Edward Reinier of the University of Southern Colorado and Jack E. Steen of Florida State University. The plans for this edition were helped by A. L. "Bart" Bartlett of Pennsylvania State University, Robert Seeley of Wilkes University, R. H. Votaw of Amber University, and Frank Balanis of San Francisco State University, and portions of the manuscript were improved substantially by suggestions from Edward Suntrup of the University of Illinois at Chicago and Bill Cooke of Wayne State University.

Reference materials are particularly important in preparing a text, and reference librarians are thus helpful in pointing out new information and locating it. I have been assisted by several in preparing this text. For the first two editions, JoAnn Sokkar, Mabel Webb, and Phyllis Hutchings of the Industrial Relations Reference Room at the University of Michigan provided this assistance. For editions three, four, and five, Georgianna Herman and Mariann Nelson of the Industrial Relations Center Reference Room at the University of Minnesota have found obscure sources and provided quick turnaround. Library services are very important in preparing a text and also important for students in making the maximum use of the exercises in this book. Research assistants are also an important resource that substantially facilitates text preparation. I was particularly fortunate to have an extremely able research assistant during the period in which this revision took place. Kimberly Scow not only found all the things I needed, she also suggested additional material and topics to emphasize. Her knowledge, thoroughness, and enthusiasm will be of great benefit to her new employer, Chevron Corporation, as she begins her professional career. I owe a great debt of gratitude to all of these individuals. Any errors or omissions in this text should not be attributed to them. I have occasionally ignored advice which was probably beneficial and may have overlooked information provided by them to me.

Finally, I owe a permanent debt to all of the parents of my family who provided me with the examples and support to undertake an academic career; to my wife, Alta, who has made the personal sacrifices of moving several times, has subordinated her interests during times when I was writing, and has offered the wisest counsel; and to my children Andy and Jean, who had to explain to their friends that their father was not "terminally weird" for spending many consecutive weekends in front of a microcomputer display after being harassed for failing to meet deadlines. And Jean, you can make one last stab at the public school library system by sneaking a copy into the high school library, but unless it circulates more frequently than the ones you put in the grade school and junior high libraries, we'll have to concede that the effort to move labor relations into the elementary and secondary school students' interests has been a failure.

John A. Fossum

CONTENTS

■ 1

INTRODUCTION   2
What Unions Do   3
Why Workers Unionize   4
   Catalyst for Organization   4
   Individuals and Union Organizing   5
Beliefs about Unions   9
   Beliefs of Employees in General   9
   Nonunion Respondents   11
   Union Members   11
Areas of Frustration   12
Collective Behavior   12
   Group Cohesiveness   13
Unions, Their Members, and Decision
   Making   14
Labor Unions in the 1990s   15
Summary and Preview   17
   Plan of the Book   17

■ 2

**THE EVOLUTION OF AMERICAN
LABOR: I**   22
Early Unions and the Conspiracy
   Doctrine   24
   Philadelphia Cordwainers   24
   Commonwealth *v.* Hunt   25
   Pre–Civil War Unions   25
The Birth of National Unions   26
   The National Labor Union   27
   The Knights of Labor   27
   The American Federation of Labor   29

Labor Unrest   31
   *The IWW and the Western Federation
     of Miners*   33
   The Boycott Cases   35
   Early Legislation   36
Trade Union Success and Apathy   37
   World War I   37
   The American Plan   37
   The End of an Era   38
   *Union Philosophies and Types in the
     United States*   39
Summary and Prologue   40
Discussion Questions   41

■ 3

**THE EVOLUTION OF AMERICAN
LABOR: II**   42
Industrial Unions   44
   The Industrial Union Leadership   44
   Organizing the Industrial Work Force   44
Legislation   46
   Norris-LaGuardia Act (1932)   46
   National Industrial Recovery Act (1933) 47
   *The Wagner Act (National Labor
     Relations Act, 1935)*   48
Employer Intransigence   49
   Constitutionality of the Wagner Act   50
Labor Power   51
   Pre–World War II   51
   World War II   53
   Reconversion   55

Changing the Balance   55
   Taft-Hartley Act   55
Retrenchment and Merger   57
   Merger   58
   Corruption   58
   Landrum-Griffin Act   60
Legislative Attempts in the 1970s   61
Public-Sector Union Growth   61
   Federal Executive Orders   62
   Civil Service Reform Act   63
   State and Local Governments   63
Passing the Torch   63
Summary   65
Discussion Questions   65

■ 4

**LABOR LAW AND FEDERAL
AGENCIES**   68
Overview   70
Railway Labor Act   70
   Overview   72
Norris-LaGuardia Act (1932)   73
Wagner and Taft-Hartley Acts (as
   Amended)   75
   Section 2, Taft-Hartley   75
   Section 3   76
   Section 7   76
   Section 8   77
   Section 9   79
   Sections 10, 11, and 12   79
   Sections 13 through 19   80
   Title II   80
   Title III   81
   Summary   81
Landrum-Griffin Act (1959)   81
   *Title I—Bill of Rights for Union
     Members*   81
   *Title II—Reports Required of Unions
     and Employers*   82
   Title III—Trusteeships   82
   *Racketeer Influenced and Corrupt
     Organizations Act*   83
   Effects of Implementation of Laws   84
Federal Departments and Agencies   85
   Department of Labor   85

   *Federal Mediation and Conciliation
     Service*   87
   National Mediation Board   88
   National Labor Relations Board   88
Summary   91
Discussion Questions   91

■ 5

**UNION STRUCTURE AND
GOVERNMENT**   94
The Local Union   96
   *Local Union Democracy and
     Participation*   98
   Functional Democracy   100
International Unions   102
National Union Goals   103
   National Union Jurisdictions   106
   National Structure   108
   National-Local Union Relationship   111
   National Union Politics   113
   National Unions and Public Policy   114
The AFL–CIO   116
State and Local Central Bodies   119
Overview of the Union Hierarchy   120
National Union Mergers   121
Union Finances   122
   *Organization Receipts and
     Disbursements*   122
   Union Officer Compensation   123
   Pension Administration   124
Summary   124
Discussion Questions   125

■ 6

**UNION ORGANIZING AND
EMPLOYER RESPONSE**   126
How Organizing Begins   128
   The Framework for Organizing   128
   Representation Elections   130
Bargaining Unit Determination   134
   Legal Constraints   135
   Jurisdiction of the Organizing Union   136
   The Union's Desired Unit   136
   The Employer's Desired Unit   136

NLRB Policy	137
Other Issues in Unit Determination	140
The Organizing Campaign	141
No Distribution or Solicitation Rules	141
Union Strategy and Tactics	142
Management Strategy and Tactics	147
The Role of the NLRB	151
Interrogation	152
Communications	152
The 24-Hour Rule	153
Employee Responses to Campaigns	153
The Effects of Unfair Practices	155
Election Certifications	155
Setting Aside Elections	157
The Impact of Board Remedies	158
Election Outcomes	158
Decertifications	159
Contextual Characteristics	
Influencing Elections	160
Organizing and Membership Trends	161
Summary	161
Discussion Questions	162
CASE GMFC Custom Conveyor Division	163

■ 7

THE ENVIRONMENT FOR BARGAINING   166

The Product and Service Market	168
Public Policy and Industrial	
Organization	170
Regulation and Deregulation	171
Foreign Competition	173
Employer Interests	173
Labor as a Derived Demand	174
Labor-Capital Substitution	175
Labor Markets	176
Employee Interests	177
Union Interests	177
Legal Requirements	179
Bargaining Power	181
Ability to Continue Operations	
(or Take a Strike)	183
Union Bargaining Power	185

Bargaining Structures	185
Multiemployer Bargaining	186
Industry-Wide Bargaining	187
National/Local Bargaining	189
Wide-Area and Multicraft Bargaining	189
Pattern Bargaining	190
Conglomerates and Multinationals	192
Coordinated and Coalition Bargaining	192
Public Policy and Court Decisions	192
Influence of Bargaining Power and	
Structure	194
Summary	195
Discussion Questions	196
CASE Material Handling Equipment Association Bargaining Group	198

■ 8

WAGE AND BENEFIT ISSUES IN BARGAINING   200

Components of Wage Demands	202
Equity	202
Ability to Pay	202
Standard of Living	204
Pay Programs	204
Pay Level	205
Pay Structure	209
Pay Form	213
Pay System	217
Union Effects on Pay	220
Union Effects on Pay Levels	220
Union Effects on Pay Structures	224
Union Effects on Pay Form	224
Union Effects on Pay Systems	225
Union Effects on Organizational	
Effectiveness	225
Productivity	225
Profitability and Returns to	
Shareholders	227
Wage Issues in Current Contracts	228
Summary	228
Discussion Questions	230
CASE Health Care Costs and Employment Levels	231

■ 9

NONWAGE ISSUES IN BARGAINING   232

Nonwage Provisions of Current Contracts   234

Union and Management Goals for Nonwage Issues   234

Design of Work   234

Hours of Work   237
   Federal Wage and Hour Laws   239
   Collective Bargaining and Work Schedules   239
   Entitlements to and Restrictions on Overtime   240
   Shift Assignments and Differentials   240
   Innovation Work Schedules   240
   Paid Time Off   241

Length of Contracts   241

Union and Management Rights   242

Discipline and Discharge   243

Grievance and Arbitration   243

Strikes and Lockouts   244

Union Security   245

Working Conditions and Safety   246

Seniority and Job Security   247
   Layoff Procedures   248
   Promotions and Transfers   249
   Equal Employment Opportunity and Seniority   249

Effects of Unions on Nonwage Outcomes   250
   Union Influences on Hiring   250
   Promotions, Transfers, and Turnover   251
   Retirement Programs   253
   Job Satisfaction   254
   Commitment to the Union   255

Summary   256

Discussion Questions   257

CASE   **GMFC Attitude Survey**   258

■ 10

CONTRACT NEGOTIATIONS   260

Management Preparation   262

Department Involvement   262
Reviewing the Expiring Contract   264
Preparing Data for Negotiations   264
Identification of Probable Union Demands   265
Costing the Contract   265
Negotiation Objectives and the Bargaining Team   269
Bargaining Books   269
Strike Preparation   271
Strategy and Logistics   272

Union Preparation   272
National-Level Activities   272
Local-Level Preparations   274
Effects of Union Characteristics on Bargaining Outcomes   275

Negotiation Requests   276

What Is Bargaining?   276
Attributes of the Parties   278
Perceptions of Bargainers   279

Theories of Bargaining Tactics   280
Bluffing   281

Behavioral Theories of Labor Negotiations   282
Integrative Bargaining   282
Attitudinal Structuring   285
Intraorganizational Bargaining   285
Use of the Components in Bargaining   287

Negotiations   289
Initial Presentations   289
Bargaining on Specific Issues   289

Tactics in Distributive Bargaining   290
Committing to a Position   291

Settlements and Ratifications   291
Nonagreement   292
Recent Changes in Bargaining Outcomes   294
Summary   296
Discussion Questions   296

Negotiating Exercise   298
   A. Contract Costing   298
   B. Approach   305
   C. Demands   305
   D. Organization for Negotiations   306
   E. Negotiations   306
   F. Additional Information   307

Agreement between General
   Manufacturing & Fabrication
   Company and Local 384, United
   Steelworkers of America   313

11
IMPASSES AND THEIR
RESOLUTION   338

Impasse Definition   340
Third-Party Involvement   340
Mediation   340
   Mediator Behavior and Outcomes   343
   Mediator Backgrounds and Training 347
   Mediator Activity   349
Fact-Finding   349
   Taft-Hartley Fact-Finding   350
   Railway Labor Boards   351
   Fact-Finding and the Issues   351
Interest Arbitration   351
Review of Third-Party Involvements   352
Strikes   352
   Strike Votes and Going Out   353
   Picketing   354
   Slowdowns   355
   Corporate Campaigns   356
   Shutdowns   356
   Continued Operations   357
   Rights of Economic Strikers   358
   Contracting Out   359
   Evidence on the Incidence, Duration,
      and Effects of Strikes   360
Overview   364
Boycotts   365
Lockouts   367
   Perishable Goods   367
   Multiemployer Lockouts   367
   Single-Employer Lockouts   368
Bankruptcies   369
Summary   370
Discussion Questions   371
CASE   GMFC Impasse   372

12
UNION-MANAGEMENT
COOPERATION   374

Labor and Management Roles and the
   Changing Environment   376
   Organizing and the Evolving Bargaining
      Relationship   376
   Preferences of Management and Labor 377
   Levels of Cooperation and Control 377
Integrative Bargaining   378
Creating and Sustaining Cooperation   380
   Methods of Cooperation   381
Area-Wide Labor-Management
   Committees   382
Joint Labor-Management Committees   383
Relations by Objectives   383
Workplace Interventions   384
   The Scanlon Plan   388
   Rucker Plans   391
   Impro-Share   392
   Quality Circles and Team Concepts 392
   Labor-Management Committees   396
   Quality-of-Work-Life and Employee
      Involvement Programs   396
   Union Political Processes and the
      Diffusion of Change   398
   Management Strategy   399
   Research on the Effects of Cooperation
      across Organizations   399
   Research on the Long-Run Effects of
      Cooperation   400
Employee Stock Ownership Plans   402
   The Diffusion and Institutionalization
      of Change   402
Summary   403
Discussion Questions   404
CASE   Continuing or Abandoning
         the Special-Order
         Fabrication Business   405

13
CONTRACT ADMINISTRATION   408
The Duty to Bargain   410

Issues in Contract Administration   410
  Discipline   410
  Incentives   411
  Work Assignments   411
  Individual Personnel Assignments   412
  Hours of Work   412
  Supervisors Doing Production Work 412
  Production Standards   412
  Working Conditions   412
  Subcontracting   413
  Past Practice   413
  Rules   413
  Prevalence of Issues   414

Grievance Procedures   414
  Steps in the Grievance Procedure   414
  Time Involved   417

Methods of Dispute Resolution   418
  Striking over Grievances   418
  Wildcat Strikes   418
  Discipline for Wildcat Strikes   420
  Grievance Mediation   421

Employee and Union Rights in
  Grievance Processing   421
  To What Is the Employee Entitled? 422
  Fair Representation   423
  Individual Rights under the Contract 423

Grievances and Bargaining   425
  *Union Responses to Management
    Action*   426
  Fractional Bargaining   426
  Union Initiatives in Grievances   427
  *Individual Union Members and
    Grievances*   429

Effects of Grievances on Employers
  and Employees   431

Summary   434

Discussion Questions   434

CASE   435

14
THE ARBITRATION OF
GRIEVANCES   436

What Is Arbitration?   438

Development of Arbitration   438

Lincoln Mills   439
Steelworkers' Trilogy   439
The 1962 Trilogy   441
*Recent Supreme Court Decisions on
  Arbitration*   441
NLRB Deferral to Arbitration   442
Exceptions to Deferral   443

Arbitration Procedures   444
Prearbitration Matters   445
Selection of an Arbitrator   445
*Sources and Qualifications of
  Arbitrators*   446
National Academy of Arbitrators   448
American Arbitration Association   448
*Federal Mediation and Conciliation
  Service*   449
Prehearing   449
Hearing Processes   452
Representatives of the Parties   452
Presentation of the Case   453
Posthearing   453
Evidentiary Rules   453
Arbitral Remedies   455
Preparation of the Award   455

Procedural Difficulties and Their
  Resolutions   456
Expedited Arbitration   457
Inadequate Representation   458

Arbitration of Discipline Cases   460
Role of Discipline   460
Evidence   460
Uses of Punishment   461

Arbitration of Past Practice Disputes 462

Arbitral Decisions and the Role of
  Arbitration   463

Summary   464

Discussion Questions   464

CASES   467

15
PUBLIC-SECTOR LABOR
RELATIONS   470

Public-Sector Labor Law   472
Federal Labor Relations Law   472

Civil Service Reform Act, Title VII — 472
State Labor Laws — 473
Jurisdictions and Employees — 474
Sources of Employment — 474
Levels of Government — 474
Types of Employee Groups — 474
Public Employee Unions — 476
Bargaining Units and Organizing — 477
Public-Sector Bargaining Processes — 478
Bargaining Structures — 478
Management Organization for Bargaining — 479
Multilateral Bargaining — 479
Bargaining Outcomes — 481
Impasse Procedures — 483
Fact-Finding — 484
Statutory Role of the Fact-Finder — 486
Fact-Finding Results — 486
Criteria for Fact-Finding Recommendations — 488
Arbitration — 488
Interest Arbitration Variants — 489
Final-Offer Arbitration — 489
Results of Final-Offer Laws — 490
What Is a Final Offer? — 492
An Alternative to Final-Offer Selection — 492
Evidence on the Narcotic Effect — 493
Arbitration and Maturing Labor Relations — 494
Arbitral Criteria — 494
The Utility of Arbitration for Unions — 495
Strikes — 496
Summary — 498
Discussion Questions — 499
CASE — 500

■ 16
EMPLOYEE RELATIONS IN
NONUNION ORGANIZATIONS — 502
What Is Employee Relations? — 504
"Union-Free" Organizations — 504
Union Avoidance — 505

Environmental Factors Associated with Union Avoidance — 505
Transient Employees and Representation — 506
A Philosophy-Laden Approach to Employee Relations — 507
Wage Policies — 507
Nonwage Policies — 509
Personnel Expenditures — 510
Employment Security — 510
Employee "Voice" Systems — 511
Other Innovative Techniques — 516
Employer/Employee Committees — 516
Developing Practices in Nonunion Employee Relations — 517
Summary — 519
Discussion Questions — 519
CASE — 520

■ 17
A SURVEY OF LABOR
RELATIONS IN DEVELOPED
MARKET ECONOMIES — 522
The Development of Labor Movements — 524
The Structure of Labor Movements — 526
Organizing and Representation — 528
Bargaining Issues — 529
Bargaining Structures — 530
Impasses — 531
Union-Management Cooperation — 531
Contract Administration — 534
Public-Sector Unionization — 534
Summary — 535
Discussion Questions — 535

GLOSSARY — 536

INDEX — 548

LABOR RELATIONS
Development, Structure, Process

1

INTRODUCTION

Labor relations and employment experienced major changes during the 1980s.[1] The proportion of employees represented by unions declined substantially; unionized employees in many industries have agreed to economic concessions; and employers became more successful in resisting union-organizing campaigns. Many commentators marked the 1981 air traffic controllers' strike and their subsequent discharge by the federal government as a major event in the recent decline in union power. The decline in union membership has been particularly marked in the United States, but membership in other western countries also has declined as the employment structure has changed from goods to service production and from manual to mental labor.[2]

Some conditions that developed in the 1980s, such as foreign competition and an emphasis on increased profitability, continue to strongly influence labor relations in the 1990s. Unlike in the 1980s, the United States faces a shortage of high-quality labor in the 1990s. This is partly because of demographic changes related to the "baby bust" of the 1960s and 1970s and because of inadequate education and training. Employers no longer have a cushion of a large number of qualified unemployed persons to fill the jobs of striking union members. Also in the 90s, unions have changed some traditional ways of serving present and potential members that could lead to their gaining strength during the decade.

WHAT UNIONS DO

Unions evoke a lot of controversy. People generally have strong opinions about their effects and tactics. As will be noted in the history sections that follow, unions have been a part of U.S. history for as long as the nation has existed. Working men and women have felt a need to collectivize to negotiate pay and working conditions with employers, believing that employers had interests that conflicted with theirs.

As also will be noted in more detail later, one reason unions are controversial is because unionization restricts labor supply and creates **monopoly power** for employees who are represented by unions. On the other hand, the public regards unions as important because they provide employees a voice in how the employment relationship is implemented in their workplaces. Thus, unions are expected to benefit their members

---

[1] For a comprehensive examination, see Thomas A. Kochan, Harry C. Katz, and Robert B. McKersie, *The Transformation of American Industrial Relations* (New York: Basic Books, 1986).

[2] Leo Troy, "Is the U.S. Unique in the Decline of Private Sector Unionism," *Journal of Labor Research* 11 (1990), pp. 111–43.

(monopoly power), possibly at the financial expense of the public, and to benefit the public at large through labor contracts and their requirement that employers must respond to employee grievances (voice power).[3]

There are large differences in the degree to which industries and occupations are unionized. Some of the differences relate to the mix of occupations by industries and some to the age and employment practices of the industries. Job attributes influence the degree of unionization; job situations in which employer-specific knowledge is required and where internal workplace governance issues more strongly influence outcomes to workers are more heavily unionized.[4]

WHY WORKERS UNIONIZE

About 15 percent of the U.S. employees belong to unions. The proportions of represented employees differs greatly across occupations and industries, as does the point in American history at which occupations and industries were organized.

Employees become union members through one of three different processes. First, nonunion employees may decide they would benefit from **representation** and organize a union to bargain collectively for them. Second, an employee working in a unit covered by a **collective bargaining** agreement may decide to join the union. Third, newly hired employees may be required by the contract to join the union as a condition of continued employment.

Catalyst for Organization

A variety of employee, economic, and job characteristics are related to unionism and unionization. The monopoly power and voice roles of unions are obviously important to employees, but other aspects such as job content, experience, age, gender, and so forth are also related to willingness to form or join a union.[5] Specific events probably trigger organizing activity for employees of any given employer. Employee dis-

---

[3] Richard B. Freeman and James L. Medoff, *What Do Unions Do?* (New York: Basic Books, 1984).

[4] Greg Hundley, "Things Unions Do, Job Attributes, and Union Membership," *Industrial Relations* 28 (1989), pp. 335–55.

[5] Jack Fiorito, Daniel G. Gallagher, and Charles R. Greer, "Determinants of Unionism: A Review of the Literature," In *Research in Personnel and Human Resources Management*, ed. Kendrith Rowland and Gerald Ferris (Greenwich, Conn.: JAI Press, 1986), pp. 269–306.

satisfaction is significantly related to both union activity and actual voting for union representation when elections are held.[6]

Employees vote for unions more often as their dissatisfaction increases. Also, employees in units with organizing activity that is not sufficient to lead to a representation election are more dissatisfied than in units where activity does not occur. Individuals are influenced to vote for unions more by dissatisfaction with employment conditions than by job task characteristics. Dissatisfaction with **job security,** economics, and supervisory practices were most predictive of a prounion vote across a set of studied elections.[7] Table 1–1 summarizes these findings. Attitudes predicting the presence and level of organizing activity in units of one large multilocation company centered around supervision, co-worker friction, amount of work required, career progression, feelings about the company, physical surroundings, and the kind of work done.

Dissatisfaction alone does not automatically mean a union-organizing campaign will result or an election will be won by the union. Two conditions have to exist to predict organizing attempts and a union win. First, individuals have to be dissatisfied and believe that they are individually unable to influence a change in the conditions causing dissatisfaction. Second, a majority of employees have to believe collective bargaining would improve conditions and the benefits outweigh the costs.[8]

The creation of unions and the tenacious struggle of some employee groups to secure collective bargaining are examined in Chapters 2 and 3. Chapter 6 studies union-organizing campaigns. Chapters 8 and 9 consider the specific demands unions and managements make in collective bargaining. All of these issues help explain why workers attempt to unionize. This introduction is concerned with a general explanation of why workers join unions and what they expect unions will accomplish that they are unable to achieve individually.

Individuals and Union Organizing

In an organizing campaign, people must decide whether unionization is in their best interest. To make this decision, individuals assess what the likely outcomes of unionization will be, whether each outcome is positive

[6] Julius G. Getman, Stephen B. Goldberg, and Jeanne B. Herman, *Union Representation Elections: Law and Reality*, (New York: Russell Sage Foundation, 1976); W. Clay Hamner and Frank J. Smith, "Work Attitudes as Predictors of Unionization Activity," *Journal of Applied Psychology* 63 (1978), pp. 415–21; and Chester A. Schreisheim, "Job Satisfaction, Attitudes toward Unions, and Voting in a Union Representation Election," *Journal of Applied Psychology* 63 (1978), pp. 548–52.

[7] Jeanne M. Brett, "Why Employees Want Unions," *Organizational Dynamics* 8, no. 4 (1980), pp. 47–59.

[8] Ibid., pp. 48–49.

TABLE 1-1

Correlation between Job Satisfaction and Voting for Union Representation

Issue	Correlation with Vote for Union
Are you satisfied with the job security at this company?	−.42
Are you satisfied with your wages?	−.40
Taking everything into consideration, are you satisfied with this company as a place to work?	−.36
Do supervisors in this company treat all employees alike?	−.34
Are you satisfied with your fringe benefits?	−.31
Do your supervisors show appreciation when you do a good job?	−.30
Do you think there is a good chance for you to get promoted in this company?	−.30
Are you satisfied with the type of work you are doing?	−.14

SOURCE: Adapted from Jeanne M. Brett, "Why Employees Want Unions," *Organizational Dynamics* 8, no. 4 (1980), p. 51. Reprinted by permission of the publisher. Copyright © 1980 by AMACOM, a division of American Management Associations. All rights reserved.

or negative, and the likelihood that their working for or voting for a union will lead to the positive or negative outcomes. An individual might first examine the present job situation and assess the possibility of receiving positive or negative outcomes as a result of holding that job. Where a job has some negative outcomes, individuals may weigh such actions as convincing supervisors or management to behave differently, doing nothing, or organizing to change the situation. A person's experience with the efficacy of a particular action determines whether that action will be pursued or abandoned. Figure 1-1 outlines a motivational model that follows this approach.[9]

Figure 1-2 depicts a hypothetical belief system for two employees in a situation where organizing is being considered. The figure suggests that each employee evaluates the likely outcomes from organization. The same set of outcomes and valuations is specified for both employees in the example, but the outcomes are not required to be the same, especially if the employees have major individual differences. Examining the outcomes and their valuations reveals differences between the two individuals. Individual A positively values a union leadership position, while B

[9] This is a variant on the expectancy model of motivation. For further information, see Victor H. Vroom, *Work and Motivation* (New York: John Wiley & Sons, 1964); Lyman W. Porter and Edward E. Lawler III, *Managerial Attitudes and Performance* (Homewood, Ill.: Richard D. Irwin 1968); and Edwin E. Lawler III, *Motivation in Work Organizations* (Monterey, Calif.: Brooks/Cole Publishing, 1973).

FIGURE 1-1

A Motivation Model

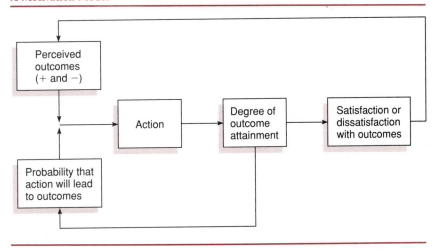

apparently attaches no positive or negative value to it. Other differences also exist, such as preferences for individual treatment.

The next explanatory component links the outcomes with the result of an action—in this case, success or failure in organizing. For individual A, success in organizing is associated with six positive and two negative outcomes. Failure to organize leads to one positive, one negative, and two neutral items. If individual A believes taking action will increase the likelihood of unionization, efforts to do so would be expected because the greater net balance of positive outcomes results from a union. Individual B, on the other hand, expects four positives and three negatives from a union and four positives and one neutral from no union. B would be predicted to oppose the union.

Some consequences could follow directly from the action taken rather than the result of the action. For example, if individual A thinks neither working for nor against the union will affect the organizing campaign outcome, then no effort would be expected. Why? It's easier. But, effort would be predicted from individual A if A thinks it's necessary for organization and believes his or her effort will contribute to winning the election.

Some might argue that this model makes it difficult to predict what people in a group will do. This is the case if group members have extremely diverse backgrounds or widely differing beliefs as to what actions will lead to results or what outcomes will follow from results. However, a number of things might reduce this diversity.

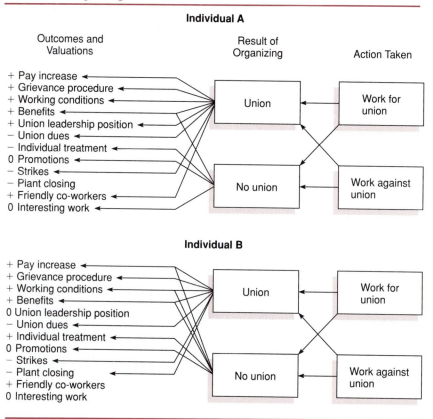

FIGURE 1-2

Beliefs about Organizing

Individual A

Outcomes and Valuations	Result of Organizing	Action Taken

+ Pay increase
+ Grievance procedure
+ Working conditions
+ Benefits
+ Union leadership position
– Union dues
– Individual treatment
0 Promotions
– Strikes
– Plant closing
+ Friendly co-workers
0 Interesting work

Union

No union

Work for union

Work against union

Individual B

+ Pay increase
+ Grievance procedure
+ Working conditions
+ Benefits
0 Union leadership position
– Union dues
+ Individual treatment
0 Promotions
– Strikes
– Plant closing
+ Friendly co-workers
0 Interesting work

Union

No union

Work for union

Work against union

Employees often see avenues other than union membership to attain valued outcomes from employment. For example, if promotions and interesting work are highly valued but seen as unattainable on the jobs likely to be unionized, then many of the employees desiring them would probably leave. Achievable, positive, past job outcomes also become increasingly important to employees. Thus, unionizing attempts may begin because management withholds rewards or changes the system so rewards differ from what people in the jobs value.

The degree to which unionization is seen as leading to the attainment of positive outcomes and the avoidance of negative outcomes may also be changed through campaign attempts. Both labor and management attempt to direct employees toward a stronger belief that unionization will have positive and negative consequences, respectively.

Examining the perceptions and choices individuals make about unions should make it clear that, before unionization is possible, employees must hold a common belief that a union will benefit them. This means a large heterogeneous unit would probably be difficult to organize, whereas a smaller, more stable employment situation should be more easily organized.

BELIEFS ABOUT UNIONS

Each of us has beliefs about the appropriate role of organized labor in society. These beliefs result from our upbringing and experiences, involvement with union members, work in union or nonunion organizations, and the gains or costs we perceive to be associated with organized labor.

Surveys conducted during the late 1970s and early 1980s give a clearer idea of how American workers view labor unions.[10] Nonunion respondents were asked whether they would vote for a union if a representation election were held where they work. Union members were asked what their unions ought to be involved in, what unions were actually involved in, their degree of participation in union affairs, and their satisfaction with the union.

Beliefs of Employees in General

Survey results suggest the public sees unions as powerful and selfish. In general, unions are seen as out for themselves, more powerful than employers, and able to strongly influence legislation. As might be expected, older persons and white-collar employees were more likely to hold these beliefs, whereas union members, women, nonwhites, public-sector employees, and Southerners were less likely. Overall, however, a majority of *both* unionized and nonunionized employees shared these beliefs.

However, the survey also found that respondents believed unions were effective in protecting workers from unfair treatment and in improving wages and job security. More positive attitudes were held by union members, more highly educated individuals, and southern residents. Table 1–2 details the respondents' beliefs.

When individuals have been asked whether they would vote for a union if they were involved in a representation election, about one third have said they would. Different sets of attitudes appear to influence feelings about a prounion vote. Perceptions of the power of the labor movement and its instrumentality for worker gains are important, but so are specific beliefs the individual has about the effects of the union on

---

[10] Thomas A. Kochan, "How American Workers View Labor Unions," *Monthly Labor Review* 102, no. 4 (1979), pp. 23–31; and a 1984 Harris poll conducted for the AFL-CIO Evolution of Work Committee.

TABLE 1-2

American Workers' Beliefs about Trade Unions (in percent)*

Beliefs	Strongly Agree	Agree	Neither Agree Nor Disagree	Disagree	Strongly Disagree
Big-labor-image beliefs:					
Influence who gets elected to public office	37.5%	46.0%	1.8%	12.7%	1.1%
Influence laws passed	24.0	56.6	3.8	14.4	1.2
Are more powerful than employers	24.8	41.6	6.2	25.4	2.0
Influence how the country is run	18.1	53.4	4.8	21.7	1.9
Require members to go along with decisions	18.5	56.0	3.9	20.1	1.6
Have leaders who do what's best for themselves	22.8	44.7	6.4	24.0	2.1
Instrumental beliefs:					
Protect workers against unfair practice	20.5	63.0	3.4	11.2	2.0
Improve job security	19.2	61.0	2.8	14.5	2.5
Improve wages	18.9	67.6	3.2	8.7	1.7
Give members their money's (dues') worth	6.9	38.5	6.3	36.9	11.3

* In the survey, 1,515 workers were polled.

SOURCE: Thomas A. Kochan, "How American Workers View Labor Unions," *Monthly Labor Review*, 102, no. 4 (1979), p. 24.

personal intrinsic and extrinsic outcomes and the introduction of more fairness into the employment setting.[11] Membership in unions has declined substantially since the middle 1950s. Some of this is due to structural change, but some is also related to changing perceptions of union members and the general public. Between 1977 and 1984, beliefs about the ability of unions to enhance employment conditions declined while job satisfaction increased for employees in nonunion employers and declined for those in unionized employers.[12]

The local community and its beliefs also affect individuals and union power. Unions influence the political makeup in the community, and the depth of union support among members and individual community members who may not be union members helps to determine the union's ability to gain important collective bargaining outcomes. Community influence is most likely when an outcome of a dispute unfavorable to labor strongly threatens the community.[13]

---

[11] S. P. Deshpande and Jack Fiorito, "Specific and General Beliefs in Union Voting Models," *Academy of Management Journal* 32 (1989), pp. 883–97.

[12] Henry S. Farber, "Trends in Worker Demand for Union Representation," *American Economic Review* 79, no. 2 (1989), pp. 161–65.

[13] James A. Craft, "The Community as a Source of Union Power," *Journal of Labor Research* 11 (1990), pp. 145–60.

Nonunion Respondents

Among individuals in occupations eligible for unionization, almost one third said they would vote for a union in a representation election. For blue-collar workers, attitudes and characteristics most strongly associated with a propensity to vote for a union included difficulty in exerting influence, severity of job dangers, inadequate income, member of a racial minority, and beliefs that unions are effective in gaining important outcomes. Factors leading to a likely vote against a union were residence in the north central United States and government employment. White-collar workers expressing dissatisfaction with bread-and-butter issues and the nature of their work showed a willingness to vote for the union. Other important issues that influenced the direction of white-collar workers' votes were desired on-the-job influence, inadequate fringe benefits, inequitable pay, being a racial minority group member, beliefs about labor's ability to gain important ends (all positive), and residence in the north central region (negative).

Persons who would vote against a union generally believed their jobs were satisfactory, and/or they preferred to deal with their employer on an individual rather than collective basis.

Union Members

Union members place the highest priorities on the following issues: the union's handling of grievances, getting feedback from their unions, additional fringe benefits, having a say in the union, better wages, and job security. The preferences of union members for bargaining outcomes will be covered in much greater detail in Chapters 8 and 9. Generally, union members are satisfied with the performance of their unions, particularly on economic issues. The 73 percent satisfaction rate is about the same as the historic job satisfaction rate in the United States.[14]

Among a sample of public-sector union members who could choose to join or not join the union that represented them, satisfaction with the union's performance was related to beliefs in the goals of the union movement and endorsement of the union's preferred positions on promotions and job security. Less favorable attitudes were found among those who joined for social reasons or who felt pressured to join.[15]

---

[14] Thomas J. Chacko and Charles R. Greer, "Perceptions of Union Power, Service, and Confidence in Labor Leaders: A Study of Member and Nonmember Differences," *Journal of Labor Research* 3 (1982), pp. 211–21.

[15] Michael E. Gordon and Larry N. Long, "Demographic and Attitudinal Correlates of Union Joining," *Industrial Relations* 21 (1981), pp. 306–11.

AREAS OF FRUSTRATION

Few employers find themselves targeted with an **organizing campaign** soon after they open their doors and hire employees. A union-organizing campaign begins when something in the employment relationship causes employees to determine their expectations are not being met or they are being treated unfairly in relation to others.

General preferences for job outcomes vary across occupations, but several classes of outcomes, including compensation policies and practices, advancements and transfers, rules and discipline, and supervisory practices and decisions, may be of considerable importance to large groups of employees.[16]

Employees may find they are earning less than comparable employees in other organizations. They may also find their employer is making considerably higher profits than in the past and has a greater ability to pay. Promotions may be awarded on the basis of favoritism or other criteria that seem irrelevant or unfair to those interested in advancement. Employees may believe seniority norms should govern advancements and transfers. Supervisors may be seen as imposing discipline or offering rewards capriciously. Differences between shifts and units in terms of supervisory behavior may be noted. All of these factors may stimulate the desire for union organization if they are perceived by a large enough group of employees.

COLLECTIVE BEHAVIOR

Groups form for a variety of reasons. Some groups evolve because of mutual interests or similarities. These common interests might be necessary for union formation. Another reason groups form is to react to perceived danger or threat. An employer who exercises a fear campaign in supervision may lead to this type of collective behavior. "Wagon-circling" behavior seems to be a pervasive phenomenon. Studies of inexperienced combat troops in World War II found they tended to group when under fire, even though spreading out reduced their vulnerability to attack. Other studies indicate that assisting or affiliating behavior requires that the danger be applicable to a majority of individuals in an area before group activities occur.[17]

When individuals are dissatisfied with their present employment, one might ask why they don't simply leave. These employees may believe they

---

[16] Lloyd H. Lofquist and Rene V. Dawis, *Adjustment to Work* (New York: Appleton-Century-Crofts, 1970).

[17] See, for example, Stanley Schachter, *The Psychology of Affiliation: Experimental Studies of the Sources of Gregariousness* (Stanford, Calif.: Stanford University Press, 1959).

have invested parts of their lives with their employers or alternative employment will be hard to find. One theory suggests that people can dissent in two ways—either by leaving an organization (exit option) or by trying to change conditions within it (voice option).[18] Forming a union enables use of a collective voice in influencing change at work.

Group Cohesiveness

A group is labeled *cohesive* when a generally low variance in behavior of the group's members is observed. Many studies show that the productivity of some work groups remains relatively constant over time and varies little among members. This indicates group members are adhering to a collectively adopted output norm.

What are the underlying reasons for cohesiveness? First, the members of the group are likely to hold the same basic values and to agree on the methods used for their attainment. Second, age, seniority, and other background characteristics are probably quite similar. Third, the group has probably informally chosen a group leader. This member often has values closest to the overall values of the group. Finally, cohesiveness may be a function of external threat.

If external threat increases cohesiveness, how does it do so, and is the relationship linear or at least monotonic? Expectancy theory can answer the first part of this question. If someone perceives that negative outcomes will occur for one who must act alone but not for one acting within a group, then acting as a group is perceived to have positive consequences. If a united front is perceived to be strong, then cohesiveness will be high. If an employer is unwilling to grant a wage increase to a single employee and dares the employee to quit, the same employer might not be willing to risk denying a collectively demanded raise if the alternative is a strike.

How far would we expect group members to go in individually sacrificing for the good of the group? When the costs of membership outweigh the benefits perceived from remaining a group member, cohesiveness will break down. As Figure 1-3 shows, the hypothetical relationship between threat and cohesiveness is an inverted U.

Unions cannot ensure background similarities among their members because management makes the hiring decisions and unions are obligated to admit all employees who desire membership. Thus, only one avenue is available to the union to maintain cohesiveness—perceived threats from management. To maintain cohesiveness through threat, an adversarial relationship is necessary. Thus, management acting against

---

[18] A. O. Hirschman, *Exit, Voice, and Loyalty* (Cambridge, Mass.: Harvard University Press, 1970).

FIGURE 1–3
Hypothesized Relationship between Threat and Cohesiveness

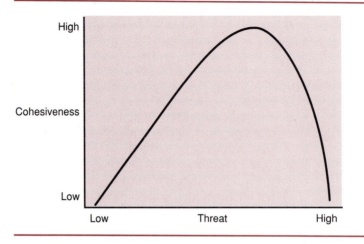

individuals or the group may be to the union's benefit because management action can then be rebuffed, modified, or rescinded through what
members perceive as group action.

UNIONS, THEIR MEMBERS, AND DECISION MAKING

It's necessary in understanding the activities of unions to recognize their
officers are elected by the members and contracts require ratification by
the members. **Local unions** are not organized until a majority of employees desire representation; officers are elected or defeated by majorities of
local union members; and contracts are ratified by a majority of the
membership. Ultimately, the policies of large national unions are influenced strongly by the actions of majorities of local union members.

For specific union decisions requiring votes, it's helpful to understand
the concept of a **median voter**.[19] To obtain a majority in any two-issue
decision, the chosen alternative must be favored by the person who
occupies the middle political position in the union on that issue since a
majority requires 50 percent plus one. Thus, to predict the outcome of an
election or ratification, an analyst must learn the preferences of the
middle person on a continuum of attitudes toward an issue. The median
voter concept will be discussed at several points in this book when
covering union decision making.

[19] Michael D. White, "The Intra-Unit Wage Structure and Unions: A Median Voter
Model," *Industrial and Labor Relations Review* 35 (1982), pp. 565–77.

LABOR UNIONS IN THE 1990s

As noted earlier in this chapter, the 1980s was a decade of decline for organized labor as economic changes, coupled with employer and governmental initiatives, surprised unions and eroded membership. The 1990s will be a decade in which unions face crucial structural and functional problems whose results will likely affect the future viability of organized labor. One set of commentators suggests the U.S. legislative climate, along with a decline in membership, has retarded organizing, representation, and bargaining outcomes relative to the past and compared to Canadian unions.[20] Another position is that the decline can be traced to aggressive actions by employers to fight organizing campaigns, build new plants where they will not be initially unionized and where antipathy toward unions probably exists, and violate or ignore labor laws aimed at protecting collective bargaining.[21] Another position is that larger numbers of employees were organized in the past than actually preferred to be represented, partly because of coercive organizing tactics in which unionized employees of an employer refused to deal with nonunion employees. Legislation outlawing this behavior coincides with the beginning of the decline in unionization.[22] Finally, it's argued that the employment relationship in union and nonunion firms is substantially different. Nonunion employees may be treated more consistently in promotions and pay increases, have more involvement in managing production, be subject to fewer rules, and have a more leisurely work pace.[23]

A historical perspective suggests the economic history of the United States is strongly related to the relatively small proportion of the work force belonging to unions. While U.S. unions have waxed and waned at various points during the past two centuries, several conditions may have prevented their empowerment.

First, employers fiercely protected and unions ceded to them the capitalist, market-driven system the United States has embraced. Thus, prices, and ultimately wages, are controlled by the market rather than by collective bargaining or administrative order. Second, with the exception of the skilled trades, employers have always controlled the content of jobs. Even the trades have been increasingly defined by employers

[20] Gary N. Chaison and Joseph B. Rose, "New Directions and Divergent Paths: The North American Labor Movements in Troubled Times," *Labor Law Journal* 41 (1990), pp. 591–95.

[21] Richard B. Freeman, "Contraction and Expansion of Unionism in the Private and Public Sector," *Journal of Economic Perspectives* 2, no. 2 (1988), pp. 63–88.

[22] Melvin W. Reder, "The Rise and Fall of Unions: The Public Sector and the Private," *Journal of Economic Perspectives* 2, no. 2 (1988), pp. 89–110.

[23] J. Evansohn, "The Effects of Mechanisms of Management Control on Unionization," *Industrial Relations* 28 (1989), pp. 91–103.

through attempts to blur trade boundaries. Third, employers have historically been involved with the U.S. educational system, especially the high schools, colleges, and universities that have the closest relationship to developing skills of future employees. Ironically, given organized labor's strong advocacy of free public education, this has occurred within the public as well as the private school systems. Fourth, business has been strongly involved with government, in advocating legislation, in providing executives for public policy positions, and in using the courts to litigate labor problems. Fifth, and probably most telling, the United States has had a large middle class that has had strong interests in efficiency and productivity. If an income distribution is perceived as fair by the middle class, then support for collective bargaining would not be strong.[24]

The fifth point—the effect of the middle class—appears to be the most important (recognizing that it's also related to the others). The future vitality of the labor movement depends on a class consciousness developing or a perception by the middle class that the income distribution *is* unfair. If the middle class decreases in size, relative to the upper and lower classes, then the lower class could exert more power through unions because efficiency claims would not be as strong. If the income distribution is perceived as unfair, the middle class may seek collective bargaining as a method for restoring an appropriate balance. These issues lead to a challenge for the labor movement in the 1990s.

The challenge involves membership. Traditionally, union membership occurred through a collective bargaining agreement in the workplace. If employment was lost, the union member often terminated membership. Only in the building trades, the maritime unions, and some entertainment unions did membership survive the end of employment with a particular employer. The reason it did was that the union was the primary source of employees through union hiring halls and other training and development activities. If employees in the future have increasingly temporary ties to an employer, industrial unions may take on the same features as the building trades. They could offer continuity in benefits and training programs to improve occupational skills and to enable members to excel in comparison to nonmembers. If industrial unions don't offer these services and act only as a collective bargaining agent, they will find it increasingly difficult to attract members in a transient employment environment.

---

[24] For a provocative expansion of these issues, see David Montgomery, *The Fall of the House of Labor* (New York: Cambridge University Press, 1987).

SUMMARY AND PREVIEW

This study of labor relations will examine the historical development of the labor movement, the structure of union organizations and federal agencies involved in labor relations, and the processes of collective bargaining, including the identification of bargaining issues, negotiations, and contract administration.

Evidence suggests that employee dissatisfaction leads to interest in organizing. For the most part, the general population sees unions and their leaders as out for their own interests but effective in achieving their goals. A significant minority of unorganized employees say they would vote for union representation if an election were held in their work unit. Feelings about unions have remained quite stable recently.

Cohesiveness appears to be a necessary property for successful organization. Similarities among group members and external threats have a positive influence on cohesiveness. The adversary role that unions take is likely to enhance the cohesiveness of their memberships.

Plan of the Book

The title, *Labor Relations: Development, Structure, Process*, was not chosen haphazardly. The first part of the title indicates a focus on the employment relationship in unionized settings. The words following the colon establish the topical flow of the book.

Development

The present state of the labor movement and collective bargaining is the result of a variety of economic and social situations in which strategic choices were made by labor leaders and managers. In examining the *development* of the labor movement, the conditions related to the initial formation of unions must be understood. Public opinion influenced the response of public officials toward both the subsequent formation of unions and their operation.

Other areas of interest concern the reactions of employers to unions. Where did unionization begin? In what industrial sectors have unions been most prevalent? How have the parties adapted to each other over the long run? What are the present stances of employers toward unions, and where are the greatest changes occurring?

Chapters 2, 3, and 4 address development issues, tracing the historical evolution and present public policy environment in which American labor operates. Although union activity has occurred throughout the history of the country, effective labor organizations are just over 100 years old. These chapters indicate that labor law and its enforcement have played an important role in the development of collective bargaining. The development chapters trace societal and economic changes and detail the statutes that have contributed to the development and particular shape of collective bargaining in the United States. In particular, legislation passed in the 1930s to protect employees in forming unions and engaging in collective bargaining contributed to union growth.

Structure

The examination of union *structure* focuses on the office and institutions that either make up the labor movement or have major impacts on it. In this regard, the last part of Chapter 4 details the federal institutions involved in regulating collective bargaining. Chapter 5 examines the various organizational levels in the labor movement and identifies the location of the power centers within the movement. Chapter 5 also discusses the organizational structure of several national unions, the roles played by union officers, and the causes and consequences of the recent increase in union mergers. The various structures within which negotiations between labor and management take place are detailed in Chapter 7.

Process

The greatest emphasis in this text is on *process*. This section concerns methods used to organize employees into unions, identifies issues of importance in bargaining, explains the organization and processes involved in negotiations, and details how labor and management deal with differences that occur during bargaining and after a contract has been signed. These areas are covered in Chapters 6 through 14.

Special Chapters

The last three chapters of the book involve special issues that cut across development, structure, and process areas. Chapter 15 covers collective bargaining in the public sector and issues unique to it. Chapter 16 examines the recent increase among private-sector employers in implementing formal policies and programs for nonunion employment relations. Chapter 17 examines some of the differences between unions and labor relations in the United States and other industrialized nations.

Preview

In this text, each chapter begins by introducing the subject and highlighting some major issues that should be explored to gain an understanding of the development, structure, or process of labor-management relations.

Most chapters end with discussion questions. These either relate to relatively broad issues raised in the chapter or ask that a position be formulated for labor or for management on one of these issues. Many chapters also conclude with case material. Most of these cases relate to a simulated organization, General Materials & Fabrication Corporation (GMFC), a heavy-equipment manufacturer. The first case involving GMFC follows Chapter 6. Later, a mock negotiation exercise, contract administration cases, and cases discussing arbitration issues arising from the contract are presented. These cases should help you gain a greater appreciation of the process involved in the collective bargaining relationship.

Point of View

Most readers of this book are or have been employed, but most have probably not been union members, and most do not expect to be union members. But readers have likely formed attitudes toward labor unions and collective bargaining through information provided by the news media. Media attention is usually focused on unusual events. In labor relations, this usually means a major negotiation, strike, lockout, or an unlawful practice charge. The media shouldn't be faulted for this— excitement draws viewers and sell newspapers, but it does not reflect day-to-day labor relations in the United States. Overt disagreement, reflected in strikes, lockouts, and unlawful practices, occurs relatively infrequently.

This text includes information to increase your ability to understand labor relations as it is practiced in the United States. This understanding must be based on the evolution and development of the labor movement to its present form, the subject matter and jurisdiction of labor law, and the practices of the two major parties in the process—management and labor.

The subject should be interesting. In teaching courses in organizational behavior, personnel/human resource management, and labor relations, I have always found that most students are more intrinsically interested in labor relations than in the other two. Perhaps this is because we are likely to have strong attitudes about what we think are the proper roles each party should take in the process and notions about which side should be blamed for the problems surrounding labor relations. I do not expect your basic posture toward labor relations to change as a result of either this book or the course you are in, but I expect you to gain a far greater understanding of why the parties act as they do. I also expect you to become more willing to agree that, in most instances, both parties do a good job of representing their constituents and settling conflicts, thereby minimizing disruptions in their organizations and, as a result, minimizing disruptions to the public.

KEY TERMS

unions

monopoly power

representation

collective bargaining

job security

organizing campaign

local unions

median voter

2

THE EVOLUTION OF AMERICAN LABOR: I

Labor relations in the United States has a history as old as the nation. Understanding the present operation and goals of the American labor movement requires an understanding of the events, personalities, and philosophies that shaped it. Among the questions that need to be asked are the following: What are the concerns of the labor movement and how do concerns in the United States differ from those in other countries? How has the movement grown, and in what occupational and industrial sectors is its strength currently growing or waning? What place has organized labor been accorded by public opinion and the development of public policy over time? The next three chapters examine the history of the American labor movement and trace the evolution, growth, and demise of major labor organizations. The American labor movement has been predominantly results oriented rather than ideologically oriented. Surviving labor organizations have adapted to change and been responsive to member needs.

This chapter concentrates on the path the labor movement traveled from the nation's founding to the end of the 1920s. Particular questions you should ask include:

1. What was the legal, public policy, and public opinion climate surrounding early American labor relations? Consider the influence of legislators, judges, and the news media on early labor relations.

2. What form did the American labor movement develop? Be aware of the properties that appear necessary for success in the United States. Ask whether the ingredients change over time.

3. What types of events contributed to and detracted from union growth? Do these still operate in the same manner?

4. How have the personalities of the major actors within the labor movement contributed to union growth?

EARLY UNIONS AND THE CONSPIRACY DOCTRINE

The genesis of the American labor movement parallels the birth of the nation. In 1778, the first successful collective action to win a wage increase was implemented by the New York **journeyman** printers.[1] However, union growth in the United States did not keep pace with the growth of the nation during most of the following 200 years. Substantial impediments were raised by legal decisions, the predominantly rural nature of 19th-century America, and the substantial number of relatively unskilled immigrants who competed for jobs at relatively low wages. In fact, most collective actions through the 19th century were aimed at resisting wage cuts rather than attempting to gain increases.

Philadelphia Cordwainers

The Federal Society of Journeyman Cordwainers (shoemakers) was organized in Philadelphia in 1794.[2] Its formation resulted from some substantial changes in the way shoes were marketed. Until about 1790, journeymen had been almost exclusively involved in the manufacture of "bespoke" (custom) work. Master shoemakers took orders and supplied material for the journeymen, who produced a pair of shoes or boots for an agreed wage. This arrangement required that the customer be willing to wait for completion of the work. Because this was inconvenient and expensive, three other market classes were developed by the masters. These were "shop," "order," and "market" work. Shop work was for the master's stock, order work was for wholesalers, and market work was to sell in the public market. Each commanded a lower price than its predecessor, and the master attempted to differentiate wage rates depending on the type of market being supplied. The journeymen cordwainers responded by attempting to fix wages for shoemaking at the rate paid for bespoke work. This attempt was a forerunner of the union demand of equal pay for equal work.

The cordwainers' refusal to work at rates that varied depending on the ultimate market for their output was seen by the employers as a criminal act. The courts found that the collective actions of the cordwainers in pursuit of their personal interests contravened the interests of citizens in general and was, hence, a criminal conspiracy. Each member of the

[1] U.S. Department of Labor, Bureau of Labor Statistics, *A Brief History of the American Labor Movement*, Bulletin 1000, rev. (Washington, D.C.: U.S. Government Printing Office, 1970), p. 99.
[2] For a thorough analysis of this group, see John R. Commons, *Labor and Administration* (New York: Macmillan, 1973), pp. 210–64.

EXHIBIT 2-1

Charge to the Jury in the Philadelphia Cordwainers Case

"What is the case before us? . . . A combination of workmen to raise their wages may be considered in a twofold point of view: one is to benefit themselves . . . the other is to injure those who do not join their society. The rule of law condemns both. . . . [T]he rule in this case is pregnant with sound sense and all the authorities are clear on the subject. Hawkins, the greatest authority on criminal law, has laid it down, that a combination to maintain one another, carrying a particular object, whether true or false, is criminal. . . ."

SOURCE: Condensed from 3 Commons and Gilmore 228–33, which was partially reprinted in Jerre S. Williams, *Labor Relations and the Law*, 3rd ed. (Boston: Little, Brown, 1965), p. 20.

union was fined $8 on conviction (see Exhibit 2–1).[3] This decision established the **conspiracy doctrine,** under which a union could be punished if either its *means* or *ends* were deemed illegal by the courts.

Commonwealth v. *Hunt*

In 1842, the conspiracy doctrine was softened substantially by the Massachusetts Supreme Court's decision in *Commonwealth* v. *Hunt*.[4] This decision set aside the conviction of members of the Boston Journeymen Bootmakers' Society for refusing to work in shops where nonmembers worked for less than the negotiated rate. The court held that the society's action was primarily to persuade nonmembers to join the organization rather than to secure criminal ends. The court refused to enjoin organizing activities, but it did not say that injunctions against other collective activities would be stopped (see Exhibit 2–2).[5]

Pre–Civil War Unions

During the first half of the 19th century, unions were faced with a number of problems, including employers who did not see them as legitimate organizations, courts that enjoined and punished collective activity, and competition from a growing supply of immigrant labor. But even in the face of these impediments, collective activity still occurred. Most was among skilled artisans, such as the cordwainers, but even unskilled textile workers in Massachusetts became involved.

---

[3] Jerre S. Williams, *Labor Relations and the Law*, 3rd ed. (Boston: Little, Brown, 1965), p. 18.

[4] 4 Metcalf 111 (1842).

[5] Williams, *Labor Relations and the Law*, p. 22.

EXHIBIT 2-2

Interpretation of Conspiracy Doctrine
under *Commonwealth* v. *Hunt*

"The manifest intention of the association is to induce all those engaged in the same occupation to become members of it. Such a purpose is not unlawful. It would give them a power which might be exerted for useful and honorable purposes, or for dangerous and pernicious ones. If the latter were the real and actual object and susceptible of proof, it should have been specially charged. . . . In this state of things, we cannot perceive that it is criminal for men to agree to exercise their acknowledged rights in such a manner as best to subserve their own interests."

SOURCE: 4 Metcalf 129, as contained in Jerre S. Williams, *Labor Relations and the Law*, 3rd ed. (Boston: Little, Brown, 1965), p. 22.

Workingmen's parties were organized and contributed to the election of President Andrew Jackson.[6] Following Jackson, Martin Van Buren promulgated an executive order decreasing the length of the workday for federal employees to 10 hours. Unions in major U.S. cities successfully used strikes to secure wage increases. Union membership swelled in the early 1830s, but poor economic conditions soon tipped the scales in favor of employers, and union activity waned where membership threatened one's continued employment.

THE BIRTH OF NATIONAL UNIONS

Beginning in the 1850s, a number of national trade unions were formed. Of those formed at this early stage, all have either disappeared or merged into other surviving unions. Until the end of the Civil War, the unions represented only certain trades or industries. This pattern ultimately prevailed in American unions, with workers joining unions representing their skills or industries. After the Civil War, however, the first major movements were organized on a national scope, without craft or industry distinctions. As will be noted, the labor movement was involved heavily in many of the major public policy issues of the 19th century. Immigration policy posed a problem for unions because while many members were immigrants, they feared the effects immigration would have on their earnings levels. Many civil organizations opposed free immigration and

---

6 See Foster Rhea Dulles, *Labor in America*, 3rd ed. (New York: Crowell, 1966), pp. 35–52.

advocated literacy tests. Trade unions gravitated toward these positions at the end of the 1800s, partly in a bid to attain mainstream legitimacy as social institutions.[7]

The National Labor Union

The **National Labor Union** (NLU) was founded at a convention in Baltimore in 1866. Its goals were largely political and reformist rather than economic or immediate. Its leader, William Sylvis, had been instrumental in organizing the National Molders' Union in 1859. NLU goals included introduction of the eight-hour workday, establishment of consumer and producer cooperatives, reform of currency and banking laws, limitation on immigration, and establishment of a federal department of labor.

The NLU was open not only to skilled trades workers but also to other interested and sympathetic individuals. Suffragists, particularly prominent at its national meetings, attempted to get the NLU to endorse their efforts to gain voting rights for women.

Sylvis was the backbone of the NLU; but, with his death in 1869 and the NLU's subsequent alliance with the Greenback party in 1872, the movement failed. The lack of leadership and inattention to worker problems contributed most to the NLU's demise.[8] However, the first attempts to coordinate labor organizations nationally had begun—and would ultimately be successful.

The Knights of Labor

The **Knights of Labor** was organized in Philadelphia in 1869. Its goals and membership, while different from those ultimately embodied in the U.S. labor movement, more closely approximated the final pattern than did the NLU. It was part labor organization and part fraternal lodge. Workers were organized on a city-by-city basis across crafts rather than primarily along craft lines. When a city assembly (the Knights' local unit) had a group of members from a particular craft large enough to be self-sustaining, another assembly was spun off. A basic position of the Knights of Labor held that all workers had common interests that blurred craft distinctions.

---

[7] C. Collomp, "Unions, Civics, and National Identify: Organized Labor's Reaction to Immigration, 1881–1897," *Labor History* 29 (1988), pp. 450–74.

[8] Dulles, *Labor in America*, pp. 100–13.

From a philosophical standpoint, the Knights of Labor was more willing to recognize the short-term legitimacy of capitalism than was the NLU. The leaders of the Knights—first Uriah Stephens, then Terence Powderly—were essentially idealists who advocated such tactics as favoring arbitration over strikes. Employers used these prestated positions to their advantage. But in confrontation situations, the rank and file were more militant than the leadership in their use of strikes to counter employer initiatives.

The Knights of Labor grew slowly. It took three years to gain enough members to establish a second assembly in Philadelphia. In 1873, the first district assembly (a collection of five assemblies) was created, and by 1875, district assemblies had headquarters in Reading and Pittsburgh, Pennsylvania, as well. Because it was a secret society, the Knights of Labor was in conflict with the Roman Catholic Church. Clergy believed that members of the Knights might be required to take secret oaths that might commit them to beliefs inconsistent with Roman Catholic dogma. Ultimately, negotiations between Terence Powderly and James Cardinal Gibbons led to a ruling that Roman Catholics could belong to the Knights.[9]

As often occurred during the 19th century, the country entered a depression in the beginning of the 1880s. These periods had usually taken their toll on labor organizations in the past, but this time the strength of the Knights of Labor grew. In a number of railroad strikes in 1882 and 1883, the Knights successfully organized workers and won their demands—a sharp contrast to the crushing defeat railroad strikers suffered in 1877. When railroad financier Jay Gould attempted to break the union by laying off its members in 1885, the union's strike on the Wabash Railroad and its refusal to handle Wabash rolling stock on other lines forced him to cease discriminating against Knights of Labor members. The nationally publicized negotiations surrounding this dispute gave added impetus to organization, so by the middle of 1886, membership in the Knights of Labor reached 700,000.[10]

There was a degree of irony in the Knights' success against Jay Gould.[11] A large influx of new members entered the ranks to gain the same types of concessions from their employers that Gould had given. But the position of Powderly and the other leaders was much more long-run oriented than just the satisfaction of day-to-day grievances. They did not espouse a collective bargaining approach that would lead to an

---

[9] Philip Taft, *Organized Labor in American History* (New York: Harper & Row, 1964), pp. 84–89.

[10] Dulles, *Labor in America*, pp. 139–41.

[11] Neil W. Chamberlain and Donald E. Cullen, *The Labor Sector*, 2nd ed. (New York: McGraw-Hill, 1971), pp. 97–98.

EXHIBIT 2-3

The Ascetic Terence Powderly on Labor Picnics

"I will talk at no picnics. When I speak on the labor question, I want the individual attention of my hearers, and I want that attention for at least two hours, and in that two hours I can only epitomize. At a picnic where the girls as well as the boys swill beer I cannot talk at all. . . . If it comes to my ears that I am advertised to speak at picnics . . . I will prefer charges against the offenders for holding the executive head of the Order up to ridicule. . . ."

SOURCE: Foster Rhea Dulles, *Labor in America: A History*, 3rd ed. (New York: Crowell, 1966), p. 136.

---

ultimate goal on a piecemeal basis. They also firmly opposed using the strike as a weapon for pressuring employers. The long-run perspective of the leadership and its belief in "rational" processes for achieving ultimate objectives is typified by these quotes from Powderly and Knights of Labor publications: "You must submit to injustice at the hands of the employer in patience for a while longer," and, "Do not strike, but study not only your own condition but that of your employer. Find out how much you are justly entitled to, and the tribunal of **arbitration** will settle the rest."[12]

The reformist and long-run objectives were inconsistent with the immediate results sought by the new membership. To some extent, the differences between the ascetic Powderly as leader (see Exhibit 2–3) and the interests of the burgeoning rank and file hastened the decline of the Knights. Besides the leadership-membership cleavages, an antagonistic press increasingly linked anarchy and radical action with the Knights of Labor. Public pressure, internal power vested in individuals with reformist sentiments, and an inability to get employers to arbitrate all contributed to the decline of the Knights' membership to 75,000 by 1893. But the withering of the Knights of Labor did not bring an end to national organizations. At the height of the Knights of Labor's success, the first enduring national federation was formed.

The American Federation of Labor

The **American Federation of Labor** (AFL) was created in a meeting of national unions in Columbus, Ohio, in 1886.[13] It was born out of the frustration **craft** unionists felt about the mixing of skilled and unskilled workers in Knights of Labor assemblies and its increasingly reformist

---

[12] Ibid., p. 98.

[13] Dulles, *Labor in America*, p. 161.

orientation. The Knights of Labor also tended toward centralization of authority, which diminished the autonomous power of individual craft unions.

Twenty-five national labor groups representing about 150,000 members initially formed the federation. The individual unions maintained autonomy and control over their trades while ceding authority to the AFL to settle disputes among them.[14] The AFL was formed by unions of skilled employees. During most of the rest of its history, it maintained a skilled-worker, or craft, orientation and an antipathy toward involving unskilled workers in its unions. The AFL concentrated on winning tangible gains for its members by entering into collective agreements with employers. It aimed at rationalizing the work place by contracting conditions of employment.

Much of the early direction of the AFL was influenced by the philosophies of its first president, Samuel Gompers. As a member of the New York local of the Cigarmakers, he had seen radical action punished by civil authorities and experienced the Knights of Labor's advocacy of unskilled demands within the Cigarmakers. As a labor leader, these experiences led Gompers to pay close attention to the workers he represented, not necessarily the interests of all laborers. Experience also led him to take a pragmatic approach, seeking gains at the bargaining table rather than through legislation. His long incumbency—from 1886 to 1924 expect for one year—is in large part responsible for the "business" orientation of U.S. unions.

Gompers and other early leaders, such as Adolph Strasser, cemented the base on which the American trade union movement stood. Their approach accepted the system as it existed and worked within it. They were primarily concerned with improving the lot of the members they represented. This approach is basically retained in the present agency role taken by unions in representation (see Exhibit 2–4).

Taking this pragmatic, business-oriented viewpoint limited the AFL in sponsoring major social reform initiatives. The AFL approach advocated legislation only in situations in which it could not bargain successfully for its objectives. The immediacy and absence of an underlying ideology is best typified in the answer, attributed to Gompers, to a question asking what labor's goals were: "More, more, more."

Another aspect of the pragmatic genius of the AFL's founders was their structural design for the federation. Its early structure, broadly maintained to the present, preserves the autonomy of the international unions and makes their locals subsidiary to them. This approach serves two purposes: first, the leaders' focus is toward the job problems unique to

---

[14] Ibid.

EXHIBIT 2–4

Testimony of Adolph Strasser, President of the International Cigarmakers' Union, before the Senate Committee on Education and Labor, 1885

Q: You are seeking to improve home matters first?

Strasser: Yes, sir, I look first to the trade I represent . . . the interests of the men who employ me to represent their interests.

Q: I was only asking you in regard to your ultimate ends.

Strasser: We have no ultimate ends. We are going on from day to day. We fight only for immediate objects—objects that can be realized in a few years.

the trade they represent; second, discipline is maintained over the activities of the locals, and thus a more united and rational front is presented when initiating actions or responding to management.

LABOR UNREST

The last three decades of the 19th century and the first decade of the 20th century saw some of the bitterest labor struggles the United States has ever experienced. This period was characterized by frequent financial panics resulting in depressions, continuing adamancy by owners refusing to recognize or negotiate with labor unions, and intervention by the government on the side of employers. Some of the unrest was localized and grew out of either radical political action or the nationalistic solidarity of immigrant groups, but much of it was of a general nature within an area or industry.

In one of the first outbursts, coal miners in Pennsylvania struck when mine operators unilaterally cut wages below an agreed minimum. As the strike lengthened, some miners returned to work, but a few diehards formed a secret organization (which became known as the Molly Maguires) to continue resisting the mine owners. This group sabotaged the mines, threatened owners and supervisors, and conducted other terrorist activities until it was infiltrated by James McParlan, a Pinkerton detective hired by the owners. In 1875, as a result of his testimony, 10 of the Molly Maguires were hanged, and another 14 were jailed, ending the mine warfare.[15]

---

[15] Ibid., pp. 117–18.

In the summer of 1877, the railroads cut wages while maintaining high dividends to their stockholders. In the East, rail employees struck and in some instances seized railway property. In Pittsburgh, federal troops were called in to retake the property, but not before 25 people had been killed. Widespread rioting broke out. Railroad property was burned, and local business establishments were looted.[16]

In 1886, violence broke out between strikers and strikebreakers at the McCormick Harvester plant in Chicago. The police intervened, and four persons were killed. To protest the use of police, a meeting was held in Haymarket Square. As the peaceful meeting was dispersing, the police arrived and ordered everyone to leave. Just then a bomb exploded among the police, killing one of them. Before the battle was over, seven more police and four workers were killed, and more than 100 persons were injured. The riot was blamed on anarchists. Eight were rounded up and charged with murder; seven were ordered hanged and the eighth imprisoned. All were pardoned six years later, and those still alive were released.[17]

Two major strikes in the 1890s helped shape the constituency of the labor movement while casting doubt on the power of industrial employees to win their demands. These were the Homestead strike in the Carnegie Steel Company in 1892 and the Pullman Company strike in 1894.

Homestead workers refused to accept a company-ordered wage cut and were then locked out by Henry Frick, Carnegie's general manager. The workers correctly assumed Frick would attempt to reopen the plant by hiring strikebreakers. To accomplish this, Frick barged 300 armed Pinkerton detectives up the Monongahela River behind the plant. As they neared the works, the entrenched workers opened fire on them. The battle raged all day. Workers attempted to sink the barges with a small cannon and poured oil onto the river and set it on fire. The Pinkertons surrendered.

The workers' victory was short lived; the governor called out the militia, which took over the plant. Frick staffed the reopened plant with strikebreakers. The union was crushed to the extent that serious attempts to organize the steel industry were not made again until the 1930s.[18]

The Pullman strike of 1894 began as a local issue, but it took on nationwide proportions before being crushed by the combined use of federal troops and court injunctions. The Pullman Company produced railroad cars. Pullman workers lived in company-owned houses and paid

---

[16] Ibid., pp. 119–20.
[17] Ibid., pp. 123–25.
[18] Ibid., pp. 166–69.

rent. They had no other choice of living accommodations; the company required them to use company-owned housing. In 1893, the company laid off half of its employees and cut the wages of those remaining up to 40 percent. However, rents were not reduced, and the company continued to pay dividends to stockholders.

Pullman employees attempted to get the owners to adjust their economic grievances, but the company refused and fired several of their leaders. The Pullman locals of the American Railway Union (ARU) reacted by striking. The company refused the union's offer to arbitrate the differences. As a result, leader Eugene Debs ordered members not to handle Pullman rolling stock.

Railroad employees throughout the country stopped trains and uncoupled cars manufactured by Pullman. The railroads retaliated by discharging employees found cutting out Pullman cars. But whole train crews quit and abandoned their trains if one of their members was fired.

One management strategy led to the end of the strike. When trains were assembled, Pullman cars were connected to U.S. mail cars. If the Pullman cars were later uncoupled, the mail car might also be cut out, thus interfering with the mail, a federal offense. When this occurred, the federal government intervened, supplying federal troops and permanently enjoining interference with mail delivery and the movement of goods in interstate commerce. Debs was sent to jail for conspiracy to obstruct the mails, and the strike was broken.[19]

The failure of these early industrial actions convinced members of one faction of the labor movement that the capitalistic system needed to be replaced by socialism if worker goals were to be achieved. Revolutionary unions were spawned in the West in mining and timbering and in textiles in the East.

The IWW and the Western Federation of Miners

The inability of the Knights of Labor to win important settlements and the antipathy of the AFL to industrial organization led to more radical approaches. Just as Eugene Debs's jail term convinced him that revolutionary unionism and the abolition of capitalism were necessary, so too did the results of numerous mine strikes and wars convince "Big Bill" Haywood that miner solidarity and resistance were the answer to employer intransigence.

Haywood played an active role in organizing the Western Federation of Miners (WFM), which had withdrawn from the AFL in 1897. After the long-smoldering Cripple Creek, Colorado, strike was crushed in 1904, the

---

[19] Ibid., pp. 171–79.

EXHIBIT 2-5

Preamble to the IWW Constitution

The working class and the employing class have nothing in common. There can be no peace so long as hunger and want are found among millions of working people and the few who make up the employing class have all the good things of life.

Between these two classes a struggle must go on until the workers of the world organize as a class, take possession of the earth and the machinery of production, and abolish the wage system.

We find that the centering of management of the industries into fewer and fewer hands makes the trade unions unable to cope with the ever-growing power of the employing class. The trade unions foster a state of affairs which allows one set of workers to be pitted against another set of workers in the same industry, thereby helping defeat one another in wage wars. Moreover, the trade unions aid the employing class to mislead the workers into the belief that the working class have interests in common with their employers.

These conditions can be changed and the interest of the working class upheld only by an organization formed in such a way that all its members in any one industry, or in all industries if necessary, cease work whenever a strike or lockout is on in any department thereof, thus making an injury to one an injury to all.

Instead of the conservative motto, "A fair day's wage for a fair day's work," we must inscribe on our banner the revolutionary watchword, "Abolition of the wage system."

It is the historic mission of the working class to do away with capitalism. The army of production must be organized, not only for the everyday struggle with capitalists, but also to carry on production when capitalism shall have been overthrown. By organizing industrially we are forming the structure of the new society within the shell of the old.

WFM realized it needed national support. Thus, in 1905, Haywood, Debs, and other leading socialists banded their unions together to form the **Industrial Workers of the World** (IWW) (see Exhibit 2-5).[20]

Immediately embroiled in internal political struggle, the IWW was decimated by the withdrawal of the WFM in 1906, but Haywood stayed with the IWW. Its rhetoric was radical, but whether its demands were is another question. When involved in collective action, the IWW's usual demands related to wages and hours rather than usurpation of the management function.[21] And although violence related to strikes occasionally broke out, these incidents were often sparked by management action

---

[20] Ibid., pp. 208–11.

[21] Joseph G. Rayback, *A History of American Labor* (New York: Free Press, 1966), p. 248.

similar to that facing the 19th-century industrial labor movement. It is important to note, however, that the *purpose* of the IWW was not to achieve better wages and working conditions—instead, it was to abolish the wage system. This may be why it encountered such resistance from employers and why it had little success in building permanent organizations.

Perhaps the most successful IWW strike occurred in Lawrence, Massachusetts, in 1912 after textile workers there had suffered a wage cut. Although most of the workers were unorganized, 20,000 walked out, and IWW organizers took over the direction of the strike. After two months, during which several violent incidents occurred (some perpetrated by the owners and local authorities, others resulting from clashes with strikebreakers), worker demands were met, and the mills reopened.[22]

Despite this union victory, the IWW lost a subsequent textile strike in 1913 in Paterson, New Jersey. This outcome coupled with the advent of World War I, during which the IWW stated that its members would fight for neither side since only the capitalists would benefit, led to the IWW's demise. Haywood and other leaders were tried and convicted of sedition for allegedly obstructing the war effort. The IWW was effectively finished.[23]

The Boycott Cases

The strike was not the only weapon labor unions used against employers before World War I. While local employees struck, national unions urged other union members and the general public to boycott struck or "unfair" products. Two major national **boycotts** to support strikes, the *Danbury Hatters* and *Bucks Stove* cases, led to sharp legal reverses for labor organizations.

In the *Danbury Hatters* case, the employer, D. E. Loewe and Company, retaliated by filing charges against the union for conspiring to restrain trade, a violation of the Sherman Antitrust Act. Under provisions of the Sherman Act, if restraint was found, actual damages could be punitively trebled. The union lost, and for a time it appeared that Loewe employees would have to pay damages, but the AFL and the United Hatters' national organization "passed the hat" and paid the fines.[24] In the *Bucks Stove* case, a federal district court enjoined the boycott and held Samuel Gompers in contempt of court. The old specter of the conspiracy doctrine reappeared in the application of court injunctions to halt union actions. Strikes, union organizing, and other union activities

---

[22] Dulles, *Labor in America*, pp. 215–19.

[23] Ibid., pp. 219–22.

[24] Ibid., pp. 197.

were increasingly interpreted by federal district courts as leading to a restraint on interstate commerce and, hence, were enjoinable and punishable.[25]

Early Legislation

Early attempts by unions to engage in collective action on an industrial scale generally had been met by a two-pronged attack: adamant resistance by employers and injunctive relief to employers by the courts. In an effort to balance the power between the conflicting parties and to substitute statutory law for court-made common law, Congress passed the Erdman Act in 1898. The statute guaranteed that railroad employees could not be discriminated against for union membership. However, it was held unconstitutional in 1908 as an abridgment of personal liberty and the rights of property.[26]

The rulings of the federal courts in the *Danbury Hatters* and *Bucks Stove* applied the Sherman Antitrust Act to union activity. Union leaders believed this application hamstrung collective activity. With the election of President Woodrow Wilson and a Democratic Congress, labor expected legislative relief to be forthcoming. In 1914, their hopes were realized with passage of the Clayton Act, hailed by Samuel Gompers as the "industrial Magna Carta upon which the working people will rear their structure of individual freedom."[27]

Sections 6 and 20 of the Clayton Act, which removed labor from the jurisdiction of the Sherman Act and limited the use of federal injunctions, contributed to Gompers's euphoria. However, enthusiasm was short lived because the act's ambiguous wording ultimately led to judicial interpretations that disappointed labor.[28] The Supreme Court held in *Duplex Printing* v. *Deering*[29] that, although the antitrust laws could not be construed as rendering trade unions illegal per se, the unions' actions might still be construed as restraining trade. The court also held that a strike terminated the normal employer-employee relationship, thereby removing the protection against injunctions for lawful employee activities.[30] Thus, the Clayton Act lost whatever teeth labor had believed it had gained.

---

[25] Rayback, *A History of American Labor*, pp. 224–26.

[26] *Adair* v. *United States*, 208 U.S. 161 (1908).

[27] Samuel Gompers, "The Charter of Industrial Freedom," *American Federationist* 31, no. 11 (1914), pp. 971–72.

[28] S. I. Kutler, "Labor, the Clayton Act, and the Supreme Court," *Labor History* 3(1962), pp. 19–38.

[29] 254 U.S. 445 (1921).

[30] Dallas L. Jones, The Enigma of the Clayton Act," *Industrial and Labor Relations Review* 10(1957), pp. 201–21.

TRADE UNION SUCCESS AND APATHY

World War I

Although World War I spelled the end of the IWW, AFL unions made solid gains at that time. During 1917, numerous strikes, many fomented by the IWW, protested static wages during a period of steadily advancing prices. To reduce the incidence of strikes, the National War Labor Board was established in 1918 and included five representatives each from labor and management, with two members as cochairpersons to represent the public interest. Labor's right to organize and bargain collectively was recognized by President Wilson's administration. By the end of the war, average earnings of even semiskilled union members exceeded $1,000 annually, and the AFL had added more than a million members, thus exceeding 4 million in 1919.[31]

The American Plan

A variety of factors combined to erode labor's growth after World War I. The 1920s was a decade of relative prosperity and freedom from economic panics. The declining flow of immigrants reduced the competition for jobs among unskilled workers. Management identified labor as politically extremist, several leaders of the IWW having been prosecuted for sedition. Although they did not represent large portions of the labor movement, they became symbols of its danger in the public's eye. At the same time, the Bolsheviks gained power in Russia, and Americans were warned that this pattern could occur in the United States as well if trade unions became too strong.

Against this backdrop, the **American Plan** was implemented. Employers subtly associated the union movement with foreign subversives and questioned whether it was appropriate for workers to be represented by union officials who were not employed at their plant. Employers also championed the **open shop,** ostensibly to preserve the freedom of employees to refrain from joining unions. But the freedom to join was not zealously protected and, in fact, was discouraged through the use of **yellow-dog contracts,** which applicants and employees were required to sign, indicating they were not nor would become union members. As the decade wore on, the yellow-dog contract was seen increasingly as an instrument of coercion, and one that severely restricted the private rights and potential economic power of employees.[32]

---

[31] Dulles, *Labor in America*, pp. 226–28.

[32] D. Ernst, "The Yellow-Dog and Liberal Reform, 1917–1932," *Labor History* 30 (1989), pp. 251–74.

EXHIBIT 2-6

Charles M. Schwab, Chairman of the Board of Bethlehem Steel, in a Speech to a Chamber of Commerce Audience, 1918

"I believe that labor should organize in individual plants or amongst themselves for the better negotiation of labor and the protection of their own rights; but the organization and control of labor in individual plants and manufactories, to my mind, ought to be made representative of the people in those plants who know the conditions; that they ought not to be controlled by somebody from Kamchatka who knows nothing about what their conditions are."

SOURCE: Charles M. Schwab, "Capital and Labor: A Reconstruction Policy," *Annals of the American Academy of Political and Social Science*, January 1919, p. 158.

Local communities organized open-shop committees to protect citizens from outside labor organizers. Reinforcing the local-control-local-concern idea, many employers improved wages and working conditions in unorganized plants. Where employees began to organize, employers encouraged them to establish a company union, autonomous from a national union but not necessarily autonomous from the employer (see Exhibit 2–6).[33]

The End of an Era

The 1920s, a decade of transition for the United States in many ways, saw changes in organized labor. The country was shifting from an agricultural to an industrial society. Henry Ford introduced the assembly line. Many new jobs required few skills, creating an industrial rather than a craft orientation. Immigration quotas limited the influx of impoverished potential employees to a trickle. And while the AFL took a stand-pat approach to industrial organization, some of its newer leaders began to see the importance of organizing unskilled workers.

Before the 1920s, public policy had generally left the development and interpretation of labor law to the courts. The court rulings were predominantly in favor of business, severely restricting the lawful boundaries of union action. The World War I experience and a more sympathetic Congress showed that the conduct of labor-management relations needed some explicit ground rules. The 1920s spawned the first permanent labor legislation and laid the groundwork for later legislation.

---

[33] See Chamberlain and Cullen, *Labor Sector*, pp. 109–10; and Taft, *Organized Labor*, chap. 27.

EXHIBIT 2-7

Samuel Gompers's Farewell Words to the AFL

"I want to live for one thing alone—to leave a better labor movement in America and in the world than I found it when I entered, as a boy. . . ."

SOURCE: *AFL Proceedings*, 1924, p. 281.

It also marked the end of the Gompers era, which spanned almost 50 years of leadership. His parting words to the AFL are capsuled in Exhibit 2-7.[34]

American labor by the end of the 1920s cannot be adequately described in terms of a stage of development. Looking at the surface of the AFL, one might describe it as a withering, elderly, senile recluse, attending only to its own interests, conserving a shrinking base. In examining the changing role of industry, it might be described as a sleeping giant awaiting the dawn. In term of internal politics, it might be seen as a festering mass of irreconcilable factions. But, regardless of the factionalism, American labor did have a mainstream and a distinctive flavor subscribed to by most that was vital and unique to its movement.

Union Philosophies and Types in the United States

Since the beginning of the union movement, certain ideas fueled its direction and development. Their intensity has varied at different times and in different labor organizations, but they underlie the actions of all. The ideas can be summarized as follows: In society there is a productive class that ultimately creates the tangible products or services people demand. Labor is thus the ultimate creator of wealth and is entitled to its returns. Society generally includes a monied aristocracy, in which society's wealth is excessively, unequally distributed. Without major efforts to avoid it, education is unequal and undemocratically provided. Class distinctions exist, and the goals of workers differ from those of employers. Thus, trade unions are necessary to protect workers' rights.[35]

In 1921, a still-useful classification of unions was developed defining them by their goals.[36] Four categories of unions were recognized: uplift, revolutionary, business, and predatory. **Uplift unionism,** concerned with

---

[34] I. Yellowitz, "Samuel Gompers: A Half-Century in Labor's Front Rank," *Monthly Labor Review* 112, no. 7 (1989), pp. 27–33.

[35] Maurice F. Neufeld, "The Persistence of Ideas in the American Labor Movement: The Heritage of the 1830s," *Industrial and Labor Relations Review* 35 (1982), pp. 207–20.

[36] Robert F. Hoxie, *Trade Unionism in the United States* (New York: Appleton-Century-Crofts, 1921).

social issues, is aimed at the general betterment of educational and monetary outcomes and labor-management systems for workers. The National Labor Union is an example of this type. **Revolutionary unionism** is primarily oriented toward changing the fabric of society, overthrowing the capitalistic system, and replacing it with worker ownership of industry. The IWW serves as the prime American example of this type. **Business unionism** relates to the representation of employees' immediate employment interests, primarily the regulation of wages, hours, and terms and conditions of employment. This philosophy was typified by Adolph Strasser, one of the AFL's founders, in 1883, when he testified in Congress, "We have no ultimate ends. We are going on from day to day. We are fighting only for immediate objects—objects that can be realized in a few years." **Predatory unionism** occurs when the union's prime goal is to enhance itself at the expense of the workers it represents.

No U.S. union exists in one of these absolutely pure forms, but most appear to duplicate the characteristics of business unionism—concerned with immediate goals, accepting the system as it is, and working for union goals within that system. This approach has contributed to the durability of the labor movement, but it has also led to missed chances to contribute to meaningful changes in the mainstream of American society.

SUMMARY AND PROLOGUE

The following major points should be apparent to students examining the early U.S. labor movement:

1. Labor organizations have been an integral part of the nation's growth at all stages.
2. Before the end of the 1920s, labor was faced with a hostile national environment.
3. Most of labor's activities could be—and were—enjoined by the courts when they were effective.
4. Most successful labor leaders were concerned about labor's role in representing their members' immediate concerns and refrained from advocating ideological positions.

In summary, labor encountered several hurdles in its early organization: the conspiracy doctrine, initial uplift union movements, the link with radicals, and injunctions aimed at union activities. Personalities who shaped the early American labor movement included Terence Powderly and Uriah Stephens, Samuel Gompers and Adolph Strasser, Eugene Debs and "Big Bill" Haywood.

The 1920s was a decade of retrenchment. Underneath the surface was a growing interest in industrial union organization, particularly by John L. Lewis, president of the United Mine Workers. Interest in labor legislation was growing. Then the Depression began. The 1930s saw most present labor legislation being shaped and many present-day industrial unions formed. It was a decade of turbulence, formation, and definition and an adolescence necessary for America's labor-management relations to endure to reach adulthood and relative maturity.

DISCUSSION QUESTIONS

1. Trace the evolution of the legal status of American unions. What activities were restricted by laws and courts? Did constraints increase or decline with time?
2. What were the major contributing causes to the failure of uplift unionism?
3. What were the advantages and disadvantages of taking a "business union" approach as opposed to advocating a labor political party?
4. Who were the leading personalities in 19th-century labor relations? Which ones contributed to the definition of labor relations in the United States?

KEY TERMS

journeyman
conspiracy doctrine
National Labor Union
Knights of Labor
arbitration
American Federation of Labor
craft
Industrial Workers of the World

boycotts
American Plan
open shop
yellow-dog contracts
uplift unionism
revolutionary unionism
business unionism
predatory unionism

3

THE EVOLUTION OF AMERICAN LABOR: II

To say the Great Depression of the 1930s caused a reorientation of many American social institutions would be an understatement. Increased regulation of private business activities resulted. The economic security of wage earners was protected. The federal government assumed the role of employing out-of-work people. Government fiscal policy was tailored to affect the economy. And American labor emerged with legislation guaranteeing its legitimacy and protecting many of its activities.

Immediately after the Depression and its labor surpluses came World War II and its labor shortages. The growth of union power resulting from legislation and employer demands for labor affected the consuming economy after the war was over. The growing power of labor led to legislation restricting union activities and encouraging labor and management to bargain collectively without outside interference as long as the public's well-being was not seriously threatened.

This chapter examines the development of industrial unions, their split with the AFL and subsequent reunification, the effect of federal labor law, the new administrative procedures occasioned by the laws and World War II, and the thrust of unionization into the public sector. This chapter emphasizes several major themes or issues that have affected the evolution of our labor relations system. Among these are:

1. The continuing opposition of the AFL to industrial organization.

2. The shift in public sentiment toward unions in the 1930s and away from them in the late 1940s and the influence of this shift on union success.

3. The conflict between revolutionary and business union factions in the newly founded industrial unions.

4. The role of legislation in creating an atmosphere for collective bargaining, seeking to balance the power of the contending parties and introducing rules constraining the behavior of both (toward each other and toward individual employees or members).

5. The reductions in the size of the organized component of the work force and the effects of concessions on the labor movement's direction.

INDUSTRIAL UNIONS

Until the 1930s, attempts to organize **industrial unions** were generally unsuccessful. A number of factors contributed to this lack of success, including the continuing supply of unskilled workers provided by immigration, the AFL's relative disinterest in industrial unions, and the tendency of industrially oriented unions to adopt revolutionary goals. By the mid-1930s, a new set of circumstances created an atmosphere more favorable for industrial organizing. The Depression and legislative initiatives in labor-management relations helped. Established union leaders with a business-union orientation took up the industrial organizing crusade. Elected officials became more tolerant of, or actively favored, union activity.

The Industrial Union Leadership

The early leadership of Eugene Debs and "Big Bill" Haywood had lapsed for more than a decade when industrial organizing efforts resumed. This time the leadership came from within the AFL. John L. Lewis and other officials of the United Mine Workers (UMW), an AFL union, spearheaded the drive over the objections of the craft unions.

An established leader within the AFL, Lewis realized his UMW was faced with membership problems in a declining industry. A pragmatist, he decided in the early 1930s that the time had come to push for industrial organizing. He was not prepared for the adamant opposition he met within the AFL. In an acrimonious debate at the 1935 AFL convention, Lewis and "Big Bill" Hutcheson, president of the Carpenters' Union, actually came to blows (see Exhibit 3–1). The convention voted 18,000 to 11,000 to uphold craft unionism and not embark on industrial organization. After the convention, Lewis and Philip Murray of the UMW, Sidney Hillman of the Amalgamated Clothing Workers, David Dubinsky of the International Ladies' Garment Workers, Charles Howard of the Typographical Union, Thomas McMahon of the Textile Workers, Max Zaritsky of the cap and millinery department of the United Hatters, Harvey Flemming of the Oil Field, Gas Well, and Refining Workers, and Thomas Brown of the Mine, Mill, and Smelter Workers met to form the **Committee for Industrial Organization** (CIO).[1]

Organizing the Industrial Work Force

Major efforts were begun to organize workers in basic industries: steel, textiles, rubber, and autos. Philip Murray headed the Steel Workers Organizing Committee (SWOC), which established 150 locals totaling

---

[1] Joseph G. Rayback, *A History of American Labor* (New York: Free Press, 1966), pp. 348–50.

EXHIBIT 3-1

Lewis and Hutcheson at the 1935 AFL Convention

The industrial union report was defeated, but the question kept recurring. Delegates from rubber, radio, mine, and mill kept urging a new policy. Their way was blocked, though, not least by the towering figure of Big Bill Hutcheson, powerful head of the Carpenters' Union. Hutcheson and Lewis had always held similar views and frequently worked together. Like Lewis, Hutcheson was a big man, 6 feet tall and 220 pounds. When a delegate raised the question of industrial unions in the rubber plants, Hutcheson raised a point of order. The question had already been settled, he contended. Lewis objected; the delegate should be heard on a problem facing his own union. "This thing of raising points of order," he added, "is rather small potatoes."

"I was raised on small potatoes," Hutcheson replied.

As Lewis returned to his seat, he paused to tell Hutcheson that the opposition was pretty small stuff. "We could have made you small," was the reply. "We could have kept you off the executive council, you crazy bastard."

Lewis swung a wild haymaker. It caught Hutcheson on the jaw; the two men grappled, crashed against a table, and fell awkwardly to the floor. President Green wildly hammered his gavel as delegates tried to separate the two heavyweights.

SOURCE: David F. Selvin, *The Thundering Voice of John L. Lewis* (New York: Lathrop, Lee, & Shepard, 1969), pp. 103–4.

over 100,000 members by the end of 1936. In early 1937, through the secret efforts of John L. Lewis and Myron Taylor, head of U.S. Steel, SWOC was recognized as the U.S. Steel employees' bargaining agent. The 8-hour day, a 40-hour week, and a wage increase were won. The other steel firms were not so readily organized. During an organizing parade at Republic Steel, violence broke out, and 10 strikers were killed by Chicago police Memorial Day, 1937.[2]

The autoworkers were next. Despite the relatively high wages pioneered by Henry Ford, the jobs were tedious and fatiguing, and the owners had established private police forces to keep the workers in line.[3] Organizing began in 1936. By the end of the year, the United Automobile Workers (UAW), under President Homer Martin, sought recognition from General Motors. GM refused, but worker sentiments were so strong that "quickie" strikes resulted.[4]

Then, in late 1936, the UAW embarked on a strategy that succeeded in forcing GM to recognize and negotiate with it—the **sit-down strike.**

[2] Foster Rhea Dulles, *Labor in America*, 3rd ed. (New York: Crowell, 1966), pp. 299–302.

[3] Martin J. Gannon, "Entrepreneurship and Labor Relations at the Ford Motor Company," *Marquette Business Review*, Summer 1972, pp. 63–75.

[4] Rayback, *History of American Labor*, p. 353.

Auto workers at GM's Fisher body plants in Flint, Michigan, refused to leave their workplaces and took over the plants. GM viewed this as criminal trespass, but the workers asserted that job rights were superior to property rights. Injunctions obtained to oust the workers were ignored (see Exhibit 3–2). Attempts to persuade Michigan Governor Frank Murphy to mobilize the militia to enforce the injunction failed. Realizing the workers could hold out, GM capitulated in February 1937, agreeing to recognize the UAW and promising not to discriminate against union members.[5]

This tactic was later used successfully to organize Chrysler workers as well as the glass, rubber, and textile industries. Industrial unionization had been achieved. By the end of 1937, the CIO unions' membership of 3.7 million exceeded membership in the older AFL by 300,000.[6]

LEGISLATION

Organized labor did not achieve overnight success in its efforts to unionize workers. But, by the 1930s, public policy toward unions had shifted radically from the previous two decades. Before the Railway Labor Act in 1926, no legislation facilitated organization or bargaining. Courts had consistently enjoined unions from striking, organizing, picketing, and other activities, even if they were peacefully conducted. State laws regulating injunctive powers of state courts were struck down by the Supreme Court in *Truax* v. *Corrigan*, a case testing an Arizona statute.[7]

Norris-LaGuardia Act (1932)

By the time the **Norris-LaGuardia Act** was passed in 1932, Congress had recognized the legitimacy of collective bargaining. In view of earlier judicial decisions, it pointed out that capital had been collectivizable through incorporation, while labor had not been allowed to collectivize. Up to that time, acceptance of a collective bargaining relationship had to devolve from a voluntary employer action.[8]

To grant organized labor relief from federal court injunctions against collective activity, the act guaranteed the rights to strike for any purpose, pay strike benefits, picket, ask other employees to strike, financially aid persons involved in court actions over labor disputes, meet on strike

---

[5] Sidney Fine, *The General Motors Strike of 1936–1937* (Ann Arbor: University of Michigan Press, 1969).

[6] Rayback, *History of American Labor*, pp. 354–55.

[7] 257 U.S. 312 (1921).

[8] Benjamin Taylor and Fred Witney, *Labor Relations Law*, 2nd ed. (Englewood Cliffs, N.J.: Prentice Hall, 1975), pp. 144–46.

EXHIBIT 3-2

Telegram from Sit-Down Strikers to Governor Murphy

"Governor, we have decided to stay in the plant. We have no illusions about the sacrifices which the decision will entail. We fully expect that if a violent effort is made to oust us many of us will be killed and we take this means of making it known to our wives, to our children, to the people of the state of Michigan and of the country that if this result follows from the attempt to eject us you are the one who must be held responsible for our deaths."

SOURCE: Sidney Fine, *Sit-Down: The General Motors Strike of 1936–1937* (Ann Arbor: University of Michigan Press, 1969), p. 278.

---

strategy, and organize using nonemployees. The act safeguarded these rights by restricting the power of federal courts to issue injunctions in labor disputes. The act also forbade federal courts from enforcing the yellow-dog contract, which required employees or job applicants to agree, as a condition of employment, not to join a labor union. Previously, if a worker joined a union after signing such an agreement and was discharged as a result, federal courts could and did uphold the discharge.[9]

While the Norris-LaGuardia Act protected numerous previously enjoinable activities, it was a neutral policy—it did not open any right to demand employer recognition. Other than the removal of the yellow-dog contract, explicit federal ground rules for employer conduct in labor–management relations still did not exist. This would change after the inauguration of President Franklin D. Roosevelt.

National Industrial Recovery Act (1933)

The National Industrial Recovery Act (NIRA), adopted in 1933, was not principally labor legislation. Its major focus was to encourage employers to band together and set prices and production quotas through industrial codes. To complete an industrial code, however, employers were required to include a provision enabling employees to bargain through representatives of their own choosing, free from employer interference.

NIRA survived for only two years before being found unconstitutional.[10] Labor is perhaps fortunate that the law did not survive because the law included no enforcement mechanism to guarantee rights to organize. It did, however, sow the seeds for the first piece of comprehensive labor legislation enacted in the United States.[11]

---

[9] *Hitchman Coal Co.* v. *Mitchell*, 245 U.S. 229 (1917).

[10] *Schechter Poultry Corp.* v. *United States*, 295 U.S. 495 (1935).

[11] Taylor and Witney, *Labor Relations Law*, pp. 147–48.

Wagner Act (National Labor Relations Act, 1935)

NIRA was bogging down even before it was ruled unconstitutional. Big business objected to being required to recognize in their codes the legitimacy of union activities, and smaller businesses objected to the monopoly powers inherent in the codes. Unions lost their safeguards when NIRA was wiped out, although the 1935 amendments to the Railway Labor Act secured them for some transportation employees. The **Wagner Act** was rolled into place to resecure organizational rights as well as to specify illegal activities by employers.[12]

Section 7, the heart of the act, specifies the rights of employees to engage in union activities: "Employees shall have the right to self-organization, to form, join, or assist labor organizations, to bargain collectively through representatives of their own choosing, and to engage in concerted activities, for the purpose of collective bargaining or other mutual aid or protection." To specify the types of actions presumed to interfere with Section 7 rights, Congress created Section 8. Section 8 broadly forbade interference with employees' rights to be represented, to bargain, to have their labor organizations free from employer dominance, to be protected from employment discrimination for union activity, and to be free from retaliation for accusing the employer of an unlawful (unfair) labor practice.

To investigate violations of Section 8 and to determine whether employees desired representation, the Wagner Act established the **National Labor Relations Board** (NLRB), whose major duties were to determine which, if any, union was the employees' choice to represent them collectively and to hear and rule on alleged unfair labor practices.

The Wagner Act also established the concept of **exclusive representation** in the agency relationship between the union and the employees. Where a union was certified as the choice of the majority of employees, all employees in that unit, regardless of union membership, would be represented by the union in issues of wages, hours, and terms and conditions of employment.

The Wagner Act did not apply to all employers and employees, although a major portion of the private sector was covered. Specifically exempted were the following employees: those who worked for federal, state, and local governments; those subject to the Railway Labor Act; and those who belonged to labor organizations (except when members were acting as another's employees). Employee groups specifically exempted were supervisors and managers, agricultural workers, domestic employees, and family workers.

---

[12] Dulles, *Labor in America,* pp. 273–75.

Passage of the Wagner Act did not immediately presage a shift in U.S. labor relations. With NIRA recently having been declared void by the Supreme Court and with Section 7 of the Wagner Act closely duplicating the NIRA section, some employers expected the courts to rule against Congress on a constitutional challenge.

EMPLOYER INTRANSIGENCE

Many employers strongly opposed unions and doubted the constitutionality of the Wagner Act. Unions saw the legislation as a legitimation of their position. The act created a mechanism for determining whether unions would represent units of employees. Almost half of the strikes between 1935 and 1937 were not over bargaining issues but rather over obtaining recognition, reflecting the adamancy of employers as well as the new militancy of unions.

Firms practiced a variety of strategies in relation to union-organizing activities. Some included establishing and fostering company unions. Other tactics included exploiting the differences existing between the AFL and CIO.[13] Companies that responded with company unions provided managerial support to them, but gradually some of these unions became relatively independent and effective as companies were scrutinized to determine whether the unions were illegally dominated by management.[14] Another device employers used was called the **Mohawk Valley formula,** aimed at linking unions with agitators and communists. Proponents of this strategy organized back-to-work drives during strikes, got local police to break up strikes, and aligned local interests against the focus of union activities.[15]

A congressional investigation into company attempts to thwart or rebuff union activities disclosed that, between 1933 and 1937, companies spent almost $10 million for spying, strikebreaking, and munitions. To prepare for potential strikes, Youngstown Sheet and Tube amassed 8 machine guns, 369 rifles, 190 shotguns, 450 revolvers, 109 gas guns, 3,000 rounds of gas, and almost 10,000 rounds of shotgun shells and bullets. Republic Steel purchased almost $80,000 worth of repellent gases and allegedly possessed the largest private arsenal in the United States.[16]

---

[13] D. Nelson, "Managers and Nonunion Workers in the Rubber Industry: Union Avoidance Strategies in the 1930s," *Industrial and Labor Relations Review* 43 (1989), pp. 41–52.

[14] S. M. Jacoby, "Reckoning with Company Unions: The Case of Thompson Products, 1934–1964," *Industrial and Labor Relations Review* 43 (1989), pp. 19–40.

[15] Dulles, *Labor in America,* p. 278

[16] Ibid., pp. 277–78.

Constitutionality of the Wagner Act

Both sides had reasons to believe their positions to be legitimate. Management had seen a long line of Supreme Court decisions adverse to labor, not the least of these being the striking down of NIRA, which was partially similar to the Wagner Act. Labor had seen sympathy for its position grow throughout the country. With President Roosevelt consolidating his position through the overwhelming electoral endorsement of the New Deal in 1936, labor believed the court would find it difficult to invalidate the law.[17]

Opposition to the Wagner Act by employers was probably related to ideological, legal, and economic factors. Employers' creation and use of the American Plan, Mohawk Valley formula, and other devices during the 1920s reflected their ideological opposition to industrial unionization. Employers reasonably expected the Wagner Act to be found unconstitutional given the earlier *Schechter Poultry* decision. Employers also believed unionization would raise their labor costs. A recent study of the economic effects of the Wagner Act on employers indicates the market value of companies that were unionized after passage of the Wagner Act was decreased. Thus, the reduced ability to avoid unionization following passage of the act had an economic cost for employers.[18]

The legitimacy of the Wagner Act was decided by the Supreme Court on April 12, 1937, in the *Jones & Laughlin* case.[19] Previously, the NLRB had determined that Jones & Laughlin had violated the act by coercing employees and discriminating against union members. It ordered 10 employees reinstated with back pay and told the firm to cease its unfair labor practices. The appeals court had held that the NLRB's action was beyond the range of federal power, but the Supreme Court agreed to review the case.

In a 5–4 decision, the Supreme Court sided with the board and upheld the validity of the act. The Court held first that Congress may regulate employer activities under the Constitution's commerce clause. Second, it reaffirmed the right of employees to organize and recognized Congress's authority to restrict employer activities likely to disrupt organization. Third, the Court ruled that manufacturing, even if conducted locally, was a process involving interstate commerce. Fourth, it was reasonable for Congress to set rules and procedures governing employees' rights to organize. Finally, the Court found that the board's conduct at

---

[17] Taylor and Witney, *Labor Relations Law*, pp. 161–64.

[18] C. A. Olson and B. E. Becker, "The Effects of the NLRA on Stockholder Wealth in the 1930s," *Industrial and Labor Relations Review* 44 (1990), pp. 116–29.

[19] *NLRB* v. *Jones & Laughlin Steel Corp.*, 301 U.S. 1 (1937).

the hearing and its orders were regular, within the meaning of the act, and protected. Thus, the Wagner Act passed the Supreme Court's test and opened an era of rapid industrial organization.

LABOR POWER

Pre–World War II

The momentum gained by the CIO in its split from the AFL continued for the remainder of the 1930s. Both federations raided each other's members, and employers were caught in the midst. These jurisdictional disputes created public hostility and led to some state legislation outlawing certain union activities.[20]

Although labor had been instrumental in getting its friends elected to public office since the Depression began, its ranks split in 1940 when John L. Lewis abandoned President Roosevelt and announced his support for Wendell Wilkie. The split began in 1937 when Lewis had expected the Democratic administration to repay labor for its campaign assistance by providing help during the GM sit-down strike. During the strike, Lewis said:

> For six months the economic royalists represented by General Motors contributed their money and used their energy to drive this administration [Roosevelt's] out of power. The administration asked labor for help, and labor gave it. The same economic royalists now have their fangs in labor. The workers of this country expect the administration to help the workers in every legal way and to support the workers in General Motors plants.[21]

President Roosevelt did nothing except urge meetings between the UAW and the company. During the strike, some of Lewis's other pronouncements were equally dramatic (see Exhibit 3–3).

Later, during the "Little Steel" campaign, Roosevelt again incurred Lewis's wrath by criticizing labor and management jointly: "a plague on both your houses." Lewis responded by chastising Roosevelt: "It ill behooves one who has supped at labor's table and who has been sheltered in labor's house to curse with equal fervor and fine impartiality both labor and its adversaries when they become locked in deadly embrace."[22]

---

[20] A jurisdictional dispute occurs when two or more unions claim to (1) simultaneously represent or attempt to bargain for the same employee group or (2) simultaneously assert that their members are entitled by contract to perform a certain class of work.

[21] Rayback, *History of American Labor*, p. 368.

[22] Ibid.

EXHIBIT 3-3

The Rhetoric of John L. Lewis

[The mid-1930s were] a time of virtual class warfare. The National Guard was called out more than a dozen times a year; strikes were broken not only by goons and ginks and company finks, in the words of the old labor song, but by tear gas and machine guns. And when a particularly disdainful Chrysler president asked for Lewis's comment in the midst of a negotiation inspired by a spontaneous sit-down at Chrysler, the six-foot-two Lewis stood up and said, "I am 99 percent of a mind to come around the table right now and wipe that damn sneer off your face." Lee Pressman, of the new CIO, later observed, "Lewis's voice at that moment was in every sense the voice of millions of unorganized workers who were being exploited by gigantic corporations. He was expressing at that instant their resentment, hostility, and their passionate desire to strike back."

. . . When F.D.R. lumped labor with management, declaring his famous "plague on both your houses" . . . Lewis intoned: "Labor, like Israel, has many sorrows. Its women weep for their fallen, and they lament for the future of the children of the race. It ill behooves one who has supped at labor's table and who has been sheltered in labor's house to curse with equal fervor and fine impartiality both labor and its adversaries when they become locked in deadly embrace."

The "sup" to which he had made reference was a $500,000 UMW contribution to F.D.R.'s 1936 campaign. Lewis was unabashed about demanding his money's worth. "Everybody says I want my pound of flesh, that I gave Roosevelt $500,000 for his 1936 campaign, and I want quid pro quo. The UMW and the CIO have paid cash on the barrel for every piece of legislation gotten. . . . Is anyone fool enough to believe for one instant that we gave this money to Roosevelt because we are spellbound by his voice?"

. . . Although Lewis was rarely photographed smiling ("That scowl is worth a million dollars," he once confided to a friend), one can see the demon gleam in his eye as he scratched out his answer (to Roosevelt's plea for a wartime no-strike pledge). "If you want to use the power of the state to restrain me, as an agent of labor, then, sir, I submit that you should use the same power to restrain my adversary in this issue, who is an agent of capital. My adversary is a rich man named Morgan, who lives in New York." Signed, in letters which ran two and a half inches tall, "Yours humbly."

SOURCE: Victor Navasky, "John L. Lewis, Union General," *Esquire*, December 1983, pp. 264–66.

The prewar period was a time of great political ferment. Many questioned the ability of the capitalist system to overcome the Depression and avoid a recurrence. A variety of radical political agendas were created, with varying degrees of government regulation or operation of the economy contemplated. However, many of the most influential new industrial union leaders gave priority to trade union matters over a political agenda.[23] As the 1930s wore on, it became apparent that an increasingly large number of industrial union staff positions were held by communists. They did not join in President Roosevelt's support for the Allies after Germany and Russia signed their nonaggression pact in 1939.

1941 was a year of crisis for labor-management relations. The ambivalent stand of some industrial union leaders toward the war caused employers to brand them nonpatriotic. While this stand shifted when Philip Murray became president of the CIO in 1940, the label was not entirely removed. Employers refused to recognize unions, although union organization of Ford and Little Steel was finally successful. For the first time, labor's goal of "more, more, more now" was becoming intolerable to the general public. More than 4,300 strikes broke out in 1941, involving more than 8 percent of the work force. This widespread industrial disruption would probably have been moderated by congressional action had not the attack on Pearl Harbor involved the United States in World War II.[24]

World War II

At the outbreak of World War II, the AFL, the CIO, and management representatives pledged to produce together to meet the war effort. Labor pledged not to strike if a board were established to handle unresolved grievances. Management did not entirely concede, and, as a result, President Roosevelt established the National War Labor Board (NWLB). As the war got under way, prices rose more rapidly than in the previous several years. Labor's demands for wage increases grew. The NWLB attempted to maintain a policy whereby wage increases (unless not recently attained) would equal changes in the cost of living. Labor objected to the dual check of collective bargaining and NWLB policy on wages, but the policy was not changed.[25]

Although no-strike pledges had been given, in 1945, 4,750 strikes involved 3,470,000 workers, and 38 million worker-days were lost. This exceeded the prewar high of 28.4 million days in 1937. Major sporadic strikes in the coal industry, led by John L. Lewis, were particularly evident to the public. At one point, the coal mines were seized and run by Secretary of the Interior Harold Ickes (see Exhibit 3-4).[26]

---

[23] K. Boyle, "Building the Vanguard: Walter Reuther and Radical Politics in 1936," *Labor History* 30 (1989), pp. 433–48.

[24] Rayback, *History of American Labor*, pp. 370–73.

[25] Philip Taft, *Organized Labor in American History* (New York: Harper & Row, 1964), pp. 546–52.

[26] Ibid., pp. 553–56.

EXHIBIT 3–4

Comments by President Roosevelt on Coal Strikes during 1943

On June 23, the president issued a statement in which he said that "the action of the leaders of the United Mine Workers coal miners has been intolerable—and has rightly stirred up the anger and disapproval of the overwhelming mass of the American people."

He declared that the mines would be operated by the government under the terms of the board's directive order of June 18.

He stated that "the government had taken steps to set up the machinery for inducting into the armed services all miners subject to the Selective Service Act who absented themselves, without just cause, from work in the mines under government operation." Since the "Selective Service Act does not authorize induction of men above 45 years into the armed services, I intend to request the Congress to raise the age limit for noncombat service to 65 years. I shall make that request of the Congress so that if at any time in the future there should be a threat of interruption of work in plants, mines, or establishments owned by the government, or taken possession of by the government, the machinery will be available for prompt action."

SOURCE: Arthur Suffern, "The National War Labor Board and Coal," in *The Termination Report of the National War Labor Board, vol. 1: Industrial Disputes and Wage Stabilization in Wartime* (Washington, D.C.: U.S. Government Printing Office, 1948), p. 1009.

The strike activity led Congress to pass the War Labor Disputes Act over President Roosevelt's veto. This act authorized the seizure of plants involved in labor disputes, made strikes and lockouts in defense industries a criminal offense, required 30 days' notice to the NWLB of a pending dispute, and required the NLRB to monitor strike votes.[27]

While this overview of World War II has not reflected accommodation and innovation, they were evident. Even unions with overtly communist political agendas such as the International Longshore Workers Union (ILWU) supported no-strike agreements because this was consistent with aiding the Soviet-American alliance in Europe.[28] In only 46 of 17,650 dispute cases before the NWLB did the parties fail to reach or accept agreements. The war experience also led to a widespread acceptance of fringe benefits in lieu of wage increases. Holidays, vacations, sick leaves, and shift differentials began to be approved by the NWLB as part of labor contracts. For the first time, labor shortages led to policies advocating equal employment opportunities for minorities and equal pay for men and women in the same jobs.[29]

---

[27] Ibid., p. 557.

[28] M. Torigian, "National Unity on the Waterfront: Communist Politics and the ILWU During the Second World War," *Labor History* 30 (1989), pp. 409–32.

[29] Taft, *Organized Labor*, pp. 559–62.

Reconversion

As the war ended, consumers anticipated the return of goods unavailable during the war. Labor looked forward to wage increases to offset the cost-of-living increases that had occurred during the war. The inevitable clash of labor and management led to the greatest single-year period of labor conflict in U.S. history. Between August 1945 and August 1946, 4,630 strikes involved 4.9 million workers and the loss of 119.8 million worker-days (or 1.62 percent of total days available). Major strikes affected the coal, rail, auto, and steel industries. These were settled with wage increases averaging about 18.5 cents per hour; and some, especially in steel, resulted in price increases as well.[30]

The end of the war, the strikes, and the election of a more conservative Congress led to legislation that balanced the power between unions and managements.

CHANGING THE BALANCE

The Wagner Act was passed when industrial organizing was just beginning and employers had an overwhelming array of weapons with which to battle labor. The act was to have struck a balance between the contenders. Over the 10 years since its passage, however, the challenger had become the champion. The strikes of 1941, the coal problems during World War II, and the labor difficulties encountered in 1946 all stimulated legislation to expand and clarify rules applied to the practice of U.S. labor relations.

The Wagner Act had addressed only employers' unfair labor practices, but critics of the labor movement argued that unions could also engage in tactics that might coerce individual employees and constitute a refusal to bargain collectively. The balancing legislation was enacted in amendments and additions to the Wagner Act entitled the Labor-Management Relations Act of 1947, better known as **Taft-Hartley.**

Taft-Hartley Act

Employee rights were expanded in Section 7 to include not only the right to join but also the right to refrain from union activities unless a contract between an employer and a union required union activity. This right to refrain allowed collective bargaining agreements to require, at most, joining a union or paying dues. But Congress went further by adding Section 14(b), which enabled states to pass more restrictive legislation

---

[30] Ibid., pp. 563–78.

regarding employees' rights to refrain from union activities. In these states, **right-to-work laws** make illegal any contract provision requiring union membership as a condition of continued employment. Most of the states passing right-to-work laws are either in the South and West or in predominantly agricultural states where union strength has never been high.[31] Efforts at passage in Ohio and California failed in 1958, and Indiana voters repealed a state statute in 1965. Right-to-work laws are highly emotional issues, both to their proponents and their opponents. Organized labor refers to them as "right-to-wreck" laws, enabling non-members to act as free riders by using union gains applicable to an entire bargaining unit without contributing money or effort to the cause. Proponents see the laws as essential to freedom of association and protective of the right to join or not join organizations. The heat of the rhetoric from both sides is probably greater than the impact of the statutes, as we will note in Chapters 5, 6, and 7.

Section 8 was amended to restrict a union's treatment of its members, recognizing the agency role the union plays for all bargaining unit members. Unions were required to bargain in good faith with employers and were forbidden to strike to gain recognition or to put pressure on uninvolved second parties to get at a primary employer.

Title II was a new addition to U.S. labor legislation. First, it established the **Federal Mediation and Conciliation Service** (FMCS) to aid settlement of unresolved contractual disputes. This assistance could be requested by the parties or offered directly by the FMCS. Second, provision was made for intervention in strikes likely to create a national emergency. A president who determined a current or pending labor dispute imperiled the nation could convene a board of inquiry to determine the issues and positions of the parties. If the president then believed it was a national emergency, the attorney general could seek to have the strike or lockout enjoined for 80 days. During the first 60 days of the injunction, the parties would continue negotiations. At the end of this period, if agreement had not been reached, the board of inquiry would report the last position of both parties. The NLRB would then hold an election in which union members would vote to accept or reject management's last offer. The results of the election would be certified by the end of the 80 days. If the membership voted to accept, the contract would be ratified; if to reject, members would be free to strike, although the president was directed to submit a report to Congress so that it could consider acting.

Title III dealt with suits by and against labor organizations. Either

---

[31] Alabama, Arizona, Arkansas, Florida, Georgia, Iowa, Kansas, Louisiana, Mississippi, Nebraska, Nevada, North Carolina, North Dakota, South Carolina, South Dakota, Tennessee, Texas, Utah, Virginia, and Wyoming.

employers or unions could be sued for violating labor contracts. Recovery of damages was restricted to the assets of the organization, not of the individual members. Union officials were forbidden to accept money from employers, and employers could not offer inducements to them. This title further provided that boycotts to force an employer to cease doing business with others (i.e., a struck or nonunion firm) were illegal. Corporations and labor unions were forbidden to make political contributions. Finally, federal employees were forbidden to strike.

The overall thrust of the legislation balanced the relative power of the contenders and provided mechanisms (the FMCS and national emergency dispute procedures) to reduce the likelihood of a recurrence of labor strife of the magnitude seen in 1946. Because the bill represented a retreat from the initiatives labor had previously enjoyed, it was not greeted with enthusiasm in that quarter. But the bill satisfied business, Congress, and the public. It passed by wide margins in both houses, was vetoed by President Truman, and repassed over his veto.

RETRENCHMENT AND MERGER

The AFL and CIO both regarded the Taft-Hartley Act as a "slave-labor" bill. They foresaw the possibility that labor disputes would again be subject to injunctions through the national emergency procedures.

In one major case where the emergency procedures might arguably have been employed, President Truman seized the nation's steel mills in 1952 rather than invoke the national emergency steps. When the Supreme Court declared his action unconstitutional, he was forced to return operations to management, and a strike ensued. We will examine the mechanisms and uses of Taft-Hartley injunctions in greater detail in Chapter 11.

Organized labor realized two things after Taft-Hartley. First, it would have to exert more influence in legislative activity and adopt a more publicly advocative stance on labor issues. Second, the strength of management and labor had been equalized by the act. The time had come to direct labor's energies toward unity rather than division. The old guard present at the sundering of the AFL was disappearing. William Green and Philip Murray both died in 1952. Their deaths resulted in the election of a new president of the AFL, George Meany, and of the CIO, Walter Reuther. John L. Lewis's UMW was unaffiliated, thus greatly reducing the historic friction.[32]

---

[32] Dulles, *Labor in America*, pp. 360–72.

Merger

The first step toward rapprochement was the ratification of a no-raid agreement by AFL and CIO conventions in 1954. A Joint Unity Committee was also established to explore ways to devise a merger. On February 9, 1955, a merger formed the combined AFL–CIO. George Meany became president of the merged federations.[33]

Meany expounded the merged federation's goals in 1955. He reendorsed Gompers's concept of "more" as it applied to a person's standard and quality of living. He reaffirmed labor's commitment to collective bargaining. He was unwilling to involve labor in management but demanded that management's stewardship be high (see Exhibit 3–5).[34] Essentially, his essay reiterated the goals and past behavior of the union movement: careful, member-oriented activity, yet with a degree of social concern, recognizing that advances for its members may lead to advances for society.

The merged AFL–CIO did not become a more powerful movement than the single federations had been in the past. In fact, union membership as a proportion of the labor force reached its peak in 1956 at about one third. By 1964, this proportion had fallen to 30 percent, and a decline of 700,000 members had been recorded. Part of the decline was due to less-aggressive organizing, to better nonunion employee relations, and to the reduced relative proportion of blue-collar manufacturing workers in the labor force. Whatever the reasons, the 1956–65 decade was one of malaise and retreat for the labor movement.[35] Unions did not gain stature in the public eye either, but they did gain some unwanted notoriety as congressional investigators uncovered gross malfeasance by some major national union officers.

Corruption

In 1957, the Senate Select Committee on Improper Activities in the Labor Management Field convened its investigations under Chairman John L. McClellan. For the next two and a half years, the American public was exposed to televised hearings in which a parade of labor officials invoked the Fifth Amendment to avoid self-incrimination.

The Teamsters Union drew the lion's share of the spotlight as witnesses disclosed that its president, Dave Beck, had converted union funds

---

[33] Ibid., pp. 372–74.
[34] George Meany, "What Labor Means by 'More,'" *Fortune* 26, no. 3 (1955), pp. 92–93.
[35] Dulles, *Labor in America*, pp. 377–81.

EXHIBIT 3-5

George Meany on Labor's Role

Plain realism dictates, therefore, that our thinking about the America of the quarter century ahead must be limited to goals rather than to predictions. Yet long-range goals, if they are meaningful, originate in the world of today and are shaped by one's tradition and one's philosophy. In a single man's lifetime, 25 years is a long time, perhaps half the span of his mature, vigorous life. Institutions, and the men who reflect them, have a longer perspective than individuals alone, and in the A.F. of L. our traditions and our philosophy have emerged from an experience of 75 years. Our goals can be understood only in terms of that experience. Moreover, the goals of a future but a quarter of a century away will not appear so unreal when measured against a philosophy hammered out by millions of Americans over the course of three quarters of a century.

Our goals as trade unionists are modest, for we do not seek to recast American society in any particular doctrinaire or ideological image. We seek an ever-rising standard of living. Sam Gompers once put the matter succinctly. When asked what the labor movement wanted, he answered, "More." If by a better standard of living we mean not only more money but more leisure and a richer cultural life, the answer remains "More."

But how do we get "more"? Imperfect in many details as our system may be, this country has adopted a flexible method for increasing the standard of living while maintaining freedom. It is the method of voluntary collective bargaining, of free decision making outside the coercions of government, in the solution of economic disagreement. And it is through the give-and-take of collective bargaining that we seek to achieve our goals.

SOURCE: George Meany, "What Labor Means by 'More,'" *Fortune* 26, no. 3 (1955), p. 92.

to his own use, borrowed money from employers, and received kickbacks from labor "consultants." James R. Hoffa was accused of breaking Teamster strikes and of covertly running his own trucking operation. "Sweetheart" contracts, offering substandard benefits and guaranteeing labor peace, were uncovered in the New York area in unions chartered by the Teamsters and operated by racketeers.

Other unions, including the Bakery and Confectionery Workers, Operating Engineers, Carpenters, and United Textile Workers, were also involved. Management contributed to the corruption by providing payoffs for sweetheart contracts that prevented other unions from organizing but that paid substandard rates.[36]

The publicity associated with the hearings cast a pall over the entire labor movement. By inference, all labor was corrupt. The AFL–CIO

---

[36] Taft, *Organized Labor*, pp. 698–704.

investigated internally and considered charges against the Allied Industrial Workers, Bakers, Distillers, Laundry Workers, Textile Workers, and Teamsters. The Textile Workers, Distillers, and Allied Industrial Workers agreed to mandated changes. The Bakers, Laundry Workers, and Teamsters did not and were expelled from the AFL–CIO in 1957.[37] Meanwhile, the congressional investigations led to legislation to reduce the likelihood of corrupt practices and also to amend the Taft-Hartley Act.

Landrum-Griffin Act

As a result of congressional investigations, considerable legislative interest in monitoring internal union affairs was expressed. In 1959, Congress passed legislation giving the U.S. Department of Labor greater power to audit union financial and political affairs. The **Landrum-Griffin Act**, formally titled the Labor-Management Reporting and Disclosure Act of 1959, also amended portions of the Taft-Hartley Act.

The Landrum-Griffin Act contained seven major titles. Title I established rights of individual union members to freedom of speech, equal voting rights, control of dues increases, and copies of labor agreements under which they worked, and it retained the right to sue. Title II required labor organizations to file periodic reports of official and financial activities and financial holdings of union officers and employees, and it required employers to report financial transactions with unions. Title III required reporting of trusteeships (in which the national union takes over a local union's operations) and specified conditions under which trusteeship would be allowed. Title IV dealt with internal union elections. Title V required bonding of officers, restricted loans, and prohibited recently convicted felons from holding office. Title VI contained miscellaneous provisions, including the prohibition of extortionate picketing.

Title VII amended the Taft-Hartley Act. Major changes strengthened the prohibitions against secondary boycotts (pressuring uninvolved employers to cease doing business with a struck or nonunion firm), restricted the use of picketing of unorganized employers to force recognition, made "hot-cargo" clauses (wherein employers agree not to use nonunion goods) illegal, reestablished the legality of what amounted to a closed shop[38] in building and construction, and established minimum levels of economic activity necessary before the NLRB would assert its jurisdiction in representation and unfair labor practice cases.

---

[37] Ibid., p. 704.

[38] A closed shop requires a worker to be a union member as a condition of obtaining employment.

LEGISLATIVE ATTEMPTS IN THE 1970s

Several legislative initiatives were undertaken in the 1970s to modify and expand Taft-Hartley. One was successful: in 1974, the Taft-Hartley Act was extended to cover employees of private nonprofit hospitals. Additional rules governing collective bargaining in private health care facilities were also fashioned.

A construction industry bargaining bill passed in late 1974 would have allowed a union in dispute with one of the contractors on a site to picket the whole site rather than only its reserved gate. This so-called *common situs picketing* would have established more pressure for settlement because all workers would likely refuse to cross picket lines established to cover all entrance gates. As an inducement to gain the support of a majority of Congress, a comprehensive construction bargaining mechanism aimed at establishing regional and national control of settlements was included. All parties predicted the bill would become law because President Ford had indicated he would sign if the comprehensive bargaining title were included. But in January 1976, he vetoed it. The bill was reintroduced without the bargaining titles after President Carter's inauguration, but it failed to pass.

In 1977, a bill amending Taft-Hartley to make organizing and representation easier for unions was introduced. The amendments would have imposed punitive damages on employers who intentionally interfered with employees' Section 7 rights. A great deal of acrimony surrounded this bill, and both labor and management exaggerated its supposed equity and punitive aspects. The labor reform bill passed the House but failed, by one vote, to survive a Senate filibuster during the summer of 1978.

Finally, attempts were made in the mid-1970s to introduce and pass a law similar to the Wagner Act for employees of federal, state, and local governments. The prime movers behind this were the National Education Association, the American Federation of Teachers, and the American Federation of State, County, and Municipal Employees. Labor's initial optimism about the law's chances of debate and passage vanished in the dust clouds surrounding the virtual financial collapse of New York City. Critics argued that public employee unions were already too powerful, as evidenced by high pay rates and heavy future pension liabilities cities and states had incurred through bargaining.

PUBLIC-SECTOR UNION GROWTH

As private-sector organizing activity sank into the doldrums of the late 1950s and early 1960s, public employees became increasingly interested in unionization. In the federal service, the Taft-Hartley Act had forbidden strikes. Most state statutes forbade strikes by public employees, generally made strikers ineligible for any gains won by striking, and included summary discharge as a penalty. Concomitantly, most federal and state statutes had no mechanism for recognizing bargaining representatives.

Federal Executive Orders

In 1962, President Kennedy issued **Executive Order 10988,** a breakthrough for federal employee unions. This order enabled a majority union to bargain collectively with a government agency. Negotiations open to the union were restricted to terms and conditions of employment, not wages. Unions could not represent employees if they advocated strikes or the right to strike. While a grievance procedure was outlined, final determination was to be made by the federal government, not an impartial arbitrator.[39]

Executive Order 11491, effective January 1, 1970, amended 10988. It required secret-ballot elections for recognition, established procedures for determining appropriate bargaining units, required Landrum-Griffin-type reporting by unions, and granted arbitration as a final settlement procedure for grievances. The order specified unfair labor practices and created procedures for redressing them. Finally, a Federal Impasse Panel was created to render binding decisions when collective negotiations reach an impasse. This provision ameliorated the statutory no-strike provisions facing federal government employees.[40]

In August 1971, Executive Order 11616 allowed professionals in an agency to decide whether to join a bargaining unit, allowed individuals to pursue unfair labor practice charges through grievance channels or through the assistant secretary of labor for labor-management relations, required a grievance procedure in exclusively represented units (while narrowing the range of issues allowed arbitration), and allowed some negotiating on government time.[41]

Executive Order 11491 required the Federal Labor Relations Council (FLRC) to review the status of labor relations at the federal level and report to the president. As a result of its recommendations, President Ford issued Executive Order 11838 in 1974. This order provided for the consolidation of some bargaining units, increased the area covered in negotiations, and dealt with structural aspects of the FLRC.[42]

---

[39] Taylor and Witney, *Labor Relations Law*, pp. 545–49.

[40] Ibid., pp. 550–53.

[41] Ibid., pp. 553–55.

[42] Murray A. Nesbitt, *Labor Relations in the Federal Government Service* (Washington, D.C.: Bureau of National Affairs, 1976), p. 133.

Civil Service Reform Act

Title VII of the Civil Service Reform Act of 1976 regulates labor-management relations in the federal service. The act codifies the provisions written into the executive orders. It also establishes the **Federal Labor Relations Authority,** which acts as the federal service equivalent of the NLRB. Requirements and mechanisms for alleviating bargaining impasses and unresolved grievances under the contract are also spelled out.[43]

State and Local Governments

Since no federal law asserts jurisdiction over state and local employees, the laws for and development of these employee unions differ substantially. For most areas, the development is a relatively recent phenomenon, with police and fire fighters more likely to have specific laws enabling organization and specifying bargaining. Employees occasionally acquired unionization when previously private employers, such as local transit companies, were taken over by public authorities. Chapter 15 details the development and growth of labor unions in public employment.

PASSING THE TORCH

The year 1982 was the 100th year since the founding of the American Federation of Labor. In that time, with the exception of a one-year period, the AFL and its successor, the AFL–CIO, had only four presidents: Samuel Gompers, William Green, George Meany, and Lane Kirkland. George Meany retired from the presidency in November 1979 at the age of 85. He died January 10, 1980. Meany's service to the labor movement was great, but his passing, like the earlier passings of Green and Murray, created opportunities for rapprochement and change. Since Lane Kirkland took office, the United Auto Workers have reaffiliated with the AFL–CIO, and the Teamsters were invited to consider rejoining.

But while organized labor changes, it maintains its ties to the past and its interest in outcomes important to its members. Exhibit 3–6 contains excerpts from George Meany's farewell address, delivered just two months before his death.

---

[43] Henry B. Frazier III, "Labor-Management Relations in the Federal Government," *Labor Law Journal* 30 (1979), pp. 131–38.

EXHIBIT 3-6

Excerpts from George Meany's Farewell Address, November 1979

Today is the last time I will have the honor of opening a convention of the AFL-CIO. By coincidence it is also an historic anniversary for the American trade union movement.

Ninety-eight years ago on this day—in Pittsburgh, Pennsylvania—107 trade unionists established the first, continuing national trade union center. The AFL-CIO is its direct descendant.

On November 15, 1881, the Federation of Organized Trades and Labor Unions was born for one simple reason—the unions of that day knew—as we know—that in unity there is strength.

Of course, there were many trade unions, assemblies and councils in many cities, even national and international labor unions in 1881. They had already made many important gains. But the founders of this great movement knew that much more could be accomplished through a combination of all those organizations.

So they organized and adopted a charter to "promote the general welfare of the industrial classes and secure that justice which isolated and separated trade and labor unions can never fully command."

Each succeeding generation of trade unions has given that charter life and breath. It has been a torch handed down from generation to generation—sometimes flickering, but never dimmed. It is now our responsibility—individually and collectively—to preserve that charter, to give it life and meaning in our time, and to pass it, intact and shining, to those who follow us; to carry that torch high, with pride, with honor.

Despite what some of my friends in the media may believe, I did not attend that convention in 1881. But I have read the proceedings and I believe Gompers, Foster, Leffingwell and all the courageous founders of our movement would look with favor upon the stewardship of their successors. . . .

*   *   *   *   *

I am confident that the labor movement is about to embark on another period of significant growth and expansion. The growth in unionization among public workers is continuing at a strong pace—and there are significant organizing breakthroughs by unions in the service trades. White-collar and professional workers are seeking organization. Farm workers are proving their strength against the most oppressive tactics used by any employers anywhere in the nation. . . .

*   *   *   *   *

Today the American trade union movement is vital, dynamic, growing. It is strong and unified.

But it needs to continue to grow, to consolidate its strength. And, I predict with certainty, it will.

SUMMARY

The 1930s provided the environment necessary for successful industrial unions. Both the Norris-LaGuardia and Wagner acts were passed, eliminating injunctions against most union activities and establishing collective bargaining as the preferred mode for resolving employment disputes.

The CIO was formed by dissident AFL leaders. It began by organizing efforts in primary industries, such as auto, steel, and rubber. Employers strongly resisted, but sit-down strikes and changes in public policy toward unions strengthened the CIO's efforts. By 1937, membership in the CIO was moving toward 4 million and had surpassed the AFL.

Industrial strife increased until the outbreak of World War II. The National War Labor Board was established to cope with employment problems during the wartime mobilization and to resolve disputes. Arbitration of grievances was introduced and later incorporated into collective bargaining agreements.

After the war, strikes reached unprecedented levels. In 1947, the Taft-Hartley Act passed over President Truman's veto, provided for national emergency dispute procedures, established the Federal Mediation and Conciliation Service, and designated several union unfair labor practices. In 1959, the Landrum-Griffin Act limited the possibility of corruption in union-management relations.

The AFL and the CIO merged in 1955; but, shortly after, the union movement reached its maximum growth as a share of the labor force. With the exception of the public sector, union membership has recently been declining. Later chapters identify the causes of these changes and their consequences for the labor movement.

DISCUSSION QUESTIONS

1. Why was the AFL reluctant to organize industrial workers during the early 1930s?
2. What were the major reasons for the rapid increase in labor's power during the 1930s and 1940s?
3. Why didn't the industrial unions embrace uplift or revolutionary unionism instead of business unionism?
4. Who were the most effective union leaders during the 1930s and 1940s? What are your criteria for effectiveness? Would these same leaders be effective now?

5. What impact did the 1988 presidential and congressional elections
    have on the growth and practices of the labor movement?

KEY TERMS

industrial unions

Committee for Industrial Organization

sit-down strike

Norris-LaGuardia Act

Wagner Act

National Labor Relations Board

exclusive representation

Mohawk Valley formula

Taft-Hartley

right-to-work laws

Federal Mediation and Conciliation Service

Landrum-Griffin Act

Executive Order 10988

Federal Labor Relations Authority

4

LABOR LAW
AND FEDERAL
AGENCIES

This chapter covers federal law related to collective bargaining. The relevant laws include the Railway Labor Act, the Norris-LaGuardia Act, the Wagner Act (as amended by Taft-Hartley and later legislation), the Landrum-Griffin Act, and the Civil Service Reform Act. Although it is not explicitly a labor law, portions of the Racketeer Influenced and Corrupt Organizations (RICO) Act will be covered since they affect both employees and unions.

These laws established several government agencies. Other agencies also influence labor relations directly. The chapter gives an overview of the statutes, major government agencies, and their organizational structures as of 1990. Finally, this chapter examines briefly some of the effects of how laws are enforced by federal government agencies, and how employees react to protections granted by some employment laws.

In studying this chapter, keep the following questions in mind:

1. What specific types of activities are regulated?
2. In what areas have regulations been extended or retracted?
3. What employee groups are excluded or exempted from various aspects of the regulations?
4. How do administrative agencies interact with employers and unions in implementing laws and regulations?

OVERVIEW

As noted in Chapters 2 and 3, statutory labor law is relatively recent in the United States. Current laws governing organizing and collective bargaining date back to 1926, when the Railway Labor Act was enacted. Since then, five other significant pieces of legislation have followed: Norris-LaGuardia (1932), Wagner (1935), Taft-Hartley (1947), Landrum-Griffin (1959), and the Civil Service Reform Act, Title VII (1978). Each was enacted to clarify and/or constrain the roles of management and labor. While six acts may not seem a significant number, it is important to remember that labor relations is generally more legislated in the United States than in most western European countries. Table 4–1 lists each piece of major legislation and the areas of labor relations to which it applies.

RAILWAY LABOR ACT

The **Railway Labor Act** applies to rail and air carriers and their employees. To be covered by the act, an employee must not be a supervisor or manager. The act claims to have five general purposes:

1. Avoiding service interruptions.
2. Eliminating any restrictions on joining a union.
3. Guaranteeing the freedom of employees in any matter of self-organization.
4. Providing for prompt dispute settlement.
5. Enabling prompt grievance settlement.

Section 2 prescribes a number of general duties: (1) carriers and employees are called on to maintain agreements relating to pay, rules, and working conditions and to settle disputes about these to avoid interrupting services; (2) disputes are to be settled by representatives of the carriers and the employees; (3) parties cannot influence the choice of the other's representative, and the chosen representative need not be an employee of the carrier; (4) employees are free to choose a representative by majority vote, and this representative shall be free from any dominance or financial relationship to the carrier; (5) no one can be forced to refrain from union membership or activities as a condition of employment; (6) a procedure for settling grievances must be established and be consistent with the provisions of the act; (7) no aspect of pay, rules, or working conditions can be unilaterally changed by the employer if covered in a contract; (8) carriers must notify employees of their intention to comply with the act; (9) the **National Mediation Board** (established by the Railway Labor Act) determines majority status of a union if disputed;

TABLE 4–1
Federal Labor Law

Law	Coverage	Major Provisions	Federal Agencies
Railway Labor Act.	Nonmanagerial rail and airline employees and employers in the private sector.	Employees may choose bargaining representatives for collective bargaining, no yellow-dog contracts, dispute settlement procedures include mediation, arbitration, and emergency boards.	National Mediation Board, National Board of Adjustment.
Norris-LaGuardia Act.	All private-sector employers and labor organizations.	Outlaws injunctions for nonviolent union activities. Makes yellow-dog contracts unenforceable.	
Labor-Management Relations Act (originally passed as Wagner Act, amended by Taft-Hartley and Landrum-Griffin acts).	Nonmanagerial employees in nonagricultural private sector not covered by Railway Labor Act; postal workers.	Employees may choose bargaining representatives for collective bargaining; both labor and management must bargain in good faith; unfair labor practices include discrimination for union activities, secondary boycotts, and refusal to bargain; national emergency dispute procedures are established.	National Labor Relations Board; Federal Mediation and Conciliation Service.
Landrum-Griffin Act.	All private-sector employers and labor organizations.	Specification and guarantee of individual rights of union members. Prohibits certain management and union conduct. Requires union financial disclosures.	U.S. Department of Labor.
Civil Service Reform Act, Title VII.	All nonuniformed, nonmanagerial federal service employees and agencies.	Employees may choose representatives for collective bargaining; bargaining rights established for noneconomic and nonstaffing issues. Requires arbitration of unresolved grievances.	Federal Labor Relations Authority.

(10) criminal penalties for violations of the act are established; and (11) if unions do not discriminate in fees and dues, **union-shop** clauses may be negotiated with the carriers.

Section 3 establishes the **National Railroad Board of Adjustment (NRBA)**. The NRBA is supposed to consist of an equal number of union and management members and is empowered to settle grievances of both parties. If the board deadlocks on a grievance, it obtains a referee to hear the case and make an award. Awards are binding, and prevailing parties may sue in federal district courts for orders to enforce the awards. In actuality, most disputes are handled by Public Law Boards and Special Boards of Adjustment, which involve ad hoc arbitrators or rotating boards of neutrals who hear and rule on deadlocked dispute cases.

Section 4 establishes the National Mediation Board (NMB), composed of three members appointed by the president. Section 5 covers the NMB's duties: mediating bargaining disputes on request, urging parties to arbitrate when mediation is unsuccessful, interpreting mediated contract agreements, and appointing arbitrators if disputing parties cannot agree on one.

Section 6 requires 30-day notice of an intent to renegotiate a contract. However, since railroad and airline contracts do not contain length of contract clauses, renegotiation only takes place after a Section 6 notice is filed. Sections 7, 8, and 9 deal with arbitration, the selection of arbitrators, procedures, and enforcement of awards.

Section 10 indicates the president is empowered to establish an emergency board of neutrals when the NMB determines a dispute will deprive a section of the country of transportation. These boards are usually convened after a substantial period of negotiation has occurred after a Section 6 notice was filed and the parties have been unable to agree on a new contract. The emergency board has a fact-finding duty in the dispute, and no party involved in the dispute may change employment conditions within 30 days of the board's filing of conclusions.

Sections 11 through 13 extend coverage of the act to air carriers.

Overview

Compared with later acts, the Railway Labor Act highly details dispute handling. Subsequent laws generally left this up to the parties. The Railway Labor Act also required employees to be organized by craft (or occupational area), forcing employers to bargain with several unions, some of which may have conflicting goals. Over time, bargaining by craft has changed somewhat as mergers have taken place forming new unions such as the United Transportation Union (UTU) and the Transportation Communications International Union (TCIU). The TCIU constitutes a merger among employees in blue- and white-collar railroad and airline occupations.

One should temper criticism of the act because the technological changes railroads faced after its passage would have engendered a great deal of controversy. The advent of diesel locomotives rendered firemen obsolete. Rather than facing slow attrition, as would occur in most industrial unions, a single craft was faced with rapid extinction. A further assessment of the Railway Labor Act's relative effectiveness will be covered in a section of Chapter 11 analyzing impasse procedures.

There have also been differences in the way the law has been implemented in the rail and airline industries. Arbitration of intracontract disputes in the airline industry is generally conducted like industries covered by the NLRA. In addition, contrary to the technical wording of the law, some railway supervisors, such as yardmasters, are represented by unions.

Norris-LaGuardia Act (1932)

The Norris-LaGuardia Act was the first law to protect the rights of unions and workers to engage in union activity. It is comprehensive in its application to workers and firms and absolute in its prescriptions. Federal courts have construed the law strictly.

The Norris-LaGuardia Act has two major purposes. First, it forbids federal courts to issue **injunctions** against a variety of specifically described union activities. Second, it makes yellow-dog contracts (in which employees agree that continued employment depends on abstention from union membership or activities) unenforceable. These contracts had been upheld by the Supreme Court.[1]

The act recognizes that freedom to associate for collective bargaining purposes is the corollary of the collectivization of capital through incorporation. Injunctions and yellow-dog contracts interfere with freedom of association.

Besides the absolute prohibition of yellow-dog contracts, a number of activities are specified as outside the scope of injunctive relief. These specifications apply regardless of whether the act is done by an individual, a group, or a union. The following cannot be enjoined:

1. Stopping or refusing to work.
2. Union membership.
3. Paying or withholding strike benefits, unemployment benefits, and the like to people participating in labor disputes.

---

[1] *Hitchman Coal & Coke Co. v. Mitchell*, 245 U.S. 229 (1917).

4. Aid or assistance for persons suing or being sued.
5. Publicizing a labor dispute in a nonviolent, nonfraudulent manner.
6. Assembly to organize.
7. Notifying anyone that any of these acts are to be performed.
8. Agreeing to engage or not engage in any of these acts.
9. Advising others to do any of these acts.

The Norris-LaGuardia Act also finally and completely laid to rest the 18th-century conspiracy doctrine. Section 5 prohibits injunctions against any of the above activities if pursued in a nonviolent manner. The effects of the *Danbury Hatters* decision (which required union members to pay boycott damages) were substantially diminished by Section 6.[2] That section mandates that an individual or labor organization may not be held accountable for unlawful acts of its leadership unless those acts were directed or ratified by the membership.

Section 7 ensures the act may not be used as a cover for violent and destructive actions. This section states that an injunction may be issued if:

1. Substantial or irreparable injury to property will occur.
2. Greater injury will be inflicted on the party requesting the injunction than the injunction would cause on the adversary.
3. No adequate legal remedy exists.
4. Authorities are either unable or unwilling to give protection.

Before an injunction can be granted, the union must be given the opportunity for rebuttal. If an immediate restraining order is sought and there is insufficient time for an adversary proceeding, the employer must deposit a bond to compensate the union for possible injuries done to it by the injunction. Section 7 also requires surgical rather than broadbrush injunctions; that is, the injunction is to be issued against only those persons or associations actually causing the problems.

Section 8 further restricts injunction-granting powers by requiring the requester to try to settle the dispute before asking for the injunction. Section 9 states that the injunction cannot be issued against all union activities in the case, only those leading to the injury. For example, mass picketing might be enjoined if it is violent; but the strike, payments of strike benefits, and so on could not be enjoined.

While the Norris-LaGuardia Act did not require an employer to recognize a union or bargain with it, it provided labor some leverage in

---

[2] *Loewe* v. *Lawlor,* 208 U.S. 274 (1908).

organizing and bargaining. Labor could, henceforth, bring pressure on the employer through strikes, boycotts, and the like without worrying about federal court injunctions.

WAGNER AND TAFT-HARTLEY ACTS (AS AMENDED)

The Wagner and Taft-Hartley acts were enacted 12 years apart, but Taft-Hartley was, to a large extent, an amendment of and extension to the Wagner Act. In 1959, the Landrum-Griffin Act extended the amending process. Finally, the Taft-Hartley Act was amended in 1974 to apply to private nonprofit health care organizations and modified some provisions for these organizations only. These acts made clear the public policy preference for collective bargaining for resolving differences in the employment relationship and for roughly balancing the power of labor and management. The Wagner Act, passed during a period of relative weakness for organized labor, only spoke to employer practices. As the pendulum swung in the other direction, the Taft-Hartley amendments added labor practices to the proscribed list. Finally, the Landrum-Griffin Act attempted to "fine-tune" the statutes consistent with day-to-day realities. The major substantive provisions of these laws follow.

Section 2, Taft-Hartley

Section 2 defines the terms used in the act. The most important definitions are related to the terms **employer, employee, supervisor,** and **professional employee.**

Employer

An employer is an organization or a manager acting on behalf of the organization. However, certain types of organizations are specifically excluded from the act's jurisdiction. These are federal, state, and local governments or any organizations wholly owned by these agencies (except the U.S. Postal Service); persons subject to the Railway Labor Act; and union representatives when acting as bargaining agents.

Employee

An employee does not necessarily have to be a member of an organization against which a labor dispute is directed. For example, if firm A is being struck and employees of firm B refuse to cross the picket lines, even though no dispute exists with B, B's workers are considered employees for labor-management relations purposes under the act. An individual also remains an employee if on strike for a contract or if on strike or discharged because of an employer's unfair labor practice. Employees remain within this definition, even if employers do not consider them employees, until they take new employment at or above a level equivalent to their previous jobs. Domestic workers, agricultural workers, independent contractors,[3] individuals employed by a spouse or parent,[4] or persons covered by the Railway Labor Act are excluded.

Supervisor

A supervisor is an employee with independent authority to make personnel decisions and to administer a labor agreement. Examples of personnel decisions include hiring, firing, adjusting grievances, making work assignments, and deciding pay increases.

Professional Employee

A professional employee is one whose work is intellectual in character, requiring independent judgment or discretion; whose performance cannot readily be measured on a standardized basis; and whose skills are learned through a prolonged, specialized program of instruction.

Section 3

Section 3 establishes the National Labor Relations Board. The board consists of five members appointed by the president and confirmed by the Senate. Members serve five-year terms and may be reappointed. One member, designated by the president, chairs the board.

The board may delegate its duties to any group of three or more members. It can also delegate authority to determine representation and election questions to its regional directors. The board has a general counsel responsible for investigating charges and issuing complaints.

Section 7

The heart of the original Wagner Act, Section 7 still embodies public policy toward the individual worker and collective bargaining. As amended, Section 7 reads:

> Employees shall have the right to self-organization, to form, join, or assist labor organizations, to bargain collectively through representatives of their own choosing, and to engage in other concerted activities for the purpose of collective bargaining or other mutual aid or protection, and shall also

---

[3] *P.Q. Beef Processors, Inc.*, 231 NLRB 179 (1977).
[4] *Viele & Sons, Inc.*, 227 NLRB 284 (1977).

have the right to refrain from any or all of such activities except to the extent that such right may be affected by an agreement requiring membership in a labor organization as a condition of employment as authorized in Section 8(a)(3).

Section 8

Section 8 specifies employer actions that violate an employee's Section 7 rights and includes union violations of Section 7 and refusals to bargain with an employer. Part (a) deals with employer practices; part (b) with those of unions.

Employer Unfair Labor Practices

An employer may not interfere with an employee engaging in any activity protected by Section 7. The employer may not assist or dominate any labor organization. For example, if two unions are vying to organize a group of workers, an employer may neither recognize one to avoid dealing with the other nor express a preference for one.

An employer may not discriminate in hiring, assignment, or other terms of employment on the basis of union membership. However, employers and unions may negotiate contract clauses requiring union membership as a condition of continued employment (a union shop agreement). But if such a clause is negotiated, the employer cannot discriminate against nonmembership if the union discriminatorily refuses to admit an employee to membership.

Employees may not be penalized or discriminated against for charging an employer with a violation of the act.

Finally, employers may not refuse to bargain with a union over issues of pay, hours, or other terms and conditions of employment.

Union Unfair Labor Practices

Unions may not coerce employees in the exercise of Section 7 rights, but this does not limit union internal rule making, discipline, fines, and so forth. Unions cannot demand or require an employer to discriminate against an employee for any reason except failure to pay union dues.

Unions are also forbidden to engage in—or encourage individuals to engage in—strikes or refusals to handle some type of product or work if the object is to accomplish any of the following ends:

1. Forcing an employer or self-employed person to join an employer or labor organization or to cease handling nonunion products (except in certain cases, detailed later).
2. Forcing an employer to bargain with an uncertified labor organization; that is, one whose majority status has not been established.

3. Forcing an employer to cease bargaining with a certified representative.

4. Forcing an employer to assign work to employees in a particular labor organization unless ordered to do so or previously bargained to do so.

5. Requiring excessive initiation fees for union membership.

6. Forcing an employer to pay for services not rendered.

7. Picketing an employer to force recognition of the picketing union if:
   a. The picketing group has not been certified as the employees' representative;
   b. Either no union election has taken place within the past 12 months or the picketing union requests a representation election within 30 days after picketing begins; but
   c. Nothing can prohibit a union's picketing to advise the public that an employer's employees are not unionized, provided the picketing does not interfere with pickups and deliveries.

Protected Concerted Activity
Where no evidence of threat, reprisal, or promise of benefit exists, the parties involved in collective bargaining activities are free to express views in any form.

Duty to Bargain
Unions and employers have a mutual duty to bargain in good faith about wages, hours, and terms and conditions of employment. Each must be willing to meet at the request of the other to negotiate an agreement, to reduce it to writing, and to interpret its meaning when a disagreement arises. Neither party is required to concede any issue to demonstrate good faith. Notification of the Federal Mediation and Conciliation Service (FMCS) is required as a condition for contract modification. Specific and more stringent requirements are laid out for health care organizations.

Prohibited Contract Clauses
Except in the construction and apparel industries, employees and unions cannot negotiate contracts providing that particular products of certain employers will not be used. This is the so-called **hot cargo** issue. For example, a trucking union could not negotiate a contract prohibiting hauling goods manufactured by a nonunion employer. But a construction union could refuse to install nonunion goods if a contract clause had been negotiated.

Construction Employment
Contractors can make collective bargaining agreements with construction unions, even without a demonstration of majority status. The agreements may also require union membership within seven days of

employment and give the union an opportunity to refer members for existing job openings. These exceptions recognize the relatively short-run nature of many construction jobs. Labor agreements may also provide for apprenticeship training requirements and may give preference in job openings to workers with greater past experience.

Health Care Picketing

A union anticipating a strike or picketing at a health care facility must notify the Federal Mediation and Conciliation Service (FMCS) 10 days in advance.

Section 9

Section 9 deals with representatives and elections. The act provides that if a majority of employees in a particular unit desires representation, all employees (whether union members or not) will be represented by the union regarding wages, hours, and terms and conditions of employment. Individuals can present and have their own grievances adjusted if the adjustment is not inconsistent with the contract.

The NLRB determines what group of employees would constitute an appropriate unit for a representation election and subsequent bargaining. Its discretion is limited, however. First, it cannot include professional and nonprofessional employees in the same unit unless a majority of the professionals agree. Second, it cannot deny separate representation to a craft solely on the basis that it was part of a larger unit determined appropriate by the board. Third, it cannot include plant guards and other types of employees in diverse units. Also, supervisors are not employees as defined by the act; so, for example, a unit of production supervisors would be an inappropriate group for representation.

In cases of questionable union majority status, the board is authorized to hold elections (subject to certain constraints, detailed in Chapter 6). The board may also conduct elections to determine whether an existing union maintains a continuing majority status.

Sections 10, 11, and 12

These sections deal with (1) the prevention of unfair labor practices and (2) procedures used by the NLRB in investigating and remedying them. If the board finds an unfair labor practice has occurred, it can issue cease-and-desist orders, require back pay to make wronged persons whole, and petition a court of appeals for enforcement of its orders.

Section 11 deals with the procedures the NLRB has available to obtain evidence, such as subpoena powers. Section 12 provides for criminal penalties for persons interfering with board activities.

Sections 13 through 19

These sections limit the applicability of other sections. Section 13 indicates that nothing in the act limits the right to strike. Section 14(a) holds that supervisors cannot be prohibited from belonging to a union but an employer need not recognize membership for bargaining purposes. Section 14(b), one of the most controversial in the act, permits passage by the states of right-to-work laws. In states with these laws, employees represented by unions cannot be compelled to join a union or pay dues as a condition of continued employment. Section 14(c) allows the NLRB to decline jurisdiction in cases where the impact on commerce is judged insignificant, but state agencies can assert jurisdiction if the board declines. Section 15 deals with bankruptcies (a subject covered in more detail in Chapter 11). Section 19 provides that employees of health care organizations whose religious beliefs preclude union membership may donate a sum equal to union dues to a nonreligious charity in lieu of the dues or agency fees.

Title II

This title begins the major additions made by the Taft-Hartley Act to the original Wagner Act. Obviously, some of those previously mentioned, such as union unfair labor practices, were important; but Title II broke new ground in public policy toward collective bargaining.

Title II, Section 201, indicates maintaining stable labor relations is in the public interest. If conflicts between the parties interfere with stability, the government should be able and willing to offer assistance. Thus, Section 202 created the FMCS (defined in Section 203) to offer mediation services whenever a dispute threatens to interrupt commerce or where it involves a health care organization. The FMCS is directed to emphasize services in contract negotiations, not grievance settlements.

A second major feature of Title II is the national emergencies sections. If, in the opinion of the president, a labor dispute imperils the nation, a board of inquiry may be appointed to investigate the issues surrounding the dispute. After the board submits its report, the attorney general may be directed to ask a district court to enjoin a strike or lockout. If the court agrees the dispute threatens national security, an injunction may be issued. If an injunction is ordered, the board is reconvened and monitors the settlement process. If an agreement is not reached after 60 days, the board reports the positions of labor and management and includes management's last offer. Over the next 15 days, the NLRB holds an election among the employees to determine whether a majority favors accepting management's last offer. Five more days are taken to certify the results. At this time (or earlier, if a settlement was reached), the injunction will be discharged. If a settlement was not reached, the president forwards the report of the board, the election results, and the president's recommendations to Congress for action.

Title III

This title addresses suits by and against labor organizations. Unions are enabled to sue on behalf of their members and to be sued and found liable for damages against organizational (but not members') assets.

The title forbids financial dealings between an organization and the representative of its employees. Union agents are forbidden from demanding payment for performing contractual duties. Certain regulations relating to the establishment of trust funds are also included.

Unions and corporations are forbidden to make political contributions in any elections involving the choice of federal officeholders.

Summary

The important aspects of the LMRA relate to the establishment, function, and powers of the NLRB; the delineation of employer and union unfair labor practices; the promulgation of rules governing representation and certification; the creation and functions of the FMCS; and the national emergency injunction procedures. These aim at balancing the power of labor and management and stabilizing industrial relations.

LANDRUM-GRIFFIN ACT (1959)

The Landrum-Griffin Act, formally the Labor-Management Reporting and Disclosure Act of 1959 (LMRDA), resulted from congressional hearings into corrupt practices in labor-management relations. It regulates internal activities of employers and unions covered by both Taft-Hartley and the Railway Labor Act.

Title I—Bill of Rights for Union Members

Section 101 provides union members with equal rights and privileges in nominating, voting, and participating in referenda, meetings, and the like. Each member has a right to be heard and to oppose the policies of the leadership insofar as this does not interfere with the union's legal obligations. Dues, initiation fees, and assessments cannot be increased without a majority vote to approve the increase. Members' rights to sue their unions are guaranteed as long as they have exhausted internal union procedures and are not aided by an employer or an employer association. Finally, members of unions cannot be expelled unless due process consistent with this section is followed.

Section 104 provides that copies of the labor agreement between the employer and the union be available to every member.

Title II—Reports Required of Unions and Employers

Section 201 requires all unions to file constitutions and bylaws with the secretary of labor. Unions must file annual reports detailing assets and liabilities, receipts, salaries and allowances of officers, loans made to officers, loans made to businesses, and other expenditures prescribed by the secretary of labor. The report must also be made available to the membership. Employees covered by union contracts have little access to information on union expenditures to influence political outcomes, litigation, and the like before it is filed with the department of labor.[5]

Section 202 requires *every* officer and employee (except clerical and custodial employees) to submit an annual report to the secretary of labor detailing any family income or transaction in stocks, securities, or other payments (except wages) made by a firm where the union represents employees; income or other payments to a business that had substantial dealings with these firms; or any payments made by a labor consultant to such a firm.

Section 203 requires employer reports on payments made to union officials (even if only to reimburse expenses); to employees to convince other employees to exercise or not exercise their rights to organize and bargain collectively; and to obtain information about unions or individuals involved in disputes with the employer. Employers must also report agreements with or payments to a labor relations consultant who is trying to influence workers in voting under Section 7 of the Taft-Hartley Act.

Title III—Trusteeships

A union may take action against a subsidiary for breaching the union's constitution or bylaws. To reduce the possibility of stifling dissent, Title III requires that a **trusteeship** be imposed only to restore democratic

---

[5] M. F. Masters, R. S. Atkin, and G. W. Florkowski, "An Analysis of Union Reporting Requirements under Title II of the Landrum-Griffin Act," *Labor Law Journal* 40 (1989), pp. 713–22.

EXHIBIT 4-1

P-9 Trusteeship Gets Judge's Approval; Local Leadership Out

A federal judge ruled Monday that the United Food and Commercial Workers (UFCW) union can take control of striking Local P-9 of Austin, Minn.

The ruling clears the way for the international union to negotiate a labor contract with Geo. A. Hormel & Co., according to the international and Hormel.

It also enforces the suspensions of P-9 officers. They contended in their fight with the international that they were elected by the membership and could not be replaced as the sole bargainers for the striking meatpackers.

Joe Hansen, an international vice president, district director of the UFCW and the international's trustee, said late yesterday that Hormel has agreed to meet later this week to resume contract negotiations in the nearly 10-month-old labor dispute.

"The trustee is the bargaining agent for Local P-9," said Hansen. "Jim Guyette (P-9's president) and all of the officers of P-9 have been suspended and all business of the local will be conducted with me or with the (two) deputy trustees."

U.S. District Judge Edward Devitt [said] . . . , "Since Local P-9 did not comply with the international's directive to cease its strike against Hormel (in March) or to cease its roving picket line activities, the international acted within its authority in appointing the trustee to manage P-9's affairs."

SOURCE: Neal St. Anthony, "P-9 Trusteeship Gets Judge's Approval; Local Leadership Out," *Minneapolis Star and Tribune*, June 3, 1986, pp. 1A, 9A.

---

procedures, correct corruption or financial malfeasance, or assure performance of collective bargaining agreements or other legitimate union functions. If a trusteeship is imposed on a subsidiary, the union must file a report with the secretary of labor detailing the reasons for the takeover. It must also disclose the subsidiary's financial situation. A union exercising a trustee relationship cannot move assets from the subsidiary or appoint delegates to conventions from it (unless they were elected by secret ballot of the membership). Recently, the United Food and Commercial Workers (UFCW) placed its local P-9, which represented employees of Hormel's Austin, Minnesota, plant, under trusteeship for refusing to end a strike. Exhibit 4-1 contains some background information on the controversy surrounding the trusteeship.

Racketeer Influenced and Corrupt Organizations Act

RICO was passed by Congress in 1970 to increase the penalties for corruption through the forfeiture of interests gained through corruption. Penalties are assessed at triple the amount gained through the corrupt activities. State laws have also been enacted to attempt to reduce or eliminate corruption. Evidence in the New Jersey casino industry suggests the laws work well in policing employers, but unions are more difficult to control because local unions may represent employees in both casinos and other service organizations. Thus, the election of corrupt union officers is possible through a majority being represented in corrupt relationships.[6] An economic analysis of corruption in the New York City construction industry and unions suggests that the level of coordination necessary in construction coupled with the potential monopoly power of unions to supply skilled labor could lead to the involvement of organized crime in monitoring or facilitating activities. The effect of possible corruption on wages of unionized New York City construction workers appears not to be significant—somewhat surprising given the relatively high unionization of New York City construction workers relative to those in the rest of the United States.[7]

Effects of Implementation of Laws

An intriguing new theory studying critical labor law and labor history suggests the courts have consistently interpreted new statutory law to reinforce market-oriented practices. For example, the Supreme Court, while agreeing with the constitutionality of the NLRA, also reiterated the rights of management to exclusively make certain decisions unless it voluntarily agreed to bargain about them. Further, it is argued that courts have generally been permissive toward employer-sponsored participation plans and have not ruled them to be dominated labor organizations. Laws and their interpretation appear to be based on a pluralist assumption that management, labor, and government operate together in a relationship in which government facilitates the operation of the market through mechanisms to deal with conflict between labor and management that permit the market to continue functioning.[8]

Employers are more likely to engage in actions that are later found to be unfair labor practices the greater the differences between union and nonunion wages. Regulatory agencies such as the NLRB have difficulty

---

[6] Barbara A. Lee and James Chelius, "Government Regulation of Union-Management Corruption: The Casino Industry Experience in New Jersey," *Industrial and Labor Relations Review* 42 (1989), pp. 536–48.

[7] Casey Ichniowski and Ann Preston, "The Persistence of Organized Crime in New York City Construction: An Economic Perspective," *Industrial and Labor Relations Review* 42 (1989), pp. 549–65.

[8] R. L. Hogler, "Critical Labor Law, Working-Class History, and the New Industrial Relations." *Industrial Relations Law Journal* 10 (1988), pp. 116–43; and R. L. Hogler, "Labor History and Critical Labor Law: An Interdisciplinary Approach to Workers' Control," *Labor History* 30 (1989), pp. 185–92.

coping with these problems because complaints cannot be processed quickly without increased staff, which must be appropriated by Congress, and the board can levy no penalties above the requirement that workers be made whole for the effects of violations.[9]

FEDERAL DEPARTMENTS AND AGENCIES

All three branches of government—legislative, executive, and judicial—are involved in labor relations. Congress writes and amends the law; the executive agencies implement and regulate within the law; and the judiciary examines the actions of the other two in light of the Constitution, the statutes, and common law. This section examines the departments and agencies concerned with labor relations functions.

Department of Labor

The Department of Labor, created as a cabinet department in 1913, has a broad charter.

> The purpose of the Department of Labor is to foster, promote, and develop the welfare of the wage earners of the United States, to improve their working conditions, and to advance their opportunities for profitable employment. In carrying out this mission, the department administers more than 130 federal labor laws, guaranteeing workers' rights to safe and healthful working conditions, a minimum hourly wage and overtime pay, freedom from employment discrimination, unemployment insurance and workers' compensation. The department also protects workers' pension rights, sponsors job training programs, helps workers find jobs; works to strengthen free collective bargaining; and keeps track of changes in employment, prices, and other national economic measurements. As the department seeks to assist all Americans who need and want to work, special efforts are made to meet the unique job market problems of older workers, youths, minority group members, women, the handicapped, and other groups.[10]

The organization of the Department of Labor is shown in Figure 4–1.

Labor-Management Services Administration

The LMSA collects reports from employers and unions as required by the Employee Retirement Income Security Act of 1974 (ERISA) and the Landrum-Griffin Act. The LMSA also provides research assistance in

---

[9] R. J. Flanagan, "Compliance and Enforcement Decisions under the National Labor Relations Act," *Journal of Labor Economics* 7 (1989), pp. 257–80.

[10] Office of the Federal Register, National Archives and Record Service, General Services Administration, *U.S. Government Manual, 1986–1987* (Washington, D.C.: Government Printing Office, 1986), p. 399.

FIGURE 4-1
Department of Labor

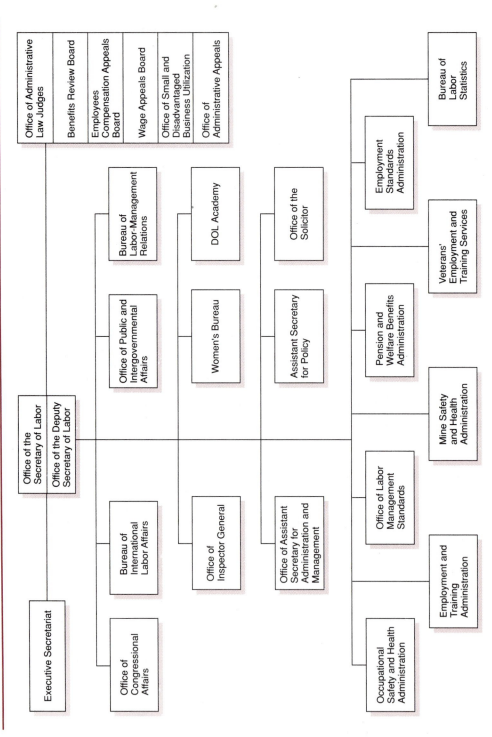

SOURCE: *U.S. Government Manual, 1989–1990*, Federal Register Office (Washington, D.C.: Government Printing Office), p. 410.

collective bargaining for long-range changes (for example, automation) and immediate negotiations. The LMSA administers legislation pertaining to federal employee labor relations by determining appropriate bargaining units, supervising representation elections, ruling on unfair labor practices, and deciding the arbitrability of grievances.

Occupational Safety and Health Administration

OSHA is responsible for the interpretation and enforcement of the Occupational Safety and Health Act of 1970. It investigates violations and assesses penalties through hearings held by Department of Labor administrative law judges. One study found that workers who are better educated or unionized were more knowledgeable about hazards, and workers who were better protected in the exercise of their rights were more likely to refuse unsafe work.[11]

Employment and Training Administration

The Bureau of Apprenticeship and Training in the ETA assists employers and unions in establishing high-quality skilled trades training programs with consistent standards.

Bureau of Labor Statistics

The BLS collects, maintains, and publishes data that interested persons use to assess the current state of the economy—nationally, regionally, or locally. It publishes the consumer price index, conducts area wage surveys, and provides unemployment data.

Employment Standards Administration

Several offices within the ESA are important to unions and employers. The Wage and Hour Division enforces provisions of the Fair Labor Standards Act governing overtime, minimum wage, and child labor. The Office of Federal Contract Compliance Programs monitors actions of companies with federal contracts in affirmatively hiring and employing women, minorities, and the handicapped. The Office of Workers' Compensation Programs administers federal programs for longshore workers and for miners suffering from black lung diseases.

Federal Mediation and Conciliation Service

The FMCS was established by the Taft-Hartley Act to help parties resolve labor disputes. In contract negotiation, it may mediate either through invitation or on its own motion. **Mediators** assist the parties in bargaining but have no power to impose settlements or regulate bargaining activity.

---

[11] V. Walters and M. Denton, "Workers' Knowledge of Their Legal Rights and Resistance to Hazardous Work," *Relations Industrielles* 45 (1990), pp. 531–45.

It also maintains lists of arbitrators to provide names from which parties may choose to settle disputes within the contract. In listing or delisting an arbitrator, the FMCS applies established qualification rules.

National Mediation Board

The NMB was established in 1934 by an amendment to the Railway Labor Act. It mediates contract disputes between carriers and their unions and certifies representatives of employees for bargaining. It refers grievances to the National Railroad Adjustment Board (NRAB). The NMB may appoint a referee to assist in making NRAB awards when the panel is deadlocked.

The NMB is also responsible for notifying the president if an unsettled, mediated dispute threatens to cripple transport in some section of the country. The president may then appoint an emergency board to study the situation and make recommendations.

National Labor Relations Board

The NLRB was established by the Wagner Act. It determines whether employees desire union representation and whether unions or companies have committed unfair labor practices as defined by federal law. The NLRB has jurisdiction over most for-profit employers; private, profit and nonprofit hospitals; and the U.S. Postal Service. Figure 4-2 shows the structure of the board.

NLRB members are appointed by the president for five-year terms and confirmed by the Senate. The general counsel determines whether to proceed against an employer or union once a complaint is filed. The board does not initiate action but only responds to complaints from the involved parties.[12]

The board receives about 50,000 cases per year through its 33 regional offices. About 80 percent are **unfair labor practice** (C) cases, with about 20 percent representation election (R) cases. When a C case is filed, the regional office investigates. If the charge appears not to be meritorious, the charging party is asked to withdraw it, or charges are dismissed. These decisions can be appealed to the general counsel, but only about 4 percent are reversed. If the case has merit, the regional director works with the parties to try to fashion a remedy and settle the case. This tactic succeeds in about 94 percent of cases. Failing that, the case is heard within one to three months by an administrative law judge. After the

---

[12] For complete details, see Kenneth C. McGuinness, *How to Take a Case before the National Labor Relations Board*, 4th ed. (Washington, D.C.: Bureau of National Affairs, 1976).

FIGURE 4-2

National Labor Relations Board

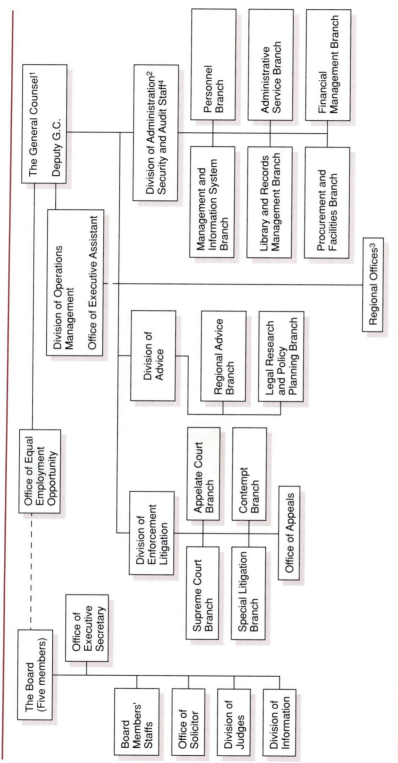

[1] The authority and responsibility of the general counsel in certain administrative matters is derived by delegation from the board.

[2] Division of Administration is also responsible to the board for administrative support services required in the performance of board functions.

[3] Includes exercise by regional director of board authority under Section 9 of the act, in representation cases, by delegation from the board.

[4] The auditor is authorized to bring findings directly to the board or G.C. as appropriate.

SOURCE: "NLRB Organizations and Functions," Rules and Regulations and Statements of Procedure (Washington, D.C.: U.S. Government Printing Office, 1987), p. 281.

judge issues a ruling, exceptions can be filed, and the case is assigned to a board member. The board must then study the case, and a three-member panel issues a ruling.[13]

If one of the parties does not comply with an NLRB decision, the board may petition a U.S. court of appeals for enforcement. Board orders must be publicized to employees and/or union members. The board may issue cease-and-desist orders, bargaining orders, and decisions making employees whole for illegal personnel actions, such as termination for union activity.

Because the NLRB makes initial decisions regarding unfair labor practices in the absence of judicial review, employers and unions might regard the decisions as establishing precedents. However, evidence suggests this is not the case. The political appointment process appears to influence the determination of unfair labor practice charges. A board member could be a Democrat appointed by a Democrat president (DD), a Democrat appointed by a Republican president (DR), a Republican appointed by a Democrat president (RD), or a Republican appointed by a Republican president (RR). A study of cases decided in 1977 by three-member panels of the NLRB had the following results: when a majority were DD members, rulings favored unions 12 percent *more* often than when the majority were RD or DR; and when the majority were RR members, unions received favorable rulings 20 percent *less* often than if RD or DR panels decided the cases.

The general counsel's political orientation may also strongly influence outcomes because that office decides which cases should be referred to the board members for decisions.[14] A comparison of unfair labor processing in Ontario and the United States found that in Ontario, charges were more likely to be heard and heard promptly. There was also a lower frequency of filings and less intervention by courts in reviewing administrative decisions. Unlike in the United States, in Ontario, the parties pay the cost of processing an unfair labor practice charge.[15]

NLRB decisions may alter the bargaining power between labor and management if a previously used practice is prohibited. Filing rates appear influenced by the level of economic activity, and they increase for *both* unions and managements when it appears that board composition will lead to more favorable decisions for management. Employers may

[13] Donald L. Dotson, "Processing Cases at the NLRB," *Labor Law Journal* 35 (1984), pp. 3–9.

[14] William N. Cooke and Frederick H. Gautschi III, "Political Bias in NLRB Unfair Labor Practice Decisions," *Industrial and Labor Relations Review* 35 (1982), pp. 539–49.

[15] P. G. Bruce, "The Processing of Unfair Labor Practice Cases in the United States and Ontario," *Relations Industrielles* 45 (1990), pp. 481–509.

increase their filings because they believe pro-management decisions may deter union tactics.[16] Much controversy surrounds recent board decisions, with union leaders suggesting they might be better off without labor legislation.[17]

SUMMARY

U.S. labor law consists primarily of the Railway Labor, Norris-LaGuardia, Wagner, Taft-Hartley, and Landrum-Griffin acts. These enable collective bargaining, regulate labor and management activities, and limit intervention by the federal courts in lawful union activities.

The legislative branch of government enacts the laws, the executive branch carries them out, and the court system tests their validity and rules on conduct within their purview.

As a cabinet department, the Department of Labor is primarily responsible for implementing human resource programs and monitoring activities. It has little direct influence on collective bargaining.

Rule-making, interpretive, and assistance agencies have major influences on employers, through either direct intervention or regulation. The FMCS and NLRB have the greatest impact on collective bargaining.

DISCUSSION QUESTIONS

1. In the absence of federal labor laws, what do you think the scope and nature of labor relations would be in the United States?
2. Should workers now under the Railway Labor Act be brought within the jurisdiction of the LMRA?
3. Are current laws strong enough to preserve individual rights in collective bargaining?
4. To what extent should the federal government have power to intervene in collective bargaining activities?

---

[16] Myron Roomkin, "A Quantitative Study of Unfair Labor Practice Cases," *Industrial and Labor Relations Review* 34 (1981), pp. 245–56.

[17] See, for example, *NLRB at 50: Labor Board at the Crossroads* (Washington, D.C.: Bureau of National Affairs, 1985).

5. Should such administrative agencies as the NLRB be allowed to render administrative law decisions that can be enforced by the courts, or should an agency be required to go directly to court?

KEY TERMS

Railway Labor Act	employee
National Mediation Board	supervisor
union shop	professional employee
National Railroad Board of Adjustment	hot cargo
injunctions	trusteeship
employer	mediators
	unfair labor practice

5
___

UNION STRUCTURE AND GOVERNMENT

Employing organizations and labor unions are governed differently. Employees are hired to perform tasks to accomplish certain objectives, and many have little voice in what the objectives will be. The objectives are determined by high-level managers who are monitored by owners or boards of directors elected by shareholders or, in the case of public agencies, by their elected or appointed boards. Managers and leaders are responsible to their constituencies: a corporation's shareholders, a city's voters, a union's members. The goals of unions, like other organizations, reflect member interests. The elected leadership must generally be responsive to member desires if they are to remain in office.

This chapter examines the organizational components of the labor movement. Functions and government of unions and how these relate to and involve the membership are described.

Union political activities are also explored. This chapter addresses the following major questions:

1. What are the major organizational levels within the labor movement?
2. What roles do the local union, the international, and the AFL–CIO play?
3. How do international union organizational structures and politics differ?
4. To what extent are unions autocratically or democratically governed?
5. How does organized labor become involved in the political process?

The U.S. labor movement is composed of three major hierarchical structures: the local union, the national union, and the labor federation. These are all discussed in the following sections.

The Local Union

The local union is the institution that represents employees in day-to-day dealings with the employer. Local union jurisdictions tend to be defined along four major dimensions: (1) the specific jobs workers perform or the industrial classification in which they are employed (craft and industrial jurisdictions), (2) a specified geographic area, (3) the specific activity involved (organizing, bargaining, and so on), and (4) the level of union government applying the jurisdiction.[1] The exact definition of a local's constituency can vary within these parameters. Many local unions operate in a specific municipality, represent workers in a single industry or job classification, and frequently bargain with a single employer. There are exceptions, however. For example, Local 12 of the United Auto Workers in Toledo, Ohio, (an amalgamated local) represents employees among several employers in different industries; Local 65 of the Retail, Wholesale, and Department Store Union in New York City represents employees in over 2,000 establishments; Local 3 of the Operating Engineers covers portions of four western states; and Local 459 of the International Union of Electrical Workers (IUE), based in New York, bargains with employers in Milwaukee, New Orleans, and Chicago.[2]

A local union's jurisdiction affects its size, constitution, officers, and organizational structure.[3] A president, vice president, recording secretary, financial secretary, treasurer, sergeant at arms, and trustees are generally elected. Unless the local is large, these posts are part time and usually unpaid. Locals interested in expanding to or dealing with several employers will often create a **business agent** position. The business agent's job is to ensure that contractual rights of members are not being violated and refer union members to available employment. Business agents are most necessary in industries in which union members often move from employer to employer as work is finished on one project and becomes available on another.

Two major committees operate within most locals: the **executive committee** (made up of the local's officers) and the grievance or **negotiation committee.** The executive committee establishes local policy; the negotiation committee reviews members' grievances and negotiates with management over grievances and contract changes. Other committees deal with organizing and membership, welfare, recreation, and political action.

---

[1] Jack Barbash, *American Unions: Structure, Government, and Politics* (New York: Random House, 1967).

[2] Ibid., pp. 12–14, 43.

[3] Leonard R. Sayles and George Strauss, *The Local Union,* rev. ed. (New York: Harcourt Brace Jovanovich, 1967), pp. 2–5.

At the work-unit level, the union elects or appoints **stewards.** Stewards are responsible for ensuring that first-line supervisors comply with the contract. When grievances are presented, the steward acts as a spokesperson. Stewards also collect dues and solicit participation in union activities. Many collective bargaining contracts recognize the vulnerability of the steward's advocative position by according it **superseniority.** As long as one remains a steward, he or she is, by definition, the most senior member of the unit. Stewards often have little experience in representative positions before their election or appointment. Union training helps them accomplish their responsibilities—particularly understanding the goals of the union movement, understanding the contract, and communicating with members.[4] Exhibit 5–1 provides an example of how one steward views his work.

The situation of the steward—as a full-time company employee and also the unit employees' representative when they have grievances against the employer—is paradoxical. To whom is the steward committed, the union or the employer or both? A study of about 200 stewards at one employer found that about 80 percent were committed to the union, 36 percent were committed to the employer, and 12 percent were committed to neither. Almost 30 percent were committed to the union and the employer simultaneously. **Dual commitment** was related to stewards' positive perceptions about the employer's supervisors, the promotional opportunities, and the union's influence on the employer; positive beliefs about the union's decision-making process; perceptions of low job opportunities with other employers; and beliefs that the grievance procedure is not a tool to punish supervisors.[5]

Commitment is also an important issue for higher-level local union officers. While their employers generally grant them leaves of absence in larger units, they still remain attached to the firm and also bear responsibility to their national unions as well as their local memberships. Local officers are committed strongly to the labor movement, but are less positive about the fairness of national union elections than they are about local elections. They are willing to advocate issues favored by their national union, but they are more closely wedded to the traditional goals of the labor movement than to new approaches.[6]

---

[4] B. Broadbent, "Identifying the Education Needs of Union Stewards," *Labor Studies Journal* 14 (1989), pp. 28–45.

[5] James E. Martin, John M. Magenau, and Mark F. Peterson, "Variables Related to Patterns of Union Stewards' Commitment," *Journal of Labor Research* 8 (1986), pp. 323–36.

[6] M. F. Masters, R. S. Atkin, and G. Schoenfeld, "A Survey of USWA Local Officers' Commitment-Support Attitudes," *Labor Studies Journal* 15, no. 3 (1990), pp. 51–80.

EXHIBIT 5-1

Example of the Role of a Shop Steward

East Chicago, Ind.—Alan Moseley, still sweating from his workday in the steel mill, lumbers into the office of United Steelworkers Local 1010 and slams his briefcase down in frustration.

Mr. Moseley is a union "griever," or shop steward, as he would be called in some unions, handling union members' complaints against his employer, Inland Steel Industries Inc. His frustration at the time results from a year of sometimes rancorous talks with Inland over whether eight new jobs in its plant should go to union or salaried workers.

Yanking the complaint from his bulging briefcase, he grouses that a tentative agreement is meeting resistance from his own members. "It's total unrest out there," Mr. Moseley says, gesturing toward Inland's sprawling mill down the street. "It's a daily battle over jobs."

. . . Mr. Moseley's recent struggle over the eight new jobs at Inland reflects the deep tension. As his negotiations with the company dragged on, workers grew angry at the delay. Last summer, they circulated a cartoon depicting Mr. Moseley as a fat hog with a hoof in the company's till. Enraged, Mr. Moseley telephoned dozens of members but failed to find out who distributed the cartoon.

"You've got to have a leather hide in this business, but that hurt me," the 41-year-old Mr. Moseley says.

After more than a year of effort, Mr. Moseley in February finally worked out a compromise with the company: Inland promised to let union members take four of the eight jobs in a new automated steel-testing laboratory.

. . . But despite all the frustrations and despite a high defeat rate among grievers who seek reelection, Mr. Moseley has continued to run every three years. Shunning the hard-hat decals many candidates pass out, Mr. Moseley laboriously handwrites a letter to each member, asking for his vote.

He continues at this often-thankless job, he says, "because of the injustices out there." He recalls handing out food last Christmas to a long line of laid-off workers: "It made me want to hold on to the jobs I have." Besides, he adds, "I enjoy defending people. If I had my life to do over, I'd probably be a lawyer."

SOURCE: Excerpted from Alex Kotlowitz, "Grievous Work: Job of Shop Steward Has New Frustrations in Era of Payroll Cuts," *The Wall Street Journal* 68, no. 118 (1987), pp. 1, 20.

Local Union Democracy and Participation

Local union governance resembles municipal politics. Union elections usually generate only moderate interest, and incumbents are usually reelected unless the rank and file believes a critical issue has been mishandled. The local typically holds regular business meetings, open to all members. Two aspects of local union government and politics bear examination: (1) the type of business conducted by unions in their meetings, and (2) the degree to which the local union is democratically operated. Local business meetings are fairly mundane unless contract negotiations are approaching. They deal mostly with reporting disbursements, communications, and pending grievances.

Attendance rates vary; rates are higher in smaller locals and among skilled workers. Typical rates might vary between 1 and 33 percent.[7] Meeting agendas also affect attendance. In a newly organized utility workers local, the highest attendance—for the contract ratification—was 42 percent. It exceeded 15 percent in only 3 of the other 16 meetings (18 percent for a discussion of contract demands, 20 percent for an election of temporary officers, and 18 percent for a report on the completed contract).[8] Low attendance at local union meetings raises questions about breadth of support and union democracy. Member involvement seems low at the local level, although most of their interests in collective bargaining are centered there.

Local union democracy is manifested in the way factions are combined into coalitions around certain issues. It is also demonstrated by two or more candidates running for an office and occasional close elections for major offices. Members of a Canadian public employee union's locals were more willing to participate in union activities and less opposed to union political positions if they believed they had strong relationships with their leaders. Centralization of authority reduced democracy. Participation in local activities declined with increases in the size and organizational complexity of the union, the amount of its formal communications to members, its age, and internal factionalism. Participation increased as the ratio of leaders to members in the local structure increased. Elections were closer in larger units, with a more specialized jurisdiction, formal communication processes, no incumbent in the race, and no hostility from management.[9]

Evidence is mixed on the relationship between participation in union activities and satisfaction with the union. Among a group of professional employees, willingness to represent the union was associated with personal financial responsibility, beliefs about the union's legitimacy, involvement in the employing organization, and the importance of having influence and being involved in decision making.[10] Another study found that members who attended union meetings were more likely to be committee activists, voters, campaigners, and union newspaper readers.

[7] Sayles and Strauss, *Local Union*, p. 97.

[8] Ibid., p. 98.

[9] John C. Anderson, "A Comparative Analysis of Local Union Democracy," *Industrial Relations* 17 (1978), pp. 278–95.

[10] William Glick, Philip Mirvis, and Diane Harder, "Union Satisfaction and Participation," *Industrial Relations* 16 (1977), pp. 145–51.

Participation was not greater among grievance filers because individual grievances are normally independent of internal union participation activities.[11] Among a U.S. sample, participation was higher among members who expressed dissatisfaction with their unions, but it was also higher when members indicated their unions were effective in gaining member goals and were interested in both intrinsic and extrinsic goals of members.[12] Race differences do not appear to be associated with participation.[13] But evidence suggests women are less likely to participate because of duties at home, underestimation of their abilities, and beliefs that men would make better union officers.[14]

Union participation may involve administrative activities; attending meetings; and voting in elections, strike authorizations, and contract ratifications. Participation in administration is predicted primarily by interest in union business, educational level, seniority, beliefs in the value of unions, and low job involvement.[15] Participation varies according to the environment in which the union operates. Democracy appears greater where unions are not faced with a hostile environment. Political processes may be more active in larger unions, but rank-and-file participation declines for many activities. The reduction in participation in larger unions may not be contrary to member desires, since participation and satisfaction do not appear linked.[16]

Unions are relatively democratic. Pressures by the membership to handle grievances and improve conditions require responses by union officers. But if management is intransigent, the pressure to maintain a united front may lead to suppression of dissent.[17]

Functional Democracy

Are local unions run democratically? If democracy required two or more relatively permanent factions, the answer must generally be no. But if democracy demands only that leaders respond to individuals and groups,

---

[11] John C. Anderson, "Local Union Participation: A Re-Examination," *Industrial Relations* 18 (1979), pp. 18–31.

[12] Thomas I. Chacko, "Member Participation in Union Activities: Perceptions of Union Priorities, Performance, and Satisfaction," *Journal of Labor Research* 6 (1985), pp. 363–73.

[13] Michele M. Hoyman and Lamont Stallworth, "Participation in Local Unions: A Comparison of Black and White Members," *Industrial and Labor Relations Review* 40 (1987), pp. 323–35.

[14] G. N. Chaison and P. Andiappan, "An Analysis of the Barriers to Women Becoming Local Union Officers," *Journal of Labor Research* 10 (1989), pp. 149–62.

[15] Steven L. McShane, "The Multidimensionality of Union Participation," *Journal of Occupational Psychology* 59 (1986), pp. 177–87.

[16] Ibid.

[17] Sayles and Strauss, *Local Union*, pp. 135–47.

the answer is generally yes. Democracy is a constitutional requirement within the local through the specifications of electoral proceedings and terms of office. Also, the Landrum-Griffin Act requires locals to conduct elections at least once every three years. Further, under exclusive representation requirements, the union must apply the terms of the contract equally to all bargaining unit employees.

Democratic operation requires individual commitment to union activity. While most members believe their union works to their benefit, many were not involved in its founding and may view the union simply as their agent in employment matters. In return for dues, many members expect the union to relieve them of the effort and detailed work involved in regulating the employment relationship. What the members may want is representation in return for their dues, not participation and involvement in the union.

In a unionized employer, an individual is simultaneously an employee and a union member. The parties in the **functional democracy** of employment are the employer and the union. Thus, democracy in unionized settings does not require two or more factions to exist and be tolerated within the union.[18]

Union members are entitled to due process under at least two sets of rules: one is in the local union's constitution, the other in the collective bargaining agreement. Each is administered by separate sets of officials: the local by the executive board and the contracts by the the negotiation committees. Thus, an internal check-and-balance system helps ensure the contract is administered fairly for all bargaining unit members and the contract is not contrary to union standards.[19]

Figure 5–1 pictures the idea of **dual governance**. Assume a local included three **bargaining units** in an open-shop industry. Three separate contracts are administered by the local through three negotiation committees. Each bargaining unit's union members are eligible to vote for the officers of the local. Each bargaining unit's employees are eligible to vote on the contract. The shaded area represents workers who are both union and bargaining unit members, while those outside the local circle are bargaining unit members only.

Local unions are probably less democratic electorally than are governmental units. But this may not be a problem because union members generally are interested in similar types of outcomes, view the union as their agent, and evaluate it on the outcomes it produces rather than on the ideological stand of a faction.[20] Union members do not generally feel

---

[18] Neil W. Chamberlain and Donald E. Cullen, *The Labor Sector*, rev. ed. (New York: McGraw-Hill, 1971), pp. 194–96.

[19] Alice H. Cook, "Dual Governance in Unions: A Tool for Analysis," *Industrial and Labor Relations Review* 15 (1962), pp. 323–49.

[20] Sayles and Strauss, *Local Union*, p. 141.

FIGURE 5-1
Dual Governance in Unions

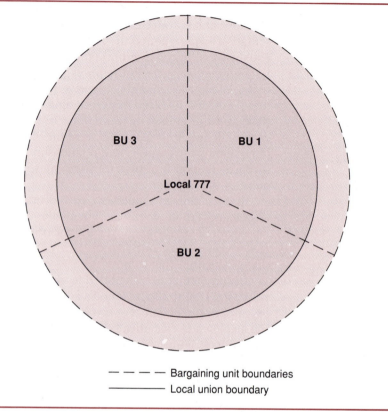

— — — — Bargaining unit boundaries
—————— Local union boundary

a need to be "protected" from their union; on the contrary, it is management they are worried about. If union members are concerned about a lack of democracy in the union, they can attempt to have it decertified. Legal safeguards are sufficient to require responsiveness, if not democracy, and that appears to be enough for most members.

The local union is not an autonomous, freestanding organization. It most often owes its existence to—and almost certainly must comply with—the directives of a parent international.

INTERNATIONAL UNIONS

International unions originally established jurisdictions over workers in specific crafts, industries, or other job territories. They are called *internationals* because many have members in Canada as well as in the United States. As noted in Chapters 2 and 3, the (inter)national union is the unit in which authority is vested within the union movement. Most local unions are chartered by a parent national, and many local activities are constrained or must be approved by the national body.

In its most recent directory, the Bureau of National Affairs lists more than 190 national unions, of which 90 are affiliated with the AFL–CIO. In 1987, about 83 percent of the total U.S. union membership of 16.9 million belonged to unions affiliated with the AFL–CIO.[21] In 1989, 29 affiliated unions had more than 100,000 members. Over half of all union members belong to the 12 largest national unions. Table 5–1 lists national unions affiliated with the AFL–CIO with 100,000 or more members in 1989. The median number of locals affiliated with the national union is about 150.

National unions are full-time operations. Officers are full-time unionists. Departments, with appointed and hired specialists, are established. Most national unions elect officials at their union conventions, required by law to meet at least every five years. Delegates to the convention are designated by each local and sent on a per capita basis or are national union officials and **field representatives.** The union convention is similar to a political convention. If the national leadership can appoint many delegates, its chances of staying in office are greatly enhanced.

NATIONAL UNION GOALS

All organizations in an economy depend on each other to a degree. But labor unions are particularly dependent since they do not have the option of vertically integrating their operations. Their primary function in the United States has been to represent employees in collective bargaining. Thus, the employment issues directly determine their major goals.

As noted in Chapter 1, individuals unionize when they believe a union would improve their employment outcomes. Chapter 2 noted that unionists have traditionally believed the inequality in income distribution in the United States is excessive.[22] Chapters 3 and 4 examined the legal environment in which labor relations occurs and recognized that U.S. labor law limits the union movement in representing employees. The exclusive agency relationship created in collective bargaining stimulates a competitive environment for employee relations services that influences how both unions and managements operate.

---

[21] C. D. Gifford, *Directory of National Unions and Employee Associations, 1988–1989* (Washington, D.C.: Bureau of National Affairs, 1988).

[22] Maurice F. Neufeld, "The Persistence of Ideas in the American Labor Movement: The Heritage of the 1830s," *Industrial and Labor Relations Review* 36 (1982), pp. 207–20.

TABLE 5-1

AFL–CIO Affiliated Labor Unions Reporting 100,000 Members or More in 1989

Organization	Number of Members
Teamsters	1,161,000
State, County, Municipal (AFSCME)	1,090,000
Food and Commercial Workers (UFCW)	999,000
Automobile, Aerospace, and Agricultural (UAW)	917,000
Service Employees (SEIU)	762,000
Electrical Workers (IBEW)	744,000
Carpenters	613,000
Teachers (AFT)	544,000
Machinists	517,000
Communication Workers	492,000
Steelworkers	481,000
Laborers	406,000
Operating Engineers	330,000
Hotel, Restaurant Employees	278,000
Plumbing and Pipefitting	220,000
Postal Workers	213,000
Paperworkers	210,000
Letter Carriers	201,000
Clothing and Textile Workers (ACTWU)	180,000
Electronic, Electrical, and Salaried	171,000
Government Employees (AFGE)	156,000
Garment Workers (ILGWU)	153,000
Fire Fighters	142,000
Retail, Wholesale Department	137,000
Painters	128,000
Graphic Communications	124,000
Ironworkers	111,000
Sheet Metal Workers	108,000
Bakery, Confectionery, and Tobacco	103,000

SOURCE: American Federation of Labor and Congress of Industrial Organizations, *Report of the AFL–CIO Executive Council* (Washington, D.C.: AFL–CIO, 1989).

National unions have two major goals: organizing an increasing number and share of the labor force and providing representation services that enhance the well-being of their members. The two goals are obviously interrelated. To an extent, organizing success depends on the success the union has had in representing employees in a manner visible to potential new members. Successful representation depends on organizing a group of employees through which bargaining power can be exerted on the employer.

National unions were formed for economic reasons. As U.S. industry became more national through the development of transportation facilities, the bargaining power of local unions declined. National unions were established to exert greater pressure on employers and to assist local unions during difficult periods in which they might not have survived on their own. Support and control thus became lodged in national unions.

National unions have their own goals. But do any common elements help predict what each might do? Unions are generally composed of members who anticipate services and permanent employees who supply them. Members evaluate whether they want continued representation by comparing the level of contract outcomes and services received from their union with those available from alternative sources (other unions or nonunion personnel departments). Leaders desire growth to enhance their power and stability, and they desire strong unionization within an industry to promote bargaining power. Elected leaders and appointed full-time unionists need membership approval to retain their posts.[23] Thus, leaders might be expected to promote organizing, while the rank and file would probably prefer services for present members first. Unions in highly organized industries spend a smaller proportion of their resources on organizing than do those in jurisdictions with lower union penetration.[24]

With the major changes that have occurred in the economy during the past decade, many national unions are beginning to develop plans and strategies for the future. National unions that paid more attention than others to planning devoted larger proportions of their resources to organizing in their traditional and new jurisdictions, participated in **corporate campaigns,** and formed **political action committees.**[25] The union movement is also beginning to look at alternative forms of representation that do not involve exclusive agency. More people will join associations than will vote for union representation. Associations have often been precursors of unions, particularly among professional and public-sector employees.[26] Also, many employees now work in part-time situations and/or for small employers who do not have personnel or other employee-relations functions. The union could act as a vehicle for counseling about workplace problems; providing information on job opportunities elsewhere; purchasing group medical, dental, and other insurance benefits; and other activities. In return, **associate,** or nonrepre-

[23] Richard N. Block, "Union Organizing and the Allocation of Union Resources," *Industrial and Labor Relations Review* 34 (1980), pp. 101–13.

[24] Ibid.

[25] K. Stratton and R. B. Brown, "Strategic Planning in U.S. Labor Unions," *Proceedings of the Industrial Relations Research Association* 41 (1988), pp. 523–31.

[26] C. Ichniowski and J. S. Zax, "Today's Associations, Tomorrow's Unions," *Industrial and Labor Relations Review* 43 (1990), pp. 191–208.

sented, **members** would pay a service fee or dues to the union.[27] Attitudes toward consumer benefits affect interest in joining an association but not a union. Strong pro-union attitudes predict a willingness to join both.[28] Exhibit 5–2 is an excerpt from the AFL–CIO's statement on the need for changing representation patterns.

National Union Jurisdictions

National unions have traditionally operated as either craft or industrial unions. Generally, the craft unions formed the AFL, and the industrial unions formed the CIO. Craft and industrial jurisdictional boundaries blurred as AFL and CIO unions competed for members before their merger and as craft and industrial employment patterns changed.

National unions often concentrate on certain jurisdictions, and many define their jurisdictions in their constitutions. For example, the jurisdiction of the Carpenters' Union is asserted as follows:

> The trade autonomy of the United Brotherhood of Carpenters and Joiners of America consists of the milling, fashioning, joining, assembling, erection, fastening or dismantling of all materials of wood, plastic, metal, fiber, cork and composition, and all other substitute materials. The handling, cleaning, erecting, installing and dismantling of machinery, equipment and all materials used by members of the United Brotherhood.
>
> Our claim of jurisdiction, therefore, extends over the following divisions and subdivisions of the trade: Carpenters and Joiners, Millwrights, Pile Drivers, Bridge, Dock, Wharf Carpenters, Divers, Underpinners, Timbermen and Core Drillers, Shipwrights, Boat Builders, Ship Carpenters, Joiners and Caulkers; Cabinet Makers, Bench Hands, Stair Builders, Millmen; Wood and Resilient Floor Layers, and Finishers; Carpet Layers; Shinglers, Siders; Insulators; Acoustic and Dry Wall Applicators; Shorers and House Movers; Loggers, Lumber, and Sawmill Workers; Furniture Workers; Reed and Rattan Workers; Shingle Weavers; Casket and Coffin Makers; Box Makers, Railroad Carpenters and Car Builders, regardless of material used; and all those engaged in the operation of woodworking or other machinery required in the fashioning, milling or manufacturing of products used in the trade, or engaged as helpers to any of the above divisions or subdivisions, and the handling, erecting and installing material on any of the above divisions or subdivisions; burning, welding, rigging and the use of any instrument or tool for layout work, incidental to the trade. When the term "carpenter(s)" or "carpenter(s) and joiner(s)" are used, it shall mean all the divisions and subdivisions of the trade.[29]

---

[27] Thomas A. Kochan, Harry C. Katz, and Robert B. McKersie, *The Transformation of American Industrial Relations* (New York: Basic Books, 1986), pp. 221–23.

[28] P. Jarley and J. Fiorito, "Associate Membership: Unionism or Consumerism?" *Industrial and Labor Relations Review* 43 (1990), pp. 209–24.

[29] *Constitution and Laws of the United Brotherhood of Carpenters and Joiners of America*, as amended (Washington, D.C.: United Brotherhood of Carpenters and Joiners, 1975), sect. 7, pp. 6–7.

EXHIBIT 5-2

New Methods of Advancing the Interests of Workers

First, unions must develop and put into effect multiple models for representing workers tailored to the needs and concerns of different groups. For example, in some bargaining units, workers may not desire to establish a comprehensive set of hard and fast terms and conditions of employment, but may nonetheless desire a representative to negotiate minimum guarantees that will serve as a floor for individual bargaining, to provide advocacy for individuals, or to seek redress for particular difficulties as they arise. In other units, a bargaining approach based on solving problems through arbitration or mediation rather than through ultimate recourse to economic weapons may be most effective.

Second, . . . unions must continually seek out and address new issues of concern to workers. For example, the issue of pay inequity has become a proper concern of women workers; collective action provides the surest way of redressing such inequities. There is a strong concern among workers about health and safety issues and a high degree of impatience with the inadequacy of government programs in this area. Again, collective action through labor unions can develop constructive steps to meet these concerns. . . .

. . . Approximately . . . 27 million workers . . . are former union members; most . . . left their union only because they left their unionized jobs. There are hundreds of thousands more nonunion workers who voted for a union in an unsuccessful organizing campaign. . . . These individuals might well be willing to affiliate with a union with which they have had contact or with which they have had some logical relationship provided that the costs were not prohibitive; this would be especially true to the extent unions offered services or benefits outside of the collective bargaining context . . . . New categories of membership should be created by individual unions or on a Federation-wide basis to accommodate individuals who are not part of organized bargaining units, and affiliates should consider dropping any existing barriers to an individual's retaining his membership after leaving an organized unit.

SOURCE: *The Changing Situation of Workers and Their Unions*, Report of the AFL–CIO Evolution of Work Committee, February 1985, pp. 18–19.

The largest U.S. nationals tend to be unions with broad jurisdictions. In 1985, these were the Teamsters; the National Education Association (NEA); the State, County, and Municipal Employees (AFSCME); the Food and Commercial Workers (UFCW); the Auto Workers (UAW); the Electrical Workers (IBEW); and the Service Employees (SEIU). The Teamsters originally organized transportation and warehouse employees employed outside the railroad industry. Now, about half of all Teamster members work in occupations and industries with no primary relationship to transportation. The NEA represents both public and private schoolteachers at primary, secondary, and postsecondary educational institutions. The UAW has expanded its organizing to nonteaching employees in colleges and universities. AFSCME organizes employees in many occupations across a broad spectrum of nonfederal public and private nonprofit employers. The IBEW began as a craft union but has successfully organized electrical workers in electrical equipment manufacturing. Where employment in traditional jurisdictions is declining, union leaders would be expected to push for expanding jurisdictions.

National Structure

The organizational structure of national unions results from the interaction of two factors: the types of services members demand and the bargaining structure that has evolved with the organizations in which the union represents employees. As the bargaining structure changes, union organization changes with it. To demonstrate these relationships and the differences between national unions, the structural properties of the UAW, Teamsters, Carpenters, and AFSCME will be examined.

Organizational Structure of the UAW

The UAW has traditionally organized workers in industries that fabricate and assemble autos and trucks, airplanes, construction and agricultural equipment, and associated parts suppliers. Final assemblers are highly concentrated (that is, relatively few manufacturers account for most of the production). Before the 1980s, virtually all U.S.-made automobiles were assembled by four manufacturers: American Motors, Chrysler, Ford, and General Motors. Honda, Mazda, and Nissan have opened U.S. assembly plants recently, and Chrysler has acquired American Motors. To best serve members in a consistent manner across operations of these major manufacturers, the UAW established **national departments.** Because U.S.-based domestic automakers' production facilities were virtually 100 percent unionized, the national departments concentrated on representation rather than organizing activities. Figure 5–2 shows a recent organizational chart of the UAW at the national level.

National departments are the line portion of the organization. This is where national-local interfaces occur. Each national department has a council consisting of delegates from that department's locals. In turn, the councils form subcommittees based on common interests of the members, such as seniority and work rules. Subcommittees designate members to take part in the national negotiation council from that department.

Staff departments provide information for the national departments and also assist locals through the UAW's international representatives. Besides having a "product-line" approach in its national departments, the UAW is also broken into geographical regions based on the concentration of UAW members in a given area. The regional staffs conduct organizing

FIGURE 5–2
Organizational Structure of the UAW

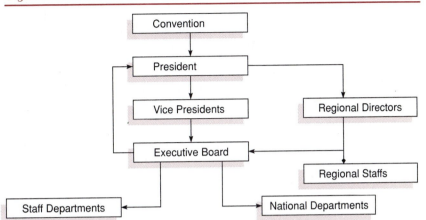

Staff Departments
Accounting
Arbitration Service
Auditing
Circulation
Community Action Program (CAP)
Community Services
Competitive Shop
Conservation and Natural Resources
Consumer Affairs
Education
Fair Practices and Anti-Discrimination
Family Education Center
International Affairs
Job Developing & Training
Legal
Organizing
Public Relations and Publications
Recreation and Leisure Time Activities
Research
Retired Workers
Skilled Trades
Social Security—Health and Safety
Social-Technical-Educational Programs
  (STEP)
Strike Insurance
Time Study and Engineering
Veterans
Washington Office
Women's and Women's Auxiliary

National Departments
Aerospace
Agricultural Implement
American Motors
Bendix
Champion Spark Plug
Chrysler
Dana
Eltra
Ford
Foundry
General Motors
Independent Parts and Suppliers
Mack Truck
Technical, Office and Professional (TOP)

SOURCE: Abstracted from *You and Your Membership in the UAW,* publication 383 (Detroit: United Auto Workers, 1978).

drives and assist remote locals or those not closely affiliated with national departments in negotiation, administration, and grievance handling. Regional staffs may also have experts in such areas as health and safety or industrial engineering.

The organizational makeup of the UAW is largely a function of employer concentration and the level at which economic bargaining occurs. Thus, it has been quite centralized. However, as automakers close older, less efficient plants, local economic concessions may be a key to job security, necessitating more concern by the UAW for local bargaining issues.

Organizational Structure of the Carpenters' Union

The Carpenters' Union differs from the typical industrial union in that it represents a narrower occupational group and generally deals with smaller employers. The construction industry tends to be locally or regionally based with several employers in a given area. Construction employers also tend to concentrate on certain types of construction (for example, business and government contracts for large buildings or residential construction).

The Carpenters' Union usually bargains at the local or regional level. The national union has responsibility to review actions of local unions against its members, authorize strikes, and adjudicate jurisdictional disputes between its locals or between the Carpenters and other unions. The national also administers its members' pension plan. This arrangement is common in the trade unions because tradespeople may work for many employers during their careers, and the union is the only employment-related organization with which they have long-run relationships.

Organizational Structure of the Teamsters

The Teamsters' Union is the closest to being a general union of any in the United States. After its expulsion from the AFL–CIO in 1960, it broadened its jurisdiction from trucking and warehousing to cover all workers. The mergers of several smaller national unions, such as the Brewery Workers, into the Teamsters made the Teamsters the dominant union force within several industries. The Teamsters reaffiliated with the AFL–CIO in 1987.

Given the early background of the Teamsters and the local or regional nature of much of the trucking industry, the union's organization is somewhat decentralized, particularly regarding representation and organizing in the transportation industry. The executive board of the Teamsters consists of the general president, the general secretary-treasurer, and 15 vice presidents. Several of the vice presidents are also international directors of the five area Teamster conferences. Twelve trade divisions address the bargaining issues associated with the industries in which Teamster members are employed: airline; automotive, petroleum, and allied trades; building material and construction; conventions and exposition centers; freight; food processing; laundry; warehouse; newspaper drivers; parcel and small package; trade show and movie making; and public employees. Four trade conferences (Bakery, Communications, Brewery and Soft Drink Workers, and Dairy) coordinate activities in these industries.

The Teamsters' Union has established 51 local joint councils. These semiautonomous bodies administer activities among affiliated locals. Each local is required to belong to a joint council and must get council permission to sign a contract or to strike. Each joint council is indirectly controlled by the executive branch. Thus, much of the grass-roots organizing and representation activity is initiated or controlled at the joint council level.

Organizational Structure of AFSCME

The American Federation of State, County, and Municipal Employees (AFSCME) is an industrial-type union asserting jurisdiction over non-elected public employees outside of the federal government and employees in private, nonprofit public-service organizations. Its structure reflects the fact that its members are employed in a variety of governmental jurisdictions and bargain under many different laws. Unlike most industrial unions, AFSCME does not require the national's approval of local contract settlements. The decision to strike is also handled at the local level. All locals are expected to affiliate with one of the regional AFSCME councils, which are operated within jurisdictions relating to the bargaining laws associated with the occupations represented.

The national executive staff provides support for the regional councils and locals. An international executive board that includes regional representatives advises the executive board.[30] AFSCME's federal nature recognizes that its affiliated locals bargain with employers who operate under a myriad of collective bargaining laws and that different laws may apply to different employee groups it represents within the same jurisdiction.

National-Local Union Relationship

National unions charter locals, provide services, and generally require that locals not strike or ratify contracts without the national's permission, reducing the possibility of competition between locals and increasing the discipline of locals when necessary to pressure a large national employer.

---

[30] *AFSCME Officers Manual* (Washington, D.C.: AFSCME, no date), pp. 31–43; and *Constitution of the American Federation of State, County, and Municipal Employees, AFL–CIO* (Washington, D.C.: AFSCME, 1980).

Service to local unions, particularly from industrial unions, is provided by international representatives, usually recruited and appointed by national union officers from local union officer positions or activists interested in a union career. There are large differences among unions in the intensity of services they provide through professional staff members. Recent figures indicate a relatively high level of staff per union member in the Steelworkers (1 to 677) while the ratio is quite low in the Teamsters (1 to 9,013).[31] Newly elected national union officers may discharge permanent staff employees as long as it doesn't interfere with their roles as union members,[32] but elected union officers are protected by the Landrum-Griffin Act's Title I free speech provision and cannot be removed for expressing dissenting opinions.[33]

International representatives, unlike many local union officers, are full-time union employees. Their major responsibilities are to organize nonunion employees in industries or occupations in which the national union has an interest, to provide assistance to employees interested in starting an organizing campaign, and to assist in representing union members, particularly in negotiating contracts and processing grievances. International representatives are typically assigned to regional staffs and may be responsible for a number of local unions. National unions employ international representatives when they want consistent policies established across employers, where locals are relatively small, where local officers lack sophistication, and where the area is thinly organized.

Union clerical and professional employees frequently organize to collectively bargain with the leaders of the unions for which they work. Organized staff units are most common in larger industrial unions. Some unions have strongly opposed the organization of their staff members, while others have welcomed organizing attempts. These unions generally bargain for the same types of employment issues that the unions in general seek, but they seldom strike in support of their demands.[34]

When local unions have a great deal of autonomy, particularly where they operate in a local labor market and where employment with a given employer is likely to be transient, a business agent is the primary contact for local union members. Business agents have many of the same responsibilities as international representatives and are concerned with employers' compliance with the contract. Since an established negotiating

---

[31] P. F. Clark, "Organizing the Organizers: Professional Staff Unionism in the American Labor Movement," *Industrial and Labor Relations Review* 42 (1989), pp. 584–99.

[32] *Finnegan* v. *Leu*, No. 80-2150, U.S. Supreme Court, 1982.

[33] *Sheet Metal Workers' International Association* v. *Lynn*, No. 86-1940, U.S. Supreme Court, 1989.

[34] Clark, "Organizing the Organizers."

committee or steward structure may not exist in transient employment, the business agent must monitor the employment relationship.

National Union Politics

National unions are ultimately governed by their constitutional conventions, which establish broad policies, may amend its constitution, and frequently elect officers. The degree of membership participation in national union activities depends on the method used to choose convention delegates and elect union officers. Although national unions are required by law to hold constitutional conventions and elect officers at least every five years, they differ greatly in the extent to which member involvement is sought and to which democratic ideals are applied to their operation.

National union democracy can be measured by identifying the degree of control union members have in the major decision-making areas unions face: contract negotiations, contract administration, service to members, union administration, and political and community activities. Members' control in each area could range from complete autocracy to consultation, veto power, or full decisional control and participation.[35] Desire for democracy may be inferred through the level of union member participation in decisions open to them and their satisfaction levels in relation to opportunities for, or actual participation in, union decision-making activities.

Most national unions do not have two-party systems, but a union's constitutional organization affects the degree to which dissent may lead to a change in the union's direction. Unions electing officers on an at-large basis among all the eligible voters (either as delegates or through a general referendum) are much less likely to be responsive to factional viewpoints than are unions that elect executive board members on a geographic basis.[36] In the Mineworkers and the Steelworkers (both of which have changed national general presidents because of internal dissent), regionally elected executive boards have served as springboards to national campaigns. In national referendum elections, unions may prevent candidates from obtaining financial assistance from outside the union to forward their campaigns.[37] If officers are elected by convention

[35] Arthur Hochner, Karen Koziara, and Stuart Schmidt, "Thinking about Democracy and Participation in Unions," *Proceedings of the Industrial Relations Research Association* 32 (1979), pp. 16–17.

[36] Sara Gamm, "The Election Base of National Union Executive Boards," *Industrial and Labor Relations Review* 32 (1979), pp. 295–311.

[37] *United Steelworkers of America, AFL–CIO–CLC* v. *Sadlowski*, No. 81-395, U.S. Supreme Court, 1982.

and if the delegates to the international convention include not only those selected at a local level but also officials appointed by the incumbent, then the chance of ousting the incumbent is virtually nonexistant.[38]

Leaders of national unions generally come from union backgrounds. Their family economic conditions are generally modest, and while most have some post–high school education, few are college graduates. Most joined unions because their employers had agreed to a union shop. They began their union careers early, usually as local union officers. Many had mentors, and most are very satisfied with their chosen careers.[39]

National Unions and Public Policy

Representation is aimed at enhancing union members' employment outcomes through collective bargaining. Unions also serve member needs through attempts to influence public policy. Some are aimed at membership interests in particular industries, while others are aimed at improving the lot of the membership as a whole or of an identifiable subgroup across industries.

Examples of public policy initiatives that cut across industries include labor's support of occupational safety and health legislation, opposition to lower minimum wages for younger workers, and reduction of pay inequality between men and women. Special interest groups within the labor movement have energized the advocacy of certain positions. For example, the Committee of Labor Union Women (CLUW) was a strong proponent of equal pay and civil rights legislation enabling women workers to be paid similarly to men in equal jobs.[40] While wage equality would lead to gains primarily for women, it's also squarely within the equalitarian approach of trade unionism. Other social issues that have strong appeal to subgroups within the labor movement, such as abortion, can lead to cleavages within the labor movement and loss of support from traditional allies if pursued but to internal strife if not aired.[41]

As competition changes within industries, unions may advocate legislation to restrict the employment-cutting options of employers. For example, the deregulation of airlines and trucking has created incentives for

---

[38] Arthur L. Fox II and John C. Sikorski, *Teamster Democracy and Financial Responsibility* (Washington, D.C.: Professional Drivers Council for Safety and Health, 1976).

[39] P. L. Quaglieri, "The New People of Power: The Backgrounds and Careers of Top Labor Leaders," *Journal of Labor Research* 9 (1988), pp. 271–84.

[40] C. Kates, "Working Class Feminism and Feminist Unions: Title VII, The UAW and NOW," *Labor Studies Journal* 14, no. 2 (1989), pp. 28–45.

[41] S. B. Garland, "How the Abortion Issue Is Shaking the House of Labor," *Business Week*, August 6, 1990, p. 39.

employer efficiency and allowed the entry of new employers. Because these new employers have neither senior employees nor labor unions, competition between union and nonunion employees is injected. Where domestic markets have opened to foreign competition (for example, autos and steel), lower wage costs among foreign competitors may reduce the demand for domestic unionized employees. Thus, unions advocate protective legislation in the form of tariffs, domestic content laws, or reregulation. Differences exist among what unions advocate. Mature unions representing skilled workers urge more legislation to protect unions as organizations, while emerging unions and those representing employees in service industries urge more attention to income redistribution.[42]

Chapter 4 noted that National Labor Relations Board decisions are related to its political composition, with Republican members appointed by Republican presidents particularly likely to rule against labor. Given that a Republican president has held office since 1981, and Republicans held a majority in the Senate from 1981 through 1986, labor would have seemed vulnerable from a public policy standpoint. An examination of the first four years of this period shows, however, that no existing labor laws were reversed, and while no improvements occurred, labor organizations won approval for several measures they supported. Education organizations, such as the American Federation of Teachers and the National Education Association, were particularly successful.[43]

Union political action efforts may result from choices about how to best deploy resources. One study finds that medium-sized unions spend more per capita on political action than do smaller or larger unions; and spending increases as dues increase. The proportion of women members in a national is also related to amount spent on political activity, although evidence suggests there is less political activity than members might desire.[44] National union political activities increased markedly in the 1980s, particularly among unions representing public employers and those in which executive boards are democratically chosen.[45] PACs were important vehicles for providing financial support to campaigns of candidates with friendly positions. The receipt of PAC contributions by a candidate who subsequently becomes or remains an incumbent appears to be related directly to roll-call voting records and indirectly to the

[42] D. B. Cornfield, "Union Decline and the Political Demands of Organized Labor," *Work and Occupations* 16 (1989), pp. 292–322.

[43] Marick F. Masters and John Thomas Delaney, "Union Legislative Records during President Reagan's First Term," *Journal of Labor Research* 8 (1987), pp. 1–18.

[44] John Thomas Delaney, Jack Fiorito, and Marick F. Masters, "The Effects of Union Organizational and Environmental Characteristics on Union Political Action," *American Journal of Political Science* 32 (1988), pp. 616–42.

[45] Marick F. Masters and John Thomas Delaney, "The Causes of Union Political Involvement," *Journal of Labor Research* 6 (1985), pp. 341–62.

number of candidates elected.[46] PACs do not, however, give contributions to all who support their causes. Contributions appear to depend on the willingness of the organization to give, the compatibility of the candidate's ideology with that of the contributing PAC, the probability of the candidate's winning (with more given when the race is close), and the magnitude of the vote margin the candidate had in the last election (if an incumbent).[47] Contributions also appear related to the closeness of an incumbent's committee assignment to interests of labor, voting record, and electoral security.[48]

While unions, and corporations, are heavily involved in PAC activities, the attitudes of their members are not monolithic, and, in most cases, seem less liberal than the positions espoused by their unions' PACs. Further, PACs appear to be more successful in influencing legislative outcomes peripheral to labor's interest, such as education, than to outcomes directly affecting it, such as labor law reform.[49] Political endorsements and get-out-the-vote campaigns by unions have some value. Union members are more likely to vote in general elections than nonmembers (or their own family members), and they vote for endorsed candidates about 15 to 20 percent more often than nonmembers. But, union members appear not to vote more often in primaries, and about 50 percent of voters split their votes between endorsed and unendorsed candidates.[50]

The AFL–CIO

When national unions attempt to speak as one voice on public policy they use the AFL–CIO. The AFL–CIO is a federation of national unions banded together to provide some overall direction to the labor movement and technical assistance to individual nationals. It also has a number of directly affiliated independent local unions. To maintain membership in the AFL–CIO, a national union must comply with the federation's Ethical Practices Code, avoid dominance by nondemocratic ideologists, and

---

[46] Gregory M. Saltzman, "Congressional Voting on Labor Issues: The Role of PACs," *Industrial and Labor Relations Review* 40 (1987), pp. 163–79.

[47] Allen Wilhite and John Theilmann, "Unions, Corporations, and Political Campaign Contributions: The 1982 House Elections," *Journal of Labor Research* 7 (1986), pp. 175–86.

[48] Kevin B. Grier and Michael C. Munger, "The Impact of Legislator Attributes on Interest-Group Campaign Contributions," *Journal of Labor Research* 7 (1986), pp. 349–59.

[49] Marick F. Masters and John Thomas Delaney, "Union Political Activities: A Review of the Empirical Literature," *Industrial and Labor Relations Review* 40 (1987), pp. 336–53.

[50] John Thomas Delaney, Marick F. Masters, and Susan Schwochau, "Unionism and Voter Turnout," *Journal of Labor Research* 9 (1988), pp. 221–36; and John Thomas Delaney, Marick F. Masters, and Susan Schwochau, "Union Membership and Voting for COPE-Endorsed Candidates," *Industrial and Labor Relations Review* 43 (1990), pp. 621–35.

agree to submit interunion disputes for mediation and adjudication by the AFL–CIO.[51] Just as changes in the structure of the labor movement after the deaths of William Green and Philip Murray helped end the conflict between the AFL and the CIO and facilitated their merger, the retirement and death of George Meany coupled with leadership changes over time in the UAW and Teamsters resulted in their recent reaffiliation with the AFL–CIO.

The AFL–CIO's organization is complex because of its federal nature and its simultaneous role as coordinator of national union interests and director of state and city central body activities. Figure 5–3 gives the general organization of the AFL–CIO. At the top is the biennial national convention. Delegates are apportioned to the convention on the basis of size and are elected or appointed according to individual national union policy. Other delegates are sent by directly affiliated locals, state and city central bodies, and national industrial and trade departments. The AFL–CIO convention amends the constitution, elects officers, and expresses official positions of the federation. The general board consists of the executive council, presidents of each affiliated national, and representatives from each constitutionally described department within the federation.

The ongoing business of the AFL–CIO is handled by the top executives, their staffs, and the constitutional departments. One set of constitutional departments—the seven trade and industrial departments— relates to jurisdictional interests of the national members: building and construction trades, maritime trades, metal trades, railway employees, industrial unions, union label and service trades, and public employees.

The staff portion of the organization consists of the standing committees and their equivalent departments. These are involved in the normal ongoing federal activities:

1. *Organizing.* Field representatives of the department of organizing and field services encourage and assist unorganized workers or local unions in unionization campaigns.

2. *Legislation.* The department of legislation prepares official positions; provides testimony on relevant legislation dealing with labor, social issues, and foreign policy; and lobbies members of Congress.

3. *Politics.* The committee on political education evaluates legislative records of federal, state, and local candidates and provides political information to the membership.

4. *Community services.* The department of community services coordinates activities with and assists local charitable and community service agencies during fund drives, local crises, and regional disasters.

---

[51] *Directory of National Unions and Employee Associations 1982–1983* (Washington, D.C.: Bureau of National Affairs, 1982), pp. 7–10.

FIGURE 5–3

Structural Organization of the American Federation of Labor and Congress of Industrial Organizations

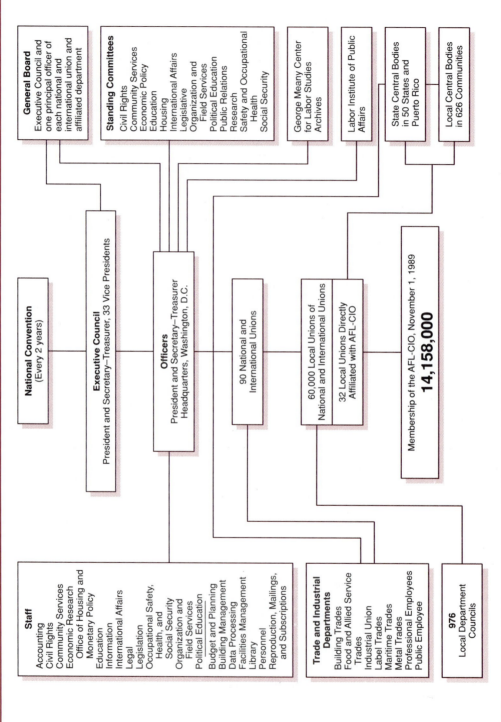

5. *International affairs.* The department of international affairs maintains a liaison with trade unions in the free world.

6. *Civil rights.* The department of civil rights polices union violations of civil rights and pursues liaison activities with state and federal civil rights agencies.

7. *Housing.* The department of housing encourages the investment of pension funds in mortgages for union members, coordinates apprenticeship programs for minorities, and works toward the increased utilization of urban human resources.

8. *Education.* The department of education prepares curricula for training union members in the principles of trade unionism.

9. *Social security.* The department of social security advises affiliates on matters related to social security, unemployment insurance, and workers' compensation.

10. *Research.* The department of economic research analyzes economic trends and the effects of legislative and economic policy on collective bargaining. It also maintains specialists in industrial engineering, consumer affairs, and natural resource problems.

11. *Public affairs.* The department of information maintains liaison with the media and communicates the official position of the federation on current issues. It also serves as the major link between the federation and the individual member through publication of the weekly *AFL–CIO News.*

12. *Economic policy.* The committee on economic policy formulates AFL–CIO positions on the development of public policy regarding wages and employment.

13. *Occupational safety and health.* This department works closely with government agencies administering health and safety legislation. It also provides technical support to unions and education programs to union members on job safety.

Political activity and lobbying are major activities of the AFL–CIO. Many issues before Congress have potential direct and indirect effects on the labor movement. Exhibit 5–3 describes some of the activities of Robert M. McGlotten, the AFL–CIO's chief lobbyist.

STATE AND LOCAL CENTRAL BODIES

In addition to its departments, the AFL–CIO has a direct relationship with almost 800 state and local **central bodies.** These bodies reflect the composition of the parent AFL–CIO and the particular industrial mix of their geographical areas. The state and local centrals are directly responsible to the AFL–CIO, not to the internationals.

State and local central bodies are primarily involved in political and

---

EXHIBIT 5-3

Labor Lobbying Activities

It is evening in the Capitol, and Robert M. McGlotten, chief lobbyist for the AFL–CIO, emerges briskly from a closed meeting with Representative Dan Rostenkowski, the Ways and Means Committee chairman.

The lobbyist jabs a finger into the air to make a point with a colleague, pauses to trade jokes with two members of Congress, then forms a tight corridor huddle with his fellow labor lobbyists to plot the next move on a trade bill.

"I've been running around like a chicken without a head," Mr. McGlotten declared, describing the quickened pace of life four months into his job of representing the interests of the AFL–CIO.

. . . Mr. McGlotten faces . . . hurdles. . . . While most lobbyists are expected to master and become influential on a certain topic, he is expected to be persuasive on dozens of issues that concern big labor, from unemployment to taxes to trade to health and, of late, the budget.

. . . Much of Mr. McGlotten's work these days is devoted to defeating the Reagan administration's proposed budget cuts. To that end, as an experienced corridor pacer, one who knows by first name a dizzying array of people involved in the day-to-day operations of Congress, Mr. McGlotten sometimes seems to be everywhere at once, working the labyrinthine halls of the Capitol, trading gossip and vital information, breathing the air, feeling the pulse.

"From day to day, from hour to hour, nothing is the same on the Hill," he said. "You have to be there, one on one. If you're not there, you're missing something."

SOURCE: Kenneth B. Noble, "Labor Lobbyist's Task: Be Everywhere at Once," *New York Times*, May 25, 1986, p. 18Y.

---

lobbying activities. However, activities in national elections must be consistent with the position taken by the AFL–CIO.[52] Endorsements of state and local candidates and testimony and lobbying on local and state legislative matters are emphasized. The major difference between the parent AFL–CIO and the state and local central bodies is that the AFL–CIO consists predominantly of affiliated internationals, while state and local centrals draw on affiliation with local unions. Figure 5–4 shows the relationship of state and local central bodies to the AFL–CIO.

OVERVIEW OF THE UNION HIERARCHY

Power in the labor movement clearly resides in the nationals, with locals and the federation deriving their authority from the nationals. Local unions are structured to handle the day-to-day activities of the

---

[52] *Rules Governing AFL–CIO State Central Bodies*, Publication No. 12 (Washington, D.C.: AFL–CIO, 1973), p. 21.

FIGURE 5-4

The Relationship of the AFL–CIO to State and Local Central Bodies

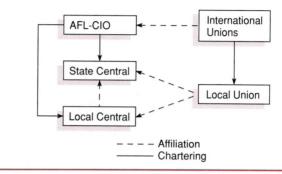

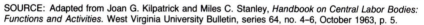

SOURCE: Adapted from Joan G. Kilpatrick and Miles C. Stanley, *Handbook on Central Labor Bodies: Functions and Activities.* West Virginia University Bulletin, series 64, no. 4–6, October 1963, p. 5.

membership. Much of their effort involves policing the contract and handling grievances.

A national union could be compared with the corporate staff division of a large company, where policies are developed, actions are audited to ensure conformity to policy, and advice is given to generalists in the plants (or locals) on specific issues. Although the convention ultimately governs the national, many presidents have broad powers to take interim actions and also to influence the delegate composition of future conventions.

The AFL–CIO serves the same function as a trade association, a chamber of commerce, or a national association of manufacturers. It coordinates activities among the nationals and amplifies their voices. The federation's prime functions are information, integration, and advocacy. Its greatest areas of autonomy relate to legislative and political processes.

NATIONAL UNION MERGERS

The recent past has witnessed a large number of corporate mergers and acquisitions. Organizational change in the labor movement has mirrored these activities, although hostile takeovers are not possible in the labor movement. Union mergers appear to take two forms: *absorption*, in which a small or rapidly declining union becomes a part of a larger national[53] (for example, the 450-member Window Glass Cutters League's 1975 merger into the 80,000-member Glass Bottle Blowers); and *amalgamation*, in which two unions of roughly equal size merge to form a new union (for example, the 1979 merger of the 500,000-member

---

[53] Charles J. Janus, "Union Mergers in the 1970s: A Look at the Reasons and Results," *Monthly Labor Review* 102, no. 10 (1978), pp. 13–23.

Amalgamated Meat Cutters and Butcher Workers with the 700,000-member Retail Clerks to form the United Food and Commercial Workers.[54]

A merger can take three forms: (1) a *symbiotic* merger, in which two unions represent workers whose outputs are interdependent; (2) a *commensalistic* merger, in which two unions have competed for the organization of the same employees; and (3) a *scale* merger, wherein a large union seeks to increase its efficiency or power. Symbiotic mergers prevail when unions are expanding membership, and commensalistic mergers are more common during contraction. Recessions are associated with greater merger activity.[55]

Mergers are complicated by duplicate national union officers and services unless staffs are consolidated. Symbiotic mergers are probably the easiest because the needs of the merged membership may have little overlap. Commensalistic mergers require agreements on the role of present union officers and the fate of local unions following the merger. Mergers are eased when few integration issues exist, such as where craft identities are preserved, the regional penetration of one union is great, important historical traditions are preserved, leadership duplication problems are accommodated, and merged structures are based on strong individual union identities.[56]

UNION FINANCES

Union finances are generally related to two different functions. The first involves the day-to-day operations of the union, and the second is associated with the fiduciary obligation of officers in some unions to the collection, trusteeship, and disbursement of pension and welfare benefits to members. The latter is usually found in craft unions or unions in which employers are too small or marginal to administer their own pension programs.

Organization Receipts and Disbursements

Three major sources of revenue are available to unions: dues from members; fees, fines, and assessments from members; and investment income. Dues and fees are collected at the local level. The nationals and the AFL–CIO levy a per capita tax on the local. The current AFL–CIO per capita tax is 13 cents monthly; many nationals require locals to remit

---

[54] Gary N. Chaison, "Union Growth and Union Mergers," *Industrial Relations* 20 (1981), pp. 98–108.

[55] John Freeman and Jack Brittain, "Union Merger Process and the Industrial Environment," *Industrial Relations* 16 (1977), pp. 173–85.

[56] Gary N. Chaison, "Union Mergers and the Integration of Union Governing Structures," *Journal of Labor Research* 3 (1982), pp. 139–51.

about 50 percent of dues for their operations.[57] Dues vary widely among unions; some require a flat fee, while others scale fees to earning levels. The parent national usually sets minimum and maximum levels, and the local can adjust within those limits. Occasionally, an assessment is added to replenish or maintain strike funds.

The most recent study available indicates about 85 percent of local unions require an initiation fee. Most new members pay $40 or less to become members. Dues vary among locals, but a common rule of thumb is to set them equal to two hours' wages per month.[58]

Although dated, the most recent U.S. Department of Labor data indicate local unions received 72 percent of their income from dues; 9 percent from fees, fines, and assessments; and 19 percent from other sources. Of disbursements, 30 percent went for per capita taxes, 26 percent for officer and employee salaries, 8 percent for office and administrative expenses, 7 percent to member benefits, and 29 percent for other items. National unions received 29 percent of their income from per capita taxes; 1 percent from fees, fines, assessments, and work permits; and 70 percent from investments and other sources. Investments in securities, real estate, and other ventures reflect the business orientation of U.S. unions. National unions spent about 7 percent of funds for affiliation payments, 8 percent for salaries, 3 percent for office and administrative expenses, less than 1 percent for loans, 11 percent for benefits, and the other 71 percent for other payments.[59]

Union Officer Compensation

The compensation of national union officers is relatively modest in comparison with executives of large private-sector corporations. During the most recent survey year, the average compensation for a national union president in one of the large national unions or associations was $118,619. The most highly paid was the late Jackie Presser, the general president of the Teamsters, with total pay from his three union jobs of $571,960.[60] Variables strongly related to national officer compensation include total expenditures of the national union, dues levels, total assets owned by the union, and number of locals.[61]

---

[57] *This Is the AFL–CIO*, Publication no. 20 (Washington, D.C.: AFL–CIO, 1980), p. 5.

[58] Charles W. Hickman, "Labor Organizations' Fees and Dues," *Monthly Labor Review* 100, no. 5 (1977), pp. 19–24.

[59] U.S. Department of Labor, *Union Financial Statistics, 1976* (Washington, D.C.: U.S. Government Printing Office, 1978).

[60] Jonathan Tasini and Jane B. Todaro, "How Much Top Labor Leaders Made in 1986," *Business Week*, May 4, 1987, p. 96.

[61] Marcus H. Sandver and Herbert G. Heneman III, "Analysis and Prediction of Top National Union Officers' Total Compensation," *Academy of Management Journal* 24 (1980), pp. 534–43.

Pension Administration

Pension plans are frequently administered by craft unions and other unions where the size of employers is small. Craft union dues are greater than those in industrial unions, with a portion set aside for benefits. Other unions require employers to make a per capita payment, as in the National Master Freight Agreement with the Teamsters (1990), which called for $169.70 per employee per week in health, pension, and welfare payments. A royalty on tonnage is negotiated in the coal industry, and this income is used to pay retirement benefits.

Administering pension programs has become an increasingly important issue for both union administrators and members. The Employee Retirement Income Security Act of 1974 requires pension administrators to follow practices to safeguard contributions made toward retirement. Certain investment practices, such as risky or low-interest loans, are illegal. Investments in one's own organization are also largely precluded.

SUMMARY

Organized labor has essentially a three-tiered structure (local, national, and AFL–CIO), with power concentrated at the second level. At the local level, the most typical structure is the single bargaining unit. Multi-employer units are perhaps most common in the construction industry. National unions are of two major types—craft, representing workers in a specific occupation; and industrial, representing occupations in a specific industry. The AFL–CIO is the only major U.S. labor federation, with over three quarters of union and association members affiliated since the Teamsters rejoined.

Although the local is the workers' direct representative, members' interests in internal affairs are generally low. They appear to view the union as their employment agent and allow a cadre of activists to control its internal politics.

National union structures, particularly the industrials, adapt to both the breadth of their constituencies and the concentration within their industries. For example, the UAW has a General Motors Department, and the USW has a basic steel component in its industry conference.

Whether unions operate democratically depends on the definition of the term. Most do not have two-party systems, and many equate dissent with attempts to undermine union goals. On the other hand, local officers are directly elected, and international officials are chosen in a manner similar to a presidential nominating convention. Unions introduce democracy into the work setting by requiring a bargaining contract. Within unions, the checks and balances initiated through its constitution and contracts increase democracy and safeguards for members.

DISCUSSION QUESTIONS

1. If you were recommending an organizational structure for a national union, what factors would you advise that it consider (industrial concentration, occupations it represents, and so on)?
2. Should unions be permitted to endorse political candidates and engage in political action?
3. How could a union local increase the involvement of its membership?
4. Defend or attack the usual method of electing an international president (through local delegates and international staff members at the convention).

KEY TERMS

business agent

executive committee

negotiation committee

stewards

superseniority

dual commitment

functional democracy

dual governance

bargaining units

international unions

field representatives

corporate campaigns

political action committees

associate members

national departments

central bodies

6

UNION ORGANIZING AND EMPLOYER RESPONSE

Chapter 1 examined some of the reasons workers desire representation. This chapter examines the flow of organizing campaigns, involvement of the National Labor Relations Board, (NLRB), effects of union avoidance programs, strategies and tactics used by employers and unions during election campaigns, and recent results in NLRB-monitored representation elections.

In studying this chapter, consider the following questions:

1. At what points and in what ways is the NLRB involved in representation elections?

2. What effects have recent employer union avoidance programs had on the incidence of union organizing?

3. What common strategies and tactics are used by employers and unions during organizing campaigns?

4. How successful are unions presently in organizing new units?

How Organizing Begins

Campaigns to organize unrepresented workers begin at either the local or national union level. National union-organizing campaigns send full-time organizers to specific sites to encourage or assist local employees in unionizing. A national union campaign often occurs when a unionized firm establishes a new nonunion plant. The national union representing employees in the firm's other plants campaigns to organize the new plant's employees to bring employment practices at the new plant into line with those in the rest of the organization. National organizing attempts may also target a nonunion firm in a predominantly unionized industry. Most organizing attempts begin at the local level when some employees decide they would be better off if they could bargain collectively with the employer.[1]

The Framework for Organizing

Union organizing begins with an **authorization card** campaign. By signing authorization cards, employees designate the union as their agent in negotiating wages, hours, and terms and conditions of employment. Figure 6–1 presents a generalized sequence of organizing events. Figure 6–2 is an example of an authorization card.

The authorization card campaign tries to enroll as many employees as possible in the work unit the union desires to represent. If a majority of employees join, the union can directly request recognition from the employer as the employees' bargaining agent. In most cases, this request is refused. The union then petitions the NLRB for a **representation election** and includes the signed authorization cards as evidence of support. The NLRB checks the signed cards against a roster of employees in the work unit. If fewer than 30 percent signed, the petition is dismissed for lack of sufficient interest. If more than 30 percent signed, the union is legally within its jurisdiction, and the employer doesn't contest the appropriateness of the proposed unit, the NLRB schedules an election. The makeup of an **appropriate bargaining unit** is frequently contested by the employer, requiring the NLRB to decide who should be included. The criteria the board uses to decide the proposed unit's appropriateness is discussed later in this chapter. Bargaining units are usually made up of employees with common interests, as determined by the board.

When an appropriate bargaining unit is defined, if at least 30 percent

---

[1] For another detailed examination of organizing activities, see John J. Lawler, "Union Organizing and Representation," in *Employee and Labor Relations*, SHRM-BNA Series, Vol. 4, ed. John A. Fossum (Washington D.C.: Bureau of National Affairs, 1990), pp. 4–134 to 4–179.

FIGURE 6-1
Sequence of Organizing Events

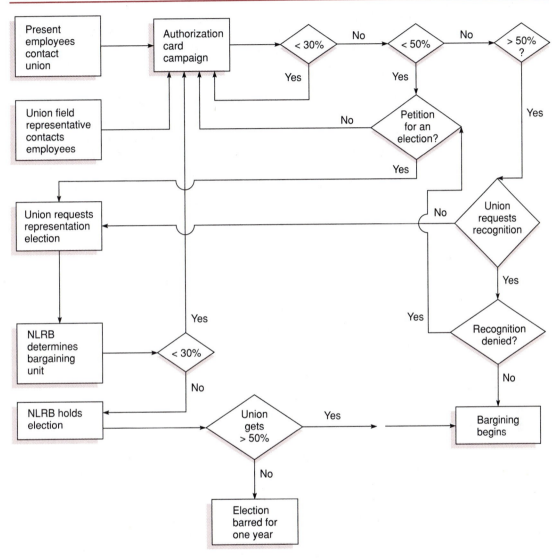

of the employees have signed authorization cards, the NLRB will order an election unless the union withdraws its petition. If the union wins a majority of the eligible votes cast in the election, the board certifies it as the employees' bargaining agent and negotiations on a contract can begin. If the union loses, the board certifies the results, and no other representation election may be conducted in that unit for one year.

FIGURE 6–2
Authorization Card

YES, I WANT THE IAM

I, the undersigned employee of

(Company) _____

authorize the International Association of Machinists and Aerospace Workers (IAM) to act as my collective bargaining agent for wages, hours and working conditions. I agree that this card may be used either to support a demand for recognition or an NLRB election, at the discretion of the union.

Name (print) _____ Date _____

Home Address _____ Phone _____

City _____ State _____ Zip _____

Job Title _____ Dept. _____ Shift _____

Sign Here X _____

Note: This authorization to be SIGNED and DATED in Employee's own handwriting. YOUR RIGHT TO SIGN THIS CARD IS PROTECTED BY FEDERAL LAW.

RECEIVED BY (Initial) _____

Representation Elections

Figure 6–3 shows that if interest in repesentation or (decertification) is sufficient, the union (or the employer in the absence of a demand for recognition) can petition the NLRB to hold an election to determine the desires of the employees. This section will trace the basic steps involved.

Recognition Requests

An election initially occurs to determine whether employees desire representation. If doubt later arises whether the union retains its majority status, a **decertification election** will be held.

A union will not usually make a recognition request unless a substantial majority of employees sign authorization cards. The union prefers a large margin because the employer will likely question the eligibility of some workers to be represented or vote in the election. Employers faced with a recognition request usually claim the union's majority status is doubtful. The union may offer to have a neutral third party match the authorization card signatures with a list of employees to establish that a majority actually exists. If a majority has signed and the employer is

FIGURE 6-3

Avenues to Election Petitions

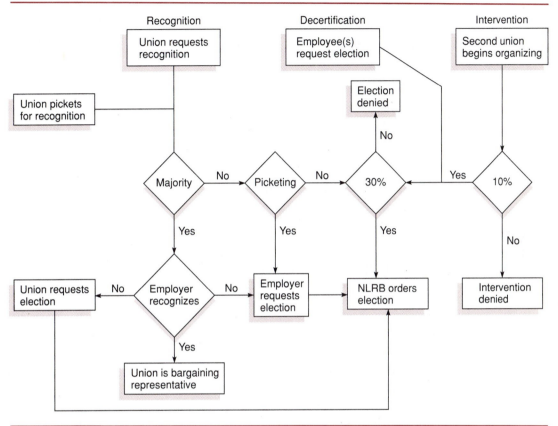

satisfied with the appropriateness of the proposed bargaining unit, recognition can be granted voluntarily.

A union may picket an unorganized employer for up to 30 days, demanding that it be recognized as the employees' bargaining representative. If this occurs, the employer can petition the NLRB to hold an election among the employees the union seeks to represent. If the union loses, further **recognitional picketing** would be an unfair labor practice.

Election Petitions

An election petition may be filed with the board by a labor organization, an employer, or an individual. In certain types of elections, however, employers are precluded from filing petitions because early petitions might find inadequate union support to pursue the election. Proof of interest must be shown in a petition or within 48 hours. The union must specify the group of employees it desires to represent. If an employer has had a recognition demand from a union (for example, recognitional picketing), it can directly petition the board to hold an election. A union or an employee (but not an employer) can file a decertification petition alleging that the present union is no longer supported by a majority of employees and its removal as bargaining agent is desired. The 30 percent interest requirement exists here as well.

Preelection Board Involvement

The NLRB determines whether it has jurisdiction in the proposed election. Jurisdiction requirements vary according to the type of business involved. For example, nonretail operations must do at least $50,000 of business in interstate commerce per year to be included. When the board takes jurisdiction, a number of avenues open. Figure 6–4 details board procedures before the election.

There are two types of elections: (1) a **consent election,** in which the parties agree on the scope of the proposed bargaining unit and which employees will be eligible to vote; and (2) a **board-directed (or petition) election,** in which the NLRB **regional director** determines, after hearings, the appropriate bargaining unit and the eligible voters.

If the board directs an election, the employer is required to provide within seven days a so-called *Excelsior* **list** containing the names and addresses of employees in the proposed bargaining unit.[2] Then after 10 days but not more than 30 days, the election will normally be held.

The Election

The NLRB supervises the secret ballot election. Both company and union observers may challenge voter eligibility but may not prohibit any individual from voting. Challenges are determined subsequent to the election. After the ballots are counted, the choice receiving a majority of votes cast is declared the winner. If more than two alternatives (for example, two different unions and no union) are on the ballot and none obtains an absolute majority, a runoff will be held between the two highest choices. Figure 6–5 is an example of an NLRB election ballot.

After the election has occurred and any challenges are resolved, the regional director will certify the results. If the union wins, it becomes the exclusive bargaining representative of the employees in the unit and may attempt to negotiate a contract. If the employer wins, no further election can take place in that unit for one year. In effect, **certification** guarantees the union or nonunion status of a bargaining unit for a period of at least one year.[3]

---

[2] *Excelsior Underwear, Inc.,* 156 NLRB 1236 (1966).
[3] *Brooks v. NLRB,* 348 U.S. 96 (1954).

FIGURE 6-4

NLRB Involvement: Petition to Election

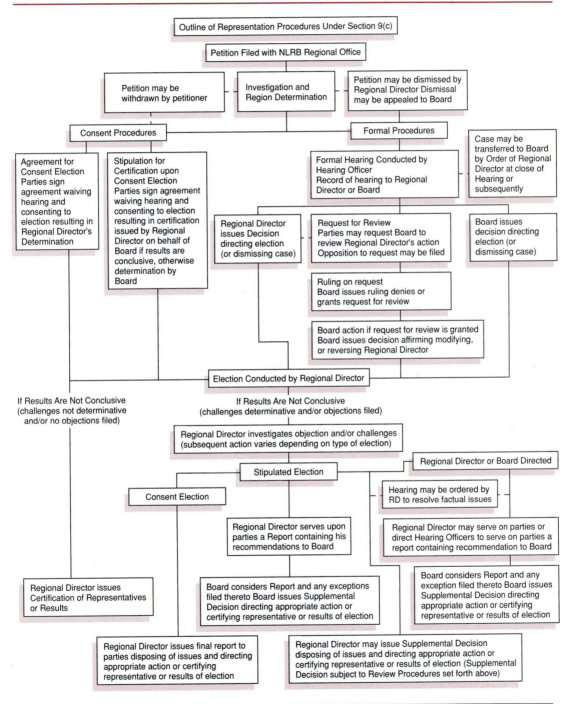

FIGURE 6-5
Specimen NLRB Ballot

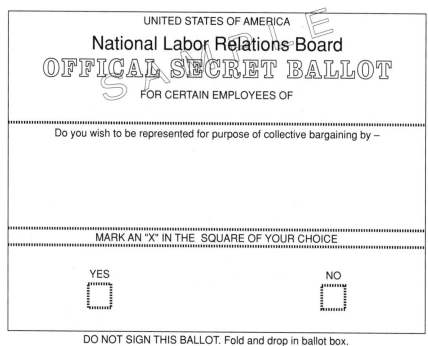

UNITED STATES OF AMERICA

National Labor Relations Board

OFFICAL SECRET BALLOT

FOR CERTAIN EMPLOYEES OF

Do you wish to be represented for purpose of collective bargaining by –

MARK AN "X" IN THE SQUARE OF YOUR CHOICE

YES   NO

DO NOT SIGN THIS BALLOT. Fold and drop in ballot box.
If you spoil this ballot return it to the Board Agent for a new one.

Bargaining Unit Determination

The NLRB determines bargaining units by considering a variety of factors, including (1) legal constraints, (2) the constitutional jurisdiction of the organizing union, (3) the union's likely success in organizing and bargaining, (4) the employer's desires in resisting organization or promoting stability in the bargaining relationship, and (5) its own philosophy in unit determination.

Bargaining units may differ depending on whether the focus is on organizing and representation or contract negotiations. For example, several retail stores in a given chain may constitute an appropriate bargaining unit for representation election purposes; while for bargaining purposes, several retail stores owned by different companies may associate in **multiemployer bargaining.** The discussion of bargaining unit determination in this chapter is concerned only with representation activities, while bargaining units for negotiations will be discussed in Chapter 7.

Legal Constraints

Legal constraints limit the potential scope of a bargaining unit, but within these, the contending parties—labor and management—are free to jointly determine an appropriate unit. If they do, a consent election results. If they don't, the NLRB is responsible for determining unit appropriateness.

Section 9(b) of the Taft-Hartley Act details the constraints placed on unit determination. First, no unit can be made up of both professional and nonprofessional employees without the express approval of a majority of the professionals. Second, a separate craft unit within an employer's operation may not be precluded from forming simply because the board had earlier included it in a broader group; however, this subsection has been broadly interpreted by the NLRB in continuing the inclusion of craft groups in larger units. Third, no bargaining unit may jointly consist of guards hired by employers to enforce the company's rules and other employees. Fourth, supervisors and managers may not be included in a unit and/or bargain collectively because their roles as agents of the employer place them outside the employee definition in Section 2. These proscriptions apply to employers outside the health care area. The 1974 amendments to Taft-Hartley permitting representation in private, non-profit health care facilities established special constraints on bargaining. Since then, the board has wrestled with the issue of appropriate bargaining units and has engaged, for the first time, in rule making rather than case-by-case rulings. Units found appropriate by the board include registered nurses, physicians, other professionals, technical employees, skilled maintenance workers, business office clericals, guards, and all other nonprofessional employees. These rules have been challenged and upheld.[4]

While this chapter does not detail organizing in employers covered by the Railway Labor Act, it should be noted that the National Mediation Board handles elections in those units. The major difference between the two jurisdictions is that the Railway Labor Board requires that bargaining units be formed on a craft basis.

---

[4] *American Hospital Association* v. *NLRB*, U.S. Supreme Court, No. 90–97, April 23, 1991.

Jurisdiction of the Organizing Union

Some unions concentrate on organizing certain occupations or industries. Many other unions organize in areas other than their traditional jurisdictions because of a shrinking employment base. If an AFL–CIO union is organizing where another affiliate already represents employees, the NLRB will notify the AFL–CIO when a petition is filed to allow it to adjudicate the problem internally according to its constitution. The problem is always resolved because a condition of affiliation is agreeing to let the federation resolve internal disputes. **"Raid" elections** have declined recently and will continue to recede now that the Teamsters have reaffiliated with the AFL–CIO.[5]

The Union's Desired Unit

The union is faced with several problems in deciding which bargaining unit configuration it desires. It must balance the optimal configuration of a unit to win an election against its objectives in later contract negotiations. A craft union would likely seek a bargaining unit that includes only workers of relatively similar skills. Industrial unions would tend to be inclusive, seeking recognition for most employees (coverable under the law) within a given plant or company.

A union must be recognized before it can bargain. Thus, it might suggest a unit in which an authorization card majority already exists or one that it believes will be easiest to organize. On the other hand, organizing a unit that would have little impact on the company's business if the union were to strike would be futile. For example, gaining a majority in a unit of custodial employees in a manufacturing plant may be relatively easy, but negotiating a favorable contract might be more difficult because the employer could readily subcontract the work for little incremental cost during the strike.

The goals of the union, then, are twofold: (1) the establishment of a "winnable" unit and (2) the definition of a unit that will have some bargaining power with the employer.

The Employer's Desired Unit

The employer's desired unit is often different from—but not necessarily opposite of—the union's desired unit. It generally prefers a unit in which the union is unlikely to win. If a craft union is organizing, the employer will generally favor a plantwide unit. In some circumstances, the em-

---

[5] C. Odewahn and C. Scott, "An Analysis of Multi-Union Elections Involving Incumbent Unions," *Journal of Labor Research* 10 (1989), pp. 197–206.

FIGURE 6–6

Conflicting Unit Desires

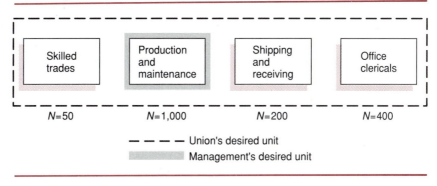

ployer will seek to narrow the unit so groups strongly in favor of the union will not lead to a majority among a variety of groups that marginally support management. Figure 6–6 details a situation in which management might argue for a smaller unit than the organizing union desires.

The firm also would like the unit configured to minimize the union's bargaining power if it obtained recognition. Thus, management might desire functionally independent units, which would allow continued operations if a strike occurred. On the other hand, it would like to avoid fragmented units, which might require continuous bargaining because of different contract expiration dates and might result in conceding to excessive demands of single units to avoid a siege of rotating strikes among the unions.

NLRB Policy

NLRB policy determines bargaining unit appropriateness where disputes exist. Although the board has not exercised completely consistent decision making in unit determination, it has applied the following criteria.[6]

1. *Community of interests.* The mutuality of interests among employees in bargaining for wages, hours, and working conditions is frequently applied.[7] However, this criterion is difficult to interpret because no benchmark is used to define the degree of similarity necessary between employee groups.

[6] John E. Abodeely, Randi C. Hammer, and Andrew L. Sandler, *The NLRB and the Appropriate Bargaining Unit*, rev. ed., Labor Relations and Public Policy Series, report no. 3 (Philadelphia: Industrial Research Unit, Department of Industry, Wharton School of Finance and Commerce, University of Pennsylvania, 1981).

[7] *Continental Baking Co.*, 99 NLRB 777 (1952).

2. *Geographic and physical proximity.*   The more separated in distance two or more locations are, the more difficult it is for a single union to represent employees. This factor may be given considerable weight when the employer's policies differ substantially across locations.

3. *Employer's administrative or territorial divisions.*   If labor relations or personnel management within a firm were uniform over a given territory (for example, 46 grocery stores located in five counties of southeastern Michigan and managed as a territorial subdivision of a multistate chain), then this unit rather than a single store or subset may be appropriate.

4. *Functional integration.*   This factor relates to the degree to which all potentially includable employees are required to maintain the company's major production processes. For example, in its decision in *Borden Co.*, the board recognized that although 20 different facilities having varying personnel policies were involved in the seemingly independent processes of manufacturing (3) and distributing (17) ice cream, an appropriate unit would contain all 20 plants because of the interrelationships among facilities necessary to market the final product.[8]

5. *Interchange of employees.*   If employees are frequently transferred across plants or offices, their community of interest may be similar, thus leading the board to designate a multiplant unit.

6. *Bargaining history.*   In applying this factor, the board may consider the past practices of the union and the employer (if it were a decertification or unit clarification election) or typical industry practices in bargaining. For example, if an employer had a companywide unit that had served the mutual bargaining interests of both the employer and the union, the board would probably leave it undisturbed.

7. *Employee desires.*   Early in the board's history, the *Globe Doctrine* was developed.[9] Where a bargaining history involving several units exists, the board may allow employees to vote for or against their inclusion in a more comprehensive unit.

8. *Extent of organization.*   The board may consider, after the foregoing factors are analyzed, the degree to which organization has occurred in a proposed unit, although this is not considered the prime factor.[10] The Supreme Court has ruled the board could consider it because Section 9(c)(5) of the Taft-Hartley Act requires consideration of allowing employees the fullest freedom in exercising their rights.

---

[8] *Borden Co., Hutchinson Ice Cream Div.*, 89 NLRB 227 (1950).

[9] Abodeely et al., *NLRB and the Appropriate Bargaining Unit*, pp. 66–68.

[10] *NLRB v. Metropolitan Life Insurance Co.*, 380 U.S. 438 (1965).

Many of these factors are interrelated. For example, employee interchange is more likely to occur within a defined administrative unit, and, in turn, an interchange should establish a broader **community of interests.** Thus the board's determination frequently rests on several factors. Although these factors are generally utilized, there have been exceptions to each.[11]

Craft Severance

The term *craft severance* means a group of employees with a substantially different community of interests within a proposed unit is allowed to establish a separate unit. **Craft severance** can occur during initial unit determination or when a group of employees votes to leave their bargaining unit.

The NLRB will allow craft severance only when the following conditions exist: (1) a high degree of skill or a functional differentiation and a tradition of separate representation; (2) a short history of bargaining in the present unit and a low degree of likely disruption if severance were granted; (3) a distinct separateness in the established unit among members of the proposed unit; (4) a different collective bargaining history in the industry; (5) low integration in production; and (6) a high degree of experience as a representative for that craft of the union desiring severance.[12]

Severance is easier during initial organization. Craft severance has been allowed in cases of a recognizable difference in the communities of interest when no prior contrary bargaining history exists.[13]

What Factors Are Used?

Except in health care, no administrative rules apply. The board determines bargaining unit appropriateness on a case-by-case basis. For severance, the overriding factor is bargaining history, buttressed by functional integration in an employer's operation. For representation, community of interest and functional integration are important. The workers' community of interest is affected by the production process, transfer policies, geographical proximity, and administrative decision making.

Judicial precedents are few; NLRB bargaining unit determinations are unappealable because they are not "final orders." If an employer were dissatisfied with the board's determination, it would refuse to bargain after losing an election and have the courts determine the appropriateness of the board's determination.[14] In most cases, the courts leave it undisturbed.

---

[11] Abodeely et al., *NLRB and the Appropriate Bargaining Unit*, pp. 11–86.

[12] *Mallinckrodt Chemical Works*, 162 NLRB 387 (1966).

[13] *E. I. duPont de Nemours & Co.*, 162 NLRB 413 (1966), and *Anheuser-Busch, Inc.*, 170 NLRB No. 5 (1968).

[14] Abodeely et al., *NLRB and the Appropriate Bargaining Unit*, pp. 28–29.

Other Issues in Unit Determination

The structures of organizations change over time. What was initially an appropriate unit may not be now. Major factors involved in the continuing definition of a unit include company growth and acquisitions, reorganization, reclassification of jobs, or purchase by another firm.

Accretion

Accretion occurs when a new facility is included in the bargaining unit or when an existing union in an organization gains representation rights for employees previously represented by another union. The NLRB generally applies the same standards to accretion as it does to initial unit determination. However, the board tends to give extra weight to the desires of employees in the unit subject to accretion.

Reorganization and Reclassification

An employer will occasionally reclassify jobs or reorganize administrative units. These changes might make a previously defined bargaining unit inappropriate, and the parties may redefine the unit by consent. Failing this, the employer would have to refuse to bargain, and the union would have to file an unfair labor practice charge in order for the board to reexamine appropriateness.

Successor Organizations

Generally, a firm acquiring or merging with another assumes the contractual bargaining obligations accrued up to the time of the merger.[15] An employer who assumes another's operations where the employees simply change employers is obligated to recognize the union but need not honor the predecessor's contract with the union.[16] But a substantial and apparent continuity in operations does not create an obligation if the union lacks majority status, even if the absence of a majority is because of layoffs and new hires by the successor.[17] When a firm is restarted by new owners after discontinuous operations, such as from a liquidation, the bargaining relationship continues if a majority of the new employees are persons who worked for the previous company and were in a represented unit.[18]

---

[15] *John Wiley & Sons, Inc. v. Livingston,* 376 U.S. 543 (1964).

[16] *NLRB v. Burns International Security Services,* 406 U.S. 272 (1972).

[17] *Howard Johnson Co., Inc. v. Detroit Local Joint Executive Board, Hotel and Restaurant Employees & Bartenders International Union, AFL–CIO,* 417 U.S. 249 (1974).

[18] *Fall River Dyeing v. NLRB,* 107 S. Ct. 2225 (1987); see also, R. F. Mace, "The Supreme Court's Labor Law Successorship Doctrine after *Fall River Dyeing,*" *Labor Law Journal* 39 (1988), pp. 102–9.

THE ORGANIZING CAMPAIGN

Organizing is a critical event, particularly from the employer's view. Besides repudiating the employer's personnel/human resource program, a successful organizing campaign also affects the value of the firm and the careers of the managers of organized units. A company's value, as measured by stock prices, falls when election petitions for initial organizing are filed.[19] Conversely, in a decertification campaign, firm value increases when the NLRB certifies a union loss.[20] In campaigns where unions succeed, managers in charge when the campaign began are frequently fired, demoted, or transferred.[21] This may explain why employers have increasingly adopted vigorous and militant programs to attempt to beat organizing campaigns.

The organizing campaign begins with attempts by the union to gain signed authorization cards. During the early part of the campaign, organizing may be done surreptitiously to avoid an employer reaction. Many employers have installed preventive measures to make organizing by nonemployees difficult.

No Distribution or Solicitation Rules

Most employers prohibit solicitations by an organization on company property or on company time. These rules prohibit labor organizers from gaining easy access to employees, because they cannot be treated differently from representatives of other organizations. An organizing campaign is much more difficult if workers must be contacted off the job, especially if the organizer does not know where they live.

No-solicitation rules do not apply to employees. Employee organizers are allowed to solicit fellow workers on company premises (during nonworking time) unless it's clearly shown that solicitation interferes with production.[22] Nonemployee organizers (e.g., international union field representatives) can, in most instances, be barred from soliciting on company property.[23] These distinctions require very early in-plant support for a drive to be successful.

---

[19] S. G. Bronars and D. R. Deere, "Union Representation Elections and Firm Profitability," *Industrial Relations* 29 (1990), pp. 15–37.

[20] W. L. Huth and D. N. MacDonald, "Equity Market Response to Union Decertification Petitions and Elections," *Journal of Labor Research* 11 (1990), pp. 193–201.

[21] R. B. Freeman and M. M. Kleiner, "Employer Behavior in the Face of Union Organizing Drives," *Industrial and Labor Relations Review* 43 (1990), 351–65.

[22] *Republic Aviation Corp.* v. *NLRB*; and *NLRB* v. *LeTourneau Co.*, 324 U.S. 793 (1945).

[23] *NLRB* v. *Babcock & Wilcox Co.*; *NLRB* v. *Seamprufe, Inc.*; and *Ranco, Inc.* v. *NLRB*, 351 U.S. 105 (1956).

In special cases, an organizer may solicit on company property where reasonable access to employees is unavailable, as in remote operations such as logging, or where workers live in a company town.[24] But organizers may not take advantage of the quasi-public nature of some of the company's property, such as retail store parking lots or shopping malls, to solicit workers.[25] Employers can lessen the chance of solicitation by requiring employees to leave working areas and plants immediately after their shifts end. In cases decided by the Supreme Court, employer property rights have generally been given precedence over the rights of employees to organize in determining the legality of campaign activities.[26]

Union Strategy and Tactics

Once the campaign begins, both parties' actions are open to scrutiny. Individuals may not be coerced or restrained in their right to engage in or avoid concerted activity or to be represented by their own chosen agents. This means neither party may legally interfere with an employee's right to join or not to join a union.

The union is faced with a delicate early strategy problem. It must publicize its activities enough to induce others to join, but conceal the activities from the employer to avoid triggering a reaction. If a union suspects that an employer will retaliate against employee union organizers, it may deliberately publish the activists' names so the company cannot later plead that any disciplinary actions taken against them were not based on antiunion feelings.[27]

To avoid unfair labor practice findings, employers must take care to not treat employees differently based on their union activity. Once a campaign begins, the employer must continue to apply personnel practices consistently with past practices and equally across workers. Exhibit 6–1 illustrates this point in a case involving a personnel practice reversal toward an employee.

The union may encounter difficulties if employees do not want to sign cards authorizing it to act as their bargaining representative. If signers do not authorize an agency relationship, the cards may not be

---

[24] *Marsh* v. *Alabama,* 326 U.S. 501 (1946).

[25] *Central Hardware Co.* v. *NLRB,* 407 U.S. 539 (1972); and *Hudgens* v. *NLRB,* 91 LRRM 2489 (U.S. Supreme Court, 1976).

[26] R. N. Block, B. W. Wolkinson, and J. W. Kuhn, "Some Are More Equal than Others: The Relative Status of Employers, Unions, and Employees in the Law of Union Organizing," *Industrial Relations Law Journal* 10 (1988), pp. 220–40.

[27] Stephen I. Schlossberg and Frederick E. Sherman, *Organizing and the Law,* rev. ed. (Washington, D.C.: Bureau of National Affairs, 1971).

EXHIBIT 6-1

Edward G. Budd Manufacturing Co. v. *NLRB*

United States Court of Appeals, Third Circuit, 1943, 138 F. 2d 86, Biggs, Circuit Judge. . . .

The complaint alleges that the petitioner, in September 1933, created and foisted a labor organization known as the Budd Employee Representation Association upon its employees and thereafter contributed financial support to the association and dominated its activities. The amended complaint also alleges that in July 1941 the petitioner discharged an employee, Walter Weigand, because of his activities on behalf of the union. . . .

The case of Walter Weigand is extraordinary. If ever a workman deserved summary discharge it was he. He was under the influence of liquor while on duty. He came to work when he chose, and he left the plant and his shift as he pleased. In fact, a foreman on one occasion was agreeably surprised to find Weigand at work and commented upon it. Weigand amiably stated that he was enjoying it. He brought a woman (apparently generally known as the "Duchess") to the rear of the plant yard and introduced some of the employees to her. He took another employee to visit her, and when this man got too drunk to be able to go home, punched his time card for him, and put him on the table in the representatives' meeting room in the plant in order to sleep off his intoxication. Weigand's immediate superiors demanded again and again that he be discharged, but each time higher officials intervened on Weigand's behalf because as was naively stated he was "a representative" (of the association, found to be a dominated union). In return for not working at the job for which he was hired, the petitioner gave him full pay and on five separate occasions raised his wages. One of these raises was general; that is to say, Weigand profited by a general wage increase throughout the plant, but the other four raises were given Weigand at times when other employees in the plant did not receive wage increases.

The petitioner contends that Weigand was discharged because of cumulative grievances against him. But about the time of the discharge it was suspected by some of the representatives that Weigand had joined the complaining CIO union. One of the representatives taxed him with this fact, and Weigand offered to bet a hundred dollars that it could not be proved. On July 22, 1941, Weigand did disclose his union membership to the vice chairman (Rattigan) of the association and to another representative (Mullen) and apparently tried to persuade them to support the union. Weigand asserts that the next day he, with Rattigan and Mullen, were seen talking to CIO organizer Reichwein on a street corner. The following day, according to Weigand's testimony, Mullen came to Weigand at the plant and stated that he, Mullen, had just had an interview with Personnel Director McIlvain and Plant Manager Mahan. According to Weigand, Mullen said to him, "Maybe you didn't get me in a jam." And, "We were seen down there." The following day Weigand was discharged.

As this court [has] stated . . . an employer may discharge an employee for a good reason, a poor reason, or no reason at all so long as the provisions of the

---

EXHIBIT 6–1

(concluded)

National Labor Relations Act are not violated. It is, of course, a violation to discharge an employee because he has engaged in activities on behalf of a union. Conversely an employer may retain an employee for a good reason, a bad reason, or no reason at all, and the reason is not a concern of the board. But it is certainly too great a strain on our credulity to assert, as does the petitioner, that Weigand was discharged for an accumulation of offenses. We think that he was discharged because his work on behalf of the CIO had become known to the plant manager. That ended his sinecure at the Budd plant. The board found that he was discharged because of his activities on behalf of the union. The record shows that the board's finding was based on sufficient evidence. . . .

---

used to gain a representation election.[28] Employees may also be concerned that their employer will find out they are personally interested in unionization.

Union campaigns stress issues important to employees and show them how a union would enable them to achieve these ends.[29] A study of 33 campaigns showed that 15 issues were raised by the union in at least half.[30] Table 6–1 displays union campaign issues and the percent of elections in which each was raised. The issues call attention to inequitable or threatening treatment by the employer and create a strong impression that the union's agency role will yield important gains to the employee, countering expected employer positions and establishing the legitimacy of the union and its activities.

After a recognition request or election petition is made, the union's tactics become more open for three reasons. First, the strongest proponents have already signed up, and thus each additional prounion vote will require increasingly concentrated collective pressure. Second, because the employer is now definitely aware of the campaign, secrecy is not needed. And third, publicity eliminates any possibility of an employer claiming ignorance of union activity as a defense if action is taken against employees.

During the preelection period, the union may show its strength by asking adherents to wear campaign buttons or union T-shirts. The union can hold meetings during nonwork time and utilize the *Excelsior* list to

---

[28] Ibid., p. 51.

[29] For a detailed plan for organizing, see Ken Gagala, *Union Organizing and Staying Organized* (Reston, Va.: Reston Publishing, 1983), pp. 95–195.

[30] Julius Getman, Stephen Goldberg, and Jeanne B. Herman, *Union Representation Elections: Law and Reality* (New York: Russell Sage Foundation, 1976), pp. 80–81.

TABLE 6–1

Prevalent Union Campaign Issues

Issue	Percent of Campaigns
Union will prevent unfairness, set up grievance procedure/seniority system	82
Union will improve unsatisfactory wages	79
Union strength will provide employees with voice in wages, working conditions	79
Union, not outsider, bargains for what employees want	73
Union has obtained gains elsewhere	70
Union will improve unsatisfactory sick leave/insurance	64
Dues/initiation fees are reasonable	64
Union will improve unsatisfactory vacations/holidays	61
Union will improve unsatisfactory pensions	61
Employer promises/good treatment may not be continued without union	61
Employees choose union leaders	55
Employer will seek to persuade/frighten employees to vote against union	55
No strike without vote	55
Union will improve unsatisfactory working conditions	52
Employees have legal right to engage in union activity	52

SOURCE: Adapted from Table 4–3 in *Union Representation Elections: Law and Reality,* by Julius G. Getman, Stephen B. Goldberg, and Jeanne B. Herman. Copyright © 1976 by Russell Sage Foundation, New York.

make personal contacts at workers' homes. Leaflets and cartoons may be distributed. Figure 6–7 is an example of a suggested late campaign leaflet.

The union will frequently stress how wages, hours, and working conditions at the target employer differ from those in unionized organizations. Unions have the advantage over management because they can speculate on changes likely to occur after organization, while the employer may not legally communicate benefits that might result if organization fails. Issues and tactics in organizing campaigns have not changed much recently. Face-to-face organizing tactics and issues involving grievance handling, job security, and economics are important. If the bargaining unit is predominantly female, face-to-face tactics are emphasized more, and opportunities for advancement and technical training become more salient.[31] Individual characteristics of organizers also influence organizing outcomes.[32]

A general model of a simple local organizing campaign has been described. Unions may also conduct area-wide, total company, or

---

[31] M. L. Lynn and J. Brister, "Trends in Union Organizing Issues and Tactics," *Industrial Relations* 28 (1989), pp. 104–13.

[32] T. F. Reed, "Do Union Organizers Matter? Individual Characteristics and Representation Election Outcomes," *Industrial and Labor Relations Review* 43 (1989), pp. 103–19.

FIGURE 6–7
Specimen Union Communication

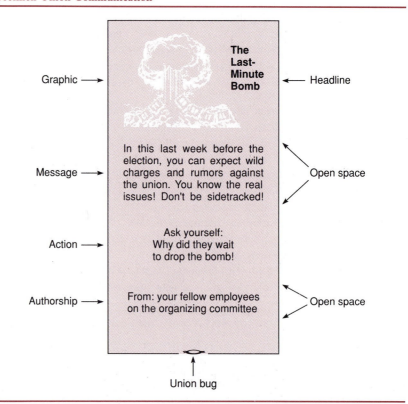

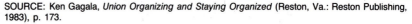

SOURCE: Ken Gagala, *Union Organizing and Staying Organized* (Reston, Va.: Reston Publishing, 1983), p. 173.

industrial campaigns. Four new strategies have been suggested to overcome employer resistance: (1) conduct corporate campaigns involving financial and product market pressures and confrontations with top-level management not closely involved in the organizing attempt, (2) use employer neutrality pledges and accretion agreements for new plants, (3) identify the union with significant community interests, and (4) pool the resources of several unions.[33]

Union organizing has been the object of substantial recent interest. In general, unions did not organize as actively or as broadly in the 1980s as earlier.[34] Union campaign success within industries is related to firm size, capital intensity, the ratio of labor to total costs, and extremes in

[33] James A. Craft and Marian M. Extejt, "New Strategies in Union Organizing," *Journal of Labor Research* 4 (1983), pp. 19–32.

[34] G. N. Chaison and D. G. Dhavale, "The Changing Scope of Union Organizing," *Journal of Labor Research* 11 (1990), pp. 307–22.

profitability. In general, large, unprofitable firms are most vulnerable.[35] Unless there are salient employee issues for unionizing, even well-orchestrated drives are likely to fail as did the AFL–CIO's efforts to organize several state Blue Cross–Blue Shield organizations.[36]

Management Strategy and Tactics

Management strategy and tactics are planned at both corporate offices and at the facility at which organizing activities occur. At the corporate level, a variety of responses is possible. Unless the organization is in the public sector, or unless it's already heavily unionized, top management almost always resists organizing. It vigorously combats organizing by sending out advisors at the first sign of union activity, and it may also try to rid itself of presently unionized situations. Many major firms have specific goals for repelling or containing union organizing activities.[37]

Many organizations periodically sample employee attitudes and ask supervisors to keep alert for signs of potential organizing activity. When organizing occurs, consultants may be hired to assist management in conducting an antiunion campaign. Uncovering union activity in a covert manner, restricting solicitations, waging an intense campaign, and opposing a consent election influence election outcomes in management's favor.[38]

If the union seeks an election, management almost always contests the proposed bargaining unit to delay the election, which works to management's advantage. On the average, the union's authorization card position erodes by 2.5 percent for each month the election is delayed.[39] Delays contribute to both reduced participation in elections and proportions of prounion votes.[40]

[35] C. L. Maranto, "Corporate Characteristics and Union Organizing," *Industrial Relations* 27 (1988), pp. 352–70.

[36] H. R. Northrup, "The AFL–CIO Blue Cross–Blue Shield Campaign: A Study of Organizational Failure," *Industrial and Labor Relations Review* 43 (1990), pp. 525–41.

[37] Audrey Freedman, *Managing Labor Relations* (New York: Conference Board, 1979), p. 33; and *The New Look in Wage Policy and Employee Relations* (New York: Conference Board, 1985), pp. 5–6.

[38] Kent F. Murrmann and Andrew A. Porter, "Employer Campaign Tactics and NLRB Election Outcomes: Some Preliminary Evidence," *Proceedings of the Industrial Relations Research Association* 35 (1982), pp. 67–72.

[39] Richard Prosten, "The Longest Season: Union Organizing in the Last Decade, a/k/a How Come One Team Has to Play with Its Shoelaces Tied Together?" *Proceedings of the Industrial Relations Research Association* 31 (1978), pp. 240–49. Delays, however, do not appear to have increased over time, see Richard N. Block and Benjamin W. Wolkinson, "Delay in Union Election Campaigns Revisited: A Theoretical and Empirical Analysis," *Advances in Industrial and Labor Relations* 3 (1986), pp. 43–81.

[40] Gary Florkowski and Michael Schuster, "Predicting the Decisions to Vote and Support Unions in Certification Elections: An Integrated Perspective," *Journal of Labor Research* 8 (1987), pp. 191–207.

The greater the differential between union wages in an industry and the employer's wage, the greater management resistance will be. Employer resistance increases more rapidly with differentials than with desires for unionization by the employees.[41] An active union avoidance strategy for new facilities decreases the likelihood of organizing from about 15 percent to 1 percent.[42] Neutrality likely leads toward representation.[43]

Management campaigns emphasize unions are outsiders less concerned than the employer with employee welfare; conditions may not improve after unionization; and employees will be unable to deal individually with employers on employment conditions. Table 6–2 shows issues emphasized most often by management in the same campaigns from which union issues were portrayed in Table 6–1. Management communicates personally with employees to oppose the union. Figure 6–8 is an example of material urging employees to vote against the union.

Consultants or campaign advisors suggest employers direct large-scale communications efforts toward employees, including mass meetings, small-group discussions with management representatives, and individual interviews to give information on *present* (not anticipated) company personnel programs.[44] Supervisors, a key management group in communicating with rank-and-file employees, need extensive briefings on the company's position and on the avoidance of unfair labor practices.[45]

A vigorous and successful management campaign uses tactics that gain early warnings of union activity and combine outside consultants, strong inside involvement, and delaying tactics.[46] Unfortunately, some managements, particularly those with low wages and poor working conditions,[47] may also purposely commit unfair labor practices to blunt an organizing drive. The cost to employers of restoring discriminatorily fired

[41] Richard B. Freeman, "The Effect of the Union Wage Differential on Management Opposition and Union Organizing Success," *American Economic Review* 76 (1986), pp. 92–96.

[42] Thomas A. Kochan, Robert B. McKersie, and John Chalykoff, "The Effects of Corporate Strategy and Workplace Innovations on Union Representation," *Industrial and Labor Relations Review* 39 (1986), pp. 487–501; see also John J. Lawler and Robin West, "Impact of Union-Avoidance Strategy in Representation Elections," *Industrial Relations,* 24 (1985), pp. 406–20.

[43] A. H. Raskin, "Management Comes Out Swinging," *Proceedings of the Industrial Relations Research Association* 31 (1978), pp. 223–32.

[44] For an overview and incidents involving consultants for both sides, see *Labor Relations Consultants: Issues, Trends, and Controversies* (Washington, D.C.: Bureau of National Affairs, 1985).

[45] Louis Jackson and Robert Lewis, *Winning NLRB Elections* (New York: Practising Law Institute, 1972).

[46] Murrmann and Porter, "Employer Campaign Tactics"; John Lawler, "Labor–Management Consultants in Union Organizing Campaigns: Do They Make a Difference?" *Proceedings of the Industrial Relations Research Association,* 34 (1981), pp. 374–80; and John J. Lawler, "Union Growth and Decline: The Impact of Employer and Union Tactics," *Journal of Occupational Psychology* 59 (1986), pp. 217–30.

[47] Freeman and Kleiner, "Employer Behavior."

TABLE 6–2

Prevalent Management Campaign Issues

Issues	Percent of Campaigns
Improvements not dependent on unionization	85
Wages good, equal to/better than under union contract	82
Financial costs of union dues outweigh gains	79
Union is outsider	79
Get facts before deciding, employer will provide facts and accept employee decision	76
If union wins, strike may follow	70
Loss of benefits may follow union win	67
Strikers will lose wages, lose more than gain	67
Unions not concerned with employee welfare	67
Strike may lead to loss of jobs	64
Employer has treated employees fairly/well	60
Employees should be certain to vote	54

SOURCE: Adapted from Table 4–2 in *Union Representation Elections: Law and Reality*, by Julius G. Getman, Stephen B. Goldberg, and Jeanne B. Herman. Copyright © 1976 by Russell Sage Foundation, New York.

union activists to their jobs with back pay is far outweighed by the potential costs of wage increases in a union contract if they were to be organized.[48] Employers appear to learn that consequences for unlawful discrimination are slight; such discrimination occurs most frequently where unionization is pervasive and among employers who previously violated the labor acts.[49] Discrimination against employees engaging in union activities decreases union organizing success by an average 17 percent.[50] Employees who perceived that their employers committed unfair labor practices in campaigns were less likely to vote for representation than those who had not, other things equal.[51] Unfair labor practice charges by unions have increased substantially since 1970 at the same time that their success in elections and the number of elections conducted have fallen. Table 6–3 is a summary of studies looking at the effects of management activity on election results.[52]

[48] Charles R. Greer and Stanley A. Martin, "Calculative Strategy Decisions during Union Organizing Campaigns," *Sloan Management Review* 19, no. 4 (1978), pp. 61–74.

[49] Morris M. Kleiner, "Unionism and Employer Discrimination: Analysis of 8(a)(3) Violations," *Industrial Relations* 23 (1984), pp. 234–43.

[50] William N. Cooke, "The Rising Toll of Discrimination against Union Activists," *Industrial Relations*, 24 (1985), pp. 421–42.

[51] T. J. Keaveny, J. Rosse, and John A. Fossum, "Campaign Tactics and Certification Election Outcomes," unpublished manuscript (Milwaukee, Wis.: Marquette University, 1989).

[52] Richard B. Freeman, "Contraction and Expansion of Unionism in Private and Public Sectors, *Journal of Economic Perspectives* 2, no. 2 (1988), pp. 63–88.

FIGURE 6–8
Specimen Employer Communication

Home mailing

Wednesday

Dear Fellow Employee:

At our plant gate yesterday, the union distributed a leaflet in which it discussed how it will back up its demands at our company.

In other words, the union is stating that it can fulfill its promise by the use of force. This is absolutely untrue. While the union can make promises and threaten to force us to do things, it is the company that pays your wages and provides you with benefits.

I think you should know some facts about what the union <u>cannot do</u> to your company, and some of the things they <u>can do</u> to you.

First, let's look at what it <u>cannot</u> force your company to do:

1. It cannot force the company to agree to any proposal that the company is unwilling or unable to meet.
2. It cannot increase any wages or benefits unless the company feels it is in its best interest to do so.
3. It cannot guarantee job security or furnish you a day's work or a day's pay.

Now let's work at what it <u>can</u> "force" employees to do.

1. It can force the employees to pay dues each and every month where there is a union-shop clause in the contract.
2. It can force members to stand trial and pay fines for violation of any of the provisions of the "book of rules" (constitution).
3. It can force members to pay assessments whenever the union treasury requires more money.

Consider the many advantages and benefits you now enjoy. These have been provided without a union. Consider the many disadvantages of union membership. When you do, I am sure you will vote "no."

Sincerely,

General Manager

SOURCE: Louis Jackson and Robert Lewis, *Winning NLRB Elections* (New York: Practising Law Institute, © 1972), p. 134.

TABLE 6-3

Effects of Management Activity on NLRB Representation Election Results

Study and Sample	Measurement of Management Activity	Does Activity Have Effect?
1. National Industrial Conference Board, 140 union organizing drives of white-collar workers, 1966–67	Amount of communication by management	Yes
2. AFL–CIO, 495 NLRB election, 1966–67	Amount of opposition by management	Yes
3. Prosten (1978), analysis of probability of union win in 130,701 elections in 1962–77	Amount of time delay between election and petition	Yes
4. Lawler (1984), 155 NLRB elections, 1974–78	Company hires consultant	Yes
5. Drotning (1967), 41 elections ordered void and rerun by NLRB	Amount of communication by management	Yes
6. Roomkin-Block (1981), 45,155 union representation cases, 1971–77	Delay between petition and election	Yes
7. Seeber and Cooke (1983), proportion of workers voting for union representation by state, 1970–78	Employers object to election district	Yes
8. US General Accounting Office (1982), analysis of 8(a)(3) illegal firings or other discrimination for union involvement in 368 representation elections	Employer committed unfair labor practice	Yes
9. Aspin (1966) study of 71 NLRB elections in which reinstatements were ordered	Employer fired worker for union activity	Yes, unless reinstated before election
10. Getman, Goldberg, and Herman (1976) analysis of 1,293 workers in 31 elections in 1972–73	Campaign tactics employer	Not statistically significant
11. Dickens (1983) study of 966 workers in 31 elections in 1972–73 (using data set in #10)	Legal and illegal campaign tactics by employer	Yes
12. Catler (1978) study of 817 NLRB elections	Unfair labor practices and delay	Yes
13. Kochan, McKersie, and Chalykoff (1986), 225 firms	Employer emphasizes union avoidance strategy	Yes

SOURCE: Richard B. Freeman, "Contraction and Expansion of Unionism in Private and Public Sectors," *Journal of Economic Perspectives* 2, no. 2 (1988), p. 83.

THE ROLE OF THE NLRB

The NLRB's responsibility is to conduct the election and certify the results. If unfair campaign practices are charged, the board must decide whether they occurred and interfered with the employee's Section 7 rights to freely choose to be represented or not. The NLRB's position has been that an election should "provide a laboratory in which an experiment may be conducted, under conditions as nearly ideal as possible, to determine the uninhibited desires of the employees."[53]

The board may examine employer conduct in interrogating employees, scheduling meetings, issuing communications, and campaigning during the day before the election. The board may also assess the **totality of conduct** of the union or the employer in an election.

Interrogation

Interrogation would probably be legal if used only to test a union's claim to majority status[54] but would likely be unfair if: (1) there was a history of employer hostility toward unions, (2) the information is likely to be used against a particular individual, (3) the questioner is a high-level manager, (4) the interrogation occurs in an intimidating atmosphere, or (5) the responses to the questions indicate fear on the part of the respondent.[55]

Communications

The employer may require employees to attend meetings on company premises during working hours to hear management representatives opposing the union.[56] However, if solicitation is barred during nonworking time (as in a retail establishment), the union may be entitled to equal access.[57]

Communication content in both employer and union campaigns has long been considered by the board. Employers cannot promise employees new benefits if the union loses, but they can point out that if the union is certified, all present levels of wages and benefits will be subject to negotiation.

"Truth in campaigning" has also been controversial. Since 1977, the NLRB has reversed itself three times on whether campaign distortions are an unfair practice requiring a remedy. Before 1977, the board followed the *General Shoe* laboratory condition rule requiring truthfulness.[58] Presently, it no longer considers the truthfulness of campaign claims, reasoning that voters have experienced political campaigns and many had voted in union representation elections. Thus, they would not easily be swayed

---

[53] *General Shoe Corp.*, 77 NLRB 127 (1948).

[54] *Blue Flash Express Co.*, 109 NLRB 591 (1954).

[55] *Bourne v. NLRB*, 322 F. 2d 47 (1964).

[56] *Livingston Shirt Corp.*, 33 LRRM 1156 (1953).

[57] *May Department Stores Co.*, 136 NLRB 797 (1962).

[58] Beginning with *Hollywood Ceramics Co.*, 140 NLRB 221 (1962), which required truthfulness; adopting *Shopping Kart Food Markets, Inc.*, 229 NLRB 190 (1977), which did not; shifting to *General Knit of California, Inc.*, 239 NLRB 101 (1978), which did; and concluding with *Midland National Life*, 263 NLRB No. 24 (1982), which did not.

by rhetoric or claims. Voters appear to make their decisions relatively early in the campaign; thus, truth or falsity may have little effect during the waning days.[59]

The 24-Hour Rule

Because it would be almost impossible for a union or an employer to rebut a last-minute campaign statement, the NLRB's *Peerless Plywood* rule prohibits employers or unions from holding a captive-audience presentation within the 24 hours directly preceding the election.[60]

EMPLOYEE RESPONSES TO CAMPAIGNS

Employees apparently respond to only a few campaign issues. Attendance at either union- or management-sponsored gatherings makes one familiar with issues but has little effect on voting unless the meeting was union sponsored. Persons who remember issues generally vote for the side expressing them.[61]

Unions seldom gain support during the campaign. They tend to win elections in units where they held clear authorization card majorities before filing a petition. Between the time of the petition and the election, union support usually erodes about 4 percent. The only activity through which unions gain support is holding union-sponsored meetings attended by noncommitted employees. Undecided employees tend to vote for the company rather than the union.[62] Unless an employee makes an effort to gain exposure to the union's position, he or she will have heard much more management information before the vote is taken.

Voters are influenced by co-worker and family member attitudes toward unionization but not by supervisors or management in general. These influences, combined with beliefs about the attractiveness of outcomes from unionization and the instrumentality of the union for achieving them, predict actual votes very well.[63] Table 6–4 shows attitudes toward the outcomes among pro- and anti-union voters in one large representation election.

---

[59] J. Malcolm and John J. Lawler, "Union Campaign Activities and Voter Preferences," *Journal of Labor Research* 7 (1986), pp. 19–40.

[60] 107 NLRB 427 (1953).

[61] Getman et al., *Union Representation Elections*, pp. 95, 98–99.

[62] Ibid., pp. 100–8.

[63] B. R. Montgomery, "The Influences of Attitudes and Normative Pressures on Voting Decisions in a Union Certification Election," *Industrial and Labor Relations Review* 42 (1989), pp. 262–79; and Joseph G. Rosse, Timothy A. Keaveny, and John A. Fossum, "Predicting Union Election Outcomes: The Role of Job Attitudes, Union Attitudes, and Coworker Preferences," unpublished manuscript (Boulder, Colo.: College of Business Administration, University of Colorado, Boulder, 1986).

TABLE 6–4

Mean Normative Beliefs, Motivations to Comply, Outcome Beliefs, and Outcome Evaluations for Respondents Voting For and Against AFSCME's Certification: University of Michigan Clerical Workers, 1984

Variable	Those Voting For (*N* = 53)	Those Voting Against (*N* = 46)	Those Voting For (*N* = 53)	Those Voting Against (*N* = 46)
Referents	*nb* **Normative Belief Strength**[a]		*mc* **Motivation to Comply**[b]	
1. Co-workers	.64	−.62***	2.47	2.20
2. Other clericals	1.02	.15***	2.75	1.96**
3. Supervisor	−.33	−.32	2.25	2.26
4. Other management staff	−.63	−.76	2.08	2.15
5. Family members	1.28	−.70***	3.43	2.67**
Outcomes of Voting for AFSCME's Certification	*b* **Outcome Belief Strength**[c]		*e* **Outcome Evaluation**[d]	
1. Increase my pay	.58	−1.39***	1.96	1.63
2. Give us someone to go to for help in resolving problems and grievances	2.09	−.09***	2.32	.95***
3. Require me to pay union dues	2.42	2.72*	.15	−1.72***
4. Give clericals a say in the determination of university policies affecting them	1.38	−.57***	2.30	1.30***
5. Result in a strong, effective union for clerical and office staff	1.36	−1.20***	2.28	−.08***
6. Improve my beliefs	.74	−1.28***	2.28	1.72***
7. Result in standard rules that would apply to all clericals	1.91	1.07***	1.98	.43***
8. Result in things being the same as they were with the last clerical union	−.85	.70***	−.50	−1.28**
9. Equalize salary increases among clericals	1.30	.57**	1.17	−.37***
10. Force supervisor to treat people more fairly	1.47	−.59***	2.43	1.04***

[a] Normative Belief *(nb)*: respondent's perception of the likelihood that the referent wants the respondent to vote for the union (scored −3 to +3, extremely unlikely to extremely likely).

[b] Motivation to Comply *(mc)*: strength of the respondent's propensity to comply with the wishes of the referent (scored 1 to 7, extremely unlikely to extremely likely).

[c] Outcome Belief *(b)*: respondent's perception of the likelihood that voting for AFSCME's certification will lead to the outcome (scored −3 to +3, extremely unlikely to extremely likely).

[d] Outcome Evaluation *(e)*: respondent's evaluation of the desirability of the outcome (scored −3 to +3, extremely bad to extremely good).

* *p* < .10; ** *p* < .05; *** *p* < .01—significant differences between proponents and opponents of the union.

SOURCE: B. Ruth Montgomery, "The Influences of Attitudes and Normative Pressures on Voting Decisions in the Union Certification Election," *Industrial and Labor Relations Review* 42 (1989), p. 268.

The Effects of Unfair Practices

The vigor of management's campaign influences its likelihood of winning the election. Unfair labor practices during a vigorous campaign influence voters away from the union and may not involve large costs to the employer, even if the employer is penalized. Using the *Union Representation Elections* data, a study simulated the relative effects of various employer practices on the outcomes of elections.[64] In the *Union Representation Elections* study, an NLRB administrative law judge was asked to review the campaigns to determine whether an unfair labor practice was committed by either party during the campaign. Actual charges were filed in some of the elections, and the NLRB issued rulings on them. In 31 campaigns that had elections, 9 resulted in the board issuing a **bargaining order** (discussed below), and 13 resulted in other remedies (such as election reruns for 12 of the campaigns). Thus, the sample showed both fair and unfair conduct.

Analysis found several campaign practices influenced election outcomes. Among the most important were one legal practice (early letters to employees) and one unfair practice (threats and actions against union supporters). Table 6–5 shows the effects of individual background, election background, and campaign measures on voting behavior. In the actual campaigns, unions won 36 percent of the elections. Table 6–6 shows the effects of various campaign types on simulated election outcomes. Compared to the average, if the company fails to campaign against the union, the union's probability of winning increases by about 31 percent. In an intense legal campaign, unions lose 14 percent more frequently; and an intense campaign using both legal and illegal approaches reduces union victories by about 32 percent to only 4 percent (or 1 in 25 elections). Although employees may not pay much attention to issues, they do respond to early employer campaign efforts and illegal tactics.

ELECTION CERTIFICATIONS

After the election, ballots are counted to determine which alternative, if any, received a majority. If no objections or unfair campaign charges are filed, the NLRB certifies the results. If a union wins the election unit, it becomes the exclusive representative of the employees and can begin bargaining with the employer. If it loses and challenges are unsuccessful, then another **election** is **barred** for one year. Even if a winning union lost its majority status within the year, the board wouldn't permit a new

---

[64] William T. Dickens, "The Effect of Company Campaigns on Certification Elections: *Law and Reality* Once Again," *Industrial and Labor Relations Review* 36 (1983), pp. 560–75.

TABLE 6–5
Estimates of the Reduced-Form Voting Model*

	Specification	
Independent Variable	Specific Violations—Average Percent Impact	NLRB Remedy—Average Percent Impact
Individual background		
1. Tenure < year	.008%	.010%
2. Part-time worker	−.064	.066
3. Age code	.047†	.044
4. Age code squared	−.011	−.010
5. Married	−.047†	−.051†
6. No. of dependents	.008	.008
7. Education code	−.018	−.021†
8. White	−.000	−.001
9. Relative a union member	.057‡	.065§
10. Initial disposition	.430§	.427§
11. Not asked to sign card	−.158§	−.159§
12. Potential wage change	.127§	.130§
Election background		
13. U.A.W.	−.213§	−.180§
14. Teamsters	−.150§	−.115§
15. Steelworkers	.173§	.226§
16. Retail clerks	−.320‡	−.316‡
17. Machinists	−.416§	−.339§
18. Percent for union	.006§	.006§
19. Average education	.264§	.354§
20. No. of workers	.003§	.003§
Campaign measure		
21. Illegal speech	−.022	—
22. Illegal actions	−.024	—
23. Threats and actions vs. union supporters	−.155‡	—
24. Early letters	.010‡	.021§
25. Late letters	−.037§	−.035§
26. Early meetings	−.052‡	−.068§
27. Late meetings	−.025	.004§
28. Percent talked to by supervisor	.001	−.001
29. Remedy is bargain	—	−.073
30. Other remedy	—	−.051†

* Dependent variable equals one if the worker voted union and zero if otherwise.
† Significant at the .10 level in a one-tailed test.
‡ Significant at the .05 level in a one-tailed test.
§ Significant at the .01 level in a one-tailed test.
SOURCE: William T. Dickens, "The Effect of Company Campaigns on Certification Elections: *Law and Reality* Once Again," *Industrial and Labor Relations Review* 36 (1983), p. 568.

TABLE 6–6

Simulated Effects of Campaigns on Election Outcomes, in Percentages of 3,100 Simulated Elections Won by the Union

		Type of Campaign					
Specification	Actual Campaign	All Violations Committed in Every Case	No Violations Committed in Any Case	No Company Campaign in Any Case	Intense Company Campaign in Every Case	Intense Legal Campaign in Every Case	Light Legal Campaign in Every Case
NLRB remedy	36%	25%	44%	66%	5%	9%	58%
Specific violations	36	17	47	67	4	22	63

SOURCE: William T. Dickens, "The Effect of Company Campaigns on Certification Elections: *Law and Reality* Once Again," *Industrial and Labor Relations Review* 36 (1983), p. 572.

election. The Supreme Court and the board reason that certification is equivalent to an elected term in office, even if the official's constituency no longer supports him or her.[65] If the union loses the election, the employer cannot legally take action against its supporters. Even though they are not represented by the union, the supporters are legally protected from discrimination.

Setting Aside Elections

If challenges are filed and the board finds the activity interfered with the employees' abilities to make a reasoned choice, the election will be set aside and rerun. If the violations are trivial, the board certifies the results.

Bargaining Orders

In some cases, the board considers employer conduct to be so coercive it erodes an already demonstrated majority. For example, assume a majority signs authorization cards and attends union-organizing meetings, and the employer interrogates employees and threatens cutbacks, possible plant closings, or strikes over bargaining issues if the union wins. If the union loses and the board finds the employer conduct undermined an actual union majority, it issues a bargaining order, requiring the employer to recognize and negotiate with the union. The remedial approach is imposed because the union would have won if not for the employer's illegal conduct.[66]

---

[65] *Brooks* v. *NLRB*, 348 U.S. 96 (1954).

[66] *NLRB* v. *Gissel Packing Co.*, 395 U.S. 575 (1969); for a case in which the NLRB issued a bargaining order where no majority had been demonstrated but where the employer's behavior was seen as preventing its establishment, see George R. Salem, "Nonmajority Bargaining Orders: A Prospective View in Light of *United Dairy Farmers*," *Labor Law Journal* 32 (1981), pp. 145–57.

The Impact of Board Remedies

Bargaining orders do not necessarily lead to a contract, however. In an examination of a large number of *Gissel*-type cases, only about 39 percent of unions were able to achieve a contract. Success in getting a contract is apparently independent of unit size, extent of organization, or type of employer Section 8 violation.[67]

Unions do not win rerun elections as frequently as elections in general. Unions were certified in less than 33 percent of rerun elections in fiscal 1987, compared to 44 percent in all elections. In 1987 reruns, 46 percent had a different outcome than the original election.[68]

In addition to election reruns or bargaining orders, the NLRB can issue cease-and-desist orders for unfair labor practices during organizing drives. If individuals have been discriminated against on the basis of union activity (e.g., being discharged), the board will order their reinstatement with back pay and interest to cover the differences between wages they would have earned and what they actually earned during their discrimination.

Election Outcomes

In 1988, 243,692 persons were eligible to vote in 4,153 NLRB-conducted representation elections. Of these, 3,509 were requested by unions, employees, or employers in initial representation (RC and RM cases), and 644 were filed by employees seeking decertification (RD cases). Table 6–7 shows the size of bargaining units, number of employees eligible to vote, total elections, and percent won by a union in 1987 initial certifications. Over half were conducted in units of less than 30 employees. Unions won about 49 percent of all certification elections.

Unions involved in elections are likely to be those that organize in industries where the proportion of employees organized is not extremely large. Where organizing has been successful in the past, the international union is more likely to presently concentrate on representation activities.[69]

Evidence also suggests the economic returns of union representation are substantially greater than the costs of organizing for employees in most industries.[70] Thus, the union may recoup its investment through

---

[67] B. W. Wolkinson, N. B. Hanslowe, and S. Sperka, "The Remedial Efficacy of *Gissel* Bargaining Orders," *Industrial Relations Law Journal* 10 (1989), pp. 509–30.

[68] *Fifty-Second Annual Report of the National Labor Relations Board* (Washington, D.C.: Government Printing Office, 1989), pp. 219, 221.

[69] Richard N. Block, "Union Organizing and Allocation of Union Resources," *Industrial and Labor Relations Review* 35 (1980), pp. 110–13.

[70] Paula B. Voos, "Union Organizing: Costs and Benefits," *Industrial and Labor Relations Review* 37 (1983), pp. 576–91.

TABLE 6–7

Election Results by Unit Size

Size of Unit	Number Eligible	Total Elections	Percent Won by Union
Under 10	4,380	788	58.8
10–19	9,760	693	54.4
20–29	10,747	442	48.0
30–39	9,780	285	42.5
40–49	9,508	215	49.8
50–69	18,321	312	46.8
70–99	19,035	229	44.5
100–149	24,584	206	49.0
150–199	21,211	124	25.8
200–299	24,738	101	37.6
300–399	17,137	51	33.3
400–499	10,089	23	34.8
500–999	23,336	33	45.5
1,000–1,999	8,812	7	16.7

SOURCE: Adapted from *Fifty-Third Annual Report of the National Labor Relations Board* (Washington, D.C.: Government Printing Office, 1990), p. 239.

dues, and the employee receives a one-time boost in wage levels compared to nonunion employees. Few differences exist between industries, unions, and geographical locations except those due to the size of the proposed unit (wins less likely for larger units) and degree of union effort in the campaign (wins more likely with greater effort).[71]

Decertifications

Once recognized, unions face a risk in continuing their representation role. If a majority of workers vote to oust the union after the one-year certification period has elapsed in which no contract is in effect, the union is decertified from its right to represent bargaining unit employees. Decertification elections tend to be more successful in small units having a lack of local leadership, low member involvement in union activities, a changing composition of represented employees, and affiliation with a large national union.[72] Economy-wide variables associated

[71] William T. Dickens, Douglas R. Wholey, and James C. Robinson, "Correlates of Union Support in NLRB Elections," *Industrial Relations* 26 (1987), pp. 240–52.

[72] See John C. Anderson, Gloria Busman, and Charles A. O'Reilly III, "What Factors Influence the Outcome of Union Decertification Elections?" *Monthly Labor Review* 102 no. 11 (1979), pp. 32–36; Anderson, O'Reilly, and Busman, "Union Decertification in the U.S.: 1947–1977," *Industrial Relations* 19 (1980), pp. 100–7; Anderson, Busman, and O'Reilly, "The Decertification Process: Evidence from California," *Industrial Relations* 21 (1982), pp. 178–96; I. Chafetz and C. R. P. Fraser, "Union Decertification: An Exploratory Analysis," *Industrial Relations* 18 (1979), pp. 59–69; and James B. Dworkin and Marian M. Extejt, "Why Workers Decertify Their Unions: A Preliminary Investigation," *Proceedings of the Academy of Management* 39 (1979), pp. 241–46.

with decertification elections include inflation, low union density in the industry, frequency of strikes, and small bargaining units.[73] Environmental variables associated with decertification include employee turnover in the unit and lowered industrial production (as in a recession).[74]

Contextual Characteristics Influencing Elections

Variables related to representation election outcomes include whether the bargaining unit is contested, the size of the bargaining unit, the region of the country in which the election is conducted, the union seeking to organize the unit, economic factors, and the like. Evidence suggests the probability of the union winning a representation election is negatively related to the size of the unit and to the length of delays between the petition and the election. The probability is also lower when the Teamsters are the organizing union and in southern right-to-work law states. The following factors are associated with union wins: high unemployment rates during the previous years, consent rather than petition elections, and high degree of unionization in the industry being organized.[75] Unions win more elections if they are larger and more democratic. Benefits directly provided to members and relatively lower dues enhance organizing success for white-collar employees but make no difference for blue-collar workers.[76] Some evidence shows that size and petition-versus-consent election differences account for North–South differences,[77] but lower organizing success in the South may result from a lower proportion of petitions filed. Passage of a state right-to-work law appears to damage the credibility of organized labor. Organizing attempts decrease about 50 percent in the first five years after passage and an additional 25 percent over the next five years. Membership is reduced between 5 and 10 percent.[78]

Research in hospitals finds previous union activity, the presence of other unions, and the opportunity to organize influence union victories.

---

[73] Dennis A. Ahlburg and James B. Dworkin, "The Influence of Macroeconomic Variables on the Probability of Union Decertification," *Journal of Labor Research* 5 (1984), pp. 13–28.

[74] Ralph D. Elliott and Benjamin M. Hawkins, "Do Union Organizing Activities Affect Decertification?" *Journal of Labor Research* 3 (1982), pp. 153–61.

[75] William N. Cooke, "Determinants of the Outcomes of Union Certification Elections," *Industrial and Labor Relations Review* 36 (1983), pp. 402–14.

[76] Cheryl L. Maranto and Jack Fiorito, "The Effect of Union Characteristics on the Outcome of NLRB Certification Elections," *Industrial and Labor Relations Review* 40 (1987), pp. 225–39.

[77] Marcus H. Sandver, "South–Nonsouth Differentials in National Labor Relations Board Certification Election Outcomes," *Journal of Labor Research* 3 (1982), pp. 13–30.

[78] D. T. Ellwood and G. Fine, "The Impact of Right-to-Work Laws on Union Organizing," *Journal of Political Economy* 95 (1987), pp. 250–73.

Nonmedical jobs and nonprofit or religious hospitals are associated with union losses. Size is generally negatively related to organizing across all hospitals, although positively related to larger cities.[79]

Organizing and Membership Trends

Recent information on union membership rates, as given in Chapter 5, clearly indicates both the absolute and relative numbers of employees who are union members have fallen recently. Membership has been falling absolutely since 1979.[80] Whether this trend will continue is open to speculation. Election results reveal many more certification than decertification elections. Although unions do not win a majority of representation elections, many more individuals initially are included in new bargaining units each year than are lost through decertification. However, countervailing explanations help resolve this apparent paradox. First, much of the change is because of declining employment in heavily unionized industries.[81] Second, the median size of bargaining units in which elections are held is declining. Third, if unionized firms existing in the same industry as nonunion firms have higher wage costs, they are either more vulnerable to closure or require productivity increases to balance increasing wage costs.[82] The frequent, long-run reaction to increased wages is to substitute capital for labor.

SUMMARY

Organizing is an extremely complex issue involving unions, employers, and the NLRB. The union's goal is to organize a majority of employees; the employer seeks to avoid unionization. The NLRB's role is to preserve the free choice of employees to be represented or to remain unorganized.

[79] Brian E. Becker and Richard U. Miller, "Patterns and Determinants of Union Growth in the Hospital Industry," *Journal of Labor Research* 2 (1981), pp. 307–28; and John T. Delaney, "Union Success in Hospital Representation Elections," *Industrial Relations* 20 (1981), pp. 149–61.

[80] Edward C. Kokkelenberg and Donna R. Sockell, "Union Membership in the United States, 1973–1981," *Industrial and Labor Relations Review* 38 (1985), pp. 497–543.

[81] William T. Dickens and Jonathan S. Leonard, "Accounting for the Decline in Union Membership, 1950–1980," *Industrial and Labor Relations Review* 38 (1985), pp. 323–34. For a more detailed look at the employment changes of unionized and nonunion workers, see Larry T. Adams, "Changing Employment Patterns of Organized Workers," *Monthly Labor Review* 108, no. 2 (1985), pp. 25–31.

[82] For a thorough presentation of union membership and representation data, see M. A. Curme, B. T. Hirsch, and D. A. Macpherson, "Union Membership and Contract Coverage in the United States, 1983–1988," *Industrial and Labor Relations Review* 44 (1990), pp. 5–33.

Crucial aspects of organization include the authorization card campaign, bargaining unit determination, the postpetition campaign, and certification. The NLRB's decisions on bargaining units and unfair campaign charges have important bearings on many election outcomes.

Recent results show that most union victories occur in smaller election units where employees may be more homogeneous or closer geographically. Recent behavioral research suggests prepetition management activity is more influential on election outcomes than postpetition activity and unfair practices do influence employee voting decisions.

DISCUSSION QUESTIONS

1. To what extent should the NLRB get involved in determining bargaining units? Shouldn't the vote be in the unit preferred by the employees?
2. Should union organizers have greater or less access to employees in organizing campaigns than they have now?
3. What do you think explains the relatively poor recent record for unions attempting to organize large bargaining units?
4. Do employers have an unfair tactical advantage in union-organizing situations?

KEY TERMS

authorization card
representation election
appropriate bargaining unit
decertification election
recognitional picketing
consent election
board-directed (or petition) election
regional director
Excelsior list

certification
multiemployer bargaining
"raid" elections
community of interests
craft severance
accretion
totality of conduct
bargaining order
election bar

CASE
GMFC CUSTOM CONVEYER DIVISION

Last year, General Materials and Fabrication Corporation (GMFC) acquired a small manufacturer of custom-built conveyer equipment used in the freight forwarding industry. The nonunion plant, renamed the Custom Conveyer Division (CCD), employs about 120 production employees, 3 supervisors, a general supervisor, a production manager, 2 engineers, 3 office clericals, and a plant manager. The production employees are in five semiskilled job classifications: fabricator, welder, prepper, painter, and assembler.

The fabricators convert raw material, such as steel plates and tubes, into parts using powered presses, sheers, numerical control cutting equipment, and the like. Welders take the fabricated parts and create frames for conveyer subassemblies. They also weld sheet metal into complex slides and chutes. Preppers clean welding slag, grind welds, degrease welded assemblies, and perform other cleaning functions preparatory to painting. Painters spray paint assemblies using a variety of paints and painting equipment, taking special care not to paint areas where additional parts will be attached. Assemblers, working in teams, use the welded subassemblies and fabricated parts—purchased parts such as rollers, chains, sprockets, belts, motors, switches, and the like—to assemble the equipment and test its operation. They then travel to the installation site to combine the subassemblies and test the completed custom installation.

The plant is located in Cumberland, a small rural city of about 2,500. All of the employees are hired in the local labor market, which comprises about a 20-mile radius around the plant. The starting wage for all classifications is $6.50 per hour, with an increase to $7.00 after a 60-day probationary period. Wages increase to a maximum of $7.75 per hour in three 25-cent increases at six-month intervals. About 75 percent of the employees are earning the maximum hourly rate. CCD pays for comprehensive health insurance for all employees and provides for 80 percent of the cost of dependent coverage. Turnover is very low, averaging about 5 percent per year from all causes. Two other plants in Cumberland hire employees with the same types of skills and pay a starting wage of $5.50 per hour. Most of GMFC's employees have been hired from those plants.

The plant has been quite profitable, with profits of over $1 million before taxes last year on gross revenues of $6 million. Five other competitors manufacture this type of equipment, but GMFC–CCD has established a strong reputation for high quality and low cost, and its share of the market is expanding. Because most of the conveyer systems are used in airports and warehouse operations in large cities, transportation is required for each unit shipped. GMFC paid about $3 million for the operation when it was purchased last year.

Union Organizing

The district director of the United Steelworkers in the region in which Cumberland is located wants to increase the number of members in the district. He received a letter today from Dave Neumeier, an employee of GMFC–CCD, who is a former Steelworker member. Dave suggested that CCD was ripe for organizing given the difference in wages between CCD ($7.75 maximum) and workers in GMFC's main Central City operation is between $2 and $3 per hour. He said some of the preppers were dissatisfied, too, because their work was much more repetitive and dirtier than the other jobs, but the pay was the same.

The district director assigned two of his newest organizers, Leslie Buss and Andy Khan, to attempt to organize the plant. Leslie was previously a maintenance mechanic in an iron mine before she was appointed to her present position. Andy drove a tow truck for an auto repossession company. The district director has given them a copy of the GMFC contract that's currently in force (see the mock negotiating exercise after Chapter 10). Leslie and Andy have been instructed to try to get jobs at the plant and begin organizing internally. If that's not possible, they are to contact Neumeier and get names and addresses. In either event, they need to formulate a strategy for organizing.

Management

James Holroyd, the plant manager, has just returned from his weekly supervisors meeting. Steve Christian, one of the supervisors, said a new employee who just moved to the area, Dave Neumeier, has a Steelworkers local sticker on the inside of his toolbox. While there has been no previous union activity at CCD, Holroyd was told by GMFC top man-

agement to make sure the CCD operation remained nonunion to keep its wage costs down.

While work has been steady lately, a layoff is possible in two months if new orders aren't received. With the economy in a mild recession, the shipping business is down somewhat, and there has been less interest in replacing old equipment or building new warehouses recently.

The plant has a generous recreational program for employees with a party every quarter, an outboard runabout and recreational vehicle that can be borrowed on weekends, and an extensive videocassette library that employees can borrow from for free.

Problem

If you have a union organizer role, develop a strategy for organizing this plant. Consider such things as the authorization card campaign, contacts with employees, campaign literature, comparisons you want employees to make, bargaining unit determination, coping with delays, and potential unfair labor practice charges.

If you have a management role, develop a strategy to maintain a nonunion employment situation. How would you determine whether an organizing threat is likely? Create employee communications, supervisory training programs, and the like. Consider how you would respond to potentially untruthful campaign literature. How will you deal with Dave Neumeier if he starts to talk up a union to employees?

7

THE ENVIRONMENT FOR BARGAINING

Organizing campaigns focus on the individual employer and the union trying to organize a bargaining unit. While the organizing campaign is in progress, both parties concentrate on the issue at hand—whether the employees desire representation. If employees decide to be represented, then the employer and the union must bargain within the realities of the environment in which they operate. Some environmental aspects that influence bargaining are the degree of competition in the product market in which the employer participates, the financial condition of the employer, the capital-labor mix used by the employer, the bargaining issue interests of the organized employees, the effects of unionization on the employer's relationship with the labor market, and any public policy issues that relate to the industry in which the employer operates or the fact that it is now unionized.

This chapter explores three major areas: the economic environment in which collective bargaining occurs, the influence of the economic environment and the **bargaining structure** on **bargaining power,** and bargaining structures that unions and managements design. The chapter serves as the basis of a four-chapter section on bargaining issues and negotiations. Chapter 8 concentrates on wage and benefit issues and evidence related to the effects of unions in these areas. Chapter 9 concentrates on nonwage issues and union members' perceptions of their unions' effectiveness. Chapter 10 covers the organizational structures in which employers and unions negotiate, the types of negotiation issues given organization and union goals, the negotiation process, and the identification and quantification of contract issue costs.

In studying this chapter, consider the following questions:

1. How does the degree of competition within the product market influence the bargaining behavior of the parties?

2. What effect does unionization have on the wage and employment decisions of employers?

3. What influence does regulation or deregulation have on collective bargaining?

4. What joint decisions do employers and unions make in their bargaining relationship to attempt to insulate themselves from market conditions?

5. How do economic conditions, product market concentration, and bargaining structure influence bargaining power?

THE PRODUCT AND SERVICE MARKET

Both private- and public-sector organizations create products and services. Some of these products and services result from responses to consumer demands, while others result from new discoveries and developments, which consumers will demand in the future. Obviously, the degree to which consumers need (demand) certain products or services, the level of competition among suppliers, and the availability of acceptable substitutes all influence how employers relate to the market.

To create products and services, employers combine raw materials, capital, and labor. To produce steel, iron ore, limestone, scrap iron, coke, and other ingredients (raw materials) are combined in a blast furnace within a steel mill (capital) operated by steelworkers and their supervisors (labor). This combination of production factors is not as obvious where services, such as education, are provided. In a university, students (raw materials) use libraries, classrooms, computers, and audio-visual equipment (capital), with the assistance of faculty, librarians, clericals, food service and residence workers, and maintenance employees (labor) to obtain a degree.

The economy is a dynamic process in which the supplies of raw materials, capital, and labor interact with the demand for the products and services that organizations supply. At various stages in the process, raw materials, capital, and labor may be demanded or supplied, depending on who the vendor and who the purchaser are. But the use of raw materials, capital, and labor is ultimately a result of the final consumers' demands for products and services that organizations produce. The producer's demand for each factor of production is said to be derived from the final demand by consumers. Therefore, the demand for each is proportionately related to the good or service produced. Other things being equal, we would expect a decrease in the quantity of any product or service sold as the price charged by the producing organizations increases.

How consumers react to price changes determines the elasticity of demand. Demand is inelastic if price changes (up or down) have relatively little effect on the amount of a product or service sold, while demand is elastic if the quantity sold is highly sensitive to price changes. Figure 7–1 shows examples of relatively elastic (D_E) and inelastic (D_I) demand schedules where Q is the quantity sold and P is the price.

Levels of demand may vary over time. Some changes in demand are cyclical (the demand for types of clothing is related to seasons), while others are secular (long-term changes related to shifts in demand or the introduction of substitutes, such as fewer women's hats or increased use of artificial fibers). Short-run (or cyclical) demand changes mean employers will change their derived demands for inputs to make the products or offer the services. In most instances, however, the use of capital cannot

FIGURE 7-1

Examples of Elastic and Inelastic Demand

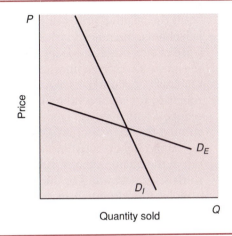

be changed rapidly. For example, when the demand for automobiles declined during the late 1970s and early 1980s, auto producers did not immediately sell plants or assembly lines in response to the reduction. Instead, they purchased less steel, fiberglass, aluminum, tires, and parts and laid off workers at various levels (production employees first) to accommodate the reduction in overall demand for motor vehicles. In the long run, some plants were shut down, but substantial reductions in raw material and labor purchases occurred first.

If there are several suppliers of relatively similar products and services, the consumer can pick and choose among them based on price. Where a relatively small capital investment is necessary to become a competitor, more competition should result. It's no accident that travel agents outnumber airlines, because the capital outlay required to operate a travel agency is far less than required to provide air travel. The more producers there are, the more elastic is the demand for the products of each individual producer (an area to be examined soon).

The willingness of consumers to substitute one product for another or the degree to which the demand for one product is influenced by the demand for another is also important to the employer. Consider fast food, for example. As menus expand, consumers have more price-quality-taste decisions to make. If hamburger prices go up and consumers switch to chicken or fish sandwiches, they are substituting chicken or fish for hamburgers. As a result, purchases of beef decrease, resulting in decreased demand for packinghouse workers, cattle, and beef-processing plants. Conversely, fishing and fishery workers, chicken-processing employees, and chicken producers will be positively influenced by the change. There are also complementary relationships between products. If the demand for fish sandwiches goes up, so will the demand for tartar sauce.

If the relative prices of the factors of production change, employers will change the ratios in which they use each one. For example, when the price of silver increased substantially in 1980, printers installed devices to recapture silver from photographic plates. Capital was substituted for raw materials. Automakers substitute capital for labor when they install robots to update assembly lines. When homeowners install insulation to reduce heating costs, labor and capital (insulating materials) are substituted for raw materials (gas, oil, or electricity).

Public policy constraints on markets have also been enacted. Some retard the changes that would occur rapidly as the result of major market shifts (e.g., rationing or allocations during fuel shortages), while others prohibit the formation or operation of monopolies.

PUBLIC POLICY AND INDUSTRIAL ORGANIZATION

Since the passage of the Sherman Antitrust Act in 1890, public policy has limited industrial concentration and collusive activities between producers in a single industry. Excessive industrial concentration is not defined in the statute, by the courts, or by the Federal Trade Commission. On the other hand, price fixing and other collusive activities have been vigorously prosecuted when discovered, and persons or organizations who have been harmed by them have been entitled to recover treble damages.

The growth and maturation of most industries seem to follow a general pattern. During an industry's infancy, the production process is labor intensive. Products and their capabilities are relatively diverse. As consumer preferences become known, some producers go out of business because their products do not meet consumers' needs. As production methods become standardized, capital and cheaper labor may be substituted for skilled craft work, and more efficient producers lower prices, thus driving less efficient producers from the industry. Over time, an industry becomes dominated by relatively few producers, and the less dominant either mimic the leader or occupy niches in which the leader chooses not to produce. In the developing microcomputer industry, several entrants have dropped out or scaled back, including Texas Instruments, Atari, and AT&T. Some survivors are concentrating on a certain market niche (Japanese manufacturers in laptop computers; Amiga in high-resolution graphics). Apple has prospered with a proprietary design, while IBM has led an open architecture approach. Technological leadership in an open approach is highly competitive and invites the entry of clones that can assemble widely available parts.

In competitive markets, pricing has a major effect on the quantities producers sell. Thus, they face a very elastic product demand curve. For example, at colleges and universities with several bookstores, prices for textbooks are lower than where there is a monopoly. If the bookstores are within a reasonable distance of campus, students' loyalties appear highly price related. Thus, a price-cutting textbook supplier will find its market share increasing rapidly. As noted later, the elasticity of demand for the individual firm has major effects on its demand for labor. However, competition will probably not increase the overall demand for textbooks in the college market unless they're seen as substitutes or complements for other products. A student will purchase only one copy of each required text.

In highly concentrated markets (only one dominant producer or a few major producers), the effect of pricing decisions on the quantity demanded is much more dependent on the demand in the overall market. For the monopolist, the effect of a price cut on total revenue is equivalent to the elasticity of demand in the total market. As corporations tend toward monopolies, price cutting is less likely because the product demand curve is less elastic than in a competitive market situation.

Concentration is a likely natural consequence in most industries, particularly when the overall demand for goods or services is inelastic. Companies with high costs as a result of inefficiency, poor management, or other factors will be forced out of business as competitors drop their prices to increase market share. This process will take longer when the product market is growing (which would lead to a more elastic demand for each), but ultimately concentration would be expected.

Regulation and Deregulation

Regulation of certain industries was a tradition in the United States for almost a century. The Interstate Commerce Act was passed in 1887 to regulate interstate rail freight rates. Congress intended to reduce or eliminate price discrimination between small and large shippers and to maintain an incentive for transportation companies to provide service to rural areas. Other industries that have had services and charges regulated include communications, banking, petroleum products and natural gas, electrical utilities, interstate trucking, and airlines. But over the past several years, federal regulation in many of these areas has been reduced or eliminated. The initial result has been the elimination of monopolies and the restoration of price competition.

Deregulation enabled new companies to enter these markets and created competition in wages between union and nonunion sectors of the industries. To this point, wages and employment have been most affected by deregulation in trucking and air carriers. Exhibit 7–1 is an example of the Teamsters' reaction to deregulation in trucking.

EXHIBIT 7-1

Testimony of Jackie Presser, General President of the Teamsters, before the Senate Committee on Commerce, Science, and Transportation, September 21, 1983

. . . We are here today to tell you that while deregulation is touted as a major success by the Interstate Commerce Commission . . . the opposite has been true for the [Teamsters] and its members in this vital industry.

Deregulation has . . . had disastrous consequences for our members in the regulated sector of the trucking industry. And it has brought incredibly bad times to a number of formerly stable motor carriers who face, instead of once-profitable operations, bankruptcy and the prospect of continuing bad times. . . .

We must note . . . that continuing actions by the Interstate Commerce Commission do more damage every day to the trucking industry—through such policies as wide-open entry, overbroad grants of jurisdiction, by ignoring the common carrier obligation in the law to service the needs of small communities and small shippers, by ignoring its mandate to minimize disruptions to the industry and by engaging in policies that clearly don't enable carriers to earn adequate profits to maintain a competitive stance or provide for fair working conditions and wages, again as provided by the [Motor Carrier] Act. . . .

[Our Layoff Survey] shows that unemployment among our regulated trucking industry membership has increased to 32.5 percent of that membership on layoff status this year, up for the third year in a row since deregulation!

We learned that few of our laid-off members have found other employment within the jurisdictions of their local unions and that it is unlikely laid-off workers covered by this survey obtained other employment at all in establishments covered by our local unions' collective bargaining agreements.

. . . These people are professional truck drivers, not doctors. Truck driving is likely their principal occupation, one not easily exchanged for another job. . . .

We're not talking about people looking for a free ride either, but about workers committed to the work ethic; about people who've spent a lifetime providing the nation with goods and services in the fastest, most efficient, most economical way possible, who've always been self-sustaining and independent, and whose jobs now have been legislated out of existence.

People who've spent a lifetime working to own a home now find themselves scraping to pay mortgage payments, car loan notes, bills for the kids' educations, and worrying about how to put food on the table. There's damn little left over, believe me.

FOREIGN COMPETITION

Many manufacturers encounter substantial foreign competition. Steel is an example. Because it's essentially a commodity, differences in the costs of production and shipping cannot be passed on to consumers. Certain fixed costs for plants and equipment, incurred whether operating or not, lead producers to sell steel at a loss for a short time rather than shut down a plant. Where excess capacity exists in the short run, the foreign firms may "dump" steel in the United States at prices below their costs.

In the auto industry, foreign competition resulted from products more suited to coping with increased fuel prices and lower costs for foreign producers. Relative costs may also increase or decrease depending on the relationship between the dollar and foreign currencies. Before fuel economy concerned consumers, the auto market was dominated by domestic producers and a few high-priced European producers (e.g., Mercedes-Benz, Rolls-Royce). Japanese producers concentrated in the economy and low-priced sports car market.

When these types of changes occur, the elasticity of demand for a particular producer's products increases substantially because the industry is no longer concentrated. Wage increases cannot be as easily passed through. The concessions that occurred in the 1980s were partly due to labor costs (combined with other costs) that would not permit U.S. manufacturers to operate at a profit. After short-run reductions in wages (labor) and parts suppliers' prices (raw materials), some obsolete plants (capital) were also shut down to reduce the cost content of new vehicles.

The advent of foreign competition in basic industries had drastic effects on the employment of unionized workers. The trend is toward a global economy and a relaxation of tariffs and other barriers to the movement of goods. Domestic producers are also moving some operations offshore or to the Mexican border to capitalize on lower labor costs. These changes will continue to be a fact of life in employment in the future.

EMPLOYER INTERESTS

As noted in Chapter 5, in the private sector, organizations' legal members are their shareholders. Labor is hired to accomplish organizational objectives. The major objective of investors is an acceptable return, which means the organization's original purpose may no longer be the one by which the investors can best realize their objectives. Organizations might be expected to leave previous markets and enter new ones as the environment changes the rates of return for various industries. With all the mergers and acquisitions of the past decade, the mobility of capital now exceeds that of labor. If an organization is not making an acceptable return on its investment, a lower-earning division can be divested, forcing unions to deal with successor organizations.

To meet these investment objectives, management seeks to achieve certain profit levels in its present operations and to move its investments from areas with declining returns to those in which anticipated returns will improve. To achieve goals, management desires the greatest amount of flexibility possible.

Labor as a Derived Demand

Labor is necessary to produce and sell products. The quantities of the products sold depend on the aggregate purchases made by consumers. Thus, the employment of labor is a derived demand influenced by the elasticity of demand for the employer's products. However, in a number of situations, the derived demand for labor tends to be inelastic, such as: (1) the more essential the given type of labor is in the production of the final product, (2) the more inelastic the demand is for the final products, (3) the smaller the fraction of total cost accounted for by the item in question, and (4) the more inelastic is the supply of competing production factors.[1] These situations indicate skilled trades in relatively small bargaining units where substitutes are not readily obtainable and where price has little influence over sales would be least likely to concern the employer when wage rates are established.

When an employer is a relatively small factor in a labor market and/or when there is substantial unemployment, the supply of labor will likely be very elastic, and hiring more employees will have little effect on the wage rate. But if several employers hire the same type of employees simultaneously and/or unemployment is low, a wage increase will be necessary to obtain a larger supply. Employers are likely to be able to pass on the cost of a wage increase if they are in a noncompetitive product market, because a price increase will not greatly reduce quantities sold if demand is inelastic.

Employers generally prefer to view labor from a short-run perspective. When more employees are needed, they can be hired; when less are needed, they can be laid off. The amount of labor hired would be determined by the firm's productivity, given the capital equipment and the product market in which the employer operated. Economic theory suggests an employer will hire additional workers until the wage rate equals the value of the additional product that the last hired worker adds. This value (the amount of the product times the price) is called the

---

[1] Alfred Marshall, *Principles of Economics*, 8th ed. (New York: Macmillan, 1920).

marginal revenue product. If the demand curve shifted or changed its elasticity, the employer would need more or fewer workers and would like to react quickly and accordingly.

In the short run, the marginal product of additional labor declines because the employer is using a fixed amount of capital. For example, a university contains a fixed number of classrooms. At some point, hiring additional faculty would not lead to more admitted students because there would be no place to teach them. The declining marginal product of labor means the demand for labor is somewhat inelastic (downward sloping), even though the demand for the company's product might be completely elastic. In concentrated industries, the demand for the firm's product is never completely elastic because the firm is a large proportion of the industry. Therefore, the demand for labor is less elastic than in the competitive situation because marginal revenue at the point where market demand intersects the labor supply price would be less than the price of labor. Figure 7–2 gives examples of the employment changes comparisons in competitive and concentrated situations.

Labor-Capital Substitution

Labor and capital are required to produce products and services. Besides being interested in moving in and out of product and service markets quickly, employers would also like to change the capital-labor mix as the relative costs of the two change. For example, inventory and checkout processes in a supermarket might be handled in two ways. In one, the checker would total prices using a conventional tape-printing cash register. Stock clerks would track shelf and back-room inventory and then tell the store manager when to order certain items. In the other, the checker would use an optical scanner that reads universal product codes, retrieves prices from a computer, prints them on the register tape, and simultaneously subtracts the purchased item from the stock in the store's inventory. When sufficient purchases had been made, the item automatically would be added to a reorder list.

Assume in the first situation one stock clerk is required for every eight checkers, and each employee is paid $25,000 in wages and benefits annually. If a store had 16 checkers, its checking and stock clerk payroll costs would be $450,000 annually. Assume with optical scanners, the checkers are slightly less productive (scanning takes slightly longer than checking), so one more checker is needed for the same volume. But stock clerks are no longer needed. Assume also the costs of the scanners is $2,000 per checker per year. But the scanners' rapid feedback and greater precision in ordering reduces stockouts, excessive inventories, and outdated goods, so the store makes an additional profit of $15,000 per year. The cost of checkers using the old capital goods was $450,000 per year.

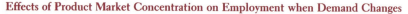

FIGURE 7–2

Effects of Product Market Concentration on Employment when Demand Changes

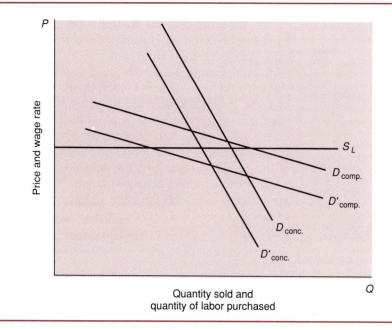

Under the new system, payroll costs would be $425,000 (17 checkers and no stock clerks), equipment costs would increase by $34,000 (17 check stands), and inventory management-related profits would increase by $15,000. The net savings of the new system would be $6,000 per year. As a result, the store would reduce its staff by one (add one checker and eliminate two stock clerks) while expanding its use of capital.

Employers would like to make adjustments whenever a different combination of factors would improve returns. Changes in the use of capital are generally based on relatively long-run payoffs. Labor contracts change labor decisions to long-run decisions and may change long-run labor-capital cost relationships, leaving the employer with what it believes is a suboptimal combination.

Labor Markets

Employers are generally assumed to compete with all other employers for labor, but this is not always the case. Where an employer is a significant factor in a given labor market (e.g., as an employer of public elementary schoolteachers in a given geographic area), if may affect wage rates. Such an employer, called a *monopsonist* (single purchaser of labor), may exist for certain occupations (e.g., schoolteachers but not janitors) or for all

FIGURE 7-3
Effects of Monopsony on Wage Rates and Employment

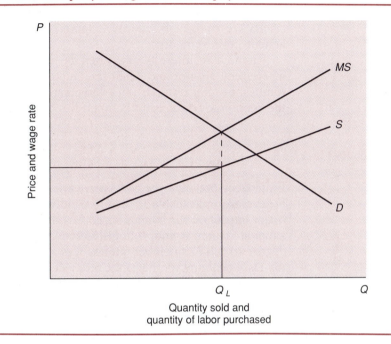

occupations in a given location (e.g., a remote mining operation). Where a monopsony exists, the employer's relevant wage rate is the marginal supply curve. It would take an overall wage increase to hire additional workers because the employer would have to increase wages in order to retain those hired at lower wages. In this case, the wage rate will be below a market equilibrium level, and the employer will be free to select among those who apply. Figure 7–3 is an example of the monopsony situation.

EMPLOYEE INTERESTS

Employee interests are different from those of employers because employee interests are realized in the long run. Employees invest in training and forgo other opportunities to receive higher benefits they associate with long-term employment. Where employees receive firm-specific training, employers increase employment ties by making some benefits contingent on seniority.

A variety of job outcomes are important to employees. Issues initially involved in the growth of the trade union movement remain important to members. A survey of members' attitudes toward unions found that grievance handling, fringe benefits, wages, and job security were the most important issues.[2] The relative importance of each probably varies with the economic and employer environment. For example, when layoffs are rising, job security is more important than wage and fringe benefit improvements.

Employees' interests can often be met in their employment, but where they are not and when the employees do not have other opportunities, forming a union can often create bargaining power by changing the economic relationship between the employer and its employees.

UNION INTERESTS

Employees organize for collective bargaining to obtain outcomes they believe are unavailable to them as individuals. Member desires have a major impact on the bargaining goals of labor organizations. The organizational structure and voting differences within unions influence the degree to which member preferences are reflected in bargaining demands. Local union officers are often elected by a single bargaining unit. Bargaining success directly influences their ability to be reelected. Similarly, labor agreements are customarily ratified by the membership. This means the contract must gain the approval of at least a majority of the membership to go into effect.

It has been suggested that contract demands reflect the preferences of the "median voter" in a unit.[3] Where local unions service several bargaining units and where ratification must be affirmatively rejected by the membership (e.g., the Master Freight Agreement negotiated by the Teamsters must be rejected by two thirds of the membership for it to fail to be ratified), local officers might be less concerned about the contents of individual contracts.

As an institution, the union desires security as the employees' representative through union shop agreements. Unions demonstrate their effectiveness by attracting new members and by organizing additional units. Effectiveness is also frequently measured by economic gains won by the union, which, in turn, have long-run effects on union membership.

Economists have suggested the two major goals of labor organizations are higher wages and increased membership.[4] Labor is presumed to

---

[2] Thomas A. Kochan, "How American Workers View Labor Unions," *Monthly Labor Review* 102, no. 4 (1979), pp. 23–31.

[3] Michael D. White, "The Intra-Unit Wage Structure and Unions: A Median Voter Model," *Industrial and Labor Relations Review* 35 (1982), pp. 565–77.

[4] Allan M. Cartter, *Theory of Wages and Employment* (Homewood, Ill.: Richard D. Irwin, 1959), pp. 88–94.

prefer both, but in its dealings with management, the union often makes trade-offs between them. If wages increase relative to those of other firms, an employer might find it necessary to reduce employment (membership) to remain competitive. To expand employment, wages must rise less rapidly than productivity. On occasion, unions may believe they can simultaneously increase wages and membership through bargaining, but this is only possible when additional capital would be less productive than additional labor.

Generally, unions would be predicted to seek wage gains for present members before pursuing expanded employment. Figure 7–4 shows the presumed direction of preferred union trade-offs. The theoretical preference path is not straight because union members may not equally value employment changes and wages. For example, members may prefer wage increases over additional membership. When facing a cutback, senior members (if they are the median voters) may prefer employment reductions to wage cuts. Evidence suggests widespread job insecurity occurred in 90 percent of the cases in which concessions were granted by unions during the first half of 1982. Concessions were tied into job security guarantees in 96 percent of these agreements.[5]

LEGAL REQUIREMENTS

Public policy establishes the ground rules for the issues the parties will discuss and the way negotiations will be conducted. Section 8(d) of the Labor-Management Relations Act of 1947 sets forth in one sentence the essence of collective bargaining in the United States.

> For the purposes of this section, to bargain collectively is the performance of the mutual obligation of the employer and representative of the employees to meet at reasonable times and confer in good faith with respect to wages, hours, and terms and conditions of employment, or the negotiation of an agreement, or any question arising thereunder, and the execution of a written contract incorporating any agreement reached if requested by either party, but such obligation does not compel either party to agree to a proposal or require the making of a concession.

This broad definition of collective bargaining affects both the process and the issues. For example, for process, what does "good faith" mean? On issues, what do "wages, hours, and other terms and condition of employment" signify? Unions, employers, the NLRB, and the courts have all grappled with these. Novel demands and bargaining tactics have been challenged to determine whether they conform to the statute.

---

[5] Peter Cappelli, "Concession Bargaining and the National Economy," *Proceedings of the Industrial Relations Research Association* 35 (1982), pp. 362–71.

FIGURE 7–4
Wage-Employment Preference Path

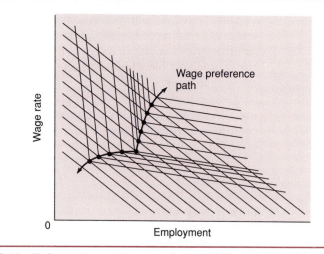

SOURCE: Allan M. Cartter, *Theory of Wages and Employment* (Homewood, Ill.: Richard D. Irwin, 1959), p. 91. Copyright © 1959 by Richard D. Irwin, Inc.

Chapters 10, 11, 13, and 14 examine **good faith bargaining** and its impact on process. Chapters 8 and 9 examine the meaning of "wages, hours, and other terms and conditions of employment" issues.

Bargaining issues can be divided into three legal categories: **mandatory, permissive,** and **prohibited.** Mandatory issues fall within the definition of wages, hours, and other terms and conditions of employment. Wages and hours are straightforward, dealing with economics and work schedules. "Terms and conditions of employment" is a more amorphous concept. A reasonable test of whether an issue is within this area asks if the practice would have a direct and immediate effect on union members' jobs and is strongly determined by labor cost factors.[6] A plant closing or a reassignment of work between job groups are examples. Permissive issues need not be responded to because they have no direct impact on management or labor costs. A demand by a union to have a say in the establishment of company product prices would be permissive. Prohibited issues are statutorily outlawed, such as demands that employers use only union-produced goods. Another distinction between mandatory and permissive issues is that neither party may go to impasse (refuse to agree on a contract) over a permissive issue. Figure 7–5 describes tests that appear to be used to distinguish between mandatory and permissive issues.

---

[6] John T. Delaney, Donna Sockell, and Joel Brockner, "Bargaining Effects of the Mandatory-Permissive Distinction," *Industrial Relations* 27 (1988), pp. 21–36.

FIGURE 7-5

How Mandatory (M) or Permissive (P) Status Is Determined

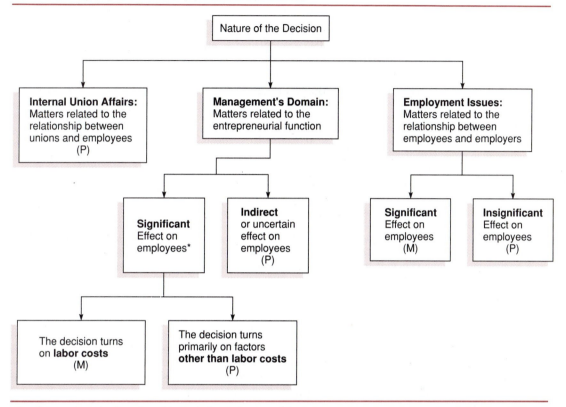

* The duty to engage in effects-bargaining typically attaches to such issues.
SOURCE: John T. Delaney, Donna Sockell, and Joel Brockner, "Bargaining Effects of the Mandatory–Permissive Distinction." *Industrial Relations* 27 (1988), p. 24

The labeling of issues as mandatory and permissive seem to affect their appearance in contracts. Permissive issues are not included as frequently in situations where the distinction is imposed. The bargaining power of the union also appears to increase the likelihood of permissive issues being included in contract clauses in the negotiated agreement.[7]

BARGAINING POWER

Bargaining power does not necessarily reside in the degree to which the employer controls its product or service market. Bargaining power is better conceptualized as "my cost of disagreeing on your terms relative to

---

[7] John T. Delaney and Donna Sockell, "The Mandatory-Permissive Distinction and Collective Bargaining Outcomes," *Industrial and Labor Relations Review* 42 (1989), pp. 566–83.

my cost of agreeing on your terms."[8] For example, a gasoline service station owner in a highly competitive market may find that agreeing to a wage demand will push the cost of the gasoline sold higher than sales receipts. Thus, the owner would object to a union wage proposal. The employees would likely pressure the union to lower its demands unless strike benefits were equivalent to present wages or unless alternative employment were available. On the other hand, an employer who sells products in a less-than-competitive market may accept a relatively large wage demand that it might otherwise resist to forgo the risk that consumers might switch to substitute products.

The elasticity of demand for products and labor has a major impact on the bargaining power of the parties. Power is enhanced by obtaining a monopoly in the product or service market. For example, customers would be at the mercy of the only food store in miles. As prices increased, they might buy less of each commodity, but total revenues would continue to rise with lower volume because the community would need to eat. Sooner or later, news about the amazing profits made by the remote food store would spread out, and a new operator would build a store to get a share of those profits. Competition would ensue, and prices would fall.

Unionization reduces the elasticity of the supply of labor, and some bargaining relationships can create characteristics of a product market monopoly. When unions are able to organize an employer in a purely competitive industry, negotiating a wage increase (other things being equal) will necessarily lead to a reduction in employment as the employer will be forced to replace labor with capital or to cut back on employment in the short run to remain in the black. Thus, it is to the union's benefit to cooperate in creating a more inelastic demand curve in the employer's product market.

A grocery clerks' union in the remote food store example should be able to gain a large wage increase because the cost could be passed through to the store's customers. But how might the union gain a wage increase in a large city with hundreds of food stores? By bargaining in a unit that includes all stores, each store will pay the same wage increase and will attempt to pass the increase through to consumers simultaneously. No competitive advantage would accrue to any store having the same capital-labor mix. Less motivation would exist for any single store to resist a wage increase because all stores would encounter the same wage outcomes, leading to relatively little impact on the volume of sales if the market demand curve is relatively inelastic. This rationale, the establishment of multiemployer bargaining units, is discussed later in this chapter.

---

[8] Neil W. Chamberlain and Donald E. Cullen, *The Labor Sector*, 2d ed. (New York: McGraw-Hill, 1971), p. 227.

Ability to Continue Operations (or Take a Strike)

In addition to the demand and supply characteristics of the product market in which a firm operates, employer bargaining power is enhanced substantially by its ability to take a strike. Many conditions influence this ability, including timing, perishability of the product, technology, the availability of replacement employees, as well as competition.

Timing

A strike will have less impact on an employer if it comes during off-peak periods. Facetiously, a strike of Santa Clauses on December 26 wouldn't faze an employer. If timing cannot be controlled, it can frequently be neutralized by the company by having large inventories or accelerating deliveries to customers for their inventories.

Perishability of the Product

A food processor would be at a relative disadvantage if a strike occurred just when the fruits or vegetables it was going to pack were ripening. There might be a window during which the produce must be processed or it will spoil. Similarly, striking transportation carriers would lose quasi-perishable goods, such as business travel, permanently because the opportunity to take them will not recur for the customer.

Technology

If the firm is highly capital intensive, it frequently can continue to operate by using supervisors in production roles. For example, if a telephone operating company were struck tomorrow, operations would likely be uninterrupted. Exhibit 7–2 describes how supervisors were involved in a telephone strike.

Availability of Replacement

Strike replacements might come from either of two sources. First, and most possible in capital-intensive firms, supervisors may be able to perform enough of the duties of strikers to maintain operations. Second, the looser the labor market and the lower the jobs' skill level, the easier it will be for an employer to hire and utilize replacements effectively. In several recent instances, hiring replacements or the threat of hiring them has influenced negotiations.

Multiple Locations and Staggered Contracts

If an employer has several plants producing the same product and different contract expiration dates, production can be shifted to the nonstruck plants and a large fraction of normal output can be continued. This is the primary reason Hormel could withstand the United Food and Commercial Workers Local P–9 strike of 1985–86.

EXHIBIT 7-2

AT&T's Managers Weather Strike Despite Long Hours, Tedious Work

The nationwide telephone strike is starting to take its toll on Linda Watson. The telephone-company supervisor says working 12-hour days as an operator is tiring and disrupts her personal life. But despite the pressures, she is determined to help keep the system functioning.

Mrs. Watson normally works a 40-hour week as an assistant manager in an engineering office of the Chesapeake and Potomac Telephone Co. . . . When three unions struck . . . on August 7, she and about 11,000 other managers and nonunion employees of C&P Telephone began doing some of the jobs of the company's 31,900 union members who walked out. Along with about 40 other workers here, Mrs. Watson is assisting those callers who dial "operator."

About 97 percent of all telephone calls are dialed directly and handled automatically by computers, according to the telephone company. Still, the striking unions insist that over time, both the company's equipment and its people will falter and the strike will more seriously affect service. To the unions, then, Mrs. Watson and her co-workers are Ma Bell's weak point—the one that will give first in the confrontation.

Despite the long hours and the tedious work, morale appears to be good. . . . William Callahan, who normally works in marketing, says the most interesting [calls] come from the city jail, where all calls must be made collect.

"The prisoners use a lot of strange names," he says. "I had a call the other day from a guy called 'The Pig' who wanted to make a collect call to his mother. I called and said 'Ma'am, will you accept a collect call from The Pig?' She said, 'Of course,'" He grins and adds: "It provides a little entertainment."

. . . Although emergency repair work and installation work is being done, routine repair work and installation work is beginning to pile up. The company is using some employees with technical backgrounds for this work, but a spokesman says that only about half of the approximately 8,000 repair and maintenance jobs have been filled by nonstrikers.

SOURCE: Robert S. Greenberger, "AT&T's Managers Weather Strike, Despite Long Hours, Tedious Work," *The Wall Street Journal*, August 17, 1983, p. 25.

Integrated Facilities

When output from one plant is necessary for production in several others, strikes in the supplier plant convey more bargaining power than usual for the union. This situation frequently occurs in the auto industry at supplier plants such as those producing electrical equipment or radiators for all vehicles in a manufacturer's line. Problems associated with strikes in supplier facilities have become more critical as manufacturers have moved toward just-in-time parts deliveries.

Lack of Substitutes

Ability to take a strike increases if no adequate substitutes for the organization's goods or services are available. Revenues are not irretrievably lost, only postponed until the firm is in production. Public education is an example of this type of product or service.

Union Bargaining Power

Just as employer bargaining power is enhanced by its ability to take a strike, union bargaining power is increased by its ability to impose costs with a strike. Union wage gains in bargaining are higher in cases of significant barriers to entry for new employers, relatively few present employers in the industry, and low foreign competition. Within the industry, high union coverage by a dominant union also facilitates bargaining power.[9]

Studies of the airlines following deregulation demonstrate the bargaining power of unions—as measured by their ability to resist concessions—is highest among those representing occupations employed in other industries (mechanics, as compared to pilots and cabin attendants), where the wage cut associated with changing employers is smaller (cabin attendants, as compared to pilots), and where the national union exerts strong control over the approval of collective bargaining agreements (International Association of Machinists).[10]

BARGAINING STRUCTURES

The election unit is not necessarily the unit in which bargaining takes place, as noted in Chapter 6. The parties may decide that a larger negotiating unit would be to their mutual interests. This section explores the types of and reasons for variations in bargaining unit structures presently used for negotiating contracts.

Bargaining structures for negotiation often aggregate employer units, either collecting numbers of small employers who operate in the same industry in a given region or lumping together various geographically separated plants or units of a single employer. Less often, unions representing employees within a single employer have coordinated bargaining. Bargaining units larger than election size occasionally bargain over wage issues only and leave nonwage issues for local determination.

---

[9] L. Mishel, "The Structural Determinants of Union Bargaining Power," *Industrial and Labor Relations Review* 40 (1986), pp. 90–104.

[10] Peter Cappelli and Timothy H. Harris, "Airline Industrial Relations in Transition," *Proceedings of the Industrial Relations Research Association* 37 (1984), pp. 437–46.

Aggregations of employer units will be explored first, followed by the union side, including public policy issues influencing the structure of the negotiating relationship.[11]

Multiemployer Bargaining

Many industries comprise large numbers of relatively small employers in any single geographic region. Examples include contract construction, garments, and retail and wholesale trade. Within the industries, the issues leading to unionization will likely be relatively common across employers, and one union is often the bargaining agent for employees in many employer units.

In the local market, these employers compete for sales. Since all employers in the local industries (e.g., grocers) offer essentially similar goods and services, the demand for each employer's products is highly elastic (price sensitive). Thus, a wage increase would be difficult to pass through to customers. To remain competitive, the employer must cut back on its use of labor and also produce less. Figure 7–6 shows why this result occurs.

From the union's standpoint, besides the political risks associated with job loss, differences in the willingness of each employer to grant wage increases will lead to a varied pattern of wages throughout the area, and union members in units where wage increases are lower than those in other units may become dissatisfied with their representation. Employers will also be more motivated to compete on the basis of labor cost differences.

To reduce these problems and to gain the monopolist's advantage in passing wage increases on to consumers, employers and unions have frequently formed **multiemployer bargaining** units. In a multiemployer unit, a single set of negotiators speaks for all employers, and the negotiated wages apply to all members of the bargaining association. The contract expires at the same time for all, so everyone faces the same economic risks of strikes. Each employer, as a member of the unit, faces a product and service demand curve essentially equivalent to the market demand curve because wage-related costs will likely be passed through by all members simultaneously. Figure 7–7 shows the effects of a wage increase in a multiemployer bargaining unit. If the market demand for the employers' goods and services is quite inelastic, most of the wage increases can be passed through with relatively minimal effects on employment.

---

[11] For a retrospective look at some of these issues, see Arnold R. Weber, ed., *The Structure of Collective Bargaining: Problems and Perspectives* (New York: Free Press, 1961).

FIGURE 7-6

Effect of a Wage Increase for a Single Employer in a Competitive Product Market

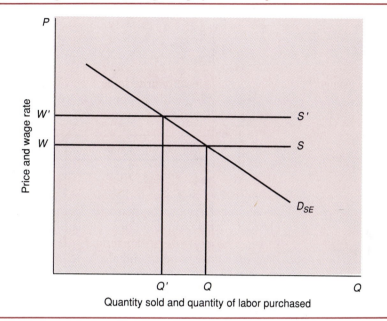

Quantity sold and quantity of labor purchased

The most successful multiemployer bargaining occurs when employers have roughly comparable nonlabor costs, all employers have been unionized, and new firms have a relatively high cost of entry. If so, an employer member of the bargaining unit would probably not be differentially affected by a wage increase, nor would the union have to compete against nonunion labor.

Industry-Wide Bargaining

While most multiemployer bargaining is done within a relatively small geographic area, it also occurs on an industry-wide basis when products or services are essentially commodities or are indistinguishable among suppliers. The two most prominent examples have been among the eastern coal-mining companies and organized interstate trucking companies.

The bargaining relationship between the Bituminous Coal Operators Association and the United Mine Workers involves bargaining between a team representing many employers in the eastern below-ground coal mining industry and the United Mine Workers. In the trucking industry,

FIGURE 7-7

Effects of a Wage Increase in a Multiemployer Bargaining Unit

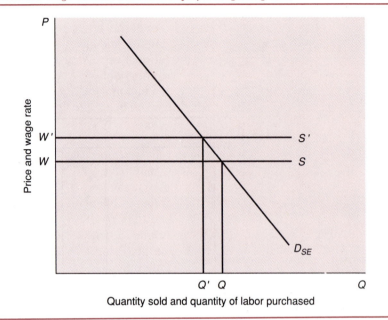

Quantity sold and quantity of labor purchased

negotiations occur between the major interstate truckers and the Teamsters Union, resulting in the National Master Freight Agreement.

Maintaining an **industry-wide bargaining** structure is a perilous proposition. As more employers are included, the sizes of each and their respective abilities to take strikes become dissimilar. In the coal industry, mining operators that also operate in other energy-producing areas may be more able to withstand a strike than bargaining unit members who concentrate on coal. In both coal and trucking, employers face significant competition from nonunion sources (in mining, from western coal; and in trucking, from owner-operators). During the 1980s, industry-wide bargaining became increasingly difficult to continue. Major erosions have occurred in the proportion of employers covered, particularly in the trucking industry.[12]

Political considerations within the union also affect bargaining structures. As unions become involved in industry-wide bargaining, the power and autonomy of local or regional officials decrease. Some commentators have suggested the Master Freight Agreement is vulnerable to regional factionalism within the Teamsters Union.

[12] Peter Cappelli, "Collective Bargaining," in *Employee and Labor Relations*, SHRM-BNA Series, Vol. 4, John A. Fossum (Washington, D.C.: Bureau of National Affairs, 1990), pp. 4–190 to 4–193. ed.

National/Local Bargaining

In some firms, bargaining occurs on a company-wide basis for wages and benefits and locally for terms and conditions of employment. In most cases, plant managements and local unions negotiate work rules and other items after a national economic agreement is reached. Work rules may be negotiated simultaneously, but the local usually may not strike over local issues until a national economic settlement is concluded. If the local represents employees in a critical plant (e.g., a sole supplier of parts necessary for all final assembly products), the local may have considerable bargaining power.

Plant labor intensity levels vary given the production technology used; thus, wage increases may have varied effects on costs across plants. In one plant, a wage increase may push costs over the limit that can be recouped in sales, leading to the plant closing. Employees represented by some locals might lose their jobs as the result of the national increase. Recently, more economic settlements have been negotiated at the plant level, especially those involving concessions. This occurred more frequently when the difficulties being experienced varied greatly among plants. When both management and labor perceive contract difficulties to be related to local problems or when the union expects to get trade-offs in response to concessions, organization-wide bargaining appears more prevalent.[13] Exhibit 7–3 reports some effects of plant-level bargaining on management and labor.

Wide-Area and Multicraft Bargaining

The construction industry has traditionally bargained at the local level. This decentralization has led to many strikes and many attempts to keep up with or exceed what some other unit has won. In most instances, each craft has bargained on its own instead of banding together. Increasingly, construction employers and unions bargain on a wide-area and multicraft basis. These configurations may involve all unions of a particular set of crafts in a given geographical market. Where unions have strong national leaders, this arrangement will likely be successful because it solidifies their positions through the use of regional staff assistance in bargaining and the appointment power of the nationals. On the other hand, internal politics at the local level become more difficult, because the rank and file may still pressure local leaders to match other settlements instead of concentrating on smoothing the bargaining process.[14]

---

[13] Cappelli, "Concession Bargaining."

[14] Paul T. Hartmann and Walter H. Franke, "The Changing Bargaining Structure in Construction: Wide-Area and Multicraft Bargaining," *Industrial and Labor Relations Review* 34 (1980), pp. 170–84.

EXHIBIT 7–3

Plant-Level Talks Rise Quickly in Importance

It is nothing new for work rules to come up in local talks, but the importance of these discussions is rising rapidly. "Almost every plant involved in the basic steel industry has made some form of accommodations in crew size and job combinations that lend to more efficient operations," says Sam Camens, a United Steelworkers official. Moreover, 12 of GM's 22 assembly plants now have "competitive" agreements, in most cases because the local unions agreed to reopen local contracts before their September 1987 expiration. The contract changes usually consist of reducing classifications (increasing the variety of jobs that one worker can do) and limiting the times workers can switch jobs. . . .

But not only are the companies benefiting from the changes. For industrial workers, job security has become the top issue. While union leaders are struggling to make some headway in that area at the national table, the companies are making it clear that a "competitive" local contract is the best thing a union can do to keep a plant open or to retain work in-house.

GM was scheduled to close its Fairfax, Kansas, plant by the end of this year, but, in 1985, it said it would replace it with a new plant that it might put near the antiquated facility. Two months after the union local signed a letter of intent saying it would consider drastic changes, the company agreed to build the new plant there. Local 31 believes its cooperation was "damn important" to preserving the 4,900 hourly jobs, says Charles Knott, the local's president. "Had we taken a hard line and said we weren't willing to look at anything, chances are we wouldn't have a $1.05 billion plant along the Missouri River."

However, unions are increasingly afraid that the emphasis on local talks is threatening their power. Workers at Mack Truck plants in Hagerstown, Maryland, and Allentown, Pennsylvania, recently approved concessionary local contracts providing various wage cuts and a no-strike clause in return for job guarantees. But the UAW International vetoed the agreements, saying they would "compel accommodations by our members . . . at present and future Mack facilities."

SOURCE: Abridged from Jacob M. Schlesinger, "Plant-Level Talks Rise Quickly in Importance; Big Issue: Work Rules," *The Wall Street Journal*, March 16, 1987, pp. 1, 13.

Pattern Bargaining

In highly concentrated industries, the dominant union chooses a major employer as a bargaining target. Negotiations are concentrated on this target firm, which is struck if agreement is not reached. When agreement is reached, the union moves on to the remaining firms in turn and usually quickly concludes an agreement along the lines of the initial bargain.

Pattern bargaining has occurred frequently in the auto and rubber industries.[15]

Another form of pattern bargaining involves a large-scale approximation of the multiemployer bargaining model, such as the old Coordinating Committee of Steel Companies (CCSC) consisting of representatives of the major steel producers, led by the chief negotiator at U.S. Steel, and their national and local union counterparts in the Basic Steel Industry Conference of the United Steelworkers (BSIC). The CCSC was dissolved in 1985 when its members—Armco, Bethlehem, Inland, LTV, and U.S. Steel—unanimously agreed to end it.[16]

Some say pattern bargaining broke down during the 1980s because of major differences in plant efficiency levels among single employers and among employers and new plants in areas with lower levels of unionization. Managers responsible for bargaining increasingly cited firm profitability and labor costs as more important than industry patterns in their bargaining stances.[17] Unions, on the other hand, are particularly interested in maintaining a pattern to avoid internal political problems and serve as a base from which to launch demands for wage increases.[18] Moving away from a pattern might result in more variance in wage settlements across employers. However, the evidence suggests that variance decreased between 1977 and 1983.[19] How, can these differences be resolved? First, during the late 1970s, inflation was increasing rapidly during a period in which labor contracts ran for multiyear periods. Thus, newly negotiated contracts tended to establish new patterns at the same time that large variances ensured. Second, during the 1980s, waves of concessions occurred within fairly short periods, resulting ultimately in low wage variance as companies and unions bargained down to a new, lower wage level. However, there were *large* differences in other contract provisions such as early retirement, job security, union-management participation, profit sharing, and employee stock ownership plans (ESOPs).[20]

---

[15] For detailed examinations of the history and present bargaining structures in these (and other) industries, see Harry C. Katz, "Automobiles," and Mark D. Karper, "Tires," in *Collective Bargaining in American Industry*, ed. David B. Lipsky and Clifford B. Donn (Lexington, Mass.: Lexington Books, 1987), pp. 13–54, 79–102.

[16] John P. Hoerr, *And the Wolf Finally Came* (Pittsburgh: University of Pittsburgh Press, 1988), pp. 474–76.

[17] Audrey Freedman, *The New Look in Wage Policy and Employee Relations* (New York: Conference Board, 1985), p. 9.

[18] Cappelli, "Collective Bargaining," pp. 4–191 to 4–193.

[19] Kathryn J. Ready, "Is Pattern Bargaining Dead?" *Industrial and Labor Relations Review* 43 (1990), pp. 272–79.

[20] Hoerr, *And the Wolf Finally Came.*

Conglomerates and Multinationals

A conglomerate is a business organization operating in a variety of distinct industries. For example, a firm may operate a chain of fast-food franchises, market data-processing time and services, manufacture and sell agricultural chemicals, and produce household appliances. This firm bargains differently from a firm specializing in a given product line, such as autos or steel. A conglomerate often bargains with several unions and has contracts with different expiration dates. By its nature, a conglomerate has high bargaining power—no single part of its business is very large relative to others, and its distinct parts do not depend on each other for components or processes. Thus, it could take a long strike at almost any subsidiary.[21]

Multinational organizations are not necessarily conglomerates in terms of product-line diversity, but they have great bargaining power because of operating in different countries. Because unions representing U.S. employees do not represent offshore employees, the firm can withstand strikes by shifting production to another country or forgoing small proportions of revenues.

Coordinated and Coalition Bargaining

Coordinated bargaining occurs where two or more national unions represent employees of a single major employer. In coordinated bargaining, the unions seek to gain comparable agreements with common expiration dates. Both agree that the other can sit in on bargaining and make suggestions to the other union's negotiators. **Coalition bargaining** involves a closer relationship between the unions in which a bargaining team is made up of members from both unions and identical pacts are negotiated with the company. The largest continuing example of coordinated bargaining involves General Electric and the Electronic Workers and United Electrical Workers. Other unions negotiate similar economic terms following the initial settlement and ratification.[22]

Public Policy and Court Decisions

Legislation has affected bargaining structure. For example, firms covered by the Railway Labor Act do not bargain with industrial-type unions because the act requires bargaining on a craft basis. Hence, airline gate

---

[21] Charles Craypo, "Collective Bargaining in the Conglomerate, Multinational Firm," *Industrial and Labor Relations Review* 29 (1975), pp. 3–25.

[22] For the terms of their 1988 settlement, see G. Ruben, "GE, Coalition Settle Dispute Union Split," *Monthly Labor Review* 111, no. 3 (1988), p. 46.

agents may be represented by the Brotherhood of Railway and Airline Clerks (BRAC); pilots, Air Line Pilots Association; and mechanics, Machinists. Craft bargaining and perishability of air travel (passages to certain destinations at certain times) enhance each union's bargaining power because a strike by any might shut a line down.[23]

In the past, airlines insulated themselves from the perishability problem by securing strike insurance through a mutual aid pact.[24] The legislation that deregulated the airline industry eliminated this tactic, but the deregulation itself reduced union bargaining power by allowing new carriers that used nonunion labor to enter the market more easily.

The NLRB permits coordinated and coalition bargaining.[25] The NLRB required General Electric to bargain with a negotiating committee comprised of representatives from several unions as long as each union represented GE employees. Outside representatives could not vote on offers but could observe and comment. Unions have also been permitted to demand common contract expiration dates among employers in a single industry.[26]

At its most elemental level, a bargaining unit is what labor and management say it is. This is a seeming tautology, but Chapter 6 noted the NLRB ordered consent elections in companies where labor and management *did not dispute* the makeup of the bargaining unit for representation purposes and no prohibited employees were included. But once past the representation stage, the parties are free to make the bargaining unit more (but not less) inclusive in negotiations, which may lead to novel bargaining structures to accommodate peculiarities of the unions, firms, or industries involved.

The expansion of a bargaining unit results only from the voluntary agreement of the parties. In a case where a union charged a company with refusing to bargain when it would not consider a company-wide fringe benefit program, the NLRB held that only the local units are certified and any expanded unit would have to be by mutual agreement.[27]

Where employers and unions have negotiated a multiemployer unit, the NLRB and the courts have generally held that employers cannot unilaterally withdraw from the unit during negotiations without the consent of the union, even if a bargaining impasse has been reached. The

[23] Wallace Hendricks, Peter Feuille, and Carol Szerszen, "Regulation, Deregulation, and Collective Bargaining in Airlines," *Industrial and Labor Relations Review* 34 (1980), pp. 67–81.

[24] S. Herbert Unterberger and Edward C. Koziara, "The Demise of Airline Strike Insurance," *Industrial and Labor Relations Review* 34 (1980), pp. 82–89.

[25] *General Electric Co.*, 173 NLRB 46 (1968).

[26] *AFL-CIO Joint Negotiating Committee for Phelps-Dodge v. NLRB* (3rd Circuit Court of Appeals, No. 19199, 1972), 313.

[27] *Oil, Chemical, and Atomic Workers v. NLRB*, 84 LRRM 2581 (2nd Circuit Court of Appeals, 1973).

FIGURE 7–8

Bargaining Patterns

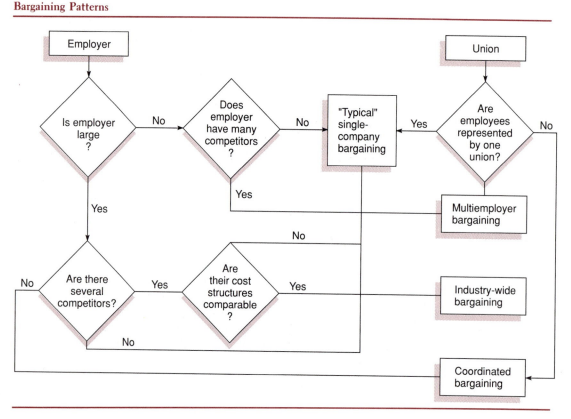

Supreme Court did not see impasses as unusual in bargaining or sufficiently destructive of group bargaining to allow the withdrawal of unit members.[28]

Figure 7–8 represents a flowchart that predicts the type of bargaining structures that could evolve in the special situations discussed.

Influence of Bargaining Power and Structure

Bargaining structures can influence bargaining power, and the relative effects for both unions and managements can be altered by the structures they agree to use. The next two chapters examine a variety of bargaining

---

[28] *Bonanno Linen Service* v. *NLRB*, 109 LRRM 2557 (U.S. Supreme Court, 1982).

FIGURE 7-9

A Conceptual Framework for the Determinants of Bargaining Outcomes

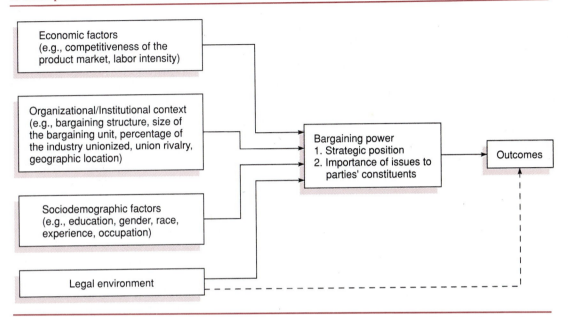

SOURCE: John T. Delaney and Donna Sockell, "The Mandatory-Permissive Distinction and Collective Bargaining Outcomes," *Industrial and Labor Relations Review* 42 (1989), p. 571

issues. Just as the inelasticity of demand for labor influences the degree to which management can grant wage increases, the inelasticity of demand related to any of the separate demands of labor will influence the outcome of the bargaining relationship. The employer is much more likely to grant in total a demand expected to have relatively little effect on overall costs than one that will broadly affect outcomes. This is one reason pension benefits and health care have grown from small-cost to large-cost items in the labor contract. Figure 7–9 is a helpful diagram of several of the variables that shape bargaining power and its effect on bargaining outcomes.

SUMMARY

Labor, capital, and raw materials combine to produce products or services. Employers generally adjust labor and raw material inputs in the short run and capital in the long run. Labor is a derived demand depending on the level of consumers' demands for the firm's goods and services. The elasticity of this demand influences wages and employment. In the United States, legislation prohibits employers from creating product or service market monopolies; thus, employers compete regarding the costs of their products and attempt to reduce labor costs. Deregulation and foreign competition have recently increased the elasticity of consumer demand for products and have allowed competition by lower-cost forms of labor: nonunion and foreign. This situation has led to concessions by unionized employees in industries affected by these changes.

Employers generally create strategies allowing them to concentrate in product and service markets with the greatest returns on investment. Where necessary, they want to be able to substitute capital for labor if its efficiency is higher. Employees, concerned about gaining a return on their investment in training and employment, require job security and wages commensurate with their investment.

Bargaining power is determined by assessing whether one's costs of agreeing are greater or less than costs of disagreeing. Bargaining power relationships are sometimes purposely altered to create more power in the product or service market vis-à-vis consumers. Multiemployer bargaining is an example of this strategy.

Several different bargaining structures exist. The election unit may be expanded as the result of mutual agreements between the employer and the union. Small employers often form multiemployer bargaining units to deal with a single union. Occasionally, nationally based employers form industry-wide units to bargain with a national union. Pattern bargaining, in which one company's settlements serve as a basis for negotiating in the rest of the industry, is declining. Conglomerates and multinationals generally have a great deal of bargaining power because of their fragmented business and bargaining relationships.

DISCUSSION QUESTIONS

1. What effect does a lower elasticity of demand have on the wage and employment outcomes for the employer and the union?
2. How is bargaining power influenced by deregulation and foreign competition? Who is most affected by these changes—labor or management?
3. Why are employers less likely to approve coalition bargaining than unions to approve of multiemployer bargaining?
4. Why does the current public policy for bargaining that applies to the Railway Labor Act sector create more bargaining impasses?

KEY TERMS

bargaining structure
bargaining power
good faith bargaining
multiemployer bargaining

industry-wide bargaining
pattern bargaining
coordinated bargaining
coalition bargaining

CASE
MATERIAL HANDLING
EQUIPMENT ASSOCIATION
BARGAINING GROUP

GMFC is a charter member of the Material Handling Equipment Association (MHEA). The organization was started in the late 1940s and now includes 30 members producing over 95 percent of all domestic material handling equipment. Presently, these manufacturers produce 70 percent of the material handling equipment sold in the United States. About 80 percent of the association's total production is for the domestic market. Primary foreign markets are in Europe and Latin America, with increasing marketing emphasis in eastern Europe.

All of the members are unionized, to some extent, with the proportions of production jobs organized ranging from 25 percent to 100 percent. GMFC is 80 percent unionized. Most of the companies bargain with the Steelworkers, the Auto Workers, or the Machinists. Some variations exist between contracts within employers and across employers in the association. Unions have been particularly interested in negotiating relatively similar contracts across employers and national-level agreements within employers.

The MHEA industrial relations executives recently studied the possibility of industry-wide bargaining. Coincidentally, the major unions representing MHEA employees explored potential coalition bargaining arrangements.

Taking either a management or union role, formulate arguments for or against:
(1) industry-wide bargaining with each separate union; (2) industry-wide bargaining with coalition bargaining; (3) single-employer bargaining with coalition bargaining; (4) single-employer bargaining at the corporate level with the union representing employees; (5) bargaining at the local level on all issues with the union that happens to represent the employees.

8

WAGE AND BENEFIT ISSUES IN BARGAINING

Since union activity began in the United States, wages have been a major issue in bargaining. Management is concerned with wage and benefit issues in bargaining because its ability to compete depends to some extent on its labor costs. Organizations producing equivalent output but with lower labor costs will have higher profits and be more able to operate during downturns.

Both labor and management are concerned about a variety of pay aspects. Each is concerned with the overall level of pay, but both are also concerned about how pay rates for different jobs in the organization and pay increases are determined and about the form of wages and benefits paid to employees.

This chapter examines the components of wage demands made by unions; bargaining on specific aspects of the pay program; the effects unions have on wage levels in both union and nonunion organizations; and the prevalence of wage and benefit issues in labor agreements.

In studying this chapter, consider the following issues and questions:

1. What are the strongest current arguments unions and/or managements use in the proposal or defense of present or future wage and benefit levels?

2. What effect do wage and benefit levels have on the economic performance of the employer and on nonunion employment of the same or other employers?

3. How does the form of wage costs influence employer and employee outcomes?

4. How does the system for allocating salary increases differ in union and nonunion organizations?

5. How does the usual structuring of union wage and benefit demands alter the structure of wage differentials in an organization over time?

COMPONENTS OF WAGE DEMANDS

In framing its justification for wage demands, the union relies on three major criteria: equity within and across employers, the company's ability to pay, and the **standard of living.** These criteria suggest the union must make a number of comparisons in formulating wage demands.

Equity

From an equity standpoint, unions desire that wages for jobs they represent exceed—or at least be consistent with—those of equivalent nonunion jobs in the firm. They also expect fringe-benefit package equivalence across jobs, particularly in insurance benefits because personal risks are generally equal regardless of job or salary level. Unions pay attention to bargains forged in other industries; but, because of increased foreign competition and deregulation (as discussed in Chapter 7), upward pattern bargaining has been substantially reduced. Unions also try to maintain uniformity in wage rates for the same jobs in different locations of the same company. For example, an auto assembly worker at Ford's Twin Cities (Minnesota) assembly plant earns the same rate as another on a similar job in Wixom, Michigan. These patterns within a single employer are eroding, however, as plant-level negotiations often lead to concessions in older, less-efficient plants to avoid shutdowns and the resulting loss of jobs.

Ability to Pay

While **ability to pay** takes two forms, the major argument relates to the profitability of the firm. When employers' profits are increasing, unions expect to receive pay increases. They are reluctant to accept reduced pay when profits decline but have recently done so when employers have incurred substantial losses and job loss would be the alternative to not conceding. Some internal union critics have condemned concessions and argued that past labor leaders would not have accepted them. Exhibit 8–1 recalls the position of Walter Reuther, long-time president of the UAW, as told by Douglas Fraser, the UAW president during the initial concessionary period in the early 1980s.

The ability-to-pay issue is also related to the proportion of labor costs in a company's total costs. Generally, the lower a firm's labor intensity (lower the share of costs going to labor), the greater the unions believe its ability to pay. This assumption is based on the relatively lower elasticity of the derived demand for labor in the capital-intensive firm. Table 8–1 shows an example of the effects of wage increases on the costs of labor- and capital-intensive firms.

EXHIBIT 8-1

Douglas Fraser Recalls Walter Reuther's Position on Concessions

. . . Fraser . . . urge[d] a change in union behavior, in speeches to UAW groups. There were always critics present who challenged him, invoking Reuther's name as the final authority.

Fraser told me about one such meeting when I visited him in 1985. . . . "I went into one lion's den last week, a union meeting," Fraser said, "and there was this old Commie there who I knew would raise that precise issue, 'Reuther spinning in his grave.'" Fraser chuckled and rummaged in a desk drawer. He pulled out a mimeographed text of a speech.

So I brought this along and read it:

> All industries and all companies within an industry do not enjoy the same economic advantages and profit ratios. We cannot blind ourselves to this fact at the bargaining table. As an employer prospers, we expect a fair share, and if he faces hard times, we expect to cooperate. . . . Our basic philosophy toward the employers we meet at the bargaining table is that we have a great deal more in common than we have in conflict, and that instead of waging a struggle to divide up scarcity, we have to find ways of cooperating to create abundance and then intelligently find a way of sharing that abundance.

Fraser showed me the first page of the text. It was an address delivered by Walter P. Reuther in 1964 at the University of Virginia. . . .

SOURCE: John P. Hoerr, *And the Wolf Finally Came* (Pittsburgh: University of Pittsburgh Press, 1988), p. 195.

Standard of Living

This component also takes on two meanings. One relates to the purchasing power of employees' pay (real wage). If prices increase by 10 percent for the things the average worker buys, but wages rise only 6 percent over the same period, real wages have been eroded by 4 percent. **Cost-of-living adjustments** (COLA) are aimed at maintaining parity between wages and prices over time. With lower inflation rates and more employer interest in knowing future wage rates, COLA is less often included in contracts now than in the past.

Standard-of-living issues also arise with unions' beliefs that their members' purchasing power needs improvement to enable them to enjoy higher qualities of goods and services; for example, owning a home rather than renting. Some comparison or equity aspects are included here, but the comparison is with society in general, not with a specific work group.

TABLE 8–1

Cost Comparisons for Labor- and Capital-Intensive Firms

	Labor-Intensive Firm	Capital-Intensive Firm
Material cost	$ 500,000	$ 500,000
Capital cost	100,000	400,000
Labor cost	400,000	100,000
Total cost	$1,000,000	$1,000,000
Cost of 10 percent wage increase	40,000	10,000
New total cost	$1,040,000	$1,010,000

Figure 8–1 represents the components of wage demands just discussed. Equity relates to both internal and external comparisons, ability to pay relates to profits and labor intensity, and standard of living relates to real wages and absolute improvement. Although equity issues were discussed first, none of these pay issues is, a priori, more important than another. Both sides will emphasize issues they believe will enhance their bargaining power.

PAY PROGRAMS

Collective bargaining alters the status quo in pay administration by substituting a collective agreement for management's unilaterally determined practices. One useful way to examine pay programs and categorize demands divides them into four major components: pay level, pay structure, pay form, and pay system.[1] **Pay level** refers to the average pay rates for a given job or for the organization as a whole. It is used to compare rates between organizations. **Pay structure** consists of the sets of wage rates applied to different jobs and the ranges of wage rates possible within specific jobs in the organization. **Pay form** is the method by which compensation is received and may include such components as money, insurance payments, deferred income, preferential discounts, payments in kind, and recreational and entertainment programs. **Pay system** refers to the methods used to determine how much each *individual* will earn within a job. The system might be based on piece rates, other productivity or performance indexes, skill level, time worked, seniority with the

---

[1] Herbert G. Heneman III and Donald P. Schwab, "Work and Rewards Theory," in ASPA *Handbook of Personnel and Industrial Relations* ed. Dale Yoder and Herbert G. Heneman Jr. (Washington, D.C.: Bureau of National Affairs, 1979), pp. 6–1 to 6–2.

FIGURE 8–1
Wage Demand Components

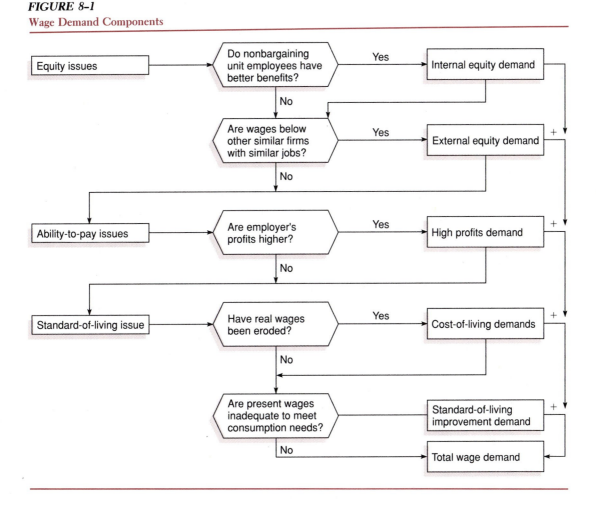

organization, or other factors. Union and management goals relating to these pay program components are examined in the following sections.

Pay Level

The basic components associated with pay level changes were those shown in Figure 8–1: ability to pay, equity, and standard of living.

Ability to Pay
A variety of considerations influence ability to pay. First, the general level of business activity influences profits. When the economy is strong, wage demands increase, and the incidence of strikes to support bargaining

demands rises. Second, in more concentrated industries, employers are more able to pass the costs of wage increases along to consumers, particularly if all firms negotiate with the same union and have relatively similar expiration dates for their contracts. Third, those employers who have relatively capital-intensive production processes or who bargain with several relatively small units do not have the incentive to avoid large wage increases that labor-intensive organizations have. The ability to pay has usually been an issue raised by the union, but recently employers have cited reduced profits (or losses) or changes in their industries' competitive level as arguments for demanding pay reductions. Pay level comparisons become more difficult to make as pay form becomes more complex.

Employers have become increasingly interested in reducing the fixed proportion of pay. Employees may also have some interest in making pay flexible if it leads to lower employment fluctuations. Profit sharing has been increasingly negotiated into contracts, particularly in return for concessions. For example, both General Motors and Ford employees have significant opportunities for profit sharing if their organizations do well. If profits are down or losses occur, the lower base-pay level enables the employer to make a profit at lower levels of output or to cut losses.

In attempting to reduce the size of employees' base wage levels, firms have been offering lump-sum bonuses for agreeing on a contract. For example, assume the union seeks a 4 percent pay increase for employees earning about $20,000 annually. If the employer pays a $1,000 bonus instead of a 4 percent increase, it may be saving money because the base for future increases remains at $20,000 and no additional benefits are paid on the $1,000. If the proportion of wage-tied benefits is greater than 20 percent, the employer saves in the first year. In 1988, half of all settlements included neither a lump sum nor COLA, and settlements with lump sums had an average annual wage adjustment of half (1.4 percent) those without lump sums (2.8 percent).[2]

Equity

Equity involves comparisons with other unions, with the same jobs in other organizations, and among regions. One comparison method searches for "wage contours" in which groups of employees receive relatively similar wages.[3] For example, a contour may consist of electricians in a given geographic area or workers in several occupations within a specific industry, such as steel production.

---

[2] W. M. Davis, "Major Collective Bargaining Settlements in Private Industry, 1988," *Monthly Labor Review* 112, no. 5 (1989), pp. 34–43.

[3] See John T. Dunlop, "The Task of Contemporary Wage Theory," in *New Concepts in Wage Determination*, ed. George W. Taylor and Frank C. Pierson (New York: McGraw-Hill, 1957), pp. 117–39.

Some have argued that major national unions respond to the bargaining success of their counterparts. To remain competitive with other unions in organizing and representation, trade union leaders will need to obtain settlements equivalent to or better than others recently wrung from management. Succeeding rounds of bargaining follow what has been called *orbits of coercive comparison*.[4] Major settlements are presumed to be key-comparison or pattern-setting agreements; however, wage imitation is likely to be decreased by (1) differences between industries in which employers operate, (2) differences in ability to pay within these industries, and (3) the time between the pattern-setting and later settlements.[5] As competition has increased in many industries recently, management bargainers have increasingly emphasized company productivity trends and profit levels and deemphasized industry patterns and settlements in other industries.[6] Table 8–2 indicates a relatively wide range in recent settlements across manufacturers whose employees are represented by the United Auto Workers.

Standard of Living

Inflation increases the importance unions place on maintaining a standard of living. The negotiation of COLA clauses increased rapidly during the 1970s when inflation was high. However, the escalation of wages in response to inflation is usually lower than the measured inflation rates.[7] During the 1980s, firms increasingly made the deferral of COLA or the modification or elimination of COLA clauses from contracts a major bargaining objective, particularly in concession situations.[8]

Where COLA clauses exist, pay levels are tied to changes in the consumer price index (CPI). Contracts usually provide for quarterly payments based on the difference between the CPI at the time the contract became effective and the index level at the end of the current quarter. As an example, assume a contract effective January 1, 1992, provided for a base wage of $8 per hour and a COLA of 1 cent for each 0.3 point increase in the CPI. If the CPI increased 6 points by December 31, 1992, then employees would receive a lump-sum payment of 20 cents for each hour worked during the preceding quarter.

A very important consideration with COLA is whether the increases

---

[4] Arthur M. Ross, *Trade Union Wage Policy* (Berkeley, Calif.: Institute of Industrial Relations, University of California, 1948), p. 53.

[5] Daniel J. B. Mitchell, *Unions, Wages, and Inflation* (Washington, D.C.: Brookings Institution, 1980), p. 50.

[6] Audrey Freedman, *The New Look in Wage Policy and Employee Relations* (New York: Conference Board, 1985), pp. 7–12.

[7] Mitchell, *Unions, Wages, and Inflation*, pp. 48–50.

[8] Freedman, *New Look in Wage Policy*, pp. 10–12.

TABLE 8–2

Recent UAW Contract Settlements (July 24 to August 6, 1990)

Bell Helicopter Textron, Fort Worth, Texas (office and clerical workers)
  3 years, with pay increases of 3%, 2%, none; lump sums of 3–6%, 2–4%, and 4%; COLA of 1 cent per 0.3 CPI rise.

Pabst Brewing Co., Milwaukee, Wis. (brewery workers)
  3 years, with pay increases of 40, 24, 11.5 cents; lump sum of 1.1% third year.

Miller Brewing Co., Milwaukee, Wis. (brewery workers)
  3 years, with increases of 0, 20, and 20 cents.

General Dynamics, Electric Boat Div., Groton, Conn. (designers, draftsmen, technicians, and engineers)
  3 years, 4%, 3%, 3%; classification adjustments, shortened progression to top of scale.

Diamond-Star Motors Corp. (Chrysler-Mitsubishi joint venture), Bloomington, Ill.
  3 years, $2.25–2.63 per hour over term; COLA of 1 cent per 0.26 CPI rise; 3% lump sum in 1990; parity with UAW-Chrysler agreement in 1991–92.

Fisher Controls, Marshalltown, Iowa (general)
  3 years, 0, 42, 42 cents per hour.

Village Voice, New York City (clerical, production, and professionals)
  $55 per week, $20, and additional classification adjustments.

Cynba International (formerly GM, 150 active and 900 laid-off workers)
  5 years, 0%, 0%, 3%, 3%, 3%.

GTE Sylvania, Winchester, Ky. (several locations)
  3 years, 0, 0, 3% lump.

SOURCE: Abstracted from *Collective Bargaining Negotiations and Contracts* (Washington, D.C.: Bureau of National Affairs, 1990).

become part of the base wage. Unions prefer to include them in the base before the current contract expires because otherwise an extremely large increase would be needed to bring the base up to a real income standard equivalent to that earned at the end of the expiring contract.

A variety of factors is associated with the inclusion of COLA clauses. They are more prevalent in multiyear contracts and concentrated industries, larger bargaining units, and heavily unionized industries.[9] While COLA clauses provide some protection for employees in inflationary periods, evidence suggests their effect on total wage changes has not been large.[10]

[9] Wallace E. Hendricks and Lawrence M. Kahn, "Cost-of-Living Clauses in Union Contracts: Determinants and Effects," *Industrial and Labor Relations Review* 36 (1983), pp. 447–60.

[10] Wayne Vroman, "Cost-of-Living Escalators and Price-Wage Linkages in the U.S. Economy," *Industrial and Labor Relations Review* 38 (1985), pp. 225–35; and R. T. Kaufman and G. Woglom, "The Degree of Indexation in Major U.S. Union Contracts," *Industrial and Labor Relations Review* 39 (1986), pp. 439–48.

Pay Structure

Pay structure refers to the pattern of wage rates for jobs within the organization. Within the bargaining unit, the union has the right to negotiate these rates with management. The union is also concerned with rate comparisons between bargaining unit jobs and the unorganized jobs in the employer's work force. However, management's adjustment of unorganized rates usually follows negotiations. Unorganized employees often hope the union receives a large settlement, which might obligate management to do the same for its nonbargaining unit employees.

Differentials among jobs may be negotiated on a job-by-job basis or may result from the use of a negotiated job evaluation system. Job-by-job negotiations often create difficulties over time because the original job structure established a hierarchy of jobs separated by specific price differences. Bargaining tends to result in across-the-board pay increases of equal magnitude for all bargaining unit jobs. While the absolute wage differentials are maintained, the relative difference shrinks, causing wage compression. For example, two jobs with original pay rates of $4 and $6 per hour have a 50 percent differential. Over time, across-the-board accruals of increases of $4 per hour shrink the relative differential to 25 percent. Establishing rates for new jobs during the contract and determining wage rates for jobs where no external comparisons are readily available are also problems. Methods have been devised to deal with both problems and are included in job evaluation systems.

Job Evaluation

Job evaluation determines the relative position of jobs within an organization.[11] The procedure has several steps and requires judgments that must be negotiated. In general, job evaluation includes the following steps: (1) the jobs to be evaluated must be specified (usually the jobs covered by the contract); (2) jobs must be analyzed to determine the behaviors required to be performed and/or the traits or skills necessary to perform the job; (3) of the behaviors or traits identified, those that vary across jobs and are agreed to be of value to the employer are grouped into compensable factors; (4) for evaluation purposes, each factor is clearly defined, and different levels of involvement for each factor are determined (degrees); (5) point values are assigned to factors and degrees within a factor; (6) job evaluation manuals used to apply the method are written; (7) all jobs are rated. Table 8–3 is an example of identified factors,

---

[11] For more information on job evaluation techniques, see George T. Milkovich and Jerry M. Newman, *Compensation*, 3rd ed. (Homewood, Ill.: Irwin, 1990), pp. 120.

TABLE 8-3
Points Assigned to Factors and Degrees

	Percent	Degrees and Points						Weight in Percent
		1st Degree	2nd Degree	3rd Degree	4th Degree	5th Degree	6th Degree	
Skill	50%							
1. Education and job knowledge		12 points	24 points	36 points	48 points	60 points	72 points	12%
2. Experience and training		24	48	72	96	120	144	24
3. Initiative and ingenuity		14	28	42	56	70	84	14
Effort	15							
4. Physical demand		10	20	30	40	50	60	10
5. Mental and/or visual demand		5	10	15	20	25	30	5
Responsibility	20							
6. Equipment or tools		6	12	18	24	30	36	6
7. Material or product		7	14	21	28	35	42	7
8. Safety of others		3	6	9	12	15	18	3
9. Work of others		4	8	12	16	20	24	4
Job conditions	15							
10. Working conditions		10	20	30	40	50	60	10
11. Unavoidable hazards		5	10	15	20	25	30	5
Total	100%	100%	100%	100%	100%	100%	100%	100%

SOURCE: Herbert Zollitsch and Adolph Langsner, *Wage and Salary Administration*, 2nd ed. (Cincinnati: South-Western Publishing, 1970), p. 186.

FIGURE 8-2
Definition of Factor and Degrees within Factor

1. Knowledge

This factor measures the knowledge or equivalent training required to perform the position duties.

1st Degree
Use of reading and writing, adding and subtracting of whole numbers; following of instructions; use of fixed gauges, direct reading instruments and similar devices; where interpretation is not required.

2nd Degree
Use of addition, subtraction, multiplication and division of numbers including decimals and fractions; simple use of formulas, charts, tables, drawings, specifications, schedules, wiring diagrams; use of adjustable measuring instruments; checking of reports, forms, records and comparable data; where interpretation is required.

3rd Degree
Use of mathematics together with the use of complicated drawings, specifications, charts, tables; various types of precision measuring instruments. Equivalent to 1 to 3 years applied trades training in a particular or specialized occupation.

4th Degree
Use of advanced trades mathematics, together with the use of complicated drawings, specifications, charts, tables, handbook formulas; all varieties of precision measuring instruments. Equivalent to complete accredited apprenticeship in a recognized trade, craft or occupation; or equivalent to a 2-year technical college education.

5th Degree
Use of higher mathematics involved in the application of engineering principles and the performance of related practical operations, together with a comprehensive knowledge of the theories and practices of mechanical, electrical, chemical, civil or like engineering field. Equivalent to complete 4 years of technical college or university education.

SOURCE: George T. Milkovich and Jerry M. Newman, *Compensation,* 3rd ed., (Homewood, Ill: Irwin, 1990), p. 127.

point assignments, and degree levels within factors. Figure 8–2 is a specimen of the types of definitions assigned to factors and degrees within a factor.

Job evaluation involves either (1) using a bilateral union-management committee to determine compensable factors and the degree to which they're required in bargaining unit jobs or (2) negotiating the point-pay relationship to apply to evaluations completed by management. Advantages associated with a well-designed and well-administered job evaluation system include (1) the reduction of compression in wage differentials if increases are given as a percentage of the total points assigned to the job and (2) the ease with which new jobs can be slotted into an existing pay structure. The primary disadvantage is the requirement for initial agreement between the union and management on the identification, definition, and point assignments associated with compensable factors.

Skill-Based Pay

Most pay structures in unionized settings base pay differences on the grade and job classification of employees. **Skill-based pay** (SBP) is a relatively recent innovation that ties pay to the skills possessed by the employee. An employee is hired at a base rate, usually lower than the average starting wage in the area. As the learning of prescribed skills is demonstrated, pay is increased. Relatively few job classifications exist, and employees can be moved within the organization based on the employer's needs. This pay plan combines structural (job or task relationships) and system (pay changes based on individual behavior or skills) aspects. The practice is usually related to team-based production, which sharply blurs job boundaries and, thus, is not found in many unionized plants. Where it exists in unionized settings, it was usually implemented before representation.[12]

Two-Tier Pay Plans

Two-tier pay plans are an effort by employers to lower wage costs by decreasing the starting rate offered to new employees. Two types of two-tier plans exist. The first starts employees at a lower rate and requires a longer period to reach top rates than for present employees. The second creates a permanent differential with newly hired employees never expected to earn the top rate of present employees. Managements benefit most when turnover is high or the company plans to expand. The rate of change is most rapid when retirement rates are also increasing. Both the employer and the union might expect problems when the lower-tier employment levels begin to exceed half of the total. Successful implementation of these plans requires careful employee communications and assurances that job security will be enhanced.[13]

Two-tier pay plans are more prevalent in unionized organizations and have usually been negotiated without significant concessions from management.[14] In the airline industry, two-tier plans were usually installed in the absence of any financial distress or market share shifts and were frequently negotiated following other union concessions. Airline employers justified the two-tier plans as more closely aligning their pay rates to comparable jobs in the marketplace for persons of equivalent skill

---

[12] Thomas A. Kochan, Harry C. Katz, and Robert B. McKersie, *The Transformation of American Industrial Relations* (New York: Basic Books, 1986), p. 158.

[13] Ibid, pp. 132, 170.

[14] Sanford M. Jacoby and Daniel J. B. Mitchell, "Management Attitudes toward Two-Tier Pay Plans," *Journal of Labor Research* 7 (1986), pp. 221–37.

levels.[15] Unless large numbers of new employees are hired, the union shouldn't incur severe political problems from new members for some time. Management may face problems, in that employees working together and doing equal work will receive unequal pay.

Comparable Worth

Pervasive evidence shows that women earn substantially lower wages than men, even when employed in similar occupations.[16] Occupations predominantly populated by women are generally paid less than those in which men predominate. Several plausible reasons account for this, including: (1) occupational choices for women may be narrower than those for men, thereby crowding their supply of labor; (2) women may be willing to accept lower pay than men; thus, jobs that offer low pay will be accepted more often by women; and (3) employers purposely pay less to jobs in which women predominate, regardless of the jobs' worth to the organization.

Some unions, particularly AFSCME, have begun to demand employers pay employees their **comparable worth.** Under this approach, all occupations in an organization should be compared with each other to determine their relative importance or contribution, regardless of the relationships found in the external market. Wages for each occupation would be established on these internal comparisons, and a base level would be negotiated. The comparable worth negotiation receiving the widest publicity was the 1984 negotiation involving clerical and technical workers at Yale University, in which the union struck to gain adjustments for occupations predominantly occupied by women. Exhibit 8–2 contains a brief summary of the results of that strike.

Unions that represent units with large numbers of women or are interested in organizing units with large proportions of women would be most likely to advocate comparable worth in negotiations.

Pay Form

Pay components not received in cash are received as either insurance or deferred compensation. Insurance typically applies to hospital and medical needs, life, disability, and dental benefits. Deferred compensation usually involves pension benefits. Nonmonetary wage forms have advantages and disadvantages. For the employee, the benefit of the form depends partly on usage. Employees with dependents need life and family

---

[15] D. J. Walsh, "Accounting for the Proliferation of Two-Tier Wage Settlements in the U.S. Airline Industry, 1983–1986," *Industrial and Labor Relations Review* 42 (1988), pp. 50–62.

[16] See, for example, Nancy F. Rytina, "Earnings of Men and Women: A Look at Specific Occupations," *Monthly Labor Review* 105, no. 4 (1982), pp. 25–31.

EXHIBIT 8–2

Labor Unrest in the Ivy League

. . . On September 25, [1984], Local 34, a newly formed union representing Yale's clerical and technical workers, went out on strike. Over the next 10 weeks, . . . Yale made the headlines and TV news spots around the nation, not as a center of enlightenment, but as an embattled employer faced with a striking union of librarians, secretaries, and lab workers, most of them women, claiming that they were being discriminated against for their sex.

. . . [F]or higher education, the struggle by Yale's clerical and technical workers may be only the first chapter in a resurgence of the union movement on college campuses around the nation. . . .

The [clerical and technical] work force was 85 percent female; its members were also, on the average, well educated. Yet their average salary was substantially less than that of Local 35 [food service worker] members, this indicated discrimination—if not overt discrimination, then at least an acceptance of the standards of the society as a whole, standards that consistently undervalued the worth of women's work. [The organizer] took these feelings of frustration and found a label for them; the label was comparable worth.

SOURCE: Excerpted from Crocker Coulson, "Labor Unrest in the Ivy League," *Arbitration Journal*, September 1985, pp. 53–54.

---

health care more than those without. On the other hand, the value of many of the benefits is untaxed income. When the company directly purchases medical insurance, the value is not reported as income to the recipient. A wage earner purchasing an equivalent amount may have already been taxed on the money paid for the individual benefit. Some benefits, such as holiday or vacation pay, are paid in cash.

Employers have been much more concerned recently about the form of pay. In the past, the form of the economic package was generally considered the union's province. An employer willing to give an equivalent of 50 cents per hour in wages (as shown in Figure 8–3) did not care how it was apportioned. As benefits became more complex and as medical, dental, and other health care costs began to escalate more rapidly than the costs of other goods, employer interests in the allocation of pay increased. Table 8–4 details what might happen to costs over the course of a contract. Given employers' desires for certainty or predictability in the contract's effects, their resistance to benefit packages with unknown future costs would be expected; these packages generally specify coverages, not costs. The example in Table 8–4 shows that a health insurance program costing 60 cents per hour at contract time becomes 90 cents per hour if the carrier increases rates by 50 percent. The second example reflects the fact that fringe benefits are not as easy to control as wages. In

FIGURE 8-3
Wage Forms

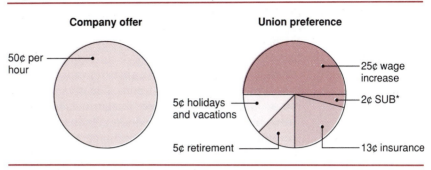

| Company offer | Union preference |

50¢ per hour

25¢ wage increase

5¢ holidays and vacations

2¢ SUB*

5¢ retirement

13¢ insurance

* Supplementary unemployment benefits (SUB).

TABLE 8-4
Cost per Employee for Wage and Fringe Increases*

	Present Rate	Total Cost/Year	Increase Offered	Anticipated Cost	Possible Cost†
Health insurance rate increase					
Wage cost	$7/hr.	$14,560	40¢/hr.	$15,392	$15,392
Health insurance	$100/mo.	1,200	30¢/hr.	1,824	2,736
Total cost		$15,760‡	($52 more/mo. in insurance)	$17,216§	$18,128#
Reduction in hours worked					
Wage cost	$7 hr.	$14,560	40¢/hr.	$ 9,707	$ 9,707
Health insurance	$100/mo.	1,200	($52 more/mo. in insurance)	1,824	2,736
Total cost		$15,760		$11,531‖	$12,443**

* Assumes standard work year of 2,080 hours.
† Assumes 50 percent increase in premiums for similar coverage by carrier.
‡ Cost per hour is $7.58.
§ Cost per hour is $8.28.
‖ Cost per hour is $8.32.
Cost per hour is $8.72.
** Cost per hour is $8.97.

this example, the employer cuts hours worked by one third. Because wages are not paid for unworked hours, costs are reduced when hours are reduced. But because health insurance is paid for each person employed, costs of this fringe benefit still increase by 50 percent, even though only two thirds as many hours are worked. Health care cost containment has increased in importance for both parties. Managements have sought to negotiate contribution limits rather than to pay for coverage, or at least to require deductibles or co-payments.[17] Unions have pressured health care providers to be more efficient so coverage costs do not escalate so rapidly.

Pensions have plagued both unions and managements. Before actuary-based funding was required by the Employee Retirement Income Security Act of 1974 (ERISA), an aging labor force could easily have resulted in staggering yearly costs for employers who paid their pensions from current earnings. Unions had the same problem. For example, increasing numbers of retired coal miners in the 1950s and 1960s, coupled with a reduction in coal production, caused the United Mine Workers to continually demand higher tonnage royalties on coal to support the pension plan. The higher royalties led to higher coal costs, which led customers to convert to alternative fuels or to conserve, thus exacerbating the effect on retirees. Contract negotiations resulting in pension increases for already retired employees create an immediate cost to mangement because it will not have time to set aside funds for the increases.

The two major types of pension plans are **defined benefit** and **defined contribution pension plans.** Defined benefit plans specify the rules used to determine the future pension benefit (for example, 2 percent of hourly pay at retirement times the number of years of service). Defined contribution plans specify what the employer will set aside for the employee's retirement (for example, 3 percent of total pay per hour). Defined benefit plans make the amount of contributions uncertain for employers because investment experience varies over time. Employees may prefer to avoid a defined contribution plan because the investment risk is shifted to them.

As work forces become increasingly demographically diversified, unions and managements will likely negotiate agreements that facilitate employment for nontraditional groups, particularly during labor shortages. The 1989 Communications Workers agreement with AT&T has new or expanded provisions to provide for newborn care, family care, tax-free dependent care reimbursement accounts, resources and referrals for professional family care, adoption assistance, flexible hours, and a fund for family care program development.[18]

Because federal wage and hour laws require that employees receive a 50 percent premium for work in excess of 40 hours per week, an employer

[17] See, for example, George Ruben, "Labor and Management Continue to Combat Mutual Problems in 1985," *Monthly Labor Review* 109, no. 1 (1986), pp. 3–15.

[18] B. B. Brown and K. Peters-Hamlin, "AT&T's Family-Care Union Agreement: A Harbinger of Change in Corporate America?" *Employment Relations Today* 16 (1989), pp. 205–10.

might reduce costs by hiring new employees when more work is needed. However, if person-tied benefits exceed 50 percent of base pay, an employer would prefer overtime unless there were a higher premium in the contract. Benefits now average about 39 percent of salaries.[19] Thus, labor's position favoring benefits restricts new entries and may reduce opportunities for its present members. Even if benefits are below 50 percent, if costs incidental to hiring and benefits exceed the overtime premium, new hiring will be resisted.[20]

Pay System

The pay system refers to the methods used to decide the pay for each employee. All of the methods for bargaining unit employees will be specified in the collective bargaining agreement. In this section, we identify many of the negotiated arrangements for individual employee pay changes.

Membership
Many contracts have provisions guaranteeing compensation simply for membership in the organization. These items are not related to length of service but are distributed equally among bargaining unit members or designated subgroups. Many employee-tied fringe benefits (such as health, life, and disability insurance) are based on membership. They are usually unrelated to the number of hours worked in a given month, as long as the employee was active at some time during a designated period.

Tenure
Several pay system features are related to seniority. **Benefit status seniority** refers to the entitlements an individual accrues as a result of continued membership. Many pay systems provide for step pay increases based on length of service within a job or grade level. These increases usually have a cap because a certain range is assigned to a given job.

Participation in pension plans also may be based on service. ERISA requires employees over age 21 to participate in an employer's noncontributory retirement plan. In a noncontributory plan, the employee makes no contributions toward future retirement benefits. However, contributions do not become vested (owned) until the employee has met certain statutorial minimum-service requirements.

---

[19] U.S. Chamber of Commerce, *Employee Benefits, 1980* (Washington, D.C.: 1981).
[20] John A. Fossum, "Hire or Schedule Overtime? A Formula for Minimizing Labor Costs," *Compensation Review*, 1, no. 2 (1969), pp. 14–22.

Frequently, entitlements to longer vacations are based on length of service. Low-service employees frequently earn only one or two weeks' vacation annually, and long-service employees may accrue five or more weeks.

Tenure may entitle employees to use accrued benefits such as retirement. Some contracts contain provisions entitling employees to retirement benefits after a defined length of service (for example, 30 years), rather than at a specific age. Autoworkers pioneered these benefits in the private sector; in the public sector, they are most prevalent in the uniformed services.

Time Worked

Most contracts base pay to a large extent on the amount of time worked and when it is worked. Wages are calculated on an hourly basis in these cases. In addition, the level of wages frequently depends on the amount of time worked during a given period (overtime) and the time of day during which the work is accomplished (shift differentials).

Productive Efficiency

Slightly more than 33 percent of contracts base wages of some bargaining unit employees on output levels.[21] These incentive plans have a bargained base output level, above which employees receive extra compensation. Depending on the plan, these additions are on a straight-line, increasing, or decreasing basis as production increases.

Negotiating an appropriate base is often difficult, and grievances frequently occur when employees are transferred to jobs where they lack sufficient experience to exceed the standard. Circumstances beyond the employees' control often intrude, eliminating their chances to achieve high output (for example, poorly fitting components on an assembly job).

Group incentive plans are often of greater interest to unions because they avoid competition among employees. Implementing the plans frequently requires significant management-union cooperation. These plans are covered in detail in Chapter 12.

Profit Sharing

To make labor costs more flexible, employers have proposed and implemented profit-sharing plans when workers agree to forgo increases in their base wages. The employee's total pay is based on both job level and employer profitability. Profit sharing has perhaps been most visible

---

[21] *Collective Bargaining Negotiations and Contracts* (Washington, D.C.: Bureau of National Affairs, 1984), tab sect. 93.

EXHIBIT 8-3

Excerpts from the GM-UAW Profit Sharing Agreement

2.09 "Minimum Annual Return" . . . means 1.8 percent of the Sales and Revenues for such Plan Year.

2.15 "Profits" . . . means income earned by U.S. Operations before income taxes and "extraordinary" items (with "extraordinary" defined as under generally accepted accounting principles). Profits are before any profit sharing charges are deducted. Profits also are before incentive program charges . . .

2.19 "Total Profit Share" . . . means an obligation of the Corporation for any Plan Year in an amount equal to the sum of:

    (a) 7.5 percent of the portion of the Profits for such Plan Year which exceeds 1.8 percent of Sales and Revenues for such Plan Year but does not exceed 2.3 percent of Sales and Revenues;

    (b) 10 percent of the portion of the Profits for such Plan Year which exceeds 2.3 percent of Sales and Revenues for such Plan Year but does not exceed 4.6 percent of Sales and Revenues;

    (c) 13.5 percent of the portion of the Profits for such Plan Year which exceeds 4.6 percent of Sales and Revenues for such Plan Year but does not exceed 6.9 percent of Sales and Revenues; and

    (d) 16 percent of the Profits for such Plan Year which exceeds 6.9 percent of Sales and Revenues for such Plan Year . . .

4.02 Allocation of Profit Sharing Amount to Participants

    The portion of the Total Profit Share for the Plan Year . . . will be allocated to each Participant entitled to a distribution . . . in the proportion that (a) the Participant's Compensated Hours for the Plan Year bears to (b) the total Compensated Hours of all Participants in this Plan entitled to a distribution for the Plan Year.

SOURCE: *Collective Bargaining Negotiations and Contracts* (Washington, D.C.: Bureau of National Affairs, 1988), pp. 93:991–93:994.

---

among U.S. auto producers. The size of an employee's bonus depends on his or her proportion of total pay in the unit, the size of the employer's profit, and the agreed formula for determining the size of the pool to share. Exhibit 8–3 contains the UAW–Ford formula for profit sharing.

Time Not Worked

Employees receive pay when not at work in a variety of situations. Contracts include provisions for paid holidays, vacations, sick leave, jury duty, and so forth. Supplementary unemployment benefits (SUB) are paid during layoffs under some contracts. SUB adds income from a trust fund to required state unemployment insurance benefits. Typically, the addition enables a worker to maintain income close to regular straight-time wages. If layoffs are pervasive and of long duration, total benefit payments may exceed the funds available to pay them, and SUB ends until the funds are restored.

UNION EFFECTS ON PAY

Unionization reduces labor supply elasticity, and the bargaining structures established by labor and management decrease competition among employers. This section examines union influences on wages and some specific environmental characteristics involving unions related to wage differences.

Union Effects on Pay Levels

There is a great deal of debate about the effect of unions on pay. If a *wage increase* is defined as an increase in the share of costs of labor as compared to capital, then economic theory argues that labor's share would not increase in the long run, because the employer could increase its return on investment by purchasing capital goods to substitute for labor unless labor productivity increased. For example, if arc welders can make 200 welds in an hour on a given product and are paid $10 per hour, the labor cost of welds is 5 cents each. If an industrial robot could produce 200 welds per hour and had a useful life of three years (ignoring interest and depreciation advantages of tax laws) and its price were less than $60,000, the employer should prefer the robot over arc welders (assuming a one-shift operation). If the robots cost $70,000, the firm would replace welders with robots whenever the welders' pay exceeded $11.66 per hour without an increase in their productivity.

Data suggest labor's relative share of the national income has slowly increased during this century. However, the share increases in the unionized sectors have been virtually nil over the past 50 years, while shares have risen substantially for nonunion employees.[22]

An exhaustive analysis of evidence on the role of unions in influencing wages finds consistent, significant positive effects for unions on employees' wages.[23] The effects of wage gains are substantially greater for increased unionization within an industry than for increased unionization within an occupation. The size of industrial effects is inversely related to the level of competition in the industry, while occupation

---

[22] F. Ray Marshall, Allan G. King, and Vernon M. Briggs Jr., *Labor Economics: Wages, Employment, and Trade Unionism* (Homewood, Ill.: Richard D. Irwin, 1980), pp. 375–82.

[23] Richard B. Freeman and James L. Medoff, *What Do Unions Do?* (New York: Basic Books, 1984), pp. 43–60.

effects are most pronounced through increased union representation at the local labor level.[24] Wage premiums do not come without a cost for labor, however. The industries with the highest union wage premium were the same ones in which employment declines were the greatest during the 1970s.[25] A variety of differential effects of unions on wages occur across definable groups. Figure 8–4 shows that individuals who have less education, are nonwhite, younger or older, male, short tenure, transport operatives, or laborers are more highly advantaged.[26] Evidence also finds that, across worker subgroups, becoming unionized, remaining unionized, or becoming employed in unionized organizations is associated with higher wages.[27] It should be recognized that unionization may have occurred because of dissatisfaction with low wages as compared to other employers or to others in one's community. Thus, unions can also raise wages from a below-average position to one of equivalence with others.[28] A study of wage levels in firms facing an organizing drive found pay levels in the year subsequent to the drive were higher than for a control group facing no union activity. The study also found firms in which organizing activity occurred had pay levels lower than comparisons before the drive began. The premium following unionization activity was nowhere near the level found between union and nonunion firms, in general, with initial contract demands focusing more heavily on workplace democracy issues.[29]

Wage Level Difference Effects over Time

The last 70 years have seen wide swings in the degree to which unionized workers are paid a premium. Premiums have ranged from a high of 46 percent in the early 1930s to a low of 2 percent in the late 1940s.[30] Premiums were greater during recessions and narrowed during inflation, perhaps because of the rigidity of rates in long-term contracts.[31]

---

[24] William J. Moore, Robert J. Newman, and James Cunningham, "The Effect of the Extent of Unionism on Union and Nonunion Wages," *Journal of Labor Research* 6 (1985), pp. 21–44.

[25] P. D. Linneman, M. L. Wachter, and W. H. Carter, "Evaluating the Evidence on Union Wages and Employment," *Industrial and Labor Relations Review* 44 (1990), pp. 34–53.

[26] Freeman and Medoff, *What Do Unions Do?* p. 49.

[27] Ibid., pp. 46–47.

[28] See Orley Ashenfelter and George E. Johnson, "Unionism, Relative Wages, and Labor Quality in U.S. Manufacturing Industries," *International Economic Review*, October 1972, pp. 488–507.

[29] Richard B. Freeman and Morris M. Kleiner, "The Impact of New Unionization on Wages and Working Conditions," *Journal of Labor Economics* 8 (1990), pp. S8–S25.

[30] George Johnson, "Changes over Time in the Union/Nonunion Wage Differential in the United States," unpublished paper (Ann Arbor: University of Michigan, 1981), Table 2.

[31] Mitchell, *Unions, Wages, and Inflation*, pp. 80–83.

FIGURE 8-4

The Union Wage Advantage by Demographic Group, for Blue-Collar Workers, 20–65, 1979

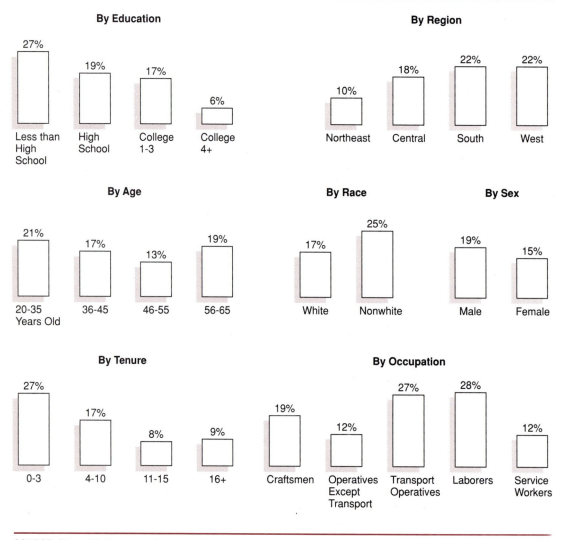

SOURCE: Richard B. Freeman and James L. Medoff, *What Do Unions Do?* (New York: Free Press, 1984), p. 49.

Improved productivity and reduced labor intensity are both associated with larger wage increases. Profits and wage increases are negatively related. This may mean that wage increases have been granted independently of profitability, causing future profits to suffer. Employers were most willing to grant increases in less concentrated industries with improving productivity. Bargaining power in these is reduced because competitive products would be easy substitutes.[32] Recently, foreign competition has influenced pay differentials for union employees. For every 10 percent increase in market share gained by imports in an industry, the differential narrowed about 2 percent. The most heavily unionized industries were most resistant to a narrowing of differentials.[33]

From 1967 to 1977, union workers received a 24 percent premium, other things equal. Particularly high returns were experienced by non-whites, Southerners, and low-educated persons. Evidence also suggests that real wages for both the union and the nonunion sector increased in tandem during this period.[34] An analysis of a large set of studies of the union-nonunion wage gap concluded the average gap is about 10 percent; narrowing occurs during periods of expansion and widening during periods of high unemployment as a result of the rigidities of contracts.[35]

Structural and Legal Factors
An analysis of a cross-sectional sample of employees surveyed in 1977 found that union members' wages increased about 18.3 percent over those who were not represented, other things equal. Other factors positively influencing wage levels were plant size (about 5.3 percent per 1,000 employees) and industrial concentration (about 7.4 percent when the largest four firms produce 50 percent rather than 30 percent of the total product of the industry).[36]

In states where right-to-work laws exist, individuals in bargaining units cannot be required to join unions as a condition of continued employment. For union members, right-to-work laws or strong campaign activity for them are associated with lower wages.[37]

Union Spillovers
Evidence shows union wage increases lead to nonunion increases, while the reverse is not the case. High unemployment rates tend to dampen the union increase rate, while upward changes in the cost of living increase them. Union-union spillovers are also found, suggesting that, where it

[32] Davinder Singh, C. Glyn Williams, and Ronald P. Wilder, "Wage Determination in U.S. Manufacturing, 1958–1976: A Collective Bargaining Approach," *Journal of Labor Research* 3 (1982), pp. 223–37.

[33] D. A. Macpherson and J. B. Stewart, "The Effect of International Competition on Union and Nonunion Wages," *Industrial and Labor Relations Review* 43 (1990), pp. 434–46.

[34] William J. Moore and John Raisian, "The Level and Growth of Union/Nonunion Relative Wage Effects, 1967–1977," *Journal of Labor Research* 4 (1983), pp. 65–79.

[35] S. P. Jarrell and T. D. Stanley, "A Meta-Analysis of the Union-Nonunion Wage Gap," *Industrial and Labor Relations Review* 44 (1990), pp. 54–67.

[36] John E. Kwoka Jr., "Monopoly, Plant, and Union Effects of Worker Wages," *Industrial and Labor Relations Review* 37 (1983), pp. 251–57.

[37] Walter J. Wessels, "Economic Effects of Right-to-Work Laws," *Journal of Labor Research* 2 (1981), pp. 55–75.

exists, pattern bargaining has influenced union settlements. Nonunion wage changes do not appear to have any subsequent effect on union wage levels.[38]

Union Effects on Pay Structures

When unionized organizations are compared with nonunion firms in the same industries, variances in wage rates are more often lower in unionized firms. In a national sample of employees, individuals who moved from nonunion to union employment had lower wage dispersions, while those who made opposite moves had increased dispersions. Compression in wages is increased by across-the-board wage increases. The average decrease in dispersions attributed to unionization is about 22 percent.[39] The results are consistent with negotiating contracts that focus on the desires of the median voters and put together coalitions best served by settlements reducing variance in wage increases. They are also consistent with the ideal that unions foster favoring a reduction in the inequality of wages.

Union Effects on Pay Form

Union members prefer larger proportions of their pay to be in the form of fringe benefits. Managements prefer a lower proportion. In terms of costs, unions have the greatest impact on small or low-wage employers; and they most greatly influence costs of insurance, followed by vacations and holidays, overtime premiums, and pensions. When compared to nonunion situations, unions have the greatest relative influence on pensions—possibly reflecting the returns to seniority included in most contracts—followed by insurance and vacations and holidays. Unions have a negative effect on the use of overtime (but not premium rates), sick leave, and bonuses. Evidence suggests the union impact is 17 percent greater for fringe benefits than it is for straight-time pay.[40]

Pension wealth for unionized employees is substantially greater than for comparable nonunion employees. Differences in plans appear greatest for collectively bargained plans having higher initial benefits, earlier retirement opportunities, and larger postretirement increases in benefits.[41]

[38] Susan Vroman, "The Direction of Wage Spillovers in Manufacturing," *Industrial and Labor Relations Review* 36 (1982), pp. 102–12.

[39] Richard B. Freeman, "Union Wage Practices and Wage Dispersion within Establishments," *Industrial and Labor Relations Review* 36 (1982), pp. 3–21.

[40] Richard B. Freeman, "The Effect of Unionism on Fringe Benefits," *Industrial and Labor Relations Review* 34 (1981), pp. 489–509.

[41] Steven G. Allen and Robert L. Clark, "Unions, Pension Wealth, and Age-Compensation Profiles," *Industrial and Labor Relations Review* 39 (1986), pp. 502–17.

Union Effects on Pay Systems

Relatively few data showing how unions influence pay systems are available, and existing data are based at the industry level. Unionized employees are much more likely to have pay increases determined by easily identifiable criteria and by automatic progressions and are less likely to have merit reviews or other forms of individual determinations. Across-the-board increases related to membership are frequent, causing compression in the pay structure.[42] Table 8–5 summarizes the effects of unions on various aspects of pay.

UNION EFFECTS ON ORGANIZATIONAL EFFECTIVENESS

Unionization and the usually resulting seniority rules change employees' orientations toward long-run employment and the benefits accruing with seniority. The effect of unionization on mobility and turnover is explored in the next chapter, but it should be recognized that unionized employees are older and more experienced, other things equal, than their nonunion counterparts. Estimates indicate human capital per worker (knowledge, skills, and abilities related to the job) is about 6 percent higher in unionized settings.[43]

Productivity

Because the evidence suggests a unionized work force increases wage costs as compared with unorganized firms in the same industries, a unionized firm should be at a competitive disadvantage, other things equal. But these other things are not equal. Recent industry-level studies have found unionized establishments to be 24 percent more productive on average than nonunion establishments. If the extent of unionization in the industry is considered, the productivity effect increases to 30 percent. Unionization also apparently has an impact on worker quality within the establishment as measured by experience, training, schooling, and the like. Evidence indicates production worker quality in union establishments is 11 percent higher, while nonproduction worker quality is lower by 8 percent.[44]

---

[42] Freeman, "Union Wage Practices."

[43] Richard B. Freeman and James L. Medoff, "The Impact of Collective Bargaining: Illusion or Reality?" in *U.S. Industrial Relations, 1950–1980: A Critical Assessment*, ed. Jack Stieber, Robert B. McKersie, and D. Quinn Mills (Madison, Wis.: Industrial Relations Research Association, 1981), pp. 47–98.

[44] Ibid.

TABLE 8–5

Recent Evidence on Union/Nonunion Differences Based on Cross-Sectional Data

Variable	Finding
Compensation	
Wage rates	All else (measurable) the same, union/nonunion hourly wage differential is between 10% and 20%.
Fringes	All else the same, union/nonunion hourly fringe differential is between 20% and 30%. The fringe share of compensation is higher at a given level of compensation.
Wage dispersion	Wage inequality is much lower among union members than among comparable nonmembers and total wage dispersion appears to be lowered by unionism.
Wage structure	Wage differentials between workers who are different in terms of race, age, service, skill level, and education appear to be lower under collective bargaining.
Cyclical responsiveness of wage rates	Union wages are less responsive to labor market conditions than nonunion wages.
Determinants of compensation differential	Other things equal, the union compensation advantage is higher the greater the percent of a market's workers who are organized. The effect of market concentration on wage differentials is unclear. The differentials appear to be very large in some regulated markets. They appear to decline as firm size increases.

SOURCE: Richard B. Freeman and James L. Medoff, "The Impact of Collective Bargaining: Illusion or Reality?" in *U.S. Industrial Relations 1950–1980: A Critical Assessment,* ed. Jack Stieber, Robert B. McKersie, and D. Quinn Mills (Madison, Wis.: Industrial Relations Research Association, 1981), p. 50.

Within industries, unionization appears to have differential effects. Research on construction industry productivity found unionized workers on private-sector projects were up to 51 percent more productive than their nonunion counterparts. The differentials decreased markedly in public-sector construction projects, however.[45] In education, student achievement was negatively affected by unionization among public schoolteachers through increased use of administrators and reductions in instruction time; but student achievement is positively influenced through increased preparation time, teacher experience, and smaller student/teacher ratios.[46] In hospitals and nursing homes, productivity was higher among unionized establishments in the private sector, but little difference was noted in the public sector.[47] A study in the auto-parts

[45] Steven G. Allen, "Future Evidence on Union Efficiency in Construction," *Industrial Relations* 27 (1988), pp. 232–40.

[46] R. W. Eberts, "Union Effects on Teacher Productivity," *Industrial and Labor Relations Review* 37 (1984), pp. 346–58.

[47] Steven G. Allen, "The Effect of Unionism on Productivity in Privately and Publicly Owned Hospitals and Nursing Homes, *Journal of Labor Research* 7 (1986), pp. 59–68.

industry found little difference in productivity levels between organized and unorganized establishments, and failure to account for firms that may have gone out of business may upwardly bias the union effects on productivity.[48]

Higher turnover in nonunion organizations is a possible explanation for productivity differentials (examined in Chapter 9). If experience is related to skill levels, unionized firms will have higher skill levels, leading to greater productivity. Because union contracts reduce the dispersion of wages within jobs in firms, employees may believe nonperformance-based compensation systems eliminate competition between workers for a wage pool and enable them to willingly share job information and train new employees.

While recent evidence shows labor productivity in the United States has grown more slowly than in other industrialized countries (the United Kingdom, France, Japan, and Germany), the U.S. employment level in manufacturing was the only one to have increased across countries during the middle 1970s.[49] This would suggest that the cost of labor relative to the cost of capital is lower in the United States than in other industrialized countries and that capital is substituted for labor at a much lower rate here. Where negative productivity rates exist, it is likely that low capacity utilization occurs and relatively large proportions of machinery and plants are unused.

Profitability and Returns to Shareholders

A substantial body of research finds unionized firms less profitable than their nonunion counterparts and less profitable subsequent to unionization.[50] Additional evidence points to lower shareholder returns as a result of unionization. Passage of the Wagner Act substantially facilitated organizing by unions. A study tracking organizing success in the 1930s found that organized firms had about a 20 percent lower rate of return to shareholders than firms that remained nonunion.[51] Firms recently involved in organizing drives and whose securities are publicly traded have experienced about a 4 percent reduction in equity value following a successful campaign—and a 1.3 percent loss even if they won the

[48] Robert S. Kaufman and Robert T. Kaufman, "Union Effects on Productivity, Personnel Practices, and Survival in the Automotive Parts Industry," *Journal of Labor Research* 8 (1987), pp. 333–50.

[49] D. Quinn Mills, "Management Performance," in *U.S. Industrial Relations, 1950–1980: A Critical Assessment*, ed. Jack Stieber, Robert B. McKersie, and D. Quinn Mills (Madison, Wis.: Industrial Relations Research Association, 1981), pp. 99–128.

[50] Freeman and Medoff, *What Do Unions Do?* pp. 181–90.

[51] Craig A. Olson and Brian E. Becker, "The Effects of the NLRA on Stockholder Wealth in the 1930s," *Industrial and Labor Relations Review* 44 (1986), pp. 116–29.

campaign.[52] The latter probably occurs because firms facing union activity have been found to increase wages more than those who don't, win or lose.[53] If unionization leads to lower rates of shareholder returns (and the evidence supports this premise), other things equal, as the agents of shareholders, top managers could be expected to embark on strategies to reduce unionization within their firms.[54] On the other hand, evidence also indicates that lower returns in unionized firms are also accompanied by lower risk in that security prices are less volatile, perhaps reflecting increased risk sharing by employees through layoff procedures.[55]

WAGE ISSUES IN CURRENT CONTRACTS

Contracts differ in the degree to which they contain particular types of wage and benefit clauses. Table 8–6 displays major types of wage and benefit clauses and the proportions in which they appear in recent U.S. collective bargaining agreements.

Between 1979 and 1989, the pervasiveness of certain types of contract clauses has changed. Dental insurance has increased, but hospitalization and other forms of medical insurance have decreased. Income maintenance has remained at about the same level, while cost-of-living allowances have declined. Concessionary situations have often been accompanied by improvements in job security clauses.

SUMMARY

Wage demands are a central part of every contract negotiation. In forming their bargaining positions, unions are often concerned with equity among employee groups, the ability of the company to pay an increase, and the change in the standard of living of its members since the last negotiation.

Pay programs, whether negotiated in contracts or formulated by the employer, address issues related to the level of pay in relation to the market, the structure of pay rates for jobs within the organization, the

---

[52] Richard S. Ruback and Martin B. Zimmerman, "Unionization and Profitability: Evidence from the Capital Market," *Journal of Political Economy* 92 (1984), pp. 1134–57.

[53] Freeman and Kleiner, "Impact of New Unionization."

[54] This and other issues are discussed and analyzed in Brian E. Becker and Craig A. Olson, "Labor Relations and Firm Performance," in *Human Resources and the Performance of the Firm*, ed. Morris M. Kleiner, Richard N. Block, Myron Roomkin, and Sidney W. Salsburg (Madison, Wis.: Industrial Relations Research Association, 1987), pp. 43–86.

[55] Brian E. Becker and Craig A. Olson, "Unionization and Shareholder Interests," *Industrial and Labor Relations Review* 42 (1989), pp. 246–61.

TABLE 8–6

Basic Wage Clauses in Contracts (1989)

Clause	Percent Containing Clause
Insurance	
Accidental death and dismemberment	74
Dental care	83
Doctor's visits	41
Hospitalization	63
Life	99
Long-term disability	21
Major medical	57
Maternity	45
Miscellaneous medical expense	50
Optical care	47
Prescription drugs	41
Sickness and accident	83
Surgical	61
Pensions	
Early retirement	96
Noncontributory plan	94
Some provision	99
Income maintenance	
Severance pay	40
Some provision	52
Supplementary unemployment benefits	14
Wages	
Deferred increases	77
Cost-of-living adjustments	35
Wage reopeners	9
Shift differentials	85
Incentive plans	33
Job classification procedures	58
Hiring rates	10
Wage progression	44
Two-tier structure	28

SOURCE: *Collective Bargaining Negotiation and Contracts* (Washington, D.C.: Bureau of National Affairs, 1989).

form in which pay is received as wages or benefits, and the system used to determine individual entitlements to varied pay treatments. A variety of concerns are subject to negotiation, with unions stressing equity and ability-to-pay issues and management favoring pay programs that positively influence employee behavior. Managements have also been increasingly interested in lowering base-pay levels and in making a larger proportion of pay flexible and responsive to changes in economic conditions.

than in nonunion organizations, with a larger proportion of pay given in benefits. Collective bargaining agreements generally contain fewer contingencies surrounding pay increases and have a larger proportion of pay in the form of deferred compensation and insurance.

Evidence suggests organized companies are about 20 percent more productive than unorganized ones. However, they are also about 20 percent less profitable. Productivity differences in favor of unionized organizations appear confined to blue-collar occupations and the private sector.

DISCUSSION QUESTIONS

1. What are the costs and benefits for management in allowing the union to decide how the economic package should be divided?
2. What demands would most likely be advocated by union leaders interested in obtaining contract ratification?
3. What information would you use to make predictions as to the economic demands and probable settlement for a particular union-management negotiation?
4. What are the economic benefits of union membership to employees, and to what extent can these benefits be increased before employers face problems?
5. What are the trade-offs among increased wages for unions, productivity effects, and profitability effects on organizations?

KEY TERMS

standard of living
ability to pay
cost-of-living adjustments
pay level
pay structure
pay form
pay system

job evaluation
skill-based pay
two-tier pay plans
comparable worth
defined benefit pension plan
defined contribution pension plan
benefit status seniority

CASE
HEALTH CARE COSTS AND
EMPLOYMENT LEVELS

During the past year, health care costs per employee provided under the GMFC-Local 384 contract have increased by 19 percent. With the increased penetration of the domestic market by foreign producers and the resulting pressure on prices, GMFC is exploring ways in which health care costs can be contained or reduced. It is concentrating on subcontracting and negotiating an arrangement to hire part-time employees who would not be eligible for health care benefits.

Local 384 would like to avoid the benefits reduction, subcontracting, and part-time workers. The first would be a concession in an environment in which reductions have already been conceded. The second would lead to a reduction in the membership of the local or a reduction in the proportion of employees who are represented.

Assuming that this issue will be a major one in the upcoming negotiations, prepare either a union or management position on the issue of health care cost containment, recognizing that the employer will be decreasingly able to compete if total compensation costs increase as they have been recently with these types of year-to-year changes in health care costs.

9

NONWAGE ISSUES
IN BARGAINING

Wage and nonwage issues are not completely separable. For example, contract provisions relating to hours of work frequently specify when entitlements to overtime premiums begin. This chapter first considers issues primarily associated with hours and terms and conditions of employment and then examines the effects of unions on nonwage outcomes for individuals and organizations.

Nonwage issues are important to both union members and management. For management, the length of the contract and the scope of management rights clauses are important. For the union member, job security provisions (particularly those related to promotions and layoffs), grievance procedures, and work schedules are important. As an institution, the union is concerned with the security level it is provided through contractual requirements for employee membership in the union. How promotions and layoffs are handled influences outcomes important to each party.

In studying this chapter, attention should be paid to the following questions:

1. What impacts do federal regulations and contract provisions have on management decision making as it relates to hours of work?
2. How do discipline and discharge procedures operate, and what procedures are available for redress of improper discipline by management?
3. How do job classification and job design affect the employment relationship?
4. What effect do seniority clauses have on employee behavior?
5. What impact does collective bargaining appear to have on the job satisfaction of represented employees?

Nonwage Provisions of Current Contracts

Just as trends and patterns exist for wage issues, certain types of contract clauses appear in a relatively large proportion of collective bargaining agreements. Table 9–1 displays the prevalence of nonwage contract terms in a sample of recent contracts.

Contract clauses relating to issues included in Table 9–1 have become more prevalent during the past four years. For example, recognition of seniority as a criterion for employment decision making and clauses related to entitlement to, restrictions on, and acceptance of overtime have increased. However, union security provisions have not increased recently.

Union and Management Goals for Nonwage Issues

Chapter 8 suggested that unions (1) are concerned with equity, ability to pay, and standards of living in formulating wage demands and (2) have simultaneous economic and membership goals. Managements are expected to resist demands that would interfere with their abilities to be flexible, to be certain of the types of costs they are likely to encounter, and to respond to changes in their operating environments through the introduction of new production technologies.

Many nonwage issues relate directly to the union's membership goals. To the degree that employer costs increase through overtime rates, hiring more employees is seen as a cost-saving alternative, leading to higher union membership. Contract provisions are negotiated to ration job opportunities during cutbacks or when employers introduce labor-saving equipment. Several issues involve management's decision-making discretion to direct and deploy its work force in ways most likely to achieve important objectives if business conditions change. To accomplish these ends, contracts frequently contain clauses recognizing the legitimacy of both parties and spelling out the rights and responsibilities of each in their day-to-day relationships.

Design of Work

Job design has important cost and flexibility implications for management and job security consequences for union members. Ironically, the job security aspects tied to work design in the past may now exacerbate layoffs, while changes toward more flexible jobs along with more flexible compensation may improve job security in the long run and employment levels in the short run.

TABLE 9–1

Basic Nonwage Clauses in Contracts (1989)

Clause	Percent Containing Clause	Clause	Percent Containing Clause
Contract term		Layoff, rehiring, and work sharing	
1 year	2	Seniority as criterion	87
2 years	9	Seniority as sole factor	46
3 years	80	Notice to employees required	49
4 years	11	No minimum	6
Contract reopeners	11	1–2 days	16
Automatic renewal	84	3–4 days	15
		5–6 days	19
Discipline and discharge		7 or more	13
General grounds for discharge	94	Bumping permitted	60
Specific grounds for discharge	75	Manufacturing contracts	72
		Nonmanufacturing contracts	32
Grievance and arbitration		Recall	81
Steps specified	99	Work sharing	18
Arbitration as final step	98		
		Leaves of absence	
Hours and overtime		Personal	76
Daily work schedules	85	Union	77
Weekly work schedules	61	Maternity	34
Overtime premiums	97	Paternity, child care, or adoption	32
Daily overtime premiums	94	Funeral	85
Sixth-day premiums	22	Civic	81
Seventh-day premiums	26	Paid sick	31
Pyramiding of overtime		Unpaid sick	53
prohibited	66	Military	70
Distribution of overtime work	67		
Acceptance of overtime	23	Management and union rights	
Restrictions on overtime	37	Management rights statement	79
Weekend premiums	67	Restrictions on management	86
Lunch, rest, and cleanup	61	Subcontracting	54
Waiting time entails	19	Supervisory work	56
Standby time	4	Technological change re-	
Travel time	22	strictions	27
Voting time	7	Plant shutdown or relocation	25
		In-plant union representation	55
Holidays		Union access to plant	55
None specified	1	Union bulletin boards	69
Less than 7	5	Union right to information	61
7, 7½	4	Union activity on company time	35
8, 8½	8	Union-management cooperation	53
9, 9½	11		
10, 10½	18	Seniority	
11, 11½	22	Probationary periods at hire	83
12 or more	32	Loss of seniority	81
Eligibility for holiday pay	88		

TABLE 9–1
(continued)

Clause	Percent Containing Clause	Clause	Percent Containing Clause
Seniority lists	70	Vacations	
As factor in promotions	74	Three weeks or more	89
As factor in transfers	59	Four weeks or more	85
Status of supervisors	28	Five weeks or more	61
Strikes and lockouts		Six weeks or more	21
Unconditional pledges (strikes)	62	Based on service	90
Unconditional pledges (lockouts)	88	Work requirement for	
Limitation of union liability	41	eligibility	53
Penalties for strikers	42	Vacation scheduling by	
Picket line observance	26	management	71
Union security		Working conditions and safety	
Union shop	62	Occupational safety and health	86
Modified union shop	13	Hazardous work acceptance	26
Agency shop	11	Safety and health committees	48
Maintenance of membership	4	Safety equipment provided	44
Hiring provisions	22	Guarantees against discrimination	
Checkoff	91	Guarantees mentioned	94
		EEO pledges	30

SOURCE: *Collective Bargaining Negotiation and Contracts* (Washington, D.C.: Bureau of National Affairs, 1989).

Part of work design involves specifying the tasks, duties, and responsibilities assigned to particular jobs. Jobs have been narrowly defined where the production process requires relatively few specific tasks and where training time is designed to be short. Jobs may also be narrowly defined where the sophistication of necessary skills is great, such as in carpentry or electrical work. Typically, manufacturing environments have had a relatively large number of jobs. These jobs are arranged to allow an employee to advance as the result of learning additional skills and/or accumulating seniority. Frequently, more senior workers bid for jobs that have better working conditions and require less physical effort.

Manufacturing employers have been particularly interested in reducing the number of distinct job classifications in both production and maintenance in order to gain flexibility in staffing and to avoid downtime for maintenance operations when a task is outside of a narrow job's jurisdiction. Broader capability requirements in broader job classifications may also require less supervision. Evidence in the auto industry indicates a reduction in job classifications is associated with a reduction in supervision required, small improvements in the quality of output, and a small increase in the total number of labor hours required for an equivalent level of output.[1] Actual reductions in the numbers of distinct jobs in the auto industry.

In return for increased job security guarantees, managements have negotiated team-oriented production designs where workers have responsibilities for several tasks and where an employee can be assigned to what would have been a variety of jobs. The GM–UAW agreement for its new Saturn division reduces job classifications substantially.

Jobs represented by the union may become relatively deskilled as new technology is introduced if management is successful in designing the jobs not to be part of the bargaining unit. Union adherence to seniority requirements may entitle jobs to employees who are not the most able to fully operate new equipment. Management is particularly unwilling to include jobs requiring programming as part of the bargaining unit when new technology is installed.[2]

Some work rule changes try to increase efficiency by more fully utilizing equipment (e.g., Teamster drivers hauling less than full load shipments).[3] Others are aimed at increasing employee flexibility through greater skills and management's ability to assign employees to an increased variety of tasks.

Work rules that reserve certain responsibilities to certain jobholders reduce efficiency, but they may preserve employment levels. One study of the construction industry found restrictive work rules increase labor costs by about 5 percent, and, in terms of their bargaining power, building trade unions appear willing to give up about 5 percent in wages to increase staffing levels by 3 percent.[4] Exhibit 9–1 covers some of these issues.

HOURS OF WORK

Hours of work are both a mandatory issue for bargaining and regulated by various federal and state wage and hour laws. As mentioned in Chapter 2, the unions' campaign for shorter work hours has been a major bargaining issue since the early 1800s, with the National Labor Union proposing a uniform eight-hour day after the Civil War. The federal government

[1] J. H. Keefe and H. C. Katz, "Job Classifications and Plant Performance in the Auto Industry," *Industrial Relations* 29 (1990), pp. 111–18.

[2] M. R. Kelley, "Unionization and Job Design under Programmable Automation," *Industrial Relations* 28 (1989), pp. 174–87.

[3] Thomas A. Kochan, Harry C. Katz, and Robert B. McKersie, *The Transformation of American Industrial Relations* (New York: Basic Books, 1986), pp. 117–18.

[4] Steven G. Allen, "Union Work Rules and Efficiency in the Building Trades," *Journal of Labor Economics* 4 (1986), pp. 212–42.

EXHIBIT 9–1

Work Rules Shape Up as Major Battleground in U.S. Labor Disputes

Work rules are turning into the next big battleground between management and labor.

Since company profits have risen from the depths of this decade's recession, further wage cuts have become less of an issue. So industry, still eager to cut costs, has turned instead to work rules—everything from the frequency of restroom breaks to who operates which machine. Unions, determined to preserve every remaining job, are digging in. . . .

"Every major strike or labor dispute today has work rules at its core," says Harley Shaiken, a labor specialist at the University of California, San Diego. . . .

Despite work rule changes' current popularity with management, some labor experts question the savings from the changes. They say that when workers do more tasks—the essence of most work rule changes—companies have to spend time teaching workers new skills. A Borg-Warner Corp. transmissions unit in Muncie, Indiana, for example, wants to create a single job classification for the workers in one part of its plant. While the company is excited about the prospect, it says that each worker will require 800 hours of training, 10 times more than at present. . . .

Nobody has done exhaustive studies on costs and savings, but companies argue that common sense says the savings are big. Cablec Corp. is a case in point.

The . . . cable maker bought a . . . plant . . . that still ran by rules adopted as long ago as the 1930s. Job categories were so rigid that when somebody classified as a millwright—essentially a mechanic—was told to repair a lift truck, he first had to call somebody classified as an electrician to disconnect the battery cables. And the seniority rules were so stiff that two years ago the plant had to rehire six high-seniority workers before it found someone with the skill to run a complicated cable-insulating machine. The five surplus workers swept floors. . . .

Jobs are at the heart of union resistance to work rule changes. Union members generally don't defend the most archaic work rules. For example, Ron Davis, the president of the . . . local at Cablec, says the old rule that allowed high-seniority workers off a job "wasn't real productive." But he and other union members fear that eliminating even the bad rules will cost them jobs. TWA says that it will need 39 percent fewer flight attendants during the off-peak season if it gets more work rule flexibility. And a Chicago-based labor-research group concluded that one third of the jobs lost in northwest Indiana's steel industry between 1981 and 1984 were due to work rule changes.

"The motive for work rule changes very often is something other than productivity—it's simply to eliminate people and increase profits," says John Zalusky, an AFL–CIO economist.

SOURCE: Alex Kotlowitz, "Work Rules Shape Up as Major Battleground in U.S. Labor Disputes," *The Wall Street Journal*, June 4, 1986, pp. 1, 19. © 1986 Dow Jones & Company, Inc. All Rights Reserved Worldwide.

regulated hours of work for civil servants during President Van Buren's administration and legislated penalties for employers for overtime beginning in the 1930s.

Federal Wage and Hour Laws

In 1937, Congress passed the Fair Labor Standards Act (FLSA), regulating wages, hours, and working conditions for private-sector employers involved in interstate commerce. Briefly, the legislation requires employees not performing supervisory roles, outside sales positions, or jobs requiring professional training be paid a 50 percent premium over their regular earnings rate for more than 40 hours per week. This premium requirement covers all employees whose work is of a routine nature or requires close supervision and direction. The legislation also establishes a minimum wage level and prohibits persons under certain ages from working in specific occupations or industries.

Congress had previously enacted the Davis-Bacon and Walsh-Healy acts, which required overtime payments for employees with similar job duties after eight hours in a given day if they were involved in government contract construction work or the production of manufactured goods for the federal government. The laws, enacted during the Depression, were designed to stimulate employers to expand their work forces, because effective rates for overtime work were set at 50 percent above regular hourly rates. Employers would save by hiring more employees rather than paying overtime to existing employees.

Collective Bargaining and Work Schedules

Unions have continually favored reductions of the workweek and workday. The 40-hour week is now typical in many union contracts, but unions have been able to reduce the workweek substantially in certain contracts. For example, Local 3 of the International Brotherhood of Electrical Workers gained a 25-hour workweek during 1962 negotiations in the construction industry. Few electricians worked only 25 hours in a given week, but overtime pay commenced after this threshold.[5] Evidence indicates that average hours worked per year for full-time employees in the more heavily unionized sectors of the economy are less than for those who are not represented, but a larger proportion of employees work full- rather than part-time schedules.[6]

[5] See Richard L. Rowan, "The Influence of Collective Bargaining on Hours," in *Hours of Work*, ed. Clyde E. Dankert, Floyd C. Mann, and Herbert R. Northrup (New York: Harper & Row, 1965), pp. 17–35.

[6] J. S. Earle and J. Pencavel, "Hours of Work and Trade Unionism," *Journal of Labor Economics* 8 (1990), pp. S150–S174.

Entitlements to and Restrictions on Overtime

Contracts usually specify rules for assigning overtime. Overtime is often rotated among workers based on their seniority, balancing hours in the work group before returning to the senior worker to begin a new cycle. Some contracts include provisions allowing employees to refuse more than a specified number of overtime hours per week. Employees who have not met this threshold would be subject to discipline for refusing to work scheduled overtime.

Shift Assignments and Differentials

In organizations where continuous-flow operations are most efficient (such as chemical manufacturers and refiners) or where product demand levels and plant investment are high enough to justify multishift operations, contracts specify which employees are entitled to which work schedules. Provisions may allow employees to transfer shifts as jobs become available in their specialties if they are more senior than other eligible employees. Shift arrangements may also be negotiated to allow rotation across shifts as work periods progress. For example, an intact shift might work from midnight until 8 A.M. for four weeks, then rotate to the 8 A.M. to 4 P.M. shift for four weeks, then move to the 4 P.M. to midnight shift for four weeks.

Innovative Work Schedules

A variety of innovative work schedules has been designed to meet employee desires and employer requirements. Most have been implemented in nonunion organizations, and most have involved the expansion of daily work hours and the shortening of the number of days in the workweek.[7]

Unions have opposed longer workday schedules because they have stressed fatigue, safety, and long-term health impact issues in arguing for shorter days. However, evidence suggests worker satisfaction improves and fatigue is not a problem in occupations that are not physically strenuous. Where employees desire to work fewer days and off-job demands in a given day are not great, compressed workweeks may benefit both employers and employees. However, employers should be aware of

---

[7] For a complete summary of these innovations, see Herbert G. Heneman III, Donald P. Schwab, John A. Fossum, and Lee D. Dyer, *Personnel/Human Resource Management*, 3rd ed. (Homewood, Ill.: Richard D. Irwin, 1986), pp. 673–77.

employee preferences before proposing the issue.[8] The union must also be aware of employee preferences. In one case, a union opposed to compressed work schedules was threatened with decertification by its members if it did not go along with the work change.[9]

Paid Time Off

Paid time off includes holidays, vacations, and other leave periods. These benefits are relatively straightforward, although management may place some restrictions on entitlement or use. For example, employees must normally work the days before and after a holiday to receive holiday pay. Employers may also exercise their discretion regarding vacation schedules. If operations are highly integrated and insufficient numbers of employees are available to continue in the absence of vacationing workers, management usually sets aside a period for vacations and shutdowns. Other organizations may require vacations to be taken during slack periods.

LENGTH OF CONTRACTS

Most contracts cover more than one year, with three years being the most common. Some provide for wage reopeners during the course of the agreement, especially when cost-of-living agreements are not included. Longer contracts are more likely to have COLAs to ensure employees against the uncertainty of wage changes, especially when inflation rates at the time of negotiation are relatively high.[10] When management seeks to eliminate them, unions usually demand shorter contracts. Evidence regarding the effects of contract length on other outcomes is relatively sparse. Employers try to avoid one-year contracts because they believe short contracts lead to more strikes and contract administration problems, lower employee morale, and higher and more unpredictable labor costs.[11] Longer-term contracts may be related to more difficult contract

---

[8] See, for example, Myron D. Fottler, "Employee Acceptance of a Four-Day Workweek," *Academy of Management Journal* 20 (1977), pp. 656–68; and Simcha Ronen and Sophia B. Primps, "The Compressed Work Week as Organizational Change: Behavioral and Attitudinal Outcomes," *Academy of Management Review* 7 (1981), pp. 61–74.

[9] Herbert R. Northrup, James T. Wilson, and Karen M. Rose, "The Twelve-Hour Shift in the Petroleum and Chemical Industries," *Industrial and Labor Relations Review* 32 (1979), pp. 312–26.

[10] W. E. Hendricks and Lawrence M. Kahn, "Contract Length, Wage Indexation, and Ex Ante Variability of Real Wages," *Journal of Labor Research* 8 (1987), pp. 221–36.

[11] Sanford M. Jacoby and Daniel J. B. Mitchell, "Employer Preferences for Long-Term Union Contracts," *Journal of Labor Research* 5 (1984), pp. 215–28.

negotiations, especially when the economic environment is changing. New agreements to replace long-term contracts were found to be harder to negotiate when foreign competition was great; where capacity utilization, selling price of the company's products, and number of vacant positions varied substantially during the contract period; where buyer or seller concentration was high in the industry among larger employers; and during periods of high inflation.[12]

UNION AND MANAGEMENT RIGHTS

Contracts specify the representation rights of the union. Most relate to the number of union stewards or representatives permitted within the bargaining unit, their rights to access employees in various plant areas, the amount of time off available for union representation activities and who is responsible for compensating this time, office space, access to bulletin boards, and access to nonemployee union officials to the organization.

Most contracts exclusively reserve to management the right to act in areas not constrained by the agreement. Typical reserved rights include the right to subcontract work even though it could be performed within the bargaining unit,[13] to assign bargaining unit work to supervisors in emergencies or to train new employees, to introduce technological changes to improve efficiency, and to determine the criteria for plant shutdowns or relocations. When management does not exclusively reserve these rights, the union is entitled to bargain during the course of the contract if changes involving job security occur. For example, if a plant shutdown would result in layoffs, the absence of a clause leaving this determination to management requires bargaining on the effects of the shutdown if the union requests it.

Management rights clauses frequently specify rights to direct the work force, to establish production levels, and to frame appropriate

---

[12] J. M. Cousineau and R. Lacroix, "Imperfect Information and Strikes: An Analysis of Canadian Experience, 1967–82," *Industrial and Labor Relations Review* 39 (1986), pp. 377–87.

[13] The Supreme Court decision in *Fibreboard Paper Products* v. *NLRB*, 379 U.S. 203 (1964) requires bargaining by management if the union requests when subcontracting is being considered, unless the union has expressly waived its right in this area; however, this rule has been relaxed somewhat by *First National Maintenance* v. *NLRB*, 107 LRRM 2705 (U.S. Supreme Court, 1981), and later by the NLRB when it held that removal of union work to another facility of the company would be permissible if bargaining had reached an impasse (*Milwaukee Spring Div. of Illinois Coil Spring Co.*, 115 LRRM 1065 [1984], enforced by the U.S Court of Appeals, District of Columbia Circuit, 119 LRRM 2801 [1985]), or for a legitimate business reason if there were no antiunion animus (*Otis Elevator Co.*, 115 LRRM 1281 [1984]).

company rules and policies. The establishment of rules and procedures and the direction of the work force form a base for clauses relating to discipline and discharge.

DISCIPLINE AND DISCHARGE

Most contracts specify that employees can be discharged or disciplined for just cause. Some reasons for discharge are spelled out in the contract, and others relate to violations of rules that the employer may promulgate under the power retained in a management rights clause.

Specific grounds in discipline and discharge clauses most often cover intoxication, dishonesty or theft, incompetence or failure to meet work standards, insubordination, unauthorized absence, misconduct, failure to obey safety rules, violations of leave provisions, or general violations of company rules.[14] Committing a violation does not necessarily mean an offender will be automatically discharged but rather will be subject to discipline. However, the organization must be consistent in the way discipline is meted out if it is to successfully defend its disciplinary actions from grievances.

Discipline and discharge clauses may also spell out the due process procedures necessary before discipline can be imposed. Renegotiation of a long-term contract frequently requires disciplinary action taken for offenses before a certain period to be removed from an employee's file.

GRIEVANCE AND ARBITRATION

Grievance procedures are a high-priority bargaining issue for unions because they allow employees to object to unilateral management action during the term of the agreement. For example, assume an employee believes a supervisor unjustly suspended him or her for a work rule violation. Without a grievance procedure, no review of the supervisor's action would be possible. Grievance procedures are also useful to management because the aggrieved employee is expected to use this forum when an alleged violation occurs, rather than refusing a work assignment or walking off the job.

Grievance procedures usually specify the person who receives a grievance, the right of employees to representation at various steps in the process, the path a grievance follows if it cannot be resolved by the parties

---

[14] For more details, see *Collective Bargaining Negotiation and Contracts* (Washington, D.C.: Bureau of National Affairs, updated as necessary), tab sect. 40.

after it has been filed, and the time limits at each step before some action is required. Chapter 13 presents grievance procedures in considerable detail.

Most contracts specify that when parties cannot agree on the disposition of a grievance, a third party will arbitrate the dispute and render a decision binding on both parties. The contract specifies how an arbitrator will be selected, how arbitrators are paid, the powers of the arbitrator, and the length of time an arbitrator has to render a decision. Arbitration of contract interpretation disputes are dealt with in Chapter 14.

High grievance rates are associated with decreased productivity. While low morale might be a hypothesized cause, productivity decreases also occur because employees and supervisors are involved during working hours in settling grievances rather than in production.[15] In situations where production rates and methods change, grievance rates might be influenced. For example, in a long-term study of grievances in an aircraft manufacturer, the level of planned production and an increase in the variety of production methods to be used, which would cause employees to change job classifications frequently, were both associated with higher grievance rates.[16] Thus, grievance rates may reduce productivity and follow from higher productivity requirements.

STRIKES AND LOCKOUTS

Pledges by unions and mangements to avoid strikes and lockouts during the term of the agreement appear in most contracts. Managements frequently demand a no-strike agreement in return for arbitrating unresolved grievances. Unions usually do not give up the right to strike during the contract if management refuses to comply with an arbitration award. Some work stoppages are permitted by contracts, including employee refusals to cross picket lines of other unions striking the same employer and to perform struck work.

Many contracts require that when unauthorized work stoppages (**wildcat strikes**) occur, the union will disavow the strike and urge the employees to return to their jobs. If employees strike in violation of the agreement, many contracts specifically indicate they can be discharged.

---

[15] Casey Ichniowski, "The Effects of Management Practices on Productivity," *Industrial and Labor Relations Review* 40 (1986), pp. 75–89.

[16] M. M. Kleiner, G. Nickelsburg, and A. M. Pilarski, "Grievances and Plant Performance: Is Zero Optimal?" *Proceedings of the Industrial Relations Research Association* 41 (1988), pp. 172–80.

UNION SECURITY

Because the union is the exclusive representative of employees in the bargaining unit, it desires that they be required to join and pay dues for the representational services the union renders on their behalf. Different levels of union security may be negotiated. Except in states with right-to-work laws, contracts may contain agency or union-shop clauses. The following are definitions of various forms of **union security.**

1. **Closed shop** requires employers to hire only union members. Although this requirement is illegal, a contract clause can require the employer to offer the union an opportunity to fill vacant assignments. These arrangements occur most frequently in the construction and maritime industries, where many employers are relatively small and have relatively short-run demands for certain occupations.

2. **Union shop** requires any bargaining unit employee employed with the firm for a specific time (not less than 30 days, 7 days in construction) to become a union member as a condition of continued employment.

3. **Modified union shop** requires any bargaining unit employee who was hired after a date specified in the agreement to become a union member within a specific time as a condition of continued employment.

4. **Agency shop** requires any bargaining unit employee who is not a union member to pay a service fee to the union for its representation activities.

5. **Maintenance of membership** requires any bargaining unit employee who becomes a union member to remain one as a condition of continued employment as long as the contract remains in effect.

Contracts also frequently provide for a dues **checkoff** whereby the employer deducts union dues from members' pay and forwards the amount directly to the union. The process benefits all parties. First, it avoids workplace disruptions involved in collection. Second, it insulates employees from union disciplinary action for nonpayment of dues. Third, it ensures a smooth cash flow for the financial operations of the local union.

Unions usually bargain for the highest form of union security attainable, but one might argue that a union or agency shop would not be in the best interests of the individual members. If union membership were not compulsory, those who joined or remained members would see to it that the union accomplished important ends efficiently. State right-to-work laws enable a preliminary test of whether union membership is influenced by the efficiency of the local union, because an individual can choose whether to join. One study found the costs of a local's operation were lower in right-to-work states; but no differences in dues levels, provision of benefits or services, compensation of union officers, or profitability of investments existed.[17] In most instances, right-to-work laws have had little effect on individual union membership decisions. Some evidence shows the proportion of union members in the bargaining unit influences the bargaining power of the union because wage levels increase with higher representation.[18]

WORKING CONDITIONS AND SAFETY

Working conditions and safety clauses are primarily concerned with the provision of safety equipment, the right to refuse hazardous work, and the creation of joint management-union safety committees. Many of the collective bargaining concerns with health and safety have been superseded by the Occupational Safety and Health Act. Unions are free to negotiate standards of hazard removal higher than what is required in the act.[19] Exhibit 9–2 details a new program introduced in one IBP plant through an agreement with the UFCW to reduce injuries in meat packing in response to OSHA findings.

Employers have also taken inititatives in this area with programs aimed at detecting and reducing substance abuse. Many employers have adopted prehire drug screening programs, over which unions have no control because applicants do not have representation rights. Unions and employers may potentially clash around bargaining over and administration of periodic or random drug tests, with unions arguing they constitute an invasion of privacy and may not be supported by just cause, while employers argue they are entitled to control the operation of the workplace and need to operate as safely as possible.[20]

---

[17] James T. Bennett and Manuel H. Johnson, "The Impact of Right-to-Work Laws on the Economic Behavior of Local Unions—A Property Rights Perspective," *Journal of Labor Research* 1 (1980), pp. 1–28.

[18] Sandra Christenson and Dennis Maki, "The Wage Effect of Compulsory Union Membership," *Industrial and Labor Relations Review* 37 (1983), pp. 230–38; for a comprehensive bibliography of right-to-work law effects, see T. R. Haggard, "Union Security and the Right to Work: A Comprehensive Bibliography," *Journal of Labor Research* 11 (1990), pp. 81–106.

[19] For an extended overview of occupational safety and health issues, see Heneman et al., *Personnel/Human Resource Management.*

[20] For more details, see E. C. Wesman and D. E. Eischen, "Due Process," in *Employee and Labor Relations*, SHRM-BNA Series, Vol. 4., ed John A. Fossum (Washington, D.C.: Bureau of National Affairs, 1990), pp. 4–96 to 4–100.

EXHIBIT 9-2

Meat-Packing Plant Acts to Curb Injuries

Cumulative trauma injuries, which have become of increasing concern in a number of industries, were addressed in a program adopted by IBP Inc. and the United Food and Commercial Workers for the company's flagship meat-packing plant in Dakota City, Nebraska. A company official explained that other IBP plants were initially excluded so that the program could be tried in a controlled environment, not helter-skelter. Some results might be seen in six months or so; other results might take two years.

Cumulative trauma injuries (carpal tunnel syndrome, for example) usually result from repetitive motions, such as those performed by workers on slaughtering lines.

The agreement calls for:

- Training certain workers as "ergonomics monitors" to identify injury-inducing jobs and recommend solutions (disputes, if any, between union and management regarding the solutions will be resolved by a joint committee).
- Training new employees in avoiding stressful work methods.
- Developing new workstation layouts to ease physical strain on employees.
- Initiating a medical program to treat and rehabilitate injured employees.

The three-year agreement came less than two years after the Food and Commercial Workers began a campaign to publicize alleged unsafe working conditions at the plant. Later, the Occupational Safety and Health Administration intensified enforcement activity in the meat-packing industry, culminating in a 1987 proposal to fine IBP $5.7 million for alleged safety and record-keeping violations. In return for the company's adopting the new safety program, OSHA reduced the fine to $975,000.

SOURCE: G. Ruben, "Developments in Industrial Relations," *Monthly Labor Review* 112, no. 4 (1989), p. 41.

SENIORITY AND JOB SECURITY

Seniority issues cut across several of the economic and noneconomic bargaining issues. Seniority may entitle employees to higher pay levels or to overtime, preferences on vacation periods, lengths of vacations, eligibility for promotions and transfers, and insulation against layoffs. Seniority provisions have been shown to positively influence the pay level of blue-collar workers represented by unions.[21]

---

[21] K. G. Abraham and H. S. Farmer, "Returns to Seniority in Union and Nonunion Jobs: A New Look at the Evidence," *Industrial and Labor Relations Review* 42 (1988), 3–19.

At the outset, a distinction should be made between two types of seniority—**benefit status** and **competitive status.** Benefit status seniority is related to the entitlement to organization-wide or bargaining unit–wide benefits established in the contract. For example, if the contract specifies that vacation length depends on seniority in the organization, then the date of hire (as adjusted by any layoffs or leaves) establishes a benefit status. Most contracts base benefit entitlements on the total length of employment.

Competitive status seniority relates to entitlement to bid on promotions and transfers and to avoid layoffs. Benefit and competitive status seniority occasionally overlap, but competitive status seniority is usually accumulated within a job or department. Assume an employee with five years' total service bids on an inspection job from a present job in assembly work. Competitive status seniority among the inspectors would begin as of the date of the job change. If a subsequent layoff occurred in which employees with four or fewer years of service on the job were furloughed, this inspector would be laid off. The inspector's benefit status seniority would be five years, but competitive status seniority would begin only from the date of obtaining the inspector job. Competitive status seniority is more likely to be company-wide than department-wide when the employer is small, capital intensive, in a single-employer bargaining unit, and when the production technology requires substantial training by the employer.[22]

Layoff Procedures

In almost 60 percent of the contracts surveyed in a recent sample, seniority was the sole provision for determining layoff or job retention rights during cutbacks.[23] In another 30 percent of the contracts, seniority was the determining factor if the individual was qualified for the remaining jobs.

Layoffs are usually in inverse order of seniority, protecting the most senior worker for the longest period. Many contracts specify layoffs will be determined on the basis of departmental seniority; some permit **bumping,** whereby a senior employee is entitled to replace a junior employee in another department or job as long as the senior employee is qualified for it.

---

[22] J. F. Schnell, "An Ordered Choice Model of Promotion Rules," *Journal of Labor Research* 8 (1987), pp. 159–78.

[23] *Collective Bargaining Negotiation and Contracts* (Washington, D.C.: Bureau of National Affairs, updated as necessary), tab sect. 60.

Promotions and Transfers

The *CBNC* survey found seniority is less frequently a criterion for promotions and transfers than for layoffs. In about half of all contracts, seniority is the sole or determining factor for promotions if qualifications are essentially equal. For transfers, seniority is also a sole or determining factor in half of the contracts.[24]

Depending on the contract, seniority for someone promoted out of the bargaining unit (for example, to first-line supervision) may continue to be accumulated, may be frozen, or may be lost after time. Employers usually desire clauses protecting accumulated seniority for supervisors because rank-and-file employees may be more willing to vie for promotions where risks of job loss are less if they fail or if employment is later reduced.

Equal Employment Opportunity and Seniority

Occasionally, competitive status seniority systems differentially affect women and minorities if they are hired more often into positions requiring training and experience before promotion to a higher level job. They are more vulnerable to layoff, even though they may have more benefit status seniority than their co-workers who remain within the department during a cutback.

Title VII of the 1964 Civil Rights Act forbids employers and unions from using race, sex, color, religion, or national origin as a basis for making employment decisions. Except under hiring-hall agreements in the construction and maritime industries, unions have no say in hiring decisions. In non-hiring-hall situations, after workers complete a probationary period, the negotiated agreement governs promotion and transfer decisions.

Superficially, seniority requirements are neutral regarding race or sex, and Section 703(h) of Title VII explicitly permits seniority to be used in making personnel decisions:

> Nothwithstanding other provisions of this title, it shall not be an unlawful employment practice for an employer to apply different standards of compensation, or different terms, conditions, or privileges of employment pursuant to a bona fide seniority or merit system . . . provided that such differences are not the result of an intention to discriminate because of race, color, religion, sex, or national origin.

---

[24] Ibid., tab sect. 68.

Supreme Court Rulings on Seniority and Discrimination

A series of Supreme Court decisions clarifies the requirements for a bona fide seniority system and the rights of unionized employees under this type of system. The Court has held that back pay is not adequate relief for victims of discrimination in unionized jobs because future decisions based on competitive status seniority would trigger a new incident in which back pay would be required. Only retroactive seniority from the date of the discriminatory action cures the problem.[25] **Constructive** (or backdated) **seniority** could not be granted before the effective date of Title VII. Persons who accumulated seniority in a job before that date, even as a result of discrimination, could continue to use it for competitive status purposes. Systems not negotiated to establish or maintain discrimination are assumed to be bona fide.

EFFECTS OF UNIONS ON NONWAGE OUTCOMES

Unions influence nonwage outcomes for both employers and the employees, predominantly in hiring, promotions, transfers, turnover, and retirement. Employee satisfaction is also related to union membership. This section explores research on the effects of unions on these types of nonwage outcomes.

Union Influences on Hiring

Lower-skilled workers prefer union jobs. Given this preference, unionization may improve the employer's ability to select more qualified job applicants. For applicants who do not initially obtain union employment, union jobs become less attractive as time passes because opportunities for promotion are at least partially related to seniority.[26] Among unemployed individuals, persons with higher reservation wages (asking pay requirements), women, minorities, and former union members are more likely to wait for a union job opening; but this tendency decreases with the overall level of unemployment and the duration of individual unemployment.[27]

---

[25] *Franks* v. *Bowman Transportation Co.,* 424 U.S. 747 (1976).

[26] John S. Abowd and Henry S. Farber, "Job Queues and the Union Status of Workers," *Industrial and Labor Relations Review* 36 (1983), pp. 354–67.

[27] J. S. Heywood, "Who Queues for a Union Job?" *Industrial Relations* 29 (1990), pp. 119–27.

Across employers, employment in unionized jobs positively influences wage levels for both black and white males. But the effects are greater for blacks than whites and much greater for young blacks. From an overall standpoint, the proportion of unionized employment in an area depresses employment opportunities for younger workers and particularly depresses wages for young black males.[28] But the proportion of newly hired employees who are minorities is greater in unionized than comparable nonunion organizations.[29]

Employers who actively avoid unionization may attempt to screen out prounion applicants. This practice, while rare, violates Taft-Hartley. Unfair labor practice charges are most likely to be upheld where the employer is involved in an organizing campaign or is openly hostile to the union, or the applicant is applying for a skilled position. Win rates for labor dropped during the Reagan administration, however.[30]

Promotions, Transfers, and Turnover

Most contracts specify the methods for filling vacant positions requiring promotions or transfers. In nonunion organizations, unless policy or custom dictates otherwise, the employer may use any legal criterion for filling jobs.

Turnover in nonunion organizations is greater than in unionized employers with equivalent jobs. Chapter 6 suggested a relatively stable work force is necessary for a successful organizing campaign. A plausible explanation for lower turnover following unionization would be the stable base preceding it. But employers with represented work forces are no more likely than other employers to hire applicants who seem innately stable.[31] Lower turnover is probably related to the fact that wage premiums for taking a unionized job are about 3 to 8 percent, but losses from leaving one are about 7 to 11 percent.[32]

One explanation of union-nonunion differences in quit rates are contract provisions requiring promotion and transfer decisions be based

[28] Harry J. Holzer, "Unions and the Labor Market Status of White and Minority Youth," *Industrial and Labor Relations Review* 35 (1982), pp. 392–405.

[29] Jonathon S. Leonard, "The Effect of Unions on the Employment of Blacks, Hispanics, and Women," *Industrial and Labor Relations Review* 39 (1985), pp. 115–32.

[30] T. L. Leap, W. H. Hendrix, R. S. Cantrell, and G. S. Taylor, "Discrimination against Prounion Job Applicants," *Industrial Relations* 29 (1990), pp. 469–78.

[31] Richard B. Freeman, "The Effect of Unionism on Worker Attachment to Firms," *Journal of Labor Research* 1 (1980), pp. 29–61.

[32] J. D. Cunningham and E. Donovan, "Patterns of Union Membership and Relative Wages," *Journal of Labor Research* 7 (1986), pp. 127–44.

on seniority. The degree to which contracts require giving weight to seniority in job assignments is associated with lower turnover rates.[33] Collective bargaining also provides employees with a voice in the operation of the organization. With grievance procedures and contract negotiations, employees can change conditions they judge unsatisfactory. Without collective bargaining, an employee must leave the organization to escape unsatisfactory conditions.[34]

When employees have grievances with their employers in nonunion organizations without established procedures for resolution, the employee must accept the employer's unilateral action or leave (assuming the action was not unlawful). In a unionized situation, the employee is entitled to due process, and the grievance might be allowed. Any lag in the grievance process will extend tenure until the grievance is finally decided against the employee. Other inducements to stay in an organized firm relate to anticipated progress in the next round of negotiations and perceptions about the likelihood of vacancies for which the individual can qualify through seniority.[35]

Unionization does not change layoff and discharge likelihoods, but laid-off unionized employees are much less likely to quit while awaiting recall than are nonunion employees.[36] Thus, in the absence of supplemental unemployment benefit packages, unionized employers should have a cost advantage—recall costs are lower because of fewer vacancies and training of new employees. Management can store labor for future demand at relatively minimal costs.[37]

Seniority provisions may also result from management attention toward the interests of senior bargaining unit members (they are much more likely to be represented on negotiating committees than are junior members) and away from the impact of the external labor market on the establishment of employment policy. Thus, where cost differences are not significant and the experience of senior employees is related to productivity, negotiated seniority clauses may benefit both the employer and longer-tenure employees. Bargaining unit members are probably more willing to ratify contracts with significant benefits for seniority, because many of them will likely have longer seniority if turnover in union situations is less; unionized employees may also anticipate achieving these benefits in later years.

[33] Richard N. Block, "The Impact of Seniority Provisions on the Manufacturing Quit Rate," *Industrial and Labor Relations Review* 31 (1978), pp. 474–88.

[34] Richard B. Freeman, "Individual Mobility and Union Voice in the Labor Market," *American Economic Review* 67 (1976), pp. 361–68.

[35] Freeman, "Effect of Unionism."

[36] Ibid.

[37] James R. Medoff, "Layoffs and Alternatives under Trade Unions in U.S. Manufacturing," *American Economic Review* 70 (1979), pp. 380–95.

If seniority clauses actually create opportunities for senior employees, tracking employees over time should demonstrate that union members have more internal job changes than nonunion employees. One study found quit rates for white union members were substantially below those of nonunion employees, and transfer and promotion rates were significantly higher. Almost all union members who had been with the same employer for more than 10 years had made at least one internal job change. Education was negatively related with a bargaining unit promotion but positively related to a promotion out of the bargaining unit. Promotions are more likely with more seniority in unionized situations, while they are less in nonunion employment. Unlike the nonunion situations in which women were less likely to receive promotions, gender made no differences in situations where employees were represented.[38]

Retirement Programs

While retirement benefits are a wage issue, the age of retirement takes on a nonwage flavor for the individual (even though it has an economic consequence for the employer). In the past, a single retirement age of 65 was established across most organizations and within most occupations, but these age rules have changed. For example, the 1979 UAW agreement with the automakers provided that an individual could retire after accumulating 30 years of service (25 in foundries) regardless of age. Although past contracts have specified mandatory retirement at age 65, no new contracts may be negotiated requiring retirement at any specific age, given the amendments to the Age Discrimination in Employment Act. Thus, employees in the auto industry could choose to retire as early as age 43 (with 25 years in foundry operations) and could not be forced to retire.

Early retirement decisions appear to be strongly influenced by the retiree's economic expectations and general health. The better the expectations and the worse the health, the more likely the individual is to retire early.[39] Married men plan to retire earlier when they expect larger pensions from both private and public sources, when their pensions have a known benefit level, when they are homeowners, when they have earned relatively higher wages, when they are in poorer health, and when they work in jobs where the retirement age was compulsory.[40]

[38] Craig A. Olson and Chris J. Berger, "The Relationship between Seniority, Ability, and the Promotion of Union and Nonunion Workers," in *Advances in Industrial and Labor Relations*, ed. David B. Lipsky and Joel M. Douglas (Greenwich, Conn.: JAI Press, 1983), pp. 1, 91–129.

[39] Richard Barfield and James Morgan, *Early Retirement: The Decision and the Experience* (Ann Arbor, Mich.: Survey Research Center, University of Michigan, 1969).

[40] Arden Hall and Terry R. Johnson, "The Determinants of Planned Retirement," *Industrial and Labor Relations Review* 33 (1980), pp. 241–54.

As benefit levels increase and as retirement decisions cover a range of time periods rather than a particular date, greater retirement planning by individuals and organizations is probable.[41] Many contracts offer social security, private pension benefits, and tax advantages that, when combined, impose an actual cash penalty on one who continues to work after eligibility for social security begins.

Job Satisfaction

The evidence surrounding the effect of union membership on job satisfaction is not at all clear-cut. Chapter 6 pointed out that dissatisfaction was a significant predictor of a vote for the union during organizing campaigns.[42] Receiving the benefits that a union might gain is expected to relate to increased job satisfaction, but a large-scale cross-sectional study found that job satisfaction of union members was lower than of nonunion employees when other variables were held constant.[43]

Job satisfaction increases for union members whose jobs change as the result of a transfer or promotion but not from a turnover. The reverse was found for nonunion employees: their satisfaction increased with turnover and did not change as the result of internal job movements.[44]

A cross-sectional study of a national sample found overall job satisfaction of unionized employees was somewhat lower than among nonunion employees; but results varied when facets of satisfaction were compared. Union members were more satisfied with their pay because they received more and because they valued pay outcomes more than nonunion employees did. Promotion satisfaction was also greater, largely because union members place lower value on promotions than other union achievements. This result can be partially accounted for by relatively lower pay differentials among jobs in unionized situations. Union members were less satisfied with supervisors and co-workers, largely through lower perceptions of supervisory behavior. They were also less satisfied with their jobs, largely as the result of lower job scope (or less varied tasks)

---

[41] For an example of the types of information that are combined to make retirement decisions for U.S. Naval officers (who generally may retire across a 10-year span), see Donald F. Parker and Lee Dyer, "Expectancy Theory as a Within-Person Behavioral Choice Model: An Empirical Test of Some Conceptual and Methodological Refinements," *Organizational Behavior and Human Performance* 17 (1976), pp. 97–117.

[42] Julius G. Getman, Stephen B. Goldberg, and Jeanne B. Herman, *Union Representation Elections: Law and Reality* (New York: Russell Sage Foundation, 1976), pp. 53–57.

[43] Richard B. Freeman, "Job Satisfaction as an Economic Variable," *American Economic Review* 69 (1978), pp. 135–41.

[44] Olson and Berger, "Relationship between Seniority."

than for nonunion employees.[45] Unions could influence the satisfaction level of employees toward supervisors and the job if they point out those features as potential sources of problems the union will help employees solve. An adversarial position might be necessary to create the need for continued representation.

Commitment to the Union

Several studies have examined the influence of commitment to an employer and its relationship to turnover.[46] The measurement of commitment to a union and the effects of commitment on behavior have also been examined. Commitment to a union is reflected in the desire to remain a member, the willingness to exert effort on behalf of the union, and the belief in and acceptance of union goals and values. Where membership is voluntary, commitment to the union appeared related to early involvement and socialization in union activities and continued participation. Satisfied union members are also more likely to be satisfied with management, although the union is seen as more important among less-satisfied employees.[47] Commitment to the union appears related, in order, to the following factors: loyalty, responsibility to the union, willingness to work for the union, and belief in unionism.[48]

During the 1980s, many local unions went through major crises with reductions in membership as plants closed or substantial layoffs occurred. Commitment to the union was positively related to the severity of job loss, indicating an increase in cohesion during a crisis. At the same time, satisfaction with both the company and the union was more likely to decline in situations where severe job loss occurred.[49]

---

[45] Chris J. Berger, Craig A. Olson, and John W. Boudreau, "Effects of Unions on Job Satisfaction: The Role of Work-Related Values and Perceived Rewards," *Organizational Behavior and Human Performance* 32 (1983), pp. 289–324; for additional confirmatory evidence, see Susan Schwochau, "Union Effects on Job Attitudes," *Industrial and Labor Relations Review* 40 (1987), pp. 209–34.

[46] Richard T. Mowday, Richard M. Steers, and Lyman W. Porter, *Employee-Organizational Linkages: The Psychology of Commitment, Absenteeism, and Turnover* (New York: Academic Press, 1982).

[47] Michael E. Gordon, John W. Philpot, Robert E. Burt, Cynthia A. Thompson, and William E. Spiller, "Commitment to the Union: Development of a Measure and an Examination of Its Correlates," *Journal of Applied Psychology* 65 (1980), pp. 479–99.

[48] Robert T. Ladd, Michael E. Gordon, Laura L. Beauvais, and Richard L. Morgan, "Union Commitment: Replication and Extension," *Journal of Applied Psychology* 67 (1982), pp. 640–44.

[49] S. Mellor, "The Relationship between Membership Decline and Union Commitment: A Field Study of Local Unions in Crisis," *Journal of Applied Psychology* 75 (1990), pp. 258–67.

Commitment to the union and to the employer has been demonstrated to be independent. Simultaneous (dual) commitment to the employer and the union has been found to be related to both individual differences[50] and a positive labor relations climate.[51] Commitment is also higher where employees perceive they have greater job influence and an active dual labor-management program is operating.[52] Union stewards were found to have dual commitment, but generally higher commitment to the union than the employer. Commitment to the employer was predicted by tenure; perceptions of immobility, supervisor support, promotion opportunities, and influence on the employer; and employment in smaller establishments. Union commitment was related to perceived immobility, belief that the union should use grievances to punish the employer, involvement in union activities and decision making, and employment in larger establishments. High dual commitment was predicted by involvement in union decision making, perceived immobility and influence on the employer, being a woman, and being unskilled. Unilateral commitment to the union was predicted by low economic outcomes, perceived involvement in the union, and lack of support from the employer.[53]

SUMMARY

Nonwage issues in contracts are related primarily to hours of work, lengths of contracts, management rights, union security, and seniority provisions. All of these have economic consequences for the employer and represented employees.

Hours of work issues primarily relate to establishment of the length of the workday, entitlements to overtime, shift assignments, and the number of days worked during given periods. Evidence suggests employers may prefer innovative schedules with fewer days and longer hours in some operations.

Management rights clauses spell out those areas in which manage-

---

[50] Cynthia V. Fukami and Erik W. Larson, "Commitment to Company and Union: Parallel Models," *Journal of Applied Psychology* 69 (1984), pp. 367–71.

[51] Harold L. Angle and James L. Perry, "Dual Commitment and Labor-Management Climates," *Academy of Management Journal* 29 (1986), pp. 31–50.

[52] P. D. Sherer and M. Morishima, "Roads and Roadblocks to Dual Commitment: Similar and Dissimilar Antecedents of Union and Company Commitment," *Journal of Labor Research* 10 (1989), pp. 311–30.

[53] James E. Martin, John M. Magenau, and Mark F. Peterson, "Variables Related to Patterns of Union Stewards' Commitment," *Journal of Labor Research* 7 (1986), pp. 323–36.

ment exercises decision-making control. It also establishes the right of the employer to make and enforce reasonable rules. Grievance and arbitration clauses provide due process rules when bargaining unit members disagree with management's interpretation and operation of the contract.

Union security clauses provide requirements related to dues payment and membership in the union. Union shops require all bargaining unit members to belong to the union, while agency-shop agreements require nonmembers as well as members to pay dues.

Seniority provisions establish entitlements to benefits (benefit status) and employment (competitive status). Benefit status seniority usually dates from hire, while competitive status seniority may begin on entry in a particular job or department. Most contracts use seniority as the prime consideration in deciding layoffs and promotions. Seniority provisions may hurt minorities and women during layoffs.

DISCUSSION QUESTIONS

1. Is it to the organization's advantage to enjoy the lower turnover rates that unionization seems to include?
2. Why would union officials likely oppose flexible work hours and other innovative work schedules?
3. What potential problems and benefits are likely with early or flexible retirement programs?
4. Should either unions or managements be concerned with the apparently little effect of higher economic outcomes on overall union member satisfaction?

KEY TERMS

management rights clauses
grievance procedures
wildcat strikes
union security
closed shop
union shop
modified union shop

agency shop
maintenance of membership
checkoff
benefit status seniority
competitive status seniority
bumping
constructive seniority

C A S E
GMFC Attitude Survey

GFMC is a member of the Heritage Group, a consortium of employers with personnel research departments who participate in employment studies and share information. All members agreed this year to administer the same attitude surveys to their employees and relate the measures to variables such as turnover and productivity. To gain agreement in Central City, GMFC agreed to share the results of the survey and the broader study with Local 384. In return, Local 384 urged members to complete the surveys they received.

When comparative information became available, the results shown in the table were sent to Central City.

If you were a union or management representative, what would you make of the results? What impact might this have on the potential for negotiations in the next round of contract talks?

	Satisfaction	
	Central City	**Total**
Pay	53	50
Promotions	36	50
Work itself	62	50
Supervision	27	50
Co-workers	86	50
	Turnover	
Rate per hundred	18	50

(Results are in percentiles for all participating establishments.)

10

CONTRACT
NEGOTIATIONS

The negotiation of a labor agreement is of critical importance to both parties. The agreement will govern the relationship between them for a definite contractual period. For the employer, the contract will have cost impacts and constrain management decision making. For the union, it will spell out the rights of union members in their employment relationships.

Why does a contract emerge in the form that it does? How do the parties prepare for bargaining? What influences do the rank and file or the various functional areas within an organization have on the demands made in the negotiations? How does each group organize for bargaining? What constitutes success or failure in negotiations? What sequence of activities usually takes place during negotiations?

In this chapter, the activities preceding the negotiations are examined first, from both union and management perspectives. Then the theory and tactics of the negotiating process are covered. The steps necessary for agreement and ratification are detailed. Finally, management's assessment of bargaining is examined.

In reading this chapter, consider the following questions:

1. How do both management and union prepare for negotiations?
2. How are negotiating teams constituted for bargaining?
3. What processes are usually involved in presenting and responding to demands in collective bargaining negotiations?
4. How are agreements reached, and what processes are necessary to obtain approval by the union rank and file for ratification?

Except for initial contracts and unusual financial conditions, when bargaining activities occur is largely determined by the expiration of a previous contract and the law. Under the law, if either party desires modification at expiration, it must give at least 60 days' notice. In all negotiations, the parties are required to meet at reasonable times to bargain.

Different strategies may be used across bargaining situations; however. Figure 10–1 portrays the general sequence of activities likely found in the bargaining process. The diagram lays out the basic prenegotiation activities, the proposals and responses in bargaining, and the possible outcomes of bargaining together with settlement procedures.

Both parties have some idea how they would like a new contract to be shaped. They either have taken positions during an organizing campaign or have some experience with an existing agreement. We will examine bargaining activities using Figure 10–1 as a general backdrop.

MANAGEMENT PREPARATION

Because labor is a very large share of the total cost of operating most organizations, management must be well aware of the cost implications of various contract proposals. The more heavily organized the firm, the more attention paid to contract terms. Ironically, less-organized firms should also be aware of contract implications because benefits won at the bargaining table are frequently passed on to unorganized employees.

Collective bargaining practices have been examined by the Conference Board, a group of collaborating organizations supporting business research projects.[1] The results of the board's research will be followed in examining management preparation.

Department Involvement

In heavily organized firms, the chief executive officer (CEO) generally establishes the limits for possible concessions and targets needed changes for the organization during bargaining. The top industrial relations executive is responsible for coordinating preparations for bargaining and may act as the leading management negotiator. Various functional departments contribute to preparations for bargaining and have interests in seeing certain issues pursued at the bargaining table. Production managers may be interested in work rules and costs. Marketing managers want a contract that will minimize shipping disruptions. Accounting personnel supply many of the cost figures useful for bargaining.

---

[1] Audrey Freedman, *Managing Labor Relations* (New York: Conference Board, 1979).

FIGURE 10–1
Bargaining Process Events

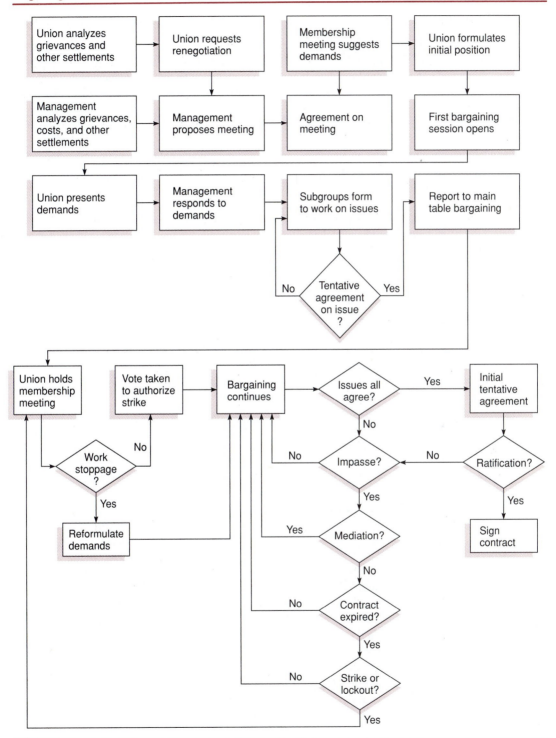

Reviewing the Expiring Contract

The expiring contract is reviewed by top management, the labor relations staff, and first-line supervisors. This review centers on contract language that contributed to cost or operating difficulties during the contract, areas in which frequent grievances were encountered, the results of arbitration over unresolved grievances, current practices not covered in the contract, and other contract supplements that affect operations.

Preparing Data for Negotiations

Pay and benefit data are necessary and include relevant comparisons, such as rates paid within the industry, local labor market rates for occupations governed by the agreement, settlements gained by unions known as pattern setters, and changes in cost-of-living figures since the last negotiations.

The characteristics of the employer's work force in terms of seniority, age, sex, job classification, shift, and race are important. Because entitlement to many benefits is related to seniority, an increasingly senior work force will incur higher benefit costs, even without an increase in benefit levels in a given negotiation. For example, if entitlement to vacations increases from two to three weeks after five years' service, a work force that had 200 employees with three years' seniority at the beginning of a three-year agreement would have 200 with six years at the end (assuming no turnover). This change in seniority would mean an increase of 200 weeks of vacation at the end of the agreement. Possible implications include paying for 200 unworked weeks and hiring four more employees to work the lost production time. Knowing the number of persons on each shift allows consideration of demands for shift differentials and their costs.

Internal economic data—such as the cost of benefits, participation in discretionary benefit plans (recreation, etc.), overall earnings levels, and the amount and cost of overtime—are important. Management prefers broadly used benefits because they improve employees' perceptions of the competitiveness of the compensation program. Competitive overall earning levels are important because some employee groups may feel underpaid. For example, skilled trades employees in industrial plants earn less per hour than their counterparts in contract construction, but they are laid off less frequently for weather or lack of work and thus may have higher gross earnings.

Legal requirements are scrutinized. While minimum wage increases would seldom affect a unionized situation, an employer also tracks the implications of other employment law modifications. For example, social security tax increases raise costs without wage increases.[2] Changes in equal employment opportunity laws and regulations may also suggest that employers negotiate changes in promotion and transfer procedures.

An examination of the union's negotiation and ratification procedures is important. The bargaining team needs to know how the union signals concessions and how it drops demands during the process. The length of time necessary for ratification and whether the union usually works after contract expiration are important from a time deadline standpoint.

Information regarding the organization's current level of operations and anticipated future changes will be important in assessing bargaining power on certain issues. For example, if little inventory is available and customer orders have increased recently but customers have different sources available for similar products and services, then a strike might be disastrous.

Identification of Probable Union Demands

Using information from grievances under the expiring contract and feedback from first-line supervision, management may be able to assess the likelihood of certain demands and the likely tenacity of the union during bargaining. In large companies where national-level negotiations will occur, attention to union bargaining conventions should inform management about the issues to which the union has committed itself. Other pattern settlements should offer clues to management.

Costing the Contract

As noted in Chapter 7, the wages and fringe benefits included in the ultimate settlement have a definite cost impact for the organization. To make rational choices among possible demands and to counteroffer with an acceptable package minimizing its costs, management must accurately cost contract demands.

A variety of costing methods can be used. Some are more sophisticated than others. A good example of a relatively simple approach highlighting many of the issues is portrayed in Table 10–1.[3] This example shows some of the important dynamics in long-term contracts. For example, social security tax rates and taxable bases may change during the

---

[2] Thomas A. Mahoney, "The Real Cost of a Wage Increase," *Personnel*, May–June 1967, pp. 22–32.

[3] Reed C. Richardson, "Positive Collective Bargaining," in *Handbook of Personnel and Industrial Relations*, ed. Dale Yoder and H. G. Heneman, Jr. (Washington, D.C.: Bureau of National Affairs, 1979), pp. 7–127 to 7–129.

TABLE 10–1

Costing Out Changes in Contract Terms

Changes in costs	Increased Cost
1. Direct payroll—annual	
Straight-time earnings—36¢ per hour general increase; 100 employees × 2,080 hours × 36¢	$ 74,800
Premium earnings—second shift established differential—10¢ per hour; 30 employees 2,080 hours × 10¢	6,240
Overtime—overtime cost increased by increased straight-time rate—average straight-time rate increases 39¢; 39¢ × 12,000 overtime hours × .5 overtime rate	2,340
Bonus	None
Other direct payroll cost increases	None
Total increase in direct payroll costs	$ 83,460
2. Added costs directly resulting from higher payroll costs— annual F.I.C.A.—5.85 times increase in average straight-time earnings below $9,000 annual; 100 employees × 36¢ × 5.85% × 2,080 hours	$ 4,380.48
Federal and state unemployment insurance tax—Number of employees × 4,200 × 2.5% tax rate	No change
Workers' compensation (total cost or estimate)	No change
Other	No change
Total additional direct payroll costs	$ 4,380.48
3. Nonpayroll costs—annual	
Insurance—company portion	
Health insurance	No change
Dental insurance	None
Eye care	None
Life insurance—added employer contribution, $100 per year; $100 × 100 employees	$ 10,000
Pension costs—fully vested pension reduced from 25 years and age 65 to 20 years and age 62	
Estimated additional cost	52,000
Miscellaneous	
Tuition reimbursement (addition)	600
Service rewards	No change
Suggestion awards (addition)	350
Loss on employee cafeteria	No change
Overtime meals	No change
Cost of parking lots	No change
Company parties	No change
Personal tools	No change
Personal safety equipment (addition)	1,200
Personal wearing apparel	No change
Profit sharing	No change
Other	No change
Total additional nonpayroll costs—annual	$ 64,150
4a. Changes in nonwork paid time	
Holidays—2 new holidays added to 6 already in contract; 100 employees × 8 hours × 2 holidays × $3.96 average new wage	$ 6,336

TABLE 10–1
(concluded)

Changes in costs	Increased Cost
Vacation—new category added—4 weeks (160 hours annual vacation) with 20 or more years service—former top was 3 weeks after 15 years. Average number of employees affected annually: 15 employees × 40 hours @ $3.96 average new wage	2,376
Paid lunch time—paid ½ lunch time added to contract; 100 employees × ½ hour × 236 days worked yearly × $3.96 average new wage	$ 46,728
Paid wash-up time	None
Coffee breaks	No change
Paid time off for union activity—new 1 hour per week per shop steward; 10 shop stewards × $4.20 shop steward average new wage × 1 hour × 52 weeks	2,184
Paid sick leave	None
Paid time off over and above worker's compensation paid time	None
Jury service time off—no change	None
Funeral leave time off—no change	None
Paid time off for safety or training—no change	None
Other	None
Total change in hours paid for but not worked—annual	$ 57,624

4b. Financial data derived from costing out (Items 1–4, above)

	Increased Cost
Total increase in contract costs: Item 1 + Item 2 + Item 3	$151,990
Average total increase in contract costs per employee payroll hour: Item 1 + Item 2 + Item 3 ÷ 2,080 hours	.73
Average total increase in direct payroll cost per labor-hour: Item 1 + Item 2 ÷ 2,080 hours ÷ 100 employees	.422
Average total increase in nonpayroll costs per payroll-hour per employee: Item 3 ÷ 2,080 hours ÷ 100 employees	.308
Average total increase in nonwork paid time expense per payroll-hour per employee: Item 4 ÷ 100 employees	.277
Average total increase in direct payroll costs per productive (worked) hour per employee: Item 1 + Item 2 ÷ 1,888 hours ÷ 100 employees	.49
Average total increase in nonpayroll costs per productive (worked) hour per employee: Item 3 ÷ 1,888 hours ÷ 100 employees	.34

SOURCE: Reed C. Richardson, "Positive Collective Bargaining," in *Handbook of Personnel and Industrial Relations*, ed. Dale Yoder and H. G. Heneman Jr. (Washington, D.C.: U.S. Bureau of National Affairs, 1979), pp. 7-127 to 7-129.

term of the contract. Unemployment insurance rates may increase or decline, depending on the economy and a firm's individual layoff rate.

The cost implications of certain contract terms are not straightforward and must be examined closely to capture the real cost impacts.[4]

---

[4] Michael H. Granof, *How to Cost Your Labor Contract* (Washington, D.C.: Bureau of National Affairs, 1973).

First, many firms do not closely track the "roll-up," or amount by which overtime and wage-tied fringes are increased by changes in the base rate. Second, overtime premiums greater than required by law should cause the firm to consider how controllable its overtime hours are and the degree to which labor cost increases can be passed on to customers. Third, the cost of vacations and holidays are seldom critically examined. For example, vacations for maintenance employees may be essentially costless if their work is postponable and if an excess of staff can accomplish it. On the other hand, production employees' vacations may require scheduling overtime, thereby increasing vacation costs by the premium rate, or hiring an equivalent number of full-time employees. Fourth, relief time may cost more if it is broken up in short periods—some time may be necessary to begin the break and then return to work. This slippage will require adding more employees to sustain production volume.[5]

Benefits costing also poses problems for organizations. Pension costs depend not only on a defined contribution requirement in some cases (for example, 5 percent of base wages) but also on experience factors, vesting (personal ownership of benefits) requirements, and possible defined benefit levels at retirement. For example, if the contract provided for vesting of benefits after five years of service but only 20 percent of employees ever accrue five years, the cost of the pension would be far less than the 5 percent of base wages used in the example. Health insurance is generally negotiated to provide a certain level of benefits (for example, all hospital and physician expenses up to $100,000 annually with $250 deductible). Unfortunately, organizations have little control over the premium charged for the benefits. Thus, their future costs can only be estimated.[6]

Organizations may not closely evaluate the costs of salary increases during the term of the agreement. For example, given interest rates and the total amount paid out, agreeing to a wage demand for increases of 50 cents, 50 cents, and 75 cents over a three-year agreement might cost the company less than giving 90 cents, 40 cents, and 30 cents. In the former case, the total increase is $1.75, while the latter is $1.60. But in the former case, an employee would earn 50 cents per hour more for three years ($1.50), 50 cents more for two years ($1.00), and 75 cents more for one year—a total of $3.25 more over the contract period. In the latter case, the employee would get 90 cents more for three years ($2.70), 40 cents for two years ($.80), and 30 cents for one year—a total of $3.80. But postponing increases to give a larger total increase during the agreement raises the base wage rate for subsequent negotiations.[7] Management should also consider the costs of wages and fringe benefits that will be granted to nonunion employees to preserve wage differentials and equity.

---

[5] Ibid., pp. 55–56.

[6] Ibid., pp. 60–69.

[7] Ibid., pp. 83–126.

A detailed example of costing contract demands is given in the introduction to the negotiating exercise at the end of this chapter. Whatever method is used for costing should allow management to calculate the effects of various union proposals quickly and provide a true estimate of their financial ramifications.

Negotiation Objectives and the Bargaining Team

Contract objectives should support the goals of the organization. For example, if production disruptions are to be avoided, clauses providing for arbitration of grievances that cannot be mutually resolved in return for no-strike agreements will serve this purpose. If cost certainty is important, avoiding fringe benefits and cost-of-living clauses and including **gainsharing,** profit sharing, and/or piece-rate pay plans provide a path to these ends. Exhibit 10–1 is an example of management objectives and preferences in bargaining.

Bargaining team members often represent areas of particular interest in the contract (for example, production) or have expertise in specific negotiated areas (for example, employee benefits manager). The leader of management's team is frequently the top industrial relations executive of the organization. The CEO may delegate responsibilities for negotiating the contract but may also retain authority to approve the ultimate agreement.

Bargaining Books

A **bargaining book** is a cross-referenced file enabling a negotiator to quickly determine what contract clauses would be affected by a demand. The book contains a general history of specific contract terms and a code to indicate the proposals' relative importance to management. Many bargaining books are now automated and tied to spreadsheets so "what if" questions can be answered, and the cost implications of demands and concessions can be rapidly calculated. Following is information likely to be contained for each clause:

1. The history and text of the particular clause as it was negotiated in successive agreements.
2. Comparisons of the company's experience with that of other companies in the industry, including comments on similarities and differences.
3. The company's experience with the clause, both in operation and in the grievances.
4. Legal issues pertaining to the clause, including both NLRB determinations and judicial decisions.

EXHIBIT 10-1

Extracts from Bituminous Coal Operators' Association Bargaining Statement

TODAY'S REALITY FOR UMWA-NATIONAL COAL AGREEMENT

1981 negotiations between the UMWA and the BCOA for a new National Bituminous Coal Wage Agreement come at a time when the reality of today's depressed economic conditions, particularly in that sector of the coal industry covered by the UMWA-National Agreement, falls far short of tomorrow's promise for the coal industry as America's growing energy source of the future.

- Over 20,000 miners are laid off.
- Many mines have closed, and more are expected to close.
- At least 100 million tons of annual production capacity lies idle for lack of a market, and most of that idle capacity is in the eastern half of the United States where most UMWA-National Agreement mines are located.

And there are no signs that these crippling conditions, especially in the UMWA-National Agreement sector of the industry, are likely to change very quickly.

*   *   *   *   *

LOW PRODUCTIVITY

The biggest reason for the failure of the UMWA-National Agreement segment of the industry to participate in the growth of the total coal market is the heavy cost burden that low productivity imposes on coal produced under the UMWA-National Agreement. Unless corrective steps are taken now to reduce this cost, coal mined under the UMWA-National Agreement cannot compete effectively in the coal market.

From 1969 to 1979, the United States experienced a period of continuing gains in industrial productivity. Every major industry enjoyed the benefits of a productivity increase; every industry, that is, except one—the coal industry.

If coal from UMWA-National Agreement mines is going to compete in the marketplace with coal from the rest of the industry, it is essential that we get our productivity back where it once was, and improve each year as other industries do. The market world will not pay for our noncompetitive costs. As we negotiate a new UMWA-National Agreement, we are in a position to take major steps toward correcting the situation. The present agreement has many provisions that contribute nothing to the well-being of the coal miner, but do stand in the way of increased productivity, such as those that:

- Restrict full use of expensive equipment in continuous operations.
- Allow employees too much lateral and downward job bidding.
- Restrict use of new employees on equipment.
- Permit largely unrestricted use of paid days off.
- Encourage featherbedding.

*   *   *   *   *

(concluded)

LABOR INSTABILITY

Another major reason, which cannot be overlooked, that has contributed greatly to the erosion of the UMWA-National Agreement share of the coal market has been labor instability—wildcat strikes.

HIGH EMPLOYMENT COSTS

In 1970, the coal miner's earnings were 41 percent higher than the earnings of workers in other industries. By 1980, however, the gap between the coal miner and other workers had widened to a full 63 percent difference in favor of the coal miner.

SOURCE: *Daily Labor Report*, January 13, 1981, pp. F1–F8.

5. Points the company would like to have changed with regard to the clause, differentiated into minimum, maximum, and intermediate possibilities.

6. Points the union may have asked for in the past with regard to changes in the clause, the union's justification for the proposed change, and the arguments used by mangement to rebut the union's position.

7. Data and exhibits with regard to the clause, including cost and supporting analysis.

8. Progress with regard to the clause in the current negotiation, together with drafts of various company proposals.[8]

Strike Preparation

As noted, anticipation of a strike or the reduction of vulnerability to a strike may substantially improve managment's bargaining power. The organization also needs to plan how it will handle a potentially disruptive situation, particularly if it expects to continue operations.

The organizations must determine the costs and benefits of remaining in operation in case of a strike. Labor relations will undoubtedly be troublesome after a contract is negotiated, particularly if replacements have been hired. Additional security may be required, and picket-line observation will be important. Suppliers, customers, and government agencies will require notification if a strike occurs. For important customers, alternative methods of supply—including supply through competitors—may be necessary.

---

[8] Meyer S. Ryder, Charles M. Rehmus, and Sanford Cohen, *Management Preparation for Bargaining* (Homewood, Ill.: Dow Jones-Irwin, 1966), pp. 65–66.

Strategy and Logistics

Finally, the strategies to be used to move toward an agreement must be constructed. Questions about who has the power to make concessions and the final positions beyond which management will not go must be answered.

A place to hold bargaining meetings must be arranged. If meetings will be held off the organization's premises, questions regarding costs must be resolved before commencing negotiations. The union will probably prefer a neutral site, given the evidence (explored later in this chapter) that concessions are more difficult for the company to make on its home ground. Table 10–2 is an example of the time frames and functions involved in preparations for negotiations.

Union Preparation

To an extent, union preparations parallel those of management's, but important distinctions exist. Traditionally, unions see contract negotiations as an event that should lead to an improvement in their outcomes. Politically, leaders are expected to gain ground or face problems from the membership. The union may not be as well prepared for possible management demands as management is for union demands, especially if the national union is not involved in the negotiations.

National-Level Activities

Research departments in national unions track settlements in contract negotiations. Research is also done to assess the employers' ability to improve economic terms of contracts.

The ability of union members to take strikes is assessed. If the union has been involved in a long strike during recent negotiations, it may not have the resources to provide subsistence strike benefits for a long strike in the present negotiations. The national must also consider the target company's ability to withstand a strike and its vulnerability to competition.

If the negotiations involve many units of a single company or are conducted on an industry-wide basis, the national is usually responsible for negotiating economic issues. The bargaining team usually comprises national officers and officers of some key locals.

Before commencing negotiations, the national union may call a **bargaining convention** at which delegates from the local unions hear the national's plans for bargaining and propose their own issues. The bargaining convention has two major purposes. First, the rank and file are heard, thus fulfilling the grass-roots political requirements for involvement in

TABLE 10–2 Management Planning for Contract Negotiations

	8 to 12 Months before Contract Expires	4 to 8 Months	1 to 4 Months before Commencement of Negotiations	During Negotiations	Postnegotiations
Local unit management	1. Assigns responsibilities for community surveys estimating union demands and employee attitude. 2. Assesses the total corporate community and union compensation/benefit plans. 3. Assesses union/employee motivation and goals for impending negotiations.	1. Division management, corporate E.R., and corporate insurance project alternate benefit proposals that are to be designed and costed. 2. Continues all steps in the planning process.	1. Secures division approval of strategy, negotiating plans, and cost estimates.	1. Continues negotiations, clears significant cost variances from plan and division management. 2. Integrates benefit negotiations with all other items. 3. Secures agreement in accord with plan. 4. Agrees with union on method and expense to inform employees of new contract terms.	1. Evaluates previous negotiations against plan within 30 days. 2. Assigns responsibilities for the planning process so as to integrate with the division's plans. 3. Identifies tentative objectives for next contract. 4. Completes wage/benefit adjustment form.
Division headquarters management	1. Assures local unit is preparing for negotiations. 2. Plans through annual financial plan projects impact of inventory build-up. Possible settlement costs, etc. 3. Identifies internal responsibilities and relationships (corporate, law, E.R. insurance, benefits, etc.). 4. Keeps corporate employee relations informed.	1. Coordinates the development of strategy and negotiating plan, consulting with corporate employee relations and benefits. 2. Develops with local management, corporate E.R., and insurance projects alternative benefit proposals that are to be designed and costed. 3. Makes broad judgment on impact of company and expected proposals in relation to division and corporate goals, strategy, and plans. 4. Evaluates plans to control costs and deviations from plan/strategy.	1. Approves negotiating plan strategy. 2. Clears benefit and corporate policy variances from plan with corporate employee relations. 3. Communicates progress to senior management and corporate employee relations. 4. Approves cost variances from plan. 5. Identifies strike issues.	1. Provides in addition to those points in "1 to 4 months" column, identification of "end" position and supports local negotiators in maintaining such position.	1. Evaluates all aspects of the previous negotiations within 45 days. 2. Identifies and communicates all long-range needs to executive management and corporate employee relations. 3. Integrates planning process in the division growth plan.
Corporate employee relations	1. Advises division and local management of union's national position on economics, benefits, and other issues. 2. Counsels on any anticipated conflict with corporate policy, other divisions, etc. 3. Provides available historical information pertinent to planning.	1. Assists division, local management, and corporate insurance in projecting and preparing alternate benefit proposals that are to be designed and costed. 2. Keeps division and local unit informed of any external developments having impact on its planning.	1. Consults with division on strategy and plans; available for on-the-scene assistance or to consult with internal union officers; recommends corporate point of view on issues. 2. Approves all variances from corporate personnel policy and benefit plan proposals. 3. Assures that all issues are resolved at the required levels.	1. Provides same as "1 to 4 months" column. 2. Identifies to division management potential problems having corporate impact; if necessary, advises corporate management of unresolved major issues.	1. Counsels with union and/or unit management on negotiating experiences and/or evaluation of new contract. 2. Informs other units of results. 3. Initiates needed objectives for study, policy change, or corporate decision.
Corporate law department	1. Counsels on request.	1. Counsels on request and reviews current contract as required. 2. Approves benefit plan drafts to assure legal compliance.	1. Counsels and drafts contract language on request. 2. Makes counsel available to review contract language before signing.	1. Provides same as "1 to 4 months" column.	1. Reviews new contracts for possible problems; advises division and corporate employee relations.

SOURCE: Audrey Freedman, *Managing Labor Relations* (New York: Conference Board, 1979), p. 24. Copyright © The Conference Board, 1979, used by permission.

the creation of bargaining issues. Second, the union leadership has a forum for publicly committing itself to certain bargaining positions. This commitment strengthens the union's bargaining power, because conceding these committed issues later at the bargaining table will be more difficult.

If the local will carry the major role in bargaining, the national will supply a representative to assist and to ensure that the local negotiates a contract consistent with the national's interest. Exhibit 10–2 is an example of how one national recently opened negotiations.

Local-Level Preparations

At the local level, the negotiating committee is usually elected with the other officers and has responsibility for negotiating contracts and processing grievances. The committee reaches some conclusions about portions of the contract (for example, allocation of overtime) susceptible to more than one interpretation or viewed as inequitable by the membership.

Locals are also served by the national union's field representatives. As a result, members learn about settlements reached by other locals in the same national. They also learn which issues the national considers critically important to include in all contracts.

The employer's performance (in terms of profitability, sales, and so on) is known if the employer is publicly owned and may be used by the union to gauge the level of its economic demands. However, in companies that participate in several industries (e.g., USX is involved in both steel making and petroleum exploration, production, and marketing), the relative contributions of each division may be difficult to separate. The union also knows the perishability of the employer's products, its competition, and its ability to operate during a strike. The union may also be aware of industry trends to move plants to other geographic regions and the likelihood the company would introduce labor-replacing equipment if high economic demands were won.

Local unions hold membership meetings before the negotiations to inform the membership about important issues and to solicit more input. These meetings also help determine local members' commitment to bargaining issues in case a strike is called.

After negotiations are under way, the union usually calls another membership meeting. The negotiating committee reports on bargaining progress and requests authorization to call a strike if necessary, which traditionally receives overwhelming approval. This vote does not mean a strike *will* occur but rather the bargainers have the authority to call one after the contract expires.

EXHIBIT 10–2

Push for COLAs for UAW Retirees in Auto Talks Accepted by Bieber

In a reversal of long-standing union policy, UAW President Owen Bieber told delegates to the union's bargaining convention last week that he is not averse to seeking cost-of-living increases for retirees when national contract talks with the Big Three automakers begin this summer.

However, a key union pension specialist said Bieber would pursue a modified inflation-protection measure rather than full-blown COLAs.

Speaking May 22 to more than 2,000 delegates gathered to help devise the union's bargaining strategy for upcoming auto talks, Bieber said language contained in the UAW's booklet of proposed resolutions does not prohibit an attempt to win expensive COLA provisions for the union's retirees. "I take great pride in being able to say that the UAW is the one single union in this country that has never forgotten its current and future retirees," Bieber said.

The labor leader's lukewarm COLA endorsement for retirees came after a convention-floor challenge regarding language included in the 120-page bargaining resolutions booklet. Bieber referred to two generally worded paragraphs on pensions that called for contract improvements for retirees. The challenge centered on whether the section specifically called for cost-of-living adjustments for pensioners. The most controversial paragraph read:

> To achieve these objectives we must improve our normal and early retirement programs, bargain increases in basic benefits and supplements for both current and new retirees and provide additional benefits to protect and maintain their purchasing power against increases in the cost of living.

SOURCE: *Labor Relations Week*, May 30, 1990, p. 515.

Effects of Union Characteristics on Bargaining Outcomes

Bargaining outcomes could be influenced by such union characteristics as size, union democracy, complexity, propensity for striking, involvement in political activities, level of dues, recent success in organizing relative to the total size of its membership, and the diversity of the workers it represents. When a variety of other characteristics is controlled, wage rates in negotiated agreements appear influenced by national control of the content of bargaining, less control of the bargaining process by the national, smaller sizes of locals in the national union, local union autocracy, membership diversity, little recent organizing, and higher dues. Higher job security outcomes result from smaller national unions, more involvement of the national in the bargaining process, higher salary levels of union officers, political activity, lower complexity, and lower dues. Overall union democracy is related to higher job security and lower wages. Higher outcomes occur when the union has a relatively small number of large locals organized in several industries. Strikes may enhance outcomes, but present attention to organizing and political activity is related to lower outcomes.[9]

Negotiation Requests

Section 8(d) of the Taft-Hartley Act requires the party desiring a renegotiation of the contract (usually the union) to notify the other party of its intention and to offer to bargain a new agreement. Notice must come at least 60 days before the end of the contract if the requesting party intends to terminate the agreement at that time.

Management's usual reply is to propose a time—usually not immediate—and place for negotiations to begin. This often means the initial demands are not being made until a month or less before the expiration date. After notice is served, both parties commence last-minute preparations for bargaining.

What is Bargaining?

Several academic disciplines have studied bargaining. Following is a description of bargaining or negotiating from an economic perspective:

1. Negotiation occurs if both parties will benefit by an agreement. In labor-management relations, the employer benefits by continued operations and the union benefits by better conditions for its members.

2. Concessions made during the negotiations are voluntary. The concessions, in number and degree, may be influenced by the magnitude of the demands and the opponent's beliefs about the demander's willingness to concede; but any movements made are still voluntary.[10]

3. Negotiations are seen as productive. They may disclose areas of agreement or alternatives not previously considered by either party.

4. Negotiations as used in labor-management relations are characterized by verbal and/or written demands and concessions.

---

[9] Jack Fiorito and Wallace E. Hendricks, "Union Characteristics and Bargaining Outcomes," *Industrial and Labor Relations Review* 40 (1987), pp. 569–84.

[10] Frederik Zeuthen, *Problems of Monopoly and Economic Warfare* (Boston: Routledge & Kegan Paul, 1930).

5. The bargaining process requires competition before the benefits available accrue to the parties involved in the bargaining.[11]

Bargaining, in its simplest format, is the communication by both parties of the terms they require for consummation of a transaction and the subsequent acceptance or rejection by both of the bargain. Negotiation is the set of techniques used to translate bargaining power into the ultimate settlement.[12]

From a psychological perspective, bargaining may be defined as "the process whereby two or more parties attempt to settle what each shall give and take, or perform and receive, in a transaction between them." For bargaining, the parties must have a conflict of interest in relation to issues jointly affecting them. For most bargaining, the parties are joined in a voluntary relationship; this may not be true in collective bargaining. The joining is relatively permanent. The activities of the parties include the division of resources and other intangible issues in which the parties have joint interests. Negotiation requires the presentation of positions, their evaluation by the other party, and counterproposals. The process requires a sequential rather than simultaneous mode because each party must have time to evaluate the other's proposals before responding.[13]

This chapter and book are not primarily concerned with bargaining per se, but rather with collective bargaining. A more specific definition from a behavioral perspective includes the following:

1. Collective bargaining includes a variety of issues, some generating conflict between the parties and others requiring collaboration to accommodate the separate interests of both.

2. The attitudes and feelings of the bargainers play a part in the outcome of negotiations over and above what occurs as a result of the rationally defined attributes of the parties. Further, the parties do not come together only for this negotiation; they must maintain an ongoing relationship. Thus, the results of the bargaining situation affect the long-run characteristics of the bargaining relationship.

3. The bargainers are often acting on behalf of others rather than for their own ends. They are representing constituents who evaluate their performance and may affect their tenure in negotiating positions.[14]

---

[11] John G. Cross, *The Economics of Bargaining* (New York: Basic Books, 1969), pp. 4–6.

[12] Carl M. Stevens, *Strategy and Collective Bargaining Negotiations* (New York: McGraw-Hill, 1963), pp. 2–4.

[13] Jeffrey Z. Rubin and Bert R. Brown, *The Social Psychology of Bargaining and Negotiation* (New York: Academic Press, 1975), pp. 2–18.

[14] Richard E. Walton and Robert B. McKersie, *A Behavioral Theory of Labor Negotiations* (New York: McGraw-Hill, 1965), pp. 3–4.

Thus, the bargaining process involves parties who are mutually interested in reaching agreement on a variety of issues. Negotiators represent others who stand to have their positions altered as a result of the bargaining. Personal characteristics of the bargainers, as well as the power of the organizations they represent, are likely to influence the outcome.

Attributes of the Parties

Much has been speculated about how the personalities of bargainers relate to bargaining power, but virtually no research on the effects of personal attributes on labor negotiations has been reported. However, some general conclusions have been reached on individual and contextual factors related to bargaining behavior in a variety of situations.

The social components of bargaining influence behavior. Labor negotiations are seldom conducted in privacy. Although the general public and most union and management constituents are excluded, the negotiating teams witness the behavior of the bargainers. Audiences make it more difficult for bargainers to concede. This difficulty increases if the bargainer is highly loyal to the group or if the group has a strong commitment to the bargaining issue. If the other party views the concession as a sign of weakness, retaliation is likely in subsequent negotiations.[15] Bargainers might use two tactics to overcome these problems. First, to promote an opponent's willingness to concede, the bargainer should respond to an opponent's concession in another area important to the opponent or should indicate a major concession required hard bargaining. Second, the negotiator should realize public commitment to an issue reduces the degree to which objective data can modify the position. But the skilled negotiator is aware that public commitment may be a tactic to justify support for an issue not really viewed as important.

The bargaining environment, the perceptions of the bargainers, and the complexity of the negotiations all influence outcomes. Neutrality in the bargaining environment is important because there is less willingness to make concessions on one's home ground. Thus, unions should not bargain at the plant. The perceived characteristics of the opponent are also important. If the opponent is perceived as nondeferring, then concessions will not be sought as vigorously. As more issues are injected into bargaining, **logrolling** (trading blocks of apparently dissimilar issues; for example, union shop for a wage increase) occurs frequently. Also, a sequence of offers, counteroffers, and issue settlement will result from bargaining on numerous issues.[16]

The interaction of personality and context variables affects the bargaining relationships. This interaction includes interpersonal orientation,

---

[15] Rubin and Brown, *Social Psychology*, pp. 43–54.
[16] Ibid., pp. 130–56.

motivational orientation, and power. Interpersonal orientation reflects responsiveness to others—reacting to, being interested in, and appreciating variations in another's behavior.[17] Motivational orientation refers to whether one's bargaining interests are individual (seeking only one's own interest), competitive (seeking to better an opponent), or cooperative (seeking positive outcomes in the interests of both).[18] Power refers to the range of bargaining outcomes through which the other party may be moved.[19]

Interpersonal orientation appears as individual differences. Motivational orientation is affected by attitudes toward bargaining, types of rewards and their attainability, and roles bargainers are told to take by their constituents.[20] Discrepancies between the parties in their bargaining power and in amounts of absolute power (ability to inflict loss on the other) are also important parameters.[21]

Given these individual differences and contextual variables, bargaining effectiveness should be greatest when interpersonal orientation is high, motivational orientation is cooperative, and power is equal and low.[22] The interaction of these variables may have no effect on how the parties structure their negotiating teams. Much of the structuring must depend on the goals of the party (for example, to break new ground on productivity issues requires cooperation) and on beliefs about the tactics an opponent may use (for example, assigning low interpersonal orientation bargainers to a team).

The type and levels of concessions from a party convey information about the party's true position. For example, a series of concessions on a given issue followed by no subsequent movement could signal that the party's resistance point has been reached. A retreat toward an original position may signal toughening a stand. Concessions appearing to reward the requester's behavior may increase cooperation between the parties and may strengthen the role of an attractive counterpart to the requester's constituency.[23]

Perceptions of Bargainers

Besides the personal attributes of the parties, the negotiators form perceptions about the bargaining situation. A variety of characteristics may influence the willingness to concede and, thus, the outcome of negotia-

---

[17] Ibid., p. 158.
[18] Ibid., p. 198.
[19] Ibid., p. 213.
[20] Ibid., pp. 201–13.
[21] Ibid., pp. 213–33.
[22] Ibid., pp. 256–57.
[23] Ibid., pp. 276–78.

tions. Perceived strategic power is one characteristic. A bargainer would have high strategic power if (1) agreement is less advantageous for the bargainer than it is for the opponent, (2) more ways exist to satisfy the bargainer's needs than to satisfy the opponent, (3) more credible threats can be made by the bargainer than by the opponent, (4) maintenance of the relationship is more important to the opponent, and (5) the opponent is under heavier time pressure.[24]

Within this framework, an example of condition 1 is an organization with a large backlog of orders. The company might be more motivated to settle, because large profits would be lost. Relatively little pressure might exist for the union, because it reasonably believes lost wages would be made up with overtime when the plant reopened. As an example of condition 2, an employer struck in one of many plants would have a distinct bargaining advantage. Condition 3 could involve beliefs that threatened actions will be taken. It reinforces the idea that a strike may have value for future bargaining situations. In condition 4, unions are expected to be more responsive because the bargaining process is necessary to maintain the relationship. Finally, condition 5 involves employers dealing in perishable goods, such as food producers and transportation companies (Christmas travel lost because of strikes). These are under greater pressure to settle on the union's terms.

THEORIES OF BARGAINING TACTICS

Bargaining occurs because either or both parties are unwilling to agree to the other's demands. The following rules govern bargaining.

Rule 1 states an impending contract expiration is necessary for the commencement of bargaining. During the course of the agreement, the parties have essentially agreed not to bargain, so the anticipated expiration allows the renewal of bargaining.

Rule 2 states the initial bargaining demand should be large. Even though both parties are fairly certain the initial positions are substantially different from what each is willing to settle for, the large initial demand creates room for bargaining and allows relatively large concessions when the time is right.

Rule 3 explains that the negotiating agenda is determined by the initial demands and counterproposals. In other words, the issues initially raised by the parties constitute the focus of the bargaining. Additions to

[24] John M. Magenau and Dean G. Pruitt, "The Social Psychology of Bargaining: A Theoretical Synthesis 1," in *Industrial Relations: A Social Psychological Approach*, ed. Geoffrey M. Stephenson and Christopher J. Brotherton (New York: John Wiley & Sons, 1979), pp. 197–99.

the initial agenda are seldom made, and offers made in regard to these items can rarely be retracted.

Rule 4 precludes strikes or lockouts before a certain time and requires notice that a strike is possible after this point.

Rule 5 provides that negotiations terminate when an agreement is reached. Within this rule may be a requirement that unresolved issues be arbitrated or operations continued to preclude an emergency while an agreement is reached.

Rule 6 requires the parties to negotiate in good faith. To do this, the parties must respond to each other's demands and take no unilateral action to change the existing conditions before the end of negotiations.[25]

Bluffing

Bluffing in contract negotiations has been studied extensively. In most negotiations, neither party expects to win its initial demands, and the other party knows a demand is greater than the expected settlement.

Bluffing serves several valuable purposes. If one stated a final position first, concessions would be impossible. A failure to concede could destroy the relationship required in collective bargaining. Bluffing also allows a bargainer to test the firmness of an opponent's demands without a full commitment to a settlement. Thus, more is learned about the opponent's expectations through bluffing.[26]

If bluffing is used to gain information for a final settlement, the union may reasonably make extreme demands on financial issues, because it lacks information on management's ability to pay. When management has a good deal of information on a settlement point, its initial offer may be close to its expected settlement point. An examination of contract settlements between the Tennessee Valley Authority and its unions show that final agreements on economic issues are closer to management proposals than union proposals in most instances. However, if management is pressured by outside forces, settlements tend to be closer to the union's positions.[27] The union runs a risk in making very high demands, because these may increase management's cost expectations and lead to a strike over points the union may ultimately be willing to concede.[28]

---

[25] Stevens, *Strategy*, pp. 27–56.

[26] Cross, *Economics of Bargaining*, pp. 169–80.

[27] Roger C. Bowlby and William R. Schriver, "Bluffing and the 'Split-the-Difference' Theory of Wage Bargaining," *Industrial and Labor Relations Review* 32 (1979), pp. 161–71.

[28] Henry S. Farber, "The Determinants of Union Wage Demands: Some Preliminary Empirical Evidence," *Proceedings of the Industrial Relations Research Association* 30 (1977), pp. 303–10.

BEHAVIORAL THEORIES OF LABOR NEGOTIATIONS

Four behavioral components are involved in bargaining. **Distributive bargaining** occurs when the parties are in conflict on a particular issue and the outcome will involve a loss for one party and a gain for the other.[29] Suppose the union wants a 60-cent hourly increase, and the parties ultimately settle for 30 cents. The 30-cent increase is a gain to the union and a loss to the company, which is not to say the loss is greater than the company expected). The company may have believed a settlement for anything less than 35 cents would be better than it expected to win. Distributive bargaining simply means some resource is in fixed supply, and one's gain is the other's loss as to that resource.

Because distributive bargaining involves the division of outcomes on a bargaining issue, much of negotiation is involved with providing the opponent information as to the importance of a particular position, the likelihood of future movement on that position, and possible trade-offs that might be made for a concession on the position. Through bargaining, both sides may pick up cues as to where the other is willing to settle. An important part of this process is identifying the commitment a bargainer attaches to a position. One bargaining strategy would be to demand most of what would constitute an acceptable outcome and then threaten the other party that a strike will follow a rejection of this demand. Evidence from bargaining experiments suggests, however, that bargainers incorporate fairness in outcomes into their sequence of offers.[30] Table 10–3 (on pp. 284–85) portrays various management and union commitment statements and analyzes them as to their finality, specificity, and consequences for ignoring them.

Integrative Bargaining

The second component is **integrative bargaining,** which occurs when the parties face a common problem.[31] For example, a company may be experiencing above-average employee turnover. As a result, union membership may be eroded, and union officials may have to spend an inordinate amount of time recruiting new members. Both parties may seek a solution to their joint problem by attacking the causes of turnover existing in their contract.

Integrative bargaining occurs in contexts where both management and union accommodate the needs of the other without cost or through a

---

[29] Walton and McKersie, *Behavioral Theory*, p. 4.

[30] J. Ochs and A. E. Roth, "An Experimental Study of Sequential Bargaining," *American Economic Review* 79 (1989), pp. 355–84.

[31] Walton and McKersie, *Behavioral Theory*, p. 5.

simultaneous gain. These contexts frequently involve management's desires to improve flexibility and union's simultaneous desires for increased job security.[32]

Attitudinal Structuring

Attitudinal structuring refers to activities the parties engage in to create such atmospheres as cooperation, hostility, trust, and respect.[33] The process primarily involves changing the parties' attitudes, expecting changed attitudes to change predispositions to act.

Relationship patterns occurring between the parties will have an effect on or be a result of one's action toward the other, beliefs about legitimacy, level of trust, and degree of friendliness.[34] The predominant patterns of these attitudinal dimensions (shown in Figure 10–2) fall within the categories of conflict, containment-aggression, accommodation, cooperation, and collusion.

Conflict occurs when both parties seek to destroy the other's base. Neither acknowledges the legitimacy of the other, and activities are pursued to interfere with the other's existence. Containment-aggression involves demonstrating a high degree of militancy while recognizing the other's right to exist. Accommodation occurs when each party accords the other a legitimate role and allows the other to represent its position as a legitimate interest. Cooperation occurs when the other's position is seen as legitimate and when common issues are of simultaneous concern to both parties. Collusion takes place when both join to subvert the goals of the parties they represent, for example, when management covertly assists a union in organizing in return for a nonmilitant stance on bargaining.[35]

Intraorganizational Bargaining

Intraorganizational bargaining is the process for achieving agreement within one of the bargaining groups.[36] For example, a management bargainer's efforts might convince fellow management representatives that a 40-cent raise is necessary to avoid a strike, although management had determined previously that the union would likely settle for 35 cents. Intraorganizational bargaining also refers to the activities union negotiators engage in to sell an agreement to the membership.

---

[32] Ibid., pp. 129ff.
[33] Ibid., p. 5.
[34] Ibid., pp. 184–280.
[35] Ibid., pp. 186–88.
[36] Ibid., p. 5.

TABLE 10-3
Interpretative Comments about the Degree of Firmness in Statements of Commitments

Statement of Commitment (1)	Degree of Finality of Commitment to a Position (2)	Degree of Specificity of That Position (3)	Consequences or Implications Associated with a Position (the Threat) (4)
From a negotiation involving a middle-sized manufacturing plant in 1953: "We have looked very seriously and must present this (10-cent package) as our final offer."	The statement "must present this as our final offer" is not as strong as, for example, "this is our final offer." The strength of the word "final" is somewhat hedged by the more tentative phrase "must present this as."	The reference to the "10-cent package" was fairly specific.	No reference to the consequences. What the other party is expected to associate with the company's position would depend on the company's reputation or other confirming tactics. It would seem to imply that company is ready to take a strike.
A union replied later, "The membership disagreed" with the company's economic proposal. "The present contract will not extend beyond 12:00 tonight."	Significantly, the membership was reported as only having "disagreed"; it did not "reject."	Reference to "economic proposal" is not specific. Hence the degree of disagreement is unclear.	By stating "the present contract will not extend," they do *not* state there would be a strike. And in the particular context it was not clear they would strike.
From the public statements regarding the 1955 negotiations between the UAW and the Ford Motor Company: Henry Ford II suggested alternate ways of achieving security "without piecemeal experimenting with dangerous mechanisms or guinea pig industries. . . ." This was a statement of opposition to the union's GAW proposal.	The statement contained no hint about the finality of his commitment of opposition.	The phrase "piecemeal experimenting . . ." clearly avoided reference to just what was objected to.	There were no references to the consequences to be associated with ultimate failure to agree.
From the transcripts of a negotiation in the oil industry: Management stated, "If you say now or never or else (on a wage increase demanded by the union), I would say go ahead; we are prepared to take the consequences."	This was an explicit, binding commitment.	The company's position was also clear in this instance—it was not prepared to make any concession on the issue at hand.	Company was indicating its readiness for a work stoppage.

TABLE 10–3
(concluded)

Statement of Commitment (1)	Degree of Finality of Commitment to a Position (2)	Degree of Specificity of That Position (3)	Consequences or Implications Associated with a Position (the Threat) (4)
Later the union spokesman replied, "My advice to your employees will be not to become a party to any agreement which binds them to present wages."	Regarding what the union leader's advice will be, that is final. It says nothing about the finality of that position of the party, however.	The advice "not to become a party to any agreement which binds them to present wages" is hardly specific. Any increase would meet the test of this statement. In fact, even a re-opening clause would avoid "binding the union to present wages."	Although at first glance this statement seems to commit the union to a wage increase "or else," it leaves them the option of continuing with no contract and with signing a contract which has a way of adjusting wages in the future. The context did nothing to clarify just what consequences were to be associated with the union's position.
"I don't believe that they (the rest of the union committee) can recommend acceptance" (of the company's offer).	"I don't believe" is more tentative than "I know they cannot."	"I don't believe that they can recommend acceptance" leaves unanswered whether the union committee would recommend that the membership not accept the offer or merely make no recommendation. Moreover, the reference is only to the company's *offer as it now stands.*	Not specified here, but the union had begun to refer to economic sanctions.

SOURCE: B. M. Selekman, S. K. Selekman, and S. H. Fuller, *Problems in Labor Relations*, 2nd ed. (New York: McGraw-Hill, 1958), pp. 221, 226, 233; Material from these pages used in formulating table by Richard E. Walton and Robert B. McKersie in *A Behavioral Theory of Labor Negotiations* (New York: McGraw-Hill, 1965), pp. 96, 97. Copyright © 1965 McGraw-Hill. Used with the permission of McGraw-Hill Book Company.

FIGURE 10–2

Attitudinal Components of the Relationship Patterns

Attitudinal Dimensions	Pattern of Relationship				
	Conflict	Containment-Aggression	Accommodation	Cooperation	Collusion
Motivational orientation and action tendencies toward other	Competitive tendencies to destroy or weaken		Individualistic policy of hands off	Cooperative tendencies to assist or preserve	
Beliefs about legitimacy of other	Denial of legitimacy	Grudging acknowledgment	Acceptance of status quo	Complete legitimacy	Not applicable
Level of trust in conducting affairs	Extreme distrust	Distrust	Limited trust	Extended trust	Trust based on mutual blackmail potential
Degree of friendliness	Hate	Antagonism	Neutralism—courteousness	Friendliness	Intimacy—"sweetheart relationship"

SOURCE: Richard E. Walton and Robert B. McKersie, *A Behavioral Theory of Labor Negotiations* (New York: McGraw-Hill, 1965), p. 189. Copyright © 1965 McGraw-Hill. Used with the permission of McGraw-Hill Book Company.

For the union, the negotiating team must be able to sell an agreement to the members once it has been reached. To do this, the team has to be sensitive to member demands while balancing competing needs of subgroups within the union. One tactic is estimating some reasonable range of contract outcomes to members. Suggesting excessive demands could damage the bargaining relations (see attitudinal structuring) can help moderate initial demands.

Another tactic, used particularly by management, limits participation of those likely to take militant stances or to be unwilling to modify positions as bargaining continues. This gives the management negotiator greater freedom to respond during the bargaining process.[37]

Negotiations are seldom settled until close to their deadline.[38] This may occur for a couple of reasons. First, the time available for bargaining may disclose additional information that might lead to a better final solution for either side. Second, and probably more important, the constituents of the bargainers may believe that settlement before the deadline constitutes poor effort and their position could have been improved.[39]

Use of the Components in Bargaining

The four bargaining processes and their degree of use may result from certain preexisting conditions and the behaviors of the negotiators.[40] Figure 10-3 shows the predictors of the processes. Conditions such as high bargaining power are expected to be related to early commitment to a position. This, in turn, should lead to the use of distributive bargaining.

Union and management negotiators' responses to questionnaires indicate distributive bargaining success was influenced by bargaining power, low probability of a work stoppage, clarity in stating issues, and the opponent's behavior when discussing the basis for its position. Integrative bargaining success depended on conditions of trust, support, and friendliness by the opponent and a clear statement of issues with open discussion and plentiful information. Success in attitudinal structuring was related to management respect for the union, generally constructive relationships toward management, and a lack of criticism of the opponent. Intraorganizational bargaining success depended on the confi-

---

[37] Ibid., pp. 281–340.

[38] A. E. Roth, J. K. Murnighan, and F. Schoumaker, "The Deadline Effect in Bargaining: Some Experimental Evidence," *American Economic Review* 78 (1988), pp. 806–23.

[39] B. P. McCall, "Interest Arbitration and the Incentive to Bargain: A Principal-Agent Approach," *Journal of Conflict Resolution* 34 (1990), pp. 151–67.

[40] Richard B. Peterson and Lane Tracy, "Testing a Behavioral Theory Model of Labor Negotiations," *Industrial Relations* 16 (1977), pp. 35–50.

FIGURE 10–3

Model of Conditions and Behaviors Related to Walton and McKersie's Four Goals of Bargaining

Conditions	Behaviors	Moderators	Goals
Bargaining power Low estimated cost and probability of a work stoppage	Early commitment of own team to a firm position Clarity and specificity of own team in stating position		(+) → Distributive bargaining
Cooperative pattern or relationships: Constructiveness, trustworthiness of other team Frequent contact between teams Large bargaining teams Ample time allowed for bargaining and preparation	Clarity and specificity of both teams in stating issues Both sides withholding commitment to a position while discussing problems and exploring solutions Freedom of negotiators from team constraints Farsightedness of both sides about future bargaining issues Necessary information made available	Side: labor, management Role: chief negotiator, other	(+) → Integrative (problem-solving) bargaining
Other team's respect and trust of your team	Recognition given to other team Farsightedness of both teams with respect to working relationship		(+) → Attitudinal structuring
Weak bargaining power High estimated cost and probability of a work stoppage High status with respect to constituents	Team solidarity Well-informed constituents Freedom of team from constituent pressure Supportiveness of other side with respect to your position with constituents		(+) → Intraorganizational bargaining

(−)   +

+

SOURCE: Richard B. Peterson and Lane Tracy, "Testing a Behavioral Theory Model of Labor Negotiations," *Industrial Relations*, February 1977, p. 17.

dence bargainers had in their constituents' endorsement and high perceived costs of a stoppage. Behaviors relevant to success were related to team solidarity and low outside pressures.

NEGOTIATIONS

This section examines the activities involved in bargaining a new contract. Issues covered include tactics, information requirements, and union and management requirements for agreements. The Taft-Hartley Act requires the parties to meet at reasonable times and places and to bargain in good faith over issues involving wages, hours, and terms and conditions of employment.

Initial Presentations

Although not legally required, the party requesting changes in its favor presents its demands first. Thus, the union will present demands when seeking improvements and management when seeking concessions. At this presentation, the side taking the initiative will specify all areas of the contract in which changes are desired. This initial session also allows the union to present all grievances or positions developed through the membership meetings. The union does not expect to gain all of these changes; but, as a political organization, it has an obligation to state the positions of individual members. It also creates new bargaining positions that alert management to expect more vigorous future demands in these areas.

Management may not reply to the union's demands at the initial session, but it will respond early in the negotiations. Its response is usually substantially below what it would be willing to settle for. If management adheres to or refuses to move past its original position, it must provide information if asked by the union to support those positions based on an inability to pay.[41]

Bargaining on Specific Issues

If the issues are complex or the company is large, the negotiating committee and company representatives will frequently divide themselves into subcommittees to negotiate specific issues. For example, the contract language on work standards may be handled by a subgroup of production employees or union stewards and production supervisors.

Usually the subgroups do not have the authority to finalize the issues

---

[41] *NLRB* v. *Truitt Mfg. Co.*, 351 U.S. 149 (U.S. Supreme Court, 1956).

they discuss, because these issues form part of a trade-off package, but they may bring tentative agreements or positions back to the main table for consideration.

At the main table, issues not forming part of a combined package or to be used as trade-offs may be initialed by the parties as finalized for the ultimate agreement. Thus, the final settlement is not necessarily a coalescence on all issues simultaneously but rather a completion of negotiations on final areas in which disagreement existed.

In most negotiations, nonwage issues—union security clauses, seniority provisions, work rules, and the like—are decided first. Wage and benefit issues are often settled as a package near the end of negotiations. As noted earlier in discussing the certainty of outcomes and the potential costs of package characteristics, wages and benefits are issues management must consider carefully.

TACTICS IN DISTRIBUTIVE BARGAINING

Each party enters the negotiations with certain positions it hopes to win. Management may have an economic position it wants to protect. The union may have specific wage and benefit demands it perceives as achievable. Bargaining is the process by which the two parties influence the perceptions of the other to adopt their positions as a final outcome.

The following represents the types of tactics both parties use to influence the resistance points of their opponents through information transmission:

> "I do not think you really feel that strongly about the issues you have introduced."
>
> "I believe that a strike will cost you considerably more than you are willing to admit."
>
> "I believe a strike will cost me almost nothing in spite of your statements to the contrary."
>
> "I feel very strongly about this issue regardless of what you say."[42]

Certain tactics may be used during negotiations to assess the actual point at which an opponent would prefer to settle. Addressing questions to various members of the negotiating team may gain an overall flavor of the important issues through their responses. To highlight the importance of a particular issue, the party proposing it may provide detailed information that clearly establish its position. For example, a firm faced with a large wage demand may provide detailed data on the wage costs of its competition and its inability to pass increases through to its consumers.

---

[42] Walton and McKersie, *Behavioral Theory*, p. 60.

One tactic gets the opponent to see that its demands will not result in as positive an outcome as it expects. For example, a demand for more paid time off may be seen by the union as a way to increase employment, but the company may show that the increased costs will result in replacing existing workers with robots.

Another successful tactic changes the costs of a strike for an opponent. For example, a strike by the UAW is much more critical if it is close to a new model year when auto companies do not have inventories of vehicles ready for delivery (as they would have in the spring). Employers may build up inventories before contract expirations by working at full capacity or by scheduling overtime to reduce the potential costs of a strike.

Committing to a Position

Commitment to a position can be a powerful bargaining tool. If the opposition perceives no more movement will be made on a specific issue, it may then be willing to concede to the offered point if within its settlement range. Three components of a position signal commitment: finality (communication indicating no further movement will be made), specificity (the clarity of the position), and the consequences (the contingent outcomes, such as a strike that will occur if the demand is not accepted as proposed).[43]

Several tactics may telegraph commitment to the opposition. Most relate to the question of consequences. For example, a strike authorization vote signals the union's commitment. A company preparing to close operations or refusing to accept new orders signals it is prepared to call the union's bluff. Consider the 1981 Federal Aviation Administration–Professional Air Traffic Controllers Organization dispute in which President Reagan committed management to a position that it would not bargain during a strike (finality) and that all strikers must return to work within 48 hours (specificity) or be permanently severed from federal employment (consequences).

SETTLEMENTS AND RATIFICATIONS

When the negotiators agree on a new contract, the union team still has responsibilities to fulfill before the final agreement is signed. In most unions, two hurdles remain to be cleared before the tentative agreement becomes permanent. First, the international union must approve the agreement. This ensures a local will not negotiate an agreement substantially inferior to other contracts in the international or other unions.

---

[43] Ibid., p. 93.

Second, most unions require a referendum among the bargaining unit's membership to ratify the contract. To do this, the bargaining team conducts a membership meeting and explains the contract gains won in negotiations. The team then generally recommends settlement, and the members vote to accept or reject.

If the negotiating committee recommends acceptance, the membership nearly always votes to ratify. However, some exceptions occur. A study of mediated negotiations in which contract rejection occurred found only 30 percent followed a unanimous recommendation by the bargaining committee to accept the contract.[44] Reasons for contract rejections included an inability to alter positions through bargaining, final positions outside the opponent's settlement range, hostile relationships between the parties, poor coordination in bargaining, or a failure to estimate correctly the priorities of the membership. Contract rejection occurred in several major **concession bargaining** situations in the 1980s, even after the national union recommended the agreement. Exhibit 10–3 displays some recent major examples.

When the negotiating committee unqualifiedly recommends ratification but the contract is rejected, union negotiators are placed in a precarious position. Management may rightfully question whether the union actually speaks for the rank and file. During the negotiations, management may have conceded on issues of seeming importance to the bargainers but of questionable relevance to the rank and file. The negotiating committee also may have difficulty selling a subsequent settlement to the membership because its credibility was undermined by the earlier rejection.

Occasionally, management will question whether the bargaining committee is representing the true wishes of the rank and file. Management bargainers may suggest a package be submitted to the membership for ratification. The company may not insist on taking a proposal to the membership, however, because this is not a mandatory bargaining issue.[45] If the negotiating committee is reasonably certain a proposal will be rejected, it may encourage the membership to reject so as to strengthen its bargaining position by putting management on notice that its position is not acceptable.

Nonagreement

Occasionally, the parties may fail to reach an agreement, either before or after the contract expires. A variety of activities may then occur, including mediation, strikes, lockouts, replacements, management's implemen-

---

[44] Donald R. Burke and Lester Rubin, "Is Contract Rejection a Major Collective Bargaining Problem?" *Industrial and Labor Relations Review* 26 (1973), pp. 820–33.

[45] *NLRB* v. *Wooster Division of Borg Warner Corp.*, 356 U.S. 342 (1958).

EXHIBIT 10-3

Major Recent Contract Rejections

WHERE WORKER DISSENT IS CAUSING PROBLEMS

Union Employer	Dispute
1983	
Auto Workers General Motors (Van Nuys, Calif.)	4,400-member Local 645 delays for three years work rule changes proposed by GM and UAW leaders.
1984	
Food & Commercial Workers Kroger (Pittsburgh)	Kroger sells 45 stores after 2,800 members of Local 23 turn down wage and work rule concessions accepted by their leaders.
1985	
Electronic Workers (IUE) General Electric (Lynn, Mass.)	The 8,500 members of Local 201, unhappy with proposed concessions in their national contract, vote out the local's executive board.
Teamsters Richard A. Shaw Inc. Watsonville Canning (Watsonville, Calif.)	Local 912's 1,700 members resist wage concessions, leading to a strike in defiance of local leaders.
Food & Commercial Workers Hormel (Austin, Minn.)	1,500-member Local P-9 rejects wage cuts in defiance of international union. Hormel breaks the ensuing strike, and the local sues its parent union, which has put P-9 in trusteeship.
1986	
State, County & Municipal Employees City of Detroit	7,000 members of Michigan Council 25 reject a wage deal accepted by their leaders, forcing continuation of a strike begun on July 16.

DATA: BW

SOURCE: *Business Week*, August 11, 1986, p. 72.

tation of its last offer, and arbitration. Impasses in negotiations lead to very complex issues, which will be detailed in the next chapter.

RECENT CHANGES IN BARGAINING OUTCOMES

The last several years have seen major changes in management objectives in collective bargaining. Figure 10–4 shows changes in management's nonwage objectives in bargaining between 1978 and 1983. Over this period, managements substantially reduced their willingness to give on virtually all objectives and expected to get improvements on all. A large

FIGURE 10-4

Shift in Management's Nonwage Objectives between 1978 and 1983

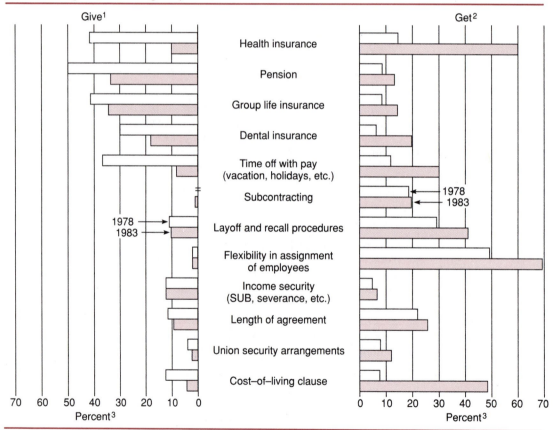

[1] Proportion of companies that were willing to use a specific item in trade for another item.
[2] Proportion of companies that wanted to tighten existing provision or get a more favorable one.
[3] 100% = all companies with the same bargaining unit for both years, with an objective in the subject area in 1978 and in 1983. (e.g., Health benefits, 130 companies; subcontracting, 86 companies.)
SOURCE: Audrey Freedman, *The New Look in Wage Policy and Employee Relations* (New York: Conference Board, 1985), p. 15.

TABLE 10-4

Management Requests for Changes in Union Contract before Expiration Date (largest bargaining unit in 133 companies reporting early openings)

Proposed Changed	Number of Companies Proposing Change[a]	Percent of All Early Openings	Proportion of Proposed Changes Accomplished (% of col. 1)
Defer ("freeze") or delay scheduled wage increases	68	51	60
Reduce wages	38	29	66
Established lower wage rates for new hires	40	30	80
Reduce fringe benefits	53	40	66
Reduce paid time off	38	29	79
Change work rules	76	57	76
Cost-of-living adjustment (COLA)			
Defer of delay effective adjustment	39	29	72
Eliminate entire clause	23	17	48
Modify formula	17	13	65
Divert COLA	15	11	93

[a] Multiple responses.

SOURCE: Audrey Freedman, *The New Look in Wage Policy and Employee Relations* (New York: Conference Board, 1985), p. 12.

share of companies recently requested changes in their contracts before the scheduled expiration dates. Table 10-4 indicates major types of changes requested and the rate at which companies were successful in obtaining them. Generally, unions responded most frequently by asking for greater job security, limits on subcontracting, or some form of profit-sharing or gainsharing program. They were most successful in obtaining job security and gainsharing but very unsuccessful in obtaining sub-contracting limits.[46]

Previous evidence has shown that companies vulnerable to strikes or struck in the past are more likely to settle above their wage targets. This trend lends credence to the suggestion that striking may constitute an investment in bargaining power for the union. Companies emphasizing union containment goals as well as bargaining goals are more likely to achieve their targets.[47] However, one must not necessarily attribute a hard-line approach to success in bargaining because a heavily unionized firm cannot readily have a credible containment policy. Containment may be related to relatively small proportions of employees being union-ized, which, in turn, increases bargaining leverage.

[46] Audrey Freedman, *The New Look in Wage Policy and Employee Relations* (New York: Conference Board, 1985), pp. 10–15.

[47] Freedman, *Managing Labor Relations*, p. 48.

SUMMARY

Managements prepare for bargaining by gathering internal and comparative data, including employee distributions by job, seniority, shift, and the like. Other data relate to wage rates granted in other negotiations, local labor market rates, and so on. Many different functional departments contribute to obtaining information and formulating a management negotiating position. Contract terms that may be renegotiated must be costed to assess their relative financial impacts on the employer. Bargaining books assist in negotiations.

Unions prepare for bargaining by determining what their memberships view as important issues. The political nature of unions requires attention be given to interests of major groups of employees. National-level preparation involves the collection and analysis of data, while local-level preparation formulates bargaining positions and involves members in forming a negotiating team.

Bargaining occccurs in situations where both parties expect the act of bargaining to improve their positions. One side may expect an improvement in benefits, while the other gains certainty through the contracting process. Attributes of the bargaining situation and the personalities of the parties involved influence outcomes. Bluffing appears important because it allows the parties to explore the significance and reasons behind demands without initially stating positions they might want to retreat from later.

Collective bargaining is suggested to have four components: distributive bargaining (one's gain is the other's loss), integrative bargaining (a settlement improves both parties' positions), attitudinal structuring (attempts to create atmospheres likely to obtain desired concessions), and intraorganizational bargaining (the parties try to convince constituents within their own organizations to change positions).

Bargaining usually begins with the party seeking a change presenting its positions. Changes will frequently be handled sequentially, although logrolling occurs on occasion. Following an agreement, the union's members must ratify the tentative agreement. Failure to ratify appears primarily related to difficulties in attitudinal structuring and intraorganizational bargaining.

DISCUSSION QUESTIONS

1. To what extent should management allow the union to select the components of an economic package in a contract negotiation?

2. What balance should exist between local- and national-level influences in negotiations? Should this balance differ by bargaining issue?

3. How could an opponent in bargaining overcome what appears to be a strong commitment to an issue by its opposite member?

4. What strategies should management use in bargaining when a settlement that was unanimously recommended by the union's bargaining team is rejected?

5. Why would it be harder for heavily unionized organizations to settle on their bargaining targets than those with a small proportion of employees unionized?

6. What attitudinal structuring and intraorganizational bargaining tactics would be different for integrative as compared to distributive bargaining?

KEY TERMS

gainsharing

bargaining book

bargaining convention

logrolling

distributive bargaining

integrative bargaining

attitudinal structuring

intraorganizational bargaining

concession bargaining

NEGOTIATING EXERCISE

This mock negotiating exercise will help you develop an appreciation of and insight into principles and problems of collective bargaining, with special emphasis on contract negotiation. Using the information covered to this point in the text, you will act as a member of a union or management bargaining team in formulating its strategies and tactics for negotiations. Following a more detailed approach to contract costing and instructions, the exercise will present a copy of the expiring contract between General Materials & Fabrication Company (GMFC) and Local 384 of the United Steelworkers of America.

A. Contract Costing

Contract costing is not straightforward. The cost changes often depend on changes in employee seniority, how increased vacations are handled, and similar issues not directly associated with the amount of an hourly wage increase. A simple costing example will be created so you can see the effects. Assume a bargaining unit containing 100 employees will renegotiate its contract. Five pay grades presently have pay rates, given length of service *in the organization*, as shown in Table MN–1.

The 100 employees are distributed by grade and seniority, as shown in Table MN–2.

Table MN–3 shows the historic turnover rates (proportion of employees who quit or retire in a given year) of bargaining unit employees by grade and seniority level.

The organization's retirement plan provides for full vesting of benefits at five years' service. Employees who quit before accruing five years of service lose their benefits. The plan is fully funded to provide for pensions for present employees taking anticipated turnover into account. The retirement program provides that employees will receive an equivalent of 5 percent of their gross pay (regular and overtime) contributed to their pension funds.

The health care program provides hospital and medical coverage paid by the employer. Twenty-five percent of the employees are single and without dependents. The other 75 percent have families, but of these, 5 percent are families in which both the husband and wife are employed by this company, so premiums need not be paid for both. Health care premiums are presently $150 per month for single employees and $250 per month for those with dependents. Premiums are expected to increase 15 percent next year for both single and family policies.

Under the contract, overtime is apportioned (within grade) on the basis of seniority, with each employee entitled to five hours of overtime before the next junior employee in that grade is entitled. If all employees within the grade have received the overtime, the cycle is repeated. During the last year, overtime was available in the following number of hours by grade: grade 1, 520 hours; 2, 840; 3, 1,640; 4, 1,020; and 5, 780. The overtime premium for all of these hours was 50 percent. Table MN–4 shows the average number of hours of overtime per employee by seniority and grade level during the past year.

All employees receive nine paid holidays and three paid sick days. The average employee takes two of these days, with no variation across grades or seniority levels. Vacations are tied to length of service. Employees with less than one year's service are

TABLE MN-1
Pay Rates

| | Seniority | | | | |
Grade	< 1 Yr.	1–2 Yr.	3–5 Yr.	6–10 Yr.	> 10 Yr.
1	5.50	6.00	6.50	6.50	6.50
2	6.50	7.00	7.50	8.00	8.00
3	7.50	8.00	8.50	9.00	9.50
4	8.50	9.00	9.50	10.00	10.50
5	9.50	10.00	10.50	11.00	11.50

TABLE MN-2
Employment Levels

| | Seniority | | | | | |
Grade	< 1 Yr.	1–2 Yr.	3–5 Yr.	6–10 Yr.	> 10 Yr.	Total
1	8	2				10
2	2	4	14			20
3		5	15	20	5	45
4			3	6	6	15
5				2	8	10
Total	10	11	32	28	19	100

TABLE MN-3
Turnover Rates

| | Seniority | | | | |
Grade	< 1 Yr.	1–2 Yr.	3–5 Yr.	6–10 Yr.	> 10 Yr.
1	.25	.10	.10	.10	.10
2	.10	.05	.05	.00	.00
3	.05	.05	.05	.00	.02
4	.00	.00	.00	.00	.03
5	.00	.00	.00	.00	.10

TABLE MN-4
Hours of Overtime

| | Seniority | | | | | |
Grade	< 1 Yr.	1–2 Yr.	3–5 Yr.	6–10 Yr.	> 10 Yr.	Total
1	51.25	55.00				520
2	40.00	40.00	42.86			840
3		35.00	35.00	37.00	40.00	1,640
4			65.00	67.70	70.00	1,020
5				75.00	78.75	780

not entitled to vacations and do not accrue vacation time. Those with 1 to 2 years are entitled to one week; 3 to 5 years, two weeks; 6 to 10 years, three weeks; and more than 10 years, four weeks.

All employees are presently working on one shift, and all have two paid break periods of 10 minutes in the morning and afternoon.

Table MN–5 shows the average wage cost per employee by grade and seniority level under the expiring contract. It is calculated by multiplying the wage rate by 2,080 (the number of hours in a normal work year) plus the number of overtime hours from the appropriate cell in Table MN–4 times 1.5 (to account for the overtime premium rate).

Social security and Medicare tax rates are 7.65 percent on the first $53,400 (1991), with the Medicare rate of 1.45 applied to any earnings between $53,400 and $125,000. Unemployment insurance is 4 percent on the first $10,000 of earnings, and worker's compensation insurance premiums are 1.2 percent of total payroll. With pensions vesting in five years, the pension contribution for persons with less than six years' service must be multiplied by the likelihood that they will remain for that period to get the total contribution required. Table MN–6 is a matrix of probabilities of an employee remaining long enough to receive vested benefits.

Present pension costs by grade and seniority (number of employees × wage cost × retention factor) are shown in Table MN–7.

Present wage costs (straight time and overtime at time and a half) are obtained by multiplying the cells in Table MN–2 by corresponding cells in Table MN–5. The results are shown in Table MN–8.

The total labor costs in the last year of the expiring contract were:

Wages	$1,858,046
Pension contributions	88,550

Social security (.0765 × Wages)	142,141
Unemployment insurance (.04 × $10,000 × number of employees)	40,000
Worker's compensation (.012 × wages)	22,297
Health insurance (25 singles × $150 × 12 months)	45,000
Health insurance (75 families × $250 × 12 months)	225,000
(Less health insurance for five husband–wife duplications)	(15,000)
Total	$2,406,034

For the coming year, assume a set of contract demands as follows:

1. A 50-cent across-the-board wage increase.
2. Five cents additional per grade from grade 2 on.
3. A 6-percent pension contribution.
4. One week additional vacation for all employees with more than five years' service.

Assume normal turnover occurs over the next year and all terminations and retirements are replaced at grade 1 and present employees are promoted to fill the vacancies left. Five employees will be lost: grade 1, less-than-1-year group, 2; grade 2, 3–5-year group, 1; grade 3, 3–5-year group, 1; and grade 5, over-10-year group, 1. Each employee will also increase one year in seniority. Assume employees are relatively evenly distributed within seniority groups and promotions are most often given to the most senior person applying, but in only two thirds of the cases is the most senior person eligible. The vacation demand will result in the loss of 56 weeks' work. Assume an additional employee must be hired at grade 1 to make up for 42 weeks of the loss and the other 14 weeks must be worked as overtime, evenly distributed among employees in grades 3 to 5 according to seniority rules. This results in 560 additional

TABLE MN-5
Average Wage Cost per Employee

			Seniority		
Grade	< 1 Yr.	1–2 Yr.	3–5 Yr.	6–10 Yr.	> 10 Yr.
1	$11,863	$12,975	$13,520	$13,520	$13,520
2	13,910	14,980	16,082	16,640	16,640
3	15,600	17,060	18,126	19,220	20,330
4	17,680	18,720	20,686	21,816	22,943
5	19,760	20,800	21,840	24,118	25,278

TABLE MN-6
Pension Vesting Probabilities

			Seniority		
Grade	< 1 Yr.	1–2 Yr.	3–5 Yr.	6–10 Yr.	> 10 Yr.
1	0.6075	0.8000	0.9000	1.0000	1.0000
2	0.8123	0.9000	0.9500	1.0000	1.0000
3	0.8574	0.9000	0.9500	1.0000	1.0000
4	1.0000	1.0000	1.0000	1.0000	1.0000
5	1.0000	1.0000	1.0000	1.0000	1.0000

TABLE MN-7
Total Pension Costs*

			Seniority			
Grade	< 1 Yr.	1–2 Yr.	3–5 Yr.	6–10 Yr.	> 10 Yr.	Total
1	$2,883	$1,038	$ 0	$ 0	$ 0	$ 3,921
2	1,130	2,696	10,695	0	0	14,521
3	0	3,839	12,915	19,220	5,083	41,055
4	0	0	3,103	6,545	6,883	16,530
5	0	0	0	2,412	10,111	12,523
Total	4,013	7,573	26,713	28,176	22,077	88,550

* Rounded to nearest dollar.

TABLE MN-8
Total Wage Costs

			Seniority			
Grade	< 1 Yr.	1–2 Yr.	3–5 Yr.	6–10 Yr.	> 10 Yr.	Total
1	$ 94,903	$ 25,950	0	0	0	$ 120,853
2	27,820	59,920	$225,150	0	0	312,890
3	0	85,300	271,894	$384,390	$101,650	843,234
4	0	0	62,059	130,893	137,655	330,607
5	0	0	0	48,235	202,228	250,463
Total	$122,723	$171,170	$559,103	$563,518	$441,533	$1,858,047

hours, with 200 hours apportioned to grade 5 and 180 each to grades 3 and 4. At the end of the contract year, the grade and seniority matrix (after turnover) could look as shown in Table MN–9.

Table MN–10 shows the seniority level and distribution of employees after promotions have been made and new hires added.

If the union wins its demands, the new wage rates would be as shown in Table MN–11, given the union's wage demands.

Overtime for the coming year (assuming same as last year except for additional hours necessary if the vacation demand is won) is shown in Table MN–12.

Table MN–13 shows the average wage cost per employee for straight time and overtime, given the proposed demands.

Multiplying Table MN–10 by Table MN–13 yields the total wage cost (less fringes) under the new contract. The results are shown in Table MN–14.

Using the turnover probability table (Table MN–6) multiplied by the total wages in Table MN–14 gives the pension costs under the new contract as 6 percent. These are shown in Table MN–15.

Pension costs increase by $28,509 (or 32 percent more than under the expiring contract) because of increased seniority, which leads to a greater likelihood of staying, combined with the 20 percent increase in contri-

TABLE MN–9
Returning Employees

			Seniority			
Grade	< 1 Yr.	1–2 Yr.	3–5 Yr.	6–10 Yr.	> 10 Yr.	Total
1	6	2	0	0	0	8
2	2	4	13	0	0	19
3	0	5	14	20	5	44
4	0	0	3	6	6	15
5	0	0	0	2	7	9
Total	8	11	30	28	18	95

TABLE MN–10
Seniority Level with Promotions and New Hires

			Seniority			
Grade	< 1 Yr.	1–2 Yr.	3–5 Yr.	6–10 Yr.	> 10 Yr.	Total
1	6	5	0	0	0	11
2	0	6	12	2	0	20
3	0	2	12	23	8	45
4	0	0	2	6	7	15
5	0	0	0	2	8	10
Total	6	13	26	33	23	101

TABLE MN-11

Postnegotiation Pay Rates

		Seniority			
Grade	< 1 Yr.	1–2 Yr.	3–5 Yr.	6–10 Yr.	> 10 Yr.
1	$ 6.00	$ 6.50	$ 7.00	$ 7.00	$ 7.00
2	7.05	7.55	8.05	8.55	8.55
3	8.10	8.60	9.10	9.60	10.10
4	9.15	9.65	10.15	10.65	11.15
5	10.20	10.70	11.20	11.70	12.20

TABLE MN-12

Postnegotiation Overtime Distribution

		Seniority				
Grade	< 1 Yr.	1–2 Yr.	3–5 Yr.	6–10 Yr.	> 10 Yr.	O/T Hours
1	45	50				520
2		40	42.5	45		840
3		40	40	40	42.5	1,820
4			80	80	80	1,200
5				95	98.75	980

TABLE MN-13

Postnegotiation Wage Cost per Employee

		Seniority			
Grade	< 1 Yr.	1–2 Yr.	3–5 Yr.	6–10 Yr.	> 10 Yr.
1	12,885	14,008	14,560	14,560	14,560
2	14,664	16,157	17,257	18,361	17,784
3	16,848	18,404	19,474	20,544	21,652
4	19,032	20,072	22,330	23,430	24,530
5	21,216	22,256	23,296	26,003	27,183

TABLE MN-14

Postnegotiation Total Wage Cost

		Seniority				
Grade	< 1 Yr.	1–2 Yr.	3–5 Yr.	6–10 Yr.	> 10 Yr.	Total
1	77,310	70,038	0	0	0	147,348
2	0	96,942	207,086	36,722	0	340,750
3	0	36,808	233,688	472,512	173,215	916,223
4	0	0	44,660	140,580	171,710	356,950
5	0	0	0	52,007	217,465	269,472
Total	77,310	203,788	485,434	701,821	562,390	2,030,743

bution rates. Following are the total costs in the first year of a new contract:

Wages	$2,030,743
Pension contributions	117,059
Social security	155,352
Unemployment insurance (101 employees)	40,400
Worker's compensation insurance	24,369
Health insurance (26 singles, 15% increase)	53,820
Health insurance (75 families, 15% increase)	258,750
(Less health insurance for 5 husband-wife duplications, 15% increase)	(17,250)
Total	$2,663,243

Under the proposed new contract, total labor costs would increase by 11.1 percent, even though average straight-time percentage wage increases would rise by grade and seniority level as shown in Table MN–16.

TABLE MN–15

Postnegotiation Total Pension Costs*

	Seniority					
Grade	< 1 Yr.	1–2 Yr.	3–5 Yr.	6–10 Yr.	> 10 Yr.	Total
1	2,818	3,362	0	0	0	6,180
2	0	5,235	11,804	2,203	0	19,242
3	0	1,988	13,320	28,351	10,393	54,051
4	0	0	2,680	8,435	10,303	21,417
5	0	0	0	3,120	13,048	16,168
Total	2,818	10,584	27,804	42,109	33,743	117,059

* Rounded to nearest dollar.

TABLE MN–16

Postnegotiation Percentage Wage Increases

	Seniority				
Grade	< 1 Yr.	1–2 Yr.	3–5 Yr.	6–10 Yr.	> 10 Yr.
1	8.6	8.0	7.7	7.7	7.7
2	5.4	7.9	7.3	10.3	6.9
3	8.0	7.9	7.4	6.9	6.5
4	7.6	7.2	7.9	7.4	6.9
5	7.4	7.0	6.7	7.8	7.5

B. Approach

Assume the GMFC-Local 384 contract is due to expire soon and the union has made a timely notification to management that it desires renegotiations. It is your responsibility to negotiate a new contract. Following are the demands of both labor and management and supplemental information that will help in choosing contract demands.

C. Demands

The union may formulate its demands from the following set, including all items from *a* through *d* and choosing any four from *e* through *k*:

a. A general wage increase of 75 cents per hour during each year of the contract, plus an additional 50 cents per hour at the effective date.

b. The company will neither subcontract work the bargaining unit is capable of performing nor close the plant or move any of its operations during the life of the agreement.

c. A 50-cent additional increase will be given to maintain wage differentials for employees outside of the assembler A and B classifications.

d. Reimplementation of a COLA based on 5 cents per hour for each one-point increase in the consumer price index.

e. The two-tier wage plan will be abolished, with lower-tier employees immediately increased to the pay rates of upper-tier employees.

f. The A jobs appear to be male-dominated occupations, while the B jobs are female-dominated occupations. Because they appear to be of comparable worth to the organization, A and B jobs will be mer-

ged, with grade 61 being equated to grade 7, 62 with 8, and so on. The B classification will be eliminated after the merger.

g. Vacations will be increased one week for employees with eight or more years of service.

h. The company's pension contribution will be increased from 5 percent of straight-time earnings to 6 percent of straight- and overtime earnings. Benefits will be 100 percent vested in three years.

i. A union-shop clause will be implemented, with membership required after 60 days of employment.

j. Double pay will be given for all overtime after nine hours in a day and for all Sunday or holiday work.

k. Company-paid dental and optical insurance will be provided.

The company's offers and demands will be formulated from the following list. All demands between *a* and *d* will be included in the offer, and any four demands between *e* and *k* may be included:

a. The length of the agreement will be three years.

b. Management shall have the right to subcontract or move to another plant any work without consulting the union.

c. Wage increases of 25 cents, 35 cents, and 40 cents will be given at the beginning of each year of the contract to graded employees. Employees in jobs with defined titles will receive increases of 2.5 percent, 3 percent, and 3.5 percent at the beginning of each year of the contract.

d. The cost-of-living allowance (Section 7.02), which was suspended during the concessions, will be eliminated.

e. The two-tier wage plan negotiated into the previous agreement will be continued. Newly hired employees will begin

at $1.25 below those of present employ-
ees. Wage increases to new employees
will occur as negotiated for all employees.

f. Persons promoted to supervisory positions will continue to accrue seniority
within the bargaining unit after their promotion.

g. Jobs will be consolidated into six different
levels. Employees will be expected to be
proficient in the duties included in all present jobs within each of the levels within
six months after the effective date of the
agreement. Level 1 includes all employees whose wage rates were at or below
$8.50 per hour at the beginning of the last
contract, level 2, those at or below $9.00,
level 3, those at or below $9.50, level 4,
those at or below $10.00, level 5, those at
or below $10.50, and level 6, those above
$10.50. Promotions to higher job levels
will require demonstration of skills required by the next level and at least one
year of service at the level immediately
below. Persons will be expected to demonstrate skills associated with all jobs at
their level.

h. Employees will pay the first $500 of health
care costs annually before the company-
paid health care plan will begin to pay
benefits.

i. All promotions will be determined by
merit and ability alone. Seniority will continue to be used for layoffs and recalls.

j. Bargaining unit members who elect to
join the union must maintain membership during the life of the agreement.
With each contract expiration, individuals who had been members will be free
to withdraw during the first week of the
subsequent agreement.

k. The losing party in arbitration shall be
responsible for all expenses of the arbitration procedure.

D. Organization for Negotiations

Each labor team will be headed by a chief
negotiator. One member of labor's team
should assume the role of international representative. Team sizes should be not less than
three nor more than eight. Each management
team will be headed by the plant labor relations director and may include experts from
other functional areas—manufacturing, accounting, shipping, and so forth. Management team sizes should be about the same as
labor's.

Before negotiations, each team should:

1. Construct its demand or offer package
and identify the relative priority of the
issues being included.
2. Identify issues it would be willing to trade
off.
3. Develop bargaining books tying demands
to provisions in the present contract.
Identify for each demand a desired settlement position, an expected settlement
position, and a maximum concession
position before bargaining.
4. Cost the provisions of the contract that
would be changed. (Both parties should
do this.)
5. Identify and develop strategies and tactics
to be used during the negotiations. Structure the roles of each member.

E. Negotiations

1. At the first bargaining session, labor and
management shall first agree on an
agenda and order of presentation. If a
mutually satisfactory agenda cannot be
achieved, the following may be used:
   a. Each demand or offer will be presented separately, with the other

party responding. Normally, where both sides will make offers on the same issue, the union will present its demand first.

  b. All demands will be presented and responded to before any concession is made.

2. As you begin to bargain, you should remember that once a concession is made, it is very difficult to retract it. Thus, carefully consider changes in your positions before announcing them.

3. During the process, it is often beneficial to suspend face-to-face negotiations to hold a caucus of your bargaining group to consider a demand or concession.

4. As you negotiate, consider the impact the bargaining outcomes you attain will have on the bargaining relationship after the contract is signed. Is this a concession the other side can live with?

5. After the contract is agreed to, management must determine the final cost impact of the agreement, and the union must develop a strategy for gaining rank-and-file ratification.

F. Additional Information

1. The terms of the contract may have some cost impact outside of the bargaining unit, because improved fringe benefits are usually passed on to nonunion white-collar workers.

2. Over the last contract, the average amount of overtime per year has been distributed as shown in Table MN–17.

3. The plant has experienced serveral layoffs since 1981. The plant population at the end of 1980 was 1,208, the largest ever achieved. In 1981, the production work force was cut by 20 percent in January and another 20 percent in March. In April 1982, 10 percent were recalled, with an additional 10 percent in October 1982, and a final 10 percent in May 1983. Maintenance and craft employment was cut 10 percent in January 1981, 10 percent in March 1981, 10 percent in June 1981, and 10 percent in September 1981. Recalls of 10 percent were made in January 1982, June 1982, and May 1983. Of those who were laid off, all were recalled except five

TABLE MN–17
Average Overtime Hours Worked per Employee under the Expiring Agreement

	Production (A and B)			Nonproduction (Maintenance and Craft)		
	1989	1990	1991	1989	1990	1991
Saturdays (9-hour shift)	144	72	54	45	18	9
Weekday 9th hours	88	37	16	29	8	4
Holidays (8 hours)	1	0	0	1	0	0
Sundays (8 hours)	0	0	0	4	2	1
Miscellaneous overtime, not elsewhere classified	2	1	0	18	6	4
Total	235	110	70	97	34	18

employees with less than one year of service at the time of the layoffs. In January 1991, after adequate contractual notice, the plant was shut down for two weeks. In June 1991, 10 percent of the maintenance work force was laid off. In July 1991, 20 percent of the production work force was laid off. All were recalled in October 1991. The present seniority list (as of January 1, 1992) is shown in Table MN–18. Turnover includes quits, retirements, and promotions and transfers out of the bargaining unit. All employees who have reached 30 years of service in the bargaining unit have retired when they became eligible.

4. The B job classification consists of 88 percent women, while the A classification consists of 96 percent men. All men in B jobs and all women in A jobs have less than 10 years' seniority.

5. The plant has been located in Central City for almost 40 years, but it expanded rapidly during the early to middle 1970s. No expansion is planned for the Central City facility at present. The company does have other similar operations in the United States and abroad, and one relatively new plant in the Sunbelt is unorganized. In total, 75 percent of production employees are represented, all by the Steelworkers.

6. Presently, 983 of the bargaining unit members belong to the union.

7. The average arbitration case cost the company and the union $5,750 each during the last contract. Arbitrators heard 18 cases and ruled for the company on 13, for the union on 5.

8. Table MN–19 gives a distribution of employees by job and seniority.

9. Productivity changes over the past five years have been as follows: 1987, up 4 percent; 1988, up 5 percent; 1989, up 3 percent; 1990, up 1 percent; 1991, up 4 percent.

10. You should consider the costs of health fringes, social security and other wage-tied benefits, and changes in the consumer price index (if applicable) when costing contract terms.

11. For wage-comparison purposes, GMFC operations are in Standard Industrial Classification (SIC) codes 3441 (Fabricated Structural Metals), 3443 (Fabricated Plate Work), 3531 (Construction Machinery and Equipment), and 3537 (Industrial Trucks, Tractors, Trailers, and Stackers).

12. Recent selected financial information for this location is shown in Table MN–20.

TABLE MN-18

Seniority of Employees and Turnover Rates by Length of Service (seniority list as of January 1, 1992

Years of Seniority	Number of Employees	Cumulative Number	Percent Turnover
30	4	4	100.0
29	19	23	1.0
28	24	47	1.0
27	16	63	1.0
26	17	80	1.0
25	19	99	1.0
24	16	115	1.0
23	14	129	1.0
22	9	138	1.0
21	11	149	1.0
20	13	162	1.0
19	98	260	1.0
18	139	399	1.0
17	102	501	1.0
16	114	615	1.0
15	26	641	1.0
14	59	700	1.0
13	93	793	1.0
12	66	859	1.0
11	17	876	1.0
10	57	933	1.0
9	8	941	1.5
8	2	943	2.0
7	0	943	2.5
6	0	943	3.0
5	6	949	4.0
4	8	957	5.0
3	2	959	6.0
2	13	972	8.0
1	11	983	10.0
<1	8	991	30.0

TABLE MN-19

Seniority Level by Job at End of Expiring Contract

Data as of 1/1/92	No. Employees																			Years of Seniority													Tot.
		<1	1	2	3	4	5	6	7	8	9	10	11	12	13	14	15	16	17	18	19	20	21	22	23	24	25	26	27	28	29	30	
Assembler B, grade 61	17	5	4	0	0	0	0	0	0	0	0	0	0	0	0	0	0	0	0	0	0	0	0	0	0	0	0	0	0	0	0	0	9
Assembler B, grade 62	88	0	0	0	0	0	2	0	0	0	3	20	6	24	32	0	0	0	0	0	0	0	0	0	0	0	0	0	0	0	0	0	87
Assembler B, grade 63	81	0	0	0	0	0	0	0	0	0	0	0	0	1	0	22	8	39	11	0	0	0	0	0	0	0	0	0	0	0	0	0	83
Assembler B, grade 64	66	0	0	0	0	0	0	0	0	0	0	0	0	0	0	0	0	0	25	41	0	0	0	0	0	0	0	0	0	0	0	0	67
Assembler B, grade 65	48	0	0	0	0	0	0	0	0	0	0	0	0	0	0	0	0	0	0	6	33	0	4	1	1	0	0	0	0	0	0	0	48
Assembler B, grade 66	27	0	0	0	0	0	0	0	0	0	0	0	0	0	0	0	0	0	0	0	0	0	2	5	5	6	6	3	0	0	0	0	28
Assembler B, grade 67	16	0	0	0	0	0	0	0	0	0	0	0	0	0	0	0	0	0	0	0	0	0	0	0	0	0	0	3	0	8	6	0	17
Assembler A, grade 7	18	2	5	0	2	0	0	0	0	1	0	0	0	0	0	0	0	0	0	0	0	0	0	0	0	0	0	0	0	0	0	0	10
Assembler A, grade 8	118	0	0	0	0	0	0	0	0	0	4	29	9	34	10	33	0	0	0	0	0	0	0	0	0	0	0	0	0	0	0	0	119
Assembler A, grade 9	78	0	0	0	0	0	0	0	0	0	0	0	0	0	37	30	13	0	0	0	0	0	0	0	0	0	0	0	0	0	0	0	80
Assembler A, grade 10	95	0	0	0	0	0	0	0	0	0	0	0	0	0	0	0	0	33	51	11	0	0	0	0	0	0	0	0	0	0	0	0	95
Assembler A, grade 11	65	0	0	0	0	0	0	0	0	0	0	0	0	0	0	0	0	0	0	61	4	1	0	0	0	0	0	0	0	0	0	0	66
Assembler A, grade 12	46	0	0	0	0	0	0	0	0	0	0	0	0	0	0	0	0	0	0	0	46	0	1	0	0	0	0	0	0	0	0	0	47
Assembler A, grade 13	37	0	0	0	0	0	0	0	0	0	0	0	0	0	0	0	0	0	0	0	0	6	5	5	7	8	4	2	0	0	0	0	37
Assembler A, grade 14	22	0	0	0	0	0	0	0	0	0	0	0	0	0	0	0	0	0	0	0	0	0	0	0	0	0	6	8	7	3	0	0	23
Assembler A, grade 15	13	0	0	0	0	0	0	0	0	0	0	0	0	0	0	0	0	0	0	0	0	0	0	0	0	0	0	0	0	9	4	0	13
Assembler A, grade 16	8	0	0	0	0	0	0	0	0	0	0	0	0	0	0	0	0	0	0	0	0	0	0	0	0	0	0	0	1	3	5	0	9
Tool and model maker	2	0	0	1	1	0	0	0	0	0	0	0	0	0	0	0	0	0	0	0	0	0	0	0	0	0	0	0	0	0	0	0	2
Tool and die maker	2	0	0	0	0	0	0	0	0	0	0	0	0	0	0	0	0	0	0	0	0	0	0	0	0	0	0	1	0	0	1	0	2
Systems control tech.	1	0	0	0	0	0	0	0	0	0	0	0	0	0	0	0	0	0	0	0	1	0	0	0	0	0	0	0	0	0	0	0	1
Jig grinder operator	4	0	0	0	0	0	0	0	0	0	0	0	0	0	0	0	0	0	0	0	0	0	1	0	1	0	0	0	0	1	1	0	4
Meas. and control tech.	1	0	0	0	0	0	0	0	0	0	0	0	0	0	0	0	0	0	0	1	0	0	0	0	0	0	0	0	0	0	0	0	1
Inst. maint. tech.	2	0	0	0	0	0	0	0	0	0	0	0	0	0	0	0	0	0	0	1	0	0	0	1	0	0	0	0	0	0	0	0	2
Electrician	2	0	0	0	0	0	0	0	0	0	0	0	0	0	0	0	0	0	1	0	0	0	0	0	0	0	0	0	1	0	0	0	2
Machinist	12	0	0	0	0	0	0	0	0	0	0	0	0	0	0	0	0	0	3	4	2	0	0	0	0	0	1	1	0	1	1	0	13
Refrig. and AC mech.	2	0	0	0	0	0	0	0	0	0	0	0	0	0	0	0	0	0	1	1	0	0	0	0	0	0	0	0	0	0	0	0	2
Steamfitter	2	0	0	0	0	0	0	0	0	0	0	0	0	0	0	0	0	0	0	1	1	0	0	0	0	0	0	0	0	0	0	0	2
Devel. electr. tech.	5	0	0	0	0	0	0	0	0	0	0	0	0	0	0	0	0	2	1	2	0	0	0	0	0	0	0	0	0	0	0	0	5
Welder	13	0	0	0	0	0	0	0	0	0	0	0	0	0	0	0	0	2	2	3	0	0	0	1	1	1	1	1	1	0	0	0	13
Millwright mechanic	5	0	0	0	0	0	0	0	0	0	0	0	0	0	0	0	0	2	0	1	0	0	0	1	1	0	0	0	0	0	0	0	5
Maintenance mechanic	6	0	0	0	0	0	0	0	0	0	0	0	0	0	0	0	0	2	1	1	0	0	0	0	0	1	0	1	0	0	0	0	6
Millwright	6	0	0	0	0	0	0	0	0	0	0	0	0	0	0	0	0	0	0	1	0	0	0	0	0	0	0	1	0	0	0	0	6

TABLE MN–19

(concluded)

Data as of 1/1/92	No. Employees	<1	1	2	3	4	5	6	7	8	9	10	11	12	13	14	15	16	17	18	19	20	21	22	23	24	25	26	27	28	29	30	Tot.
																																	Years of Seniority
Precision grinder	2	0	0	0	0	0	0	0	0	0	0	0	0	0	0	0	0	0	0	0	1	0	0	0	0	0	0	0	0	0	0	0	2
Layout & setup worker	6	0	0	0	0	0	0	0	0	0	0	0	0	0	0	0	1	0	1	1	1	0	1	0	1	0	0	0	0	0	0	0	6
Painter	3	0	0	0	0	0	0	0	0	0	0	0	0	0	1	0	0	0	1	1	0	0	0	0	0	0	0	0	0	0	0	0	3
Profile mill operator	2	0	0	0	0	0	0	0	0	0	0	0	0	0	0	1	0	0	0	0	0	0	1	0	0	0	0	0	0	0	0	0	2
Machinist trainee	1	0	0	0	0	0	0	0	0	0	0	0	0	0	0	0	0	0	0	1	0	0	0	0	0	0	0	0	0	0	0	0	1
Capital assy. worker	3	0	0	0	0	0	0	0	0	0	0	0	0	1	0	0	0	1	0	1	0	0	0	0	0	0	0	0	0	0	0	0	3
Weldment finisher	2	0	0	0	0	0	0	0	0	0	0	0	0	0	1	1	0	0	0	0	0	0	0	0	0	0	0	0	0	0	0	0	2
Metal fabricator	4	0	0	0	0	0	0	0	0	0	0	0	0	1	0	1	0	1	1	0	0	0	0	0	0	0	0	0	0	0	0	0	4
Grinder operator	5	0	1	0	0	0	0	0	0	0	0	0	0	0	0	1	1	0	1	1	1	0	0	0	0	0	0	0	0	0	0	0	6
Milling machine oper.	3	0	0	0	0	0	0	0	0	0	0	0	0	0	1	0	0	1	1	0	1	0	0	0	0	0	0	0	0	0	0	0	4
Lathe operator	4	0	0	0	0	0	0	0	0	0	0	0	0	0	0	1	1	1	1	0	0	0	0	0	0	0	0	0	0	0	0	0	4
Cabinet maker	2	0	0	0	0	0	0	0	0	0	0	0	0	0	0	1	1	0	0	0	0	0	0	0	0	0	0	0	0	0	0	0	2
Head assembly worker	1	0	0	0	0	0	0	0	0	0	0	0	0	0	0	0	1	0	0	0	0	0	0	0	0	0	0	0	0	0	0	0	1
Locksmith	1	0	0	0	0	0	0	0	0	0	0	0	0	0	0	0	0	1	0	0	0	0	0	0	0	0	0	0	0	0	0	0	1
Specialist	1	0	0	0	0	0	0	0	0	0	0	0	0	0	1	0	0	0	0	0	0	0	0	0	0	0	0	0	0	0	0	0	1
Devel. assembler	1	0	0	0	0	0	1	0	0	0	0	0	0	1	1	1	1	2	0	0	0	0	0	0	0	0	0	0	0	0	0	0	7
Oiler	6	0	0	0	0	0	0	0	0	0	0	0	0	0	0	0	0	2	0	0	0	0	0	0	0	0	0	0	0	0	0	0	2
Steelroom handlers	2	0	0	0	0	0	0	0	0	0	0	0	1	1	0	1	0	1	0	0	0	0	0	0	0	0	0	0	0	0	0	0	4
Machine operator	4	0	0	0	0	0	0	0	0	0	0	0	0	1	0	0	0	1	0	0	0	0	0	0	0	0	0	0	0	0	0	0	2
Head stockroom clerk	2	0	0	0	0	0	0	0	0	0	0	0	1	0	0	0	0	0	0	0	0	0	0	0	0	0	0	0	0	0	0	0	1
Yard worker	1	0	0	0	0	0	0	0	0	0	0	0	0	0	1	0	0	0	0	0	0	0	0	0	0	0	0	0	0	0	0	0	1
Stock service worker	1	1	0	0	0	0	0	0	0	0	0	0	1	0	0	0	0	0	0	0	0	0	0	0	0	0	0	0	0	0	0	0	2
AC cleaner	1	0	1	0	0	0	0	0	0	0	0	0	0	0	0	0	0	0	0	0	0	0	0	0	0	0	0	0	0	0	0	0	1
Truck driver	2	0	0	0	0	0	0	0	0	0	0	1	0	0	0	0	0	0	0	0	0	0	0	0	0	0	0	1	0	0	0	0	2
Experimental assembler	1	0	0	0	0	0	0	0	0	0	0	1	0	0	0	0	0	0	0	0	0	0	0	0	0	0	0	0	0	0	0	0	3
Tool crib attendant	3	0	0	0	0	0	0	0	0	0	0	1	0	1	0	0	0	0	0	0	0	0	0	0	0	0	0	0	0	0	0	0	2
Trades helper	1	0	0	0	0	0	0	0	0	0	1	1	0	0	0	0	0	0	0	0	0	0	0	0	0	0	0	0	0	0	0	0	2
Stockroom clerk	2	0	0	0	0	1	0	0	0	0	0	0	0	0	0	0	0	0	0	0	0	0	0	0	0	0	0	0	0	0	0	0	1
Assembler	1	0	0	0	0	0	0	0	0	0	1	1	0	0	0	0	0	0	0	0	0	0	0	0	0	0	0	0	0	0	0	0	2
Waste hauler	2	0	1	0	0	0	0	0	0	0	0	0	0	0	0	0	0	0	0	0	1	0	0	0	0	0	0	0	0	0	0	0	1
Yard laborer	2	0	0	1	0	0	0	0	0	0	0	0	0	0	0	0	0	0	0	0	0	0	0	0	0	0	0	0	0	0	0	0	2
Janitor	11	0	0	0	0	0	0	0	0	0	0	2	0	1	1	1	1	0	1	0	1	1	0	0	0	0	0	0	0	0	0	0	12
Total by seniority level	991	8	11	13	2	8	6	0	0	2	8	57	17	66	93	59	26	114	102	139	98	13	11	9	14	16	19	17	16	24	19	4	991

311

TABLE MN–20

Selected Financial Information for This Location

	Income Statement (000s)				
	1987	**1988**	**1989**	**1990**	**1991**
Net sales	108,019	127,864	138,219	142,218	132,679
Deductions					
Cost of materials	59,898	74,890	81,374	84,229	74,082
Depreciation	3,475	3,214	3,556	3,618	4,286
Compensation	34,150	35,293	37,010	39,337	41,127
Interest expense	1,626	1,721	1,806	2,219	2,107
Extraordinary charges	0	0	167	0	227
Profit sharing	887	1,275	1,431	1,282	1,085
Income before taxes	7,983	11,471	12,875	11,533	9,765
Provision for taxes	3,193	4,588	5,227	4,682	4,140
Net income	4,790	6,883	7,648	6,851	5,625
	Balance Sheet (Simple)				
Current assets	2,093	4,567	4,864	5,016	4,293
Plant and equipment	66,219	67,086	70,022	71,319	77,086
(less: accum, depr.)	34,942	38,156	41,712	45,330	49,616
Investments	31,226	40,066	47,639	60,732	64,879
Total assets	64,596	73,563	80,813	91,737	96,642
Current liabilities	2,026	3,108	2,799	2,588	3,291
Long-term debt	17,111	18,113	18,024	22,308	20,885
Retained earnings	45,459	52,342	59,990	66,841	72,466
Total liabilities and capital	64,596	73,563	80,813	91,737	96,642
	Employment				
Avg. number of					
employees	1,174	1,153	1,149	1,152	1,137
Bargaining unit					
employees	1,008	1,002	1,002	998	991

AGREEMENT

between

GENERAL MANUFACTURING & FABRICATION COMPANY

CENTRAL CITY, INDIANA,

and

LOCAL 384, UNITED STEELWORKERS OF AMERICA

AFL–CIO/CLC

Effective March 1, 1989

CONTENTS

Article 1. Purpose   315

Article 2. Recognition   315

Article 3. Checkoff of Union Dues   315

Article 4. Management   316

Article 5. Representation   316

Article 6. Hours   316

Article 7. Wages   318

Article 8. Seniority   321

Article 9. Grievance Procedure and No-Strike
           Agreement   326

Article 10. Vacations   328

Article 11. Sick Leave   329

Article 12. General   331

Article 13. Renewal   336

Appendix   Classified Base Rates   337

ARTICLE 1.   PURPOSE

1.01   It is the intent and purpose of the parties hereto that this Agreement will promote and improve industrial and economic relations between the employees and the COMPANY, and to set forth herein a basic agreement covering rates of pay, hours of work, and other conditions of employment to be observed by the parties and to insure the peaceful settlement of disputes and to prevent stoppages of work.

ARTICLE 2.   RECOGNITION

2.01   The COMPANY recognizes Local Union No. 384, United Steelworkers of America, AFL–CIO/CLC, as the exclusive bargaining agent for all hourly paid employees designated in the bargaining unit by the National Labor Relations Board for the Central City plant and warehouses, which includes all production and maintenance employees including machine shop employees and receiving department and warehouse employees but excluding boiler room employees, clerical employees, watchpersons, guards, assistant supervisors, supervisors, and any other supervisory employees with authority to hire, promote, discharge, discipline, or otherwise effect changes in the status of employees or effectively recommend such action.

2.02   Any employee who is a member of the UNION on the effective date of this Agreement shall, as a condition of employment, maintain his/her membership in the UNION to the extent of paying membership dues.

2.03   Any employee who on the effective date of this Agreement is not a member of the UNION shall not be required to become a member of the UNION but shall be required to pay an amount equal to the UNION's regular monthly dues. Any such employee, however, who during the life of the Agreement joins the UNION must remain a member as provided in Section 2.02.

ARTICLE 3.   CHECKOFF OF UNION DUES

3.01   Upon individual authorization from members, monthly UNION DUES in an amount to be determined by the UNION shall be deducted by the COMPANY from each member's first pay in each month. Such sums shall be forwarded by the COMPANY to the financial secretary of the UNION before the 15th day of the month.

ARTICLE 4.   MANAGEMENT

4.01   The UNION and its members recognize that the successful and efficient operation of the business is the responsibility of management and that management of the plant and the direction of the working force is the responsibility of the COMPANY, provided, in carrying out these management functions, the COMPANY does not violate the terms of this Agreement.

4.02   The COMPANY retains the sole right to discipline and discharge employees for cause, provided that in the exercise of this right it will not act wrongfully or unjustly or in violation of the terms of this Agreement.

ARTICLE 5.   REPRESENTATION

5.01   The UNION shall designate a UNION COMMITTEE of no more than 10 members who shall represent the UNION in meetings with the COMPANY, with no more than 7 employees actively working in the plant as members of the committee.

5.02   The COMPANY agrees that during meetings held with management members of the UNION required to attend shall be paid at their regular hourly base rate plus their departmental incentive for all time lost from their regularly assigned work schedule.

ARTICLE 6.   HOURS

6.01   *Work day*   A day starts at the beginning of the first shift and ends at the close of the third shift. The first shift is any shift that starts after midnight. Normally the first shift starts at 7:00 A.M. or 8:00 A.M. Present shift schedules will continue unless changes are mutually agreed to by the COMPANY and the UNION.

6.02   *Payroll week*   The payroll week starts at the beginning of the first shift on Monday and ends at the end of the third shift on Sunday.

6.03   *Daily overtime*   Time and one half shall be paid for all hours worked in excess of eight in any one day. Time and one half shall be paid for all hours worked in excess of eight in any 24-hour period whenever provisions of the Walsh Healy Act apply.

6.04   *Weekly overtime*   Time and one half shall be paid for all hours worked in excess of 40 in any one payroll week for which overtime has not been earned on any other basis.

6.05   *Saturday work*   Time and one half shall be paid for work performed on Saturday between the hours of 7:00 A.M. or 8:00 A.M. Saturday to 7:00 A.M. or 8:00 A.M. on Sunday.

6.06	***Sunday work*** Double time shall be paid for work performed on Sunday between the hours of 7:00 A.M. or 8:00 A.M. Sunday to 7:00 A.M. or 8:00 A.M. Monday.

6.06   ***Sunday work***   Double time shall be paid for work performed on Sunday between the hours of 7:00 A.M. or 8:00 A.M. Sunday to 7:00 A.M. or 8:00 A.M. Monday.

6.07   ***Consecutive hours over 8***   Time and one half shall be paid for all hours worked over 8 but less than 12.

6.08   ***Consecutive hours over 12***   Double time shall be paid for all consecutive hours worked over 12.

6.09   ***Distribution of overtime***   Overtime shall be distributed on an equitable basis within the department in a manner to be decided by the supervision and the UNION representatives in that department, giving consideration to seniority and ability to perform the work. Refused overtime hours shall be credited as overtime hours worked for purposes of distributing overtime.

6.10   ***Shift premium***

a. A shift premium of 30 cents per hour will be paid to all employees for all hours worked on a particular day if 50 percent or more of the hours worked on that day fall between the hours of 3:00 P.M. and 11:00 P.M.

b. A shift premium of 40 cents per hour will be paid to all employees for all hours worked on a particular day if 50 percent or more of the hours worked on that day fall between the hours of 11:00 P.M. and 7:00 A.M.

c. The incentive premium will not be applied to the shift premium.

6.11   ***Holidays***

a. After completion of the probationary period an hourly employee not working on the holiday will be granted holiday benefit consisting of eight hours' straight-time pay at his/her regular hourly base rate on the following holidays:

New Year's Day   Thanksgiving
Memorial Day   Christmas
Independence Day   December 24
Labor Day   December 31
Floating Holiday

b. Double time in addition to the holiday pay, as stated in Section 6.11a, will be paid for all hours worked on the above holidays.

c. The floating holiday will be designated by the COMPANY. The UNION will be notified at least 90 days prior to the day set by the COMPANY.

d. A holiday starts at the beginning of the first shift and ends at the close of the third shift. When one of these holidays falls on Sunday, the holiday shall be observed on Monday. When one

of these holidays falls on Saturday, the holiday shall be observed on Friday.

e. To be eligible, the employee must be at work on the day for
which he/she is scheduled prior to the holiday and following the
holiday unless absence is established for any of the following
reasons:
1. Unavoidable absence caused by sickness or injury.
2. Emergencies in the immediate family.
3. Any other justifiable absence previously approved by his/her
supervisor.

ARTICLE 7.   WAGES

7.01	Effective March 1, 1986, all hourly rates will be contained in the Appendix.
7.02	Effective March 1, 1990, all hourly rates will be increased by $.35.
7.03	Effective March 1, 1991, all hourly rates will be increased by $.45.
7.04	Effective March 1, 1982, all cost-of-living adjustments contained in previous Agreements are suspended.
7.05	Effective March 1, 1982, 10 percent of profits (net income before provision for income taxes) generated by the plant for the calendar year ending on December 31, 1982, and continuing thereafter on December 31 of each calendar year will be divided among members of the bargaining unit. Each employee will receive an amount equal to his/her hours worked divided by the total number of hours worked by the bargaining unit during the calendar year times the profit proportion (if any). Profit-sharing payments will be made not later than January 31 of the following year for distributions earned for the preceding calendar year.
7.06	Effective March 1, 1989, all cost-of-living adjustments, suspended or accrued, are cancelled. In return, each employee will receive a lump sum bonus on December 31, 1989, equal to 5 percent of 1989 straight-time pay.
7.07	*Job classification plan* The principle of like pay for like work shall prevail. The rates for production jobs throughout the plant shall continue to be established or reviewed by the COMPANY and the UNION after careful rating under the job classification plan in proportion to all factors of skill, responsibility, effort, and working conditions of each individual job. When a new job is established or the duties and responsibilities of any job have changed sufficiently to place that job in a different pay bracket, a special job rating to determine the proper rate will be made no later than 30 days from

the rating request. A special form for this purpose will be supplied by the COMPANY.

7.08   ***Rates retained above classified rates***

    a. If, as a result of job classification, the classified rate for a job is lowered, the employee on the job will retain his/her current rate for that job. In the event of a wage increase, he/she will participate to the extent that it does not bring his/her rate above the classified rate. Future transfers, promotions, and demotions will conform to the new rate schedule established as a result of job classification. If the higher rate is established as a result of job classification, the employee on the job will advance to the proper classified rate as provided in Section 7.07 unless the job increases two pay grades, in which case it will be posted.

    b. An employee who retains a rate above the classified rate on a job that has been reclassified will be expected to accept promotion to a higher classified job within his/her department in accordance with his/her seniority when a vacancy occurs and he/she is considered qualified to handle the job. In the event the employee who is offered the promotion chooses to remain on his/her present job, he/she will receive the new rate for his/her job on the following Monday, except in cases where the promotion would result in changing from a fixed day shift to a shift operation.

7.09   ***New employees***   Employees hired after March 1, 1986, shall be paid at $1.25 per hour less than the rates for their jobs stated in the Appendix to this Agreement during the life of this Agreement.

7.10   ***Promotional increases***   When an employee is promoted to a higher-classified job, he/she will receive the classified rate for the job the first Monday on or after his/her promotion. Employees hired on or after March 1, 1986, will receive $1.25 per hour less than the classified rate.

7.11   ***Temporary service in higher jobs***

    a. Temporary work or part-time service in a higher classified job for periods of less than one full payroll week will not be classified as a promotion or a change in classification. Wherever possible, departmental seniority will be given due consideration in assigning such temporary work.

    b. When an employee has worked temporarily on a higher classified job for 50 percent or more of his/her scheduled hours in the week, he/she will receive the higher rate during the week. When an employee is assigned temporary work in a higher classification, he/she shall, whenever possible, be allowed to complete 50 percent or more of the week on the higher classified job.

7.12   ***Transfers to lower jobs***   When an employee is permanently transferred to a lower classified job, he/she will receive the rate for the lower classification the first Monday on or after transfer to the lower classified job.

7.13   ***Temporary service in lower jobs***   The COMPANY agrees that, while an employee is assigned temporarily to a lower classified job, he/she shall receive his/her regular higher classified rate.

7.14   ***Temporary transfers between departments***   When in the interest of effective and economical operation or as a means of deferring layoffs it is desirable to transfer employees temporarily from one department to another, such temporary transfers may be made for a maximum period of four weeks, if mutually agreeable to both the COMPANY and the UNION. Wherever possible, departmental seniority will be given due consideration in determining employees to be transferred. The UNION agrees to cooperate with the COMPANY in arranging such temporary interdepartment transfers. The COMPANY agrees not to request temporary interdepartment transfers except in the interests of efficient and economical operation or as a means of deferring layoff.

7.15   ***Employee reporting and no work available***   Employees reporting for work according to their regularly assigned work schedules without being notified in advance not to report and work is not available shall be allowed a minimum of four hours' pay at the employees' regular straight-time hourly base rate except in cases beyond the control of the COMPANY.

7.16   ***Call-in pay***   Employees who have been recalled to work after they have completed their regularly scheduled shift and have left the plant shall be given a minimum of four hours' work if they so desire. If four hours' work is not available, the employee shall be paid the hours worked according to the wage and premium pay policy, and the remainder of the four hours not worked shall be paid at the employee's regular straight-time hourly rate.

7.17   ***Jury duty***   The COMPANY agrees to pay the difference between jury duty pay and the employee's straight-time hourly base rate earnings when called for jury duty. When called, the employee will be scheduled to work on the first shift whenever possible. The employee shall be required to report for work whenever he/she is able to work four consecutive hours or more of the first shift.

ARTICLE 8. SENIORITY

8.01   *Plant seniority*   Plant seniority shall be determined from the employee's earliest date of continuous employment with the COMPANY and shall apply to divisional and plant layoffs and plant recalls after layoff.

8.02   *Departmental seniority*   Departmental seniority shall be determined from the employee's earliest date of continuous employment in the department and shall apply to promotions, demotions, and reductions in force within the department.

8.03   *Termination of seniority*   Seniority shall terminate for the following reasons:

a.   Voluntary resignation.

b.   Discharge for proper cause.

c.   Absence for three successive working days without notice, unless satisfactory reason is given.

d.   Failure to report to work after layoff within five working days after being notified by registered letter (return receipt requested) at the employee's last available address, unless satisfactory reason is given. A copy of the written offer shall be sent to the UNION.

8.04   *Employees on layoff*

a.   Employees who are or shall be laid off due to lack of work and later reemployed shall retain their seniority as of the time of the layoff but will not accumulate seniority during the layoff period. If an employee after the first six months of layoff declines to return to work when contacted by the production personnel office regarding an opening, his/her seniority rights shall be terminated.

b.   Employees shall be given three working days' notice of impending layoff from the plant or three days' pay in lieu thereof.

8.05   *Probationary employees*

a.   A new employee shall be on probation without seniority for 40 days actually worked after date of employment by the COMPANY, during which period the COMPANY shall determine the employee's ability to perform satisfactorily the duties and requirements of the work. Layoff or discharge of an employee during such probationary period shall not be subject to the grievance procedure.

b.   Upon satisfactorily completing the probationary period, the employee will be placed on the department's seniority list, and his/her departmental seniority shall date from the beginning of the probationary period. If an employee is transferred to another department during his/her probationary period, his/her departmental seniority shall date back to the date of transfer to the new department upon completion of the probationary period.

8.06 *Promotions and vacancies*   When vacancies are to be filled and increases are to be made in the work force, it shall be done on the following basis:

a. *Departmental postings*
1. When vacancies occur in a department, notices shall be posted by the COMPANY for three working days in the department in which the vacancy occurs and a copy of the posting provided to the UNION representatives of the department. Any employee in the department wishing to fill the vacancy shall make written application on the form provided by the COMPANY containing the following information: (a) department and location, (b) date and hour of posting, (c) serial number of notice, (d) job title and classified rate of vacant job, (e) date job becomes effective, and (f) date and hour of closing time for application.
2. The employee making application with the most departmental seniority shall be given the job, provided he/she is qualified and has the experience to handle the job.

b. *Plant postings*   In the event the vacancy is not filled from the employees in the department as outlined above, the COMPANY agrees to post the vacancy in the plant entrances for three working days, and employees will be selected in accordance with Section 8.06a–2. To expedite the processing time, the opening adjudged to be the resulting vacancy may be posted concurrently with the departmental posting. To be eligible for consideration, an employee must make written application on the form provided for the purpose, a copy of which shall be retained by the production personnel office and a copy to be given to the UNION. The rate of pay for the job and the date the employee's seniority shall commence in the new department will be included in the posting.

c. Transfers between "A" and "B" seniority groups will not be allowed.

d. A qualified applicant shall be given a chance to qualify on the job by a fair trial. Any employee who is disqualified for any reason may have his/her qualifications acted upon in accordance with the grievance procedure.

8.07 *Transfers*
a. When an employee leaves his/her department to accept a job in

another department, his/her seniority rights in the department that he/she left shall not be forfeited for a period of 90 days. If the employee chooses to return to his/her home department (home department is where he/she has recall and return rights) within 90 days from the date of such transfer, he/she shall be returned to his/her former job not later than the third Monday following his/her request, provided he/she has enough seniority; otherwise he/she will be placed in a classification to which his/her seniority entitles him/her, provided it is not higher than the job grade he/she left. If he/she requests transfer to another department within 12 months of his/her return to his/her home department, he/she shall, upon being transferred, forfeit all departmental seniority rights.

b. When an employee has been reduced from his/her home department and is working in another department, he/she may sign plant postings, but the above clause does not apply.

c. If an employee signs a plant posting and during the 90-day period in that job signs another plant posting, he/she has the original 90 days to return to his/her home department but has no right of return to the second department he/she left.

8.08   **Layoffs**

a. *Departmental* When the number of employees in a department is reduced, reduction to lower jobs or layoffs shall be made on the basis of departmental seniority, providing those remaining are qualified to perform the work.

b. *Divisional* The employee ultimately laid off from a department shall be entitled to bump into the department of the least senior employee in the division on the basis of plant seniority, provided he/she has the necessary qualifications to perform the job to which he/she is assigned. In multiple reductions involving the displacement of employees in the department in which reduction is taking place, the employees with the most departmental seniority of those on the original reduction schedule will be retained in the department, providing employees in the reducing department do not have sufficient plant seniority to allow them to remain in the division. Others reduced from the department will be assigned to one or two shifts according to plant seniority. Upon notification to the production personnel department, special shift requests will be given consideration.

c. *Plant* The employee laid off from his/her division shall be entitled to bump into the department of the least senior employee in the plant, providing the claiming employee has the necessary qualifications to perform the job to which he/she is assigned and has more than six months of plant seniority to his/her credit. In case any of the jobs vacated by the least senior employees in the plant are on a one- or two-shift basis as opposed to the ordinary three-shift basis, the employees being laid off from a division who have the most plant seniority shall automatically be given these one- or two-shift jobs. Upon notification to the production personnel department, special shift requests will be given consideration.

d. The employee so reduced or transferred shall accept, according to his/her seniority, the position vacated to make room for him/her. The supervisor shall have the right to place the crew as he/she sees fit on jobs carrying the same classified rate in all cases of emergencies and vacancies, taking into account the most efficient utilization of his/her working force.

e. When a classification is eliminated, the employee(s) occupying that classification may exercise his/her seniority to claim any classification within the department to which his/her seniority entitles him/her. The employee(s) then affected will follow the normal layoff procedure.

f. Bumping shall not be allowed between "A" and "B" seniority groups.

8.09   ***Recall after layoff***

a. When it is necessary to employ additional employees, employees laid off due to lack of work will be recalled in order of their plant seniority, providing they are qualified to handle the jobs, before new employees are hired.

b. When an employee is recalled after layoff for a job in another department and accepts, he/she will retain his/her home departmental seniority until such time as he/she declines an opportunity to return to his/her home department, subject to Section 8.07. If a laid-off employee declines, he/she shall remain on recall to his/her home department for a period not to exceed six months after layoff date. If, during the six months' period, the employee wishes to be considered for an opening in another department, he/she may do so by notifying the production personnel office. Thereafter, he/she must return to work when offered employment by the COMPANY or his/her seniority will be terminated.

8.10   ***Leaves of absence***

a. Members of the UNION, not to exceed three in number at any one time, shall be granted leaves of absence for the duration of this Agreement to work directly for the local UNION. It is further agreed that four additional leaves shall be granted to any employees of the COMPANY covered by this Agreement who have been or who may in the future be elected to or appointed to a full-time office in the international union or the state federation of labor, AFL–CIO, providing that such leaves do not exceed the duration of this Agreement. Upon being relieved of their official positions, they will be entitled to full seniority rights as though they had been employed by the COMPANY continuously.

b. Employees, not to exceed 1 percent of the UNION's membership, who are members of the UNION when delegated or elected to attend a UNION convention or conference shall be granted such leaves of absence as may be necessary, providing reasonable notice is given the COMPANY.

c. Any employee elected to or appointed to any federal, state, or city public office shall be granted a leave of absence during the period he/she is actively engaged in such service.

d. Maternity leave.

   1. An employee who becomes pregnant will be granted a leave of absence upon request at any time during pregnancy and extending for three months after the birth of the child. Where leave of absence is taken, such employee shall not lose seniority that was acquired before the beginning of such leave of absence.

   2. All employees placed on maternity leave of absence shall have their seniority dates adjusted upon their return by an amount of time equal to the number of days absent prior to and after the birth of the child.

8.11 *Supervisory and other salaried positions*

a. It is recognized that all supervisory employees are representatives of management and the assignment of their duties, promotions, demotions, and transfers is the responsibility of the COMPANY and cannot be determined on the basis of seniority.

b. Any supervisory employees, including quality supervisors, promoted from any hourly job shall maintain seniority as follows:

   1. Hourly employees promoted to supervisory positions prior to January 1, 1980, shall continue to accumulate seniority while holding a supervisory position.

   2. Hourly employees promoted to a supervisory position after January 1, 1980, shall accumulate seniority until such a time that he/she holds a supervisory position continuously for six months. After six continuous months his/her seniority in the bargaining unit shall be frozen as of the date of promotion. If

later reduced to an hourly job, he/she shall be assigned to the job to which his/her accumulated or frozen seniority entitles him/her in the department that he/she left to become a supervisor, providing he/she is qualified to perform the job and providing the job is not in a higher job grade than the job he/she left to become a supervisor. No supervisor as herein defined shall have posting privileges until 30 days following his/her reassignment to an hourly production job. In return for protecting an employee's seniority while he/she is in a supervisory position as well as allowing him/her the right to claim a job in the bargaining unit if reduced from his/her supervisory position, supervisors who are reduced to hourly jobs shall become members of the UNION within 30 days.

c. Supervisory and other salaried employees will not perform the work of hourly production employees except in cases of emergency.

ARTICLE 9.   GRIEVANCE PROCEDURE AND NO–STRIKE AGREEMENT

9.01   *Departmental representatives*   The UNION may designate representatives for each section on each shift and in each department for the purpose of handling grievances that may arise in that department. The UNION will inform the production personnel office in writing as to the names of the authorized representatives. Should differences arise as to the intent and application of the provisions of this Agreement, there shall be no strike, lockout, slowdown, or work stoppage of any kind, and the controversy shall be settled in accordance with the following grievance procedures:

9.02   *Grievances*

Step 1.   The employee and the departmental steward, if the employee desires, shall take the matter up with his/her supervisor. If no settlement is reached in Step 1 within two working days, the grievance shall be reduced to writing on the form provided for that purpose.

Step 2.   The written grievance shall be presented to the supervisor or the general supervisor and a copy sent to the production personnel office. Within two working days after receipt of the grievance, the general supervisor shall hold a meeting, unless mutually agreed otherwise, with the supervisor, the employee, and the departmental steward and the chief steward.

Step 3. If no settlement is reached in Step 2, the written grievance shall be presented to the departmental superintendent, who shall hold a meeting within five working days of the original receipt of the grievance in Step 2 unless mutually agreed otherwise. Those in attendance shall normally be the departmental superintendent, the general supervisor, the supervisor, the employee, the chief steward, departmental steward, a member of the production personnel department, the president of the UNION or his/her representative, and the divisional committee person.

Step 4. If no settlement is reached in Step 3, the UNION COMMITTEE and a national representative of the UNION shall meet with the MANAGEMENT COMMITTEE for the purpose of settling the matter.

Step 5. If no settlement is reached in Step 4, the matter shall be referred to an arbitrator. A representative of the UNION shall meet within five working days with a representative of the COMPANY for the purpose of selecting an arbitrator. If an arbitrator cannot be agreed upon within five working days after Step 4, a request for a list of arbitrators shall be sent to the Federal Mediation and Conciliation Service. Upon obtaining the list, an arbitrator shall be selected within five working days. Prior to arbitration, a representative of the UNION shall meet with a representative of the COMPANY to reduce to writing wherever possible the actual issue to be arbitrated. The decision of the arbitrator shall be final and binding on all parties. The salary, if any, of the arbitrator and any necessary expense incident to the arbitration shall be paid jointly by the COMPANY and the UNION.

9.03 In order to assure the prompt settlement of grievances as close to their source as possible, it is mutually agreed that the above steps will be followed strictly in the order listed and no step shall be used until all previous steps have been exhausted. A settlement reached between the COMPANY and the UNION in any step of this procedure shall terminate the grievance and shall be final and binding on both parties.

9.04 The arbitrator shall not have authority to modify, change, or amend any of the terms or provisions of the Agreement or to add to or delete from the Agreement.

9.05 The UNION will not cause or permit its members to cause or take part in any sit-down, stay-in, or slowdown in any plant of the

9.06

COMPANY or any curtailment of work or restriction of production or interference with the operations of the COMPANY.

The UNION will not cause or permit its members to cause or take part in any strike of any of the COMPANY's operations, except where the strike has been fully authorized as provided in the constitution of the international union.

ARTICLE 10. VACATIONS

10.01

The vacation year shall be from April 1 to and including March 31. Wherever possible, however, vacations shall be taken before December 31 of any one year. Vacations for any two years shall not be taken consecutively.

10.02

One week's vacation One week's vacation with pay (see Section 10.07) will be granted to an employee who has accumulated 12 months or more of service credit prior to September 30 of the vacation year, provided he/she has accumulated a minimum of 6 months' service credit during the 12-month period immediately preceding April 1 of the vacation year and is actively working on or after April 1 of the vacation year.

10.03

Two weeks' vacation Two weeks' vacation with pay (see Section 10.07) will be granted to an employee who has accumulated 36 months or more of service credit by December 31 of the vacation year, provided he/she has accumulated a minimum of 6 months' service credit during the 12-month period immediately preceding April 1 of the vacation year and is actively working on or after April 1 of the vacation year.

10.04

Three weeks' vacation Three weeks' vacation with pay (see Section 10.07) will be granted to an employee who will complete 120 months or more of service credit by December 31 of the vacation year, provided he/she has accumulated a minimum of 6 months' service credit during the 12-month period immediately preceding April 1 of the vacation year and is actively working on or after April 1 of the vacation year.

10.05

Four weeks' vacation Four weeks' vacation with pay (see Section 10.07) will be granted to an employee who will complete 180 months or more of service credit by December 31 of the vacation year, provided he/she has accumulated a minimum of 6 months' service credit during the 12-month period immediately preceding April 1 of the vacation year and is actively working on or after April 1 of the vacation year.

10.06

Five weeks' vacation Five weeks' vacation with pay (see Section

10.07) will be granted to an employee who will complete 300 months or more of service credit by December 31 of the vacation year, provided he/she has accumulated a minimum of 6 months' service credit during the 12-month period immediately preceding April 1 of the vacation year and is actively working on or after April 1 of the vacation year.

10.07   One week of vacation pay shall consist of 40 hours' pay at the employee's regular straight-time hourly base rate plus the average incentive percentage of the eight weeks prior to April 1 of the department in which he/she is working at the time the vacation is taken.

10.08   If a holiday recognized with this Agreement falls within an employee's vacation period, he/she shall be granted an extra day of vacation, provided the employee is eligible for holiday pay on that holiday.

10.09   Any employee who is discharged for proper cause will not be eligible for vacation.

10.10   Vacations shall be granted at such times of the year as the COMPANY finds most suitable, considering both the wishes of the employee according to plant seniority and the requirements of plant operation.

10.11   Employees who are laid off will be granted the vacation to which they are otherwise ineligible if they have worked a minimum of 1,600 straight-time hours since the previous April 1.

ARTICLE 11.   SICK LEAVE

11.01   *Employees with one- to five-year service credit*   Employees who have accumulated 12 months but less than 60 months of service credit shall be entitled to a maximum of four working days' sick leave (32 hours straight-time pay at the employee's regular hourly base rate) in any one year calculated from April 1 to March 31, inclusive. Such benefits, not to exceed eight hours in any day, will apply only to time lost from scheduled work for reasons of personal illness or injury except that no benefits will be paid for the first two scheduled working days of any period of such absence.

11.02   *Employees with five or more years of service credit*
   a. Eligibility   A five-year employee who has accumulated 60 months of service credit will receive the difference between sickness and accident insurance or worker's compensation benefits for which he/she is eligible and his/her regular hourly base

rate for time lost due to unavoidable absence as defined in Section 11.02e, which occurs during the first 40 hours he/she is scheduled to work in any week, not to exceed 8 hours in any one day, and subject to Section 11.02d.

b. *Amount of benefits* The benefits made available each year shall be 80 hours. The year starts April 1. Combined benefits on any day of qualified absence shall total the amount equal to the number of qualified hours multiplied by the employee's base rate. In no instance shall this payment total more than base rate earnings of 8 hours per scheduled work day nor more than base rate earnings of 40 hours per scheduled work week. In other words, the COMPANY shall supplement with sick leave payments any compensation or insurance payments from a company-financed private or government plan with an amount of money sufficient to make the combined total payment equal to 8 hours of base rate pay per day of qualified absence or 40 hours per week of qualified absence.

1. If the employee qualifies for compensation from a company-financed private or governmental plan, his/her available sick leave benefits will be charged 19.9 hours per 40-hour week or 49.8 percent of the eligible working hours absent for part weeks. If the employee does not qualify for compensation from a company-financed private or governmental plan, his/her available sick leave benefits will be charged with 100 percent of the eligible working hours absent.

c. *Accumulation*
1. Sick leave benefits unused in any year of the plan may be accumulated for possible use in the next two years. When fourth-year benefits become available, the unused benefits from the first year automatically cancel and so on for each succeeding year. Order of sick leave usage is, first, the current year's benefits and second, the oldest year's benefits. Employees out sick before April 1 whose absence due to that illness extends through April 1 will first use those benefits that were available at the commencement of the absence.

d. *Waiting period* There shall be no waiting period for the first five days (40 hours) of sick leave usage in a benefit year. However, no benefits shall be payable for the first normally scheduled working day in any period of absence commencing thereafter.

e. Unavoidable absence is defined as follows:
1. Unavoidable absence caused by sickness or injury.
2. Emergencies in the immediate family.

f. Immediate family shall consist of the following with no exceptions:

Spouse	Son	Sister
Mother	Daughter	Mother-in-law
Father	Brother	Father-in-law

In addition, the death of the employee's grandfather or grandmother will be recognized as an emergency in the immediate family to the extent of allowing one day's benefit, provided it is necessary that he/she be absent.

11.03   a. A 15-year hourly employee will receive straight-time pay at his/her regular hourly base rate for time lost due to hospitalization in a recognized hospital or convalescence thereafter that occurs during the first 40 hours he/she is scheduled to work in any week not to exceed 8 hours in any day. The total amount of such allowance will not exceed 80 hours in any one year, calculated from year to year. Benefits provided in this paragraph will not apply to days of unavoidable absence for which benefits are paid under the provisions of Section 11.02.

b. A 25-year hourly employee will receive straight-time pay at his/her regular hourly base rate for time lost due to hospitalization in a recognized hospital or convalescence thereafter that occurs during the first 40 hours he/she is scheduled to work in any week not to exceed 8 hours in any day. The total amount of such allowance will not exceed 160 hours (an additional 80 hours to [a] above) in any one year, calculated from year to year. Benefits provided in this paragraph will not apply to days of unavoidable absence for which benefits are paid under the provisions of Section 2 above.

11.04   In order to obtain these benefits, the employee shall, if required, furnish his/her supervisor satisfactory reason for absence.

11.05   The COMPANY and the UNION agree to cooperate in preventing and correcting abuses of these benefits.

ARTICLE 12.   GENERAL

12.01   ***Bulletin boards***   The COMPANY shall provide bulletin boards that may be used by the UNION for posting notices approved by the industrial relations manager or someone designated by him/her and restricted to:

a. Notices of UNION recreational and social affairs.
b. Notices of UNION elections.
c. Notices of UNION appointments and results of UNION elections.

d. Notices of UNION meetings.

e. And other notices mutually agreed to.

12.02 **Relief periods**

a. Relief periods of 25 minutes for every eight-hour work period will be on COMPANY time at such times in each department as will be most beneficial to the employees and the COMPANY. A lunch period on COMPANY time may be substituted for relief period, provided the total time allowed for lunch and relief period in an eight-hour work period does not exceed 25 minutes.

b. The relief and lunch periods in each department will be determined by the department supervisors and the UNION stewards, considering both the wishes of the employees and the requirements of efficient departmental operations.

12.03 All benefits now in effect and not specifically mentioned in this Agreement affecting all hourly paid employees of the COMPANY shall not be terminated for the duration of this Agreement.

12.04 **Sickness and accident** The COMPANY agrees to maintain its current sickness and accident insurance plans, as amended, effective December 1, 1985. Benefits begin one month after the sickness and accident initially occurred and continue for six months. Benefits will be equal to 60 percent of the employee's straight-time wage at the time of the sickness or accident.

12.05 **Long-term disability plan** Subject to the provisions and qualifications of the long-term disability plan, there will be available monthly income benefits commencing after 26 weeks of continuous disability and continuing until recovery or death but not beyond the normal retirement date. The monthly amount will be $25 per $1,000 on the first $10,000 of group life insurance.

12.06 **Group life insurance**

a. The COMPANY will pay for the first $1,000 of group life insurance available to employees. Employees will have the option of purchasing an additional amount of insurance in accordance with their earnings class schedule.

b. The present permanent and total disability benefit is replaced by a disability waiver-of-premium provision under which coverage will be continued during periods of total disability, while long-term disability payments are being made, but reduced each month by the amount of the long-term disability benefit. Reductions will cease when the amount of insurance in force is equal to the greater of (a) 25 percent of the original amount or (b) the employee's postretirement life amount calculated as of the date of commencement of LTD payments. Coverage will be reduced to the latter amount at the earlier of (a) normal retirement age or (b) commencement of any income under ERI.

12.07   *Retirement income plan*

a.   The COMPANY will contribute an amount equal to 5 percent of each employee's straight-time earnings to the retirement trust fund administered by Commonwealth National Bank, Central City, Indiana.

b.   The COMPANY will provide for 100 percent vesting in pension benefits after five (5) years' service.

c.   Contributions and any investment income earned on them that are forfeited by employees who terminate prior to the vesting of pension benefits will be returned to the COMPANY.

12.08   The COMPANY will contract with Indiana Blue Cross–Blue Shield to provide hospitalization and medical insurance for all employees and their family members residing at home (except children over 21). The COMPANY will pay all premiums necessary to provide full coverage of necessary surgical, medical, and hospital care under Blue Cross–Blue Shield fee schedules when performed in a participating hospital.

12.09   Departmental agreements between COMPANY and UNION representatives shall not supersede provisions contained in this Agreement should controversies arise. In no case, however, shall any retroactive adjustment be made if and when such a departmental agreement is cancelled. Wherever possible, the UNION shall receive a copy of the agreement.

12.10   *Safety*

a.   The COMPANY will make reasonable provisions for the safety and health of the employees of the plant during the hours of their employment. Such protective devices and other safety equipment as the COMPANY may deem necessary to protect employees from injury properly shall be provided by the COMPANY without cost to the employees. The supervisor in each department will arrange for this equipment.

b.   Gloves and uniforms required on such jobs and in such departments as the COMPANY may deem necessary shall be furnished and maintained by the COMPANY.

c.   The UNION agrees in order to protect the employees from injury and to protect the facilities of the plant that it will cooperate to the fullest extent in seeing that the rules and regulations are followed and that it will lend its wholehearted support to the safety program of the COMPANY.

d. Rotating UNION departmental representatives chosen by the UNION will participate in periodic safety inspections conducted by departmental supervision and safety staff.

e. The COMPANY agrees that it will give full consideration to all suggestions from its employees of their representatives in matters pertaining to safety and health, including proper heating and ventilation, and if these suggestions are determined to be sound, steps will be taken to put them into effect.

f. It shall be considered a regular part of each employee's regular work to attend such safety meetings as may be scheduled by the COMPANY. Hours spent at safety meetings will be compensated for as hours worked.

g. It is understood that the COMPANY shall not be required to provide work for employees suffering from compensable or other injuries; the COMPANY, however, will offer regular work that may be available to such employees, provided that they can perform all duties of the job.

12.11   Other than for the recall provisions of the Agreement and the privileges accorded an employee under the COMPANY group insurance plans, employees on layoff shall not be entitled to the benefits of this Agreement.

12.12   *Supplementary unemployment benefit plan*

a. *Objective*   To provide a greater measure of income protection during periods of unemployment for all eligible employees by supplementing state unemployment benefit payments.

b. *Principles*

1. To provide income protection for permanent full-time employees as mentioned in (*a*) above.

2. To preserve the necessary differential between amount received while unemployed and straight-time weekly earnings while working so as to provide an incentive for the unemployed to become employed. This differential is defined to be 65 percent of straight-time weekly earning less any normal deductions that are not of the savings variety.

3. The COMPANY will pay the difference between 65 percent of straight-time weekly earnings less normal deductions and the state unemployment benefit for which the employee qualifies. In the event the state benefit check is reduced because of ineligibility, the SUB payment will be reduced in the same proportion. The straight-time weekly earnings will

be based on the week of layoff. The number of weeks an employee qualifies for would depend on length of service.

  c. *Eligibility*

    1. Permanent, full-time employees covered under this Agreement.

    2. Five years or more of service.

    3. On layoff from the COMPANY as per seniority provisions in the UNION-MANAGEMENT Agreement and with the following conditions present:

      a. Be able and available for work.

      b. Maintain an active and continuing search for work.

      c. Register and maintain constant contact with the State Employment Office.

      d. Accept referral by the COMPANY to other employers in the area and accept resulting employment offers if deemed suitable under terms of the existing state system.

      e. Layoff not due to a strike, slowdown, work stoppage, or concerted action.

      f. Layoff not due to a labor dispute with the COMPANY or labor picketing conducted on the COMPANY premises which interferes with the COMPANY's operations.

      g. Layoff not due to voluntary quit.

      h. Layoff not due to discipilinary suspensions or discharges.

      i. Layoff not due to leaves of absence.

    4. Weeks of eligibility.

      0–5 years' service credit—0 weeks of SUB.

      5–26 years' service credit—1 week of SUB for each full year of service credit.

      26 or more years service credit—26 weeks of SUB.

  d. *Reinstatement* When an employee has received any benefits for which s/he is eligible under this plan as per the schedule, s/he will have his full benefits reinstated after 6 months of continuous service.

  e. *To obtain benefits* To obtain benefits, the employee must initiate the claim by preparing the necessary forms and presenting his/her state unemployment check weekly to the personnel office for verification and process of claim.

12.13 In the event any section or any article of this Agreement shall be found to be illegal or inoperable by any government authority of competent jurisdiction, the balance of the Agreement shall remain in full force and effect.

12.14   *Nondiscrimination agreement*

    a. The COMPANY and the UNION agree that the provisions of this agreement shall apply to all employees covered by the Agreement without discrimination, and, in carrying out their respective obligations, it will not discriminate against any employee on account of race, color, national origin, age, sex, or religion.

    b. In an effort to make the grievance procedure a more effective instrument for the handling of any claims of discrimination, special effort shall be made by the representatives of each party to raise such claims where they exist and at as early a stage in the grievance procedure as possible. If not earlier, a claim of discrimination shall be stated at least in the third-step proceedings. The grievance and arbitration procedure shall be the exclusive contractual procedure for remedying discrimination claims.

ARTICLE 13. RENEWAL

13.01   This Agreement shall become effective as of March 1, 1989, and shall continue in full force and effect until 11:59 P.M., February 29, 1992, and thereafter from year to year unless written notice to modify, amend, or terminate this Agreement is served by either party 60 days prior to the expiration of this Agreement, stating in full all changes desired.

13.02   After receipt of such notice by either party, both parties shall meet for the purpose of negotiating a new agreement within 30 days from the date of service of said notice, unless the time is extended by mutual agreement.

APPENDIX

Job title	Wage rate	Job title	Wage rate
Assembler B, grade 61	8.40	Maintenance mechanic	10.99
Assembler B, grade 62	8.465	Millwright	10.99
Assembler B, grade 63	8.53	Precision grinder	10.99
Assembler B, grade 64	8.595	Layout and setup worker	10.90
Assembler B, grade 65	8.66	Painter	10.90
Assembler B, grade 66	8.725	Profile mill operator	10.57
Assembler B, grade 67	8.79	Machinist trainee	10.57
Assembler A, grade 7	8.905	Capital assembly worker	10.38
Assembler A, grade 8	9.00	Weldment finisher	10.38
Assembler A, grade 9	9.095	Metal fabricator	9.30
Assembler A, grade 10	9.19	Grinder operator	9.30
Assembler A, grade 11	9.285	Milling machine operator	9.30
Assembler A, grade 12	9.38	Lathe operator	9.30
Assembler A, grade 13	9.475	Cabinet maker	9.30
Assembler A, grade 14	9.57	Head assembly worker	9.23
Assembler A, grade 15	9.665	Locksmith	9.16
Assembler A, grade 16	9.76	Specialist	9.07
Tool and model maker	11.74	Developmental assembler	8.93
Tool and die maker	11.53	Oiler	8.88
Systems control technician	11.35	Steelroom handler	8.855
Jig grinder operator	11.26	Machine operator	8.855
Measurement and control		Head stockroom clerk	8.855
technician	11.17	Yard worker	8.73
Instrument maintenance		Stock service worker	8.73
technician	11.17	Air conditioning cleaner	8.73
Electrician	11.17	Truck driver	8.60
Machinist	11.08	Experimental assembler	8.60
Refrigeration and air		Tool crib attendant	8.60
conditioning mechanic	11.08	Trades helper	8.60
Steamfitter	11.08	Stockroom clerk	8.60
Development electronics		Assembler	8.385
technician	11.08	Waste hauler	8.36
Welder	10.99	Yard laborer	8.36
Millwright mechanic	10.99	Janitor	8.315

11

IMPASSES AND THEIR RESOLUTION

Negotiations do not always result in an agreement. If one is trying to buy a car and the dealer is unwilling to sell at the highest offer, a sale is not made. The same thing happens in labor-management negotiations when management and the union can't agree on the terms of a new contract. The inability to agree is called an **impasse.** Unlike a car purchase, the union isn't free to seek a new employer to deal with, and the company must still be willing to negotiate with the union representing its employees.

Most negotiations do not result in an impasse. The parties usually find a common ground for settlement; strikes or interventions by third parties are not required. Data from 1989 find about 17 million workdays were lost to strikes—only about 0.07 percent of time available.[1]

This chapter examines the causes of impasses, the tactics used to resolve impasses, and the interventions of third parties. This chapter focuses on the private sector. Public-sector impasse resolution procedures, which are generally more complex and often applicable only to certain occupational classifications, are covered in Chapter 15.

In reading this chapter, attention should be focused on these issues:

1. How are impasses handled in employers covered by the Railway Labor Act?
2. What actions can labor and management legally take after an impasse is reached?
3. What is involved in **mediation**?
4. What steps do the parties take to reduce the incidence of impasses?

IMPASSE DEFINITION

A bargaining impasse occurs when the parties are unable to move further toward settlement. The impasse may result from nonoverlapping settlement ranges—the least the union is willing to take is more than the most the employer is willing to offer— or from the inability or unwillingness of the parties to communicate enough information about possible settlements for an agreement to be reached. The first type is more difficult to overcome because it requires at least one party to adjust its settlement range to reach a solution. The second type may be helped by mediators who facilitate communication and keep the parties working toward a settlement.

Mediated impasses are dealt with first by examining the procedures used to open communications to allow reassessment and adjustment of bargaining stances that lead toward settlement. Because employees in most public-sector jobs are legally precluded from striking, third parties are used more frequently there. General types of third-party interventions used across both public and private sectors are covered here, and their application in public jurisdictions is explained in greater detail in Chapter 15.

THIRD-PARTY INVOLVEMENT

Major types of third-party interventions include mediation, **fact–finding,** and arbitration. Each becomes progressively more constraining on the freedom of the parties; but in most non–Railway Labor Act private-sector negotiations (except for health care organizations under federal legislation), parties must agree voluntarily before any third-party involvement can occur. The only major exception involves national emergency disputes under the Taft-Hartley Act, in which outside fact-finding is required. However, Taft-Hartley procedures have not been imposed for more than a decade.

MEDIATION

In mediation, a neutral third party tries to assist principals to reach an agreement. Procedures are tailored to the situation and aimed at opening communications and identifying settlement cues the parties may have missed.

While some parties use mediation before an impasse, the mediator most often deals with parties who have been unable to agree on their own, are at impasse, and have broken off negotiations. The mediator may have trouble not only in getting a settlement but also in resuming bargaining. To show strength, both sides may refuse to propose a bargaining session; if one appeared willing to reopen bargaining, the other might interpret it as weakness.

The mediator must ultimately get the parties face to face to reach a settlement, but often many sessions will be held between the mediator and a party to assess possibilities of movement. Changing the location of a meeting to the mediator's office may increase the mediator's strength in the process. Mediation requires the parties to continue to communicate and negotiate, but not at an intensity leading to a hardening of positions.[2]

Because the parties have reached an impasse, the mediator has to not only keep communications open but also move the parties toward settlement, if possible. Mediators apparently use one of two approaches. In the public sector, if bargainers are less experienced, mediators may try to create an acceptable package by obtaining the facts in dispute and the priorities of the parties regarding a settlement. With this information, they attempt to "make a deal" that both parties can accept. In private-sector mediation involving federal mediators, settlements are "orchestrated" through information exchange to build a settlement parties recognize as acceptable. Mediators let parties establish their own priorities and help them prepare negotiating proposals.[3]

To get an assessment of settlement possibilities, the mediator may try out hypothetical settlements to see the parties' reactions. The relative rigidity of a party's position must be assessed so the mediator knows whether the party is willing to compromise on given issues. As a strike deadline approaches, the mediator communicates assessments of the likelihood of a strike, the possible settlement packages available, and the costs of striking versus settling on one of the present proposals.

A few excerpts from Ann Douglas's classic work on mediation helps show the role of the mediator in resolving disputes.[4] In Exhibit 11–1, the mediator gives the union caucus some background on negotiating to make members see the processes necessary to reach a settlement. (**M** stands for the mediator; **U1** is the union's chief negotiator; **U2** is second in line; and so forth. **C1, C2,** and so on are company negotiators).

In Exhibit 11–2, the mediator meets with company negotiators. He asks them to examine positions, sees where movement can be made, and stresses the difficulties that lie ahead. Notice he refuses to tip his hand about information he may have on the union's position.

---

[2] William E. Simkin, *Mediation and the Dynamics of Collective Bargaining* (Washington, D.C.: Bureau of National Affairs, 1971).

[3] Deborah M. Kolb, "Strategy and the Tactics of Mediation," *Human Relations* 36 (1983), pp. 247–68.

[4] Ann Douglas, *Industrial Peacemaking* (New York: Columbia University Press, 1962).

EXHIBIT 11-1

M: Well, look, fellows, to get this started, I don't know how much I rea—how much time I really need with you. I had a pretty good idea last time of just what you wanted, what were the basic demands, and most prob'ly, I have more work to do with the company at this point than with you. However, I do want to do one thing tonight. I wanta go over with you what the company has responded with respect to each of the nine basic demands you substituted, plus get your thinking on each of the company's counterproposals. Now, before we get into that, I want to spend a minute or two with something else. I wanta remind you of something I used as a comparison of one of the early cases we had. You recall at that time I said that, in a sense, we all do bargaining in one form or another on many occasions, and I used the example of any one of you who might have an automobile that ya wanted to sell. What ya did was dress the thing up, make it look as attractive as possible, and put the highest price you felt you could reasonably ask on it. When a prospective purchaser came around, you gave him the best sales talk you could give, but ordinarily you did not expect he was going to say "Yes." Ya expected he was going to haggle a little bit, and when he did, ya tried to think up some arguments to counter those that he advanced. Ya try to indicate to him that the lower price he was offering was not a proper price. Maybe you would even go back in the garage and dig up another spare tire or something else to make the car a little bit more attractive, and you would keep on haggling with him over price. And eventually he would offer something that was worthwhile to you, for which you would make the swap. Now, in that sort of thing, you didn't get overly mad. Ya took it as part of the game you were playing. I'm not saying, that in collective bargaining, where you're dealing with—with much more serious things, and things which are not quite within your control as is the sale of an automobile. You can either sell it or not sell it; you don't have to. With a contract, though, ya do have to conclude it, and ya have some compulsion here which was not present in any individual bargaining you might do over a personal effect. But there are a lot of elements of sameness; and just as you would do in a private transaction, so, in part, you must do here. When you make a proposal, until ya come right down to the end of the wire, where ya have most everything settled and it's a matter of saying "Yes" or "No" to a couple of final propositions, ya got to expect that what you're going to get is a tentative "Maybe," usually ah— to which is usually added a couple of other propositions, and it becomes a switch back and forth, a jockeying to try and get the most of what you want, knowing that the company is going to do the same thing. Now, I mention these things because I want to remind you that last time I said that I did not think the company counterdemands, which you felt pretty strongly about, were things to get too seriously concerned with, for, as far as I knew at that point—they may be, but as far as I know, they do not represent a final company position. If they did, then I think that you would be logically entitled to say—and holler every sort of implication you could think of. But I don't think that that's what they represent. I think what is called for after this is some further thinking, some further proposals on your part. What I want to do is to find out, how much that the company offered in connection with the counterproposals they made to your nine proposals is acceptable to you, either as they have stated it or in some modified form. I want to find out, secondly, what there is in the company's additional nine proposals you think have any merit or that you're willing to go along with, either as they stated or in some modified form. This for my information. Tomorrow I have to do the same thing with management. How much of what the union—of what they said in their counterproposals did they say for bargaining purposes, how much closer to what they know the union wants are they willing to go?—that, again, is confidential with me. When I have those two things, then I can see how really far apart you are, and it becomes a problem, then, of trying to get you to go a little bit this way on that business, gettin' the company to go a little bit your way on some other matter, until we reach the point where it looks like we have something that is an agreeable thing with you, something that's agreeable with them. And the only way we can do that is through this point-by-point discussion. I want to repeat that what you have to say concerning it is between you and I. Concessions that you tell me you are prepared to make are not told to the company. Concessions the company tell me they are prepared to make are not told to you at this point. For what you will be willing to do, what they will be willing to do will be perhaps to make concessions on one item, providing they get a counter-, or you get a counter-, concession on another item. So until the whole thing is squared up, I have to be the repository of your confidence and of theirs. So, to get to this, then (pause), let's start with their response in connection with No. 1, two-year contract. And this is what I want to know. If you gave them a two-year contract, what would you want in return? Of what advantage is it to you to say, "We'll give you a two-year contract"? What can you get out of them in return?

SOURCE: Ann Douglas, *Industrial Peacemaking* (New York: Columbia University Press, 1962), pp. 56–58.

Returning to the union caucus, the mediator is still not specific about the positions taken by management but does say a gap exists in the settlement range. He also continues his lessons on bargaining in Exhibit 11–3.

The exchanges depicted in the exhibits and the crisis atmosphere in which mediators operate require a special mix of experience, talents, and behaviors.

Mediator Behavior and Outcomes

While the mediation scenarios presented in the exhibits cast the mediator in the roles of teacher and communicator, not all mediations follow this approach. Mediators may be either "deal makers" or "orchestrators," with the former approach used more when mediators believe their clients are inexperienced in negotiations. Deal makers are more likely than orches-

---

EXHIBIT 11–2

From the Second Management Caucus with the Mediator:

M: Well, what I'd like to do today is go over the company's counterproposals to the union's proposals and see how much it means, actually, how much room there is to move around in connection with the various points you have made, and I want this for my own information. I've already discussed a good bit of this with the union, so I have some notions on what they will and will not do. I wanta get similar notions from you and see whether or not actually you're really closer together than you appear on the surface. I'll say this pretty frankly, that quite probably there's goin' ta have ta be a lot of shaking down before you get to an agreement. The union is undoubtedly holding out for more now than you're prepared to give, and they're going to have to come down (*C2:* Uh-huh) in a number of respects.

C2: Any particular areas?

M: U1—(slight pause) I won't say now. Just (*C2:* Uh-huh) as a general position, they would appear to be holding to some things which are unlikely to come their way. I mention this because I think in part they're holding to them out of a belief that you, in your counterproposals, have advanced some rather unreasonable notion.

C1: You mean unreasonable to them.

M: Oh, of course (laughing). Not to me, never? (*C1, C2,* and *M* all laugh) Not for recording on tape.

C1: What you're tryin' to do is find out where the soft spots are.

M: Yeah, and without presenting as notions the union might have to you, I shall discuss these things from the point of view of softening your position. Again I say that this is between us and for my information to see where I can then approach the union to get them to do likewise, and if we can get enough of that done, why, the thing may not look quite as black as it appears to the union to be.

SOURCE: Ann Douglas, *Industrial Peacemaking* (New York: Columbia University Press, 1962), p. 91.

---

trators to run into problems in consummating their deals and getting agreements.[5]

In general, the role of mediators involves establishing a working relationship between the parties, improving the negotiating climate be-

---

[5] Deborah M. Kolb, "Roles Mediators Play: Contrasts and Comparisons in State and Federal Mediation Practice," *Industrial Relations* 20 (1981), pp. 1–17.

EXHIBIT 11-3

From the Mediator's Third Caucus with the Union:

U1: What's their attitudes on—their position as to our minimum demand? Are they altering those?

M: Well, you have their counterproposal, which is very definitely not acceding to your minimum demand. See, I—I don't understand minimum demand (*U1:* Well, you gotta remember that—)—what you mean by minimum demands. If you have to have everything such as this, then there's no room for bargaining.

U1: No. But we'd like to know if their counterproposal to ours is their final position.

M: Well, I just explained it. I've just told you the answer to that.

U2: Which?

M: That I've found that there is things in their position (*U2:* That's what—) that are bargainable (*U2:* Well—), which merely means that they are not saying to you, or they're not saying to me that "What we have answered the union is as far as we'll go."

U2: See what's happened, U1? We—when we went through—pract'ly went through all of these here and gave 'em our minimum demands, now what they're doin' is just knockin' them down to where—

U1: Yeah!

U2: The way it is now, we want all of ours.

U3: That's were the stalemate is.

M: No! The stalemate is that after you gave the company this offer, the company made a counteroffer and then you quit bargaining.

U1: We didn't quit bargaining. They did.

U3: They did.

M: All right. There was no cause for further reaction on your part directly to what they had said and that's what I am trying to get. Ordinarily in these things, it's a series. You demand, they reply; you demand, they reply; you demand, they reply; you demand, they reply. Somewhere in there—and this is exactly the way it looks—you start here with your demand. They reply. Then on down, each counterdemand is met with a counterreply until you reduce the difference (*U2:* Well, the—) the point where you reach an agreement. Now—

U4: Fact, all the time we're in there, M, we're t—all the time we were talking about their proposals. We hardly, if ever, mentioned our own proposals, because we figured when they got through we'd have our chance, and we never got our chance to talk.

U5: (Over *U4* above) U4, as far as language is—is concerned, the whole thing is in a package and what—C1 is sittin' back, little ah—oh, one of these here chess players with the idea he just—he can take and move us fellows like we's just pawns or somethin' there. He just tryin' to—

continued

U4: We never ran into that before. I mean—

M: (Over **U4** above) Well, look. How—how would you propose that you go about—about reaching an agreement? What's your idea of how you do these things?

U1: They never once discussed any of our demands, never (**M:** Well—), and that's what we were asking for. (**M:** And—) Uh—

M: If they didn't discuss them, it was because you didn't insist on it, because you certainly have a right to discuss your own demands. (**U1:** We insisted on those.) If you start, then they got to respond. You'll haggle back and forth until you get what is reasonably satisfactory. Now, when you tell me that you'll take 4 cents plus—4-cent improvement factor each year plus the cost-of-living adjustment, I am not going to tell them that. If anything, I might tell 'em, well, you'll take 10 cents plus their—no, I won't tell them you'll take. I'll ask them, "Well, what do you say—give 'em 10 cents plus the cost-of-living, huh?" to give me some room to move around. I gotta bargain with them, so I can't—I'm not gonna give them minimums. (Laughs) I'll stretch the minimum so I can come back a little bit.

SOURCE: Ann Douglas, *Industrial Peacemaking* (New York: Columbia University Press, 1962), pp. 59–60.

---

tween the parties by facilitating communications and using single-party caucuses, addressing issues, and applying pressure for settlement.[6]

Other variables influencing mediator behavior and bargaining outcomes revolve around intensity of the dispute and intensity of mediator activities. Dispute intensity reduces the likelihood a mediator can achieve a settlement, particularly for impasses involving the employer's inability to pay the increase demanded. Mediators are more effective in achieving settlements when they act aggressively and where negotiations have broken down.[7] Intense impasses characterized by such conditions as a new bargaining relationship, dislike between key negotiators, conflict within the management or union team, high union strength, pattern bargaining, and an inability to pay are more frequently resolved by mediators who become intensely involved in the process. High-intensity mediation includes a willingness to get true feelings before the parties and discuss real costs of the proposed packages. Low-intensity mediation is more successful when an impasse also is low intensity.[8]

---

[6] K. Kressel and D. G. Pruitt, "Conclusion: A Research Perspective on the Mediation of Social Conflict," in *Mediation Research*, ed. K. Kressel, D. G. Pruitt, and associates (San Francisco: Jossey-Bass, 1989), pp. 394–435.

[7] Thomas A. Kochan and Todd Jick, "A Theory of the Public Sector Mediation Process," *Journal of Conflict Resolution* 22 (1978), pp. 209–41.

[8] Paul F. Gerhart and John E. Drotning, "Dispute Settlement and the Intensity of Mediation," *Industrial Relations* 19 (1980), pp. 352–59.

Mediation facilitates settlement by (1) reducing hostility by focusing on bargaining objectives, (2) enhancing understanding of the opponent's position, (3) adjusting the negotiating format through chairing, subcommittee creation, and the like, (4) assuming the risk in exploring new solutions, (5) affecting perceptions regarding the cost of conflict, and (6) contributing to face-saving facilitating concessions.[9] A study examining reactions of managements and unions to mediated settlements found management believed mediator expertise and impartiality increased the likelihood of settlements, while the union attributed settlements to mediator neutrality and persistence. Mediation strategies most often cited by management as facilitating settlement included discussions of costs of disagreement, suggestions of face-saving proposals, and gains in the parties' trust. Unions said changing expectations and devising an improved negotiating framework hastened settlement.[10]

Although mediation is an art, behaviors of mediators and levels or types of disputes can be classified; thus, an appropriate style of mediation can be selected to match the intensity of the dispute to exert the greatest likelihood of a settlement. Alternatively, mediators whose styles best fit the impasse could be assigned to the case.[11]

Mediator Backgrounds and Training

No specific requirements are needed for selection as a mediator or for appointment to the Federal Mediation and Conciliation Service. This is not to say that FMCS mediators are not carefully selected or are untrained. Persons with experience in negotiating contracts are preferred, regardless of whether they were on the side of managements or unions. This mixture of backgrounds and the independence of the FMCS was ensured by its first director, Cyrus Ching.[12] Exhibit 11–4 displays the toughness and impartiality of the position he established for the FMCS.

One report finds less than half of mediators have college degrees, but they do have experience. In 1969, 69 percent of 295 FMCS mediators had significant experience as management or union negotiators, and an additional 25 percent had been neutrals in labor relations disputes. Mediators

---

[9] Ahmad Karim and Richard Pegnetter, "Mediator Strategies and Qualities and Mediation Effectiveness," *Industrial Relations* 22 (1983), pp. 105–14.

[10] Ibid.

[11] See Janette Webb, "Behavioral Studies of Third-Party Intervention," in *Industrial Relations: A Social Psychological Approach*, ed. Geoffrey M. Stephenson and Christopher J. Brotherton (New York: John Wiley & Sons, 1979), pp. 309–31; and James A. Wall Jr., "Mediation: A Categorical Analysis and a Proposed Framework for Future Research," *Academy of Management Proceedings* 40 (1980), pp. 298–302.

[12] A. H. Raskin, "Cyrus S. Ching: Pioneer in Industrial Peacemaking," *Monthly Labor Review* 112, no. 8 (1989), pp. 22–35.

EXHIBIT 11-4

Cyrus Ching and the 1949 Steel Negotiations

In 1949, when the United Steelworkers and the large steel producers were approaching the showdown over employer-subsidized pensions, Ching felt the only way to avert a strike was through appointment of a presidential fact-finding board. Truman, whose early experiences with labor in the White House made him reluctant ever to get back into the middle of a major industrial confrontation, was cool to the idea. . . . Philip Murray assured Ching that his union would keep its members at work if the companies agreed to appear before the fact-finders. Ching anticipated no difficulty on that score, because any recommendations made by the panel would not be binding.

The board of directors of U.S. Steel proved wary, however, and the rest of the industry held off, awaiting "Big Steel's" response. The first word from the board was a telegram to Truman raising questions about the function of the fact-finders. Ching regarded all of these inquiries as legitimate, and he had a telegram designed to overcome U.S. Steel's apprehensions sent over the president's signature. The company directors came back with a second telegram to Truman, raising further questions, and Ching was called to the White House for a decision on what the government's next step should be. Ching advised Truman not to answer the wire, but instead to empower the FMCS chief to call Benjamin Fairless, the company's chairman, and tell him he was speaking in the president's name. Given a green light by Truman to proceed, Ching was blunt in his conversation with Fairless the next day.

"My conversation is going to be very short this morning," Ching said. "Number one, I want to tell you that you can't bargain with the president of the United States and, number two, will you send an answer, yes or no, this morning. Either you will or you won't, no more exchanging of telegrams." Fairless gasped. "You're quite plainspoken this morning," he said. "Yes, I intended to be. And that is the message I'm giving you from the president in answer to your telegram." That conversation ended the holdout, and the fact-finding panel began its vain effort to head off a strike.

SOURCE: A. H. Raskin, "Cyrus S. Ching: Pioneer in Industrial Peacemaking," *Monthly Labor Review* 112, no. 8 (1989), pp. 33–34.

---

in the FMCS are most often over 45 and many have long experience in the service.[13]

A new FMCS mediator generally begins with a two-week training program in Washington and then is sent to a regional office to learn procedures and to work with experienced mediators. By the end of the first year, a first case has probably been assigned. Summaries and specialized training supplement experience as the mediator is assigned to increasingly complex cases.

---

[13] Simkin, *Mediation*, pp. 57–69. Recent work suggests the pattern hasn't changed. See Kolb, "Roles Mediators Play."

Mediator Activity

Under Taft-Hartley, the parties are required to notify the FMCS 30 days before the expiration of a contract when negotiations are under way and an agreement has not been reached. Table 11–1 shows notification and caseloads for the FMCS during fiscal years 1983–88. The figures indicate the FMCS is involved in just under 12 percent of cases in which 30-day notifications had been received. The proportion of cases requiring assistance has remained about the same over several years, as Table 11–2 indicates.

Most cases are settled without the intervention of mediators. Data from the FMCS *Annual Report* series show mediation is used more frequently when the parties are negotiating their first contract and when the term of the contract is for three years. Thus, the negotiator inexperience and/or the permanency of the agreement appear to inhibit agreement without outside assistance.

Mediation is one method of third-party intervention in labor disputes. It is an active process of keeping the parties together using a neutral approach. Mediation allows the parties to settle on their own terms when they have been unable to do so on their own.

FACT-FINDING

Fact-finding has a long history in U.S. labor relations. In the 19th century, it was used to fix blame on one party rather than finding the underlying causes of the dispute.[14] In present-day fact-finding, a neutral party studies the issues in dispute and renders a public recommendation for settlement.[15]

Fact-finding uses neutrals who act on behalf of the public.[16] If the fact-finders' published findings are not adopted in a settlement, private-sector parties are free to return to bargaining as they see fit.

In the United States, fact-finding has been used primarily to meet Taft-Hartley emergency dispute requirements (in which it has been relatively ineffectual) and in railroad disputes where presidential emergency boards have been created under the Railway Labor Act.[17] Fact-finding in the public sector is covered in Chapter 15.

---

[14] Thomas J. McDermott, "Fact-Finding Boards in Labor Disputes," *Labor Law Journal* 11 (1960), pp. 285–304.

[15] Charles M. Rehmus, "The Fact-Finder's Role," *The Proceedings of the Inaugural Convention of the Society of Professionals in Dispute Resolution*, 1973, pp. 34–44.

[16] Jean T. McKelvey, "Fact-Finding in Public Employment Disputes: Promise of Illusion?" *Industrial and Labor Relations Review* 22 (1969), p. 529.

[17] Rehmus, "Fact-Finder's Role," pp. 35–36.

TABLE 11-1

Analysis of Dispute Notifications (Number of Dispute Notifications Received by FMCS for the Years 1983 through 1988)

Receipt of Notifications	Fiscal 1983	Fiscal 1984	Fiscal 1985	Fiscal 1986	Fiscal 1987	Fiscal 1988
30-day notices required by the LMRA	101,541	98,770	108,751	86,720	85,292	80,774
Requests from union and/or company	5,426	3,667	1,168	2,137	2,049	1,817
NLRB and FLRA certifications	1,767	1,896	1,803	1,736	1,711	1,622
Intercessions by FMCS	61	5	5	8	2	1
Public-sector board requests*	—	—	184	450	370	307

* Data for years before 1985 were included in other figures.
SOURCE: U.S. Federal Mediation and Conciliation Service, *Forty-First Annual Report* (Washington, D.C.: Government Printing Office, 1988) p. 13.

TABLE 11-2

Analysis of Assigned Mediation Cases (Number of Closed Dispute, Preventive Mediation, and Public Information Cases for Fiscal Years 1983 through 1988)

Type of Case	1983	1984	1985	1986	1987	1988
Closed dispute cases	25,409	26,568	26,308	25,462	24,293	25,344
Joint conference cases	8,617	9,052	8,019	8,200	7,620	7,289
Separate conference cases	200	217	143	155	116	117
No conference cases	9,767	11,652	14,574	15,799	15,158	16,215
Consolidated cases	6,825	5,647	3,572	1,308	1,399	1,723
Preventive mediation cases	1,006	730	960	895	981	1,308
Public information and educational cases	876	725	822	721	826	860

SOURCE: U.S. Federal Mediation and Conciliation Service, *Forty-First Annual Report* (Washington, D.C.: Government Printing Office, 1988), p. 13.

Taft-Hartley Fact-Finding

Section 206 of the Taft-Hartley Act specifies the president may name a fact-finding board to prepare a report in a national emergency dispute. No recommendations are made in the report, which is filed with the FMCS. Under Section 208, after the fact-finders report, the president can ask a federal district court to enjoin a strike or lockout if *the court* finds the dispute is within the national emergency criteria. Thus, use of fact-finding appears redundant because a court must conclude an emergency exists. Neither the reports nor the injunctions appear to succeed in resolving impasses.

Railway Labor Boards

Presidential emergency boards have succeeded in resolving impasses in critical transportation disputes. Fact-finders have facilitated the settlement of nonoperating craft job security issues, made recommendations on phasing out the fireman job in diesel engines, and worked on the introduction of new equipment in the airline industry.[18]

In the past, the availability of fact-finding may have led to increasing numbers of railroad negotiations being designated emergencies with the boards acting in a politically expedient fashion. The use of boards may reduce the parties' willingness to bargain.[19] While Congress continues to legislate some settlements in railroads, national emergency boards and Taft-Hartley fact-finding have become virtually nonexistent.[20]

Fact-Finding and the Issues

Private-sector fact-finders are relatively unsuccessful on distributive bargaining issues. They have little authority beyond recommendations and do not personally facilitate bargaining. Neither party may accord legitimacy to an outside group in determining or recommending what either is entitled to.

On the other hand, presidential emergency board fact-finders appear to have had some success in integrative bargaining areas. In the rail industry, new technology has raised job security issues for the union and survival issues for management. The parties can implement solutions proposed by a neutral group without bearing as great an individual responsibility to their constituents. Thus, fact-finding boards facilitate integrative bargaining through the proposal of solutions and encourage intraorganizational bargaining by legitimizing positions the principal negotiators may be willing to raise but see as unacceptable to the memberships.

INTEREST ARBITRATION

Interest arbitration is an impasse resolution method that has seen considerable use in a variety of forms in the public sector. Arbitration differs substantially from mediation and fact-finding. While mediation assists

[18] Ibid., p. 36.

[19] Herbert R. Northrup and Gordon F. Bloom, *Government and Labor* (Homewood, Ill.: Richard D. Irwin, 1963), pp. 327–30.

[20] Charles M. Rehmus, "Emergency Strikes Revisited," *Industrial and Labor Relations Review* 43 (1990), pp. 175–90.

the parties to reach their own settlement, arbitration hears the positions of both and decides on binding settlement terms. While fact-finding recommends a settlement, arbitration dictates it.

Two classes of arbitration are central to labor relations—rights and interest. Interest arbitration occurs where no agreement exists or a change is sought and where the parties have an interest in the outcome because the contract will specify future rights. **Rights arbitration** involves the interpretation of an existing agreement to determine which party is entitled to a certain outcome or to take a certain action.[21]

In the United States, interest arbitration was used by the National War Labor Board during World War II and has been imposed on the railroad industry by Congress on a number of occasions since the 1960s. If interest arbitration is mandated, it eliminates the parties' need to settle on their own. Some believe the availability and use of interest arbitration has a "narcotic" effect. This controversy will be explored in greater detail in Chapter 15.

REVIEW OF THIRD-PARTY INVOLVEMENTS

Of the three methods of third-party involvements, only one—arbitration—guarantees a solution to an impasse. However, interest arbitration has not been embraced by the private sector. Fact-finding also has a relatively checkered past. It has generally been imposed on the parties, who are then free to ignore its recommendations. Actually, fact-finding doesn't involve facts, only values associated with the possible positions taken on outcomes in the dispute. Mediation is neutral in that it generally requires the parties to bargain their own terms. It has been relatively successful in keeping parties at the table, given the FMCS case load and success rate reported earlier.

Sometimes parties are not involved with mediation, fact-finding, or arbitration at impasse. And sometimes mediation and fact-finding don't break impasses. Strikes pressure employers to settle on union terms. Lockouts or hiring replacements are attempts to get unions to settle on employer terms. Their use, effectiveness, and legality are examined next.

STRIKES

The four major types of strikes have one thing in common: a withholding of effort by employees. An **economic strike** occurs after a failure to agree on the terms of a contract. It is called to pressure the employer to settle

---

[21] *Elgin, Joliet, & Eastern Railway Co.* v. *Burley*, 325 U.S. 71 (1945).

on the union's terms. The union believes the cost of the strike (both economic and political) will be less to it than to the employer, and benefits of the expected solution are greater than the strike's costs. Even though it is called an *economic strike*, the disputed issues do not always involve wages. An economic strike can occur over any mandatory bargaining issue. But if a union insists on going to impasse and strikes over a permissive issue, it commits an unfair labor practice.[22] An economic strike involves unique rules, which are explained later.

Unfair labor practice strikes protest employer violations of the labor acts. If an employer commits illegal acts, the employees' right to strike in protest and be reinstated after it's over is absolutely protected by NLRB and court interpretations of the labor acts. A **wildcat strike** is an unauthorized stoppage during the contract. Employees may face disciplinary action if the strike breaches a no-strike clause. A **sympathy strike** occurs when one union strikes to support another's strike. These occur where more than one union represents employees in a single establishment. The union's right to support another union is guaranteed by the Norris-LaGuardia Act, *even* if its contract contains a no-strike clause and provides for arbitration of unresolved grievances.[23]

Strike Votes and Going Out

As noted in Chapter 10, the union generally takes a strike vote during negotiations to strengthen its bargaining position. This doesn't mean a strike will occur, only that the union may go on strike at the contract's expiration. A local union usually needs its parent national's approval to strike. If it strikes without approval, the local and its officers may be disciplined, the international may place the local under trusteeship, or strike benefits may not be paid.

Unions usually require members to participate in strike activities, such as **picketing,** to receive strike benefits. Unions may also discipline members refusing to strike. A strike may increase cohesiveness and solidarity of the union. UAW members involved in contract negotiations in 1976 and 1977 were surveyed four times. During the talks, Ford was struck, but GM and Chrysler were not. While on strike, Ford employees' attitudes toward their international union and its leaders were more positive than before the strike and more positive than fellow union members at GM and Chrysler.[24]

---

[22] *Detroit Resilient Floor Decorators Union,* 136 NLRB 756 (1962).

[23] *Buffalo Forge Co. v. United Steelworkers of America, AFL–CIO,* 92 LRRM 3032 (U.S. Supreme Court, 1976).

[24] Ross Stagner and Boaz Eflal, "Internal Union Dynamics during a Strike: A Quasi-Experimental Study," *Journal of Applied Psychology* 67 (1982), pp. 37–44.

Picketing

Picketing is one of the most noticeable strike activities. In picketing, the union informs the public about the dispute and may appeal to others to stop doing business with their employer during the dispute. Before Norris-LaGuardia, state and federal courts often enjoined picketing. Since then, federal courts have been forbidden to enjoin strikes unless a clear and present danger to life or property is shown. States may not restrict peaceful picketing because it is protected by the First Amendment.[25] Some restrictions, however, are imposed on **recognitional picketing** under Landrum-Griffin.

To be protected from employer reprisals, employees must publicize that they are involved in a labor dispute when they picket or inform the public about the employer or its products and services.[26] The site and manner of the picketing is also of concern, because the union can be accused of illegal secondary activity in certain instances. The next sections examine various types of picketing. Legal picketing is not necessarily associated with strikes; it may also involve informational and recognitional activities.

Common Situs Picketing

The place where picketing occurs may affect secondary employers and the effects associated with picketing. This issue is highly important in construction, where a prime contractor and subcontractors may work simultaneously on a common site. Each utilizes different trades, may or may not be unionized, and may have different wages, terms, and expiration dates in contracts. If unions strike in sympathy with a primary dispute and if a dispute exists with one contractor, a whole site may be shut down.

A primary employer is one involved in a dispute, and a neutral employer is one affected by the picketing activity of the primary's employees. The rules governing common situs picketing in construction were established in the *Denver Building Trades Council* cases.[27] Picketing began when the union learned that the prime contractor on the site had employed a nonunion subcontractor. An object of the picketing was to force the general contractor to drop the subcontractor. When picketing began, all other union workers refused to cross the picket line. The prime contractor maintained the dispute was with the subcontractor and general picketing of the site was an illegal secondary boycott designed to force neutral parties to cease dealing with the subcontractor. The court

---

[25] *Thornhill* v. *Alabama*, 310 U.S. 88 (1940).

[26] *NLRB* v. *Local Union, 1229, International Brotherhood of Electrical Workers*, 346 U.S. 464 (1953).

[27] *NLRB* v. *Denver Building Trades Council*, 341 U.S. 675 (1951).

agreed, and since then, construction unions have been forbidden to picket sites to force a primary employer to cease doing business with a nonunion subcontractor. The usual practice at construction sites is to establish reserved gates for each employer. Primary dispute pickets may then patrol only the gate of their employer.

Ambulatory Site

Sometimes the objects of a strike move from place to place, such as a ship being struck by a seafarers union. In one case, when the ship was moved to dry dock for repairs, the union sought to picket by the ship. The dry-dock management refused to allow this, and a picket line was set up at the entrance to the dock. The NLRB ruled that such picketing would be legal if (1) the object is currently on the secondary employer's site, (2) the primary employer continues to engage in its normal business, (3) the picketing is reasonably close to the strike object, and (4) the picketing discloses that the dispute is with the struck employer and not the site owner.[28]

Multiple-Use Sites

In the past, an employer's site was usually easily identified. But recent changes in retailing, for example, have blurred this concept. Enclosed shopping centers make picketing a primary employer without disrupting secondary businesses difficult. And the employer has usually leased the site from another company that owns the shopping mall. The Supreme Court originally held a mall owner could stop pickets from publicizing a labor dispute with a store located in the mall.[29] However, the Court reversed itself in holding that a union does not interfere with a neutral owner and other stores by peacefully informing the public about a labor dispute with one of the stores within the mall.[30]

Slowdowns

The incidence of strikes has declined markedly recently. Employers have occasionally replaced economic strikers and have become more automated and thus better able to operate for extended periods with only supervisory employees. Unions, for their part, are increasingly using slowdowns to put pressure on employers to settle contracts. A slowdown most often involves **working to rules.** Employees refuse to perform activities outside of their job descriptions, follow procedures to the letter,

---

[28] *Sailor's Union of the Pacific (Moore Dry Dock Co.)*, 92 NLRB 547 (1950).

[29] *Hudgens* v. *NLRB*, 91 LRRM 2489 (U.S. Supreme Court, 1976).

[30] *Edward J. DeBartolo Corp.* v. *Florida Gulf Coast Building and Construction Trades Council and NLRB*, U.S. Supreme Court, No. 86-1461, 1988.

and refuse overtime and other employment duties that might be voluntary. Because they are complying with the contract and company work rules, they can seldom be disciplined.[31]

Corporate Campaigns

In a **corporate campaign,** the union looks for points where the employer might be vulnerable and exerts pressure on those to support the collective bargaining effort. A corporate campaign successfully forced the J. P. Stevens Company to negotiate a first contract with the Clothing and Textile Workers, which had won representation rights several years earlier.

The first phase of a corporate campaign explores the corporation's business activity to uncover any possible regulatory violations recorded by government agencies, such as the Environmental Protection Agency or Occupational Safety and Health Administration. The campaign will also determine which other corporations are closely linked as suppliers, customers, financial backers, and the like. Corporate investigations will also include detailed analyses of the firms' publicly reported financial data.

The second phase involves publicity of material detrimental to the employer's interests and supportive of the union's demands. The campaign tries to get outsiders in the dispute to pressure the employer to settle with the union, and especially to settle on terms beneficial to the employees. Some of the activities may be held to motivate consumer boycotts.[32]

Shutdowns

A variety of responses are available to the employer when struck. These responses generally fall into three categories: (1) shut down the affected area, (2) continue operating, or (3) contract out work for the duration. Each has its own consequences and can cause retaliatory action.

Shutdowns are designed to have the least consequences in terms of union activity. But a shutdown has consequences the employer would like to avoid. First, production revenues are lost during this period.

---

[31] "Labor's Shift: Finding Strikes Harder to Win, More Unions Turn to Slowdowns," *The Wall Street Journal,* May 22, 1987, pp. 1, 6; see also a new publication for union members, *The Inside Game: Winning with Workplace Strategies,* Industrial Union Department, AFL–CIO, 1987.

[32] Harold Datz, Leo Geffner, Joseph M. McLaughlin, and Susan Kellock, "Economic Warfare in the 1980s, Strikes, Lockouts, Boycotts, and Corporate Campaigns," *Industrial Relations Law Journal* 9 (1987), pp. 82–115.

Second, competitors may gear up to take over the lost production, thus permanently reducing the struck company's market share. Third, if a firm is a sole supplier, its customers may encourage others to enter the market as alternative sources of supply, thus reducing the possibilities of temporary shortages. And fourth, during periods of scarcity, the firm may lose its suppliers as they fill orders from more reliable customers.

Continued Operations

Continued operations may be accomplished by two strategies. Neither is relished by the union, but the second will almost certainly lead to militant action. The first strategy is to continue operations using supervisors and other nonproduction workers, which is feasible if the firm is not labor intensive and if maintenance demands are not high. Automated and continuous-flow operations, such as those found in the chemical industry, fall into this category. If this strategy is used, supervisory-employee relations may be strained after the strike because the supervisors' work may have enabled the company to prolong the strike.

The second strategy is to hire replacements for the strikers. Because this places the strikers' jobs in direct jeopardy, difficulties usually ensue. During the early 1980s, employers were much more likely to continue operations by hiring replacements, given their availability when unemployment was high. Exhibit 11–5 describes the responses of some employers to work stoppages. The company's ability to attract replacements substantially reduces the bargaining power of the union. Strike replacements face a difficult situation. They are reviled as "scabs" by the strikers (see Exhibit 11–6 for a definition almost invariably used when strike replacements are hired) and, due to low seniority, may be vulnerable to layoff after a new contract is signed. On the other hand, if the employer can operate without settling the strike for a year, the new employees may succeed in decertifying the union representing the strikers. Major strikes involving violence occur when employers either attempt to continue operations with supervisors or replacement workers. Recent examples include the United Mine Workers and Pittston Company and the New York Daily News strike.

A strike would be a true economic strike if the company bargained in good faith to an impasse. Then, if neither the company nor the union refused to move further, the gulf would remain permanently, and new employees would have to be hired to remain in business. Employers can legally replace economic strikers, and operations can then resume.[33]

---

[33] *NLRB* v. *MacKay Radio & Telegraph*, 304 U.S. 333 (1938).

EXHIBIT 11-5

More Firms Get Tough and Keep Operating Despite Walkouts

To an increasing number of companies, "strike" is no longer a frightening word. These companies are prepared to continue operating right through a labor walkout.

The latest example is Continental Airlines, which decided to keep flying on a curtailed schedule despite strikes by its pilots, flight attendants, and ground personnel. When the Machinists union struck Continental last summer, the carrier immediately hired replacements. And when the company recently filed a bankruptcy petition to bail itself out of its labor and financial problems, it rehired about 35 percent of its former work force at drastically reduced pay and then resumed flights.

Operating during strikes is nothing new for many companies. . . . But now many labor-intensive concerns are adopting the strategy as a continuation of the hard-nosed concession bargaining pressed during the recession. Companies that have chosen to operate despite strikes recently have included, in addition to Continental, Phelps Dodge Corp., Magic Chef, Inc., and Whirlpool Corp.

Labor experts say the time is ripe for such aggressive management tactics . . . "We have a president who says let's confront them, fire them, and keep on rolling. That makes it legitimate to operate during strikes, and private employers have followed the lead," says John Zalusky, an economist in the AFL–CIO's research department.

SOURCE: Robert S. Greenberger, "More Firms Get Tough and Keep Operating in Spite of Walkouts." Reprinted from *The Wall Street Journal*, October 11, 1983 p. 1. © 1983 Dow Jones & Company. All Rights Reserved Worldwide.

However, strike replacements become members of the bargaining unit and are represented by the striking union. Decertification is necessary to remove the bargaining representative.

Rights of Economic Strikers

If replacements are hired, the strikers may still get their jobs back. First, if they unilaterally offer to return to work and if their jobs or others for which they are qualified are unfilled, refusing to rehire them would be an unfair labor practice because a strike is protected by Section 7. Second, if employees ask for reinstatement when the strike is concluded, they are entitled to their jobs, if open, or to preference for rehiring when positions become open.[34] However, employers are not required to reinstate

---

[34] *NLRB* v. *Fleetwood Trailer Co., Inc.*, 389 U.S. 375 (1967).

EXHIBIT 11-6

What Is a Scab?

After God had finished the rattlesnake, the toad, and the vampire, he had some awful substance left with which He made a *scab*. A *scab* is a two-legged animal with a corkscrew soul, a water-logged brain, and a combination back-bone made of jelly and glue. Where others have hearts, he carries a tumor of rotten principles.

When a *scab* comes down the street, men turn their backs, and angels weep in heaven, and the devil shuts the gates of hell to keep him out. No man has a right to *scab* as long as there is a pool of water deep enough to drown his body in, or a rope long enough to hang his carcass with. Judas Iscariot was a gentleman compared with a *scab*. For betraying his Master, he had character enough to hang himself. A *scab hasn't!*

Esau sold his birthright for a mess of pottage. Judas Iscariot sold his Savior for 30 pieces of silver. Benedict Arnold sold his country for a promise of a commission in the British Army. The modern strikebreaker sells his birthright, his country, his wife, his children, and his fellow men for an unfulfilled promise from his employer, trust, or corporation.

Esau was traitor to himself, Judas Iscariot was a traitor to his God. Benedict Arnold was a traitor to his country.

A strikebreaker is a traitor to his God, his country, his family, and his class!

SOURCE: Philip S. Foner, *Jack London, American Rebel* (New York: Citadel Press, 1947), pp. 57–58.

---

employees involved in breaking rules, such as sabotage and picket line violence, during the strike. But discharges must be for cause, and the grievance procedure would be open for hearing disputes over these discharges.

Contracting Out

Strikes have serious consequences for an employer with major customers whose business requires output on a fixed schedule, particularly if competitive firms offer the same services. One strategy is to arrange for a competing firm to handle the work temporarily.

On its face, this seems foolproof: no problems exist with strikebreakers and the union, and customers get their work done on time by a subcontractor. It's not, however. If the subcontractor is unionized, its employees legally can refuse to perform subcontracted work when a struck employer has initiated the order. Such refusals are allowed under the so-called **ally doctrine.**

For example, a printing firm responsible for providing Sunday supplements to newspapers was struck by its employees. To maintain its ability to meet the weekly schedule, it subcontracted the work to another firm. When the second firm's employees learned why they were doing the work, they refused to perform it. The first employer charged that this was a secondary boycott, but the NLRB reasoned the dispute became primary through the handling of the struck work for the primary employer.[35]

An exception to the ally doctrine is granted to health care providers. Sick patients can't wait for care until a strike is over. Hospitals accepting struck work (patient care) cannot risk the extension of the strike to them. Congress modified Section 8(b)(4) of the Taft-Hartley Act to allow a limited exemption to the ally doctrine for health care providers. If a hospital is struck and another supplies an occasional technician to assist, an ally relationship is not established. But if shifts of nurses were provided by a group of hospitals, they would become allies. Thus, magnitude of assistance is the determining factor in whether a strike could spread to other providers.

Evidence on the Incidence, Duration, and Effects of Strikes

Strikes are popularly viewed as counterproductive. Those not directly involved might be inconvenienced, and often a winner is not apparent. Companies lose profits on lost sales, and workers lose wages that take years to make up even if the strike secured a wage rate higher than offered before the walkout. But striking or taking a threatened strike may be a long-term investment. If a union never takes militant action to support its demands, the employer may doubt the credibility of its threats. Short strikes may be a relatively low-cost investment in gaining larger future demands. From a management standpoint, taking a strike may be necessary for gaining permission to introduce new work methods or for lowering expectations.[36]

Incidence of Strikes

Several studies identify the variables associated with the incidence of economic strikes. Situations in which costs of disagreeing have changed from earlier negotiations or where relative risks to the parties have changed substantially are associated with increased incidence of strikes. For example, declining real wages or failing to win wage increases comparable

---

[35] *Blackhawk Engraving Co.*, 219 NLRB 169 (1975).

[36] For arguments supporting this position, see Charles R. Greer, Stanley A. Martin, and Ted E. Reusser, "The Effect of Strikes on Shareholder Returns," *Journal of Labor Research* 1 (1980), pp. 217–29; and Martin J. Mauro, "Strikes as a Result of Imperfect Information," *Industrial and Labor Relations Review* 35 (1982), pp. 522–38.

to other contracts increase the likelihood of strikes.[37] Strike incidence is procyclical; that is, strikes increase as unemployment falls and inflation rises.[38] Employer and union stability[39] and stability in the employer's supplier markets is associated with lower incidence rates.[40] Where risks to strikers are lower, such as where striking employees are entitled to unemployment compensation[41] or, as in Canada, where employers cannot legally replace striking employees, the incidence rate is higher.[42] For employers, strikes are longer when companies are not performing well relative to competitors or other industries.[43] Economic strikes in the auto industry were more prevalent when productivity was low, while intracontractual strike frequency was higher when productivity was increasing.[44] Strikes of 14 days or less during the last negotiation increase the odds of strikes in present negotiations.[45] Higher proportions of unionized employees in an industry are associated with higher strike and wage levels, reflecting successful use of union bargaining power.[46]

---

[37] See Orley Ashenfelter and George E. Johnson, "Bargaining Theory, Trade Unions, and Industrial Strike Activity," *American Economic Review* 59 (1969), pp. 35–49; Daniel J. B. Mitchell, "A Note on Strike Propensities and Wage Developments," *Industrial Relations* 20 (1981), pp. 123–27; M. I. Naples, "An Analysis of Defensive Strikes," *Industrial Relations* 26 (1987), pp. 96–105; and C. L. Gramm, "The Determinants of Strike Incidence and Severity: A Micro-Level Study," *Industrial and Labor Relations Review* 39 (1986), pp. 361–76.

[38] See John Kennan, "Pareto Optimality and the Economics of Strike Duration," *Journal of Labor Research* 1 (1980), pp. 77–94; Bruce E. Kaufman, "The Determinants of Strikes over Time and across Industries," *Journal of Labor Research* 4 (1983), pp. 159–75; C. L. Gramm, W. E. Hendricks, and L. M. Kahn, "Inflation Uncertainty and Strike Activity," *Industrial Relations* 27 (1988), pp. 114–29; S. B. Vroman, "A Longitudinal Analysis of Strike Activity in U.S. Manufacturing: 1957–1984," *American Economic Review* 79 (1989), pp. 816–26; and S. McConnell, "Cyclical Fluctuations in Strike Activity," *Industrial and Labor Relations Review* 44 (1990), pp. 130–43.

[39] Bruce E. Kaufman, "The Determinants of Strikes in the United States: 1900–1977," *Industrial and Labor Relations Review* 35 (1982), pp. 473–90.

[40] J. M. Cousineau and R. Lacroix, "Imperfect Information and Strikes: An Analysis of Canadian Experience, 1967–82," *Industrial and Labor Relations Review* 39 (1986), pp. 539–49.

[41] R. Hutchens, D. Lipsky, and R. Stern, *Strikes and Subsidies: The Influence of Government Transfer Programs on Strike Activity* (Kalamazoo, Mich.: Upjohn Institute for Employment Research, 1989).

[42] M. Gunderson and A. Melino, "The Effects of Public Policy on Strike Duration," *Journal of Labor Economics* 8 (1990), pp. 295–316.

[43] McConnell, "Cyclical Fluctuations."

[44] Sean Flaherty, "Strike Activity, Worker Militancy, and Productivity Change in Manufacturing, 1961–1981," *Industrial and Labor Relations Review* 40 (1987), pp. 585–600; and Sean Flaherty, "Strike Activity and Productivity Change: The U.S. Auto Industry," *Industrial Relations* 26 (1987), pp. 174–85.

[45] D. Card, "Longitudinal Analysis of Strike Activity," *Journal of Labor Economics* 6 (1988), pp. 147–76.

[46] J. M. Abowd and J. S. Tracy, "Market Structure, Strike Activity, and Union Wage Settlements," *Industrial Relations* 28 (1989), pp. 227–50.

Canadian legal mandates for conciliation and strike votes reduce incidence rates.[47]

Several individual and industry variables are related to strike incidence. Urban, southern, and female-dominated bargaining units are less likely to strike.[48] Unions in high-injury industries strike more frequently, perhaps reflective of risk-taking behavior among workers in those occupations or industries.[49]

The greater the involvement of the rank-and-file employee, the greater the propensity to strike, as shown in increases in strike activity following passage of the Landrum-Griffin Act, which increased guarantees of union democracy.[50] Younger members appear more willing to be militant, while personal hardship decreases militancy.[51]

Public policy has a mixed relationship with strikes. The availability of Aid to Families with Dependent Children or welfare payments is unassociated with strikes.[52] Right-to-work laws, on the other hand, are related to higher strike rates.[53]

Duration of Strikes

The duration of strikes and their settlement are related to a number of variables. Duration is countercyclical, increasing during poor economic times.[54] Costs do not necessarily increase at the same rate as duration. For the employer, costs for a short strike may be small if shipments can be made from inventory or if customers have stocked up in anticipation. As the strike lengthens, loss of revenue from forgone orders increases rapidly, and long-run costs are ultimately incurred as market share is lost to more reliable competitors. However, duration is longer in booming industries, suggesting that strong earnings by both companies and union members may allow them to holdout for longer periods.[55] For the union member, direct marginal costs rise rapidly as savings are exhausted and as

---

[47] Gunderson and Melino, "Effects of Public Policy."

[48] Kaufman, "The Determinants of Strikes over Time."

[49] J. Paul Leigh, "Risk Preferences and the Interindustry Propensity to Strike," *Industrial and Labor Relations Review* 36 (1983), pp. 271–85.

[50] Ashenfelter and Johnson, "Bargaining Theory."

[51] James E. Martin, "Predictors of Individual Propensity to Strike," *Industrial and Labor Relations Review* 39 (1986), pp. 214–27; see also Alan W. Black, "Some Factors Influencing Attitudes toward Militancy, Solidarity, and Sanctions in a Teachers' Union," *Human Relations* 36 (1983), pp. 973–85.

[52] Hutchens et al., *Strikes and Subsidies.*

[53] Gramm, "Determinants of Strike Incidence and Severity."

[54] Kennan, "Pareto Optimality"; Kaufman, "Determinants of Strikes over Time and across Industries"; Vroman, "Longitudinal Analysis of Strike Activity"; and A. Harrison and M. Stewart, "Cyclical Fluctuations in Strike Duration," *American Economic Review* 79 (1989), pp. 827–41.

[55] McConnell, "Cyclical Fluctuations."

the disparity between strike benefits and wages becomes apparent. Strikes last longer where union members have relatively low debt-to-income ratios.[56] Striker job security is important; durations are longer in Canada where workers are protected against replacement.[57]

Issues are related to duration; strikes involving plant administration and job security are of the shortest duration. General wage disputes result in longer strikes, with an average length from 7 to 15 days.[58] Renegotiation strikes are almost always over economics (85 percent of cases), while intracontract strikes are almost always noneconomic (90 percent of cases). The median duration of renegotiation strikes in one studied sample was 15 days, while the median for intracontract strikes was just 3 days.[59] Wildcat strikes most frequently involve plant administration issues and generally last three days or less. They are predicted by high unionization rates within the industry, unsafe working conditions, low inventories, liberal political environment, and moderate degree of bargaining experience. Wildcat strikes are inhibited by the employer's likelihood of filing an unfair labor practice charge, high unemployment rates, high real wages in the industry, a higher percentage of women in the bargaining unit, location in the South, and a long-term bargaining relationship.[60]

Ironically, the shorter the strike, the more easily it appears to be settled. Almost 13 percent of strikes are settled in the first day. At the 10th day, the rate drops to 4.8 percent; at 30 days, to 3.2 percent; and at 50 days, only 2.4 percent of the remaining strikes are settled. The data show once a strike has exceeded this length, the probability of settling does not change, indicating the costs of continuing the strike for both sides after this do not change relative to the other.[61]

Effects of Strikes

Some argue that strikes are strictly random events not known before they occur. If this were true, outsiders who could be hurt by strikes could not take any action to insulate themselves. During the 1960s and early 1970s, steel customers learned to stock up before contract expirations in the expectation of strikes. Studies of shareholder behavior suggest investors anticipate strikes; rates of return on shares of struck companies decline in value *before* a strike occurs. Investors discount stocks as the duration

[56] Gramm, "Determinants of Strike Incidence and Severity."

[57] Gunderson and Melino, "Effects of Public Policy."

[58] Kennan, "Pareto Optimality."

[59] Sean Flaherty, "Contract Status and the Economic Determinants of Strike Activity," *Industrial Relations* 22 (1983), pp. 20–33.

[60] Dennis M. Byrne and Randall H. King, "Wildcat Strikes in the U.S. Manufacturing, 1960–1977," *Journal of Labor Research* 7 (1986), pp. 387–401.

[61] Kennan, "Pareto Optimality."

increases over relatively short runs.[62] However, only about one third of the total decline in share price is discounted before the strike is announced.[63] Very long strikes appear related to situations in which firms have done better than average before the strike (ability to pay), and investors bid these stocks up after the strike (perhaps anticipating that management gained major concessions).[64] This appears rational because data indicate wages negotiated after a strike are about 3 percent lower than when no strike occurs.[65] From the standpoint of an individual employer in the lumber industry, work stoppages do not appear to appreciably affect supplies of products or prices.[66]

Negotiators may make subjective estimates of the effects of striking in deciding on bargaining tactics. In a study of the perceived results of striking, chief negotiators believed management appeared to gain more from strikes than did unions. The ability to remain in operation and/or to have a large proportion of a plant's employees involved in the strike increased management's perceived advantage.[67] Unions may also use strikes to influence internal politics. For example, locals that voted against ratifying the 1981 United Mine Workers–Bituminous Coal Operators Association agreement were very likely to vote to replace the international's leadership during the next election. Dissidents campaigned actively against the contract.[68]

Overview

Depending on which data are examined, one could argue that involvement in strikes is higher than we've suggested. This chapter's introduction noted that time lost due to strikes was not large in comparison to total time worked. Past evidence suggests, however, about 15 of every 100 workers covered by a contract strike in a given year.[69] The

---

[62] George R. Neumann, "The Predictability of Strikes: Evidence from the Stock Market," *Industrial and Labor Relations Review* 33 (1980), pp. 525–35.

[63] Brian E. Becker and Craig A. Olson, "The Impact of Strikes on Shareholder Equity," *Industrial and Labor Relations Review* 39 (1986), pp. 425–38.

[64] Greer et al., "Effect of Strikes."

[65] S. McConnell, "Strikes, Wages, and Private Information," *American Economic Review* 79 (1989), pp. 810–15.

[66] H. J. Paarsch, "Work Stoppages and the Theory of the Offset Factor: Evidence from the British Columbian Lumber Industry," *Journal of Labor Economics* 8 (1990), pp. 387–411.

[67] Arie Shirom, "Strike Characteristics as Determinants of Strike Settlements: A Chief Negotiator's Viewpoint," *Journal of Applied Psychology* 67 (1982), pp. 45–52.

[68] T. Ghilarducci, "The Impact of Internal Union Politics on the 1981 UMWA Strike," *Industrial Relations* 27 (1988), pp. 114–29.

[69] Mitchell, "Note on Strike Propensities."

relatively low number of days lost and the decline in the percentage of days lost may be attributed to short strike durations and the declining percentage of employees covered by collective bargaining agreements.

BOYCOTTS

Boycotts are used infrequently with mixed results. As noted in Chapter 2, the Danbury Hatters' and Buck's Stove boycotts were declared violations of the Sherman Antitrust Act, exposing unions to treble damages until the Clayton Act exempted them from antitrust provisions.

This exemption has not led to increased use of boycotts for a number of reasons: (1) boycotts require a great deal of publicity to alert customers, (2) customers may not respond to union requests unless a clear-cut social issue is involved, (3) keeping a primary boycott from becoming a secondary boycott is sometimes difficult, and (4) boycott effects are not turned off as easily as strike effects because the public may continue identifying the producer with poor labor relations after a settlement. Boycotts are generally seen as having little economic effect; stock prices of boycotted companies fall for only about 15 days before returning to their preboycott levels.[70]

One boycott technique informs the general public of a labor dispute at a location where the struck business's products are sold. However, this type of activity risks being declared a secondary boycott.

Consider the following: A major televison and radio receiver manufacturer is struck by its production employees. In an attempt to pressure the employer to settle, the union pickets retail stores selling the TV sets. The signs read, "Don't shop here. This store sells XYZ TV sets produced under unfair conditions. ABC union on strike for justice against XYZ." Suppose the union uses a different message on its signs: "ABC on strike against XYZ Co. Don't buy an XYZ TV while shopping here today. ABC has no dispute with this store." Only the second strategy is legal. In the second instance, the picket calls attention to the labor dispute and the struck product but does not ask persons to boycott the neutral store. If the union follows the second strategy and does not impede customers or deliveries, the action is considered primary and legal.[71]

During the 1980s boycotts were used against Adolph Coors Company

---

[70] S. W. Pruitt, K. C. J. Wei, and R. E. White, "The Impact of Union-Sponsored Boycotts on the Stock Prices of Target Firms," *Journal of Labor Research* 9 (1988), pp. 285–90.

[71] *NLRB* v. *Fruit & Vegetable Packers, Local 760*, 377 U.S. 58 (1964).

(to force recognition) and J. P. Stevens & Co., Inc. (to force recognition and bargaining on initial contracts). The Coors boycott had some effect on the ultimate willingness of the firm to recognize the union, but the J. P. Stevens action was much more difficult because many of its products are sold under labels that are hard to identify with the employer.

An unanswered concern in boycotts is what responsibility unions have to secondary employers. If boycotted products are sold in a large department store, the impact may be minimal. But if the secondary employer was a franchisee of the primary and the boycott was successful, the impact could be great.

The question of degree of impact was dismissed as an improper test of a boycott's legality in the *Tree Fruits* case, but it was raised later when a successful boycott had a much greater impact on the secondary employer. Steelworkers Local 14055 struck the Bay Refining division of Dow Chemical Company at Bay City, Michigan, in 1974. Gasoline produced by the struck refinery was marketed through Bay stations in Michigan. To pressure Dow, pickets informed customers in heavily unionized areas that Dow supplied Bay gasoline and asked consumers not to buy it when patronizing Bay stations. Over 80 percent of station revenues came from gasoline sales, so, where the boycott was effective, the impact on the secondary employer was great. Because gasoline refining was only a small part of Dow's business, any sales loss from the boycott was minimal. Furthermore, gasoline was easily marketed through other firms. The appeals court dismissed unfair labor practice complaints against the Steelworkers because *Tree Fruits* said impact was not a proper test. The Supreme Court overruled the appeals court and remanded the issue to the NLRB. The board did not reconsider its decision because Local 14055 had been disestablished.[72] Thus, the impact test has not been decided.

Unions cannot use a boycott to make political statements. The International Longshoremen's Association refusal to handle Soviet goods following its invasion of Afghanistan constituted an illegal secondary boycott because no primary dispute existed with the dockworkers' employer.[73]

So far, our coverage of impasses has involved primarily union initiatives. One tactic has also been used by employers—the lockout. Although the strike has been protected since Norris-LaGuardia, the lockout has a much murkier legal background.

---

[72] *Daily Labor Report* (Washington, D.C.: Bureau of National Affairs, May 5, 1977), p. A-4.

[73] *International Longshoremen's Association, AFL–CIO* v. *Allied International, Inc.*, No. 80-1663, U.S. Supreme Court, 1982; for a critique of this decision, see John Rubin, "The Primary-Secondary Distinction: The New Secondary Boycott Law of *Allied International, Inc.* v. *International Longshoremen's Association*," *Industrial Relations Law Journal* 6 (1984), pp. 94–124.

LOCKOUTS

Lockouts can be thought of as the flip side of the strike coin. After passage of the Wagner Act, the NLRB declared lockouts unfair labor practices. The board said lockouts interfered with employees' rights to engage in protected concerted activities. As such, any refusal to provide work as the result of a labor dispute presumably related to and interfered with workers' protected rights. Over time, this broad approach has been redefined by specific situational variables and court interpretations. Lockouts are legal in three distinct situations if specific conditions are met: (1) perishable goods, (2) multiemployer bargaining units, and (3) single-employer units.

Perishable Goods

An employer dealing with perishable goods is frequently at the mercy of the union. For example, the California vegetable canners were struck in 1976 just before the harvest. Because their revenues depended on packing and selling the produce when it was available, a strike during the pack itself would have caused the produce to rot. Thus, the employers were under great pressure to settle quickly.

Similar situations occur when the employer's goods and services are perishable, but the employer has more control over their perishability. For a packer, the timing of the crop's maturity is not within the firm's control. But a brewer can decide when to start a new batch of beer, and a contractor can elect when to begin a tract of houses. In the brewer's case, if the beer is started, it must be bottled on a certain date or the batch will spoil, resulting in immediate economic loss. For the contractor, customers may become dissatisfied waiting for an unfinished house and spread their displeasure by communicating to others. Thus, the long-term business interests of the contractor and the short-term economic losses suffered by the brewer can be minimized only by capitulating to the union on its terms. The lockout is a legitimate employer tactic to neutralize or decrease union power in situations involving perishable goods when it is done to avoid economic loss[74] or to preserve customer goodwill.[75]

Multiemployer Lockouts

Frequently, several small employers engaged in the same business with employees represented by the same union form a multiemployer bargaining unit to reduce the bargaining power the union would have with a

---

[74] *Duluth Bottling Association,* 48 NLRB 1335 (1943).
[75] *Betts Cadillac-Olds, Inc.,* 96 NLRB 268 (1951).

small single employer. If this were not done, the union might, in a **whipsawing** manner, win increasingly favorable settlements. To counteract this union tactic, the employers band together and bargain as one. But what happens if the union strikes only one employer or attempts to break the solidarity of the group by using a whipsaw strategy? Is a lockout then an appropriate and legal weapon for the multiemployer group?

In the *Buffalo Linen* case, the Supreme Court held that when one member of a multiemployer unit is struck and the remaining members lock out their employees, the lockout is defensive in nature and without its use the continued integrity of the bargaining unit could not be assured.[76]

Buffalo Linen recognizes the lockout's legality in multiemployer units when a bargaining impasse is reached and a strike follows against one of the members. As we learned earlier, employers involved in economic strikes are free to replace strikers. Also, the court has ruled multiemployer groups can lock out employees and temporarily replace them for the duration of the lockout to continue operations.

In *NLRB* v. *Brown*, a group of retail food stores was bargaining with clerks. When an agreement could not be reached, the clerks struck one store, and the other employers responded by locking out their clerks. All stores continued operating, using temporary replacements. When an agreement was reached, the replacements were discharged, and the clerks were reinstated. The Supreme Court held the action was legal and was simply one economic weapon the parties might use in persuading the other to agree to its bargaining positions. The legitimate interest of the group in continuing multiemployer bargaining, given the tactics used here, outweighed any harm done to the employees through their loss of wages.[77]

Single-Employer Lockouts

In a single-employer negotiation, there is no need to defend against a whipsaw. Thus, the question of whether a lockout interferes with employee rights to engage in concerted activities must be scrutinized more closely for single employers.

In a case involving no impasse or imminent strike, Quaker State Oil followed through with threats to shut down operations, even though the union had given written assurances that members would work while bargaining continued. The NLRB held the lockout by the company was coercive because the union had always abided by its word on continued

[76] *NLRB* v. *Truck Drivers' Local 449*, 353 U.S. 87 (1957).
[77] *NLRB* v. *Brown*, 380 U.S. 278 (1965).

work in the past and the threat and action were taken before an impasse was reached.[78]

The flagship decision in the single-employer lockout area was handed down by the Supreme Court the same day it established the prevailing precedent in multiemployer lockouts (*NLRB* v. *Brown*).[79] American Ship Building operated four shipyards on the Great Lakes. Most of the work involved ship repair on a schedule during the winter and emergency problems encountered during the heavy summer shipping season.

The company bargained with eight unions and had been struck several times. In 1961, it feared a repeat, especially likely to occur if a ship entered its yards for emergency repairs or during the winter when work loads were heaviest. On August 11, after bargaining reached an impasse and 10 days after the contract expired, the Chicago yard was shut down, the Toledo work force was reduced to two, and the Buffalo work force was gradually laid off as work was completed. The Lorain, Ohio, facility remained open to work on a major project.

The NLRB found this action illegal, believing it was done only to enhance a bargaining position. The Supreme Court overruled, holding the employer does not necessarily discriminate against union membership or coerce workers in the exercise of their rights by the use of lockouts. The Court held the lockout was the corollary of the strike and that unions had no legislated right to determine the starting date and duration of a work stoppage. Justice Goldberg suggested in his concurring opinion that the legality of lockouts should be assessed in relation to the length, character, and prevailing relationships in the bargaining relationship. For instance, a refusal to bargain simply to gain an impasse allowing the use of a lockout would be unlawful.

Recently, the NLRB substantially liberalized rules for single employers in holding that temporary replacements can be hired to pressure the union after a lockout has been imposed.[80]

BANKRUPTCIES

While bankruptcies are not impasses, some firms have used them to end impasses over concessions or to escape existing contracts without negotiating. Bankruptcy law allows companies to abrogate contracts with suppliers and renegotiate on more favorable terms. Under Chapter 11, the firm cannot cease operations but may gain protection from its

---

[78] *Quaker State Oil Refining Corp.*, 121 NLRB 334 (1958).
[79] *American Ship Building Co.* v. *NLRB*, 380 U.S. 300 (1965).
[80] *Harter Equipment, Inc.*, 122 LRRM 1219 (1986).

creditors while trying to reorganize. Bankruptcy courts oversee the changes made to contracts to safeguard the interests of both the creditors and the debtor-in-possession.

When companies attempt to abrogate labor agreements, unions have generally filed refusal-to-bargain charges with the NLRB. The NLRB has usually upheld these complaints and ordered the companies to reinstate the contract, pending the negotiation of a revised agreement. Bankrupt companies, however, have sought protection from the bankruptcy courts, arguing that labor agreements do not differ from other supplier contracts the firms have made and can be abrogated under the same authority.

Early in 1984, the Supreme Court ruled bankruptcy courts may approve the rejection of collective bargaining agreements if the debtor-in-possession shows their continued operation is burdensome to the business. The bankrupt firm may also unilaterally modify the terms after filing for bankruptcy but before formal approval is received from the bankruptcy court.[81]

Some argue relatively liberal provisions of Chapter 11, which don't require insolvency, and the Supreme Court decision allowing abrogation of labor agreements will lead to "going concerns" electing to file bankruptcy to escape contract terms unavoidable through collective bargaining. Conflicts between labor legislation and bankruptcy law lead to controversy whenever bankruptcy is declared.[82]

SUMMARY

Impasses occur when the parties fail to reach an agreement during negotiations. Several methods are used to break impasses. The parties may strike or lock out, agree to mediation, or invoke interest arbitration.

Mediation brings the parties together through a third party who helps to reopen communications, clarify issues, and introduce a realistic approach to bargaining issues that continue to separate the parties. Interest arbitration turns the dispute over to a neutral party to decide the terms of a final settlement.

Typical tactics used by unions in impasses include strikes, picketing, boycotts, and corporate campaigns. Employers respond by hiring replacements, locking out employees, or declaring bankruptcy.

---

[81] *NLRB* v. *Bildisco & Bildisco*, 115 LRRM 2805, U.S. Supreme Court, 1984.

[82] For further details, see Thomas R. Haggard and Mark S. Pulliam, *Conflicts between Labor Legislation and Bankruptcy Law*, Labor Relations and Public Policy Series, No. 30 (Philadelphia: Industrial Relations Unit, The Wharton School, University of Pennsylvania, 1987).

Strikes usually occur as the result of a disagreement on the terms of a new agreement. These strikes are called economic strikes. Other strikes occur over unfair labor practices, in sympathy with other unions, and in violation of no-strike clauses. The strikers' rights to employment in each category have been clearly defined by the courts.

Lockouts involve a refusal to provide work. Although strikes can occur anytime after the termination of the contract, lockouts seldom occur because the employer loses revenues when not in operation. Most lockouts involve multiemployer bargaining units whose members seek to preserve the bargaining relationship by countering the strike of a single member.

Strikes occur more often when unions have failed to keep up with relevant comparison settlements. Good economic conditions are also associated with more strikes. Strikes are longer if economic issues are the major concern.

Bankruptcies allow employers to abrogate labor agreements. Present interpretations of bankruptcy laws permit employers who undergo reorganization to unilaterally dissolve labor agreements just as they do other contracts.

DISCUSSION QUESTIONS

1. Why don't more firms use lockouts to break impasses?
2. What conditions are necessary for mediation to assist in settling an impasse?
3. Do you believe the present rights given to strikers by the NLRB are appropriate? Should they be increased or decreased?
4. What are the potential consequences for labor relations of the present interpretation of the bankruptcy statutes?

KEY TERMS

impasse
mediation
fact-finding
interest arbitration
rights arbitration
economic strike
unfair labor practice strikes
wildcat strike

sympathy strike
picketing
recognitional picketing
working to rules
corporate campaign
ally doctrine
whipsawing

CASE
GMFC IMPASSE

Assume you are director of industrial relations for GMFC. The company and the union have failed to agree on a new contract, and the old contract expired last week. Two issues are unresolved, and no movement has been made on these for more than 10 days. The union is demanding 10 cents an hour more than the company is willing to offer, and management continues to demand some copayment by employees for medical care. This is the first negotiation in 15 years in which a new contract has not been ratified before the expiration of the old one.

Local 384 voted a strike authorization about a month ago, but the leaders have not indicated at this point whether they intend to strike. In your organization, production managers are lobbying for a lockout to avoid material losses if the heated steel treating process must be shut down rapidly. Marketing manag-

ers want production maintained to meet orders scheduled for shipment. They argue the union doesn't intend to strike because it hasn't already done so.

In the executive council meeting this morning, financial officers briefed the top executives of GMFC and indicated the company could accept a wage settlement of 5 cents an hour more, but only if this were a firm figure and not subject to increases over the term of the contract. Unfortunately, the union appeared adamant that it will not agree to any health care copayment.

It is now your turn to recommend strategy to the company in this impasse. Considering the evidence, what action should the company take? Outline the action, including processes used and timetables. Consider the possibility that your strategy may trigger a strike or other union activity.

12

UNION-MANAGEMENT COOPERATION

Many labor relations practices are adversarial—organizing, bargaining over wages, disputing contract interpretations, and the like. But it has been increasingly argued that unions and managements can achieve improved outcomes for both through cooperation. As noted earlier, the bargaining unit depends on employment for its existence. If the viability of the employer is threatened and the union perceives this threat as credible, both are likely to cooperate to devise a survival strategy. Recent union concessions in many of the nation's primary industries were rooted in a recognition that union members' jobs were on the line.

This chapter explores the mechanisms and programs involved in union-management cooperation, including regional labor-management cooperation projects, joint union-management productivity programs, employee involvement programs, gainsharing, and innovative methods for improving negotiations. In reading this chapter, consider the following questions:

1. How are the mechanisms for problem solving different from those for adversarial situations?

2. When do cooperative projects become incorporated into the contract, and when are they operated by more informal relationships?

3. What are some results of cooperative programs? Are they equally likely to lead to successes for both unions and managements?

4. What types of outside assistance might be necessary for unions and managements to implement cooperative programs?

LABOR AND MANAGEMENT ROLES
AND THE CHANGING ENVIRONMENT

Chapters 2 and 3 examined the history of labor relations in the United States. A number of economic cycles influenced the outcomes for labor and management. Labor supply and the power of the labor movement were altered by several waves of immigration from Europe and the Far East. Legislation such as the Railway Labor Act, the Norris-LaGuardia Act, and the Wagner Act strengthened the ability of the labor movement in organizing. Taft-Hartley and Landrum-Griffin acts increased managements' powers. At various points, new production technologies substantially reduced the need for certain skills of represented employees.

A major difference between previous eras and the present is the increasing role of international competition in influencing the profitability of employers and the stability of employment. During the past 20 years, industries that virtually monopolized domestic consumption markets have encountered heavy foreign competition: steel, motor vehicles, consumer electric and electronic products, textiles, shoes, and others. Foreign competitors succeeded because costs of domestic producers increased faster than productivity. Some of this was due to unions' abilities to increase wages and some was due to employers' failures to invest in technology. Jointly, there was a lack of attention to the way in which work and production were organized as foreign producers implemented the latest in American and international production design.[1] Some companies failed and local unions were decimated, while others survived and prospered. This chapter examines mechanisms to meet the challenge and adapt, recognizing the different roles and objectives of each. In looking at the new processes that have evolved, goals and objectives of both labor and management need to be reiterated, and the interests of organized individuals must be covered.

Organizing and the Evolving Bargaining Relationship

Unionization has traditionally been fought by U.S. employers. Even in heavily unionized industries, beginning in the 1970s, employers avoided accommodating unions and implemented active union avoidance programs by fighting new organizing, shifting production from unionized plants to new **greenfield operations,** and eliminating investment in unionized plants.[2]

---

[1] J. Hoerr, *And the Wolf Finally Came* (Pittsburgh: University of Pittsburgh Press, 1989).

[2] Thomas A. Kochan, Harry C. Katz, and Robert B. McKersie, *The Transformation of American Industrial Relations* (New York: Free Press, 1986).

The adversary stage carries over to bargaining and contract implementation. The union needs to gain in bargaining to sustain itself from an internal political standpoint and to avoid decertification. Its exclusive representation right and agency responsibility require it to be responsive to all bargaining union members. The legal specification of mandatory bargaining issues increases the union's emphasis on immediate economic issues and away from employer and union survival issues. As noted earlier, managers have generally been judged on their ability to avoid unionization or to limit its impact. Thus, neither party's leaders would be initially motivated to seek cooperation.

Evidence also suggests that unions win initial certification as the result of employees' interests in exercising "voice" in the employment relationship. Creating opportunities for this to occur through cooperation may seem to management as a legitimation of union efforts.

Preferences of Management and Labor

Management seeks the highest profit level it can achieve from its production of goods and services. It is also interested in shifting investments from product lines with lower returns to those with higher profits. To do this, it needs to be able to adapt. From an unconstrained standpoint, it would prefer to open, close, and retool plants as needed; hire labor on a flexible basis; and adjust wage rates to meet changing product market conditions and respond to shifts in the labor market.

Employees are generally assumed to be risk averse, while employers are assumed to be risk neutral. This means employers are looking for the highest rate of return, consistent with the risks it expects to encounter; while employees are assumed to accept a lower pay rate in situations where they can avoid individual risk. Employees are also interested in improving their economic outcomes—particularly when it can be demonstrated that the employer is able to do so. This means employers would prefer great flexibility in employment, while employees would prefer employment security and wages that are not contingent on employer performance.

Levels of Cooperation and Control

Given the mandatory bargaining issues mentioned in the labor acts and the antipathy of management toward organized labor, managers have sought to retain as much control of the workplace as possible. Labor has generally been reluctant to seek shared responsibility for decision making with management given its adversarial role and the economic gains it might have to give up to gain a greater say in decision making. This has given way somewhat during the 1980s in bargaining situations where companies or facilities have been *in extremis*.

Unions recently have won greater claims on the rights to control processes and share in returns on investment. Employers have negotiated provisions to increase the proportion of pay at risk to individual employees, usually to help ensure the survival of the employer and the employment it offers. Participation of labor with management in gaining rights can flow along two dimensions: control and return rights. Control rights involve the degree to which labor participates in organizational decision making. Unionization, in itself, introduces a degree of control rights because the employer can no longer unilaterally determine terms and conditions of mandatory bargaining issues. At the extreme, control rights would include works council arrangements (as in Germany—covered in Chapter 17) and representation on corporate boards of directors. Return rights begin with wage payments at the minimum, and progress through incentive plans, profit-sharing and gainsharing programs, and ultimately to employee stock ownership of the enterprise.[3]

Conflicts over participation rights, along with the historical antipathy of management and adversarial relationships in bargaining, have exacerbated the difficulty in creating joint problem-solving mechanisms. This chapter explores initiatives in union-management cooperation to jointly accomplish their separate goals. Part of this is done through integrative bargaining during contract negotiations and part through developing ongoing cooperative relationships during the contract. Many cooperation experiments are initiated through side letters in the contract or through agreements to suspend contract provisions to experiment with new methods.

INTEGRATIVE BARGAINING

Integrative bargaining is a set of activities leading to the simultaneous accomplishment of unconflicting objectives for both parties. The objectives are related to the solution of a common problem.[4] Conflict occurs when parties have different goals and either the sharing of resources or the interdependencies of tasks block one party's goal attainment if the other party pursues a certain course.[5] For example, shared resources may be available hours of work, and different goals may be overtime premium earnings for the union and high profits for management. One's

---

[3] A. Ben-Ner and D. C. Jones, "On the Effects of Employee Ownership: A New Conceptual Framework and a Review of the Evidence," unpublished paper (Minneapolis: Industrial Relations Center, University of Minnesota, 1991).

[4] Richard E. Walton and Robert B. McKersie, *A Behavioral Theory of Labor Negotiations* (New York: McGraw-Hill, 1965), p. 5.

[5] Stuart M. Schmidt and Thomas A. Kochan, "Conflict: Toward Conceptual Clarity," *Administrative Science Quarterly*, 1972, pp. 359–70.

accomplishment will interfere with another's. Integrative bargaining occurs when one party's goal will not block the other's. Integrative issues may not be immediately known to the parties or may emerge as the result of distributive bargaining's failure to achieve the goals the parties anticipated.

Two major types of integrative solutions are suggested. The first is a situation in which both parties experience an absolute gain over their previous positions. As an example, autoworkers at GM and Ford in the 1980s achieved permanent job security in return for new work rules allowing the industry to reduce costs. Second, integrative bargaining may occur when both parties sacrifice simultaneously (in distributive bargaining, one's gain is the other's loss).[6] Wage concessions in the steel industry in the early 1980s reduced labor costs enough in several situations to keep certain plants open that had been considered for closure, thus increasing the likely job security of many steelworkers.

Change processes within union-management situations may require certain conditions to exist. Increasing internal or external pressures should lead to the consideration of new joint ventures. Multiple constituencies within the union and/or management would stimulate new efforts to arrive at innovative procedures for dealing with joint problems. Where the normal collective bargaining process and its attention to crisis situations is used exclusively, innovation is less likely. Joint commitments are more likely when a program is seen as accomplishing important ends for both and when both are willing to compromise on the goals they desire. Programs should allow for early measurable progress toward goals for both to maintain support from their constituencies. Many of each group's members must experience benefits, and these benefits should not detract from the accomplishment of other important goals. Programs should be insulated from the formal bargaining process, and the usual methods for distributive bargaining would be expected to continue.[7]

A three-step integrative bargaining model requires that: (1) the problem as perceived by each party is identified and each conveys information germane to the problem; (2) parties discover how they will reach their individually important goals simultaneously; (3) parties compare and evaluate the alternatives for reaching simultaneous goals to determine the actions having the greatest benefits to both.[8]

Several conditions are necessary for facilitating problem solving. First, parties must be jointly motivated to reach a solution. Second, communications between parties must reveal as much information

---

[6] Walton and McKersie, *Behavioral Theory*, pp. 128–29.

[7] Thomas A. Kochan and Lee Dyer, "A Model of Organizational Change in the Context of Union-Management Relations," *Journal of Applied Behavioral Science* 12 (1976), pp. 59–78.

[8] Walton and McKersie, *Behavioral Theory*, pp. 137–39.

addressing the problem as possible. Third, parties must have created a climate in which they can trust each other to deliberate over the issues without taking advantage over disclosed information.[9]

Integrative bargaining is appropriate for both immediate and long-run problems. For example, an integrative solution may be appropriate when a contract issue causes grievances during the agreement. Rather than waiting until the next negotiation, addressing the problem immediately may lead to positive outcomes for both parties. On the other hand, anticipated consequences of technology changes may be long run and require the parties to enter into an open-ended relationship extending beyond the contract period.

CREATING AND SUSTAINING COOPERATION

Evidence strongly supports the premise that U.S. employers basically oppose unions, particularly union involvement in decision making.[10] For 60 years, efforts have been made to implement union-management cooperation in a variety of situations, but most have not been sustained.[11] Recently, however, an increased number of collaborative initiatives outside contracts and integrative bargains within contracts have enhanced firm performance and improved job security, with studies indicating efforts are going forward in about half of all unionized firms in the private sector.[12] Given management's long-standing antipathy toward unions, it's reasonable to expect it to collaborate only where improved performance is expected.

Figure 12–1 depicts a model of the proposed impact of collaboration on performance. It suggests that once a cooperative structure is established, the relative power of the company and the union, as modified by organizational constraints, influences the intensity of cooperation. Over time, the developing labor-management relations climate also influences intensity. In turn, changing labor-management relations, the relative power of the company, and organizational constraints lead to changes in

---

[9] Ibid., pp. 139–43.

[10] David Lewin, "Industrial Relations as a Strategic Variable," in *Human Resources and the Performance of the Firm*, ed. Morris M. Kleiner, Richard N. Block, Myron Roomkin, and Sidney W. Salsburg (Madison, Wis.: Industrial Relations Research Association, 1987), pp. 1–41.

[11] W. N. Cooke, *Labor-Management Cooperation* (Kalamazoo, Mich.: W. E. Upjohn Institute for Employment Research, 1990), pp. 4–5.

[12] Kochan et al., *Transformation*; J. T. Delaney, C. Ichniowski, and D. Lewin, "Employee Involvement Programs and Firm Performance, *Proceedings of the Industrial Relations Research Association* 41 (1988) 148–58; and P. B. Voos, "Managerial Perceptions of the Impact of Labor Relations Programs, *Industrial and Labor Relations Review* 40 (1987) 556–68.

FIGURE 12–1

Model of the Effect of Cooperation on Performance and Labor Relations Outcomes

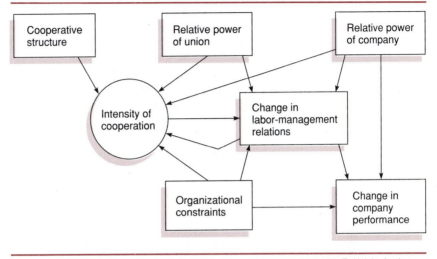

SOURCE: W. N. Cooke *Labor-Management Cooperation* (Kalamazoo, Mich.: W. E. Upjohn Institute for Employment Research, 1990), p. 94.

company performance. The availability of power to the union and company implies they will use it to influence cooperation. The application of relatively equal power should enhance cooperation efforts where both parties prefer it as a mode for achieving important ends for each.[13]

Methods of Cooperation

The next section examines methods of cooperation, covering assumptions about types of cooperation, mechanisms used to achieve cooperation, union and management personnel involved, and results of cooperative efforts. Several generic types of approaches to improving labor-management cooperation, including **area-wide labor-management committees,** improvement of the atmosphere in contract negotiations, productivity improvement and employee involvement plans, gainsharing, and employee stock ownership plans, are examined. Within bargaining relationships, several of these may be combined to enhance joint outcomes. This will be followed by examining the changing roles of management and union officials, political changes that occur, and the processes involved in the diffusion and institutionalization of innovation in workplace design.

---

[13] Cooke, *Labor-Management Cooperation*, pp. 93–95.

Area-Wide Labor-Management Committees

Area-wide labor-management committees (AWLMCs) are jointly sponsored organizations created in particular geographic areas or industries. They neither engage in collective bargaining nor form multiemployer or multiunion bargaining units. Instead, they serve as advisory units to deal with employment issues jointly experienced by their constituents.

AWLMCs are most often a response to significant employment problems. They have been concentrated in the northeastern and midwestern areas experiencing significant industrial and employment declines. There is often a history of plant closings with parent companies expanding elsewhere. High wages and/or union-management relations may have led to some of the employment problems.

A health care labor-management council was recently established in Minneapolis-St. Paul to enhance communications between labor and management in what has been an increasingly adversarial situation. Supported by the Minnesota Bureau of Mediation Services, the group's charter aims at building trust between the parties to improve labor-management relations.[14]

The primary assumption behind the creation of AWLMCs is that labor and management's peer members may pressure each to identify sources of problems and use cooperative methods to reduce or avoid conflict. The identification of joint issues, such as reduced profits and declining job security, may lead to joint efforts to resolve them.

AWLMCs are typically managed by an executive director hired by a coalition of top-level business and union leaders. Approximately equal numbers of members are from labor and management. AWLMCs engage in four major types of activities: (1) sponsoring social events to improve labor-management communications, (2) establishing labor-management committees in local plants, (3) providing assistance in negotiations, and (4) fostering local economic development.[15] These activities are aimed at creating an environment in which problems can be solved and an outward appearance of labor and management cooperation for the betterment of both.

The effectiveness of AWLMCs is difficult to assess because they do not encompass all employers and all are not facing the same types of problems. In Buffalo, New York, in-plant committees were established to facilitate negotiations in a utility company having a 17-week strike and in

---

[14] "Nearly 30 Twin Cities Area Hospitals, Unions Form Labor-Management Council," *Labor Relations Week*, July 18, 1990, p. 681.

[15] Richard D. Leone, *The Operation of Area Labor-Management Committees* (Washington, D.C.: U.S. Department of Labor, Labor-Management Services Administration, 1982).

four cargo-handling firms facing declining shipping volumes. Progress toward the negotiating and cargo volume objectives has been achieved.

In Jamestown, New York, several committees were begun in small to medium-size plants. The community had little success in involving the two largest local employers. Early evidence suggests in-plant committees were successful in improving productivity and reducing overhead; but because inadequate attention was paid to implementation and gaining agreement on the effects of changes, many of the efforts have foundered.

Generally, evidence suggests AWLMCs need the backing of major employers who have visibility in the community and a competent executive director who is willing and able to stay in the post for an extended period to be able to accomplish the goals.[16]

JOINT LABOR-MANAGEMENT COMMITTEES

An examination of the **joint labor-management committee** (JLMC) in the retail food industry indicates the forum involving top union and management leaders has helped managers to understand the national-local union relationship in a decentralized industry. Successful projects have involved research in occupational safety and health issues, the introduction of new technology, health care cost-containment, and competitiveness issues.[17] AT&T and the Communications Workers of America (CWA) developed a corporate-national union method for helping local unions and managements cope with cutbacks and job changes resulting from the divestiture of the telephone operating companies and the introduction of new technology. Many of the projects involved retraining for new jobs in AT&T or with other local employers.[18] Generally, JLMCs are implemented in industries with many employers and a dominant union with locals in many employers and locations.

RELATIONS BY OBJECTIVES

The FMCS has initiated **relations by objectives** (RBO) to assist bargaining relationships that have chronic negotiating difficulties. The program is designed to increase the skills of union and management negotiators in

---

[16] Ibid.; and Robert W. Ahern, "Discussion of Labor-Management Cooperation," *Proceedings of the Industrial Relations Research Association* 35 (1982), pp. 201–6.

[17] Kochan et al., *Transformation*, pp. 182–89.

[18] C. Alexander, "The Alliance for Employee Growth and Development," *Labor-Management Cooperation Brief*, No. 17, U.S. Department of Labor, Bureau of Labor-Management Relations and Cooperative Programs, 1989.

communication, mutual goal setting, and goal attainment. These programs assume that improving problem-solving skills and obtaining increased information will enable each side to better appreciate the other's positions and to specify the issues over which negotiations should occur. The techniques bring union and management members together outside of the negotiating situation to mutually plan actions to reduce future conflict.

Initial experiments with RBO were conducted where bargaining had experienced severe difficulties. Both managements and unions were motivated to improve relations because of disruptions in production and union members' impatience over failure to solve contract disputes and grievances without strikes. Members of bargaining committees for both sides were taken off-site and taught problem identification and solving skills. Then mixed groups were given practice in problem solving. After the training, joint labor-management committees monitored progress within the RBO programs, and some reduction in friction was reported.[19]

However, the efficacy of third-party intervention programs for the reduction of strikes has been questioned. In a continuation of work begun on wildcat strikes in the coal mining industry, it was suggested that the organizational development approach inherent in RBO is inappropriate because the elimination of conflict is inconsistent with collective bargaining. The parties might be better off constructing a system allowing the conflict to be resolved in a structured manner, written out and known by both parties before conflicts.[20] One method for accomplishing this may be to use RBO to structure new relationships after difficult negotiations.[21]

WORKPLACE INTERVENTIONS

The prevalence of joint programs varies widely across manufacturers. Table 12–1 shows the prevalence of a variety among over 200 company and union situations. Of these, quality and productivity are most frequently addressed by work-team-based programs, while productivity and labor-management climate are more frequently handled by committee-

---

[19] Denise T. Hoyer, *Relations by Objectives: An Experimental Program of Management-Union Conflict Resolution*, unpublished doctoral dissertation (Ann Arbor: University of Michigan, 1982).

[20] Jeanne M. Brett, Stephen B. Goldberg, and William Ury, "Mediation and Organizational Development: Models of Conflict Management," *Proceedings of the Industrial Relations Research Association* 33 (1980), pp. 195–202.

[21] U.S. Federal Mediation and Conciliation Service, *Fortieth Annual Report* (Washington, D.C.: Government Printing Office, 1988), p. 15.

TABLE 12–1

Type and Extent of Joint Programs across Manufacturing

Type of Program	Percent of Plants with Program*
Quality circles	31
Quality-of-work-life/employee involvement	19
Work teams	18
Productivity committees	17
Labor-management committees	15
Scanlon or other gainsharing (with employee involvement)	7
Employee stock ownership (with employee involvement)	6
Profit sharing (with employee involvement)	6
Other than above	12

* Based on 194 company responses and 40 unique responses.
SOURCE: William N. Cooke, "Improving Productivity and Quality: Juxtaposing Relative and Collaborative Power," unpublished paper (Ann Arbor: Graduate School of Business Administration and Joint Labor-Management Relations Center, University of Michigan, 1988), p. 4.

based structures. Programs were generally initiated by the company without outside assistance. U.S. government agency support was the most frequently used outside help.[22]

A variety of workplace interventions has been implemented in American industry. Table 12–2 summarizes key program dimensions for six major types of methods. The methods can be divided roughly into gainsharing and nongainsharing plans. Gainsharing plans increase pay when labor becomes more productive following an intervention than during a base period. Nongainsharing approaches may include a changed reward structure (primarily nonmonetary) in the intervention, but no contingency between productivity and pay is established. The table summarizes each intervention method's guiding philosophy, primary change goal, degree of worker participation, role of supervisors and management, any bonus formulas, role of the union, and other method characteristics.

Scanlon, Rucker, and **Impro-Share plans** are designed to improve productivity. Scanlon and Rucker plans depend on employee suggestions. The Scanlon plan allows employee groups to screen and implement suggestions, while management controls the suggestion system in Rucker plans. The Impro-Share plan shares savings resulting from performance improvements over an engineered standard and allows employers to make "buy outs" of productivity improvements if new technologies

---

[22] William N. Cooke, "Labor-Management Collaboration: New Partnerships or Going in Circles," unpublished manuscript (Ann Arbor: University of Michigan, 1988).

TABLE 12-2
Comparative Analysis of Six Workplace Interventions

	Intervention					
	Gainsharing			No Gainsharing		
Program Dimension	Scanlon	Rucker	Impro-Share	Quality Circles	Labor-Management Committees	Quality-of-Work-Life Projects
Philosophy/theory	Org–single unit; share improvements; people capable/willing to make suggestions, want to make ideas	Primarily economic incentive; some reliance on employee participation	Economic incentives increase performance	People capable/willing to offer ideas/make suggestions	Improve attitudes; trust	Improve working environment (physical, human, systems aspects)
Primary goal	Productivity improvement	Productivity improvement	Productivity improvement	Cost reduction, quality	Improve labor-management relations, communications	Improve psychological well-being at work; increase job satisfaction
Subsidiary goals	Attitudes, communication, work behaviors, quality, cost reduction	Attitudes, communication, work behaviors, quality, cost reductions	Attitudes, work behaviors	Attitudes, communication, work behaviors, quality, productivity	Work behaviors, quality, productivity, cost reductions	Attitudes, communication, work behaviors, quality, productivity, cost reduction
Worker participation	Two levels of committees: screening (1), production (many)	Screening (1), production (1) (sometimes)	Bonus committee	Screening (1), circles (many)	Visitor subcommittees (many)	Steering committees; ad hoc to work on problem; informal
Suggestion making	Formal system	Formal system	None	Context of committee	None, informal	Possibly informal, depending on project

TABLE 12-2
(concluded)

	Intervention					
	Gainsharing			No Gainsharing		
Program Dimension	**Scanlon**	**Rucker**	**Impro-Share**	**Quality Circles**	**Labor-Management Committees**	**Quality-of-Work-Life Projects**
Role of supervisor	Chair, production committee	None	None	Circle leaders	None	No direct role
Role of managers	Direct participation in bonus committee assignments	Ideas coordinator evaluates suggestions, committee assignments	None	Facilitator evaluates proposed solutions	Committee members	Steering committee membership
Bonus formula	$\dfrac{\text{Payroll}}{\text{Sales}}$	$\dfrac{\text{Bargaining unit payroll}}{\text{Production value (sales-materials, supplies, services)}}$	$\dfrac{\text{Engineered std.} \times \text{BPF}}{\text{Total hours worked}}$	All savings/improvements retained by company	All savings/improvements retained by company	All savings/improvements retained by company
Frequency of payout	Monthly	Monthly	Weekly	Not applicable	Not applicable	Not applicable
Role of union	Negotiated provisions, screening committee membership	Negotiated provisions, screening committee membership	Negotiated provisions	Tacit approval	Active membership	Negotiated provisions, steering committee membership
Impact on management style	Substantial	Slight	None	Somewhat	Somewhat	Substantial

SOURCE: Michael Schuster, *Union-Management Cooperation: Structure, Process, and Impact* (Kalamazoo, Mich.: W. E. Upjohn Institute for Employment Research, 1984), p. 73.

are introduced. **Quality circles** enable employees to solve production problems and implement solutions. No bonus is explicitly tied to improvements; however, under Japanese systems, all employees share in bonuses resulting from the organization's performance at six-month or yearly intervals. Labor-management committees are formed to deal with pervasive employment problems within the organization. **Quality-of-work-life** programs aim at improving the workplace environment and increasing the satisfaction of employees, with productivity changes as a welcomed by-product if they are positive.

The Scanlon Plan

The Scanlon plan was born in the late 1930s in an obsolete steel mill. With profits close to zero and employees demanding higher wages and better working conditions, their union leader, Joseph Scanlon, saw that gaining the demands would force the company out of business. To meet the profit goals of the company and the wage and working condition demands of the employees, he proposed the parties work together to increase productivity while postponing a wage increase. But later, if productivity were improved, the gains would be shared with the workers. The program's two underlying foundations are participation by all organization members and equity in reward distribution.[23]

The participation system is based on a recognition that abilities are widely distributed in the organization and that change in the organization's environment is inevitable. Because change occurs and because persons at all levels may have solutions to problems or may suggest changes to improve productivity, the system includes an open suggestion procedure. These suggestions are evaluated and acted on by joint-management committees who make recommendations up the line. Figure 12–2 details the typical composition of a committee and its actions.

A suggestion is evaluated by a work unit's **production committee.** If the suggestion is able to be implemented and has merit in that unit, the production committee can place it into effect. If the suggestion is questionable or has wide impact, it is forwarded to the screening committee (comprising executives and employee representatives) for evaluation and possible implementation.

The **screening committee** is also responsible for determining the bonus to be paid each month or quarter. The bonus is calculated by comparing the usual share of product costs attributed to labor against the

---

[23] Carl F. Frost, John H. Wakeley, and Robert A. Ruh, *The Scanlon Plan for Organization Development: Identity, Participation, and Equity* (East Lansing: Michigan State University Press, 1974), pp. 5–26.

FIGURE 12–2

Scanlon Plan Production Committee

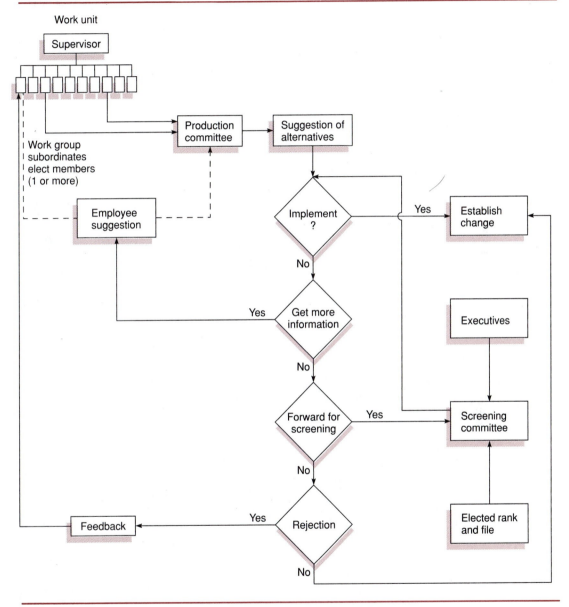

TABLE 12-3
Simple Labor Formula

Sales	$ 98,000
Returned goods	3,000
Net sales	95,000
Inventory +	5,000
Production value	$100,000
Labor bill	
Wages	$ 16,000
Salaries	8,000
Vacations and holidays	1,800
Insurance	1,700
Pensions	500
Unemployment	500
F.I.C.A.	1,500
Total labor bill	$ 30,000
Ratio	.30

SOURCE: Carl F. Frost, John H. Wakeley, and Robert A. Ruh, *The Scanlon Plan for Organization Development: Identity, Participation, and Equity* (East Lansing: Michigan State University Press, 1974), p. 103.

most recent actual costs. For example, if each $1 of sales has traditionally required 30 cents worth of labor, then any improvement, to say 29 or 25 cents, would represent a productivity improvement. Table 12–3 represents a simple formula in which labor costs are 30 percent of the total production value.

Company-wide and individual bonuses can be calculated after the screening committee receives operating results for the previous period. Table 12–4 gives an example of a company and an employee report.

The plan's major purposes are to increase rewards to both parties for productivity gains, encourage and reward participation, and link rewards to employee performance. The plan focuses on reducing labor costs for a given level of output—a factor more directly within workers' control. Thus, the behavior-outcome relationship is higher than for profit sharing or other similar types of gainsharing systems. Productivity gains are shared across work groups, encouraging solutions that mutually benefit several departments.

When one Scanlon plan was intensively tracked over nine years, investigators found it failed to pay a bonus only 13 times. While productivity changes and improvements were not significantly better, their direction was up. Employment at the site decreased over time but not as rapidly as in the industry in which it participated.[24] Another more

---

[24] Christopher S. Miller and Michael Schuster, "A Decade's Experience with the Scanlon Plan: A Case Study," *Journal of Occupational Behavior* 8 (1987), pp. 167–74.

TABLE 12–4

Bonus Report

a. Scanlon ratio	0.40/1.00
b. Value of production	$100,000
c. Expected costs (*a* × *b*)	40,000
d. Actual costs	30,000
e. Bonus pool (*c* − *d*)	10,000
f. Share to company—20% (*e* × 0.20)	2,000
g. Share to employees—80% (adjusted pool) (*e* × 0.80)	8,000
h. Share for future deficits—25% of adjusted pool (*g* × 0.25)	2,000
i. Pool for immediate distribution (*g* − *h*)	6,000
j. Bonus for each employee* as a percentage of pay for the production period (*i* ÷ *d*)	20%

The June pay record might look like this for a typical employee:

Name	Monthly Pay for June	Bonus Percent	Bonus	Total Pay
Mary Smith	$900	20%	$180	$1,080

* This example assumes all employees are participating in the plan at the time this bonus is paid; for example, there has been no turnover and no employees are in their initial 30-, 60-, or 90-day trial periods.

SOURCE: Modified from Carl F. Frost, John H. Wakeley, and Robert A. Ruh, *The Scanlon Plan for Organization Development: Identity, Participation, and Equity* (East Lansing: Michigan State University Press, 1974), p. 15.

recently implemented plan often fails to pay bonuses because of declining prices for its services, but employee suggestions for savings have continued to increase.[25]

Although comparing results across plants with Scanlon plans has limitations, the evidence suggests: (1) perceived participation by employees is necessary for successful implementation, (2) company or plant size does not appear to be a factor in plan success, (3) managerial attitudes toward the plan predict its success, (4) successful implementation takes considerable time, (5) plans are more successful where expectations are high but realistic, (6) a high-level executive must be a leader in the implementation for it to be successful, and (7) the type of production technology used does not appear to be related to success or failure.[26]

Rucker Plans

Rucker plans have some of the participative elements of the Scanlon plan, but management usually has an idea coordinator who handles the suggestion process. The bonus formula is calculated in much the same

[25] G. Pearlstein, "Preston Trucking Drives for Productivity," *Labor-Management Cooperation Brief*, no. 13. U.S. Department of Labor, Bureau of Labor-Management Relations and Cooperative Programs, 1988.

[26] J. Kenneth White, "The Scanlon Plan: Causes and Correlates of Success," *Academy of Management Journal*, June 1979, pp. 292–312.

way as the Scanlon plan except it allows employees also to share in savings in materials and other purchases for production. On the other hand, their increased costs, even in the face of improved productivity, could result in an inability to pay bonuses. Rucker plans might be suggested for an organization that is not ready to participate to the degree a Scanlon plan requires, but they may be difficult to obtain in a collective bargaining agreement.[27]

Impro-Share

Impro-Share ties improved productivity to pay. While consultative management is suggested in the plan, union participation is minimal except through a bonus committee responsible for determining some of the aspects of the bonus formula. The bonus formula is somewhat complex, but the result subtracts the actual hours employees work from the "base value earned hours" of their productivity. If the result is positive, the employee's share (say, 50 percent) is divided by the actual number of hours worked to obtain a bonus percentage. For example, if an employee worked 1,000 hours during a period and the base value earned hours were 1,100 with a 50 percent share, the Impro-Share bonus would be 5 percent.

Impro-Share allows the organization to pinpoint incentives toward specific jobs or groups and decreases competitors' ability to determine wage costs based on bonus formulas. However, employees have difficulty calculating what they will receive.[28] Table 12–5 lists characteristics assumed to improve the likelihood of a gainsharing program's success.

Quality Circles and Team Concepts

Quality circles (QCs) are a nongainsharing workplace intervention method. QCs are teams of employees supported by management who periodically meet to focus attention on product and service quality or other issues. In both union and nonunion settings, the leaders or facilitators in the QCs typically have not been the supervisors of the work group, particularly where the circle cuts across functional areas (for example, production and quality assurance). Exhibit 12–1 shows the typical characteristics of QCs. One study found the opportunity for participation in quality circles was most attractive to employees who were

---

[27] Michael Schuster, *Union-Management Cooperation: Structure, Process, and Impact* (Kalamazoo, Mich.: W. E. Upjohn Institute for Employment Research, 1984).
[28] Ibid.

TABLE 12-5
Conditions Favoring Gainsharing Plans

Characteristic	Favorable Condition
Size	Less than 500 employees
Age	Old enough so that learning curve has flattened and standards can be set based on performance history
Financial measures	Simple, with a good history
Market for output	Good, can absorb additional production
Product costs	Controllable by employees
Organizational climate	Open, high level of trust
Style of management	Participative
Union-management relationship	Cooperative
Overtime history	Limited to no use of overtime in the past
Seasonality of business	Relatively stable across time
Work floor interdependence	High-to-moderate interdependence among jobs
Capital investment plans	Little investment planned
Product stability	Few product changes
Comptroller/CFO	Trusted, able to explain financial measures
Communication policy	Open, willing to share financial results
Plant manager	Trusted, committed to plan, able to articulate goals and ideals of plan
Management	Technically competent, supportive of participative management style, good communications skills, able to deal with suggestions and new ideas
Work force	Technically knowledgeable, interested in participation and higher pay, financially knowledgeable and/or interested
Plant support services	Maintenance and engineering groups competent, willing, and able to respond to increased load

SOURCE: Adapted from E. E. Lawler, *Pay and Organizational Development* (Reading, Mass.: Addison-Wesley Publishing, 1982), p. 144.

younger, believed the union should be involved, were less likely involved in union activities, were more often involved in on-the-job activities such as suggestion programs, desired more participation, and had more information on quality circles. The results of the study suggest unions should not be concerned about employee involvement programs as a means of weakening union control. Rather, employees will identify increasingly with the company if the union doesn't support an opportunity for interested employees to be involved.[29]

---

[29] Anil Verma and Robert B. McKersie, "Employee Involvement: The Implications of Noninvolvement by Unions," *Industrial and Labor Relations Review* 40 (1987), pp. 556–68.

EXHIBIT 12-1

Typical Characteristics of Quality Circles

Objectives:
  To improve communication, particularly between line employees and management.
  To identify and solve problems.

Organization:
  The circle consists of a leader and 8 to 10 employees from one area of work. The circle also has a coordinator and one or more facilitators who work closely with it.

Selection of circle members:
  Participation of members is voluntary.
  Participation of leaders may or may not be voluntary.

Scope of problems analyzed by circles:
  The circle selects its own problems.
  Initially, the circle is encouraged to select problems from its immediate work area.
  Problems are not restricted to quality but also include productivity, cost, safety, morale, housekeeping, environment, and other spheres.

Training:
  Formal training in problem-solving techniques is usually a part of circle meetings.

Meetings:
  Usually one hour per week.

Awards for circle activities:
  Usually no monetary awards are given.
  The most effective reward is the satisfaction of the circle members from solving problems and observing the implementation of their own solutions.

SOURCE: Reprinted, by permission of the publisher, from F. M. Gryna, Jr., *Quality Circles; A Team Approach to Problem Solving* (New York: AMACOM, 1981), p. 10. Copyright © 1981 by AMACOM, a division of American Management Associations. All rights reserved.

Team concepts include aspects of quality circles but go beyond them in the way work is organized. Members of the team are expected to learn all of the skills required by jobs performed by the team. The team decides how work will be accomplished. Supervisors act as facilitators rather than directing work. In organizations where team concepts have been implemented, relatively small numbers of distinct jobs exist. Employee-supervisor relations improve more when there is substantial union leader participation and teams are very active. They do best where employment has not changed appreciably, where workers are experienced, and where management does not subcontract.[30]

While team approaches to job designs have been broadly implemented, they have been most controversial in the auto industry, particularly GM. GM's initial foray into cooperation involved quality-of-work-life (QWL) programs (discussed below), which were begun before major economic downturns hit the industry. Since then, the introduction of teams has been primarily aimed at improving productivity with more positive worker outcomes a potential by-product.

Team approaches have been quite successful in New United Motors Manufacturing, Inc. (NUMMI), the GM-Toyota joint venture in Fremont, California, which is managed by Toyota. Before the joint venture, the plant was a GM assembly plant with the worst absentee and quality record in the corporation. When NUMMI started, the UAW remained as the employees' representative, and most of the newly hired employees had previously been with the plant. The team concept was agreed to before hiring and startup, and extensive training in statistical process control and teamwork approaches was undertaken. Ultimately, the pace is faster than when GM ran the plant, but there is also a no-layoff policy. Absentee rates are very low.[31]

At GM-Van Nuys, California, however, a bare majority of employees voted to adopt the team concept in return for keeping the assembly plant open. Some union members saw the vote as pitting workers in different plants against each other to have their plants remain open. Opponents of the team concept see it as eroding the power of the local and national union and reducing returns to seniority through the virtual elimination of promotion opportunities.[32] At Van Nuys, implementation involved training in interpersonal skills, but no employment security was promised, unlike at NUMMI.[33]

Teams have seemed to be most productive where workers have the requisite skills, particularly in statistical process control, and where management has designed the maximum amount of autonomy for the

[30] W. N. Cooke, "Factors Influencing the Effect of Joint Union-Management Programs on Employee-Supervisor Relations," *Industrial and Labor Relations Review* 43 (1990), pp. 587–603.

[31] C. Brown and M. Reich, "When Does Union-Management Cooperation Work? A Look at NUMMI and GM-Van Nuys," *California Management Review* 31, no. 4 (1989), pp. 26–37.

[32] E. Mann, *Taking on General Motors* (Los Angeles: Center for Labor Research and Education, Institute of Industrial Relations, University of California, 1987).

[33] Brown and Reich, "Union-Management Cooperation."

teams.[34] Teams have more trouble when they are working with problems that might occur outside the organization, such as supplier quality and shipping schedules and inventory management. Product-line changes might disrupt teams as employment levels change.[35] Because teams were implemented about the same time wage concessions were granted, they are very controversial in many plants. Dissidents claim concessions haven't saved jobs and that teamwork is harder than the assembly line approach. They also claim their locals discourage grievances and a layer of union bureaucrats who are not in elected office, and thus not accountable, is created.[36]

Labor-Management Committees

Labor-management committees are the plant-level corollary of the AWLMC. They tend to focus on particular problems of the organization if labor-management relations have been deteriorating and may lead to one of the more formal plans previously described. Representatives and methods are determined on an ad hoc basis. Their success probably depends on the degree to which the parties can focus on joint problems threatening their mutual interests.

Quality-Of-Work-Life and Employee Involvement Programs

Quality-of-work-life (QWL) is seen as involving not only job satisfaction but also an opportunity for growth and self-development, freedom from tension and stress, and an avenue to the fulfillment of basic needs.[37] Work environments offering security, equity in treatment, opportunities for individual adaptations, and democracy are assumed to be of high quality.[38] Where QWL programs have been implemented, integrative bargaining methods have been used to begin the programs. The actual

---

[34] J. Hoerr, "The Cultural Revolution at A. O. Smith," *Business Week*, May 29, 1989, pp. 66–68.

[35] W. Zellner, "GM's New 'Teams' Aren't Hitting Any Homers," *Business Week*, August 8, 1988, pp. 46–47.

[36] W. Zellner, "The UAW Rebels Teaming up against Teamwork," *Business Week*, March 27, 1989, pp. 110–14.

[37] Edward E. Lawler, "Measuring the Psychological Quality of Working Life: The Way and How of It," in *The Quality of Working Life*, vol. 1, ed. Louis E. Davis and Albert B. Cherns (New York: Free Press, 1975), pp. 124–25.

[38] Neal Q. Herrick and Michael Maccoby, "Harmonizing Work: A Priority Goal of the 1970s," in *The Quality of Working Life*, vol. 1, ed. Louis E. Davis and Albert B. Cherns (New York: Free Press, 1975), pp. 64–66.

QWL experiment is frequently conducted outside the contract, or the contract itself is suspended within the unit in which changes are occuring. **Employee involvement** programs have also been integratively bargained but more often in a crisis situation where plant or company survival is in question. Involvement is seen as a vehicle for enhancing productivity and job security, and QWL-type outcomes might be possible secondary effects if these are realized.

From an overall standpoint, QWL programs apparently include three components: (1) improving climate, (2) generating commitment, and (3) implementing change. However, three alternative developmental patterns involving these three components exist. In planned programs, climate and commitment lead to change; in evolved programs, climate leads to change, which leads in turn to commitment; and in induced programs, change leads to appropriate climate and commitment.[39] Union willingness to become involved in QWL programs appears related to the progressiveness of the company and increased foreign competition. Increased involvement in traditional workplace decisions is related to deregulation, changing demographics, and support by a parent national union (but not pressure). Cooperation in strategic decision making is related positively to foreign competition and negatively to domestic competition—especially likely because the same national union probably represents employees in other companies in the industry.[40]

A study examining industrial relations performance, quality, productive efficiency, and QWL components in GM-UAW plants found grievances, discipline, absenteeism, number of local contract demands, and negotiating time were significantly related. Grievances and absenteeism also tended to rise during periods of strong demand for automobiles. Product quality and productivity-efficiency measures were negatively related to industrial relations problems. Managerial attitudes were positively related to both labor relations and productivity-efficiency measures. Evidence also suggests QWL programs were associated with higher product quality and reduced grievance rates. Absenteeism, ironically, was associated with higher quality, possibly because less-careful workers were absent more often. QWL program ratings were not associated with productivity-efficiency changes.[41]

---

[39] Robert W. Keidel, "QWL Development: Three Trajectories," *Human Relations*, 1982, pp. 743–61.

[40] I. Goll, "Environment, Corporate Ideology, and Employee Involvement Programs," *Industrial Relations* 29 (1990), pp. 501–12.

[41] Harry C. Katz, Thomas A. Kochan, and Kenneth R. Gobeille, "Industrial Relations Performance, Economic Preformance, and QWL Programs: An Interplant Analysis," *Industrial and Labor Relations Review* 37 (1983), pp. 3–17.

Union Political Processes and the Diffusion of Change

Collaboration is a foreign process in an adversarial environment. Major political changes are necessary for cooperation to be implemented at the national and local union levels. This is one of the reasons a stable plant environment and progressive management is necessary to ensure the safety net union leaders need to advocate change. Unions apparently adopt one of five different approaches to innovative workplace changes: "just say no," let management take the lead and see what results, become involved to protect itself politically, cooperate or collaborate, or use to assert union interests.[42] The defensiveness of local unions is not irrational because managers interpret cooperation as meaning a willingness to make economic concessions and increase productivity even as management efforts to undermine the union might continue.[43] Where unions see themselves in an unequal power relationship with management, cooperation is hard to introduce. At Western Airlines, participation became effective only when the unions gained power to constrain management rights and jointly formed a vision for survival.[44] Union leaders can take advantage of increased communication about economic problems to further worker interests. Cooperative programs also offer an opportunity to negotiate permanence to participation in contracts.[45]

The development of programs is enhanced by international union education efforts and the willingness of the local to be involved.[46] Participation programs can be beneficial to the union because active participants are more satisfied with their unions and involved in union activities. Union support is not undermined by member involvement.[47] Proactive behavior of leaders toward participation increases commitment of members to the union, but members who are negative toward the company and union before participation programs are not changed regardless of the programs' success.[48]

---

[42] A. E. Eaton and P. B. Voos, "The Ability of Unions to Adapt to Innovative Workplace Arrangements," *American Economic Review* 79, no. 2 (1989), pp. 172–76.

[43] P. B. Voos and T-Y Cheng, "What Do Managers Mean by Cooperative Labor Relations?" *Labor Studies Journal* 14 (1989), pp. 3–18.

[44] K. R. Wever, "Toward a Structural Account of Union Participation in Management: The Case of Western Airlines," *Industrial and Labor Relations Review* 42 (1989), pp. 600–9.

[45] J. Cutcher-Gershenfeld, Robert B. McKersie, and K. R. Wever, *The Changing Role of Union Leaders* (Washington, D.C.: Bureau of Labor-Management Relations, U.S. Department of Labor, 1988).

[46] A. E. Eaton, "The Extent and Determinants of Local Union Control of Participative Programs," *Industrial and Labor Relations Review* 43 (1990), pp. 604–20.

[47] A. Verma, "Joint Participation Programs: Self-Help or Suicide for Labor? *Industrial Relations* 28 (1989), pp. 401–10.

[48] M. W. Fields and J. W. Thacker, "The Effects of Quality of Work Life on Commitment to Company and Union: An Examination of Pre-Post Changes," *Proceedings of the Industrial Relations Research Association* 41 (1988), pp. 201–9.

Management Strategy

Labor-management cooperation efforts are frequently carried out at the local or plant level although there have been some corporate-wide strategies such as the Ford-UAW Employee Involvement program. Management may also frequently encounter situations in which its employees, across plants, are represented by several different international unions, each with its own approach toward union-management cooperation.

Initial research results on management strategies toward collective bargaining, cooperation, union avoidance, and firm performance suggest firms improve profitability through extensive collaboration between management and labor. The study also found that overall performance is improved by closing existing unionized facilities and opening or acquiring new nonunion plants. Deunionizing activity in any given existing plant had a negative effect of performance.[49]

Research on the Effects of Cooperation across Organizations

A study of several hundred organizations has yielded important information on the effects of various contextual and cooperative structures on productivity and quality. The more active team-based programs are, the greater their effect. Top union leader participation is important as well. Larger plants have more difficulty improving productivity through cooperative efforts. Technology changes improve productivity at a rate faster than any negative effects from unilateral management implementation. Higher union security predicts more positive results. Subcontracting apparently reduces the possibility of gains, as do situations where layoffs occur more frequently. Interestingly, the larger the proportion of women in the work force, the greater are productivity gains.[50]

A study examining performance of 24 units in the same organization found work areas with traditional adversarial labor-management relations had higher costs, more scrap, lower productivity, and lower returns to direct labor hours than areas with increased cooperation and improved grievance handling.[51] A study across many firms found that employee involvement programs were equally likely in both union and nonunion

[49] D. G. Meyer and W. N. Cooke, "Labor Relations in Transition: Strategic Activities and Financial Performance," unpublished paper (College of Business Administration, University of Akron, 1990).

[50] Cooke, "Improving Productivity and Quality."

[51] J. Cutcher-Gershenfeld, "The Impact of Economic Performance of a Transformation in Workplace Relations," *Industrial and Labor Relations Review* 44 (1991), pp. 241–60.

settings, but unionized firms allowed employees less authority. The programs, in themselves, were not related to measures of returns on assets.[52]

Another study looking at outcomes across a set of organizations found that union officer-management relations were positively related to involvement with general committees but not to return decisions such as profit sharing or **employee stock ownership plan** (ESOP) issues. Grievances were reduced where committees or gainsharing plans were implemented. General labor-management committees kept grievance handling more informal and resolved problems more quickly. Flexibility and reduced absenteeism and turnover were related to all types of participation as catalogued in workplace interventions (above).[53] Table 12–6 summarizes the results of this study.

Research on the Long-Run Effects of Cooperation

Surprisingly little research on the long-run effects of union-management cooperation has been reported. However, one study of several types of union-management cooperation initiatives offers some evidence of the effects.[54] Large differences are apparent in the philosophies underlying cooperation projects. Scanlon and quality circle programs have the greatest participation, while Rucker and Impro-Share programs are mostly associated with economic incentives. The plans cannot substitute for good management, but where that does not exist, labor-management committees can be a springboard for progress. In the absence of management's commitment to participation, Scanlon and other types of high-participation programs will fail. Critical factors for the ongoing success of the programs are the training and commitment of supervisors and the construction and understanding of the bonus formulas.

Companies and unions generally begin programs to improve labor relations, to increase the amount of compensation available, and so on. The motives will influence the type of cooperation plan chosen. Gainsharing influences productivity more than labor-management committees or QWL programs. And no matter which method is chosen, it will not be necessary if traditional collective bargaining methods are successful. Companies and unions both appear to bargain rather than use cooperative alternatives unless difficulties arise in accomplishing their goals.

---

[52] J. T. Delaney, C. Ichniowski, and D. Lewin, "Employee Involvement Programs and Firm Performance," *Proceedings of the Industrial Relations Research Association* 41 (1988), pp. 148–58.

[53] P. B. Voos, "The Influence of Cooperative Programs on Union-Management Relations, Flexibility, and Other Labor Relations Outcomes," *Journal of Labor Research* 10 (1989), pp. 103–17.

[54] Schuster, *Union-Management Cooperation.*

TABLE 12–6

Managers' Mean Evaluations of the Impact of Selected Committees and Programs on Six Labor Relations Outcomes (standard errors in parentheses)

	Union Officer-Management Relations	Grievance Rate	Ability to Resolve Grievances Informally	Flexibility in Utilizing Labor	Absenteeism	Turnover
General plant committees	1.23* (.08)	1.03* (.08)	1.24* (.08)	.54* (.08)	.41* (.07)	.31* (.06)
Specialized plant committees	.77* (.07)	.71* (.06)	.66* (.05)	.25* (.05)	.32* (.05)	.25* (.04)
Local area cooperation committees	.82* (.25)	.18 (.12)	.36* (.14)	.00 (.00)	.00 (.00)	.00 (.00)
Employee participation programs	.47* (.10)	.53* (.08)	.55* (.07)	.47* (.06)	.30* (.06)	.27* (.05)
Gainsharing plans	.57* (.17)	.76* (.20)	.76* (.19)	.76* (.18)	.57* (.16)	.47* (.16)
Profit-sharing plans	.36* (.12)	.17 (.09)	.28* (.09)	.20* (.10)	.25* (.10)	.46* (.12)
Employee stock-ownership plans	.38* (.13)	.12 (.08)	.12 (.08)	.12 (.08)	.12 (.08)	.23* (.11)

*Significant at the .05 level on a 2-tailed test.
All mean evaluations have been based on the following scaling of responses: Large positive effect = 2, small positive effect = 1, no effect = 0, small negative effect = –1, and large negative effect = –2.
SOURCE: P. B. Voos, "The Influence of Cooperative Programs on Union-Management Relations, Flexibility, and Other Labor Relations Outcomes," Journal of Labor Research 10 (1989), p. 109.

A study of cooperation at 23 sites found productivity improvements in 12 and no change in 10 others. In 16 of the sites, the subsequent experience enabled union members to earn bonuses supplementing what they would have earned solely as a result of collective bargaining. Evidence suggests bonus levels are directly influenced by the rate of suggestions generated by the employees.[55] Employment levels are relatively unaffected by cooperative programs, and labor relations are seen as improved.[56]

Finally, evidence suggests productivity improvements are associated primarily with a one-shot increase rather than a long, steady improvement. And the workplace intervention most likely to produce the productivity improvement appears to be the Scanlon plan.

[55] Michael Schuster, "The Scanlon Plan: A Longitudinal Analysis," Journal of Applied Behavioral Science 20 (1984), pp. 23–38.

[56] Michael Schuster, "The Impact of Union-Management Cooperation on Productivity and Employment," Industrial and Labor Relations Review 37 (1983), pp. 415–30.

EMPLOYEE STOCK OWNERSHIP PLANS

Employee stock ownership plans (ESOPs) were first permitted by the Employee Retirement Income Security Act (ERISA) of 1974. Under the legislation, employees may participate in the ownership of their employing firms through profit sharing, productivity improvements, or subtractions from their wages. Since the early 1980s, several companies (such as Chrysler Corporation, Eastern Air Lines, and National Steel Corporation) have agreed to give employees stock in the firm in exchange for labor concessions. In some companies, such as Weirton Steel, the employees became majority owners.

Employee ownership sometimes occurs as a result of progressively declining organizational performance. Rath Packing in Waterloo, Iowa, is an example in which a local labor-management committee helped arrange a government grant that provided loans for new equipment while employees bought 60 percent of the company through wage reduction contributions.[57] The company was able to move into the black for a short while but has since gone bankrupt due to continued cost pressures on the older segments of the meat-packing industry.

No evidence exists to show that ESOPs will, in themselves, improve productivity. Workers are generally productive regardless of the source of ownership.[58] Workers may not automatically favor ESOPs either. The firm governance role involved in ESOPs may induce fear and anxiety as well as expanded commitment. Where performance of the firm is linked to retirement security, workers may wish to avoid ESOPs.[59]

The Diffusion and Institutionalization of Change

An important issue for both labor and management is how successful changes get diffused throughout the organization and become institutionalized. Participation needs a stable environment to grow. The parties need to avoid or isolate collective bargaining shocks and strategic shocks. Layoffs create problems for teams because workers may bump in and out given competitive seniority rights. Changes are aided by implementing them in new facilities and with new workers. Diffusion of successful experiments can then move toward established settings. Unions can markedly assist change when they have a role in strategic decision making such as plant locations. They may also provide needed concessions and

[57] Warner Woodworth, "Collective Bargaining: Concessions or Control?" *Proceedings of the Industrial Relations Research Association* 35 (1982), pp. 418–24.

[58] J. R. Blasi, "The Productivity Ramifications of Union Buyouts," *National Productivity Review* 9 (1990), pp. 17–34.

[59] J. L. Pierce, S. A. Rubenfeld, and S. Morgan, "Employee Ownership: A Conceptual Model of Process and Effects," *Academy of Management Review* 16 (1991), pp. 121–44.

work rule changes to make retrofitting of existing facilities economically feasible. Training in the introduction of new technology and increasing employment security are important to employees and can help to make change permanent. Gainsharing will probably follow as a logical consequence of innovative participation.[60]

The ability to institutionalize change depends on high levels of trust and commitment by union leaders and members, supervisors, plant managers, and corporate executives. Evidence shows there are substantially different perceptions in many situations held by labor and management regarding the degree of commitment, feelings of manipulation and cooptation, and delivery on promises that the efforts undertaken have not always followed their planned course. Establishing and continuing trust is an underlying critical factor to the success of cooperation programs.[61]

SUMMARY

Cooperation between unions and managements occurs in specifying the bargaining relationship regarding the working environment of employees and the goals of employers. The mechanism for establishing cooperative relationships is integrative bargaining. This approach differs from distributive bargaining in that both parties are jointly seeking a solution to a problem instead of contesting for an outcome.

In the United States, cooperation usually occurs outside of the negotiated relationship but involves representatives of the union and management. Experiments have involved improving the bargaining relationship through such programs as relations by objectives or workplace interventions such as gainsharing plans (the Scanlon plan, Rucker plan, and Impro-Share) and nongainsharing interventions (labor-management committees, quality circles, and quality-of-work-life programs).

Employee stock ownership plans aim to increase employee commitment to the company through the long-run improvement of the value of ownership gained through higher productivity.

Evidence suggests increasing numbers of companies are implementing (with unions) team-based action groups to improve productivity and quality. Perceived productivity seems to increase most where the union is secure, where top union officials are involved in the process, and where significant numbers of union members are involved in team-based activities. Employer introduction of new technology continues to lead the

---

[60] T. A. Kochan and J. Cutcher-Gershenfeld, *Institutionalizing and Diffusing Innovations in Industrial Relations* (Washington, D.C.: U.S. Department of Labor, Bureau of Labor-Management Relations and Cooperative Programs, 1988).

[61] Cooke, *Labor-Management Cooperation*, pp. 121–36.

way in improving productivity. Unions are learning how to participate in and benefit from cooperation while retaining their distributive bargaining roles. Innovation is institutionalized through success and stability in organizations where experiments are tried.

DISCUSSION QUESTIONS

1. Why would including such programs as QWL in the collective agreement be difficult?
2. Under what conditions would a Scanlon plan be likely to be effective over relatively long periods?
3. What are the potential long-run problems for unions in agreeing to labor-management cooperation programs?
4. Should unions be guaranteed a seat on an organization's board of directors?

KEY TERMS

greenfield operations
area-wide labor-management
  commitees
joint labor-management
  committee
relations by objectives
Scanlon plan
Rucker plan
Impro-Share

quality circles
quality-of-work-life
production committee
screening committee
team concepts
labor-management committees
employee involvement
employee stock ownership plan

CASE

CONTINUING OR ABANDONING THE SPECIAL-ORDER FABRICATION BUSINESS

It is about three months since the effective date of the GMFC–Local 384 contract. In GMFC's executive council meeting this morning, financial officers reported on an in-depth study on the profitability of the special-order fabrication operations. Their recommendation was that GMFC take no more orders for this area and, when present commitments were shipped, close the operation. Their data showed the operations lost money two out of the last three years, and they argued the Speedy-Lift assembly lines could be expanded into that area for meeting the increasing demand for GMFC forklift trucks.

Top-level management in the special-order fabrication operations conceded that profits, when earned, were low but pointed out that, from a return-on-investment standpoint, they had been among the best in the company during the 1968–73 period. Besides, they argued many of the special orders were from some of the largest customers in the standard product lines, and GMFC could ill afford to lose that business if it was dependent on occasional custom orders as well.

The finance people reiterated their recommendations to terminate the operation, pointing out that labor costs had risen over the past several contracts and, because of the custom nature of the work, productivity gains had been small because new technologies could not be introduced.

After both sides presented their final summations, the chief executive officer announced the firm should prepare to terminate operations. After the announcement, the industrial relations director pointed out that GMFC would have to negotiate the termination with Local 384. The union might demand severance pay, job transfers, and so forth. The point was also raised that this decision offered the union and the company the opportunity to devise a method for reducing and controlling labor costs.

The CEO designated the vice president of finance, the general manager of special-order fabrications, and the industrial relations director as the bargaining team to present the company's decision and bargain a resolution. The CEO made it clear that the company intended to abandon these operations but could reverse its position with the right kind of labor cost reductions.

Although this meeting was not publicized, Local 384's leadership had been concerned about the special-order fabrications area for some time. Management had frequently grumbled about low productivity, and stewards were frequently harassed about alleged slowdowns. Union members in the shop often grieved about work rule changes. The stack of grievances, coupled with management's inaction on them, led the leadership to request a meeting with the industrial relations director to solve the problems.

Chapter 12

Directions

1. Rejoin your original labor or management bargaining team.

2. Reach an agreement for continuation or termination of the special-order fabrication operations.

   a. Company negotiators must reduce labor costs by 10 percent and stabilize them for project bids if operations are to continue (labor costs are 30 percent of the total costs, and ROI would be 7 percent if costs were cut by 10 percent).

   b. Union members are unwilling to have their pay rates cut.

   c. All of the employees in this area are grade 15 or 16 production workers, and most have more than 20 years' experience.

3. Use the agreement you previously reached or the contract in Chapter 10 to specify current terms for these workers.

13

CONTRACT
ADMINISTRATION

After the contract is negotiated and ratified, the parties are bound by its terms. But parties may interpret contract clauses differently, so mechanisms are needed to resolve disputes. Almost all contracts contain a grievance procedure to resolve intracontractual disputes. This chapter identifies types and causes of disputes and contractual means used for resolving them.

In reading this chapter, keep the following questions in mind:

1. What areas of disagreement emerge while the contract is in effect?

2. What actions by the parties violate the labor acts?

3. To what extent are disagreements solved by bargaining or by evaluating the merits of a given issue?

4. What obligation does the union owe its individual members in grievance processing?

THE DUTY TO BARGAIN

Parties do not end the obligation to bargain by concluding an agreement. The NLRB and courts have interpreted the duty to bargain to cover the entire labor relationship from recognition onward. Any disputes regarding wages, hours, or terms and conditions must be mutually resolved. Disputes are resolved through the grievance procedure in the contract.

Management generally takes the initiative in **contract administration.** It determines how it will operate facilities, and the union reacts if it senses a result inconsistent with its interpretation of the contract.

When a grievance procedure exists and management changes its operations, employees are expected to conform to the change. If the change is considered unjust, employees must file a grievance rather than refuse to follow orders. If the latter occurred, employees can be discharged for insubordination even if the management practice was later found to be in violation, unless the violation was flagrant.

ISSUES IN CONTRACT ADMINISTRATION

A number of issues are the focus of disputes during the contract. These disputes result from initiatives taken by the employer. The employer usually does not file a grievance when the union or a worker allegedly violates the contract; it simply acts and waits for a union response. For example, if a worker swears at a supervisor, the company may suspend the worker for five days. The company does not contact the union and ask it to discipline its members. If the union believes this is unjust, it protests the action through a grievance. Some of the major contract areas leading to grievances will be examined next.

Discipline

Discipline imposed by the employer for infractions of rules is one of the most frequently disputed issues. Discipline often involves demotion, suspension, or discharge, and it is meted out for insubordination, dishonesty, absenteeism, rule violations, or poor productivity. Rule violations include issues such as substance abuse and sexual harassment. A discharge is the industrial equivalent of capital punishment and often results in a grievance, regardless of its ultimate merit, because political solidarity often requires the union to extend itself in trying to save a member's job.

Discipline follows from departures from standards of behavior expected by employers. Employees must be aware of the standards to be able to conform to them. Employers use discipline to deter employees from behaving in ways that damage the employers' performance. To lead to discipline, unsatisfactory behaviors must be observed by or reported to an authority who can act. The authority must decide whether behaviors are sufficiently important for action to be taken. If behaviors exceed the threshold the authority perceives as sufficient for requiring punishment, discipline is imposed.[1] Unions are particularly interested that authorities, when imposing discipline, have reliably observed the unsatisfactory behaviors and have consistently applied similar penalties in similar situations and that the magnitude of the penalties is commensurate with the violations.

Incentives

A contract may have an incentive scheme where employees are paid by the piece or receive bonuses for productive efficiency. Frequently, these contracts will establish groups of jobs that work on incentive rates and identify others that don't. If an employee is moved from an incentive to a nonincentive job, wages will probably decrease. If the job seems highly similar to the incentive job, grievances may result. A grievance might also result if the assignment is considered arbitrary or punitive.

Problems also may arise if a new production process is introduced and management seeks to establish higher base rates or time standards before incentive earnings begin. New standards must be bargained collectively.

Work Assignments

A variety of job classifications might create disputes as to which classification is entitled to perform certain work. For example, assume an electrical generating plant powered by coal-fired boilers for steam generation has a boiler shut down for rebricking. To do this, a wall has to be knocked down with some care to avoid damaging other boiler parts. Who should do the work? If a general helper category existed, it might do the work under a supervisor's direction. But because some care is required and the work is preparatory to rebricking, the job could rightfully be assigned to skilled masonry workers. The company may assign the job to helpers because the cost is less and skill requirements are believed to be low. But the masons may believe the task is an integral part of their job and so file a grievance.

---

[1] R. D. Arvey and A. P. Jones, "The Use of Discipline in Organizational Settings: A Framework for Future Research," in *Research in Organizational Behavior*, ed. L. L. Cummings and B. M. Staw (Greenwich, Conn: JAI Press, 1985), pp. 367–408.

Individual Personnel Assignments

These grievances are most often related to promotion, layoffs, transfers, and shift assignments. Most contracts specify that seniority, seniority and merit, or experience on a particular job will be the governing factor in personnel assignments. Disputes often relate to layoffs and shift preference. People who are laid off may believe they are entitled to the jobs of more junior workers in another department who have been retained. While contracts normally specify that persons must be qualified for a job if they are "bumping" junior employees, opinions may differ as to whether the claimed qualifications are actually possessed.

Hours of Work

Grievances in this area relate to overtime requirements and work schedules. For example, if the firm has maintained an 8 A.M. to 4 P.M. shift to mail customer orders and finds its freight companies have moved their shipping schedule from 4 P.M. to 3 P.M., then a 7 A.M. to 3 P.M. shift would better meet its needs. However, the change will affect employees, and grievances may result.

Supervisors Doing Production Work

Most contracts forbid supervisors to do production work except when demonstrating the job to a new employee or handling an emergency. Absence of an employee is usually not considered an emergency. Like the work assignment area, this is basically a job security issue.

Production Standards

Management and the union often agree on the rate of output in assembly line technologies or the standard for an incentive in piece-rate output. If management speeds up the line or reengineers the standards, then more effort is required for the same amount of pay, and grievances often result.

Working Conditions

These issues often relate to health and safety concerns. For example, if the workers believe excessive amounts of fumes are present or if an existing convenience such as heating fails, grievances often result.

Subcontracting

Unless the contract specifies complete discretion to the company in subcontracting, work done by bargaining unit members may not be subcontracted before bargaining with the union.[2] Subcontracting can affect job security, and if a grievance results, management would be involved in a refusal to bargain if it did not discuss the subcontracting issue.

Past Practice

Many employment practices are not written into contracts but unions consider them to be obligations. For example, a company may provide food services to workers at less than the cost of commercial operations. If the employer closes a cafeteria, the union may grieve even though there is no contract language on food services, and management must respond.[3] If stopping work 15 minutes before the end of a shift to wash up is common practice, then extending working time to the shift's end is a change in past practice.

Rules

Employers occasionally institute rules to improve efficiency or to govern the work force. Many contracts establish the employer's right to do so under the management rights clause. Employees may grieve the establishment of rules as altering a term or condition of employment. For example, employer changes requiring random drug testing or prohibiting or sharply restricting smoking might be grieved as changing a term or condition of employment.

---

[2] The Supreme Court decision in *Fibreboard Paper Products* v. *NLRB*, 379 U.S. 203 (1964), requires bargaining by management if the union requests when subcontracting is being considered, unless the union has expressly waived its right in this area; however, this rule has been relaxed somewhat by *First National Maintenance* v. *NLRB*, 107 LRRM 2705 (U.S. Supreme Court, 1981), and later by the NLRB when it held that removal of union work to another facility of the company would be permissible if bargaining had reached an impasse (*Milwaukee Spring Div. of Illinois Coil Spring Co.*, 115 LRRM 1065 [1984], enforced by the U.S. Court of Appeals, District of Columbia Circuit, 119 LRRM 2801 [1985]), or for a legitimate business reason if there were no antiunion animus (*Otis Elevator Co.*, 115 LRRM 1281 [1984]).

[3] *Ford Motor Co.* v. *NLRB*, No. 77-1806, U.S. Supreme Court, 1979.

Prevalence of Issues

Grievances occur across a number of areas, as noted above. There are some differences in the extent to which they relate to different issues. A study of four organizations in different industries found that grievances were distributed as follows: pay (17 percent), working conditions (16 percent), performance and permanent job assignments (16 percent), discipline (14 percent), benefits (14 percent), management rights (7 percent), and discrimination (6 percent)[4]

GRIEVANCE PROCEDURES

Most contracts specify procedures for resolving interpretive disagreements. While contracts vary, most procedures contain four or five steps. In the absence of a grievance procedure, the employee is still entitled to press grievances individually under guarantees contained in Section 9 of the Taft-Hartley Act. Individual employees may also file grievances if the contract has such a procedure, but they generally do not, leaving the union the right to participate in the process.

Steps in the Grievance Procedure

The usual steps in the grievance procedure are as follows:

Step 1   This step varies considerably across companies. In some, an employee who believes the company has violated the contract complains to the union steward, who may accept or assist in the writing of a grievance. Then the steward will present the grievance to the grievant's supervisor, who has the opportunity to answer or adjust it.

In some companies, few grievances are settled at Step 1. The company won't delegate power to supervisors because their decisions can establish precedents in similar grievances filed by the union. Thus, supervisors simply "deny" grievances and refuse the relief asked. In other companies, the grievant orally presents the complaint directly to the supervisor, and settlements can be negotiated immediately. (Figure 13–1 is an example of a fairly complex grievance at its first step.)

Supervisory style affects grievance rates and their disposition. In a large manufacturing plant, autocratic supervisors had lower grievance rates and fewer discipline, overtime, and supervisor-related grievances

---

[4] D. Lewin and R. B. Peterson, *The Modern Grievance Procedure in the United States* (Westport, Conn.: Quorum, 1988).

FIGURE 13-1

Example of a Written Grievance

"I have just been given a job review, as a result of which I am now on the second highest eligibility list as against the top list. I now want clear and accurate answers with supporting information to the following questions:

"1. Why was this job review given five months after its effective date and on the day before my vacation?

"2. Why change my rating for 'manner and interest' from excellent to good? It was admitted that I am excellent in this category, but only to those whom I think will buy, and that the reviewer did not know of any mistakes in judgment I had made.

"3. Why change 'alertness to service' from excellent to good? Since I was told by the reviewer that I was too 'selective' in both this and the previous category, I think that (a) one or the other should be eliminated, or (b) perhaps they should be combined, or (c) both reviewer and employees should be made aware of whatever difference there may be.

"4. Why change 'cooperation' from excellent to good? Since I was told that my co-operation with the other eight people in the department was excellent, I should like to know exactly what incidents took place and who was involved, resulting in this change.

"It also seems that there is a clear, consistent pattern of downgrading everyone in the department from their previous ratings and that job reviews will be given just prior to going on vacation. It is my distinct impression that the present reviewers not only are ignorant of previous reviews but also feel that they do the job much better than the previous reviewers. If they can't come up with some better reasons for the changes than those I have heard, then I think they are doing a remarkably poor job."

SOURCE: Maurice S. Trotta, *Handling Grievances: A Guide for Labor and Management* (Washington, D.C.: Bureau of National Affairs, 1976), pp. 141–42.

than democratic supervisors. Management was less likely to reverse grievance settlements at higher levels for autocratic supervisors.[5] Stewards may have more knowledge of the contract if they are experienced and contract administration is their full-time job. But supervisors and stewards usually do not understand the contract well. About 7 to 10 grievances examined in one study were screened by stewards, and about half used their authority to adjust grievances. Steward training is equally likely to be provided by the employer or the union.[6]

Step 2   Many grievances are settled before this step. If a grievance is denied at Step 1, the steward will present it to a plant industrial relations representative. Both are very familiar with the contract, and both are

[5] Robert L. Walker and James W. Robinson, "The First-Line Supervisor's Role in the Grievance Procedure," *Arbitration Journal* 32 (1977), pp. 279–92.

[6] Steven Briggs, "The Steward, the Supervisor, and the Grievance Process," *Proceedings of the Industrial Relations Research Association* 34 (1981), pp. 313–19.

aware of how grievances have been settled in the past. In routine cases, the company is willing to let the IR representative apply and create precedents.

Step 3   If the grievance has major precedent-setting implications or involves possibilities of major costs, the IR representative may deny it and send it to Step 3. The Step 3 participants may vary substantially depending on the contract. The grievance may be settled locally, with the union represented by its local negotiating committee and management by its top IR manager or plant manager. In more complex situations or in larger firms, the parties may be an international union representative with or without the local negotiating committee and a corporate-level IR director. Most unresolved grievances are settled here.

Step 4   When a grievance is unresolved at the third step, the parties submit the dispute to a neutral arbitrator who hears evidence from both sides and renders a decision in favor of one side. A number of methods for choosing an arbitrator are available. First, the parties may designate the name of a permanent arbitrator in their contract. Second, the parties may petition a private agency, such as the American Arbitration Association, for an arbitration panel. A panel consists of an odd number of members (usually five) from which each party rejects arbitrators in turn until one remains. He or she becomes the arbitrator unless one party objects, in which case a new panel is submitted. Third, the same process may be followed by petitioning the Federal Mediation and Conciliation Service, which also supplies panels of arbitrators listed by this agency. A hearing date is set, and the arbitrator renders a decision some time after the evidence is presented. The next chapter examines arbitration as a separate topic. Figure 13–2 is an example of a contract clause dealing with grievance handling.

Grievance rates in unionized employers probably run about 10 per 100 employees per year. Of each 100 grievances, between 0.5 and 2.5 require arbitration for settlement.[7] Estimates indicate that about half of all written grievances are settled at Step 1, 60 percent of the remaining grievances at Step 2, and 80 percent of the remainder at Step 3.[8] Settling at higher levels is associated with a requirement that grievances be in writing, rules requiring that procedures be closely followed, larger bargaining units, adversarial bargaining relationships, low costs, and low supervisor and steward knowledge of the contract.[9]

---

[7] Lewin and Peterson, *Modern Grievance Procedure*, p. 89.

[8] Ibid., p. 170.

[9] Ibid., pp. 98–100.

FIGURE 13–2
Grievance Procedure Clause

9.02	Grievances

Step 1 The employee and the departmental steward, if the employee desires, shall take the matter up with his supervisor. If no settlement is reached in Step 1 within two working days, the grievance shall be reduced to writing on the form provided for that purpose.

Step 2 The written grievance shall be presented to the supervisor or the general supervisor and a copy sent to the production personnel office. Within two working days after receipt of the grievance, the general supervisor shall hold a meeting, unless mutually agreed otherwise, with the supervisor, the employee, the departmental steward, and the chief steward.

Step 3 If no settlement is reached in Step 2, the written grievance shall be presented to the departmental superintendent, who shall hold a meeting within five working days of the original receipt of the grievance in Step 2 unless mutually agreed otherwise. Those in attendance shall normally be the departmental superintendent, the general supervisor, the supervisor, the employee, the chief steward, departmental steward, a member of the production personnel department, the president of the UNION or his representative, and the divisional committeeman.

Step 4 If no settlement is reached in Step 3, the UNION COMMITTEE and an international representative of the UNION shall meet with the MANAGEMENT COMMITTEE for the purpose of settling the matter.

Step 5 If no settlement is reached in Step 4, the matter shall be referred to an arbitrator. A representative of the UNION shall meet within five working days with a representative of the COMPANY for the purpose of selecting an arbitrator. If an arbitrator cannot be agreed on within five working days after Step 4, a request for a list of arbitrators shall be sent to the Federal Mediation and Conciliation Service. Upon obtaining the list, an arbitrator shall be selected within five working days. Prior to arbitration, a representative of the UNION shall meet with a representative of the COMPANY to reduce to writing wherever possible the actual issue to be arbitrated. The decision of the arbitrator shall be final and binding on all parties. The salary, if any, of the arbitrator and any necessary expense incident to the arbitration shall be paid jointly by the COMPANY and the UNION.

Time Involved

Generally, contracts aim for a speedy resolution of grievances. Typical contracts allow 2 to 5 days for resolution at the first two steps and 3 to 10 days at Step 3. If management denies the grievance at this point, the union has 10 to 30 days to demand arbitration. If the union doesn't, the dispute may not be arbitrable later because it was not referred to arbitration in time. After arbitration is demanded, the time frame is less rigid because an arbitration panel must be requested and received, an arbitrator selected, hearing dates arranged and the hearing held, and the final award written and rendered. While an arbitrated dispute could conceivably be resolved in two months or less, the time lapse is considerably longer in most cases. One study found the average grievance was settled in between 10 and 14 days.[10] Settlements take longer where bargaining units are large, the union requires written grievances, both parties follow procedures closely, an adversarial bargaining relationship exists, and supervisory knowledge of the contract is low.[11] Figure 13–3 presents the flow of decisions in a typical grievance process.

METHODS OF DISPUTE RESOLUTION

Disputes not resolved by negotiations are handled in two major ways: arbitration and strikes. Arbitration is used far more often, but strikes are traditionally used by some unions or in some types of disputes.

Striking over Grievances

Disputes where time is of the essence are most likely to involve strikes. Arbitration usually involves a considerable time lag, so certain unions (such as building trades) seldom use it because their members frequently work short periods for a given employer. By the time a grievance is arbitrated, the job would be completed, with the employer dictating the working conditions.

The same holds for grievances over safety and working conditions in industrial situations where a stable employment relationship exists. When these conditions occur, a strike may be used by the union to force the company to interpret the contract as it demands. With a contract in effect, these strikes may or may not be breaches of the agreement and may or may not be enjoinable by the courts.

Wildcat Strikes

If the union and management have negotiated a no-strike clause, a strike during the agreement period is a wildcat strike, because it contradicts the contract and is unauthorized by the parent national union. Wildcats are particularly prevalent in coal mining.[12]

---

[10] Ibid., p. 89.

[11] Ibid., pp. 98–100.

[12] Jeanne M. Brett and Stephen B. Goldberg, "Wildcat Strikes in Bituminous Coal Mining," *Industrial and Labor Relations Review* 32 (1979), pp. 465–83.

FIGURE 13-3
Grievance Procedure Steps

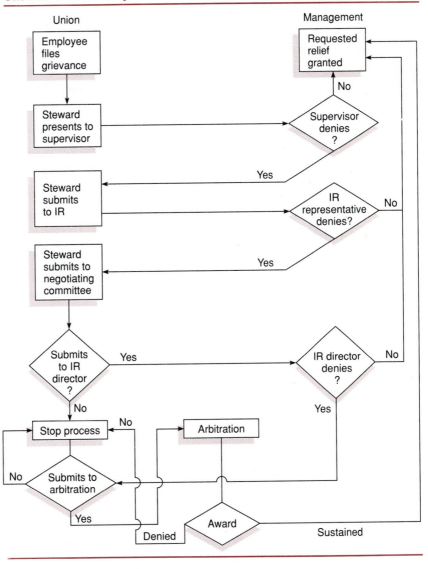

Research on the characteristics of wildcat strikes in coal mining found high-strike mines were larger than low-strike mines, perhaps reflecting the increased formality of grievance handling in large mines. Working conditions were not related to wildcat strikes, but supervisory friction was. Strikes were higher where miners perceived supervisors as being unable to handle grievances and in mines where disputes could not be dealt with locally. Confidence in the grievance procedure did not relate to strike incidence. Miners at both high- and low-strike mines believed strikes resolved disputes in the miners' favor, but high strike incidence rates appeared related to perceptions that this was the best method for getting management to listen.[13]

When companies agree to submit unresolved grievances to arbitration, they are giving up some of their initiative in changing conditions. As a quid pro quo, they usually demand and win a no-strike clause. Under that provision, the union agrees not to strike during the term of the contract, because it has an arbitral forum available. But what if the union strikes? Does the company have a legal recourse? The answer was no for a number of years. The Supreme Court interpreted the Norris-LaGuardia Act in an absolute manner, holding unions could not negotiate away protections included in the legislation.[14] But this interpretation was modified in the *Boys Markets* case, in which the Supreme Court held, where a bona fide no-strike clause existed with a grievance procedure available and where the union has not sought to arbitrate its dispute, federal courts could enjoin a wildcat strike in violation of the contract.[15] The Court explained it would not apply this doctrine when the employer had been unwilling to include an arbitration agreement along with the no-strike clause.

Discipline for Wildcat Strikes

One question frequently encountered asks what tool management has to counteract a wildcat strike? First, if the strike were over an unfair labor practice and the union were correct in its judgment that the action was illegal, the strike would be protected concerted activity under the labor acts, and the employer could not legally retaliate. But if the strike were in violation of a no-strike clause, several factors would come into play.

Both the national and local unions participate in the ratification of the agreement. Both also share in the joint responsibility for enforcing it.

---

[13] Ibid.
[14] *Sinclair Refining Co.* v. *Atkinson*, 370 U.S. 195 (1962).
[15] *Boys Markets, Inc.*, v. *Retail Clerks Union Local 770*, 398 U.S. 235 (1970).

Unfortunately for management, little in damages can be gained unless a union's leadership clearly fomented a wildcat strike.[16] However, if a union demands its members return and they fail to obey, they are subject to union discipline as well as to employer retaliation. But employers cannot sue individual union members for breach of contract for violating a no-strike clause.[17]

Grievance Mediation

As noted earlier, wildcat strikes have been a troublesome feature of labor relations in coal mining. An experiment in the mediation of grievances found costs and time to settlement were reduced by using a mediation-like process to deal with contract disputes. A large share of the grievances headed for arbitration were settled with the help of mediation. The union, in particular, was highly satisfied with mediation, especially as it related to the union's belief regarding the mediator's understanding of the grievance. Mediation may allow the parties to uncover and deal with the real reason for the conflict rather than require framing the reason as a specific contract violation. Mediation did not increase the likelihood of settlements at lower levels and was used neither for discharge grievances nor for those involving financial claims of more than $5,000.[18] In a utility setting where suspension and discharge grievances were included in grievance mediation, managements were equally satisfied with mediation and arbitration except with the settlements. About two thirds of all final step grievances were settled by mediation; thus, the number going to arbitration was cut to one third. The overall level of grievances did not decline as a result of mediation.[19]

EMPLOYEE AND UNION RIGHTS IN GRIEVANCE PROCESSING

One important issue in grievances concerns an employee's right to union representation in disciplinary proceedings. For example, if a supervisor suspects an employee of quitting early, which normally merits a suspen-

---

[16] *Carbon Fuel Co.* v. *United Mine Workers*, 444 U.S. 212 (1979).

[17] *Complete Auto Transit* v. *Reis*, 107 LRRM 2145, U.S. Supreme Court, 1981.

[18] Stephen B. Goldberg and Jeanne M. Brett, "An Experiment in the Mediation of Grievances," *Monthly Labor Review* 106, no. 3 (1983), pp. 23–30.

[19] M. T. Roberts, R. S. Wolters, W. H. Holley Jr., and H. S. Feild, "Management Perceptions of Grievance Mediation," *Arbitration Journal* 45, no. 3 (1990), pp. 15–23.

sion, can the supervisor confront and interrogate the employee without granting union representation for the employee? The Supreme Court ruled employees who are suspected of offenses that could result in discipline are entitled to union representation if they request it.[20] The employer cannot proceed with the interrogation unless a union steward is present to advise its member.

To What Is the Employee Entitled?

Not every grievance constitutes a bona fide contract violation, and not every legitimate grievance is worth pursuing to arbitration. For example, suppose a supervisor performed bargaining unit work during a rush—but not an emergency—period. The union may have a legitimate grievance, and the workers entitled, as a group, to pay for the period the supervisor worked. If it is an isolated incident, bringing it to management's attention should reduce the likelihood of its recurrence, even if management denies the relief requested.

Individual cases vary on the merits of particular facts. For example, a discharge case is more serious than when a grievant claims entitlement to two hours' pay for overtime given to another. How far can an individual union member pursue a grievance or force a union to process it through arbitration if necessary? This subject is not entirely resolved, but opinions of legal experts and court discussions provide some direction. The issue is referred to by terms such as *individual rights* and **fair representation.** In the discussion, the latter term is applied to the vigor of the union's advocacy, not necessarily its competence (the competence issue is covered in Chapter 14). A vigorous approach by the union in the face of management opposition will inevitably cause an unresolved grievance to arrive at arbitration.

Occasionally, an employer disciplines an employee for a rule violation more harshly than similar offenders were punished before union activity. If the individual charges the company with violating his or her rights to engage in union activity, the NLRB will apply the following test. First, the general counsel for the board must make a prima facie case that the discipline was motivated by the employee's union activity. Then, the employer could rebut an unfair labor practice charge if it can show the same punishment would have occurred in the absence of union activity.[21]

---

[20] *NLRB* v. *J. Weingarten, Inc.,* 420 U.S. 251 (1975).
[21] *Wright Line,* 251 NLRB No. 150 (1980).

Fair Representation

The question of fair representation is a complex issue in which the rights and duties of those involved are not completely spelled out. Generally, however, representation rights of nonunion employees are substantially less, unless employers grant them by policy.[22] All employees, represented or not, are able to seek redress for employer actions violating civil rights, wage and hour, or health and safety laws; but in other areas, unrepresented employees have no legal right to review an arbitrary decision.

Individual Rights under the Contract

Many decisions have clarified individual rights under collective bargaining agreements. Major decisions before passage of the Taft-Hartley Act helped to specify the rights of groups or minorities in grievance processing. In *Elgin, Joliet, and Eastern Railway* v. *Burley*, the Supreme Court held an employer is not immune from an employee's action simply because the union concedes a grievance.[23] The employees must have authorized the union to act for them, and some vigorous defense must be shown. Because the union is the exclusive bargaining agent for all employees, the courts will watch to ensure that all classes and subgroups are entitled to and receive equal protection and advocacy from their representatives.

Taft-Hartley enables represented employees to take grievances directly to employers. However, employers cannot process grievances without union observation, if demanded by the union, or adjust the grievance in a manner inconsistent with the contract. For example, if the contract entitles senior employees to promotions, a junior employee cannot personally insist on receiving a promotion to which a senior employee is entitled.

An individual's rights under the contract are not clearly established. Three possible positions might be suggested: (1) individuals have a vested right to use the grievance procedure through arbitration if they choose; (2) individuals should be entitled to grievance processing for discharge, seniority, and compensation cases; and (3) the union as a collective body should have freedom to decide what constitutes a meritorious grievance and how far the grievance should be pursued.[24]

---

[22] Jack Stieber, "The Case for Protection of Unorganized Employees against Unjust Discharge," *Proceedings of the Industrial Relations Research Association* 32 (1979), pp. 155–63.

[23] 325 U.S. 711 (1945).

[24] Benjamin Aaron, "The Individual's Legal Rights as an Employee," *Monthly Labor Review* 86 (1963), pp. 671–72.

The NLRB and courts seldom assert jurisdiction over grievances, particularly on issues of merit. However, a few pivotal cases help to explain union member entitlements and employer and union responsibilities. In *Miranda Fuel Company*, an employee was permitted to start vacation before the date in the contract.[25] Then, after returning late because of illness, other bargaining unit members demanded the union require he be discharged. The NLRB ruled this was an unfair labor practice because the union acquiesced to a majority demand even though the discharged employee had seniority. The case was not taken to higher courts but is in line with a subsequent Supreme Court decision.

The second case involved a merger.[26] Here the same union represented employees of the acquired and surviving companies. After the merger, the union credited seniority of the workers from the acquired company rather than starting at the acquisition date. Several employees from the surviving company claimed they were unfairly represented because their union granted seniority to new employees coming from the other firm. The Supreme Court held the employees must use Taft-Hartley remedies for breach of contract rather than state court actions to gain redress for unfair representation.

In *Vaca* v. *Sipes*, an employee returning from sick leave was discharged because the employer believed he was no longer capable of holding a job.[27] A grievance was filed and the union pressed his case, obtaining medical evidence and requesting he be given a less physically demanding job. The doctors' reports conflicted on the question of whether the discharged employee could safely continue working. Although the union vigorously pursued the grievance through the final prearbitration step, it did not demand arbitration when the company refused to reinstate the grievant.

The grievant sued his union for unfair representation and his employer for breach of contract. The Court held an employee may not go to court on a grievance unless contractual remedies have been exhausted, except where the employer and/or the union have refused to use these remedies. If the grievant contends the union has unfairly represented him or her, he or she must prove this. The Court found individual bargaining unit members have no inherent right to invoke arbitration. In representing all bargaining unit members, the union is both an advocate and an agent that must judge whether claims are frivolous or inconsistent with past practice or contract interpretation. If the union weighs the grievance's merit and treats the grievant similar to others in the same situation, then it isn't unfair representation.

---

[25] 140 NLRB 181 (1962).

[26] *Humphrey v. Moore*, 375 U.S. 335 (1964).

[27] 386 U.S. 171 (1967).

An appeals court decision can place the union "between a rock and a hard place."[28] In this case, the contract provided that promotions would be based on seniority and merit. When the company promoted junior employees, the union processed grievances of senior employees to arbitration. The arbitrator awarded the senior employees the jobs. The displaced junior employees sued their union for failing to represent their positions in the arbitration. The court held the union owed equal obligations to both groups. Although the union certainly favored seniority as the basis for promotion, it must advocate management's position as well because the contract provides benefits to two potential groups with opposite interests.

Another case extends liability for damages to the union. If an employee can prove the employer violated the contract to the employee's detriment and the union dealt with the grievance in an arbitrary and capricious manner, the employee can collect damages from both. The employee collects damages from the employer up to the point at which the union fails to process a meritorious claim and from the union until relief is granted.[29]

A review of Supreme Court decisions on fair representation has extracted the following six principles: (1) employees have the right to have contract terms enforced to their benefit; (2) an individual employee has no right to insist on his or her personal interpretation of a contract term; (3) no individual can require a union to process a grievance to arbitration, but each should have equal access to grievance procedures; (4) settlement on the basis of personal motives by union officials constitutes bad faith; (5) the individual should have a grievance decided on its own merits, not horse-traded for other grievance settlements; and (6) while the union is entitled to judge the relative merit of grievances, it must exercise diligence in investigating the situation that led to the grievance.[30]

GRIEVANCES AND BARGAINING

As noted in the chapters on union structure, organizing, and negotiation, the processes involved can be specified, but the actual behavior does not always duplicate the model. The grievance procedure, as described,

---

[28] *Smith* v. *Hussman Refrigerator Co. & Local 13889, United Steelworkers of America* (U.S. Court of Appeals, 8th Circuit, 1979); certiorari denied by U.S. Supreme Court, 105 LRRM 2657 (1980).

[29] *Bowen* v. *U.S. Postal Service*, 112 LRRM 2281, U.S. Supreme Court, 1983.

[30] Clyde W. Summers, "The Individual Employee's Rights under the Collective Agreement: What Constitutes Fair Representation?" in *Duty of Fair Representation*, ed. Jean T. McKelvey (Ithaca, N.Y.: New York State School of Industrial and Labor Relations, Cornell University, 1977), pp. 60–83.

provides a method for resolving disputes over the contract's meaning. The process consigns the union to the role of responding to management's actions and management to the role of initiating some action leading to the dispute. Grievance resolution has been dealt with as a serial process, from both the steps involved (which duplicate reality rather closely) and the presentation order (first in, first out; which is an unlikely duplication). This section looks at grievances from a political standpoint and as a bargaining tool.

Union Responses to Management Action

In many cases, grievances have a number of ramifications for the union. A novel grievance may establish a precedent for or against the union if it is arbitrated. In the past, the situation may have been informally handled on a case-by-case basis usually favorable to the union, but now the risks of losing may be too great. Other grievances may lead to internal disputes, such as entitlements to work or overtime. Politically powerful minorities within the union may also need accommodation. Upcoming election activity may also influence grievance activity and its resolution. Candidates may take militant positions, and management may grant fewer grievances or take more time, particularly in areas where it sees strength in campaigning candidates it expects will be difficult to deal with in the future.

Besides the responses of union officials to grievances, rank-and-file members may engage in tactics affecting the grievance process. If a large number of grievances build up or if settlement is slow (particularly for those alleging a continuing violation), then pressure tactics such as slowdowns, quickie strikes, and working to rules may be used to pressure management to settle or grant the grievances.[31] Grievants might not passively wait for an ultimate response but rather use tactics to speed a favorable settlement.

Fractional Bargaining

Because most grievances concern an individual employee or a single work group and relate only to one or a few contract terms, tactics aimed at modifying the practice of contract administration are called **fractional bargaining**.[32] Fractional bargaining affects work groups in the same way

---

[31] James W. Kuhn, *Bargaining in Grievance Settlement* (New York: Columbia University Press, 1961).

[32] Ibid., p. 79.

an employer with multiple bargaining units suffers a reduction in bargaining power. An organization consists of interdependent parts, and one part being embroiled in disputes that lessen its productivity will affect the remainder.

Fractional bargaining occasionally poses problems for the union because one critical group may win grievances others fail to achieve. If a union negotiating committee stops grievances of a powerful small group, internal political pressures will increase. A steward of a powerful small group may successfully pressure for settlement at lower levels to avoid local officer involvement. The company may accede to this pressure to lessen chances of production disruptions.

Management may also take the initiative by assigning work to political opponents of the existing union leadership and by handling some disciplinary cases by the book and being lenient with others. These practices may increase internal political pressures and cause more of its energies to be devoted to healing these rifts rather than to additional grievance activity. Thus, as in contract negotiations, each side pressures the other, but some mutual accommodation enabling survival of both is usually reached.

Union Initiatives in Grievances

The union may take the initiative with grievances in a number of ways. The union steward may solicit grievances, looking for situations where the rank and file see a contract violation.[33] For a grievance to be filed, a violation need not actually occur. Only the belief that one did and a linking of that belief to some contract clause is needed. If the union believes it has problems with one area or supervisor, it may simply flood management with grievances. These create work for management, because they must be answered in a certain time under the contract. If higher management has to spend more time on grievances, it may simply tell supervision to "clean up its act," usually resulting in a more lenient approach to demonstrate to management that supervision has "cured" the grievance problem.

Union stewards may also stockpile grievances as threats or trade-offs for larger issues. If an important issue comes up that the steward wants, the supervisor may be told informally that unless a change is made, grievances on a variety of matters will be filed with higher-ups later in the day.

In large plants, the steward has an advantage over the supervisor.

---

[33] Ibid., p. 14.

Many contracts specify that the steward is a full-time union representative, although paid by the company. As such, a steward's full-time work involves contract administration, while the supervisor is responsible for personnel, equipment, production, and other matters. The two are usually no match on interpreting the contract because the contract is a much more integral part of the steward's job and the steward has studied it in greater detail.

The steward's personality may also play a role. One study found stewards who informally settled grievances with supervisors were likely to have higher needs for autonomy, affiliation, and dominance than those who used formal processes. The study also found stewards who were higher in needs for achievement and dominance were involved in greater numbers of grievances.[34] Higher commitment to the union predicted higher grievance activity levels, while higher company commitment and job satisfaction were related to lower grievance activism.[35]

Grievance rates within unions are related to inexperience among union representatives, union policies that influence grievance filing, and periods close to negotiations or political choice within the union.[36] A longitudinal study of auto plant grievances for a single union local found grievances with high factual clarity were decided for the union more frequently during periods of high production importance such as model changeovers and heavy production schedules, when few grievants were involved, when the steward was politically entrenched, and in nonassembly plants. In cases where grievances had low factual clarity, political issues had more effect, such as the shorter the time until the next union election, the lower the settlement rate; the more grievances, the lower the union win rate; the more likely the grievance claimed a right given to another bargaining unit member, the lower the union win rate; and the more entrenched the steward, the lower the win rate. Other factors involved with low clarity outcomes for the union included high production pressure situations and skilled trades occupations.[37] All of these indicate management's response could be seen as pressuring the union politically and facilitating the production process.

---

[34] Dan R. Dalton and William D. Todor, "Manifest Needs of Stewards: Propensity to File a Grievance," *Journal of Applied Psychology* 64 (1979), pp. 654–59.

[35] Dan R. Dalton and William D. Todor, "Antecedents of Grievance-Filing Behavior: Attitude/Behavioral Consistency and the Union Steward," *Academy of Management Journal* 25 (1982), pp. 158–69.

[36] Chalmer E. Labig Jr. and Charles R. Greer, "Grievance Initiation: A Literature Survey and Suggestions for Future Research," *Journal of Labor Research* 9 (1988), pp. 1–27.

[37] D. Meyer and W. Cooke, "Economic and Political Factors in Formal Grievance Resolution," *Industrial Relations* 27 (1988), pp. 318–35.

Individual Union Members and Grievances

Chapter 1 noted individuals may unionize to exercise voice in governing the workplace.[38] Negotiating a contract and obtaining ratification by the bargaining unit creates an employment equilibrium. This equilibrium represents the exercise of bargaining power by both parties and their preferences for the structure of the agreement. In grieving, an individual member exercises voice and expresses dissatisfaction or takes advantage of an opportunity for gain that a specific situation such as increased production rates might allow. Figure 13–4 portrays a model of the grievant's choices and potential outcomes. Some grievance opportunities occur because of workplace changes or actions taken against the grievant. The model suggests negative outcomes will occur to the employee and employer unless the process leading to the ultimate outcome is perceived to be procedurally just.[39]

Differences exist among employees in grievance behavior and characteristics. Generally, demographic and job-related aspects are poor predictors of grievance activity,[40] although evidence exists that younger,[41] male,[42] minority,[43] and better educated employees[44] have higher rates. An attitudinal study examining employees across many organizations found grievants more likely to have lower job satisfaction and higher satisfaction with the union and to be an active participant in union affairs.[45] Another study using the same sample found employees whose job satisfaction declined during the four years between the two waves of the study, who were in larger plants, who perceived themselves as expending lower effort, and who anticipated working for the same employer in five years filed more grievances. Factors relating to perceived union

---

[38] R. B. Freeman and J. L. Medoff, *What Do Unions Do?* (New York: Basic Books, 1984).

[39] B. S. Klaas, "Determinants of Grievance Activity and the Grievance System's Impact on Employee Behavior: An Integrative Perspective," *Academy of Management Review* 14 (1989), pp. 445–58.

[40] Labig and Greer, "Grievance Initiation."

[41] Philip Ash, "The Parties to the Grievance," *Personnel Psychology* 23 (1970), pp. 13–38; John Price, James Dewire, John Nowack, Kenneth Schenkel, and William Ronan, "Three Studies of Grievances," *Personnel Journal* 55, no. 1 (1976), pp. 32–37; Lewin and Peterson, *Modern Grievance Procedures*, p. 174; and M. E. Gordon and R. L. Bowlby, "Reactance and Intentionality Attributions as Determinants of the Intent to File a Grievance," *Personnel Psychology* 42 (1989), pp. 309–29.

[42] Lewin and Peterson, *Modern Grievance Procedures*, p. 174.

[43] Ibid., and Ash, "Parties to the Grievance."

[44] Ash, "Parties to the Grievance"; Lewin and Peterson, *Modern Grievance Procedures*, p. 174; and Price et al., "Three Studies."

[45] Robert E. Allen and Timothy J. Keaveny, "Factors Differentiating Grievants and Nongrievants," *Human Relations* 38 (1985), pp. 519–34.

FIGURE 13-4

An Integrative Model of Individual Grieving Behavior

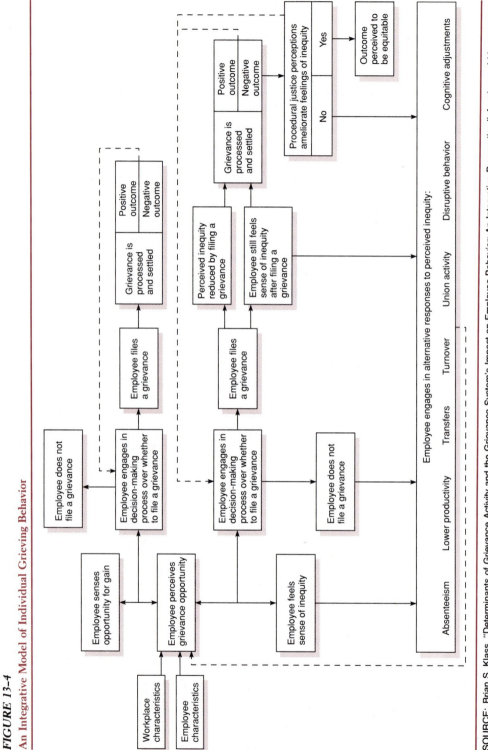

SOURCE: Brian S. Klass, "Determinants of Grievance Activity and the Grievance System's Impact on Employee Behavior: An Integrative Perspective," *Academy of Management Review* 14 (1989), p. 449.

effectiveness, poor or changing working conditions, or the opennness of the supervisor did not influence grievance filing behavior.[46] An experimental study using a hypothetical situation found union members more likely to indicate they would file grievances when the situation evoked strong reactions and when management's action was perceived to be intentional.[47]

EFFECTS OF GRIEVANCES ON EMPLOYERS AND EMPLOYEES

Both employers and employees may be influenced by the filing, processing, and outcome of grievances. A study of grievances in a government agency found that filing two grievances within one rating period was associated with receiving a lower performance rating. However, winning or losing the grievance was not associated with the rating. Employees who grieved were no more likely to transfer; however, employees who filed a second grievance were more likely to receive a disciplinary sanction, and a second negative adjustment to a grievance was associated with an increased probability of quitting. From the employer's standpoint, grievance filing was associated with higher absenteeism and fewer production hours.[48] In a study of a steel mill, grievants were usually better employees during the year in which they grieved and, if their grievance was settled at a low level and/or they lost the grievance, they were more likely to be rated higher, have better attendance, lower turnover, and more likely to be promoted in the subsequent year.[49] Managers and supervisors of units in which grievance rates were higher were somewhat more likely to be rated lower in the next period.[50]

From the perspective of the ongoing bargaining relationship, grievance levels might be expected to be associated with a more conflictual labor relations climate. Evidence across 118 bargaining units in 1976–77 followed up by a study of 18 units in 1979–80 found high grievance rates associated with conflictual rather than cooperative labor relations.[51]

---

[46] Brian Klaas and Gregory G. Dell'Omo, "The Determinants of Grievance Filing Behavior: A Psychological Perspective," paper presented at the Academy of Management Meetings, Anaheim, Calif., 1988.

[47] Gordon and Bowlby, "Reactance and Intentionality."

[48] Brian S. Klaas, Herbert G. Heneman III, and Craig A. Olson, "Grievance Activity and Its Consequences: A Study of the Grievance System and Its Impact on Employee Behavior," unpublished paper (Columbia: University of South Carolina, 1988).

[49] Lewin and Peterson, *Modern Grievance Procedures*, pp. 185–87.

[50] Ibid., p. 189.

[51] Jeffrey Gandz and J. David Whitehead, "The Relationship between Industrial Relations Climate and Grievance Initiation and Resolution," *Proceedings of the Industrial Relations Research Association* 33 (1981), pp. 320–28.

A study of public-sector management and union representatives found explicit performance and disciplinary standards were associated with higher grievance rates. Rivalry between unions within the same employer increased grievances. Positive management attitudes and management willingness to compromise were related to lower rates, but consultation with the union about items of mutual interest did not reduce grievances.[52]

Grievance resolution provides information to the parties to assist in resolving subsequent cases at lower levels. Evidence suggests only management used prior decisions to guide initial decisions on a grievance. The higher the level of settlement of a grievance, the more likely the parties were to use formal settlements of previous grievances as settlements. Earlier decisions are used most frequently as precedents in discipline and work assignment cases.[53] In a Canadian public-sector union, grievances were more likely to be settled favorably in the early steps, for more highly paid employees, and for working condition rather than work assignment issues.[54] (Management may settle grievances to the grievant and union's benefit "without precedent" for subsequent similar cases.)

This review suggests employees who frequently grieve do not necessarily have better work outcomes. But what effect do grievances have for employers? Each grievance requires time for settlement involving stewards, the grievant, and supervisors at the first step; industrial relations representatives, international union representatives, and the union negotiating committee at subsequent steps; and attorneys or representatives, witnesses, and an arbitrator at arbitration. A study of 10 paper mills (9 union and 1 nonunion) found higher grievances were associated with lower plant productivity. The presence of a grievance procedure (only in the union mills) was associated, however, with higher productivity, perhaps because employees had an outlet for complaints that would operate while production occurred.[55]

Grievances have meaning for the grievants and also for union leaders and managers. Exhibit 13–1 gives perspectives of managers and union officials on their supervisors and members and the meaning of grievances.

[52] Chalmer E. Labig Jr. and I. B. Helburn, "Union and Management Policy Influences on Grievance Initiation," *Journal of Labor Research* 7 (1986), pp. 269–84.

[53] Thomas R. Knight, "Feedback and Grievance Resolution," *Industrial and Labor Relations Review* 39 (1986), pp. 585–98.

[54] I. Ng and A. Dastmalchian, "Determinants of Grievance Outcomes: A Case Study," *Industrial and Labor Relations Review* 42 (1989), pp. 393–403.

[55] Casey Ichniowski, "The Effects of Grievance Activity on Productivity," *Industrial and Labor Relations Review* 40 (1986), pp. 75–89.

EXHIBIT 13-1

Reactions of Managers and Unions to High Grievance Rates

A hospital manager stated:

> Grievances are tricky things. On the one hand, we've got a structured procedure for resolving disputes with our nurses, and the procedure is helpful to us in spotting certain problems and in correcting certain abuses. On the other hand, the grievance procedure is often used for frivolous purposes and unwarranted claims, and we don't think that nurses who continually file grievances are the type of people we want to put in charge of things. As a matter of fact and despite the fact that, like most hospitals, we sometimes have nursing shortages, an unhappy nurse is probably better off leaving here, and we've occasionally taken steps to see that that happens.

A manager of a department store offered this observation about the grievance process:

> A supervisor who is the subject of grievances creates red flags for us. We expect supervisors to be able to handle most employee relations issues, and if they can't, then we question whether or not they have a future with us. I know that grievances are sometimes filed with no jusification whatsoever, but on the whole a supervisor who avoids formal grievances looks a lot better to management than a supervisor who's tying up his and our time in grievance hearings.

A teacher's union official commented as follows:

> I've been involved in grievance handling for a long time. After a while, you learn that certain teachers come to understand how to get things done informally, while others go by the book. Now, the same is true of school administrators, but I represent teachers and I would admit privately that a teacher who constantly raises grievances is, in effect, telling me that he doesn't understand how things operate. You're better off settling these things informally, and if you can't maybe you ought to look into another line of work. I certainly wouldn't promote such a teacher if I were running a school.

A steelworkers' union official had this to say about the grievance process:

> It's true that management brings a lot of grievances on itself, but this isn't one-sided by any means. Some workers insist on filing grievances even when they are without merit, and some workers can't understand why a case is decided against them. I know that I wouldn't want these people working for me if I were running the business, especially when you have other employees who are able to settle their grievances without making a big thing of it. When you think about it, the grievances that are really important to use are the ones that we can use in collective bargaining. In those cases, the grievance process is very valuable to us.

SOURCE: D. Lewin and R. B. Peterson, *The Modern Grievance Procedure in the United States* (Westport, Conn.: Quorum, 1988), pp. 194–95.

SUMMARY

Contract administration is the joint activity in which labor and management spend the most time. Not only do the parties respond voluntarily to differences in interpretation, but they also must, by law, bargain on practices related to mandatory items over the life of the contract.

Both sides deal with a variety of issues; job security, seniority, and discipline are among the most important. Methods for handling disputes involve the presentation and resolution of grievances in a step-wise manner, culminating in arbitration if necessary.

Unions must represent employees in a consistent manner in grievance proceedings, and employees who can show they were not accorded fair treatment may hold the union and the employer in breach of contract.

All grievances are not equally meritorious, and political factions within unions may obtain power to gain more favorable outcomes. Grievances also may accompany periodic union political elections. Management may influence these by the way in which it responds to the source of grievances during campaigning.

Grievants have been found less satisfied with their jobs, more satisfied with their unions, and more involved in union activities. They are also more likely to grieve if they see fewer alternatives (such as quitting) available to them. Grievances, in general, do not lead to stronger positive outcomes for employees. Employers with high grievance rates appear to have slightly lower productivity.

DISCUSSION QUESTIONS

1. Should management be required to consult with the union about discipline before it is imposed rather than simply providing for grievance processing after its imposition?
2. Should unions be allowed to drop an employee's grievance if the employee desires arbitration?
3. How does the grievance procedure make subtle changes in the meaning of the contract possible over time?
4. What are the advantages and disadvantages of a program to reduce the number of written grievances?

KEY TERMS

contract administration   fractional bargaining
fair representation

CASE

Carolyn Foster had just returned to her office from the weekly plant IR representatives' meeting. Her secretary had left a note to call George Lowrey, the superintendent of the forklift assembly operation. She called back and immediately recognized from the seriousness of George's tone that a major problem must be brewing in his area. They both agreed she would come right over.

After George had welcomed her into his office, he leaned forward and, putting his chin in his hands, said, "Carolyn, I feel like I'm sitting on a powder keg here. Last year we put in the new Simplex Process assembly line for our forklifts. It had a rated capacity of 35 units an hour. When we installed it, we started up at 28 units, which is the same as the old line, to shake it down and get the bugs out. The new line automates more of the assembly, so each worker has less of a physical demand than before. Well, last week we figured we had everything ironed out on the bugs, so we raised the speed to 35. We figure each worker has to put out about the same amount of effort as under the old system.

"This morning, Ed Zeller, the shop steward, and three of my general supervisors came in, all arguing. Zeller had a fistful of grievances and was yelling about a 'speedup.' Anyway, the upshot is that he wants the job reclassified under Section 7.04 of the contract because he says effort and working conditions have changed.

"Carolyn, we can't give them a penny more and remain competitive. Besides that, if they get a raise, the whole plant will paper us with classification grievances. Zeller is running for union president because Matt Duff is retiring, and if he's successful with this grievance, he's a shoo-in. All we need for a long strike over some penny-ante issue is a bunch of hotheads like him running the show. What can you do to help me?"

Carolyn had been busy taking notes about the problem. She asked, "Do you have the grievances?" George nodded and handed them to her. Then she said, "I'll study the grievances, the contract, and the union situation and get back to you in time for us to plan a Step 3 response. I'll be back to you this afternoon."

Directions

1. Draft a strategy for the company to follow. Consider the immediate problem and the possibilities of precedents being set by your action. List the advantages and disadvantages of your chosen strategy.

2. Prepare a scenario in which your response is presented to Ed Zeller. How is he likely to react? What steps do you expect he will take as a result of your response?

3. What conditions do you consider necessary for these grievances to be resolvable at Step 3?

14

THE ARBITRATION
OF GRIEVANCES

This chapter is about the final step in most grievance procedures—arbitration. Arbitration is not solely a labor relations process, and within labor relations it does not deal solely with grievances. The chapter covers the definition of arbitration, its legal place in labor relations, the process itself, difficulties associated with the practice of arbitration, and results associated with arbitration of employee discharge and discipline cases.

In reading this chapter, consider the following questions:

1. What influences have the Supreme Court's decisions had on arbitration?

2. How is arbitration aided or interfered with by the NLRB?

3. What procedures are used during arbitration?

4. What problems do critics of arbitration point out?

WHAT IS ARBITRATION?

Arbitration is a quasi-judicial process in which the parties agree to submit an unresolved dispute to a neutral third party for binding settlement. Both parties submit their positions, and the arbitrator decides which party is entitled to what types of relief. This chapter is concerned with labor arbitration, but the method is also applied to disputes between buyers and sellers, contractors and real estate developers, and doctors and patients.

Two major types of labor arbitration are *interest* and *rights*. This chapter is primarily concerned with rights arbitration. The next chapter covers interest arbitration. The Supreme Court distinguishes between interest and rights arbitration this way:

> The first relates to disputes over the formation of collective agreements or efforts to secure them. They arise where there is no such agreement or where it is sought to change the terms of one, and therefore the issue is not whether an existing agreement controls the controversy. They look to the acquisition of rights for the future, not to assertion of rights claimed to have vested in the past.
>
> The second class, however, contemplates the existence of a collective agreement already concluded or, at any rate, a situation in which no effort is made to bring about a formal change in terms or to create a new one. The dispute relates either to the meaning or proper application of a particular provision with reference to a specific situation or to an omitted case. In the latter event the claim is founded upon some incident of the employment relation, or asserted one, independent of those covered by the collective agreement. . . . In either case the claim is to rights accrued, not merely to have new ones created for the future.[1]

Thus, rights arbitration applies to interpreting and applying the terms of an existing contract, and interest arbitration decides future issues that have not been resolved.

DEVELOPMENT OF ARBITRATION

The Knights of Labor suggested arbitration as their preferred method for resolving interest differences. No federal law requires arbitration of private-sector labor disputes. However, rights arbitration was boosted by the World War II National War Labor Board by requiring labor agreements to provide for arbitration of disputes during the contract.[2] Beginning in 1957, the role and scope of arbitration has been defined by the Supreme Court and NLRB.

---

[1] *Elgin, Joliet & Eastern Railway Co.* v. *Burley*, 325 U.S. 711 (1945).

[2] Frank Elkouri and Edna Asper Elkouri, *How Arbitration Works*, 3rd ed. (Washington, D.C.: Bureau of National Affairs, 1973), p. 15.

Lincoln Mills

Lincoln Mills was the first case establishing arbitration as the final forum for contract disputes.[3] In *Lincoln Mills*, the Supreme Court held Section 301 of the Taft-Hartley Act required federal courts to enforce agreements between labor and management, including those providing for the arbitration of future grievances. If the contract called for arbitration and if the court agreed with the arbitrator, the award would be enforced by the court if either party failed to comply with it.

Steelworkers' Trilogy

The cornerstone of the legal basis of rights arbitration was decided by the Supreme Court in 1960.[4] The question facing the Court was whether arbitrators' decisions were subject to judicial review. The Court essentially said no in this set of decisions, laying down three basic protections for arbitration. First, arbitration clauses require the parties to arbitrate unresolved grievances. Second, the substance of the grievance and its **arbitrability** is to be determined by the arbitrator, not the courts. And third, if an arbitration clause exists, unless the dispute is clearly outside the scope of the contract, the courts will order arbitration. The decisions state that the arbitrator is presumed to have special competence in labor relations and is thus better able than courts to resolve labor disputes.

In the *Warrior and Gulf* case, the Court held, where a broad arbitration clause is included in the contract, even a dispute not covered in other sections is arbitrable. In this case, the employer subcontracted work while the firm's employees were in a partial layoff status. While lower courts held subcontracting to be a potential management right, the Supreme Court held the broad arbitration agreement coupled with the no-strike provision brought the dispute within the arbitral arena.

The *American Manufacturing* case involved an employee who had been disabled and had accepted worker's compensation. Later, his doctor certified his ability to return to work. When the company refused to reinstate him, he grieved, and the company refused to process the grievance, claiming it was frivolous. The Supreme Court, however, ordered arbitration.

The *Enterprise Wheel* case involved several employees who had been fired for walking out in protest of the firing of another employee. After the company refused to arbitrate the discharge grievances, the federal

---

[3] *Textile Workers Union v. Lincoln Mills*, 355 U.S. 448 (1957).

[4] *United Steelworkers of America v. Warrior & Gulf Navigation Co.*, 363 U.S. 574; *United Steelworkers of America v. Enterprise Wheel and Car Corp.*, 363 U.S. 593; and *United Steelworkers of America v. American Manufacturing Co.*, 363 U.S. 564 (1960).

district court ordered it. The arbitrator reinstated the employees with back pay for all but 10 days' lost time. The award was rendered five days after the contract expired, but the Supreme Court ordered the company to comply.

Four propositions follow from the decisions in the Steelworkers' trilogy.

1. The existence of a valid agreement to arbitrate and the arbitrability of a specific grievance sought to be arbitrated under such an agreement are questions for the courts ultimately to decide (if such an issue is presented for judicial determination) unless the parties have expressly given an arbitrator the authority to make a binding determination of such matters.

2. A court should hold a grievance nonarbitrable under a valid agreement to use arbitration as the terminal point in the grievance procedure only if the parties have clearly indicated their intention to exclude the subject matter of the grievance from the arbitration process, either by expressly so stating in the arbitration clause or by otherwise clearly and unambiguously indicating such intention.

3. Evidence of intention to exclude a claim from the arbitration process should not be found in a determination that the labor agreement could not properly be interpreted in such manner as to sustain the grievance on its merits, for this is a task assigned by the parties to the arbitrator, not the courts.

4. An award should not be set aside as beyond the authority conferred upon the arbitrator, either because of claimed error in interpretation of the agreement or because of alleged lack of authority to provide a particular remedy, where the arbitral decision was or, if silent, might have been the result of the arbitrator's interpretation of the agreement; if, however, it was based not on the contract but on an obligation found to have been imposed by law, the award should be set aside unless the parties expressly authorized the arbitrator to dispose of this as well as any contract issue.[5]

These decisions enable arbitrators to determine, first, whether a dispute is arbitrable; and second, if arbitrable, to decide what the award should be, free from federal court intervention.[6] This approach has basically been followed to the present time. Where companies or unions have gone to court over arbitration procedures or awards, courts have most often compelled arbitration where one of the parties has tried to avoid it or enforced awards where one of the parties has failed to

---

[5] Russell A. Smith and Dallas L. Jones, "The Supreme Court and Labor Dispute Arbitration," *Michigan Law Review* 63 (1965), pp. 759–60.

[6] Ibid., p. 761.

implement them. Only about 25 percent of postarbitration appeals are successful, with less than 1 percent of arbitration cases ultimately involved in court proceedings.[7]

The Steelworkers' trilogy protects a union's right to insist on arbitration and to have arbitral awards enforced without review by the courts. But could management also expect the same treatment, particularly if it agreed to arbitrate and received a favorable award and the union struck to prevent enforcement (given that the Norris-LaGuardia Act broadly prevents federal courts from enjoining most labor organization activities, including strikes for any purpose as long as they do not threaten life or property)?

The 1962 Trilogy

The 1962 trilogy involves the requirement for arbitrating damages for violating a no-strike clause rather than taking the disputes directly to the federal courts.[8] The *Drake* decision held that management should request arbitration when a no-strike clause exists to determine whether the contract has been violated. In the *Sinclair* cases, the Court held the federal courts could not enjoin a strike in violation of a no-strike clause because the Norris-LaGuardia Act prevented injunctions against labor activities.

The decision in *Sinclair* v. *Atkinson* raised an important consideration for employers and for the interpretation of no-strike clauses. Without court enforcement of no-strike clauses, nothing could stop a union from striking over a grievance if an arbitrator ruled against it or from striking rather than using the agreed grievance procedure. But the Supreme Court has reversed itself. In *Boys Markets*, it held a strike in violation of a no-strike clause before arbitration is enjoinable if the company is willing to arbitrate the dispute.[9]

Recent Supreme Court Decisions on Arbitration

Two cases involving arbitration procedures and awards modified and reaffirmed basics of the **Steelworkers' trilogy**. In the first case, the company and the union couldn't agree on whether the disputed situation

---

[7] P. Feuille and M. LeRoy, "Grievance Arbitration Appeals in the Federal Courts: Facts and Figures." *Arbitration Journal* 45, no. 1 (1990), pp. 35–47.

[8] *Sinclair Refining Co.* v. *Atkinson*, 370 U.S. 195 (1962); *Atkinson* v. *Sinclair Refining Co.*, 370 U.S. 238 (1962); and *Drake Bakeries* v. *Local 50*, 370 U.S. 254 (1962).

[9] *Boys Markets, Inc.*, v. *Retail Clerks Union Local 770*, 398 U.S. 235 (1970).

involved the contract. The union argued a decision on coverage should be made by the arbitrator after appointment, while the company maintained arbitrability should be up to the courts. The Supreme Court agreed with the company and declared the courts ultimately are responsible for deciding the arbitrability of contract disputes. This doesn't mean an arbitrator can't rule on arbitrability, but a decision is subject to court review, and, if a dispute existed, a party could petition the courts to decide arbitrability before the case was heard.[10]

The second case involved a situation in which an arbitrator had reinstated an employee who had been fired for smoking marijuana. The company appealed the decision, which was later overturned by the courts as inconsistent with public policy on drug use. The Supreme Court reversed, however, holding that in the absence of fraud or dishonesty, courts may not review a decision on its merits, or for errors of fact, or possible contract misinterpretations. Further, to overturn an award on the basis of public policy, the court must show that the policy is well defined, dominates the interests of the employee or employer, and has a history of laws and legal precedents to support it.[11]

NLRB Deferral to Arbitration

Occasionally, a dispute involves both a grievance and an unfair labor practice charge. For example, certain work that seems to belong to bargaining unit members may have been given to nonunion employees outside the bargaining unit. The grievance would allege a violation of the contract on work assignments, and the union might charge the employer with discrimination based on union membership. To prevent "forum shopping" and to reduce its caseload, the NLRB has adopted rules for deferring to arbitration in cases in which a contract violation and an unfair labor practice are alleged simultaneously.

In developing its policy, the NLRB first held that where a grievance also alleged an unfair labor practice and the arbitration award had been adverse to, say, the union, the union could not then pursue the unfair labor practice.[12] The board decreed it would defer to arbitral awards if the parties had agreed in the contract to be bound by the decisions, the proceedings were fair and regular, and the results were consistent with the provisions of the labor acts.

In 1971, the NLRB went further by deferring hearings on pending unfair labor practice charges until arbitration had been completed, as

[10] *AT&T Technologies, Inc., v. Communications Workers of America*, 106 Supreme Court, 1415 (1986).

[11] *United Paperworkers International Union, AFL–CIO v. Misco, Inc.*, 108 Supreme Court 364 (1987).

[12] *Spielberg Manufacturing Co.*, 112 NLRB 1080 (1955).

long as the process was consistent with *Spielberg*.[13] In 1977, the NLRB retreated somewhat from the **Collyer doctrine.** In two cases, the board limited deferral to cases where the alleged unfair labor practice is not a violation of an employee's Section 7 rights.[14] Ironically, a study of several awards in cases where the board deferred to arbitration in 1977 and 1978 in the Detroit region found decisions on unfair labor practices involving violation of Section 7 rights were seldom incompatible with board decisions, while refusal to bargain unfair labor practices were frequently incompatible. Unions frequently received more favorable treatment from arbitrators than they would have before the NLRB.[15] In 1984, the board extended deferral to arbitration awards unless the decision was "palpably wrong."[16] The NLRB declared it would defer to arbitration if the arbitrator had adequately considered the alleged unfair labor practice and contractual and unfair labor practice issues were essentially parallel. Even before *Olin*, regional directors of the NLRB deferred about 90 percent of cases alleging unfair labor practices. Following *Olin*, this rate increased even though appeals courts have not enforced cases similar to *Olin*.[17]

Exceptions to Deferral

Although the Supreme Court led the way in endorsing the finality of arbitration in contract disputes, and the NLRB allowed arbitrators to decide cases simultaneously alleging violations of federal labor relations law and the contract, two cases have set limits on deferral.[18] These cases indicate individual rights granted under other statutory employment laws cannot be decided in a collectively bargained arbitral procedure if a party objects to the outcome. Thus, if the grievant is dissatisfied with an arbitrator's ruling, the case could be started again by complaining to the appropriate federal compliance agency.

In *Alexander*, a black maintenance employee bid on a skilled job. After his promotion, he was warned that his performance was not up to standards; and, after completing the probationary period (during which his right to revert to his former position expired), Alexander was

---

[13] *Collyer Insulated Wire Co.*, 192 NLRB 150 (1971).

[14] *Roy Robinson Chevrolet*, 228 NLRB 103 (1977); *General American Transportation Corporation*, 228 NLRB 102 (1977).

[15] Benjamin W. Wolkinson, "The Impact of the *Collyer* Policy of Deferral: An Empirical Study," *Industrial and Labor Relations Review* 38 (1985), pp. 377–91.

[16] *Olin Corporation*, 268 NLRB 573 (1984).

[17] P. A. Greenfield, "The NLRB's Deferral to Arbitration before and after *Olin*: An Empirical Analysis," *Industrial and Labor Relations Review* 42 (1988), pp. 34–49.

[18] *Alexander* v. *Gardner-Denver Co.*, 415 U.S. 36 (1974); and *Barrentine* v. *Arkansas-Best Freight System*, 2 WH Cases 1284, U.S. Supreme Court, 1981.

terminated. He charged his termination had been racially motivated. However, the arbitrator ruled it had been performance motivated and upheld the decision.

Alexander complained to the Equal Employment Opportunity Commission (EEOC). Early in the process, the company refused conciliation because the arbitrator had ruled in its favor. The district court dismissed the suit because the contract had an EEO clause and an arbitrator had ruled. Ultimately appealed to the Supreme Court, the case was remanded when the Court ruled the law would not permit deferral to an arbitral award. On remand, the district court determined Alexander had been discharged for performance reasons.

Employers and unions could still use arbitration in discrimination cases if a grievance alleged a violation of *both* contract and law. Appropriate procedure would require a single grievant to charge only the employer discriminated and not argue the contract is discriminatory. Individuals would be entitled to counsels of their own choosing, and a transcript would be kept. Arbitrators would be required to render awards in writing. Thus, courts might be willing to defer to the award on a case-by-case basis because the procedure would meet the suggested Supreme Court requirements indicated in *Alexander.*[19]

Few EEO grievances are relitigated, and, where they are, arbitrators' awards are seldom overturned or modified. A survey of management or union advocates suggests they prefer more attention to arbitration procedures than the extension of Title VII law to the adjudication of the grievance.[20]

In some public-sector situations, employees are subject to both the labor agreement and rules of administrative agencies. A recent Supreme Court decision requires arbitrators to apply the same standards as administrative bodies in deciding employee performance cases.[21] This prevents the grievant from shopping for the most hospitable forum.

ARBITRATION PROCEDURES

This section examines the processes leading to arbitration, selection of an arbitrator, conduct of the arbitration hearing, preparation and rendering of an award, and magnitude of arbitration in the United States.

---

[19] Harry T. Edwards, "Arbitration as an Alternative in Equal Employment Disputes," *Arbitration Journal* 33, no. 12 (1978), pp. 23–27.

[20] Michele M. Hoyman and Lamont E. Stallworth, "Arbitrating Discrimination Grievances in the Wake of *Gardner-Denver*," *Monthly Labor Review* 106, no. 10 (1983), pp. 3–10.

[21] *Cornelius* v. *Nutt*, 472 U.S. 648 (1985).

Prearbitration Matters

The contract specifies how a dispute goes to arbitration. Normally, cases are handled through the preceding steps of the process. At the last step, if management denies a grievance or fails to modify its position sufficiently for the union to agree, the union can demand arbitration.

If the parties have agreed to some concessions before arbitration, these do not necessarily become the basis from which the arbitrator works. In most cases, the parties can return to their own initial positions without establishing precedents. Also, in cases settled before arbitration, the company may explicitly state in its settlement offer to the union that it will not consider the granting of that specific grievance as precedent setting.

The contract usually specifies time periods for each step. For example, a grievance usually must be filed within five days of its occurrence. A first-line supervisor may have three days to answer it, and so on up the line. If management denies the grievance at the last prearbitration step, the union has a certain time to demand arbitration. If it does not exercise its rights within this period, management's decision becomes final.

Selection of an Arbitrator

Procedures for selecting an arbitrator are in the contract. The usual forms for arbitration hearings are either to (1) use one impartial arbitrator who hears the evidence and renders an award or (2) have a tripartite board consisting of company and union representatives and an impartial chairperson. In large organizations or where a long-term bargaining relationship exists, the contract may name a specific individual or group of persons from whom arbitrators are selected. When a specific individual is named, the position is called a **permanent umpire.** Permanence, however, is relative, because the arbitrator continues to serve only as long as both parties rate performance satisfactory. Permanent umpires may be more vulnerable in situations with a militant union that presents less meritorious cases than with a union that saves arbitration for very important issues. The arbitrator would likely, in dealing with a militant union, rule much more frequently for management; and as a result, the union might rate performance unsatisfactory quite soon.[22]

A common type of selection is the **ad hoc arbitrator,** appointed to hear only one case or set of cases. The appointment expires when the award is rendered, and the company and the union may coincidentally appoint other ad hoc arbitrators to hear unrelated cases at or near the same time.

---

[22] Robben W. Fleming, *The Labor Arbitration Process* (Urbana: University of Illinois Press, 1965), pp. 219–20.

Both methods of arbitrator selection have advantages and disadvantages. Less may be known about an ad hoc arbitrator, although some information about potential arbitrators is usually available through résumés, previously published decisions, fields of expertise, and so on. But the appointment constitutes no continuing obligation by the parties. The permanent umpire has a better grasp of the problems the parties encounter because of continuing experience with both. But because the relationship is continuous, whether the umpire will engage in award splitting may always be open to question.

In a study of arbitrator acceptability based on the caseloads they carried, the visibility of the arbitrator rather than personal background or practice characteristics was the factor most highly related to caseload. Also particularly important for acceptability were a listing with referral agencies, publication of awards, membership in professional organizations, and background as a permanent umpire.[23] Another study suggests managements and unions should not pay too much attention to the personal background characteristics of arbitrators in making choices for a particular case because these characteristics account for little variance in arbitrators' rulings for the union or the company.[24] Exhibit 14-1 reports a conversation between two experienced arbitrators on gaining acceptability.

Sources and Qualifications of Arbitrators

There are no absolute qualifications to be an arbitrator. Any one could simply declare himself or herself to be an arbitrator and seek appointments. However, an arbitrator must be selected by the parties to a grievance. Where do arbitrators come from? Arbitrators are those who have arbitrated. Parties involved in ad hoc arbitration want someone with experience and expertise because some of the participants have done little arbitrating and need an experienced arbitrator to assist them in procedural matters. They also look for someone with a background in handling the disputed area. For parties with much arbitration experience, a permanent umpire may be named, and this individual is likely to have an outstanding reputation in arbitration.

Arbitrators are generally from two groups, with the first increasingly used. The first group consists primarily of attorneys whose full-time occupation is labor arbitration. The second source is academics who

[23] Steven S. Briggs and John C. Anderson, "An Empirical Investigation of Arbitrator Acceptability," *Industrial Relations* 19 (1980), pp. 163–74.

[24] Herbert G. Heneman III and Marcus H. Sandver, "Arbitrators' Backgrounds and Behavior," *Proceedings of the Industrial Relations Research Association* 35 (1982), pp. 216–23.

EXHIBIT 14–1

Gaining Acceptability as an Arbitrator

"Paul, you've been an active arbitrator for over 25 years. For several of those years arbitration was your principal means of livelihood. You're an old-timer. How did you get started?"

"Like many if not most of the old-timers, I started with the War Labor Board. I was a graduate of the Wharton School at the University of Pennsylvania and studied under Prof. George W. Taylor. When Dr. Taylor was appointed in 1942 to be vice chairman of the War Labor Board, he recruited a number of his students to the WLB, including me."

"Did most of the WLB staff continue as arbitrators after the war?"

"No, only a small fraction survived the rough-and-tumble of voluntary arbitration in the postwar years. Throughout this book, Pete, we've frequently referred to the 350 members of the National Academy of Arbitrators who do most of the arbitrating. 'Mainline' arbitrators, they're often called, to distinguish them from 'fringe' arbitrators trying to get into the main current."

"At what point did you personally cease to be a fringe arbitrator and consider yourself a mainliner?"

"Not on any one single case, I can assure you. A fringe arbitrator can be broken by a bad opinion on just one arbitration, but becoming a mainliner is a process rather than the result of a single spectacular case."

"Is there any condition or status you can describe which clearly defines a mainline arbitrator?"

"When you put it that way, Pete, I can make the line of demarcation between a fringe arbitrator and a mainliner quite distinct. When I was a fringe arbitrator, the losing party would scrutinize my opinion to find out where *I* was wrong. I knew I had arrived at the mainline stage when in many cases the loser would study my opinion to find out where *he* was wrong."

SOURCE: Paul Prasow and Edward Peters, *Arbitration and Collective Bargaining: Conflict Resolution in Labor Relations* (New York: McGraw-Hill, 1970), pp. 284–85.

---

teach labor law, industrial relations, and economics. Another source of arbitrators is new entrants. However, many offer their services but are never chosen. One method for getting started is to serve an informal apprenticeship under an experienced arbitrator, gaining practice in writing decisions and learning hearing techniques. This exposure with a highly regarded neutral may lead to later appointments. Another method is to attend training courses for arbitrators; however, few of these are available. A few recent training programs have been successful, particularly for minority arbitrators.[25] Evidence suggests arbitrator acceptability of those who complete training is quite high.

---

[25] William A. Nowlin, "Arbitrator Development: Career Paths, a Model Program, and Challenges," *Arbitration Journal* 43, no. 1 (1988), pp. 3–13.

Three major sources or bodies refer arbitrators in the United States. Each serves a slightly different function, but all have interests in providing arbitrator services in labor disputes.

National Academy of Arbitrators

The National Academy of Arbitrators consists of the most highly regarded arbitrators in the country. Membership is limited to active arbitrators who are invited to join. The academy holds meetings and conventions and issues proceedings, which comment on current difficult problems in arbitration and offer alternative solutions. For example, its membership has offered a variety of approaches in handling arbitration of matters having racial overtones, given the *Alexander* v. *Gardner-Denver* decision.[26] The group largely comprises full-time arbitrators, law school professors, and professors of industrial relations in major universities.

The academy does not offer arbitration panels to disputants, but its directory provides a source of recognized, highly qualified arbitrators the parties can contact directly.

American Arbitration Association

Many contracts specify that the parties will use the services of the American Arbitration Association (AAA) for its unresolved grievances. The AAA does not employ arbitrators but acts more as a clearinghouse to administer matters between the parties and the arbitrators.

If a contract specified AAA to assist in choosing an arbitrator, the following occurs: First, AAA is notified that a dispute exists. AAA responds with a list of arbitrators (usually five, and almost always an odd number). The arbitrators may have particular expertise in the disputed area (e.g., job evaluation) or may practice in a particular geographic area. Second, names are rejected alternately until only one remains. This person will be the nominee unless either party objects. In that case, AAA sends out another panel. Generally, referral agencies usually refuse to send more than three panels for any dispute. Third, after a name has been agreed on, AAA contacts the appointee to offer the dispute, and the appointee accepts or declines. If accepted, arrangements are made directly with the parties for a hearing date. Fourth, AAA will provide hearing facilities and court reporters if the parties request. Finally, AAA follows up to see what decisions were rendered.

---

[26] Harry T. Edwards, "Arbitration of Employment Discrimination Cases: A Proposal for Employer and Union Representatives," *Labor Law Journal* 27 (1976), pp. 265–77.

Federal Mediation and Conciliation Service

The FMCS maintains a roster of arbitrators from which it can select panels. The arbitrators are not FMCS employees but rather private practitioners. If FMCS assistance is specified in a contract, it would provide panels as AAA does but would not have reporting or facilities assistance available.

FMCS screens persons who seek listing with it as arbitrators. People with obvious conflicts of interest (union organizers, employer labor consultants, and the like) are not included, and listees who fail to be selected are purged from subsequent lists.[27] Figure 14–1 contains some of the requirements for being listed.

FMCS follows up on referral by requiring arbitrators to render awards within 60 days of the hearing's close and the receipt of posthearing briefs.

Once the arbitrator has been selected, processes related to the scheduled hearing begin. From a time standpoint, the procedure involves three distinct phases: prehearing, hearing, and posthearing processes.

Prehearing

Elkouri and Elkouri detail a number of steps both parties should go through before an arbitration hearing:

a. Review the history of the case as developed at the prearbitral steps of the grievance procedure.

b. Study the entire collective agreement to ascertain all clauses bearing directly or indirectly on the dispute. Also, comparison of current provisions with those contained in prior agreements might reveal changes significant to the case.

c. So as to determine the general authority of the arbitrator, and accordingly the scope of the arbitration, examine the instruments used to initiate the arbitration.

d. Talk to all persons (even those the other party might use as witnesses) who might be able to aid development of a full picture of the case, including different viewpoints. You will thus better understand not only your own case but your opponent's as well; if you can anticipate your opponent's case, you can better prepare to rebut it.

e. Interview each of your own witnesses (a) to determine what they know about the case; (b) to make certain they understand the relation of their testimony to the whole case; (c) to cross-examine them to check their testimony and to acquaint them with the process of cross-examination. Make a written summary of the expected testimony of

---

[27] Title 29, Chapter 12, Part 1404, *Code of Federal Regulations*.

FIGURE 14-1

Requirements for Listing as an Arbitrator with the FMCS

§1404.5 Listing on the Roster; Criteria for Listing and Retention

Persons seeking to be listed on the Roster must complete and submit an application form which may be obtained from the Office of Arbitration Services. Upon receipt of an executed form, OAS will review the application, assure that it is complete, make such inquiries as are necessary, and submit the application to the Arbitrator Review Board. The Board will review the completed applications under the criteria set forth in paragraphs *(a)*, *(b)*, and *(c)* of this section, and will forward to the Director its recommendation on each applicant. The Director makes all final decisions as to whether an applicant may be listed. Each applicant shall be notified in writing of the Director's decision and the reasons therefore.

(a) General Criteria. Applicants for the Roster will be listed on the Roster upon a determination that they:

(1) Are experienced, competent, and acceptable in decision-making roles in the resolution of labor relations disputes; or

(2) Have extensive experience in relevant positions in collective bargaining; and

(3) Are capable of conducting an orderly hearing, can analyze testimony and exhibits, and can prepare clear and concise findings and awards within reasonable time limits.

(b) Proof of Qualification. The qualifications listed in paragraph *(a)* of this section are preferably demonstrated by the submission of actual arbitration awards prepared by the applicant while serving as an impartial arbitrator chosen by the parties to disputes. Equivalent experience acquired in training, internship or other development programs, or experience such as that acquired as a hearing officer or judge in labor relations controversies may also be considered by the Board.

(c) Advocacy—(1) Definition. An advocate is a person who represents employers, labor organizations, or individuals as an employee, attorney, or consultant, in matters of labor relations, including but not limited to the subjects of union representation and recognition matters, collective bargaining, arbitration, unfair labor practices, equal employment opportunity, and other areas generally recognized as constituting labor relations. The definition includes representatives of employers or employees in individual cases or controversies involving worker's compensation, occupational health or safety, minimum wage, or other labor standards matters. The definition of advocate also includes a person who is directly associated with an advocate in a business or professional relationship as, for example, partners or employees of a law firm.

(2) Eligibility. Except in the case of persons listed on the Roster before November 17, 1976, no person who is an advocate, as defined above, may be listed. No person who was listed on the Roster at any time who was not an advocate when listed or who did not divulge advocacy at the time of listing may continue to be listed after becoming an advocate or after the fact of advocacy is revealed.

(d) Duration of Listing, Retention. Initial listing may be for a period not to exceed three years, and may be renewed thereafter for periods not to exceed two years, provided upon review that the listing is not cancelled by the Director as set forth below. Notice of cancellation may be given to the member whenever the member:

(1) No longer meets the criteria for admission;

(2) Has been repeatedly and flagrantly delinquent in submitting awards;

(3) Has refused to make reasonable and periodic reports to FMCS, as required in Subpart C of this part, concerning activities pertaining to arbitration;

FIGURE 14-1 (concluded)

(4) Has been the subject of complaints by parties who use FMCS facilities and the Director, after appropriate inquiry, concludes that just cause for cancellation has been shown.

(5) Is determined by the Director to be unacceptable to the parties who use FMCS arbitration facilities; the Director may base a determination of unacceptability on FMCS records showing the number of times the arbitrator's name has been proposed to the parties and the number of times it has been selected.

No listing may be canceled without at least 60 days' notice of the reasons for the proposed removal, unless the Director determines that the FMCS or the parties will be harmed by continued listing. In such cases an arbitrator's listing may be suspended without notice or delay pending final determination in accordance with these procedures. The member shall in either case have an opportunity to submit a written response showing why the listing should not be cancelled. The Director may, at his discretion, appoint a hearing officer to conduct an inquiry into the facts of any proposed cancellation and to make recommendations to the Director.

each witness; this can be reviewed when the witness testifies to ensure that no important points are overlooked. Some parties outline in advance the questions to be asked each witness.

f. Examine all records and documents that might be relevant to the case. Organize those you expect to use and make copies for use by the arbitrator and the other party at the hearing. If needed documents are in the exclusive possession of the other party, ask that they be made available before or at the hearing.

g. Visit the physical premises involved in the dispute to visualize better what occurred and what the dispute is about. Also, consider the advisability of asking at the hearing that the arbitrator (accompanied by both parties) also visit the site of the dispute.

h. Consider the utility of pictorial or statistical exhibits. One exhibit can be more effective than many words, if the matter is suited to the exhibit form of portrayal. However, exhibits which do not "fit" the case and those which are inaccurate or misleading are almost certain to be ineffective or to be damaging to their proponent.

i. Consider what the parties' past practices have been in comparable situations.

j. Attempt to determine whether there is some "key" point on which the case might turn. If so, it may be to your advantage to concentrate on that point.

k. In "interpretation" cases, prepare a written argument to support your view as to the proper interpretation of the disputed language.

l. In "interests" or "contract-writing" cases, collect and prepare economic and statistical data to aid evaluation of the dispute.

m. Research the parties' prior arbitration awards and the published awards of other parties on the subject of the dispute for an indication of how similar issues have been approached in other cases.

n. Prepare an outline of your case and discuss it with other persons in your group. This ensures better understanding of the case and will strengthen it by uncovering matters that need further attention. Then too, it will tend to underscore policy and strategy considerations that may be very important in the ultimate handling of the case. Use of the outline at the hearing will facilitate an organized and systematic presentation of the case.[28]

In addition, the parties may continue to meet to seek a settlement or to reduce the time necessary to settle a case. Anytime during the prehearing phase, the party initiating the arbitration may withdraw it with the consent of the other party. Frequently, the contract will specify how this is to be done, whether the withdrawal is "with prejudice" (nonresubmittable), and whether its withdrawal is precedent setting. The parties may also stipulate certain facts in the case, agree on applicable contract terms, and prepare joint exhibits. Evidence suggests settlement before arbitration after a case has been scheduled to be heard occurs more frequently when the parties' representatives are not attorneys.[29]

Hearing Processes

The actual hearing may take many forms. From the most simplified standpoint, a case may be completely stipulated, with the arbitrator simply ruling on an interpretation of the written documents submitted. This option is not entirely up to the parties, however, because the arbitrator may insist on calling witnesses and examining evidence on site.

Representatives of the Parties

The parties' positions may be advocated by anyone they choose, which means the representatives may be attorneys, company or union officials, the grievant, and so on. In most cases involving smaller companies, a national union field representative or local union officer and an industrial relations director or personnel officer are the advocates. Attorney representation and so-called *equal qualifications across advocates* are not required. A party appears to have an advantage when it is represented by an attorney and the other side is not. When only one side retains an attorney, it is more frequently management that does so.[30]

---

[28] Elkouri and Elkouri, *How Arbitration Works*, pp. 198–99.

[29] Clarence R. Deitsch and David A. Dilts, "Factors Affecting Pre-Arbitral Settlement of Rights Disputes: Predicting the Methods of Rights Dispute Resolution," *Journal of Labor Research* 7 (1986), pp. 69–78.

[30] Richard N. Block and Jack Stieber, "The Impact of Attorneys and Arbitrators on Arbitration Awards," *Industrial and Labor Relations Review* 40 (1987), pp. 543–55.

Presentation of the Case

Because the union generally has initiated the grievance, it is responsible for presenting its case first, except in discipline and discharge cases. A union presents joint exhibits relevant to its case and calls witnesses. Management's representative may object to exhibits and cross-examine witnesses. When the union has completed its case, management offers its evidence in a similar manner. Rules of evidence in arbitration cases are more liberal than in courts of law. These differences will be examined shortly.

At the end, both sides may have an opportunity to present closing arguments. During the earlier presentation, the arbitrator may question witnesses but is not required to do so.

Posthearing

Following the hearing, the parties may submit additional material in the form of briefs to support their positions. If these are received, the arbitrator will study the evidence, take the briefs into account, and perhaps examine similar cases in which arbitrators were called on for an award.

The arbitrator then prepares an award and forwards it to the parties for implementation. In some cases, the arbitrator maintains jurisdiction until the award has been implemented in case additional proceedings are necessary to iron out differences in its application.

The receipt of evidence at the hearing and the form and preparation of the award are examined next.

Evidentiary Rules

Where AAA rules apply, Rule 28 states: "The arbitrator shall be the judge of the relevancy and the materiality of the evidence offered, and conformity to legal rules of evidence shall not be necessary."[31] However, arbitrators must weigh the relevance or credibility of evidence when considering a grievance.

Two basic types of evidence are *direct* and *circumstantial*. Direct evidence is information specifically tying a person to a situation. The search for the "smoking gun" is an attempt to find direct evidence. Circumstantial evidence suggests a connection between events and an individual. For example, if shortages in a cash register occur only when one particular employee is scheduled, that circumstance, when connected with others, may establish guilt.

---

[31] 30 LA 1086, 1089.

Evidence is relevant if it addresses the issue at hand. For example, if an arbitrator hears a case involving drinking on the job, evidence related to the subject's work assignment is not highly relevant. The evidence must also be material. For example, testimony that the subject bought a six-pack of beer the week before the alleged offense has little impact on establishing a connection with the offense.

In arbitration hearings, the union must prove management violated the contract, except in discipline cases. The level of proof required in discipline cases may vary among arbitrators, but it is usually greater if the potential consequences to the employee are more severe.

Generally speaking, employees are expected to know that published rules apply and prior written warnings they received were correctly given unless challenged. Past discipline may be used to corroborate that an employee committed this type of offense; but the longer the time since the discipline, the less weight it is usually given.

If evidence shows another arbitrator has ruled on the same issue in this company and no contract changes have occurred in the area, the present arbitrator will probably rule the issue has already been decided. In discipline cases where criminal proceedings have also taken place, the arbitrator is not bound by the same rules for obtaining evidence that prove the offense beyond a reasonable doubt.

Arbitrators must also assess the credibility of witnesses. Persons who have little inherent interest in the case might be considered more credible, and one's reputation for honesty may also be considered.[32]

Occasionally, one party has information that would aid the other in the preparation of a case. Four rules have been suggested for the production of material held by one party: (1) if the arbitrator requests it; (2) if refused, the arbitrator may weigh the refusal as he or she sees fit in the award; (3) the document or information could be used to attack the credibility of a witness; and (4) the arbitrator may admit only the parts relevant to the hearing.[33]

For cross-examination and confrontation, the following have been recommended: (1) depositions and previous testimony be admitted if a witness is unavailable; (2) hearsay be accepted when a direct witness declines to testify against a fellow employee; (3) investigation should generally not be attempted by the arbitrator; (4) where exposing the identity of a witness would damage legitimate interests of either party, the witness should be questioned by counsel in the sole presence of the arbitrator.[34]

---

[32] Marvin Hill Jr. and Anthony V. Sinicropi, *Evidence in Arbitration* (Washington, D.C.: Bureau of National Affairs, 1980), pp. 1–108.

[33] Fleming, *Labor Arbitration Process*, p. 175.

[34] Ibid., p. 181.

Self-incrimination is prohibited in criminal trials and may also be an issue in arbitral proceedings. The arbitrator probably will not grant an absolute immunity against self-incrimination but will weigh the refusal to testify as if it were evidence. However, the arbitrator should not consider a refusal to testify as sufficient to sustain a case by itself.[35]

Arbitral Remedies

When a case is submitted to an arbitrator, the issues usually are specified and the grievant has indicated what relief is desired. The relief requested tends to vary given the type of case, but generally arbitrators will grant relief when it is found that the aggrieved party has been wronged, up to but not exceeding the relief desired.

In discipline and discharge cases, requested relief is usually for back pay for periods of suspension and discharge, restoration of employment, recision of a demotion or transfer, elimination of reprimands from personnel files, and the like. If reinstatement and/or back pay is to be granted, the arbitrator needs to determine the amount through the likely job history of the grievant, pay that he or she has earned on other jobs, and the like. Arbitrators might also reduce disciplinary measures taken if they exceed what the offense would merit, given similar situations in the grievant's organization or in other workplaces with the same settings.

More difficult cases to remedy involve such issues as subcontracting, plant closures, entitlements to overtime, assignment of work, and other economic issues. Usual remedies may require the restoration of work to the bargaining unit and payment of wages forgone by employees who would have been entitled to the work.[36]

Preparation of the Award

The award conveys the arbitrator's decision in the case, including (in most cases) a summary of the evidence presented, the reasoning behind the decision, and what action must be taken to satisfy the decision.

To prepare the award, the arbitrator must determine whether the dispute was actually arbitrable. Did the grievance allege an actual violation of the contract? Were the grievance procedure steps followed in a prescribed manner so the grievance and union followup were timely? If these criteria are met, the arbitrator examines the merits.

---

[35] Ibid., p. 186.

[36] Marvin Hill Jr. and Anthony Sinicropi, *Remedies in Arbitration* (Washington, D.C.: Bureau of National Affairs, 1981).

While the arbitrator has no statutory obligation to do so, it is important that the reason for a particular award be included to guide the parties in the future. Even though the grievance may appear trivial, the decision will govern employer and union conduct for a substantial time, so it is important for them to know why the issue was decided as it was.

The arbitrator must be careful to ensure that an award draws from the essence of the contract. Most contracts prohibit the arbitrator from adding to, subtracting from, or modifying the agreement. The arbitrator must show how the interpretation is within the four corners of the contract.

Occasionally, an arbitrator will find a conflict between contract language and federal labor or civil rights laws or interpretations. No clear-cut guidance for this situation exists. Some argue the arbitrator is to give primacy to a contractual interpretation,[37] while others suggest federal employment laws must supersede contract terms and influence the shape of an award where they would govern.[38]

PROCEDURAL DIFFICULTIES AND THEIR RESOLUTIONS

A major problem in arbitration is the same one found in the legal system: time delays. In 1976, the average time from filing a grievance through the submission of an arbitral award was 223 days.[39] There is no reason to believe this has improved substantially since. Although this was an average figure, it is not unusual to see some cases take up to two years for resolution. Table 14–1 provides the time data reported by the AFL–CIO.

The arbitral process can take more time, but the data show an average of 104 days from appointment to award. The 43 days from the termination of the hearing to the award date is greater than the 30-day limit previously established by the FMCS, but it may include time during which briefs are submitted. Thus, arbitrators may come close to rendering decisions within 30 days of receiving all case material. One arbitrator recently noted time delays between the close of the hearings and rendering a decision for about 150 cases varied from zero to 94 days with a mean of 30 days or less in every industry except railroads. For these cases, the time lapse between the grievance and the hearing was zero to 1,426 days,

---

[37] Bernard Meltzer, "Ruminations about Ideology, Law, and Labor Arbitration," in *The Arbitrator, the NLRB, and the Courts: Proceedings of the National Academy of Arbitrators* (Washington, D.C.: Bureau of National Affairs, 1967), p. 1.

[38] Robert Howlett, "The Arbitrator, the NLRB, and the Courts," in *The Arbitrator, the NLRB, and the Courts: Proceedings of the National Academy of Arbitrators* (Washington, D.C.: Bureau of National Affairs, 1967), p. 67.

[39] John Zalusky, "Arbitration: Updating a Vital Process," *American Federationist* 83, no. 11 (1976), pp. 1–8.

TABLE 14–1
Arbitration Time Delays

	Days
Grievance date to request for panel	68
Between request for panel and panel sent out	6
Panel sent out to appointment of arbitrator	45
Appointment of arbitrator to hearing date	61
Hearing date to arbitrator award	43
Total: Grievance date to award	223

SOURCE: John Zalusky, "Arbitration: Updating a Vital Process," *American Federationist,* November 1976, p. 6.

with a mean of over 100 days in all industries and a mean of over one year in steel, railroads, the federal government, and miscellaneous situations.[40]

Problems still exist with the length of time. The quote "justice delayed is justice denied" is not an empty platitude. It is important to individuals who have been disciplined to have their cases decided so they can make a new employment life or return to work made whole. For firms, a grievance involving many employees can lead to heavy back pay liabilities if long-delayed findings are adverse.

Arbitration costs also cause problems, particularly for unions. Because managements and unions usually share arbitration costs, a poorly financed union may be reluctant to use arbitration as much as it would like. Table 14–2 estimates the costs for a typical, relatively uncomplicated arbitration case, using 1990 per diem figures for arbitrators and doubling most other costs from when the table was first constructed in 1976.[41]

Expedited Arbitration

Since the early 1970s, some larger companies and unions have used **expedited arbitration,** to reduce time delays and costs. Rather than hearing a single case in a day, arbitrators hear several and submit very short written awards. Most expedited arbitration cases are individual discipline and discharge cases or emergency cases. Expedited arbitration also will provide for the entry of new arbitrators because relatively simple and straightforward cases are generally handled by this process. Table 14–3 contains examples of expedited arbitration procedures.

---

[40] Garth Mangum, "Delay in Arbitration Decisions," *Arbitration Journal* 42, no. 1 (1987), p. 58.

[41] D. F. Jennings and A. D. Allen, "Labor Arbitration Costs and Case Loads: A Longitudinal Analysis," *Labor Law Journal* 41 (1990), pp. 80–88.

TABLE 14–2

The Union's Cost of Traditional Arbitration for a One-Day Hearing

Prehearing
Lost time: Grievant and witnesses @ $15/32 hours	$ 480
Lawyer:	
Library research @ $50/4 hours	200
Interviewing witnesses @ $150/4 hours	600
Filing fee: AAA (shared equally) $200	100
Total prehearing costs	$1,380

Hearing expense
Arbitrator:
Fee (shared equally) 1 hearing day @ $450	$ 225
Expenses for meals, transportation, etc. (shared equally)	200
Travel time one-half day (shared equally)	112
Transcript: $10 per page with two copies and 10-day delivery of 200 pages	
(shared equally)	1,000
Lawyer: Presentation of case @ $150 per hour	900
Lost time: Grievant and witnesses @ $15/32 hours	480
Hearing room: Shared equally	100
Total hearing	$3,017

Posthearing expense
Arbitrator: 1¾ days study time (shared equally)	$ 619
Lawyer: Preparation of posthearing brief @ $150/8 hours	1,200
Total posthearing	$1,819
Total cost to union	$6,216

Inadequate Representation

Chapter 13 noted employees in certain situations have successfully argued they were not fairly represented by their unions in the grievance procedure. In arbitration, inadequate representation can arise. Inadequate representation could be malicious, or it could occur through ineptitude. Because arbitration proceedings are viewed as final determinations by the courts, the quality of the advocacy one receives is of substantial concern.

The Supreme Court reversed an arbitration award in the discharge of an over-the-road trucker who was accused of padding expenses.[42] An adequate prehearing investigation would have disclosed that the seeming dishonesty was a result of a motel clerk charging more than the published rate and pocketing the difference. The trucker was actually blameless.

Within the hearing itself, the arbitrator may become aware of differences in the quality of representation. Although the arbitrator may

---

[42] *Hines* v. *Anchor Motor Freight, Inc.*, U.S. Supreme Court, 74-1025, 1976.

TABLE 14–3

Examples of Expedited Methods

	Steelworkers—Basic Steel Industry	American Arbitration Association Service	AIW Local 562 Rusco, Inc.	American Postal Workers—U.S. Postal Service	Miniarbitration Columbus, Ohio
Source of arbitrators	Recent law school graduates and other sources	Special panel from AAA roster	FMCS roster	AAA, FMCS rosters	Its own "Joint Selection and Orientation Committee" from FMCS roster
Method of selecting	Preselected regional panels; administrator notifies in rotation	Appointed by AAA regional administrators	Preselected panel by rotating FMCS contracts	Appointed by AAA regional administrators	FMCS regional representative by rotation
Lawyers	No limitation, but understanding that lawyers will not be used	No limitation	No lawyers	No limitation but normally not used	No limitation
Transcript	No	No	No	No	May be used
Briefs	No	Permitted	No	No	May be used
Written description of issue	Last step grievance report	Joint submission permitted	No	Position paper	Grievance record expected
Time from request to hearing date	10 days	Approximately 3 days depending on arbitrator availability	10 days	Approximately 7 days depending on arbitrator availability	Not specified
Time of hearing to award	Bench decision or 48 hours	5 days	48 hours	Bench decision; written award, 48 hours	48 hours
Fees (plus expenses)	$100/½ day $150/day	$100 filing fee Arbitrator's normal fee	$100/½ day $150/day	$100 filing fee $100 per case	$100/½ day, 1 or 2 cases; $150/full day, 1 or 2 cases; $200/day, 3 or 4 cases

SOURCE: John Zalusky, "Arbitration: Updating a Vital Process," *American Federationist*, November 1976, p. 4.

question witnesses and probe into other matters, the umpire's impartiality in an essentially adversary hearing could be questioned as a result. Is it ethical for an arbitrator to "make a case" for an advocate who has inadequately prepared a case? This issue has not been settled. However, if it's clear to the arbitrator that the grievant's rights are not adequately represented, a later appeal could reverse the award.[43]

ARBITRATION OF DISCIPLINE CASES

A large number of cases heard by arbitrators are appeals made by employees to reconsider the evidence related to employer discipline or to reassess the severity of the punishment. Any punishment, including discharge, is particularly likely to go to arbitration. What principles do arbitrators apply to the evaluation of evidence and the establishment of fair punishment in industrial discipline cases?

Role of Discipline

Under the contract, employees have certain rights and obligations—as do employers. Employees have rights to their jobs as the contract reads, and employers are entitled to performance from their workers. An employer expects employees to carry out orders, regardless of the employees' interpretation of the rightness of the orders, unless they are unsafe, unhealthful, or illegal.[44] If employees believe the orders violate the contract, they are entitled to file grievances and seek relief. On the other hand, if the employees take matters into their own hands, they are guilty of insubordination and may be punished. The punishment can serve two basic purposes: (1) to motivate the individuals to avoid similar conduct in the future and (2) by example, to deter others.

Evidence

Because discipline cases are extremely important to the grievant, arbitrators require the company to present evidence showing the grievant actually committed the offense and the punishment is consistent with the breach of the rules. The company must also show it is not dealing with this employee in an arbitrary manner when compared to others involved in similar situations.

---

[43] See Jean T. McKelvey, "The Duty of Fair Representation: Has the Arbitrator a Responsibility?" *Arbitration Journal* 41, no. 2 (1986), pp. 51–58, for one arbitrator's opinion.

[44] Dallas L. Jones, *Arbitration and Industrial Discipline* (Ann Arbor, Mich.: Bureau of Industrial Relations, University of Michigan, 1961), pp. 17–18.

On the basis of this evidence, arbitrators may uphold or deny the punishment or modify it downward (but not upward) to follow the disciplinary breach more closely. Arbitrators also require the discipline to be given for just cause and not on some capricious basis.

Uses of Punishment

Punishment can be thought of in two contexts as it relates to discipline. The first sees punishment as a legitimate exercise of authority as a consequence of a breach of rules. The second sees punishment as a corrective effort to direct the employees' attention to the consequences but also to change their attitudes toward the punished behaviors.[45] Arbitrators may be concerned with these approaches, but they are perhaps more concerned with the procedural regularity of the discipline in the case at hand, in the evenness of its application across persons within the same firm, and in its fundamental fairness given societal norms.[46]

A study of arbitral decisions in discipline cases found cases divided equally in applying authoritarian or corrective discipline, with a small additional proportion using humanitarian discipline (using rules only as guidance and taking into account individual intentions). Table 14–4 shows the results. Corrective discipline is used more often for absenteeism and incompetence, while authoritarian approaches are used more often for dishonesty and illegal strike activity.[47] In the increasingly important area of substance abuse, arbitrators appear to use corrective discipline for alcohol abuse cases and punishment for drug abuse when solid evidence exists the offense occurred in the workplace.[48]

Given that corrective discipline is applied in about 50 percent of reported cases, is it effective? One intensive study concluded in no case did corrective discipline turn an unsatisfactory employee into one whose performance was satisfactory. A number of reasons are suggested for this finding. First, the individual is often restored to the original work group, where behavior that resulted in the punishment is reinforced. Second, the grievant may be unclear which behavior the punishment was related to. And third, in some cases, placing an employee in a probationary status rather than punishing him or her may be reasonable, so the contingency is on future rather than past behavior.[49]

---

[45] Ibid., pp. 2–4.

[46] Ibid., pp. 16–20.

[47] Hoyt N. Wheeler, "Punishment Theory and Industrial Discipline," *Industrial Relations* 15 (1976), pp. 235–43.

[48] K. W. Thornicroft, "Arbitrators and Substance Abuse Discharge Grievances: An Empirical Assessment," *Labor Studies Journal* 14 (1989), pp. 40–65.

TABLE 14-4

Analysis of Arbitration Decisions Relating to Discharge and Discipline by Theory of Discipline and Type of Offense, as Reported in *Labor Arbitration Reports,* May 1970 through March 1974

	Humanitarian	Corrective	Authoritarian	Total
Absenteeism, tardiness, leaving early	2	20	8	30
Dishonesty, theft, falsification of records	2	13	28	43
Incompetence, negligence, poor workmanship, violation of safety rules	1	27	9	37
Illegal strikes, strike violence, deliberate restriction of production	0	12	19	31
Intoxication, bringing intoxicants into plant	1	10	7	18
Fighting, assault, horseplay, troublemaking	3	16	15	34
Insubordination, refusal of job assignment, refusal to work overtime, also fight or altercation with supervisor	2	42	54	98
Miscellaneous rule violations	2	20	26	48
Totals	13	160	166	339
Percent	4%	47%	49%	

Source: Hoyt N. Wheeler, "Punishment Theory and Industrial Discipline,"*Industrial Relations,* May 1976, p. 239.

An employee's previous work record is apparently predictive of job performance after reinstatement. Poor performance after reinstatement among a large sample of employees was predicted by the number of warnings and other disciplinary action before being discharged and by discharges for absenteeism or dishonesty.[50] Among another group of reinstated employees, the evidence suggested most discharges had been for attendance problems, and the performance of reinstated employees was about average.[51]

ARBITRATION OF PAST PRACTICE DISPUTES

Certain work practices or benefits may not be mentioned explicitly in the contract but may have been applied so consistently there is an understanding they will continue to be applied in a similar manner. Unions may frequently negotiate clauses into contracts stating that both parties agree existing conditions will not be lowered during the present agreement.

In a variety of situations, arbitrators have ruled certain practices not

[50] Chalmer E. Labig Jr., I. B. Helburn, and Robert C. Rodgers, "Discipline History, Seniority, and Reason for Discharge as Predictors of Post-Reinstatement Job Performance," *Arbitration Journal* 40, no. 3 (1985), pp. 44–52.

[51] William E. Simkin, "Some Results of Reinstatement by Arbitration," *Arbitration Journal* 41, no. 3 (1986), pp. 53–58.

mentioned in the contract are protected to the initiator, union, or management. If management confers a benefit but announces special circumstances each time it confers it, the employer does not establish a continuing practice. On the other hand, if management mentions a benefit as a reason for not conceding in some area during negotiations, the benefit tends to assume binding characteristics. If conditions change and management decides to drop a practice, it must do so within a reasonably short time after the change to defend itself against **past practice** grievances.[52]

One arbitrator suggested eight criteria should be examined in ruling on past practice grievances.

1. Does the practice concern a major condition of employment?
2. Was it established unilaterally?
3. Was it administered unilaterally?
4. Did either party seek to incorporate it into the body of the written agreement?
5. What is the frequency of repetition of the practice?
6. Is the practice of long standing?
7. Is it specific and detailed?
8. Do the employees rely on it?[53]

If the answers to these questions are yes or frequent, the condition will likely take on the same legitimacy as a negotiated benefit.

ARBITRAL DECISIONS AND THE ROLE OF ARBITRATION

For arbitration to be accepted by the parties, neither expects to fare worse in the results. In a survey of published decisions, win rates for union and managements were divided evenly. The party with the burden of proof (management in discipline cases, the union in others) wins in 43 percent of cases.[54]

The parties negotiate the agreement and include in their grievance procedure provisions for arbitration. Most contracts indicate the arbitrator cannot add to the agreement or decide a case using criteria outside the agreement. Yet the parties encounter situations in which they

---

[52] Paul Prasow and Edward Peters, *Arbitration and Collective Bargaining: Conflict Resolution in Labor Relations* (New York: McGraw-Hill, 1970), pp. 96–121.

[53] *Jacob Ruppert* v. *Office Employees International Union Local 153*, October 19, 1960, 35 LA 505; Arbitrator, Burton B. Turkus.

[54] D. A. Dilts and C. R. Deitsch, "Arbitration Win/Loss Rates as a Measure of Arbitrator Neutrality," *Arbitration Journal* 44, no. 3 (1989), pp. 42–47.

cannot agree on the interpretation of the contract. One commentator suggests the role of the arbitrator is to add to the agreement by setting terms to cover one of a number of infinite work situations the parties could not contemplate when the agreement was negotiated.[55] The method continues to be the choice of parties to resolve intracontractual differences that cannot be negotiated or mediated.

The FMCS gathers data on the number of cases going to arbitration and the issues involved for panels it supplies. Table 14–5 shows the progression from 1973 through 1988.

SUMMARY

Arbitration is a process for resolving disputes through the invitation of a neutral third party. The use of arbitration is encouraged by the courts, and the outcome of arbitral awards is generally considered nonreviewable. Supreme Court decisions in the Steelworkers' trilogy laid the groundwork for the present status of arbitration.

Arbitral hearings are quasi-judicial in nature and involve allegations of contract violations. The arbitrator hears evidence from both parties and rules on the issue in dispute.

A large number of arbitration proceedings are associated with individual discipline and discharge cases. Arbitration cases appear to be split about evenly in applying authoritarian or corrective standards in the use of punishment.

Arbitration has been criticized for its time delays and costs and because some decisions seem to go outside the scope of the contract or dispute. But opponents and proponents are relatively satisfied with the system.

DISCUSSION QUESTIONS

1. Given the Supreme Court and NLRB rulings, what is the scope and finality associated with rights arbitration proceedings in the private sector?
2. What possible drawbacks do you see associated with the expansion of expedited arbitration?

---

[55] D. Feller, "The Remedy Power in Grievance Arbitration," *Industrial Relations Law Journal* 5 (1982), pp. 128–37.

TABLE 14-5

Number and Percent Change in Number of Issues Reported in Applicable FMCS
Closed Arbitration Award Cases for Fiscal Years 1973, 1977, 1981, 1985, and 1988;
Percent Change from 1981

Specific Issues	Total Number of Issues					Percent Change from FY 1981
	1973	1977	1981	1985	1988	
Total	4,255	6,935	8,126	5,380	5,934	−27.0%
General issues	1,130	1,922	1,962	1,378	1,480	−24.6%
Overtime other than pay						
Distribution of overtime	187	183	202	112	133	−34.2
Compulsory overtime	17	31	23	17	23	− 0.0
Other	—	29	49	25	56	+14.3
Seniority						
Promotion and upgrading	203	253	215	156	202	− 6.0
Layoff, bumping, and recall	264	320	361	267	241	−33.2
Transfer	96	96	92	61	67	−27.2
Other	90	102	93	73	57	−38.7
Union officers	27	24	41	27	25	−39.0
Strike and lockout	19	33	13	1	6	−53.8
Working conditions	48	54	57	33	55	− 3.5
Discrimination	—	56	63	51	41	−34.9
Management rights	—	201	199	139	151	−24.1
Scheduling of work	179	137	150	105	116	−22.7
Work assignments	—	403	404	311	307	−24.0
Economic—wage rates and pay—issues	581	922	930	546	680	−26.9%
Wage issues	—	86	107	54	90	−15.9
Rate of pay	—	176	176	105	140	−20.4
Severance pay	—	19	18	19	19	+ 5.6
Reporting, call-in, and call-back pay	86	82	72	47	43	−40.3
Holidays and holiday pay	119	127	129	76	94	−27.1
Vacations and vacation pay	113	150	142	92	107	−24.6
Incentive rates or standards	82	93	74	41	41	−44.6
Overtime pay	181	189	212	112	146	−31.1
Fringe benefit issues	161	219	228	156	223	− 2.2%
Health and welfare	51	81	86	58	92	+ 7.0
Pensions	24	25	23	20	21	− 8.7
Other	86	113	119	78	110	− 7.6
Discharge and disciplinary issues	1,302	2,520	3,231	2,050	2,654	−17.8%
Technical issues	400	395	380	296	283	−25.5%
Job posting and bidding	—	112	108	99	77	−28.7
Job evaluation	400	88	75	65	71	− 5.3
Job classification	—	195	197	132	135	−31.5
Scope of agreement	186	197	231	136	205	−11.3%
Subcontracting	95	109	127	98	137	+ 7.9
Jurisdictional disputes	40	51	49	14	32	−34.7
Foreman, supervision, etc.	42	32	47	23	30	−36.2
Mergers, consolidations, accretion other plants	9	5	8	1	6	−25.0

TABLE 14–5

(Continued)

Specific Issues	Total Number of Issues					Percent Change from FY 1981
	1973	1977	1981	1985	1988	
Arbitrability of grievances	223	495	734	584	154	−79.0%
Procedural	143	311	434	301	105	−75.8
Substantive	70	115	218	146	36	−83.5
Procedural and substantive	10	69	82	67	11	−86.6
Other	—	—	—	70	2	NM
Not elsewhere classified	243	215	320	234	255	−20.3%

NM = not meaningful.
SOURCE: U.S. Federal Mediation and Conciliation Service, *Thirty-Eighth Annual Report, Fiscal Year 1986* (Washington, D.C.: U.S. Government Printing Office, 1986), pp. 38–39; U.S. Federal Mediation and Conciliation Service, *Forty-First Annual Report, Fiscal Year 1988* (Washington, D.C.: U.S. Government Printing Office, 1988), p. 21.

3. What duty, if any, does an arbitrator owe to the parties to see that both are competently represented?
4. Give arguments for and against the greater involvement of attorneys in arbitration, as both advocates and umpires.
5. Forecast what you see as the future of labor arbitration in terms of the expansion or contraction of issues within its jurisdiction and the finality of its decisions.

KEY TERMS

arbitrability   ad hoc arbitrator
Steelworkers' trilogy   expedited arbitration
Collyer doctrine   past practice
permanent umpire

CASES

About six months after the new GMFC-Local 384 contract was ratified, three grievances were sent to arbitration by the union. The company and the union agreed that all three grievances would be heard on separate dates by the same arbitrator. Your name was on the panel the FMCS sent to the parties, and they selected you to hear the grievances. You agreed and have heard all three over the past three days. Now you have to prepare your awards.

Case 1

George Jones was a grade 8 production worker in the heavy-components assembly department. He worked with six other assemblers of the same grade, constructing cabs for power shovels. The supervisor, Ralph Barnes, was in charge of three of these heavy-assembly crews. George Jones had been with the company for about four years, but over two of these he had been laid off. Over the past six months, he had spent all of his time with his present work crew. His work record had been unremarkable. He had two unexcused absences but no problems with supervision.

On May 6, Jones struck a co-worker, Elliot Johnson, with his fist, rendering him unconscious. As soon as Barnes arrived on the scene and gave first aid, he asked the work crew what had happened. They had only seen Jones strike Johnson. After Johnson regained consciousness, Barnes asked him what happened. Johnson stated he and Jones had been talking when Jones suddenly turned and swung at him. Barnes then asked Jones what

happened. Jones, who is the only black employee in his work group, said Johnson had been making racial slurs toward him ever since he joined the crew, and this morning he had been pushed over the brink when Johnson said, "If it weren't for affirmative action, welfare would be the only thing that would keep a shirt on your back."

From his supervisor training course, Barnes knew it was company policy to discharge anyone who struck another employee or started a fight. Thus, he sent Jones to the personnel department for termination. On the way, Jones filed a grievance with Ralph Murphy, the union steward in his area, alleging the company had violated Section 4.02 of the contract by discharging him without cause. His grievance stated the attack on Johnson was justified given his past harassment and punching him seemed to be the "only way to get him off my back."

When Murphy gave the grievance to Barnes, it was immediately denied. Barnes said, "The rule is ironclad, as far as I'm concerned. They said we supervisors didn't have any latitude on this issue."

Murphy then presented copies of the grievance to the shift IR representative, Carolyn Foster, and Neal Young, the general supervisor. In her examination of the grievance, Foster called Johnson and Cronholm, Jensen, and Albers (three other employees in the work group) to her office separately. When questioned, Johnson repeated his allegation that Jones's attack was unprovoked and adamantly denied ever making racial slurs toward him. Information from Jensen and Albers supported Johnson's denial of racial slurs, but

Cronholm said he had repeatedly heard Johnson make disparaging remarks to Jones and Jones had asked him to stop. After weighing this information and considering company policy on fighting, she upheld Barnes's action.

The union continued to demand Jones's reinstatement with full back pay, and management adamantly refused.

When the case was heard, the union's grievance alleged that not only had Jones been discharged without cause (Section 4.02) but that the discharge had also been racially motivated, violating the EEO section (12.14a). In its opening argument, the company asked you to find the grievance nonarbitrable because Jones could file a charge with the EEOC under Title VII if your award upheld the discharge. The company also said the discrimination issue was not arbitrable because it had not been raised in Step 3 as provided in 12.14b. You noted the arguments but reserved your ruling on arbitrability for the decision you would prepare.

Both sides presented their evidence. All of it was in substantial agreement with what Barnes and Foster had found in their investigation. Jones and Johnson held to their stories, as did Jensen, Albers, and Cronholm. The company introduced evidence to show that without exception employees had been terminated for fighting. It also provided statistics showing 12 percent of the 8 employees discharged for fighting over the past three years were black and 14 percent of the production labor force was black.

In this case, your award should contain:

1. Your ruling on the arbitrability of the grievance.
2. Your rationale in finding on the merits of the case (if arbitrable).
3. If arbitrable, the degree to which you would grant the relief Jones is asking or uphold management.

Case 2

This case has the greatest ramifications for the firm from a cost standpoint. In the past, the company has always used its own janitors for cleaning and maintenance. Because of operational requirements, most of this work is performed on the third shift. About 20 janitors are required to maintain the Central City facilities. GMFC has always had problems with absences among its janitors, but since the last contract was signed, the absence rate has increased from about 5 percent per day to 15 percent. Because of this increase, housekeeping lagged, and GMFC officials were starting to worry about fire code violations resulting from the superficial cleaning. Management considered discharging those who were chronically absent but found on investigation that absences seemed to rotate systematically among members of the crew, as if they were planned.

As a result of management's investigation, Carolyn Foster contacted Matt Duff, Local 384's president, and asked him to enforce the contract and get the janitors' absence rate down. She told Duff the company considered the action the equivalent of a slowdown, and strong action would be taken if absence rates were not reduced. Duff protested, saying there was not concerted activity behind the absences.

When the high rate and rotating pattern persisted, the company discharged the janitors and subcontracted their work to Dependa-Kleen, a full-time janitorial service. To the company's pleasure, Dependa-Kleen was able to take over the entire operation at a lower cost than the in-house operation had incurred before the absence problem.

On behalf of the janitors, Duff filed a grievance arguing the discharges violated Section 4.02. He also filed an unfair labor practice charge with the NLRB, claiming the company violated Section 8(a)(5) of the Taft-Hartley Act through its unilateral action in sub-contracting the work without consulting or bargaining with the union.

The company argued it was justified in replacing the janitors because their systematic absences were a violation of the contract's no-strike or slowdown clause (Section 9.05). The company argued it was entitled to replace the participants consistent with the management rights clause, Section 4.02.

Assume the testimony at the hearing does not seriously challenge the evidence management has gathered on the increase in absences among the janitors. In this case, decide the following:

1. Would you find the grievance arbitrable given the unfair labor practice charge filed by the union?
2. Assuming you find the grievance arbitrable, frame an award and justify it.

Case 3

The maintenance electricians in the unit are assigned to repair jobs around the Central City facilities shortly after they report to work at their central shop at the beginning of a shift. Before ratification of the most recent contract, electricians traditionally returned to the shop for their afternoon coffee breaks. All of the electricians left their work so they would arrive at the shop to begin the break and left the shop at the end of the break to return to work.

The electrical shop supervisor, Ken Bates, issued a new policy after the new contract was approved, stating the break would commence once work stopped at the assigned location and end when work was restarted. This policy change meant some electricians would have insufficient time to return to the shop for their breaks.

The union filed a grievance alleging that the company had revoked a prevailing practice that had the effect of a contract term. It also argued it had not been consulted as Article 12.03 required. The company denied the grievance, citing the language in Section 12.02.

As the arbitrator, frame an award in this dispute.

15

PUBLIC-SECTOR
LABOR RELATIONS

This chapter provides information on the settings within which collective bargaining is practiced in the public sector and highlights differences in practices between public and private sectors and within public-sector levels. The public sector consists of the myriad of separate groups of levels and jurisdictions (federal, state, municipal, and so on) among governmental units. The "customer" group affected by the outcomes in public-sector labor relations is generally much larger (for example, homeowners and apartment dwellers in a garbage collection strike) and the costs of settlements are much more likely to be directly passed on to the customer in the short run than in private-sector issues. Little public-sector collective bargaining occurred before the early 1960s, as compared to the middle to late 1930s for private-sector relations.

This evolution of laws in the federal and state sectors, differences in coverages among jurisdictions and across occupations, union structure and organizational issues, bargaining methods and outcomes, and impasse procedures and their effectiveness are covered.

In reading this chapter, consider the following questions:

1. How do the public and private sectors differ in their bargaining relationships, particularly concerning impasse procedures?

2. How do laws regulating labor relations in the public sector differ across both states and occupations?

3. How successful has the application of fact-finding been in the public sector?

4. How do the conduct of collective bargaining and the determinants of bargaining power differ in the public and private sectors?

5. What variables seem to have the greatest effect on bargaining outcomes?

Public-Sector Labor Law

As Chapter 4 noted, public-sector employees are not governed by the Taft-Hartley and Railway Labor acts. Federal employees are covered by a separate law, and state and local employees are governed by laws of states in which they work, if legislation has been passed to permit collective bargaining.

Federal Labor Relations Law

Federal employees have been involved in union activities since the 1830s. However, not until the 1880s, when postal employees began to organize, did the federal government oppose unionization. Before the Lloyd-LaFollette Act, federal employees were forbidden to communicate with Congress about employment conditions. Union activities increased during the 1930s, but President Roosevelt asserted normal collective bargaining could not occur at the federal level.

After President Kennedy was elected, the federal government promulgated the first in a line of executive orders governing federal employment labor relations. A bill to allow collective bargaining for federal employees was pending in Congress when the president preempted the legislation with Executive Order 10988. The order enabled unions representing a majority of federal employees within a unit to negotiate exclusive written agreements with an agency. However, these agreements could cover only noneconomic and nonstaffing issues. Other labor organizations representing less than a majority but more than 10 percent of employees in a unit were entitled to consultation with the employer but could not negotiate agreements. Arbitration of grievances was allowed but was advisory to agency heads rather than binding. Most employees were entitled to organize, with the exception of managers and nonroutine personnel workers.

Civil Service Reform Act, Title VII

In January 1979, executive orders of Presidents Kennedy, Nixon, and Ford were supplanted by the Federal Service Labor-Management Relations statute. The act applied to federal agencies except the Postal Service (covered under Taft-Hartley), the FBI, the General Accounting Office, the National Security Agency, the CIA, and agencies dealing with federal employee labor relations. Employees of the legislative and judicial branches were also excluded.

A Federal Labor Relations Authority (FLRA) was created with responsibilities similar to those of the NLRB. The FMCS assists the agencies involved in bargaining impasses, and unresolved impasses are referred to the Federal Services Impasses Panel (FSIP).

Bargaining rights remain limited under the statute. Federal employees cannot bargain on wages and benefits, participation in political activities, classification of positions, missions or budgets of agencies, hiring or promotion, or subcontracting. They are, however, allowed consultation rights in these areas and may negotiate on these issues if the agency allows.

Federal labor organizations may not advocate the use of strikes, and unauthorized strikes may lead to decertification and discipline of individual members. Picketing is also unlawful if it disrupts an agency's activities.

Grievance procedures must be negotiated and must provide for binding arbitration of unresolved issues. The FLRA may review appealed arbitration awards and set them aside if they conflict with laws, rules, or regulations.

The law enumerates a variety of unfair labor practices similar to those in the private sector, except employers and unions must not refuse the use of impasse procedures if necessary. Unions may not call strikes, work stoppages, or slowdowns. If violations occur, the FLRA may issue cease-and-desist orders, require the renegotiation of agreements, reinstate employees with back pay, or initiate other actions necessary to redress unfair practices.[1]

State Labor Laws

Public-sector labor relations differ widely among the 50 states. Several states have no public-sector bargaining laws, a few prohibit collective bargaining in at least some nonmanagerial occupations, and most states prohibit strikes by public-sector employees. State labor laws are generally more comprehensive and were passed earlier in states in which private-sector unionization is heaviest. Unlike the private sector, some states permit collective bargaining for supervisory and managerial employees. Many states have established public employment labor relations boards to act in the same role as the NLRB in recognition and unfair labor practice situations.

---

[1] Henry B. Frazier III, "Federal Employment," in *Portrait of a Process—Collective Negotiations in Public Employment*, ed. Muriel K. Gibbons, Robert B. Hersby, Jerome Lefkowitz, and Barbara Z. Tener (Fort Washington, Pa.: Labor Relations Press, 1979), pp. 421–34.

JURISDICTIONS AND EMPLOYEES

While exceptions or exemptions from coverage for the private sector are relatively few under federal labor law, this is not the case in the public sector. For example, in the private sector, the law exempts only agricultural workers, domestic workers, and supervisors and managers as industrial and occupational classes covered by the act. In the public sector, differences in coverage exist by types of employees and political jurisdictions.

Sources of Employment

Some states may distinguish between employees within a statutory civil service system and those outside its protection. Persons receiving jobs as the result of political appointments are usually unprotected, although the Supreme Court has limited the ability of public officials to use political party membership as a criterion for maintaining a public position.[2] In some states, civil service employees are not permitted to bargain collectively.

Levels of Government

Large differences also exist in the jurisdictions of bargaining units involved. Within states, a variety of lesser jurisdictions and semiautonomous agencies exist. For example, a statewide university system may be largely autonomous from a legislature in terms of its governance. Counties, cities, school boards, sewer districts, transportation authorities, and the like are all publicly governed, but each is responsible to a different constituency and perhaps dependent on a different source of funding.

Types of Employee Groups

Frequently, state labor laws have different provisions for employees by occupation and jurisdiction, such as teachers, police, fire fighters, state employees, and local employees. Large differences exist among states and across employee groups in terms of collective bargaining rights and restrictions.

---

[2] *Elrod* v. *Burns*, U.S. Supreme Court, No. 74-1520 (1976).

Teachers

Teacher bargaining laws primarily apply to elementary and secondary public school teachers. Most states with laws permitting collective bargaining for teachers also confer exclusive recognition on a majority union; impose a mutual duty on both the employer and the union to bargain; have defined impasse procedures, normally including mediation and fact-finding; and prohibit strikes. Some states allow strikes when the school district refuses to arbitrate at a bargaining impasse.

Police

Most police statutes pertain to uniformed officers employed by cities or counties. Most states permit collective bargaining for police and grant exclusive recognition to a majority union. Where bargaining is allowed, most impose a mutual duty on both union and employer, but some allow only meet-and-confer privileges to the union. Most states have impasse procedures involving mediation and fact-finding, and many have arbitration statutes for dealing with impasses. Only Hawaii allows police a limited right to strike.

Fire Fighters

The International Association of Fire Fighters is one of the oldest public-sector unions and has been very successful in obtaining bargaining rights. Most states exclusively recognize a majority union and require a mutual duty to bargain. Impasse procedures are generally similar to those for police, and fire fighters are forbidden to strike (except in Idaho).

State Employees

Fewer states permit bargaining for state employees than for other special occupational groups. Where permitted, bargaining is generally a mutual duty. There are fewer formal procedures for breaking impasses than there are for teachers, police, and fire fighters; and some states allow strikes if an impasse has been reached.

Local Employees

Provisions for local employees in other occupational classifications are largely similar to those of state employees. More states permit strikes for local employees than for other classifications.

Although most states forbid strikes, enforcing this prohibition is often difficult. A long history of public employee strikes shows that legally permissible steps to end strikes are not taken in many cases, and statutorily mandated reprisals, such as discharges, have seldom been invoked.

Public Employee Unions

Public-sector unions parallel those in the private sector in terms of their constituencies because several unions representing employees in the private sector also organize in the public sector.

The public sector contains several major, exclusively public-sector employee unions. The American Federation of State, County, and Municipal Employees, AFL–CIO (AFSCME), represents state and local unit employees across occupations (see Chapter 5 for a description of its structure). The American Federation of Government Employees, AFL–CIO (AFGE), represents federal employees. Postal service employees are represented by several national unions, such as the National Association of Letter Carriers (NALC).

Some public employees are represented by industrial-type unions such as AFSCME, while craft unions represent others. Craft unions are less likely to be affiliated with the AFL-CIO. The government-oriented craft unions and associations are generally older than industrial-type unions, but they vary greatly in their original adoption of traditional trade union bargaining approaches.

A variety of public-sector bargaining representatives began as professional associations and were primarily involved in establishing standards and occupational licensing requirements and lobbying for improved funding and facilities. Others began as civil service employee associations before collective bargaining rights were granted to their members. These organizations were primarily involved in meeting and conferring with employer representatives and lobbying with legislatures. Some, like the California State Employees Association, were of sufficient size to exercise political influence through large blocs of voters in districts where state employment was high. Associations continue to be most prevalent where laws forbid bargaining but where legislative lobbying representing numerical strength is important. Professional associations are usually organized on occupational bases and have begun to bargain more recently than unions, often as a response to organizing by unions that demanded to bargain collectively rather than to meet and confer with employers.

There are four major classifications of nonfederal public-sector labor organizations: (1) all-public-sector employee unions, (2) mixed public- and private-sector unions, (3) state and local employee associations, and (4) unions and associations representing uniformed protective services.[3] The major mixed unions are the Service Employees International Union

[3] Jack Stieber, *Public Sector Unionism* (Washington, D.C.: Brookings Institution, 1973).

(SEIU), which is increasingly involved in health care, and the Teamsters. In the uniformed services, the IAFF and the Fraternal Order of Police (FOP), formerly a benevolent organization, are among the largest.

As mentioned in Chapter 5, unions tend to be organized to fit the jurisdictions in which employers operate. Most national organizations bargaining at the state and local levels are organized along a federal model, such as the National Education Association. Because education laws and funding methods vary by state and most bargaining occurs at the local school board level, state-level services are mostly devoted to lobbying and assisting negotiations. Local districts or state organizations have fewer requirements to get approval from the national association for actions than private-sector unions do. Membership in public-sector unions has increased during the late 1980s, while private-sector unionization has declined. About 36 percent of public-sector employees are union members. Organizing has become more intense in the public sector, while management resistance to unions is lower.[4] Prospects for future growth depend on the level of demand for public services, a move away from a trend toward privatization, and the increasing adoption of state laws permitting expanded bargaining rights.[5] Duty-to-bargain laws substantially increase unionization beyond other public policy measures favorable to public-sector unions.[6]

The union's organization also depends to an extent on the structure of bargaining units permitted under governing legislation. The next section explores more issues in organizing in the public sector.

BARGAINING UNITS AND ORGANIZING

Due to the variety of unions and associations involved and differences in dates when organization occurred, employers frequently bargain with several unions. Bargaining units are generally not as inclusive as those in industry but more akin to the building trades in construction. In a given geographical area, public employees may also bargain with a variety of statutory agencies. For example, a large city may have a local government, school board, transit authority, sewer district, public utility, and so forth; all having autonomous powers to bargain, levy taxes, and provide

---

[4] John F. Burton Jr. and Terry Thomason, "The Extent of Collective Bargaining in the Public Sector," in *Public Sector Bargaining*, 2nd ed., ed. Benjamin Aaron, Joyce M. Najita, and James L. Stern (Washington, D.C.: Bureau of National Affairs, 1988), pp. 1–51.

[5] L. N. Edwards, "The Future of Public Sector Unions: Stagnation or Growth," *American Economic Review* 79, no. 2 (1989), pp. 161–65.

[6] J. S. Zax and C. Ichniowski, "Bargaining Laws and Unionization in the Local Public Sector," *Industrial and Labor Relations Review* 43 (1990), pp. 447–62.

specific services. Separate bargaining units may exist within each. For example, a school board may bargain with an AFT local representing teachers, a SEIU local representing custodians, an AFSCME local representing clericals, and a Teamsters local representing bus drivers. This situation makes whipsawing an unsophisticated management possible, but the costs ultimately result in higher taxes, which bring either legislative or taxpayer referendums, or both, into play.

Given the generally broader occupational mix and relatively fewer number of employees in a given occupation, it is unlikely that public-sector unions will seek to represent them using an industrial model. Balancing competing desires of various occupational groups in a collective agreement using an industrial approach is too difficult. From the employer's standpoint, the scope of a bargaining unit is likely to be limited by the extent of the taxing authority. For example, a statewide clerical bargaining unit would be appropriate for state employees but not for local government clericals, because the city may not have the revenue-producing capabilities necessary to finance wages negotiated at a state level.

PUBLIC-SECTOR BARGAINING PROCESSES

This section examines the differences between public- and private-sector bargaining and evolving bargaining structures found in nonfederal negotiations. Management in most public-sector bargaining consists of two levels: appointed civil service officials (such as city managers and school superintendents) and elected officials (such as mayors, city councils, and school boards). Although appointed managers may be directly responsible for negotiations, elected officials can pressure them to modify positions toward the union. Intraorganizational bargaining may need to be intense among management parties in public-sector negotiations.

Bargaining Structures

Bargaining in public employment has been much more fragmented than in the private sector. Part of this is because of legislation imposing different recognition, bargaining, impasse, and strike rules on various jurisdictions and occupations. Another reason relates to the relatively narrow governmental jurisdictions involved. For example, although teachers are a relatively homogeneous occupational group, a rather small geographic area may have several municipalities with separate school boards and separate negotiations.

On the local level, some changes have occurred, particularly among teachers. Several National Education Association (NEA) affiliates have begun programs to increase their bargaining power vis-à-vis local districts. In Michigan, locals are expected to match a standard contract before ratifying. When strikes occur, substantial financial aid to strikers is made available. Regional activities also put more pressure on school boards to settle, because replacements cannot fill all openings simultaneously. Local school boards object to this tactic because it reduces local autonomy in negotiations.

In Illinois, coordinated bargaining in 45 southern counties has apparently led to higher salary levels. Efforts have also gone forward in the East San Francisco Bay and Portland, Oregon, areas.

Management Organization for Bargaining

Unlike the private sector, the public sector has an ambiguous management structure. The top leadership is politically elected, while the ongoing management is frequently operated by career civil servants. In addition, these civil servants may belong to their own bargaining units. Bargaining structures become increasingly centralized over time to gain budgetary control and coordinate bargaining within an office with an expert bargainer who will have long-run responsibility for the collective bargaining agreement.[7]

Multilateral Bargaining

One major distinction exists between public- and private-sector contract negotiations. In the public sector, employees may strongly influence management because they also vote, and organizations to which they belong may be part of a political power bloc. Also, relatively large numbers of people in a defined geographic area may utilize services provided or see their taxes affected by the outcome of an agreement. Elected public officials may have an influence on negotiations and may in turn have been endorsed by labor organizations representing their employees. Thus, public-sector collective bargaining may not be bilateral but rather multilateral, with public officials being approached to influence negotiating positions of management members who are ultimately responsible to these elected officials.

Some have suggested public-sector bargaining is becoming less like private-sector labor relations. Opportunities for a sophisticated union to apply pressure along a variety of fronts move it toward a multilateral

---

[7] Milton Derber, "Management Organization for Collective Bargaining in the Public Sector," in *Public Sector Bargaining*, 2nd ed., ed. Benjamin Aaron, Joyce M. Najita, and James L. Stern (Washington, D.C.: Bureau of National Affairs, 1988), pp. 90–123.

approach. Unions may exercise more political power and be more able to bring community interest or public pressure to bear in public-sector bargaining.

Multilateral bargaining occurs when more than two groups with particular interests engage in the process simultaneously. It more likely occurs where there is internal conflict among management bargainers, where the union is politically active and involved, and where the union attempts to use a variety of impasse procedures. Activities involved in multilateral bargaining include (1) public officials influencing the negotiations outside the process, (2) union representatives discussing contract terms with management members who are not on the bargaining team, (3) community interest groups being involved, (4) city officials not implementing the agreement, and (5) mediation attempts by elected officials. With data collected from 228 fire fighter negotiations in cities nationwide, multilateral bargaining was most strongly related (in order of importance) to: (1) general conflict among city officials, (2) union political pressure tactics, (3) union impasse pressure tactics, and (4) management commitment to collective bargaining. The incidence of multilateral bargaining increased with the age of the bargaining relationship, but comprehensiveness of state laws and experience of management negotiators had little impact.[8]

In Texas, where state law allows cities to vote to hold referenda to decide whether police and fire fighters can bargain collectively, communities with high union membership were more likely to permit bargaining, unions endorsed police and fire fighter positions, and good police and fire fighter cooperation existed. Unfavorable votes were associated with active business opposition, active opposition by the present governing body or an ad hoc group, and a concurrent city council election.[9] Thus, not only are bargaining and employment outcomes affected by a multilateral approach, but also the ability to bargain may be influenced multilaterally.

Because public-sector unions appear to attempt multilateral bargaining, an assessment of its effectiveness is important. An examination of fire fighter contracts finds six variables were significantly related to positive union outcomes: (1) compulsory arbitration at impasse, (2) fact-finding at impasse, (3) comprehensiveness of the state's bargaining law, (4) the decision-making power of management's negotiator, (5) city council-negotiator goal incompatibility, and (6) elected official intervention at

---

[8] Thomas A. Kochan, "A Theory of Multilateral Collective Bargaining in City Government," *Industrial and Labor Relations Review* 28 (1974), pp. 525–42.

[9] Darold T. Barnum and I. B. Helburn, "Influencing the Electorate: Experience with Referenda on Public Employee Bargaining," *Industrial and Labor Relations Review* 35 (1982), pp. 330–42.

impasse. The first three variables reflect the legal environment, the next two reflect management characteristics, and the last is a multilateral bargaining component. Union pressure tactics were not significantly related to outcomes.[10]

The scope of public-sector bargaining laws reflects the relative wealth of a state.[11] The coincidence of comprehensive laws and greater ability to pay may influence bargaining outcomes toward the union. A comprehensive law legitimizes the union, reduces management's costs of recognition, and may legally decrease management's use of contract rejection, refusals to bargain, and other similar tactics.[12] Environmental characteristics affect not only the makeup of the bargaining teams and their interrelationships but also the power and tactics available to the parties during negotiations.

Statutory law lags public opinion because legislators enact laws after they are elected. Using legislation as a lagged variable, bargaining outcomes for unions in medium-sized municipalities were better (1) where only certain trades were involved, rather than a large general unit; (2) where no statutory penalty for striking existed; (3) where the union was affiliated with a public-sector national; (4) where strike activity in the state was above average; and (5) where public opinion had led to or favored a bargaining law.[13]

Bargaining Outcomes

Bargaining outcomes may have immediate effects for the employment relationship or long-run effects on the occupation as a whole. This section examines several studies of public-sector bargaining outcomes.

Public employees who bargain are often part of a monopoly. Their service is provided only by the government (for example, police protection); thus, obtaining better contracts should be easier because the government can more easily pass on the costs to the consumer (at least in the short run). In a study of cities with either public or private waste management systems, the effect of unions on wages in privately managed systems was not significant; but in publicly managed systems, the effects were between 10 and 17 percent. In privately managed systems, several com-

---

[10] Thomas A. Kochan and Hoyt N. Wheeler, "Municipal Collective Bargaining: A Model and Analysis of Bargaining Outcomes," *Industrial and Labor Relations Review* 29 (1975), pp. 46–66.

[11] Thomas A. Kochan, "Correlates of State Public Employee Bargaining Laws," *Industrial Relations* 12 (1973), pp. 322–37.

[12] Paul F. Gerhart, "Determinants of Bargaining in Local Government Labor Negotiations," *Industrial and Labor Relations Review* 29 (1976), pp. 331–32.

[13] Ibid., p. 349.

peting waste haulers were usually involved in the market.[14] These results indicate monopoly power available to public employers can be used to increase wages.

Research on the effects of collective bargaining on wages, employment, and productivity of unionized versus nonunion government employees finds union wages and benefits are about 8 to 12 percent higher, but differences are greater in the private sector.[15] Wage differences increase as employees gain recognition and bargaining rights. Spillovers to unorganized areas also occur.[16] Evidence on specific occupations finds state bargaining laws and mandatory impasse procedures increase police wages. Nonunion police receive almost as much due to the threat of organizing.[17] Fire fighter unionization influenced total compensation, entry, and maximum salary levels. The greatest impact was for fringe benefits, similar to findings in the private sector.[18] For teachers, greater union activity is related to lower male/female and elementary/secondary pay differences. Unionization also increased pay for advanced education, years of experience, and years of experience in the district. Measurable, job-related aspects assumed a greater value for pay outcomes in situations where more union activity was present.[19] In higher education, unionized faculty received about 2 percent higher pay, with greater returns to length of service and less to publications than in nonunion colleges and universities.[20] Employment in represented units increased 3 percent faster than in nonunion units around 1980. While employment usually falls as wages increase, lobbying and other activities to influence the electorate led to net expansions.[21] Productivity results are not clear; but

[14] Linda N. Edwards and Franklin R. Edwards, "Wellington-Winter Revisited: The Case of Municipal Sanitation Collection," *Industrial and Labor Relations Review* 36 (1982), pp. 307–18.

[15] H. G. Lewis, "Union/Nonunion Wage Gaps in the Public Sector," *Journal of Labor Economics* 8 (1990), pp. S260–S328.

[16] J. S. Zax, "Wages, Nonwage Compensation, and Municipal Unions," *Industrial Relations* 27 (1988), pp. 301–17.

[17] P. Feuille and J. T. Delaney, "Collective Bargaining, Interest Arbitration, and Police Salaries," *Industrial and Labor Relations Review* 39 (1986), pp. 228–40; and Casey Ichniowski, Richard B. Freeman, and H. Lauer, "Collective Bargaining Laws, Threat Effects, and the Determination of Police Compensation," *Journal of Labor Economics* 7 (1989), pp. 191–209.

[18] Casey Ichniowski, "Economic Effects of the Firefighters' Union," *Industrial and Labor Relations Review* 33 (1980), pp. 198–211.

[19] Alexander B. Holmes, "Union Activity and Teacher Salary Structure," *Industrial Relations* 18 (1979), pp. 79–85.

[20] D. A. Barbezat, "The Effect of Collective Bargaining on Salaries in Higher Education," *Industrial and Labor Relations Review* 42 (1989), pp. 443–55.

[21] L. M. Spizman, "Public Sector Unions: A Study of Economic Power," *Journal of Labor Research* 1 (1980), pp. 265–74; and J. S. Zax, "Employment and Local Public Sector Unions," *Industrial Relations* 28 (1989), pp. 21–31.

in the private sector, only unionized blue-collar occupations were more productive. During the 1980s, concessions were much larger in the private sector, but the union wage advantage was also greater there previously.[22] Collective bargaining increases expenditures in municipal departments that are covered, but it does not appear to influence property taxes, total revenues, or total expenditures.[23]

The advent of collective bargaining in the federal government has affected supervisors' uses of personnel policies. Organizations may have several personnel policies not part of the collective agreement that are the focus of grievances, given the manner in which supervisors implement them. Figure 15–1 suggests the supervisor is influenced by the union's presence and his or her perception regarding the union's position on specific policies. In a federal government study, supervisors who worked where the union was well entrenched and where it had negotiated certain policies into contracts were more aware of the unions' positions and used the policies more often.[24]

IMPASSE PROCEDURES

Because strikes are generally prohibited for public-sector employees, the following may occur when an impasse is reached: management may continue the past contract, mediation may occur, employees may legally or illegally strike or have a "sickout," fact-finding may take place, interest arbitration may decide remaining differences, or a legislative body may mandate an agreement. Fact-finding, arbitration, and strikes will be examined, with an emphasis on the first two because they don't normally occur in the private sector.

What leads to impasses in public-sector negotiations? A study of New York state police and fire fighter negotiations proposed the model shown in Figure 15–2. Environmental characteristics most strongly related to impasses included previous impasse experience, percentage of the local electorate voting Democratic in 1972 (for police), and previous starting salary (for police). Structural characteristics associated with impasses were union pressure tactics, adherence to pattern settlements (police),

[22] Daniel J. B. Mitchell, "Collective Bargaining and Compensation in the Public Sector," in *Public Sector Bargaining*, 2nd ed., ed. Benjamin Aaron, Joyce M. Najita, and James L. Stern (Washington, D.C.: Bureau of National Affairs, 1988), pp. 124–59.

[23] R. G. Valletta, "The Impact of Unionism on Municipal Expenditures and Revenues," *Industrial and Labor Relations Review* 42 (1989), pp. 430–42.

[24] Janice M. Beyer, Harrison M. Trice, and Richard E. Hunt, "The Impact of Federal Sector Unions on Supervisors' Use of Personnel Policies," *Industrial and Labor Relations Review* 34 (1980), pp. 212–31.

FIGURE 15–1

Union Impact on Supervisor Policy Usage

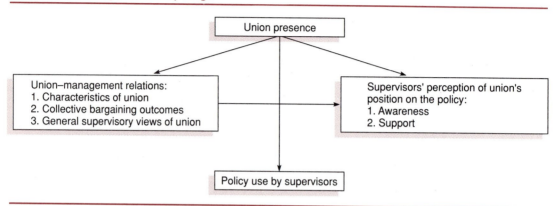

SOURCE: Janice M. Beyer, Harrison M. Trice, and Richard E. Hunt, "The Impact of Federal-Sector Unions on Supervisors' Use of Personnel Policies," *Industrial and Labor Relations Review* 34 (1980), p. 214.

lack of authority for the management negotiator, internal management conflict, and pressure on union leaders (police). Interpersonal/personal factors included hostility, lack of management negotiator skills (fire), lack of union or management in-house negotiators, and management negotiator experience.

Negotiations requiring formal procedures at or beyond fact-finding were more likely with higher starting salaries, with previous impasse experience, in large cities (police), when union pressure tactics were used, and when management negotiators had little authority. Hostility and negotiator experience were also related, while negotiator skill (for fire) was negatively related.[25]

Fact-Finding

Fact-finding began in the private sector through the establishment of fact-finding boards in Taft-Hartley and emergency board procedures in the Railway Labor Act. However, it is presently far more prevalent in the public sector.

In a private-sector impasse, the fact-finder's role is to establish a reasonable position for a settlement by objectively studying the context and issues and preparing a report of conclusions based on the setting. A

---

[25] Thomas A. Kochan, Mordehai Mironi, Ronald G. Ehrenberg, Jean Baderschneider, and Todd Jick, *Dispute Resolution under Fact-Finding and Arbitration* (New York: American Arbitration Association, 1979), pp. 32–33.

FIGURE 15-2

Determinants of Impasses

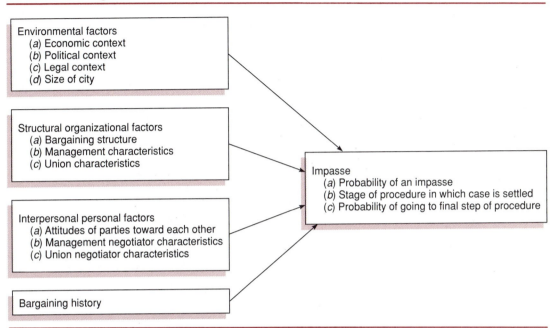

SOURCE: Thomas A. Kochan, Mordehai Mironi, Ronald G. Ehrenberg, Jean Baderschneider, and Todd Jick, *Dispute Resolution under Fact-Finding and Arbitration: An Empirical Evaluation* (New York: American Arbitration Association, 1979), p. 32.

primary end result sought by this process is the publication of the disputed issues and recommended settlement. In this way, public opinion may be galvanized to pressure a settlement on this factual conclusion. Fact-finding may also lead to economizing a legislature's time when it expects to impose a solution.[26]

The role of providing facts for a legislature is not very appropriate in the public sector, because legislators are frequently a party in the dispute (school boards, city councils, and so on). Here the fact-finder's role is to educate the public as to the costs of a reasonable settlement. Fact-finding may be sought by parties who fear adverse public opinion if they bargain a settlement. They might reason a fact-finder would probably recommend something similar to a negotiated settlement, but the "facts" from a neutral party seem more reasonable and less collusive.[27]

---

[26] Jean T. McKelvey, "Fact-Finding in Public Employment Disputes: Promise or Illusion," *Industrial and Labor Relations Review* 23 (1969), pp. 528–30.

[27] Ibid., pp. 530–31.

Statutory Role of the Fact-Finder

Wisconsin was one of the first states to pass a comprehensive fact-finding statute. While this law was in effect, fact-finding could be initiated by either party if an impasse existed or if the other party refused to bargain. The Wisconsin Employee Relations Board (WERB) investigated the request and attempted to mediate. If the mediation failed, a neutral was appointed to examine the evidence and recommend a settlement. The recommendation was sent to the parties and the WERB, which publicized it. Although the parties may have asked for fact-finding, they were under no obligation to accept the report's recommendations.[28]

Fact-finding cases in Wisconsin took from three months to two years from the initial request until a recommendation was issued. Fact-finders had to fit cases into their schedules, because they were usually university professors or attorneys appointed on an ad hoc basis.[29] On the other hand, in Michigan, where a strike situation led to a request for fact-finding, only about 26 days elapsed from a request to the fact-finder's report.[30] If dispute resolution is the criterion, the success of fact-finding is much lower than other methods once an impasse has been reached.

Fact-Finding Results

Does fact-finding accomplish what it was designed to do (that is, lead to a settlement acceptable to both parties without a work stoppage)? The answers depend on where the issue is examined and how the procedure works.

Wisconsin

A study of early Wisconsin experiences concluded fact-finding was effective because only 11 percent of the petitions for fact-finding weren't resolved. But not all cases ultimately went to fact-finders. Of those that did, about one quarter were not resolved after the fact-finder's report was issued. Both parties were relatively positive about the procedure; however, some managements complained the fact-finder was not sufficiently aware of local problems, and some union officials decried management's ability to disregard the findings in areas where the union had little political power.[31] Since the study, arbitration has replaced fact-finding in Wisconsin.

---

[28] James L. Stern, "The Wisconsin Public Employee Fact-Finding Procedure," *Industrial and Labor Relations Review* 20 (1966), pp. 4–5.

[29] Ibid., pp. 7–8.

[30] Russell Allen, "1967 School Disputes in Michigan," *Public Employee Organization and Bargaining* (Washington, D.C.: Bureau of National Affairs, 1968), chap. 9.

[31] Stern, "Wisconsin Public Employee."

Michigan

In Michigan schools, fact-finding was negatively viewed by the parties where strikes were under way. Parties were not experienced enough with the procedure to present their cases adequately, and time pressures were great. Unlike Wisconsin, the state paid for the process, reducing any cost-based reluctance by the parties to use it.[32]

New York

About 50 percent of the early cases referred to the Public Employee Relations Board were settled by mediation before fact-finding was ordered. Of the other half, 22 percent were mediated before a report was issued, 45 percent were settled by accepting the fact-finding report, and the other third required additional mediation or were unilaterally modified by the employer. Of 316 impasses, nine resulted in strikes. However, the statute defines an impasse as an inability to agree within 60 days of the required adoption of a budget, so the parties may still have experienced some movement in bargaining positions after an official impasse was declared.[33]

Fact-finding probably works better when parties are unsophisticated in collective bargaining because they may have difficulty defining a reasonable settlement. This may be reconciled with the Michigan findings, because a strike has not been called. Some labor advocates complain an employer may request the process and then reject the recommendations. Because the employer is often the legislative body that sets the rules, the union may be vulnerable if fact-finding is the only available impasse resolution procedure.

Iowa

The Iowa statute includes fact-finding, binding arbitration, and final-offer selection for all bargaining units. One major difference in Iowa's law is that the arbitrator may select from management's, the union's, or the fact-finder's recommendations as the final offer. In Iowa, the Public Employee Relations Board, rather than the parties, requests the fact-finding. Early experience suggests fact-finding reduces the number of issues taken to arbitration.[34] Parties may formulate more reasonable positions if required to use fact-finding because fact-finders often choose one of the parties' positions rather than formulate their own. Fact-finders

---

[32] Allen, "1967 School Disputes."

[33] McKelvey, "Fact-Finding," pp. 536, 538.

[34] Daniel G. Gallagher and Richard Pegnetter, "Impasse Resolution under the Iowa Multistep Procedure," *Industrial and Labor Relations Review* 32 (1979), pp. 327–28.

often act like arbitrators because they know the party may go to arbitration if it does not like the findings. About 70 percent of impasses presented to Iowa fact-finders were resolved without going to arbitration.[35]

Florida

In a variation on fact-finding, Florida has implemented nonbinding interest arbitration. The arbitrator may mediate to resolve the impasse and, if unsuccessful, prepare a report that would serve as the basis for a contract. While these are frequently rejected, parties often adopt a majority of the arbitrator's recommendations on individual issues.[36]

Criteria for Fact-Finding Recommendations

In early Wisconsin experiences with fact-finding, wage comparisons were most frequently used for economic recommendations. The governmental unit's ability to pay was also frequently considered. Some fact-finders decided what the wage settlement would have been if the union were permitted to strike. Productivity and cost-of-living issues were seldom mentioned, although management and labor raised them in their presentations.[37]

Arbitration

Some laws provide mandatory arbitration of contract negotiation disputes. Where these exist, they apply more often to public safety divisions, primarily for uniformed services, and are considered in lieu of granting the right to strike. With arbitration at impasse, the union is not faced with the prospect of management unilaterally continuing past terms without recourse to some other bargaining weapon. Other laws allow unions and managements voluntarily to agree to interest arbitration as a means for settling negotiating impasses.

Arbitrators who handle public-sector interest cases are normally selected in the same way as in private-sector ad hoc rights cases. The hearing procedure is also similar. Both sides present evidence supporting their positions, and the arbitrator determines the contract on the basis of the evidence and whatever criteria are to be used for the award.

---

[35] Daniel G. Gallagher and M. D. Chaubey, "Impasse Behavior and Tri-Offer Arbitration," *Industrial Relations* 21 (1982), pp. 129–48.

[36] K. O. Magnusen and P. A. Renovitch, "Dispute Resolution in Florida's Public Sector: Insight into Impasse," *Journal of Collective Negotiations in the Public Sector* 18 (1989), pp. 241–52.

[37] Stern, "Wisconsin Public Employee," pp. 15–17.

Interest Arbitration Variants

A number of different methods are used in public-sector interest arbitrations. In a typical situation, the arbitrator hears the case and determines an appropriate settlement. However, it has been argued this approach has a **chilling effect** on bargaining because parties believe an arbitrator will split differences between them. For example, if a union wants 90 cents an hour and management is willing to give 30 cents, they may believe an arbitrator will settle on 60 cents—halfway between. It is also argued arbitration becomes habit forming. Parties supposedly skip negotiations and go directly to impasse, thereby availing themselves of an effortless and less risky remedy: arbitration. This is the so-called narcotic effect. Beliefs regarding the presence of a narcotic effect have led to implementation of several variants of interest arbitration. Early evidence suggests a narcotic effect existed because negotiations in states providing for arbitration more frequently went to impasse.[38] Current evidence regarding the repeated use of arbitration will be examined later.

Final-Offer Arbitration

To reduce the use of arbitration, final-offer arbitration has been implemented in some states. Final-offer arbitration was proposed as a "medicine" to cure parties from using arbitration. In final-offer arbitration, each party presents its positions and the arbitrator is required to choose the positions of one or the other without compromise. This supposedly results in an extreme contract the loser would do anything to avoid in the future.[39]

Some jurisdictions opt for entire-package approaches (Massachusetts and Wisconsin), while others use issue-by-issue methods (Michigan). Entire-package selections increase the responsibility for making a reasonable final-offer submission because one unreasonable issue in an otherwise reasonable package may tip the arbitrator's preferences toward the other party's offer. Evidence suggests where final-offer selection is available on an issue-by-issue basis more unresolved issues reach the arbitrator.[40]

---

[38] Hoyt N. Wheeler, "Compulsory Arbitration: A 'Narcotic Effect'?" *Industrial Relations* 14 (1975), pp. 117–20.

[39] Carl M. Stevens, "Is Compulsory Arbitration Compatible with Bargaining?" *Industrial Relations* 5 (1966), pp. 38–50.

[40] Peter Feuille, *Final-Offer Arbitration* (Chicago: International Personnel Management Association, 1975), pp. 35–48.

One way interest arbitration differs from rights arbitration is many collective agreements and statutes permit parties to settle after the process begins and to alter final offers. Since public-sector interest arbitration is often conducted before a tripartite board (one labor, one management, and one neutral member), partisans may sense which direction the neutral appears to be leaning and concede an issue rather than lose entirely.[41]

Results of Final-Offer Laws

Final-offer procedures can be evaluated by examining whether parties accept and comply with awards and whether the process chills or encourages future bargaining.[42] Several studies have examined this issue.

Eugene, Oregon
The early experience with an entire-package, final-offer approach worked well in Eugene. No rejections of the awards occurred, fewer arbitrations were invoked in succeeding years, and the number of issues in the impasse packages decreased.[43] Table 15–1 contains the details.

Michigan
Michigan uses issue-by-issue offers for economic aspects and a conventional approach for others. The process has had no appreciable effect on the number of cases going to arbitration in the uniformed services. There has been a slight tendency for deputy sheriff negotiations to use the procedure more often than police or fire, but this was partially attributed to a relatively newer collective bargaining relationship.[44]

Wisconsin
Wisconsin uses a package-type final-offer procedure. The Wisconsin experience does not support the idea that arbitration use declines in a package-selection environment over time.[45] But evidence does indicate its use decreases when management wins.[46] The relative use of arbitration in Wisconsin is less than in Michigan, an issue-by-issue state.

---

[41] Ibid.

[42] Ibid., pp. 15–16.

[43] Gary Long and Peter Feuille, "Final-Offer Arbitration: 'Sudden Death' in Eugene," *Industrial and Labor Relations Review* 27 (1974), pp. 186–203.

[44] James L. Stern, Charles M. Rehmus, J. Joseph Loewenberg, Hirschel Kasper, and Barbara D. Dennis, *Final-Offer Arbitration* (Lexington, Mass.: Lexington Books, 1975), pp. 37–75.

[45] Ibid., pp. 77–115.

[46] Craig A. Olson, "Final-Offer Arbitration in Wisconsin after Five Years," *Proceedings of the Industrial Relations Research Association* 31 (1978), pp. 111–19.

TABLE 15-1
Eugene Negotiation—Arbitration Experience (1971–1975)

Employee Group	Arbitration Invoked?	Items Submitted to Arbitrators	Outcome
1971–72 negotiations			
Fire fighters	Yes	Entire contractual package	City first offer selected
Police patrolmen	Yes	Entire contractual package	Agreement negotiated during arbitration proceedings
AFSCME	Yes (binding fact-finding)*	Union security; all other items agreed to in negotiations	Union position (agency shop) selected
1972–73 negotiations			
Fire fighters	Yes	Longevity pay dispute; all other items agreed to in negotiations	City alternate offer selected
Police patrolmen	No	—	Negotiated agreement
AFSCME	Yes	One-year economic package; non-economic issues agreed to in negotiations	City alternate offer selected but was moot because of three-year agreement negotiated during arbitration proceedings.
1974–75 negotiations			
Fire fighters	No	—	Negotiated agreement
Police patrolmen	No	—	Negotiated agreement
AFSCME	No	—	Negotiated agreement

* The two sides agreed to use the fact-finding services provided free by the state and to be bound by the fact-finder's decision. Because this arbitration did not take place under the city procedure, the final-offer selection criteria did not apply in this case.

SOURCE: Peter Feuille, *Final-Offer Arbitration* (Chicago: International Personnel Management Association, 1975), p. 17.

Massachusetts

The Massachusetts law is a package final-offer procedure. After passage of the law, arbitrations increased almost 70 percent. Almost 40 percent of negotiations went to impasse, but only 7 percent were ultimately decided by arbitrators. Arbitrator's awards paralleled closely the reports fact-finders issued earlier during the impasse.[47]

[47] David B. Lipsky and Thomas A. Barocci, "Final-Offer Arbitration and Public-Safety Employees: The Massachusetts Experience," *Proceedings of the Industrial Relations Research Association* 30 (1977), pp. 65–76.

New Jersey

Bargainers can elect to use conventional arbitration, final-offer arbitration on a single package, final-offer on an issue-by-issue basis, final-offer on the economic package and issue-by-issue on others, or two forms of fact-finding. Parties choose which they want to use. Results indicate relatively fewer negotiations have arbitrated settlements, and arbitrators are acting more frequently in mediating roles.[48]

The evidence suggests states with issue rather than package approaches have more arbitrations and more issues going before arbitrators.

What Is a *Final* Offer

One problem frequently encountered in final-offer arbitration is "What is a *final* offer?" In Wisconsin, parties are required to state their positions to the WERB when an impasse is declared. But it has been the practice there and in Michigan (where mediation by the arbitrator appears to be encouraged) to allow negotiations to narrow differences subsequent to an arbitration request. Some see this as an advantage because the parties settle the issues. But others see it as a no-win situation because, if they adhere to a well-thought-out final position and only the opposition expresses a willingness to move, the arbitrator may award the point to the opponent because of the apparent intransigence of the adamant party. Thus, a party may provoke an impasse to achieve what it believed it could not get from true bargaining. Research has concluded that unions gained 1 to 5 percent more in economic settlements as a result of arbitration than they would have in bargaining a settlement.[49]

An Alternative to Final-Offer Selection

One argument levied against final-offer arbitration is the arbitrator has knowledge of the parties' positions in bargaining through public reports and their final offers. Some argue arbitrators should be given only information on each party's desired outcome and not evidence from previous negotiations.[50] Thus, either party might risk getting less than it had already been offered in negotiations. As such, they may have a greater motive to settle on their own. No test has been made of this procedure in the United States, but some British experiences suggest it reduces the incidence of arbitration.

---

[48] R. A. Lester, "Analysis of Experience under New Jersey's Flexible Arbitration System," *Arbitration Journal* 44, no. 2 (1989), pp. 14–21.

[49] Stern et al., *Final-Offer Arbitration*, pp. 77–115.

[50] Hoyt N. Wheeler, "Closed Offer: Alternative to Final Offer Selection," *Industrial Relations* 16 (1977), pp. 298–305.

Another argument suggests where parties know final- or closed-offer selection is the consequence of an impasse, they will position their demands symmetrically around where they believe an arbitrator will rule. They are expected to use the same types of information an arbitrator would use as criteria for determining a settlement. Thus, splitting the difference may not be an arbitral strategy but a negotiation strategy that leaves this as a logical solution.[51]

Evidence on the Narcotic Effect

A study of New York police and fire fighter impasses found after the impasse law was changed to allow arbitration rather than legislative action as the final step, negotiations increasingly went to impasse and were likely to proceed to the final step. However, there was no evidence parties were less likely to move before bargaining and little evidence that the awards were different from outcomes in similar situations where bargaining was completed.[52] The availability of arbitration seemed to chill the ability to reach a bargained settlement but not the ability to bargain.

A longitudinal examination of the New York law's effect found a positive narcotic effect during early negotiation rounds later became negative.[53] A study of negotiations following changes in the Minnesota public-sector law in 1979 suggests the narcotic effect was an "epidemic effect" with units using arbitration largely because other units in the same bargaining round used it. In subsequent rounds, parties appeared to avoid arbitration.[54]

Recent evidence on the narcotic effect is mixed. Cross-sectional evidence finds arbitration used more widely when it becomes available but less often when it has been experienced. A longitudinal study of collective bargaining in Iowa, Indiana, and Pennsylvania supports the premise that once the novelty of arbitration has dissipated, there are neither negative nor positive effects in its use level.[55] In a situation where

[51] Henry S. Farber, "Splitting the Difference in Interest Arbitration," *Industrial and Labor Relations Review* 34 (1981), pp. 70–77.

[52] Kochan et al., *Dispute Resolution*, pp. 158–59.

[53] Richard J. Butler and Ronald G. Ehrenberg, "Estimating the Narcotic Effect of Public Sector Impasse Procedures," *Industrial and Labor Relations Review* 34 (1981), pp. 3–20.

[54] Paul L. Schumann, Mario F. Bognanno, and Frederic C. Champlin, "An Empirical Study of the Narcotic and Epidemic Effects of Arbitration Use," unpublished paper (Minneapolis: Industrial Relations Center, University of Minnesota, 1983); and Frederic C. Champlin and Mario F. Bognanno, "Chilling under Arbitration and Mixed Strike-Arbitration Regimes," *Journal of Labor Research* 6 (1985), pp. 375–87.

[55] James R. Chelius and Marian M. Extejt, "The Narcotic Effect of Impasse Resolution Procedures," *Industrial and Labor Relations Review* 38 (1985), pp. 629–38.

arbitration has been available for many years, use of arbitration in the last round increases its likelihood in the next round, but aggregate use across bargaining situations reduces its use in the next round in total.[56]

Arbitration and Maturing Labor Relations

Public-sector labor legislation has almost always prohibited strikes. Because the private-sector model included them and little experience existed with other mechanisms, a great deal of experimentation has occurred. The use of fact-finding has decreased, both statutorily and at the individual impasse level. Several forms of arbitration have been implemented. Surveys suggest the usage is low and decreasing.[57] Arbitration's effectiveness or failure may also depend on prehearing processes. Where experienced negotiators are in place, mediation may be much more helpful than arbitration in fashioning an acceptable settlement.[58]

It is difficult for the parties to determine an appropriate settlement point where third-party determinations exist. Neither party knows for certain what an arbitrator would view as a correct solution. They also may have doubts as to an imposed solution's workability. The choices may also vary substantially given what constitutes a last offer.

Arbitral Criteria

Just as rights arbitrators apply criteria in deciding awards in grievance cases, so do arbitrators in interest cases. Some criteria are specified by law; others are specified by the arbitrators. These criteria can cause problems for both the arbitrators and disputants.

One fact often considered is ability to pay. Nevada statutorily requires its assessment in arriving at an award.[59] During New York City's acute financial crisis, an arbitrator in a hospital interest arbitration mentioned ability-to-pay criteria for her low wage award.[60] The ability-to-pay issue

---

[56] J. Currie, "Who Uses Interest Arbitration? The Case of British Columbia's Teachers, 1947–1981," *Industrial and Labor Relations Review* 42 (1989), pp. 363–79.

[57] Craig A. Olson, "Dispute Resolution in the Public Sector," in *Public-Sector Bargaining*, 2nd ed., ed. Benjamin Aaron, Joyce M. Najita, and James L. Stern (Washington, D.C.: Bureau of National Affairs, 1988), pp. 160–88.

[58] Paul F. Gerhart and John F. Drotning, "The Effectiveness of Public-Sector Impasse Procedures," in *Advances in Industrial and Labor Relations*, vol. 2, ed. David B. Lipsky and Joel Douglas (Greenwich, Conn.: JAI Press, 1985), pp. 143–95.

[59] Joseph R. Grodin, "Arbitration of Public-Sector Labor Disputes," *Industrial and Labor Relations Review* 27 (1974), pp. 89–102.

[60] Margery Gootnick, arbitrator, award in *League of Voluntary Hospitals and District 1199, Hospital and Health Care Employees, RWDSU*, reprinted in *Daily Labor Report*, September 16, 1976, pp. D1–D7.

may retard wage gains when revenues do not support wage demands. However, there are suggestions arbitrators are less concerned about the actual ability to pay than are elected officials.[61] (This is hardly surprising since officials are generally closer to their managements than to their rank and file, who are coincidentally constituents.) A study of Wisconsin interest arbitrators found economic awards were most frequently shaped by internal and external comparability of pay packages, less so by cost of living, and least by ability to pay.[62] Comparability was stressed by police impasse arbitrators, and offers by the city had greater influence than the union.[63]

Managements and unions have some common and dissimilar preferences about their choice of an arbitrator. Of 69 arbitrators listed by the New Jersey Employment Relations Commission in 1980, employers and unions distinctly preferred certain arbitrators. While management and union preferences were moderately similar and stressed arbitrators' experience levels, unions preferred arbitrators with legal backgrounds while managements preferred economists. Both sides were influenced by the direction of the arbitrator's previous awards.[64]

The Utility of Arbitration for Unions

Public safety unions have been strong advocates of binding arbitration to resolve impasses. While it is obvious that arbitration does provide a method for resolving interest differences when strikes are prohibited, less information is available on the impact of the process on bargaining outcomes. Two studies found relatively minimal wage effects (0 to 5 percent) associated with arbitration.[65] However, arbitration should serve to raise management offers, particularly in final-offer selection states. Management might be expected to concede toward what an arbitrator's award might be, rather than to risk the choice of a union's extreme position. For the union's part, it might likely take a harder line where it has a final resolution available that does not entail the risk of an illegal strike. Studying fire fighter arbitration laws found that arbitration was

[61] Raymond D. Horton, "Arbitration, Arbitrators, and the Public Interest," *Industrial and Labor Relations Review* 27 (1975), pp. 497–507.

[62] G. G. Dell'Omo, "Wage Disputes in Interest Arbitration: Arbitrators Weigh the Criteria, *Arbitration Journal* 44, no. 2 (1989), pp. 4–13.

[63] S. Schwochau and P. Feuille, "Interest Arbitrators and Their Decision Behavior," *Industrial Relations* 27 (1988), pp. 37–55.

[64] David E. Bloom and C. L. Cavanagh, "An Analysis of the Selection of Arbitrators," *American Economic Review* 76 (1986), pp. 408–22.

[65] Stern et al., *Final-Offer Arbitration*, pp. 77–115; and Kochan et al., *Dispute Resolution*, pp. 158–59.

associated with higher salaries and shorter working hours the longer the law was in effect. Wage increases averaged about 11 to 22 percent higher in arbitration states.[66]

The expected utility of arbitration to settle a dispute depends on the perceived threat presented by arbitration to both sides. The lower the expected utility from arbitration, the less favorable a settlement a party would be willing to accept.[67] Part of utility is related to direct costs. The highest the costs, the more likely parties are to negotiate their own settlement. Where this occurs, the less risk averse party achieves higher outcomes.[68] In some situations, a union bargainer chooses arbitration where a satisfactory settlement might be negotiated to signal to members that it isn't shirking negotiations and settling for less than it could have gotten.[69]

Strikes

Most states prohibit public employee strikes and have injunction and penalty provisions if strikes occur. However, the right to strike is granted to certain public employees in Alaska, Hawaii, Idaho, Minnesota, Montana, Oregon, Pennsylvania, Vermont, and Wisconsin in certain situations. Although most states forbid strikes, prohibiting them and enforcing the prohibition are two different things. The long history of public employee strikes shows legally permissible steps to end them are not taken in most cases, and statutorily mandated reprisals, such as discharges, have often not been invoked. Table 15–2 shows the relative incidence of strike activity across occupations and jurisdictions in the public sector.

The table shows the largest number of strikes occurred at the local level, with school employees involved in more strikes than any other jurisdictional level. More days are lost from strikes by school employees, and the duration of strikes is longest for school disputes. One reason for the level and duration of school strikes is that they are often essentially costless to both employers and employees. Legislatures establish school years of certain lengths, so if a strike disrupts the first three weeks of

---

[66] Craig A. Olson, "The Impact of Arbitration on the Wages of Firefighters," *Industrial Relations* 19 (1980), pp. 325–39.

[67] Frederic C. Champlin and Mario F. Bognanno, "A Model for Arbitration and the Incentive to Bargain," in *Advances in Industrial and Labor Relations*, ed. David Lipsky and Joel Douglas (Greenwich, Conn.: JAI Press, 1986), pp. 153–90.

[68] H. S. Farber, M. A. Neale, and M. H. Bazerman, "The Role of Arbitration Costs and Risk Aversion in Dispute Outcomes," *Industrial Relations* 29 (1990), pp. 361–84.

[69] B. P. McCall, "Interest Arbitration and the Incentive to Bargain: A Principal-Agent Approach," *Journal of Conflict Resolution* 34 (1990), 151–67.

TABLE 15–2

Work Stoppages in the Public Sector, 1970–1988*

Employer and Year	Number	Employees Involved (000)	Number of Days Lost (000)
Federal			
1970	3	155.8	648.3
1975	0	—	—
1980	1	.9	7.2
1985	0	—	—
1988	0	—	—
State			
1970	23	8.8	44.6
1975	32	66.6	300.5
1980	45	10.0	99.7
1985	1	6.8	13.6
1988	2	6.4	91.6
Local			
1970	386	168.9	1,330.5
1975	446	252.0	1,903.9
1980	493	212.7	2,240.9
1985	7	50.0	208.6
1988	2	7.4	42.4

* 1985–88 data includes only strikes that involved 1,000 or more employees.
SOURCE: "1983 Work Stoppages in Government," *Government Employee Relations Report* (Washington: Bureau of National Affairs, 1983), p. 71:1011; U.S. Bureau of Labor Statistics, *Handbook of Labor Statistics* (Washington: Government Printing Office, 1989), p. 545.

school, the year is simply extended three weeks. The only cost to the school or the teachers is the delay in school aid receipts and wages. The incidence and duration of school strikes is associated with state laws governing the length of the school year and the local district's willingness to tax itself for greater educational costs.[70]

There is mixed evidence regarding the incidence of strikes. For police, the evidence suggests strikes occur less often when there is a provision for collective bargaining and arbitration to settle impasses.[71] On the other hand, strikes appear to be used when they are legal or not prevented as vehicles for increasing public employee bargaining power. Well-enforced penalties or threats of firing reduce public-sector strikes, while

---

[70] Craig A. Olson, "The Impact of Rescheduled School Days on Teacher Strikes," *Industrial and Labor Relations Review* 38 (1984) pp. 515–28.

[71] Casey Ichniowski, "Arbitrators and Police Bargaining: Prescriptions for the Blue Flu," *Industrial Relations* 21 (1982), pp. 149–66; and Robert N. Horn, William J. McGuire, and Joseph Tomkiewicz, "Work Stoppages by Teachers: An Empirical Analysis," *Journal of Labor Research* 3 (1982), pp. 487–95.

poorly enforced laws have no effect, and permissive laws increase their frequency.[72] Strike incidence declines with both the length of experience of the bargainers and the relative equality of their experience level.[73]

Generally, strike activity in the public sector appears positively influenced by the rate of wage increase for private-sector employees, increases in the cost of living, and fiscal belt-tightening. Unemployment in the private sector and recession appear to be related to reduced public-sector strike activity.[74]

Recent studies of teacher strikes suggest they are not used as an offensive weapon to improve outcomes more than other comparison groups but are used as defensive weapons to maintain a relative position or to reverse erosion. Among Illinois and Iowa teachers, strikes are worth only about $285 annually. Evidence suggests the availability of impasse resolution procedures influences wages by about 10 percent.[75]

SUMMARY

The legal environment is a critical factor in public employee unionization because management determines ultimately the scope of bargaining rights. Public opinion predicts changes in these laws in some states, but generally rights are more restrictive than in the private sector. Legislation is most conducive to bargaining in the industrialized North and East and is least in rural or southern areas. Right-to-work laws for the private sector predict statutes prohibiting union activity in the public sector.

Where bargaining is permitted, issues are much the same as in the private sector. Unionization varies, with AFSCME taking an industrial-union approach and the uniformed services generally organized on a craft basis.

Impasse resolution varies widely by jurisdiction and occupation. In the federal government, the Federal Services Impasses Panel resolves disputes. In states providing for impasse resolution by statute, arbitrators usually handle uniformed services disputes. In other areas, fact-finding, mediation, and other methods are prescribed. Strikes are forbidden in most jurisdictions.

---

[72] Craig A. Olson, "Strikes, Strike Penalties, and Arbitration in Six States," *Industrial and Labor Relations Review* 39 (1986), pp. 539–51.

[73] E. Montgomery and M. E. Benedict, "The Impact of Bargainer Experience on Teacher Strikes," *Industrial and Labor Relations Review* 42 (1989), pp. 380–92.

[74] William B. Nelson, Gerald W. Stone Jr., and J. Michael Swint, "An Economic Analysis of Public Sector Collective Bargaining and Strike Activity," *Journal of Labor Research* 2 (1981), pp. 77–98.

[75] John Thomas Delaney, "Strikes, Arbitration, and Teacher Salaries: A Behavioral Analysis," *Industrial and Labor Relations Review* 37 (1983), pp. 431–46.

Evidence suggests unions benefit from interest arbitration and other designated impasse procedures. Final-offer selection may reduce reliance on arbitration, but more recent evidence suggests any experience with arbitration may lessen its future usage.

DISCUSSION QUESTIONS

1. If government employees were to be given a limited right to strike, which occupations should be prohibited from striking, and under what conditions should the prohibition be enforced?
2. Since arbitrators are not responsible to the electorate, should they be allowed to make binding rulings on economic issues?
3. Civil service rules provide many public employees with a large measure of protection from arbitrary action, so why should public employees be allowed to organize?
4. Because fact-finding publicizes the major areas in dispute and a proposed settlement, why has it not been more successful, given the public's stake in the outcome?

KEY TERMS

chilling effect

CASE

The annual contract negotiations between the Pleasant Ridge Board of Education and the Pleasant Ridge Classroom Teachers Association (PRCTA) are due to begin July 1, one week from now. Under state law, the new contract has to be signed by September 1, or an impasse will be declared. Following an impasse, state law provides for simultaneous mediation and fact-finding. The fact-finder's report must be published no later than September 20. Under the law, the parties could arbitrate unresolved contract issues using a total-package final-offer selection approach if both agree arbitration would be binding. The state law prohibits teachers from striking, but about 10 short strikes occurred in the state last year at the time school opened.

The contract at Pleasant Ridge was not signed until November 10 last year, even though mediation and fact-finding occurred. The PRCTA had repeatedly requested arbitration of the contract dispute, but the board refused. Although no strike occurred, two "sickouts" took place in October when teacher absence rates exceeded 90 percent and schools had to be closed. For the upcoming contract, apparently considerable sentiment exists for "hitting the bricks" if negotiations are unsatisfactory.

About 5,000 students are enrolled at Pleasant Ridge in kindergarten through 12th grade. There are 250 teachers, of whom 240 are PRCTA members. Like many other established school systems, enrollment at Pleasant Ridge has been declining in recent years because of the baby bust. The impact has been greatest in the secondary grades (with a recent drop of about 6 percent annually). Now with the baby boomlet, enrollments are increasing in the elementary grades by about 10 percent annually.

The school system's operating budget is funded from two sources: state school aid based on student enrollments and local property taxes. The legislature has passed a 5 percent increase in per student funding for the upcoming school year. Local property taxes presently provide the other 60 percent, based on a 22 mill levy against assessed market value. Fifteen mills are permanently required by state law. The other seven are supplemental and are periodically reconsidered by local voters. Five of the seven mills expire this November and will be subject to reapproval by the voters in the general election. Property values are presently appreciating by 2 percent annually.

School costs are approximately equally divided between salaries and plant, equipment, and supplies. Of the 50 percent allocated to salaries, 80 percent is paid to the instructional staff represented by the PRCTA. Nonwage costs are increasing at an annual rate of 3 percent.

The PRCTA bargaining committee has just completed its contract demands. Major areas in which it demands changes include an 8 percent salary increase, a reduction in maximum class size from 30 to 25 in the elementary grades (K-6), and the granting of tenure after the second year of teaching, instead of the fourth. Because about 2,500 students are in the K-6 program, a reduction in class sizes would boost teacher employment. The tenure change would affect 25 second-year and 25 third-year teachers now uncovered. In case of staff reduction, tenured employees who are terminated are entitled to one year's pay under the contract. As part of its preparations for negotiations, the PRCTA surveyed comparable schools and found that its members' pay is about 5 percent below the market rate, that tenure is normally granted after three years, and that the median elementary class size (by contract) is 27.

As the school's governing body, the Pleasant Ridge Board of Education must ultimately approve the contract if arbitration is not used, but the school system's superintendent, personnel director, high school principal, and two elementary principals form the management bargaining team. The school board consists of five persons. Two of these are union members, and three (including these two) were endorsed by the Pleasant Ridge Central Labor Union (PRCLU) at the last election. Two others endorsed by the PRCLU lost to the other present members. At that last election, two mills of the supplementary tax were approved, but the margin was only 500 out of 10,000 votes cast.

Questions

1. What should be the initial bargaining position of the school board? What data justify this position?

2. What should the PRCTA consider a reasonable settlement?

3. If fact-finding occurs, what should the fact-finder use as criteria in recommending a settlement? What should the recommendation be?

4. Should the board go to arbitration if an agreement cannot be negotiated?

5. What strategies should the management and union negotiators use to win their demands?

6. If the negotiations go to arbitration as a final-offer package, what should each party's offer be for the arbitrator?

16

EMPLOYEE RELATIONS IN NONUNION ORGANIZATIONS

Organized labor achieved a high-water mark in the proportion of the labor force that belonged to unions in the middle 1950s and in the number of members in the early 1960s. It is difficult to predict whether these will be peaks in the history of the U.S. labor movement.

This chapter explores some characteristics of organizations with no substantial proportion of their employees belonging to unions. Even unionized organizations have many employees who aren't union members. Nonunion employees in unionized firms often are not only those statutorily forbidden from collective bargaining. Few private-sector white-collar employees have unionized. This examination focuses on attempts to avoid organizing, the economic and noneconomic policies of nonunion organizations, grievance or complaint procedures in nonunion organizations, and the formation and operation of nonunion joint management-employee committees.

In reading this chapter, consider the following issues:

1. What characteristics differentiate union from nonunion organizations?

2. How do the roles of supervisors and the operation of complaint procedures differ in nonunion organizations?

3. What legal boundaries exist regarding the mechanisms for involving employees in nonunion organizations?

4. How do the operations of personnel departments differ in nonunion organizations from those of unionized firms?

WHAT IS EMPLOYEE RELATIONS?

This book has focused to this point on the development, structure, and process of labor relations. Thus, a strong base has been established for understanding labor relations. While union and nonunion organizations have been compared in terms of certain characteristics or outcomes, practices in unionized organizations have been emphasized.

This chapter focuses on distinctive differences in nonunion organizations, as compared to union settings. In nonunion organizations, employee relations is the corollary of labor relations. One can think of employee relations as:

> . . . the reciprocal expectations and behaviors between employers and employees. In practice, employee relations encompasses the operational processes implementing an employer's philosophical or policy approaches to employment. . . . Among other things, employee relations would specify the manner in which the workplace is governed.[1]

"UNION-FREE" ORGANIZATIONS

A "union-free" organization is one that is entirely unorganized in its U.S. operations. Many companies fit this label, but among extremely large companies, they are more often in the financial services industry. Among firms with manufacturing operations, IBM is the best example of a large organization without organized employees in the United States. Some organizations with bargaining units have goals to reduce or eliminate employee representation in the future.[2] These goals can be achieved as a result of decertification elections in organized facilities or through closing, selling, or moving operations from organized locations to new facilities.

A study of large nonunion organizations concluded two types of firms can operate without unions. The first type is called *doctrinaire*. A doctrinaire organization explicitly desires to continue operating without unions and implements personnel policies it believes will lead employees to resist unions. Its personnel policies frequently mimic what unions have won in similar organizations through collective bargaining. The second type is called *philosophy-laden*. Such companies have no unions, but the lack of organizing is because of the employee relations climate of the organization. Management engages in personnel practices it believes are

---

[1] John A. Fossum, "Employee and Labor Relations in an Evolving Environment," in *Employee and Labor Relations*, SHRM-BNA Series, vol. 4, ed. John A. Fossum (Washington, D.C.: Bureau of National Affairs, 1990), pp. 4–11 to 4–12.

[2] Audrey Freedman, *Managing Labor Relations* (New York: Conference Board, 1979), p. 5.

right.[3] The policies are evidently congruent with employee desires because union-organizing activities in these firms are practically nonexistent. These two approaches will be examined as the personnel policies of both are explored.

Union Avoidance

Employer organizations have recently become more vocal in their beliefs about the legitimacy of labor organizations. Some of their leaders have questioned whether employees want union affiliation, whether unions are the friend of the poor, or whether unions have significant political influence.[4] Management typically campaigns strongly against union representation, and partially represented companies are seldom neutral in elections in nonunion plants. This approach apparently occurs without any analysis of whether the organization would be benefited or harmed by unionization and is done simply to avoid unionization whatever the costs or benefits.[5] Earlier evidence in Chapter 6 indicated profitability and share prices are negatively affected by unionization, and managers who are in charge when unions successfully organize a facility are frequently fired or demoted. Thus, while formal analysis of the effects of unionization are not undertaken by managers, they act in their own self-interest in avoiding unionization.

Environmental Factors Associated with Union Avoidance

A variety of environmental factors are associated with union avoidance, some of which can be influenced by employer choices. Employers generally believe locational choices can affect their ability to remain nonunion. Union penetration is highest in the Northeast and Midwest and lowest in the South and rural areas of the United States. Employers may make locational decisions to avoid highly unionized areas for two reasons. First, employers may believe that employees in areas where unions have relatively little membership may be less willing to join unions. Mixed evidence exists on this point, as discussed in Chapters 1 and 6. Second, plants located in areas without unions seldom enable employees to compare economic benefits provided by union and non-

---

[3] Fred K. Foulkes, *Personnel Policies in Large Nonunion Companies* (Englewood Cliffs, N.J.: Prentice Hall, 1980), pp. 45–57.

[4] R. Heath Larry, "Labor Power: Myth or Reality," *MSU Business Topics*, Winter 1979, pp. 20–24.

[5] D. Quinn Mills, "Management Performance," in *U.S. Industrial Relations, 1950–1980: A Critical Assessment*, ed. Jack Stieber, Robert B. McKersie, and D. Quinn Mills (Madison, Wisc.: Industrial Relations Research Association, 1981), pp. 114–16.

union organizations and, as a result, the employees may not become involved in organizing campaigns. This assumption rests on the belief employees will choose local plants as a logical comparison, not other plants in the industry.

Plant size may be viewed by employers as a factor associated with avoiding unions. The evidence on union election success covered in Chapter 6 found plants with fewer than 100 employees more vulnerable to unionization than larger plants. While very large plants are difficult to organize, employers may also believe the type of personnel management they would prefer to implement is difficult to inculcate in a large plant. Thus, the trend appears to be toward siting plants in labor market areas able to support medium-sized operations and planning they will generally not exceed 500 employees unless returns to scale are large. Plants also should not be smaller than 200 employees because a union can capitalize quickly on an issue in a smaller plant, and the plant population may be relatively homogeneous, enabling quicker and more nearly unanimous agreement among employees on whether to be represented.

Regardless of industry, companies founded earlier have tended to be more readily organized, reflecting what might have been the prevailing environment for personnel practices at their founding. The period during which the organization's predominant growth occurred influences unionization. For example, organizations that were founded before 1950 but grew most rapidly after that are less likely to be organized.[6]

Differences also exist among and within industries. Industries with a large proportion of white-collar workers (for example, finance) are less likely to be unionized. But within industries, some firms have not been organized while others are completely unionized. In construction, relatively new organizations remain nonunion through guaranteed employment during usual layoff periods and through the implementation of personnel policies on the organizational level. Newly incorporated, technically oriented industries also have had a relatively low level of unionization, even when they have been located in traditionally highly unionized areas. Some of this is probably due to employment security resulting from rapid growth, while other aspects of resistance to organization may be related to progressive employee relations policies and practices.

Transient Employees and Representation

Another situation in which unionization is unlikely is with a highly unstable employee population. As noted in Chapter 6, at least 50 percent of employees must agree a union is necessary before representation can

---

[6] See Arthur Stinchcombe, "Social Structure and Organizations," in *Handbook of Organizations*, ed. James G. March (Chicago: Rand McNally, 1965), pp. 142–93.

be gained. Where turnover is extremely rapid, that level of agreement might be impossible to achieve. Administration of the bargaining unit will also be difficult for the union unless a contract is negotiated containing a checkoff. With high turnover, the desires of the bargaining unit for certain contract provisions could also change rapidly. Little interest in structuring a contract to reward seniority would be likely. Unionization is also unlikely in marginal operations with very few advancement opportunities because many employees view such employment as temporary until something better comes along. Employees need to believe something is worth gaining in the employment relationship through unionization before they would be willing to expend the effort to organize.

A PHILOSOPHY-LADEN APPROACH TO EMPLOYEE RELATIONS

A model has been constructed that helps explain how a philosophy-laden approach to employee relations results in a variety of outcomes, one of which is the likely absence of a union. The model shows that environmental factors similar to those mentioned above may be involved in the location and demographics of the organization's establishments, the variety of substantive policies implemented, and company characteristics that promote the ability to achieve specific outcomes. These, in turn, lead to a particular climate or culture. The by-products of this culture are a variety of behaviors and attitudes associated with a reluctance to join unions, an avoidance of industrial conflict, and a belief the company is a good place to work. Figure 16–1 depicts the model and its interrelationships. This model will be explored in some detail in the following sections.

Wage Policies

Large nonunion organizations generally try to lead the market in their pay levels. They try to anticipate what unions will gain at the bargaining table and provide pay increases equaling or exceeding that level, awarding them at dates before unions gain theirs. Nonunion organizations may also implement merit pay policies, using performance measures to differentiate pay increases. Attention is paid to communicating pay and benefit levels and practices to employees.[7] More recently, companies are likely to have implemented skill-based pay programs to support new organiza-

---

[7] Foulkes, *Personnel Policies*, pp. 158–63.

FIGURE 16-1

Top Management's Stated Beliefs in the Worth of the Individual, Equity, Leadership by Example, and Other Attitudes, Values, Philosophies, and Goals Concerning Employees

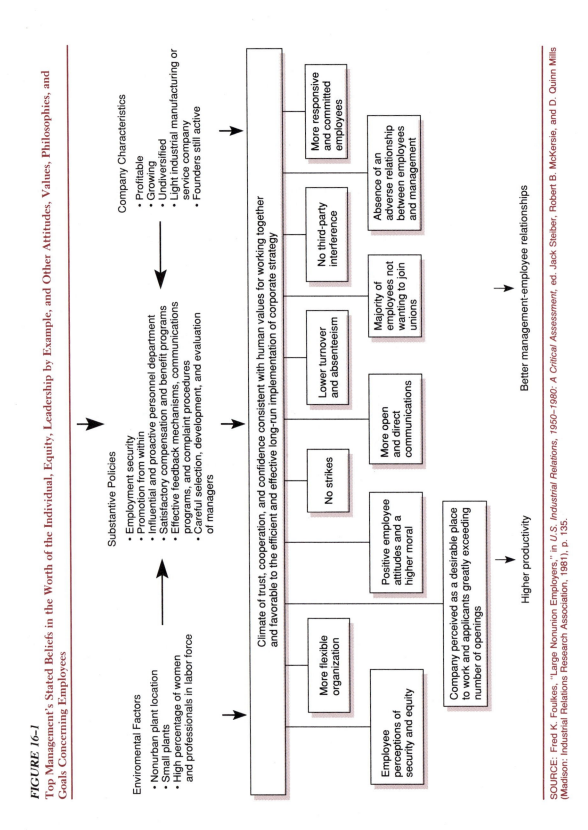

SOURCE: Fred K. Foulkes, "Large Nonunion Employers," in *U.S. Industrial Relations, 1950–1980: A Critical Assessment*, ed. Jack Steiber, Robert B. McKersie, and D. Quinn Mills (Madison: Industrial Relations Research Association, 1981), p. 135.

tional structures stressing team designs. Additionally, increasing numbers of companies are considering or implementing profit-sharing or gainsharing programs.

To accomplish these wage goals, an organization must compare favorably with others in its ability to pay.[8] Location in a growing industry with relatively high profits or a position as market leader in the industry should enable an organization to maintain its ability to pay. In turn, a high-paying employer may have an advantage in recruiting and retaining high-quality employees who are motivated to retain their high-paying jobs.[9]

If employee preferences are considered, as a philosophy-laden organization is expected to do, then benefit levels in nonunion organizations should closely lead those in union organizations because there won't be any "stickiness" associated with contractual provisions. Companies might be expected to react quickly to changing needs associated with changing age and gender mixes in its work forces.

Nonwage Policies

Union organizations generally have lower turnover and higher rates of internal promotion and transfer than nonunion organizations. If an organization sought to emulate the conditions employees desire, it would have a rationalized internal labor market with high levels of information on job opportunities available to employees.

Nonunion firms studied generally had formalized job-posting systems, with clearly communicated and unambiguous promotion criteria emphasizing both seniority and skills. Development opportunities were emphasized so that employees could develop the skills necessary to take advantage of openings likely to occur.[10]

Philosophy-laden firms generally take a career-oriented approach toward employment. Full-time nonprobationary employees are normally assumed to be likely to spend their entire careers with the organization. Thus, nonunion firms frequently require longer probationary periods or hire substantial numbers of part-time employees to provide a buffer for permanent employees during periods of fluctuating product demand.[11] Increasingly, retirement programs are structured to support earlier retirement from full-time employment coupled with part-time or seasonal work with the same employer.

---

[8] Ibid., pp. 165–67.

[9] J. Yellen, "Efficiency Wage Theory," *American Economic Review* 74, no. 2 (1984), pp. 200–5.

[10] Foulkes, *Personnel Policies*, pp. 123–45.

[11] Ibid., pp. 99–122.

Personnel Expenditures

In unionized organizations, union representation and the negotiated contract take the place of many personnel/human resource programs devised by nonunion organizations. Management has less need to attend closely to employee desires because this is the union's responsibility, and the contract spells out how employee relations will be handled. Staffing and development needs are handled through on-the-job training, and retention of employees is gained through negotiated seniority clauses and the employees' initial and continuing interest in being represented.

Nonunion organizations have higher personnel expenditures, and more personnel workers are involved in employee relations. The organization must pay more attention to compensation because it usually tries to match or exceed what unions negotiate or to construct a particular package to attract and retain employees. Development activities are emphasized. Supervisory support for problem solving is offered through the personnel department instead of the grievance system.

EMPLOYMENT SECURITY

Union members have the basis for their relative degree of employment security spelled out in the contract. Almost always, increasing competitive status seniority is associated with greater rights to continued employment in a present job or another job for which one is qualified. Recently, these rights have been of lower value where organizations have opted to close entire facilities—but even there, entitlements to transfers and severance pay are often spelled out in contracts and benefit levels increase with seniority.

Employees in nonunion organizations have their employment rights determined by their employers. Unless otherwise provided, it's legally assumed an employee is hired at the will of the employer and can be terminated for a good reason, a bad reason, or no reason at all as long as the termination is not for a reason prohibited by an employment law. Courts have increasingly narrowed employers' rights to terminate at will, particularly where employers are judged to have acted in bad faith.[12] Even where employers have contracts with employees and where a discharge could lead to a breach of contract suit, employers may be vulnerable to heavier tort damages for bad faith behavior associated with a discharge.[13]

[12] E. C. Wesman and D. C. Eischen, "Due Process," in *Employee and Labor Relations*, SHRM-BNA Series, vol. 4, ed. John A. Fossum (Washington, D.C.: Bureau of National Affairs, 1990), p. 4–117.

[13] M. J. Keppler, "Nonunion Grievance Procedures: Union Avoidance Technique or Union Organizing Opportunity," *Labor Law Journal* 41 (1990), pp. 557–62.

In the reciprocal relationship that develops in employment, employees may come to feel an implied contract exists between them and their employer. With an employee's investment in developing skills needed by his or her present employer and through conscientious application of effort, the employee sees himself or herself producing benefits for the employer. In turn, the employee may build expectations of continued employment and a willingness by the employer to provide long-term employment in return for effort and loyalty.[14]

A variety of methods are used by nonunion employers to enhance employment security for at least some employees. Given increasing needs for flexibility in the work force, employers are increasingly subcontracting or allocating jobs needing relatively little training about the employer's specific mode of operation to supplemental or complementary work forces of temporary employees. Frequently, these employees are hired on a contract basis for a particular term—usually a year or less. These employees are explicitly told they have no employment security guarantee beyond the period for which they are hired. When faced with a need for major employment reductions, employers have increasingly implemented expanded separation incentives, redeployment to other facilities with or without retraining, training programs for new occupational assignments, expanded personal leaves, and work-sharing programs involving salary and hours cuts to save jobs or provide incentives for those willing to terminate employment.[15]

Employee "Voice" Systems

Chapter 9 noted lower turnover in unionized situations might be related to an opportunity to voice needs for change through the grievance and negotiation processes. Where these mechanisms are absent, employees who desire change may be able to achieve it only by "voting with their feet."[16]

In unionized organizations, employees are able to exercise their voice on immediate matters through grievance procedures and on long-run matters through participation in negotiation committees. Those having the greatest disagreements with the organization's operations might be expected to have the most motivation to be involved in union activities at the employer level.

In nonunion organizations, the employee has no contractual entitle-

---

[14] Fossum, "Employee Relations," pp. 4–12 to 4–14.

[15] Fred K. Foulkes, "Employment Security: Developments in the Nonunion Sector," *Proceedings of the Industrial Relations Research Association* 41 (1988), pp. 411–17.

[16] A. O. Hirschman, *Exit, Voice, and Loyalty* (Cambridge, Mass.: Harvard University Press, 1970).

ment to have grievances redressed or to have a voice in how the organization should be run. Some nonunion organizations, particularly those with philosophy-laden backgrounds, have constructed elaborate systems enabling employees to voice complaints and get action on them.[17]

A model system enables an employee to communicate directly with the chief executive officer of the organization, who has a department that directly investigates causes of complaints and reports its findings. The complaining employee's superiors may be a focus of the investigation, but the employee is not identified, and no reprisals may be taken against the group from which the complaint is made. Exhibit 16–1 is a commentary on how one of these systems works.

Several methods have been devised to reduce the possibility of employee cynicism about management's commitment to neutral grievance procedures in nonunion organizations. For example, IBM operates a system that allows employees direct anonymous access to high-level management on complaints. When complaints are received, investigations are required, and the remedial action to be taken, if any, is communicated back to the grievant. Followup is monitored by high-level management.

These so-called *open-door* policies vary substantially in their real access to higher-level managers—in terms of the types of complaints or questions that can be taken up and also the degree to which employees must first contact lower-level supervisors and managers before higher-level managers will see a complaint.[18]

Many firms have created an ombudsman position to resolve grievances. The ombudsman, while technically an employee of the firm, has certain prescribed latitudes for taking action or requiring certain decisions to be made. If a complaining employee is not satisfied with a proposed management solution, the employee can ask the ombudsman to investigate the situation.[19]

Another innovative approach is creating an employee review board to act as an impartial group to resolve outstanding grievances. Where this is used, a review board of randomly chosen employees or persons at the same relative organizational level as the grievant hears evidence and renders a decision binding on the employer and the grievant.

Employees may have concerns about due process. For due process to operate, a procedure must necessarily include an objective investigator

---

[17] For an overview, see R. Bernbeim, *Nonunion Complaint Systems: A Corporate Appraisal* (New York: Conference Board, 1980).

[18] D. M. McCabe, "Corporate Nonunion Grievance Procedures: Open Door Policies—A Procedural Analysis," *Labor Law Journal* 41 (1990), pp. 551–56.

[19] D. M. McCabe, *Corporate Nonunion Complaint Procedures and Systems* (New York: Praeger Publishers, 1988).

EXHIBIT 16-1

The Open-Door Policy

The Open-Door Policy is deeply ingrained in [the company's] history. This policy is a reflection of our belief in respect for the individual. It is also based on the principle that every person has a right to appeal the actions of those who are immediately over him in authority. It provides a procedure for assuring fair and individual treatment for every employee.

Should you have a problem which you believe the company can help solve, discuss it with your immediate manager or your location's personnel manager or, in the field, with the manager of your location. You will find that a frank talk with your manager is usually the easiest and most effective way to deal with the problem.

Second, if the matter is still not resolved, or is of such a nature you prefer not to discuss it with your immediate manager or location personnel manager, you should go to your local general manager, regional manager, president or general manager of your division or subsidiary, whichever is appropriate.

Third, if you feel that you have not received a satisfactory answer, you may cover the matter by mail, or personally, with the Chairman of the Board.

SOURCE: Fred K. Foulkes, *Personnel Policies in Large Nonunion Companies* (Englewood Cliffs, N.J.: Prentice Hall, 1980), p. 300.

---

and decision maker who has the power to make a binding decision on both employee and employer.[20] Unless the employee believes the employer's procedures allow a valid appeal, the employee may prefer to take an employment grievance to court as a tort issue.[21] Nonunion procedures in the public sector are relatively similar to union grievance procedures. Peer review panels are sometimes included. Their effectiveness is related to encouraging employees to use them, training in their operation, assistance by management in processing complaints and obtaining information for grievants, and full and fair hearings together with an explanation of the decision.[22] Table 16-1 is a summary of characteristics found in several comprehensive nonunion employee grievance programs.

Several large nonunion organizations also periodically conduct attitude surveys to obtain an early identification of potentially troublesome areas. These might include certain employee groups or certain employee relations policies such as advancement, pay, or development

---

[20] D. W. Ewing, *Justice on the Job: Resolving Grievances in the Nonunion Workplace* (Boston: Harvard University Press, 1989).

[21] Keppler, "Nonunion Grievance Procedures."

[22] G. W. Bohlander and K. Behringer, "Public Sector Nonunion Complaint Procedures: Current Research," *Labor Law Journal* 41 (1990), pp. 563–67.

TABLE 16–1
Data on Boards in 11 Companies

Company	Citicorp	Control Data	Donnelly Corporation	Federal Express	General Electric (Columbia, Maryland, plant)
Name of board	Problem Review Board	Review Board	Equity Committee (5 in company)	a. Boards of Review b. Appeals Board	Grievance Review Panel
Years established	1977	1983	Late 1970s	1981	1982
Number of voting members	5	3	ca. 10–25 each	a. Boards of Review: 5 b. Appeals Board: 3	5
Terms	Ad hoc	Ad hoc	2 years	a. Boards of Review: ad hoc b. Appeals Board: ex officio	Ad hoc
Cases per year	ca. 12	ca. 8	3–4	a. Boards of Review: 37 (1986) b. Appeals Board: 209 (1986)	ca. 19
Number of cases per 1,000 employees	0.23	0.25	3	a. Boards of Review: 1 (1986) b. Appeals Board: 5 (1986)	20
Arbitration allowed as final step?	No	No	No	No	No
Reversal rate	n/a	22% (1985)	n/a	a. Boards of Review: 67% (1986) b. Appeals Board: 28% (1986)	n/a
Complaints processed by personnel staff	1982: 293 1984: 374 1986: 700	n/a	n/a	726 (1986) 62% of decisions appealed overturned	n/a

SOURCE: D. W. Ewing, *Justice on the Job: Resolving Grievances in the Nonunion Workplace* (Boston: Harvard University Press, 1989), pp. 80–81.

TABLE 16–1
(concluded)

Honeywell (DSD-USD)	John Hancock	Northrop	Polaroid	SmithKline Beckman (Pharmaceutical Division)	TWA
Management Appeal Committee	Employee Relations Committee	Management Appeal Committee	Personnel Policy Committee	Grievance Procedure	System Board of Adjustment
1981	1981	1946	1946	ca. 1971	Early 1950s
7	5	3	3	3	3
3 years	Indefinite	Ex officio	Ad hoc	Ad hoc	Ad hoc
ca. 2	15–20	15–20	ca. 20	ca. 8	50–75
0.33	1.5–2.0	0.33	2	1.3	7.1–10.7
No	No	Yes—1 case in 1984, 13 in 1986	Yes	No	No
n/a	n/a	60% (1984)	n/a	n/a	Over 50% in 1985; less than 25% in 1987–88
n/a	ca. 120 (1985)	n/a	ca. 1,000–2,000	n/a	n/a

opportunities. Given that attitudes may be precursors of subsequent behaviors, the diagnosis of potential problem spots allows management to conduct remedial activities to eliminate the potential areas of contention.

In some organizations, supervisors and managers are evaluated by their subordinates as well as by other performance indicators. They are expected to maintain a work environment leading to positive employee attitudes as measured by periodic surveys. When attitude surveys point out a problem, they may be required to devise action plans to eliminate difficulties.

Other Innovative Techniques

Some organizations have begun to hold mass meetings between employees and top-management officials to get a sense of possible problems. One approach involves meetings between top managers and groups of lower-level employees to present current problems and gripes. This "deep-sensing" approach may give top managers a better reading on the pulse rate of employee morale, and employees in turn might expect more action on their problems.

Another approach, called *vertical staff meetings*, has been implemented by the Rocketdyne Division of Rockwell International. About a dozen employees from various levels are picked at random to meet with the division's president at a monthly meeting. Problems disclosed by the attendees are followed up by the president's report to the participants.[23]

EMPLOYER/EMPLOYEE COMMITTEES

A number of organizations have formed various types of management-employee committees. Quality circles are one example of this type of device. But other situations involve employees in making recommendations to management regarding hiring, personnel assignments, hours, terms and conditions of employment, and other similar issues, which are the subject of collective bargaining in unionized organizations.

The Taft-Hartley Act forbids dominance of a labor organization by an employer. A critical question then becomes: Does an employer dominate a labor organization if it establishes and meets with employee committees and considers (among other things) some of these issues? The answer is not totally settled, but if an employer uses these committees as

---

[23] "Vertical Staff Meetings Open Lines of Communications at Rocketdyne Plant," *World of Work Report* (1979), pp. 27–28.

mechanisms for communication between employees and management but not as a means to avoid being organized, it is unlikely to be considered a dominated labor organization.[24]

The communicative activities in some of these committees may be similar to collecting attitude survey data from a sample of the plant population and using these data as a representation of the employees' attitudes. It also enables both groups to enrich their understanding of what each perceives as problems in the workplace and their causes.

In some situations, employers have also vested some supervisory activities in work groups. For example, General Foods established work groups in one plant in which the group made its own work assignments, created and operated training programs, and made recommendations on staffing decisions.[25] These were found not to be employer-dominated labor organizations.[26]

DEVELOPING PRACTICES IN NONUNION EMPLOYEE RELATIONS

An increasing number of companies have explicit union avoidance policies and tailor employee relations practices to support these goals. Several of the areas in which differences exist between companies with an explicit union avoidance policy and those without include providing more information to employees regarding their work group's productivity; more work group discussion of quality or productivity issues; more encouragement of participative mechanisms, such as quality circles and autonomous work teams; work sharing in preference to layoffs; and the development and operation of formal complaint systems.[27] Table 16-2 shows the number of positive responses toward a variety of employee relations practices among a sample of large employers.

In addition to differences in communication and participation, a major difference between new nonunion situations and traditional unionized facilities is the organization of the workplace. In an effort to increase flexibility, employers have substantially reduced the number of

---

[24] Raymond L. Hogler, "Employee Involvement Programs and *NLRB* v. *Scott & Fetzer Co.*: The Developing Interpretation of Section 8(a)(2)," *Labor Law Journal* 35 (1984), pp. 21–27.

[25] Richard E. Walton, "The Diffusion of New Work Structures: Explaining Why Success Didn't Take," *Organizational Dynamics* 3, no. 3 (1975), pp. 2–22.

[26] *General Foods*, 231 NLRB 1232 (1977).

[27] Audrey Freedman, *The New Look in Wage Policy and Employee Relations* (New York: Conference Board, 1985), pp. 16–20.

TABLE 16–2
Company Practices among Nonunion Employees

Company Initiative	Number of Companies in which:	
	Managers Are Encouraged to Develop or Sustain	Practice Exists
Information-related		
Employees are given information about competitive or economic conditions of plant or business		431
Employees track their group's quality or productivity performance		264*
Participation-related		
Employee-participation programs (quality circles, quality-of-work-life programs)	364*	
Autonomous work teams	107*	
Employees meet in small work groups to discuss production or quality		340*
Compensation-related		
Profit-sharing, gainsharing, or bonus programs for non-exempt employees	191	
Employees receive productivity or other gainsharing bonuses		121
"Payment for knowledge" compensation systems	107	
All-salaried compensation systems	173	
Miscellaneous		
Formal complaint or grievance system	378*	
Work sharing instead of layoffs	176*	
Flextime or other flexible work schedules	162	

* Statistically significant relationship with a company preference for union avoidance, at .05 or better.
SOURCE: Audrey Freedman, *The New Look in Wage Policy and Employee Relations* (New York: Conference Board, 1985), p. 17.

job classifications in manufacturing facilities. In many situations, employees are organized into teams and the team is responsible not only for production but also for maintenance of its equipment. The team may have only one or two different jobs, which are defined on the basis of skill level rather than the functional specialty of the jobholder.[28]

---

[28] Thomas A. Kochan, Harry C. Katz, and Robert B. McKersie, *The Transformation of American Industrial Relations* (New York: Basic Books, 1986), pp. 81–108.

SUMMARY

The proportion of organized employees has declined markedly over the past 30 years. Part of this is because of changing employment patterns by occupation and industry, but some is related to improved employee relations practices by employers.

Many employers have an explicit goal of avoiding unions or ridding themselves of unions presently representing employees. Employers appear to adopt one of two approaches toward unions if they are successful in remaining union free. In the doctrinaire approach, the organization maintains employee relations systems equal to or better than what unions have negotiated in comparable organizations. In a philosophy-laden approach, the organization is not explicitly concerned about unions but provides an excellent employee relations environment that makes unions superfluous. Increasingly sophisticated programs to support employment security have been designed.

A variety of recently evolved systems enable managements to communicate more readily with employees and to learn earlier about issues that might make unionization attractive to employees. These early information systems can assist organizations in making an employee relations response that eliminates the issue as a source of employee frustration.

DISCUSSION QUESTIONS

1. What conditions are necessary before a union-free environment can exist in U.S. labor relations?
2. Does it make sense for an organization to establish an explicit goal to remain union free? What costs and benefits are associated with this type of goal?
3. Think about the local area in which you reside. What characteristics appear associated with organizations that are union or nonunion in your area? Would you predict present organizing patterns to continue in the future? Why or why not?

CASE

Solroy Genetic Engineering is a five-year-old biomedical company pioneering in the production of highly purified and genetically engineered pharmaceuticals. Two products and one process have been patented, essentially assuring the long-run viability of the company. As a result of these early successes, Solroy became profitable in its fourth year.

The company now employs 325 at its newly constructed site in an industrial park in the greater St. Louis, Missouri, area. The scientific staff consists of 25 biologists, biochemists, biophysicists, and physiologists with advanced degrees. A development staff includes another 10 biomedical engineers. The administrative and professional staff consists of 20 sales representatives and 15 administrative professionals in accounting, finance, marketing, and other support areas. The top executive structure consists of the two founders and three vice presidents. Eighty employees are nonprofessional technicians, equally divided between jobs assisting the scientific staff and production activities. Production is accomplished by 140 operatives who monitor equipment and pack the completed products. They are supervised by 10 lead people who have been promoted from production ranks. There are 10 process engineers who supervise the technicians and design and oversee the production equipment.

The founders and their vice presidents have just returned from their annual fishing trip to Long Lake, Wisconsin. While this trip offers a respite from the pressure of daily activities at the plant and competition within the industry, it also involves a time for reflection and "battery recharging." On the last night of the trip, after returning to their lodge at Marawaraden Resort from the annual "bragging dinner" at Spring Waters Inn where Alvin Richards, their host, serves them their catch (occasionally needing supplementation—depending on their luck and skill), the founders reminisced about how close all of the Solroy employees had been as it grew through the first four years, and how success had seemed to lead to both growth and a loss of a family feeling. They lamented that they were losing touch with the workplace.

The group talked about a number of things they could do to restore the sense of community, including the abolition of the term *employee*, replacing it with *associate*. They also talked about how they could increase communications with employees and responsiveness to problems in the workplace. Finally, they also talked about their compensation program and its ability to reward organizational performance while holding down costs and remaining competitive.

It's now the Monday after the group has returned. Rebecca Oldmeier, the vice president for marketing, has called you (founder of a new consulting firm dealing with organization and employment issues) to consider offering a proposal to assist Solroy with developing a state-of-the-art employee relations program. What would you recommend—given cost constraints, training required, likely motives of owners and present employees, and the future growth potential and risks the organization faces?

17

A SURVEY OF
LABOR RELATIONS
IN DEVELOPED
MARKET
ECONOMIES

This chapter provides an overview of labor relations in modern industrial market economies around the world. Labor organizations vary substantially in their involvement in political activity, collective bargaining, and decision making within societies, industries, and enterprises. Labor unions differ in their organization as well. The previous chapters have dealt with a variety of development, structure, and process issues that influence and describe U.S. labor relations. The present chapter is an overview of differences in the development of labor movements and structures and the manner in which processes are implemented in market economies. The chapter will emphasize the basics in nations such as Australia, France, Germany, Japan, Sweden, and the United Kingdom; provide information on some specific aspects in Italy, the Netherlands, New Zealand, and Spain; and contrast practices with those in the United States.

By its brief nature, the chapter provides a sketchy overview that should acquaint and direct the reader to more detailed and analytical treatments.

In reading this chapter, consider the following issues:

1. What are the major differences in the prevalence and operation of labor unions in North America and Western Europe?

2. How are the plant-level needs of workers addressed in countries where bargaining occurs at the industry and employer association level?

3. How does the role of the government in labor-management relations differ across developed market-base economies?

4. What are the advantages and disadvantages to workers, unions, and employers of the various structures of labor-management relations examined?

THE DEVELOPMENT OF LABOR MOVEMENTS

In comparing industrial relations systems across countries and economies, an examination of the societies in which they develop and the periods in which they came into being helps explain current approaches. In the United States, uplift, revolutionary, business, and predatory unions were identified as representing a typology of unions. Another basis for classification identified unions as utilitarian (rational or instrumental values), idealistic (commitment or identification values), affective (emotional values), or traditional (values based on the results of previous outcomes such as utilitarian or idealistic approaches). Cultural values, ideologies, and political policies strongly influence the approach chosen by a union.[1] Table 17–1 explains this typology in greater detail.

The development of European labor unions roughly paralleled developments in the United States, with some variations across countries depending on political activities. German unions began to form with the 1848 revolution, which united the various semi-independent German states. Swedish unions gained adherents in the late 19th and early 20th centuries. British unions began to organize about the same time and in the same manner as the Knights of Labor in the United States. As this chapter will note, only British collective bargaining bears much semblance to U.S. labor relations evolving with bargaining at the plant level.

As in the United States, several variations of union activity emerged during the formative period. In the United States, the National Labor Union and the Knights of Labor espoused an uplift approach; while later the Industrial Workers of the World (IWW), anarchists, and syndicalists advocated revolutionary unionism. Germany and England were early spawning grounds of revolutionary approaches to government and employment. Karl Marx advocated the takeover of the state by the proletariat (rank and file) together with state ownership of the means of production to end the exploitation of workers. Under this approach, the goals of unions and the state would be synonymous. Anarchists and syndicalists advocated the abolition of the state and/or capitalistic ownership of the means of production. The Fabians in Great Britain and other socialists favored state ownership and planned economies to better allocate wealth among a population and to choose desired outputs.

In Sweden, labor began to organize into a variety of federations that formed the Swedish Confederation of Trade Unions (LO) in the late 1890s. This was followed by employers forming the Swedish Employers' Confederation (SAF) around 1900. In 1906, the SAF recognized the LO's right to unionize and the LO recognized managerial prerogatives. Industry-wide agreements were negotiated during the 1900–10 decade after

---

[1] M. Poole, *Industrial Relations: Origins and Patterns of National Diversity* (London: Routledge and Kegan Paul, 1986).

TABLE 17-1

Strategies and Categories of Social Action

General Categories of Social Action (orientations)	Strategies
1. *Instrumental-rational* (Zweckrational)— that is, determined by expectations as to the behavior of objects in the environment and of other human beings; these expectations are used as 'conditions' or 'means' for the attainment of the actor's own rationally pursued and calculated ends	Utilitarian, based on material interests and a 'will to power'
2. *Value-rational* (Wertrational)—that is, determined by conscious belief in the value for its own sake of some ethical, aesthetic, religious, political, or other form of behavior, independently of its prospects of success	Idealistic, based on identification and commitment
3. *Affectual* (especially emotional)—that is, determined by the actor's specific affects and feeling states	Not strategic but sentiments and emotions can enhance value-rational commitments
4. *Traditional*—that is, determined by in-grained habituation	The institutionalization of previous strategic decisions of an utilitraian or idealistic character

SOURCE: M. Poole, *Industrial Relations: Origins and Patterns of National Diversity* (London: Routledge and Kegan Paul, 1986), p. 14.

major strikes.[2] Substantial conflict continued between labor and management until the 1930s when the government moved into the hands of the Social Democrats. Labor's agenda meshed closely with the Social Democrats, separating the political and economic power of employers for the first time. After some adjustments, an era of consultation and cooperation was begun that continues to some extent today.

Japanese unions emerged in the 1890s after its industrial revolution. They were active before World War II and were encouraged during the martial law period after the war in which the United States ruled Japan. Following the war, unions exhibited Marxist tendencies while real wages were low, but became more enterprise oriented as productivity and wages increased. As in most industrialized countries, unions in Japan affiliate with federations.[3]

---

[2] W. Korpi, "Industrial Relations and Industrial Conflict: The Case of Sweden," in *Labor Relations in Advanced Industrial Societes: Issues and Problems*, ed. B. Martin and E. M. Kassalow (Washington, D.C.: Carnegie Endowment for International Peace, 1980), pp. 89–108.

[3] K. Koike, *Understanding Industrial Relations in Modern Japan* (New York: St. Martin's Press, 1988).

While many unions have supported socialist agendas and have been affiliated with labor parties in European politics, the trend has been increasingly toward accommodation of capitalism and free market economies. In Germany, unions have moved from having Marxist perspectives toward acting as intermediaries representing worker interests and ameliorating the effects of changes in supporting a dynamic economy within democratic capitalism.[4] At the same time, where the economic system of the country implies less shareholder interest in the organization, managers appear to be more pluralistically oriented.[5]

THE STRUCTURE OF LABOR MOVEMENTS

In the United States, the primary locus of authority in the labor movement is in the individual national unions, organized on a craft or industrial basis. This model does not hold for most of the rest of the industrialized world with market economies. Many of the other industrialized countries' unions concentrate their control in labor federations or at the local level.

As noted above, Swedish unions concentrate power in the LO, which, in turn, deals with the employers' SAF. In Germany, a relatively small number of national unions retain most of the power in bargaining. British unions are organized into nationals, but locals retain a fair amount of authority. Local unions in many countries have primarily geographic rather than corporate relationships.[6] Italy, France, and the Netherlands have politically or religiously based national federations. Employers in the Netherlands are also organized along religious lines.[7] Generally, national unions are increasingly merging in the European Economic Community (EEC), similar to the United States.[8] In Japan, although unions generally conduct most important business at the local or enterprise level, most affiliate with a national union.[9] Enterprise unions in Japan usually include both blue- and white-collar workers.[10]

---

[4] O. Jacobi, "World Economic Changes and Industrial Relations in the Federal Republic of Germany," in *Industrial Relations in a Decade of Economic Change*, ed. H. Juris, M. Thompson, and W. Daniels (Madison, Wis.: Industrial Relations Research Association, 1985), pp. 211–46.

[5] Poole, *Industrial Relations*.

[6] J. P. Windmuller, "Comparative Study of Methods and Practices," in *Collective Bargaining in Industrialized Market Economies: A Reappraisal*, ed. J. P. Windmuller (Geneva: International Labour Office, 1987), pp. 3–158.

[7] T. Kennedy, *European Labor Relations* (Lexington, Mass.: Lexington Books, 1980).

[8] Windmuller, "Comparative Study."

[9] Koike, *Understanding Industrial Relations*.

[10] Ibid.

There is greater entrenchment of leadership in European unions than in U.S. unions, particularly at the local level, because many officers face recurrent elections.[11]

In the United States, a variety of characteristics were related to interest and participation in union activities. The activities of Japanese union members is predicted relatively similarly. For example, length of membership in the union, pay levels, dissatisfaction with pay and working conditions, interaction with others in the work group, and perceptions of union effectiveness and democracy predict participation in Japan. Contrary to the United States, age and educational attainment were negatively related and job status was unrelated.[12]

Because members in many European countries may have little involvement in bargaining and contract negotiations at the plant or enterprise level, there is less rank-and-file participation in union activities. In Germany, most establishments are required to have **works councils.** These councils advise the establishment's management on employment matters and may also be involved in knowing the overall strategy of the organization. There may be an operational conflict between unions and works councils; evidence suggests works councils may be more interested in preserving plant interests than those of the union to which many of its employees are associated.[13] Table 17–2 shows the types of issues and level of authority works councils have in Germany. In Germany, movement has been made toward labor and management operating as "social partners." Substantial technical expertise exists in German unions with a strong permanent professional administration component. German unions are highly consolidated; only 17 major unions are currently established.[14]

When a distinction is made between craft and industrial unions, most German unions could be classified as industrials, as would those in Sweden. British and Australian unions tend to follow a craft model, which is consistent with the Australian Arbitration Court method of setting occupational wage rates.[15]

---

[11] Poole, *Industrial Relations.*

[12] S. Kuruvilla, D. G. Gallagher, J. Fiorito, and M. Wakabayashi, "Union Participation in Japan: Do Western Theories Apply?" *Industrial and Labor Relations Review* 43 (1990), pp. 374–89.

[13] K. R. Wever, "Industrial Relations Developments in France, West Germany, the U. K., and Sweden: An American Assessment," *Proceedings of the Industrial Relations Research Association* 41 (1988), pp. 361–64.

[14] C. Lane, *Management and Labour in Europe* (Hampshire, England: Edward Elgar, 1989).

[15] B. Dabscheck and J. Niland, "Australian Industrial Relations and the Shift to Centralism," in *Industrial Relations in a Decade of Economic Change,* ed. H. Juris, M. Thompson, and W. Daniels (Madison, Wis.: Industrial Relations Research Association, 1985), pp. 41–72.

TABLE 17–2

Important Participation Rights of the Works Council

Kind of Right	Social Concerns	Personnel Issues	Economic Matters
Co-determination rights (can be enforced)	Beginning and end of daily working time; planning of holidays; design of payment system; piecework and premium rates; humane organization of work in accordance with established scientific knowledge	Staff file; selection criteria; in-firm training	Social plan
Veto rights		Recruitment; redeployment; assignment to wage group; dismissal	
Consultation and Information rights	Labor protection; accident prevention	Personnel planning; Right to be heard before dismissal	Information about major business plans or changes in the firm; Consultation about: building or extending plant and changing/introducing equipment; changes in work processes or places; economic committee.

SOURCE: C. Lane., *Management and Labour in Europe* (Hampshire, England: Edward Elgar, 1989), p. 230.

ORGANIZING AND REPRESENTATION

Organizing and representation in the rest of the industrialized world outside of North America is quite unlike what occurs in the United States. With the exception of Great Britain, members of the EEC have no mechanism for workers to vote on representation. Rather, unions are recognized at the national or federation level by their employer counterparts and bargaining over a basic contract occurs at that level.

Exclusive representation is also uncommon outside of the United States. In several European countries, employers may deal with several unions in the workplace, each with slightly different representational agendas. This type of situation is particularly prevalent in countries with unions having religious ties. As will be noted below, this multiplicity in representation and the lack of exclusive jurisdiction do not appear to be problems.

Union security differs substantially across Europe. Closed shops can be negotiated in Great Britain, but in most other countries, union security is not an issue because several unions may represent employees in what would be considered a bargaining unit in the United States.[16]

BARGAINING ISSUES

Bargaining issues in other countries are both broader and narrower than in the United States. Because most countries do not have a statute enabling collective bargaining, they do not specify modes for bargaining or issues to be included. Thus, there is no definition of or distinction among mandatory, permissive, or prohibited issues. The issues chosen and the outcomes of negotiations also differ from country to country depending on the economic policies of the government and the degree to which central planning or income policies exist.[17] Further, except in Sweden and France, there is no legal duty to bargain, although it is implied in employer recognition of unions.[18] Work rules and seniority issues are seldom found in contracts and may evolve from tradition, particularly in Great Britain. These clauses are less necessary in most EEC countries because there is substantial social legislation to deal with redundancy due to economic reverses and technological changes.[19]

From an economic standpoint, the bargaining power of employers is reduced in Australia because the arbitration courts have moved toward wage indexation. A form of multilateral bargaining also occurs because Australian states can legislate directly on wages and working conditions.[20]

In France, contracts are usually negotiated annually, but the length of agreements may be indeterminate in some countries.[21] This is very contrary to U.S. approaches where contracts have tended toward longer periods and the only intracontract issues open to change are wages, and then only annually.

In Japan, unions have little say on promotion procedures, but they do

---

[16] T. Kennedy, *European Labor Relations* (Lexington, Mass.: Lexington Books, 1980).

[17] Poole, *Industrial Relations.*

[18] Windmuller, "Comparative Study."

[19] A. Sturmthal, *Comparative Labor Movements* (Belmont, Calif.: Wadsworth, 1972).

[20] Dabscheck and Niland, "Australian Industrial Relations."

[21] S. Dayal, "Collective Bargaining and Contemporary Management-Labor Relations: Analysis and Prospects," in *Advances in International Comparative Management*, ed. S. B. Prasad (Greenwich, Conn.: JAI Press, 1989), pp. 45–59.

exert control on transfers between workshops or employee groups. The group's supervisor has great influence in promotion decisions and is usually a member of the union. Regular and contract workers are from noncompeting groups. Because there is no distinction between classes of bargaining issues in Japan, unions have more influence in managerial decision making than in the United States. Issues requiring consultation or consent at the enterprise level involve improvement in production methods, conditions of labor, shop-floor environment and safety, and fringe benefits. Occasionally, consultation occurs regarding investments, product development, financial situations, recruiting, mergers, and training policies.[22]

BARGAINING STRUCTURES

With the exception of Great Britain, bargaining in most EEC countries occurs at the industry level involving national unions or federations and employer associations. In Italy, unions may bargain with the government on social issues, at the employer association and industry levels on economics, and at plant levels on working conditions.[23]

It's suggested that industry-level bargaining, coupled with works councils, enhances the ability to introduce technological change because the contract would likely address issues of redundancy. The union may take a broader look at employment security, and employers may be able to take economic adjustments to cope with retraining out of competition since all in the industry would be vulnerable for the same levels. Great Britain's tendency to negotiate at the plant and local union level has been cited as one reason British firms may be less able to incorporate technological change than other EEC members.[24] The fact that several unions frequently represent employees and obtain contracts in British firms also leads to employer and employee resistance to workplace concessions involving technological issues.

While most union-management relationships have occurred within national boundaries, the increasing importance of multinational organizations may lead to changes. Changes in local economic climates that increase global competition will make the availability of information increasingly critical for both labor and management in the future. In turn, this should increase the use of multinational consultation. But because of their interests in maintaining geographical and national differ-

---

[22] Koike, *Understanding Industrial Relations*.

[23] Kennedy, *European Labor Relations*.

[24] W. Brown, "The Effect of Recent Changes in the World Economy on British Industrial Relations," in *Industrial Relations in a Decade of Economic Change*, ed. H. Juris, M. Thompson, and W. Daniels (Madison Wis.: Industrial Relations Research Association, 1985), pp. 151–75.

entials in pay, employers will likely resist multinational negotiations.[25] In multinational companies, union officials frequently have difficulty getting access to executives who make overall industrial relations policy for their companies.[26]

IMPASSES

Strikes vary substantially in incidence and duration across industrialized nations. Incidence rates are high in Australia and New Zealand. Australia, Italy, New Zealand, Finland, Spain, Israel, Portugal, and New Zealand are high in involvement levels per 1,000 workers. Strikes are longest in the United States, Ireland, and Canada; while number of days lost per 1,000 to strikes are highest in Italy, Spain, Canada, Ireland, and Australia.[27] Strikes of any particularly long duration are unlikely in socialist economies, where they would be seen as meaningless and destructive because the workers own the means of production and strikes would rob the state (and citizens) of goods that would otherwise be produced.[28]

In Australia, conciliation and arbitration are available to settle disputes.[29] Arbitration courts establish wage rates for occupations across a broad class of employers. Ironically, strikes may follow arbitration awards to lead toward their implementation. These strikes are relatively frequent, but also short.

France requires conciliation when agreements can't be reached. Italy frequently has intracontract strikes.[30]

UNION-MANAGEMENT COOPERATION

Different mechanisms have been developed to enhance union-management or worker-manager cooperation. This has been particularly well developed in Germany through the implementation of works councils.

In Japan, enterprise-level labor councils frequently exist in the steel and auto industires. Managements and unions have negotiated profit-

---

[25] H. R. Northrup, D. C. Campbell, and B. J. Slowinski, "Multinational Union-Management Consultation in Europe: Resurgence in the 1980s?" *International Labour Review* 127 (1988), pp. 525–43.

[26] D. Kujawa, "Labor Relations of U.S. Multinationals Abroad," in *Labor Relations in Advanced Industrial Societies: Issues and Problems*, ed. B. Martin and E. M. Kassalow (Washington: Carnegie Endowment for International Peace, 1980), pp. 14–42.

[27] Poole, *Industrial Relations*.

[28] J. Wilczynski, *Industrial Relations in Planned Economies, Market Economies, and the Third World* (New York: St. Martin's Press, 1983).

[29] B. Dabscheck and J. Niland, "Recent Trends in Collective Bargaining in Australia," in *Collective Bargaining in Industrialized Market Economies: A Reappraisal*, ed. J. P. Windmuller (Geneva: International Labour Office, 1987), pp. 161–76.

[30] Kennedy, *European Labor Relations*.

TABLE 17-3
A Comparative Analysis of the Main Types of Industrial Democracy

Type	Defining Characteristics	Structural Properties	Range of Incidence	Key Examples
1. Workers' self-management	Occurs in decentralized socialist economies; a substantial degree of workers' participation on the main decision-making bodies and the overall right of the work force to use but not to own the assets of the enterprise	Typical organs of administration include workers' assemblies, workers' councils, and representation on management committees	Algeria, Peru, Poland, Yugoslavia, and various Third World and eastern European societies	Yugoslavia
2. Producer co-operatives	Occur in a variety of political economies; workers' ownership with market mechanisms	Many workers own stock, ownership is widely distributed, workers participate in enterprise management and control and share in the distribution of the surplus (profits)	Very wide-ranging, including many Third World countries, France, Italy, Spain, USA, and UK	Mondragon (Basque provinces of Spain)
3. Co-determination	Rights of workers' representatives to joint decision making on actual enterprise boards in predominantly private enterprise economies	Single- or two-tier boards (supervisory and management), varying rights to veto and proportion of workers' representatives on main board(s)	Widely practised in western Europe (e.g. Italy, Norway, Sweden, West Germany) Africa (e.g. Egypt), and South America (e.g. Argentina)	West Germany
4. Works councils and similar institutions	Varying political economies, bodies which regularly meet with management on enterprise issues	Representatives of work force elected, varying degree of legalism or voluntarism and extent to which committees are constituted solely by employees and are joint bodies	Broad-ranging, including Finland, Indonesia, Netherlands, Spain, Sri Lanka, West Germany, and Zambia	Netherlands West Germany

TABLE 17-3
(concluded)

Type	Defining Characteristics	Structural Properties	Range of Incidence	Key Examples
5. Trade union action				
a. Disjunctive via collective bargaining	Pluralist societies, acknowledgment of conflicting interests accommodated through trade union-management negotiations	Trade union channel of representation on workers' side, varying degrees of legalism and voluntarism and levels at which bargaining is conducted	The most common form of participation in pluralist societies. Examples include Australia, Canada, USA, and UK	United States United Kingdom
b. Integrative	State socialism or corporatism; trade union rights to determine various issues within a framework of harmoniously conceived interests of management, trade union, and the state	Trade unions have responsibility for areas such as holiday arrangements and influence decisions over dismissals, safety, welfare, and working conditions but are integrated into both management and the state	The typical role for trade unions in a planned economy whether under state socialism or corporatism	USSR Eastern Europe
6. Shop-floor programs	Workers' initiatives and new concepts of work organization; participation by employees in the organization of work in various political economies (e.g., autonomous work groups and quality-of-work-life programs)	Influence of workers varies depending on program, though usually task-based	Very wide-ranging worker practices and accommodative management techniques in First, Second, and Third Worlds	Scandinavia USA

SOURCE: M. Poole, *Industrial Relations: Origins and Patterns of National Diversity* (London: Routledge and Kegan Paul, 1986), pp. 154–56.

sharing arrangements that help to make pay more flexible and to enhance worker job security. Many plants may periodically have large-scale job shifts to introduce variety and enhance the breadth of employee skills.[31]

Industrial democracy has developed to a much higher degree in most industrialized countries than in the United States. There is also a greater incidence of worker-owned cooperatives, input into managerial selection, and other consultations of unions. Table 17–3 shows types of industrial democracy in industrialized nations.

CONTRACT ADMINISTRATION

Large differences exist in contract administration because there are such great differences in bargaining structure and because the contract is simply a basic agreement in many countries and individual plants and employees may add to it.

In Canada, labor law forbids intracontract strikes and requires binding arbitration of unresolved grievances even if the parties have not negotiated it into an agreement.[32] Where unresolved grievances remain in France, conciliation is required; while in Italy, they are referred to the courts.[33]

In Germany, disputes may arise occasionally within works councils with worker and management representatives at odds. Strikes are not permitted to pressure a settlement. By law, disputes over works council discussions must be settled by arbitration.[34]

PUBLIC-SECTOR UNIONIZATION

Collective bargaining in the public sector internationally is somewhat akin to the differences found among states in the United States. Its level and practice depends largely on the relative development of private-sector unionism and the friendliness of the ruling political party. For example, public-sector unions were defensive during most of Margaret Thatcher's term as prime minister in the United Kingdom. As in the United States, a variety of impasse procedures are used and significant differences exist as to what are considered permissible bargaining issues.[35]

---

[31] K. Kawahito, "Labor Relations in the Japanese Automobile and Steel Industries," *Journal of Labor Research* 11 (1990), pp. 231–38.

[32] R. J. Adams, B. Adell, and H. N. Wheeler, "Discipline and Discharge in Canada and the United States," *Labor Law Journal* 41 (1990), pp. 596–600.

[33] Kennedy, *European Labor Relations.*

[34] International Labour Office, *World Labour Report*, 2 (Geneva: International Labour Office, 1985), pp. 5–52.

[35] International Labour Office, *World Labour Report*, 1989 (Geneva: International Labour Office, 1989), pp. 105–25.

SUMMARY

Labor relations in other industrialized countries is conducted in a variety of modes. Generally, union power tends to reside in labor federations on the continent and at the enterprise level in Great Britain and Japan. Works councils are most prominent in Germany and Sweden. Employees may be represented by more than one union in a workplace, and recognition is gained through the bargaining process.

Bargaining issues are much more broadly defined than in the United States because there is no legislation in most EEC countries differentiating between so-called *mandatory* and *permissive* issues. Bargaining structures are more centralized; employer associations represent a large number of employers within an industry, and federations or national unions bargain with them. By contrast, in Japan, most decisions are made on the enterprise level.

Most European countries have strikes of shorter duration than in the United States, but strike incidence rates are higher in Australia and New Zealand, Italy, and Finland. Conciliation is mandated in some countries, and arbitration precedes contracting for wages in Australia.

DISCUSSION QUESTIONS

1. Given the degree of democracy found in U.S. political jurisdictions, why isn't there more democracy in the workplace?
2. Why are there such large differences in Germany and Japan in the structure of unions and managements for negotiation, yet such similar levels of consultation in the workplace?
3. Could religious or politically affiliated unions have an effective role in labor relations in the United States?
4. Are the concepts of exclusive representation and mandatory bargaining issues anachronisms in a modern industrial society?

KEY TERMS

works councils

GLOSSARY

ability to pay   The economic ability of the employer to grant a wage increase.

accretion   The adding of a group of employees to an existing bargaining unit.

across-the-board increase   An equal cents-per-hour increase for all jobs in a bargaining unit.

ad hoc arbitrator   An arbitrator appointed to hear a particular case or set of cases.

administrative law judge   A judge charged with interpreting the application of federal labor law in unfair labor practice cases that are not settled between the parties.

agency shop   A union security clause that requires employees who are not union members to pay a service fee to the bargaining agent.

ally doctrine   The employees of a secondary employer do not commit an unfair labor practice by refusing to perform struck work.

American Federation of Government Employees (AFGE)   An industrial-type union asserting jurisdiction over employees of the federal government.

American Federation of Labor   The first permanent national labor organization. It brought together a set of craft unions in 1883 and evolved a business unionism approach toward influencing employers and public policy.

American Federation of Labor–Congress of Industrial Organizations (AFL–CIO)   The primary labor federation for international union affiliation in the United States. It coor-

dinates national public policy initiatives for the labor movement.

American Federation of State, County, and Municipal Employees (AFSCME)   The dominant industrial-type union organizing nonfederal public-sector employees.

American plan   A strategy used by employers in the 1920s that aimed at casting organized labor in an outsider role to employees. It fostered company unions and opposed nonemployees from being able to act as bargaining representatives.

appropriate bargaining unit   A group of employees the National Labor Relations Board determines to be a reasonable unit in which a representation election will be held.

arbitrability   A grievance is arbitrable if it alleges a violation under the contract and if the contract terms allow it to be settled through arbitration.

arbitration   A dispute resolution procedure in which a neutral third party hears the positions of the parties and renders a decision binding on both. The arbitrator draws his or her power from the agreement of the parties to abide by the decision and/or the creation of the position in a contract to handle any disputes arising under the contract.

Area-Wide Labor Management Committee (AWLMC)   An organization of industrial and trade union leaders in a given geographical region whose goal is to deal with employment problems of common concern. Usually these are aimed at promoting labor-management cooperation to enhance job security and

536

competitiveness, especially in an area experiencing economic decline.

associate member   A proposed status for union membership in which an individual who is not in a bargaining unit can receive group benefits through union membership.

attitudinal structuring   The techniques and processes aimed at changing a party's position toward bargaining issues in negotiations.

authorization card   A card signed by an employee to authorize the union to act as his or her bargaining representative. It is necessary for establishing a sufficient interest to request an election from the NLRB.

bad faith bargaining   A practice by an employer or union that constitutes a refusal to bargain, a refusal to discuss mandatory issues, or to insist until impasse on a permissive issue.

bargaining book   A collection of contract clauses and their history, the desired position of the party on an issue in negotiation, and acceptable levels for settlement.

bargaining convention   A meeting of union delegates to determine the union's position on mandatory bargaining issues in an upcoming negotiation.

bargaining order   An order from the NLRB requiring an employer to bargain with a union where a representation election failed, but the employer's egregious conduct eroded the union's majority.

bargaining power   The ability of one side in a dispute to inflict heavier loss on the other than it will suffer.

bargaining structure   The organizational nature of the relationship between union(s) and employer(s) in contract negotiations including a specification of the employees and facilities covered.

bargaining unit   A collection of employees with similar interests who are represented by a single union representative. For organizing purposes, bargaining units would be within the same employer. For bargaining purposes, they might involve several employers.

benefit status seniority   The seniority in a bargaining unit entitling an employee to a certain level of benefits, usually dating from date of hire (adjusted by layoffs or leaves).

board-directed (or petition) election   A representation election in which the NLRB determines the bargaining unit in which the election will be conducted.

boycott   A refusal by individuals not directly involved in a labor dispute to deal with the employer directly involved. For example, if a clerks' union struck a store, a boycott would occur when some segment of the general public (usually union members) refused to patronize the store until the dispute was settled.

bumping   The assertion of a competitive status seniority right of an employee who is going to be laid off to claim a different job held by another employee who has lower competitive status seniority.

business agent   A permanent union employee who administers the contract and provides services to union members in a local union representing employees across several employers, particularly in the construction industry.

business unionism   An approach in which collective bargaining is the union's primary objective, leading to the betterment of the workers they represent.

"C" (charge) cases   The NLRB cases involving allegations of unfair labor practices against an employer or union.

cease and desist orders   The orders by the NLRB to stop conduct that violates labor law.

central bodies   The collections of local

unions at the city or state level for the purposes of political activity. Their support is directly from the AFL–CIO.

certification   This occurs when the NLRB determines the results of a representation election. Certification bars an election in the same unit for one year.

checkoff   A collective bargaining agreement provision in which the employer agrees to deduct union dues from employees' pay.

"chilling" effect   The assumption that the availability of interest arbitration decreases the willingness of the parties to negotiate an agreement.

civil service system   A public-sector employment system defining rules for hiring and promotion. It insulates employees from political patronage by preserving certain jobs as not vulnerable to loss when political parties change.

closed shop   A collective bargaining clause requiring that a prospective employee be a union member before employment. It is unlawful under federal labor law.

coalition bargaining   A bargaining structure in which a group of unions simultaneously bargains with a single employer.

collective bargaining   The collective aspect of collective bargaining is the exclusive representation by the union of the collection of people in a bargaining unit. Bargaining represents the negotiation of labor agreements and their administration during the period in which they are in effect.

Collyer doctrine   The NLRB's policy of deferring the disposition of unfair labor practice charges to pending arbitration.

Committee for Industrial Organization (later Congress of Industrial Organizations)   A group of trade unionists interested in the early 1930s in organizing unskilled workers by industry. Later, as they were successful, the unions that were created formed the Congress of Industrial Organizations.

common situs picketing   The picketing of a facility used by several employers. An action aimed at a single employer may cause unionized employees of other employers to refuse to cross the picket line.

community of interests   The degree to which the employees in a proposed unit have common interests in bargaining outcomes. It is one of the most frequent criteria the NLRB uses to determine the scope of a bargaining unit in petition elections.

company union   An employer-established labor organization established for a single firm's employees. It is unlawful under federal labor law.

comparable worth   A concept under which work of comparable value, generally as measured by job evaluation, would be paid equally. Its net effect is essentially to raise the pay of comparably rated female-dominated occupations to levels of male-dominated occupations.

competitive status seniority   The seniority levels of employees that entitle them to certain jobs, bid on certain jobs, bump, or avoid layoffs. It is usually calculated from the date of promotion into a given job or job group.

concession bargaining   A negotiating situation in which the union is asked to give back previously won economic levels.

consent elections   A representation election in which there is no dispute between the employer and union about which employees would be represented if the union won.

conspiracy doctrine   The legal approach holding that any union activity among a collection of individuals was ultimately aimed to restrain trade through the fixing of wages.

constitutional conventions   Periodic national meetings required by the constitutions of labor unions to elect officers, adopt positions, and amend their constitutions (as necessary).

constructive seniority The establishment of a basis for seniority that would exist if an employee were not the victim of illegal discrimination.

contract administration The process a union and management pursue in complying with the contract during its term.

coordinated bargaining The cooperation between two or more unions in bargaining with a single employer. This method may involve observation of bargaining by other unions or coordinating bargaining demands.

corporate campaign An activity by unions in difficult organizing or bargaining situations to pressure companies whose officers are members of the board of directors of the target company with public relations campaigns. It is frequently used against banks and aimed at informing the public of the connection between the target company and potential supporting companies.

cost-of-living adjustments The contract terms that adjust pay in response to changes in the level of the consumer price index. These terms are aimed at keeping the real value of pay constant over the term of the agreement.

craft A skilled occupation or trade.

craft severance An action by the NLRB to remove craft employees from a bargaining unit because their community of interests is dissimilar.

craft union A national union representing predominantly employees in one occupation, such as the Carpenters Union.

decertification election An election to determine whether a majority of bargaining unit employees still favors union representation.

defined benefit pension plan A pension plan guaranteeing a certain payment level at retirement. It is usually based on the average of the final two or three years' pay and length of service.

defined contribution pension plan A pension plan with a specific formula for calculating employer contributions toward retirement. The ultimate level of benefits depends on the amount of contributions and the investment experience of the plan.

distributive bargaining The bargaining over issues in which one party's gain is the other party's loss.

dual commitment The notion that an individual can be simultaneously committed to his or her employer and union.

dual governance The notion that individuals have opportunities for the governance of their workplace through electing officers of their bargaining unit representatives and voting on contract ratification.

duty to bargain The duty by both parties under federal labor law, following recognition or certification of a union, to bargain over wages, hours, and terms and conditions of employment.

economic strike A strike following the expiration of a contract over an impasse on any mandatory bargaining issue. Strikers may be replaced.

election bar The certification of an election prohibits another election in the same unit for a year.

employee Any person who is not an employer or supervisor and who is involved in a labor dispute, according to Taft-Hartley.

employee involvement A name for a variety of plans in which employers provide more employee voice in the operation of the work setting. It is usually included with problem-solving activity.

employee stock ownership plan　A plan in which employees acquire part or all of the shares of stock in a private-sector organization.

employer　An organization or manager acting for an organization within the jurisdiction of the labor acts.

***Excelsior* list**　A list of employees and their addresses that employers must turn over to the union when the NLRB authorizes a representation election.

exclusive representation　All individuals within a bargaining unit are represented by the union for purposes of collective bargaining regardless of whether they voted for representation or whether they are union members.

executive committee　The elected executive officers of a local union.

Executive Order 10988　An order issued by President Kennedy allowing federal employee bargaining units where a majority of employees vote for representation. Bargaining was limited to terms and conditions of employment.

expedited arbitration　An arbitration method that speeds the process and reduces the formality of the proceedings.

fact-finding　A third-party method used to develop information about the issues in dispute and recommend a potential settlement.

fair representation　The requirement that the union treat all bargaining unit members equally in processing grievances.

Federal Labor Relations Authority　The federal employment equivalent of the National Labor Relations Board. It oversees representation elections and rules on unfair labor practice allegations.

Federal Mediation and Conciliation Service　A federal agency created by the Taft-Hartley Act to assist employers and unions in bargaining through mediation, particularly in situations where they have reached impasses.

Federal Service Labor-Management Relations Statute　Title VII of the Civil Service Reform Act of 1978 codifying the right of federal employees to organize. Bargaining rights do not extend to economic or staffing issues. It created the Federal Labor Relations Authority.

field representatives　The full-time international union employees who provide organizing services and services to local unions in negotiations and grievance processing.

final-offer arbitration　A variant of interest arbitration in which the arbitrator must choose one of the offers of the parties. Variants of final-offer arbitration may require an arbitrator to select the entire package or to select one or the other party's offers on each issue.

fractional bargaining　A tactic a union might use in contract administration to pressure the employer to make concessions on issues that could not be won in bargaining.

Fraternal Order of Police　A major collective bargaining representative for police. It began as a benevolent organization and turned to collective bargaining when legislation enabled it and unions to begin to organize police.

functional democracy　The availability of union member checks on their environment through voting for local union members and ratification of contracts in their establishments.

gainsharing　A flexible compensation system in which employees receive bonuses based on labor and/or material savings as compared to a base period.

good faith bargaining   The willingness of the parties to meet at reasonable times and places to discuss mandatory bargaining issues.

greenfield operation   A newly opened plant in a location in which the employer has never had operations previously. It is usually part of an employer strategy to avoid unions or reduce the proportion of employees represented.

grievance   Any complaint any employee has against an employer. In collective bargaining, an allegation that the employer has violated the collective bargaining agreement.

hiring hall   The union office, in the building trades, at which tradespeople congregate to take available jobs for which employers have asked the unions to provide workers.

hot cargo   The goods made by nonunion labor that unionized employees refuse to transport or install.

impasse   An inability to agree on a contract which follows an unwillingness by both parties to concede further.

implied contract   A pattern of practices and expectations that lead employees to assume employers will continue to treat them in an established manner.

Impro-Share   A gainsharing plan in which groups of employees receive bonuses as a result of producing products in fewer hours than standards require.

industrial union   A national union representing predominantly employees employed in a single industry, such as United Auto Workers.

Industrial Workers of the World   A revolutionary union founded in the late 1800s that urged the end of the capitalistic system and worker control of the means of production. It was strongly opposed by employers, and its leaders were jailed during World War I for opposing the war.

industry-wide bargaining   A bargaining structure in which all (or many) employers in an industry bargain simultaneously with a single union.

injunctions   The court orders requiring that certain actions be stopped.

integrative bargaining   Bargaining over issues in which both parties may achieve a better position than the one held previously.

interest arbitration   Arbitration over the contents of the contract.

internal labor market   The pattern of rules and practices governing promotions and transfers within an organization among the set of jobs for which employees are not hired externally.

International Association of Fire Fighters (IAFF)   The dominant craft-type union organizing fire fighters. The IAFF has been highly successful in influencing public-sector legislation enabling bargaining for municipal employees.

international unions   The organizations chartering local unions representing certain crafts, industries, or as general unions. International unions are the level at which control ultimately resides in the labor movement.

intraorganizational bargaining   The activities that occur within a bargaining team that lead to agreements on positions and concessions in negotiations.

job evaluation   A procedure used to measure the relative value of jobs to an organization. It usually examines factors such as skill, effort, responsibility, and working conditions.

job posting   A procedure for publicizing to employees the availability of open positions and eligibility rules for being considered for them.

job security   The retaining of employment with a given employer until the employee voluntarily retires or quits once a probationary period is completed.

Joint Labor-Management Committee   An organization of employers and a labor union designed to deal with common industry-wide problems in an integrative manner.

journeyman   The job level in a skilled trade one attains following successful completion of an apprentice program.

Knights of Labor   A post–Civil War national union movement in which employees joined city central unions. Leaders advocated arbitration to settle disputes. The knights declined rapidly after the formation of the American Federation of Labor in 1883.

labor-management committee   A form of consultation in which representatives of a local bargaining unit and management confer on employment and production problems that are not included within the contract.

laboratory conditions   The environment the NLRB has desired to surround union representation elections to allow the employee to make a free and uncoerced choice regarding representation.

Landrum-Griffin Act   A law passed in 1959 aimed at increasing democracy in unions and ensuring individual rights. It also modified Taft-Hartley.

local union   The union body closest to the members. It is usually established in a particular geographic location to represent employees in either one employer or one industry. Officers are elected and frequently remain employed full-time.

logrolling   A practice in bargaining in which sets of dissimilar issues are traded.

maintenance of membership clause   A union security clause in which employees who become union members during the agreement are required to remain members.

make-whole orders   The orders by the NLRB to restore employment and back pay to employees who are victims of unfair labor practices.

management rights clause   A contract clause specifying certain areas in which management reserves the right to make and implement decisions.

mandatory bargaining issue   An issue that is statutorily required to be discussed if one of the parties in bargaining raises it.

median voter   The middle person, from an opinion perspective, in a bargaining unit. For any two alternate decisions, assuming that voter opinions lie along a continuum, the median voter must vote for the winning alternative.

mediation   A process involving a neutral party who maintains communications between bargainers in an attempt to gain agreement.

mediators   The neutral people who attempt to help parties to settle disputes. Mediators have no power to impose solutions but rather focus on keeping lines of communication open and exploring alternative settlements with disputing parties.

modified union shop   A union security clause in which employees who are hired after a specified date are required to become union members.

Mohawk Valley formula   An employer approach toward organizing campaigns in the 1930s in which organizers were branded as outsiders and communists, and local public interests were stirred against organizing.

monopoly power   The ability of a union to increase wages as a result of controlling the labor supply to the firm.

multiemployer bargaining   A consensual relationship between employers and a union in which bargaining on a contract involves all employers in the unit and the terms and conditions of the ultimate agreement apply equally to all employers.

multilateral bargaining   The tendency of elected officials to become involved in public-sector labor negotiations, thus creating a tripartite bargaining situation in which the employer, the union, and elected officials are the parties.

narcotic effect   the assumption that parties who have experienced interest arbitration will be more likely to use it in the future than those who have not.

national departments   The offices within unions created to bargain and administer contracts with major national employers.

National Education Association (NEA)   A professional association of elementary and secondary public school teachers with chapters in all states that is now involved in organizing and collective bargaining where permitted and has expanded its jurisdiction to higher education.

National Labor Relations Board   The federal agency created by the Wagner Act that has responsibility for investigating and ruling on unfair labor practice charges and holding and certifying the results of representation elections.

National Labor Union   A post–Civil War uplift union.

National Mediation Board   The agency that mediates contract disputes between employers and unions covered by the Railway Labor Act. It holds representation elections.

National Railroad Board of Adjustment   The group originally designed to handle unresolved grievances under the Railway Labor Act. Since there were equal numbers of management and union representatives, an independent arbitrator renders the decision.

national union   *See* international union.

negotiation committee   The local union committee responsible for contract negotiations and decisions on grievance handling above the entry-level steps.

Norris-LaGuardia Act   An act passed in 1932 prohibiting federal courts from enjoining lawful union activities and forbidding enforcement of yellow-dog contracts.

ombudsman   An individual designated to expedite the settlement of disputes within an organization. The person usually has investigative powers and powers to impose settlements.

"open door" policy   A policy in which employees have access to higher-level management to complain about problems in their work unit. These programs are usually accompanied by investigative units and formal feedback to the employee about the disposition of the problem raised.

open shop   An employment arrangement in which an employee would never be required to join a union as a condition of continued employment.

organizing campaign   The set of activities involved in attempting to gain recognition for a union and representation for employees to collectively bargain with their employer.

past practice   A traditional work practice or rule on which the employees rely even though not a part of the collective agreement.

pattern bargaining   A bargaining tactic in which employers or unions seek agreements that imitate those previously concluded in other bargaining rounds in the industry.

pay form   The manner in which pay is provided, such as cash, deferred compensation, insurance, paid time off, etc.

pay level   A comparison between the average pay rates of a given employer and the market averages for comparison jobs.

pay structure   The rates and ranges of pay assigned to different jobs in the organization.

pay system   The set of rules used by an organization or included in a contract to determine how an individual employee's pay will change.

permanent umpire   An arbitrator named in a contract who hears all cases within his or her area that may come up under the agreement.

permissive bargaining issue   An issue that does not statutorily require bargaining and one that cannot be used to go to impasse.

picketing   The act of parading at an employer's site to inform the public about the existence of a labor dispute and asking other union members and the public not to cross.

Political Action Committee (PAC)   An employer or union organization to raise and disburse funds to support political candidates.

predatory unionism   A situation in which the primary goal of the union is to gain the dues of the employees and extract side payments from employers in return for beneficial contracts.

production committee   A work unit-level committee consisting of rank-and-file employees and the unit's supervisor that acts on employee suggestions in the Scanlon plan.

professional association   An organization formed to pursue the interests of professional employees without functioning as a collective bargaining representative.

professional employee   An employee, under the Wagner Act, with substantial education and working without close supervision in a professional job. The employee cannot be included in a nonprofessional bargaining unit without majority vote of the professionals.

profit sharing   A flexible compensation system in which employees receive bonuses based on the profitability of a unit or firm.

prohibited bargaining issue   An issue the parties are statutorily forbidden to include in their contract.

quality circles   A group of employees who meet to apply statistical process control methods to improve the quality of production.

quality-of-work-life   The programs aimed at improving the work environment to enhance employee safety and satisfaction. They usually involve joint labor-management committees.

"quickie" strikes   Short strikes an employer can't anticipate designed to disrupt production and force an employer to bargain with or recognize a union.

"R" (representation) cases   Petitions for certification elections.

"raid" elections   An election to determine whether a new union should succeed the present bargaining agent.

Railway Labor Act   The labor act passed in 1926 that applies to the rail and airline industries. It establishes craft-oriented bargaining units and requires bargaining with majority representatives who have exclusive rights to bargain for employees in unit. The act established the National Mediation Board and the National Railroad Board of Adjustment.

recognitional picketing   The act of picketing to inform the public that the employer is not represented and requesting recognition. It is prohibited after 30 days if the employer requests and wins an election.

regional director   The top NLRB official in each of its regions, having broad power to deal with representation election certifications and unfair labor practice charges and investigations.

relations by objectives   A program initiated by the FMCS to train parties who have strained bargaining relationships to improve communications and focus more closely on desired bargaining outcomes.

representation   The union's role as the employees' agent in employment matters.

representation election   An election to determine whether unrepresented employees desire to be represented by a union for the purposes of collective bargaining.

revolutionary unionism   An approach in which the union movement mobilizes to change the ownership of the means of production, commonly toward a socialist approach.

right-to-work law   A state law, permitted under section 14b of the Taft-Hartley Act, prohibiting the negotiation of union or agency shop clauses, thereby forbidding the requirement of union membership as a condition of continued employment.

rights arbitration   The arbitration over interpretation of the meaning of contract terms or entitlements to outcomes.

roll up   The amount by which overtime payments and fringe benefits increase as the base wage rate is increased.

Rucker plan   A gainsharing program in which employees, as a group, receive bonuses for improvements in labor productivity and reductions in material costs.

Scanlon plan   A gainsharing program in which employees, as a group, receive bonuses for improvements in labor productivity.

screening committee   A committee of employee and management representatives under the Scanlon plan that handles suggestions referred to it from lower-level production committees.

secondary boycott   An action asking the public not to patronize an uninvolved party doing business with an employer who is involved in a labor dispute. It is unlawful under federal labor law.

seniority   The period of time between when an individual was hired or moved into a current job and the present.

"sick-out"   A concerted action to withhold labor in situations where strikes are not permitted.

sit-down strike   An illegal strike in which employees cease work in place and refuse to leave. This type of strike also denies the employer the use of the facility.

skill-based pay   A pay plan basing pay rates on the acquired skills of employees specific to the work environment. Pay is based on skills or knowledge rather than the job the person happens to be assigned to.

spillover effect   The tendency for economic gains won in collective bargaining to influence pay practices for nonunion employees and employers.

standard of living   The absolute level of goods and services an individual can purchase with his or her pay.

Steelworkers' trilogy   A set of three Supreme Court decisions essentially establishing arbitration as the *final* decision-making step in the grievance procedure when the parties have agreed to include it in a contract.

stewards   The elected or appointed shop floor union representatives responsible for interpreting the contract for union members and processing grievances.

subcontracting   Contracting with another employer to perform work that bargaining unit employees could perform.

superseniority   The state of having greater seniority than any other individual in the bargaining unit. It is usually conferred on stewards to protect union governance in case of layoffs.

supervisor   An employee who is an agent of management and who has the power to effectively hire, fire, and make compensation decisions for subordinates.

supplementary unemployment benefits An employer-provided benefit added to unemployment benefits to bring an employee's payments during unemployment closer to pay for work.

sympathy strike   A strike by a union not involved in negotiations in support of a union that is.

Taft-Hartley Act   The act amending and extending the Wagner Act to include union unfair labor practices. It also established the FMCS, provided for dealing with national emergency strikes, and regulated suits by union members against their unions.

team concept   A work design in which groups of employees are assigned to produce a given product, assembly, or service. All employees in the group are expected to be able to perform all tasks. Worker autonomy is increased because the group is responsible for supervising its own activities.

totality of conduct   The sum total of conduct of employers or unions, rather than each individual act, in organizing campaigns or bargaining may be determinative of unfair labor practices.

trusteeship   A situation in which a national union takes over operation of a local union as a result of its violation of the union constitution.

twenty-four-hour rule   The NLRB rule forbidding union and management campaigning in certification elections in the last full day before the election.

two-tier pay plan   A pay structure variant in which groups of employees are paid different rates for performing the same job. It is usually included as a concessionary clause with newly hired employees being paid at lower rates. Some plans merge employees after a period of time, while others create permanent differences.

unfair labor practice strike   A strike by employees to pressure an employer to stop an unfair labor practice. Employees are entitled to reinstatement if they are fired or replaced.

unfair labor practices   The activities by a management or union that violate Section 8 of the Taft-Hartley Act.

union   An organization established to represent the interests of employees. Under U.S. statutes, to be considered as a union, an organization must seek to represent groups of nonsupervisory employees, and after being designated as a representative, collectively bargain for the employees it represents.

union security   The level of permanency in representation negotiated into a labor agreement, such as a union shop.

union shop   A contract clause requiring that all employees who are members of the bargaining unit must become union members following completion of a probationary period as new employees.

uplift unionism   An approach in which the labor movement's primary goal is to better society as a whole.

voice power   The ability of the union as a collective group of employees to influence employment policies and redress grievances.

Wagner Act   The law that provided for collective bargaining for handling labor disputes, recognized the right to representation, established the National Labor Relations Board, initiated exclusive representation within bargaining units, defined employer unfair labor practices, and specified rights and duties of employers and unions in bargaining.

whipsawing A bargaining tactic in which a union settles contracts sequentially, demanding a higher settlement in each subsequent negotiation.

wildcat strike An intracontract strike in violation of a no-strike clause.

working to rules The act of meticulously following the contract and work rules to degrade productivity and pressure an employer to settle on the union's terms.

works council A bipartite board in Germany involving employee and management representatives in consultation over issues involving staffing, strategy, health and safety, technological change, and other issues of concern to workers in the organization.

yellow-dog contract An agreement between an employee and an employer in which the employee indicates that he or she is not a member of a labor union and that joining a labor union in the future will be sufficient grounds for dismissal.

AUTHOR INDEX

A

Aaron, B., 423, 477, 479, 483, 494
Abodeely, J. E., 137–39
Abowd, J.S., 250, 361
Abraham, K. G., 247
Adams, L. T., 161
Adams, R. J., 534
Adell, B., 534
Ahern, R. W., 383
Ahlburg, D. A., 160
Alexander, C., 383
Allen, A. D., 457
Allen, R. E., 429
Allen, R., 482
Allen, S. G., 224, 226, 237
Anderson, J. C., 99–100, 159, 446
Andiappan, P., 100
Angle, H. L., 256
Arvey, R. D., 411
Ash, P., 429
Ashenfelter, O., 221, 361–62
Atkin, R. S., 82, 97

B

Baderschneider, J., 484, 493, 495
Barbash, J., 96
Barbezat, D. A., 482
Barfield, R., 253
Barnum, D. T., 480
Barocci, T. A., 491
Bazerman, M. H., 496
Beauvais, L. L., 255
Becker, B. E., 50, 161, 227–28, 364
Behringer, K., 515
Benedict, M. E., 498
Ben-Ner, A., 378
Bennett, J. T., 246
Berger, C. J., 253–55
Bernbeim, R., 514
Beyer, J. M., 483, 485

Black, A. W., 362
Blasi, J. R., 402
Block, R. N., 105, 142, 147, 158, 228, 253, 380, 452
Bloom, D. E., 495
Bloom, G. F., 351
Bognanno, M. F., 493, 496
Bohlander, G. W., 515
Boudreau, J. W., 255
Bowlby, R. C., 281
Bowlby, R. L., 429, 431
Boyle, K., 53
Brett, J. M., 5–6, 384, 420–21
Briggs, S., 415, 446
Briggs, V. M., Jr., 220
Brister, J., 145
Brittain, J., 122
Broadbent, B., 97
Brockner, J., 180–81
Bronars, S. G., 141
Brotherton, C. J., 280, 347
Brown, B. B., 216
Brown, B. R., 277–79
Brown, C., 395
Brown, R. B., 105
Brown, W., 530
Bruce, P. G., 90
Burke, D. R., 292
Burt, R. E., 255
Burton, J. F., Jr., 477
Busman, G., 159
Butler, R. J., 493
Byrne, D. M., 363

C

Campbell, D. C., 531
Cantrell, R. S., 251
Cappelli, P., 179, 185, 188–89, 191
Card, D., 361
Carter, W. H., 221
Cartter, A. M., 179–80
Cavanagh, C. L., 495
Chacko, T. J., 11, 100
Chafetz, I., 159

Chaison, G. N., 15, 100, 122, 146
Chalykoff, J., 148
Chamberlain, N. W., 28–29, 38, 101, 182
Champlin, F. C., 493, 496
Chaubey, M. D., 488
Chelius, J., 84, 493
Cheng, T-Y, 398
Cherns, A. B., 396
Christenson, S., 246
Clark, P. F., 112
Clark, R. L., 224
Cohen, S., 271
Collomp, C., 27
Commons, J. R., 24
Cook, A. H., 101
Cooke, W. N., 90, 149, 160, 380–81, 385, 395, 399, 403, 428
Cornfield, D. B., 115
Coulson, C., 214
Cousineau, J. M., 242, 361
Craft, J. A., 10, 146
Craypo, C., 192
Cross, J. G., 277, 281
Cullen, D. E., 28–29, 38, 101, 182
Cunningham, J. D., 221, 251
Curme, M. A., 161
Currie, J., 494
Cutcher-Gershenfeld, J., 398–99, 403

D

Dabscheck, B., 527, 529, 531
Dalton, D. R., 428
Daniels, W., 526–27
Dankert, C. E., 239
Dastmalchian, A., 432
Datz, H., 356
Davis, L. E., 396
Davis, W. M., 206
Dawis, R. V., 12

548

Dayal, S., 529
Deere, D. R., 141
Deitsch, C. R., 452, 463
Delaney, J. T., 115–16, 161, 180–81, 195, 380, 400, 482, 498
Dell'Omo, G. G., 431, 495
Dennis, B. D., 490, 492, 495
Denton, M., 87
Derber, M., 479
Deshpande, S. P., 10
Dewire, J., 429
Dhavale, D. G., 146
Dickens, W. T., 155–57, 159, 161
Dilts, D. A., 452, 463
Donn, C. B., 191
Donovan, E., 251
Dotson, D. L., 90
Douglas, A., 341, 343–44, 346
Douglas, J. M., 253, 496
Drotning, J. E., 346, 494
Dulles, F. R., 26–34, 37, 45, 48–49, 57–58
Dunlop, J. T., 206
Dworkin, J. B., 159–60
Dyer, L. D., 240, 246, 254, 379

E

Earle, J. S., 239
Eaton, A. E., 398
Eberts, R. W., 226
Edwards, F. R., 482
Edwards, H. T., 444, 448
Edwards, L. N., 477, 482
Eflal, B., 353
Ehrenberg, R. G., 484, 493, 495
Eischen, D. E., 246, 510
Elkouri, E. A., 438, 452
Elkouri, F., 438, 452
Elliott, R. D., 160
Ellwood, D. T., 160
Ernst, D., 37
Evansohn, J., 15
Ewing, D. W., 512, 515
Extejt, M. M., 146, 159, 493

F

Farber, H. S., 10, 250, 281, 493, 496
Farmer, H. S., 247
Feild, H. S., 421
Feller, D., 464
Ferris, G. H., 4

Feuille, P., 193, 441, 482, 489–91, 495
Fields, M. W., 398
Fine, G., 160
Fine, S., 46–47
Fiorito, J., 4, 10, 106, 115, 160, 276, 527
Flaherty, S., 361, 363
Flanagan, R. J., 85
Fleming, R. W., 445, 454–55
Florkowski, G. W., 82, 147
Foner, P. S., 359
Fossum, J. A., 128, 149, 153, 188, 216, 240, 246, 504, 510–11
Fottler, M. D., 241
Foulkes, F. K., 505–9, 511, 515
Fox, A. L., II, 114
Franke, W. H., 189
Fraser, C. R. P., 159
Frazier H. B., III, 63, 473
Freedman, A., 147, 191, 207, 262, 273, 294–95, 504, 517–18
Freeman, J., 122
Freeman, R. B., 4, 15, 141, 148–49, 151, 220–22, 224–28, 251–52, 254, 429, 482
Frost, C. F., 388, 390–91
Fukami, C. V., 256
Fuller, S. H., 284

G

Gagala, K., 144
Gallagher, D. G., 4, 487–88, 527
Gamm, S., 113
Gandz, J., 431
Gannon, M. J., 45
Garland, S. B., 114
Gautschi, F. H., III, 90
Geffner, L., 356
Gerhart, P. F., 346, 481, 494
Getman, J. G., 5, 144–45, 149, 153, 254
Ghilarducci, T., 364
Gibbons, M. K. 473
Gifford, C. D., 103
Glick, W., 99
Gobeille, K. R., 397
Goldberg, S. B., 5, 144–45, 149, 153, 254, 384, 420–21
Goll, I., 387
Gompers, S., 36
Gootnick, M., 494
Gordon, M. E., 11, 255, 429, 431

Gramm, C. L., 361–63
Granof, M. F., 367–68
Greenberger, R. S., 184, 358
Greenfield, P. A., 443
Greer, C. R., 4, 11, 149, 364, 428–29
Grier, K. B., 116
Grodin, J. R., 494
Gryna, F. M., Jr., 394
Gunderson, M., 361–63

H

Haggard, T. R., 246, 370
Hall, A., 253
Hammer, R. C., 137–39
Hamner, W. C., 5
Hanslowe, N. B., 158
Harder, D., 99
Harris, T. H., 185
Harrison, A., 362
Hartmann, P. T., 189
Hawkins, B. M., 160
Helburn, I. B., 432, 462, 480
Hendricks, W. E., 193, 208, 241, 276, 361–62
Hendrix, W. H., 251
Heneman, H. G., Jr., 204, 265, 267
Heneman, H. G., III, 123, 204, 240, 246, 431, 446
Herman, J. B., 5, 144–45, 149, 153, 254
Herrick, N. Q., 396
Hersby, R. B., 473
Heywood, J. S., 250
Hickman, C. W., 123
Hill, M., Jr., 454–55
Hirsch, B. T., 161
Hirschman, A. O., 13, 511
Hochner, A., 113
Hoerr, J., 191, 203, 376, 396
Hogler, R. L., 84, 517
Holley, W. H., Jr., 421
Holmes, A. B., 482
Holzer, H. J., 251
Horn, R. N., 497
Horton, R. D., 495
Howlett, R., 456
Hoxie, R. F., 39
Hoyer, D. T., 384
Hoyman, M. M., 100, 444
Hundley, G., 4
Hunt, R. E., 483, 485
Hutchens, R., 361–62
Huth, W. L., 141

I

Ichniowski, C., 84, 105, 244, 380, 400, 432, 477, 482, 497

J

Jackson, L., 148, 150
Jacobi, O., 526
Jacoby, S.M., 49, 212, 241
Janus, C. J., 121
Jarley, P., 106
Jarrell, S. P., 223
Jennings, D. F., 457
Jick, T., 346, 484, 493, 495
Johnson, G. E., 221, 362
Johnson, M. H., 246
Johnson, T. R., 253
Jones, A. P., 378
Jones, D. C., 378
Jones, D. L., 36, 440, 460–61
Juris, H., 526–27, 530

K

Kahn, L. M., 208, 241, 361
Karim, A., 347
Karper, M. D., 191
Kasper, H., 490, 492, 495
Kassalow, E. M., 525, 531
Kates, C., 114
Katz, H. C., 3, 106, 191, 212, 237, 376, 380, 383, 397, 518
Kaufman, B. E., 361–62
Kaufman, R. S., 227
Kaufman, R. T., 208, 227
Kawahito, K., 534
Keaveny, T. J., 149, 153, 429
Keefe, J. H., 237
Keidel, R.W., 397
Kelley, M. R., 237
Kellock, S., 356
Kennan, J., 361–63
Kennedy, T., 526, 529–31, 534
Keppler, M. J., 510
Kilpatrick, J. G., 121
King, A. G., 220
Klaas, B. S., 429–31
King, R. H., 363
Kleiner, M. M., 141, 148–49, 221, 228, 244, 380
Knight, T. R., 432
Kochan, T. A., 3, 9–10, 106, 148, 177, 212, 237, 346, 376, 378–80, 383, 397, 403, 480–81, 484, 493, 495, 518
Koike, K., 525–26, 530
Kokkelenberg, E. G., 161

Kolb, D. M., 341, 343
Korpi, W., 525
Kotlowitz, A., 98, 238
Koziara, E. C., 193
Koziara, K., 113
Kressel, K., 346
Kuhn, J. W., 142, 426–27
Kujawa, D., 531
Kuruvilla, S., 527
Kutler, S. I., 36
Kwoka, J. E., Jr., 223

L

Labig, C. E., Jr., 428–29, 462
Lacroix, R., 242, 361
Ladd, R. T., 255
Lane, C., 527–28
Langsner, A., 210
Larson, E. W., 256
Larry, R. H., 505
Lauer, H., 482
Lawler, E. E., III, 6, 393, 396
Lawler, J. J., 128, 148, 153
Leap, T. L., 251
Lee, B. A., 84
Lefkowitz, J., 473
Leigh, J. P., 362
Leonard, J. S., 161, 251
Leone, R. D., 382 –83
LeRoy, M., 441
Lester, R. A., 492
Lewin, D., 380, 400, 414, 416, 418, 429, 431, 433
Lewis, H. G., 482
Lewis, R., 148, 150
Linneman, P. D., 221
Lipsky, D. B., 101, 253, 361–62, 491, 496
Loewenberg, J. J., 490, 492, 495
Lofquist, L. H., 12
Long, G., 490
Long, L. N., 11
Lynn, M. L., 145

M

McCabe, D. M., 514
McCall, B. P., 287, 496
Maccoby, M., 396
McConnell, S., 361, 364
McDermott, T. J., 349
MacDonald, D. N., 141
McGuinness, K. C., 88
McGuire, W. J., 497
McKelvey, J. T., 349, 425, 460, 485, 487

McKersie, R. B., 3, 106, 148, 212, 225–27, 237, 277, 282, 284–87, 290–91, 376, 378–79, 383, 393, 398, 505, 508, 518
McLaughlin, J. M., 356
McShane, S. L., 100
Macpherson, D. A., 161, 223
Magenau, J. M., 97, 256, 280
Magnusen, K. O., 488
Mahoney, T. A., 265
Maki, D., 246
Malcolm, J., 153
Mangum, G., 457
Mann, E., 395
Mann, F. C., 239
Maranto, C. L., 147, 160
March, J. G., 506
Marshall, A., 174
Marshall, F. R., 220
Martin, B., 525, 531
Martin, J. E., 97, 256, 362
Martin, S. A., 149, 360, 364
Masters, M. F., 82, 97, 114, 116
Mauro, M. J., 360
Meany, G., 58–59
Medoff, J. L., 4, 220–21, 225–27, 253, 429
Melino, A., 361–63
Mellor, S., 255
Meltzer, B., 456
Meyer, D. G., 399, 428
Milkovich, G. T., 209, 211
Miller, C. S., 390
Miller, R. U., 161
Mills, D. Q., 225–27, 505, 508
Mironi, M., 484, 493, 495
Mirvis, P., 99
Mishel, L., 185
Mitchell, D. J. B., 207, 212, 221, 241, 361, 364, 483
Montgomery, B. R., 153–54
Montgomery, D., 16
Montgomery, E., 498
Moore, W. J., 221, 223
Morgan, J., 253
Morgan, R. L., 255
Morgan, S., 402
Morishima, M., 256
Mowday, R. T., 255
Munger, M. C., 116
Murnighan, J. K., 287
Murrman, K. F., 147–48

N

Najita, J. M., 477, 479, 483, 494
Naples, M. I., 361
Navasky, V., 52
Neale, M. A., 496

Nelson, D., 49
Nelson, W. B., 498
Nesbitt, M. A., 62
Neufeld, M. F., 39, 103
Neumann, G. R., 364
Newman, J. M., 209, 211
Newman, R. J., 221
Ng, I., 432
Nickelsburg, G., 244
Niland, J., 527, 529, 531
Noble, K. B., 120
Northrup, H. R., 147, 239, 241, 351, 531
Nowack, J., 429
Nowlin, W. A., 447

O

Ochs, J., 282
Odewahn, C., 136
Olson, C. A., 50, 227–28, 253, 255, 364, 431, 490, 494, 496–97

P

Paarsch, H. J., 364
Parker, D. F., 254
Pegnetter, R., 347, 487
Pearlstein, G., 391
Pencavel, J., 239
Perry, J. L., 256
Peters, E., 447, 463
Peters-Hamlin, K., 216
Peterson, M. F., 97, 256
Peterson, R. B., 287–88, 414, 416, 418, 429, 431, 433
Philpot, J. W., 255
Pierce, J. L., 402
Pierson, F. C., 206
Pilarski, A. M., 244
Poole, M., 524, 526–27, 529, 531, 533
Porter, A. A., 147–48
Porter, L. W., 6, 255
Prasad, S. B., 529
Prasow, P., 447, 463
Preston, A., 84
Price, J., 429
Primps, S. B., 241
Prosten, R., 147
Pruitt, D. G., 280, 346
Pruitt, S. W., 365
Pulliam, M. S. 366

Q

Quaglieri, P. L., 114

R

Raisian, J., 223
Raskin, A. H., 148, 347–48
Rayback, J. G., 34, 36, 44–46, 51, 53
Ready, K. J., 191
Reder, M. W., 15
Reed, T. F., 145
Rehmus, C. M., 271, 349, 351, 490, 492, 495
Reich, M., 395
Renovitch, P. A., 488
Reusser, T. E., 360, 364
Richardson, R. C., 265, 267
Roberts, M. T., 421
Robinson, J. C., 159
Robinson, J. W., 415
Rogers, R. C., 462
Ronan, W., 429
Ronen, S., 241
Roomkin, M., 91, 228, 380
Rose, J. B., 15
Rose, K. M., 241
Ross, A. M., 207
Rosse, J. G., 149, 153
Roth, A. E., 282, 287
Rowan, R. L., 239
Rowland, K., 4
Ruback, R. S., 228
Ruben, G., 192, 216, 247
Rubenfeld, S. A., 402
Rubin, J., 366
Rubin, J. Z., 277–79
Rubin, L., 292
Ruh, R. A., 388, 390–91
Ryder, M. S., 271
Rytina, N., 213

S

St. Anthony, N., 83
Salem, G. T., 157
Salsburg, S. W., 228, 380
Saltzman, G. M., 116
Sandler, A. L., 137–39
Sandver, M. H., 123, 160, 446
Sayles, L. R., 96, 99–101
Schachter, S., 12
Schenkel, K., 429
Schlesinger, J. M., 190
Schlossberg, S. I., 142, 144
Schmidt, S., 113, 378
Schnell, J. F., 248
Schoenfeld, G., 97
Schoumaker, F., 287
Schreisheim, C. A., 5
Schriver, W. R., 281
Schumann, P. L., 493

Schuster, M., 147, 387, 390, 392, 400–401
Schwab, C. M., 38
Schwab, D. P., 204, 240, 246
Schwochau, S., 116, 255, 495
Scott, C., 136
Selekman, B. M., 284
Selekman, S. K., 284
Selvin, D. F., 45
Sherer, P. D., 256
Sherman, F. E., 142, 144
Shirom, A., 364
Sikorski, J. C., 114
Simkin, W. E., 341, 348, 462
Singh, D., 223
Sinicropi, A. V., 454–55
Slowinski, B. J., 531
Smith, F. J., 5
Smith, R. A., 440
Sockell, D. R., 161, 180–81, 195
Sperka, S., 158
Spiller, W. E., 255
Spizman, L. M., 482
Stagner, R., 353
Stallworth, L. E., 444
Stanley, M. C., 121
Stanley, T. D., 223
Steers, R. M., 255
Stephenson, G. M., 280, 347
Stern, J. L., 477, 479, 483, 486, 488, 490, 492, 495
Stern, R., 361–62
Stevens, C. M., 277, 281, 489
Stewart, J. B., 223
Stewart, M., 362
Stieber, J., 225–26, 423, 452, 476, 505, 508
Stinchcombe, A., 506
Stone, G. W., Jr., 498
Stratton, K., 106
Strauss, G., 96, 99–101
Sturmthal, A., 529
Suffern, A., 54
Summers, C. W., 425
Swint, J. M., 498
Szerszen, C., 193

T

Taft, P., 28, 38, 53–55, 59–60
Tasini, J., 123
Taylor, B., 46–47, 50, 62
Taylor, G. S., 251
Taylor, G. W., 206
Tener, B. Z., 473
Thacker, J. W., 398
Theilmann, J., 116
Thomason, T., 477
Thompson, C. A., 255

Thompson, M., 526–27, 530
Thornicroft, K. W., 461
Todaro, J. B., 123
Todor, W. D., 428
Tomkiewicz, J., 497
Torigian, M., 54
Tracy, J. S., 361
Tracy, L., 287–88
Trice, H. M., 485
Trotta, M. S., 415
Troy, L., 3
Turkus, B. B., 463

U

Unterberger, S. H., 193
Ury, W., 384

V

Valletta, R. G., 483
Verma, A., 393, 398
Voos, P. B., 158, 380, 298, 400–401
Vroman, S. B., 224, 361–62
Vroman, W., 208
Vroom, V. H., 6

W

Wachter, M. L., 221
Wakabayashi, M., 527
Wakeley, J. H., 388, 390–91
Walker, R. L., 415
Wall, J. A., Jr., 347
Walsh, D. J., 213
Walters, V., 87
Walton, R. E., 277, 282, 284–87, 290–91, 378–80, 517
Webb, J., 347
Weber, A. R., 186
Wei, K. C. J., 365
Wesman, E. C., 246, 510
Wessels, W. J., 223
West, R., 148
Wever, K., 527
Wheeler, H. N., 461–62, 481, 489, 492, 534
White, J. K., 391
White, M. D., 14, 178
White, R. E., 365
Whitehead, J. D., 431
Wholey, D. R., 159
Wilczynski, J., 531
Wilhite, A., 116
Williams, J. S., 25–26

Wilson, J. T., 241
Windmuller, J. P., 526, 529, 531
Witney, F., 46–47, 50, 62
Woglom, G., 208
Wolkinson, B. W., 142, 147, 158, 443
Wolters, R. S., 421
Woodworth, W., 402

Y

Yellen, J., 509
Yellowitz, I., 39
Yoder, D., 204, 265, 267

Z

Zalusky, J., 456–57, 459
Zax, J. S., 105, 477
Zellner, W., 396
Zeuthen, F., 276
Zimmerman, M. B., 228
Zollitsch, H., 210

CASE INDEX

A

Adair v. United States, 36
AFL-CIO Joint Negotiating
    Committee v. NLRB, 193
Alexander v. Gardner-Denver
    Co., 443
American Hospital Association
    v. NLRB, 135
American Ship Building Co. v.
    NLRB, 369
Anheuser-Busch, Inc., 139
Atkinson v. Sinclair Refining
    Co., 441
AT&T Technologies, Inc. v.
    Communication Workers,
    442

B

Babcock & Wilcox Co., NLRB
    v., 141
Barrentine v. Arkansas-Best
    Freight System, 443
Bets Cadillac-Olds, Inc., 367
Bildisco & Bildisco, NLRB v.,
    370
Blackhawk Engraving Co., 360
Blue Flash Express Co., 152
Bonanno Linen Service v.
    NLRB, 194
Borden Co., Hutchinson Ice
    Cream Div., 138
Bourne v. NLRB, 152
Bowen v. U.S. Postal Service,
    425
Boys Markets, Inc. v. Retail
    Clerks Union Local 770,
    420, 441
Brooks v. NLRB, 132, 157
Brown, NLRB v., 368
Budd Manufacturing Co. v.
    NLRB, 143–44
Buffalo Forge Co. v. United
    Steelworkers of America, 353
Burns Int'l Security Services,
    NLRB v., 140

C

Carbon Fuel Co. v. United Mine
    Workers, 421
Central Hardware Co. v. NLRB,
    142
Collyer Insulated Wire Co., 443
Commonwealth v. Hunt, 25–26
Complete Auto Transit v. Reis,
    421
Continental Baking Co., 137
Cornelius v. Nutt, 444

D

DeBartolo Corp. v. Florida Gulf
    Coast Building and
    Construction Trades
    Council and NLRB, 355
Denver Building Trades Council
    v. NLRB, 354
Detroit Resilient Floor
    Decorators Union, 353
Drake Bakeries v. Local 50, 441
Duluth Bottling Association, 367
Duplex Printing v. Deering, 36
du Pont & Co., 139

E

Elgin, Joliet, & Eastern Railway
    Co. v. Burley, 352, 423, 438
Elrod v. Burns, 474
Excelsior Underwear, Inc., 132

F

Fall River Dyeing v. NLRB, 140
Fibreboard Paper Products v.
    NLRB, 242, 414
Finnegan v. Leu, 112
First National Maintenance v.
    NLRB, 242, 414
Fleetwood Trailer Co., Inc.,
    NLRB v., 358
Ford Motor Co. v. NLRB, 413

Franks v. Bowman
    Transportation Co., 250
Fruit & Vegetable Packers, Local
    760, NLRB v., 365

G

General American
    Transportation Corp., 443
General Electric Co., 193
General Foods, 517
General Knit of California, Inc.,
    152
General Shoe Corp., 152
Gissel Packing Co., NLRB v.,
    157

H

Harter Equipment, Inc., 369
Hines v. Anchor Motor Freight,
    Inc., 458
Hitchman Coal Co. v. Mitchell,
    47, 73
Hollywood Ceramics Co., 152
Howard Johnson v. Detroit Local
    Joint Exec. Board, 140
Hudgens v. NLRB, 142, 355
Humphrey v. Moore, 424

I

Int'l Longshoremen's Ass'n v.
    Allied International, 366

J

John Wiley & Sons, Inc. v.
    Livingston, 140
Jones & Laughlin Steel Corp.,
    NLRB v., 50

L

LeTourneau Co., NLRB v., 141
Livingston Shirt Corp., 152
Local Union, 1229, IBEW v.
    NLRB, 354
Loewe v. Lawlor, 35, 74

M

MacKay Radio & Telegraph,
    NLRB v., 357
Mallinckrodt Chemical Works,
    139
Marsh v. Alabama, 142
May Department Stores Co., 152
Metropolitan Life Insurance Co.,
    NLRB v., 138
Midland National Life, 152
Milwaukee Spring Div. of
    Illinois Coil Spring Co.,
    242, 414
Miranda Fuel Co., 424
Moore Dry Dock Co., 355

N

NLRB v. various defendants (see
    defendant's name)

O

Oil, Chemical, and Atomic
    Workers v. NLRB, 193
Olin Corp., 443
Otis Elevator Co., 242, 414

P

P. Q. Beef Processors, Inc., 76
Peerless Plywood, 153

Q

Quaker State Oil Refining
    Corp., 369

R

Ranco, Inc. v. NLRB, 141
Republic Aviation Corp. v.
    NLRB, 141
Roy Robinson Chevrolet, 443

S

Sailor's Union of the Pacific, 355
Schechter Poultry Corp. v.
    United States, 47
Seamprufe, Inc., NLRB v., 141
Sheet Metal Workers
    International Ass'n. v.
    Lynn, 112
Shopping Kart Food Markets,
    Inc., 152
Sinclair Refining Co. v.
    Atkinson, 420, 441
Smith v. Hussman Refrigerator
    Co. and Local 13889,
    United Steel Workers of
    America, 425
Spielberg Manufacturing Co.,
    442

T

Textile Workers Union v.
    Lincoln Mills, 439
Thornhill v. Alabama, 354
Truax v. Corrigan, 46
Truck Drivers' Local 449, NLRB
    v., 368
Truitt Manufacturing Co.,
    NLRB v., 289

U

United Dairy Farmers, 157
United Paperworkers v. Misco,
    Inc., 442
United Steelworkers of America
    v. American Mfg. Co., 439
United Steelworkers of America
    v. Enterprise Wheel and Car
    Corp., 439
United Steelworkers of America
    v. Sadlowski, 113
United Steelworkers of America
    v. Warrior & Gulf
    Navigation Co., 439

V

Vaca v. Sipes, 424
Viele & Sons, Inc., 76

W

Weingarten, J., Inc., NLRB v.,
    422
Wooster Div. of Borg Warner
    Corp., NLRB v., 292
Wright Line, 422

SUBJECT INDEX

A

Ability to pay, 202
Accretion, 140
AFL-CIO, 116–19
  activities, 117–19
  early goals, 30–31
  merger, 58
Agency shop, 245
Ally doctrine, 359–60
Ambulatory site picketing, 355
American Arbitration
  Association, 448
American Federation of
  Government Employees,
  476
American Federation of Labor,
  29–31, 37
  founding, 29–31
American Federation of State,
  County, and Municipal
  Employees, 476
  structure, 111
American Plan, 37–38
American Railway Union, 33
Arbitration, 244
  criteria used, 494–95
  defined, 438
  deferral to, 442–44
  discipline cases, 460–62
  evidentiary rules, 453–55
  expedited, 457
  hearing process, 452
  inadequate representation,
  458–60
  past practice, 462–63
  procedures, 444–56
  public sector, 488–96
  representatives, 452
  use of punishment, 461–62
Arbitrator
  ad hoc, 445
  permanent umpire, 445
  selection of, 445–46
  sources of, 446–49
Area-wide labor-management
  committees, 382–83
Associate membership, 105
Attitude surveys, 515–16

Attitudinal structuring, 283
Authorization cards, 128

B

Bankruptcies, 369–70
Bargaining,
  attributes of parties, 278–79
  behavioral theories, 282–89
  bluffing, 281
  defined, 276–78
  employer interests, 177
  legal requirements, 179–81
  multilateral, 479–81
  pattern, 190–91
  union interests, 177–79
Bargaining books, 269–71
Bargaining conventions, 272–73
Bargaining issues
  developed economies, 529–30
  mandatory, 180
  permissive, 180
  prohibited, 180
Bargaining orders, 157
Bargaining power, 181–85
  union, 185
Bargaining process
  attitudinal structuring, 285
  distributive bargaining, 282,
  290–91
  integrative bargaining, 282–84,
  378–80
  intraorganizational bargaining,
  285–87
Bargaining structures, 185–95
  coalition bargaining, 192
  conglomerates, 192
  coordinated bargaining, 192
  European Economic
  Committee members, 530
  industry-wide, 187–88
  legal decisions, 192
  multicraft, 189
  multiemployers, 186
  national/local, 189
  public sector, 478–79
  United Kingdom, 530
  wide-area, 189

Bargaining tactics, 280–81
Bargaining units
  accretion, 140
  determination by NLRB,
  134–40
  community of interests, 137
  craft severance, 139
  legal constraints, 135
  public sector, 477–78
  reorganization, 140
  successor organizations, 140
Beck, Dave, 58
Benefit status seniority, 217, 248
Bluffing, 281
Board-directed elections, 132
Boycotts, 35, 365–66
  Bucks Stove, 35
Bucks Stove boycott, 35
Bureau of Labor Statistics, 87
Business agent, 96

C

California State Employees
  Association, 476
Carpenters' Union, 110
Certifications, 132
Checkoff, 245
Civil Rights Act, Title VII, 249
Civil Service Reform Act, 63,
  472
Clayton Act, 36
Closed-offer selection, 493
Closed shop, 245
Coalition bargaining, 192
Commitment to the union,
  255–56
Common situs picketing, 354
Community of interests, 137
Comparable worth, 213
Competitive status seniority, 248
Components of wage demands
  ability to pay, 202
  equity, 202
  standard of living, 204
Consent elections, 132
Conspiracy doctrine, 24–25

Contract administration
    developed countries, 534
    issues, 410–14
Contract costing, 265–69
Contract length, 241–42
Contract negotiations
    bargaining books, 269–71
    costing, 265–69
Contract ratifications, 291–94
Cooperation
    effects of, 399–401
    management strategy, 399
    methods, 381
    union politics, 398
Coordinated bargaining, 192
Corporate campaigns, 105, 356
Corruption, 58–59
Cost of living allowances, 206–8
Craft severance, 139

D

Danbury Hatters, 35
Debs, Eugene, 33
Decertifications, 159–60
Deferral to arbitration, 442–44
Department of Labor, 85–87
Deregulation, 171
Derived demand, 171–74
Development of labor
        movements
    developed countries, 524–26
    Germany, 526
    Japan, 525
    Sweden, 524–25
Discipline, 410–11
Discipline and discharge, 243
Distributive bargaining, 282,
        290–91
Dual commitment, 97
Dual governance, 101
Duration of strikes, 362–63
Duty to bargain, 78

E

Economic strikes, 352
    rights of strikers, 358–59
Elections
    certifications, 155–57
    petitions, 131–32
Employee defined, 75
Employee involvement
        programs, 397
Employee relations defined, 504
Employee review boards, 514–15
Employee stock ownership
        plans, 402

Employee "voice" systems,
        511–17
Employer defined, 75
Employer unfair labor practices,
        77
Employment Standards
        Administration, 87
Employment and Training
        Administration, 87
Equal employment opportunity,
        249
Equity, 202
Erdman Act, 36
Excelsior list, 132
Exclusive representation, 48
Executive committee, 96
Executive Order 10988, 62, 472
Executive Order 11491, 62
Executive Order 11616, 62
Expedited arbitration, 457

F

Federal Mediation and
        Conciliation Service, 56,
        87–88, 449
Fact-finding, 349–51
    Florida, 488
    Iowa, 487–88
    Michigan, 487
    New York, 487
    public sector, 484–88
    railway labor boards, 351
    Taft-Hartley, 350
    Wisconsin, 486
Fair representation, 423
Federal Labor Relations
        Authority, 63, 473
Federal Labor Relations
        Council, 62
Federal Services Impasses Panel,
        473
    Field representatives, 103
    Final-offer arbitration, 489
        laws, 490–92
    Foreign competition, 173
    Fractional bargaining, 426–27
    Fraternal Order of Police, 477
    Frick, Henry, 32
    Functional democracy, 100–102

G

Gompers, Samuel, 30–31, 37
Grievance mediation, 421
Grievance procedures, 243–44,
        414–18

Grievances
    effects of, 431–32
    employee rights, 421–25
    striking over, 418–19
    union initiatives, 427–28
Grievances and bargaining,
        425–31
Group cohesiveness, 13–14

H

Haywood, "Big Bill," 33–34
Health care costs, 215–16
Health care picketing, 79
Hoffa, James R., 59
Hot-cargo clauses, 78
Hours of work, 237–41, 412

I

Impasses
    defined, 340
    incidence in developed
        countries, 531
    public sector procedures,
        483–98
Impro-Share, 392
Incentives, 411
Incidence of strikes, 360–62
Individual personnel
        assignments, 412
Industrial Workers of the World,
        34–35, 37
Industrial democracy, 531–34
Industrial unions, 44–46
Industry-wide bargaining, 282–84
Integrative bargaining, 282–84,
        378–80
Interest arbitration, 351–52,
        488–96
    effects of, 495–96
    final-offer, 489–92
    narcotic effect, 493–94
International Association of Fire
        Fighters, 477
Interrogation, 152
Intraorganizational bargaining,
        385–87

J

Job evaluation, 209–12
Job security, 247–50
Joint labor-management
        committees, 383
Jurisdictional disputes, 136

K

Knights of Labor, 27–29

L

Labor-capital substitution,
    175–76
Labor-management committees,
    396
Labor Management Services
    Administration, 85
Labor markets, 176–77
Landrum-Griffin Act, 60, 81–83
Layoffs, 248
Lewis, John L., 51–53, 57
Little steel violence, 49
Local unions, 14, 96–102
    committees, 96
    democracy, 98–102
    executive committee, 96
    jurisdictions, 96
    negotiation committee, 96
    participation of members,
        99–100
    relationships with national
        unions, 111–12
    stewards, 97
Lockouts, 244, 367–69
    multiemployer, 367–68
    perishable goods, 367
    single-employer 368–69

M

Maintenance of membership,
    245
Management preparation for
    bargaining, 262–72
    contract costing, 265–69
    cost of living allowances,
        206–8
    health care costs, 215–16
    strike preparations, 271
Management rights, 241–42
Mandatory bargaining issues,
    180
Markets, 168–70
Meany, George, 57–59, 64
Median voter, 14
Mediation, 340–49
Mediator qualifications, 347
Methods of cooperation, 381
Modified union shop, 245
Mohawk Valley Formula, 39, 49
Molly Maguires, 31
Multicraft bargaining, 189

Multiemployer bargaining, 186
Multiemployer lockouts, 367–68
Multilateral bargaining, 479–81
Multiple-use site picketing, 355

N

Narcotic effect
National Academy of
    Arbitrators, 448
National Association of Letter
    Carriers, 476
National Education Association,
    477
National emergency strikes, 56,
    80–81
National Industrial Recovery
    Act, 47
National Labor Relations Act,
    48–49
    constitutionality of, 50
National Labor Relations Board,
    48, 76, 88–89
    bargaining orders, 157
    board-directed elections, 132
    campaign unfair labor
        practices, 155
    certifications, 132, 155–57
    consent elections, 132
    decertifications, 159–60
    deferral to arbitration, 442–44
    petitions, 131–32
    politicization of, 90
    role in organizing campaigns,
        151–53
National Labor Union, 27
National/local bargaining, 189
National Mediation Board,
    70–72, 88
National Molders' Union, 27
National Railroad Board of
    Adjustment, 72
National unions, 102–16
    field representatives, 103
    goals, 103–4
    jurisdictions, 106–8
    mergers, 121–22
    politics, 113–14
    relationships with local
        unions, 111–12
    structures, 108–11
National War Labor Board,
    53–54
Negotiation committee, 96
Negotiations, 289–90
Norris-LaGuardia Act, 46–47,
    73–75
No-solicitiation rules, 141–42

O

Occupational Safety and Health
    Administration, 87
Ombudsman, 514
Open-door policies, 514
Organizing campaigns, 128–51
    authorization cards, 128
    employee responses, 153
    Excelsior list, 132
    management strategy, 147–50
    NLRB role, 151–53
    no-solicitation rules, 141–42
    petition elections, 132
    recognition requests, 130–31
    truthfulness of campaign,
        152–53
    unfair labor practices, 155
    union strategy, 142–47
    violence, 49
Overtime, 240

P

Paid time off, 219–20, 241
Past practice, 413, 462–63
Pattern bargaining, 190–91
Pay programs, 204–20
    form, 213–17
    level, 205–8
    structure, 209–13
    system, 217–20
Pensions
    defined benefit plan, 216
    defined contribution plan, 216
Perishable goods lockouts, 367
Permanent umpire, 445
Permissive bargaining issues, 180
Petition elections, 132
Philadelphia cordwainers, 24–25
Philosophy-laden employee
    relations, 507–10
Picketing, 354–55
    ambulatory site, 355
    common situs, 354
    health care organizations, 79
    multiple-use sites, 355
Political action committees, 105,
    115–16
Powderly, Terence, 28
Production standards, 412
Productive efficiency, 218
Productivity, 225–27
Professional employee defined,
    76
Profit sharing, 218
Prohibited bargaining issues, 180
Promotions and transfers, 249
Public employee unions, 476–77

Public sector bargaining outcomes, 481–83
Public sector bargaining structures, 478–79
Public sector bargaining units, 477–78
Public sector strikes, 496–98
Public sector unions, 61
  developing countries, 534

Q

Quality circles, 392–93
Quality of work life, 396–97

R

Racketeer Influenced and Corrupt Organizations Act, 83–84
Railway Labor Act, 46, 70, 72–73
Railway labor boards, 351
Recognition requests, 130–31
Relations by objectives, 383–84
Remedies, bargaining orders, 157
Representation
  right to organize, 48, 76–77
  western Europe, 528–29
Representation elections, 79, 130–34
  board-directed, 132
  campaign truthfulness, 152–53
  certifications, 155–57
  consent elections, 132
  decertifications, 159–60
  outcomes, 158–89
  petitions, 131–32
  right-to-work laws, 160
Reuther, Walter, 57
Right-to-work laws, 56, 80, 160
Rights arbitration, 444–63
Rucker Plan, 391–92
Rules, 413

S

Safety, 246
Scanlon Plan, 388–91
Seniority, 247–50
  benefit status, 217, 248
  competitive status, 248
  discrimination, 250
Service Employees International Union, 476
Sherman Antitrust Act, 36, 170

Shift assignments, 240
Shift differentials, 240
Shutdowns, 356–57
Single-employer lockouts, 368–69
Sit-down strike, 45–46, 51
Skill-based pay, 212
Slowdowns, 355–56
Standard of living, 204
State labor laws, 473–75
  fire fighter, 475
  police, 475
  state employees, 475
  teachers, 475
Steel Workers Organizing Committee, 45–56
Steelworkers trilogy, 439
Stephens, Uriah, 28
Stewards, 97
Strasser, Adolph, 30–31
Strikes, 28, 244, 352–65
  ability to take, 183–85
  Cripple Creek of 1904, 33
  duration, 362–63
  economic, 352
  economic striker rights, 258–59
  effects of 363–64
  over grievances, 418–19
  Homestead Steel of 1892, 32
  incidence of 360–62
  Lawrence, Massachusetts of 1912, 35
  McCormick Harvester of 1886, 32
  national emergency, 56, 80–81
  of 1945, 53
  of 1946, 55
  operating during, 357–58
  Paterson, New Jersey of 1913, 35
  preparations, 271
  public sector, 496–98
  Pullman of 1894, 32–33
  railroad of 1877, 28, 32
  shutdowns, 356–57
  sit-down, 45–46, 51
  sympathy, 353
  unfair labor practice, 353
  wildcat, 244, 353, 420–21
Subcontracting, 413
Successor organizations, 140
Suits by union members, 81
Supervisor
  defined, 76
  doing production work, 412
Sylvis, William, 27
Sympathy strikes, 353

T

Taft-Hartley, 55, 75
  suits by unions members, 81
Team concepts, 394–96
Teamsters Union, 110–11
Trusteeships, 82–83
Two-tier pay plans, 212-13

U

Unfair labor practices
  employer, 77
  hot cargo clauses, 78
  union, 78–79
Unfair labor practice strikes, 353
Union avoidance, 505–6
Union central bodies, 119–20
Union commitment, 255–56
Union finances, 122–23
Union in contract negotiations
  bargaining convention, 272–73
  bargaining power, 285
  local-level preparation, 274
  ratifications, 291–94
Union security, 245–46
  agency shop, 245
  checkoff, 245
  closed shop, 245
  maintenance of membership, 245
  modified union shop, 245
  union shop, 245
Union typologies, 39
Unionization, 5–8
  dissatisfaction, 5–6
  motivation, 6–8
Unions
  beliefs about, 9–11
  corruption, 58–59
  effects on
    bargaining outcomes, 275–76
    future of, 15–16
    hiring, 250–51
    job satisfaction, 254–55
    nonwage issues, 250–56
    pay form, 224
    pay levels, 220–24
    pay structure, 224
    pay system, 225
    pre-Civil War, 25–26
    productivity, 227
    profits, 227–28
    retirement, 253–54
    shareholders, 227–28
    spillover on pay, 223–24

Unions—*Cont.*
  effects on—*Cont.*
    transfers, 251–53
    turnover, 251–53
  finances, 122–23
  industrial, 44–46
  locals, 14, 96–102
  officer compensation, 123
  preparation for bargaining,
    272–76
  public sector, 61
  rights, 242
  strategy in organizing
    campaigns, 142–47
  structure
    Germany, 527
    Sweden, 526

United Auto Workers, 45–46
  structure, 108–10

V

Vertical staff meetings, 516

W

Wage and hour laws, 239
Wage contours, 207
Wagner Act, 48–51
Western Federation of Miners,
  33–34

Wide-area bargaining, 189
Wildcat strikes, 244, 353, 420–21
Work assignments, 411
Work design, 234–37
Work schedule innovations,
  240–41
Work schedules, 239–41
Working conditions, 246, 412
Workingmen's parties, 26

Y

Yellow-dog contract, 37, 47